THE LUNATIC
EXPRESS

Charles Miller was a popular author and journalist, specialising in historical books on East Africa. His titles include *An Entertainment in Imperialism, Battle for the Bundu* and *The First World War in East Africa.*

THE LUNATIC
EXPRESS

CHARLES MILLER

WITH A FOREWORD BY CHRISTIAN
WOLMAR AND NICHOLAS FAITH

First published in 1971 by The Macmillan Company

This revised edition published 2016 by Head of Zeus
© Charles Miller, 1971
Foreword copyright © Christian Wolmar & Nicholas Faith, 2015

Illustrations:
p10, DeAgostini/Getty Images; p120, Shutterstock;
p332, Field Museum Library/Getty Images,
p412, SPL/Getty Images;

Every effort has been made to trace
or contact all copyright holders.

1 3 5 7 9 10 8 6 4 2

A catalogue record for this book is available from the British Library.

Printed and bound in Germany
by GGP Media GmbH, Pössneck

ISBN(HB) 9781784977382
ISBN (E) 9781784972714

Head of Zeus Ltd
Clerkenwell House
45–47 Clerkenwell Green
London EC1R 0HT
WWW.HEADOFZEUS.COM

For
Nancy and Jim
Aunt Mary
Phil and Steve

AUTHOR'S NOTE

I wish to thank the following organizations and individuals for their kindness in permitting me to reproduce textual material or illustrations: Edward Arnold Ltd., William Blackwood & Sons, The British Museum, Chatto & Windus, Dr. Theresa Clay, William Collins Sons, Culver Pictures, East African Railways Corporation, Faber & Faber, Mr. F.H. Goldsmith, Robert Hale & Co., The Hamlyn Publishing Group, Historical Pictures Services, Hodder & Stoughton, Houghton Mifflin Co., Hutchinson & Co., The Imperial War Museum, Macmillan London, The Mansell Collection, Methuen & Co., John Murray Ltd., A.D. Peters & Co., Punch, Radio Times Hulton Picture Library, The Royal Commonwealth Society, Sampson Low, Marston & Co., Underwood & Underwood, Vanity Fair and H.F. & G. Witherby. A word of more personal gratitude is also very much in order. Three good friends, Robert K. Allen, Latham Leslie-Moore and Jan V. Meininger, have not only been lavish in their hospitality during recent visits I made to east Africa but also—perhaps without knowing it—provided helpful data and perspective. If Dr. J.R. Gregory of Nairobi had not been kind enough to give me an out-of-print copy of a delightful memoir which he wrote, I should have missed a rich layer of background to my own account of European settlement in the Kenya highlands. Vic Preston, also of Nairobi, took considerable time off from his busy doings as one of Kenya's foremost racing drivers to tell me a great deal about his grandfather, Ronald O. Preston, and to let me have two otherwise unavailable works written by the latter. I feel a special debt to D.P.K. Makwaia, Public Relations Officer of the East African Railways Corporation, and to R.L. Young, formerly Chief Photographer with the line, for cooperation above and beyond the call of their normal duties in furnishing many of the illustrations shown herein. John Heminway of New York displayed uncommon generosity in the calculated risk he took when he lent me what I believe to be the only existing copy of a very useful unpublished work, while Kenneth Rose of London was most thoughtful in steering me on to one of my key sources. And the last shall be first: warmest thanks to my editor, Alick Bartholomew, for his invaluable professional advice on the organization of my material, and to Gunther Stuhlmann, paragon among agents, for just about everything—including the idea for this book.

It should go without saying that no one mentioned above is responsible for any factual errors that may have been committed; I alone am accountable in that department. The same applies to any interpretations or conclusions. This book is an informal history, its protagonist the British Empire. Writing an informal history permits a certain latitude of opinion, and it is hardly possible not to have an opinion about the British Empire. Thus, while I have tried to come up with an objective account, I have not slammed the door entirely on my own views. For the record, I think that the British Empire, with all its horrendous failings, was on balance a good thing. I mourned its passing.

CONTENTS

ILLUSTRATIONS

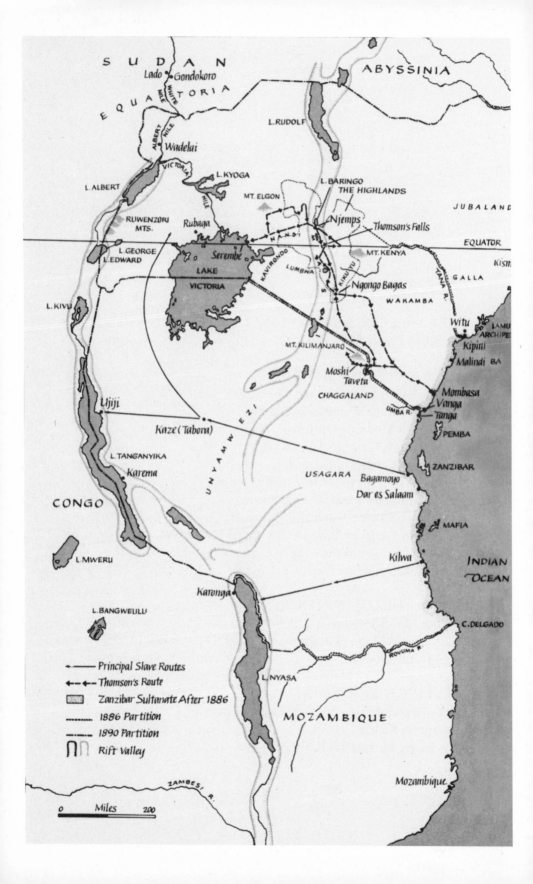

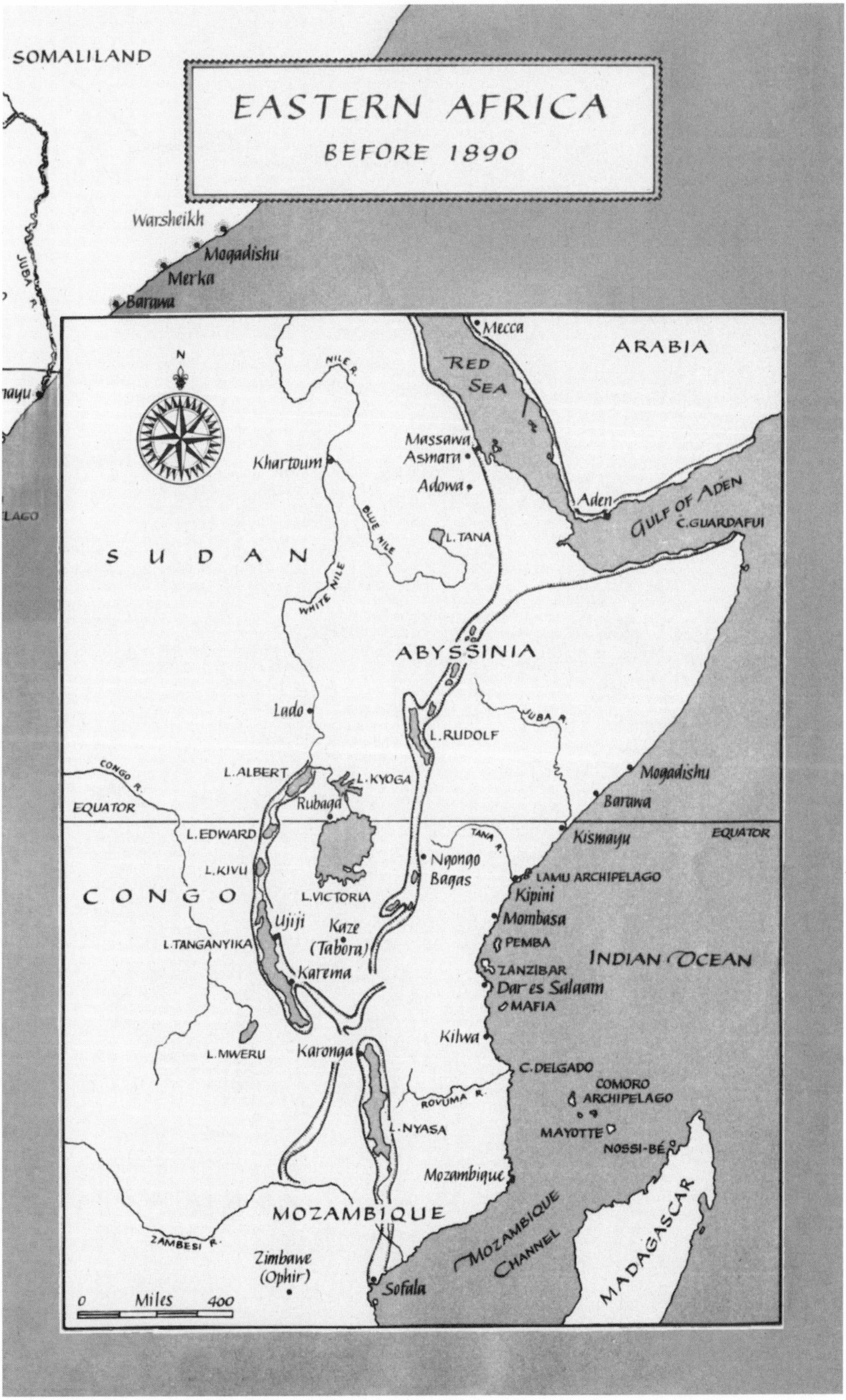

EASTERN AFRICA
BEFORE 1890

SOMALILAND

Warsheikh
Mogadishu
Merka
Barawa

N

Mecca

ARABIA

RED
SEA

NILE R.

Khartoum

Massawa
Asmara
Adowa

Aden

GULF OF ADEN

C.GUARDAFUI

S U D A N

BLUE NILE

L.TANA

WHITE NILE

ABYSSINIA

Lado

L.RUDOLF

JUBA R.

CONGO R.

L.ALBERT

L.KYOGA

Mogadishu

Barawa

EQUATOR

Rubaga

EQUATOR

L.EDWARD

TANA R.

Kismayu

L.KIVU

Ngongo
Bagas

C O N G O

L.VICTORIA

LAMU ARCHIPELAGO

Kipini

Ujiji

Kaze
(Tabora)

Mombasa

L.TANGANYIKA

PEMBA

INDIAN OCEAN

Karema

ZANZIBAR

Dar es Salaam

MAFIA

L.MWERU

Karonga

Kilwa

C.DELGADO

ROVUMA R.

COMORO
ARCHIPELAGO

L.NYASA

MAYOTTE

NOSSI-BÉ

Mozambique

M O Z A M B I Q U E

MOZAMBIQUE CHANNEL

MADAGASCAR

ZAMBESI R.

Zimbawe
(Ophir)

Sofala

0   Miles   400

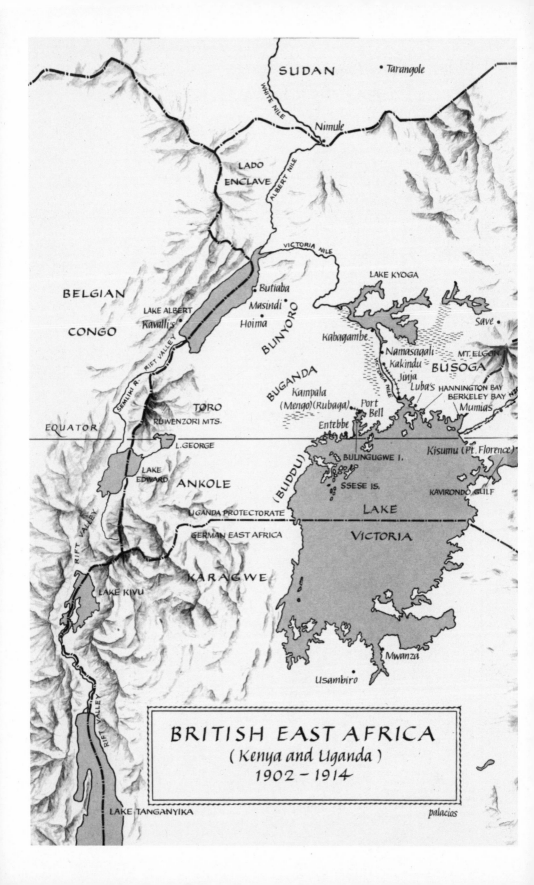

BRITISH EAST AFRICA
(Kenya and Uganda)
1902–1914

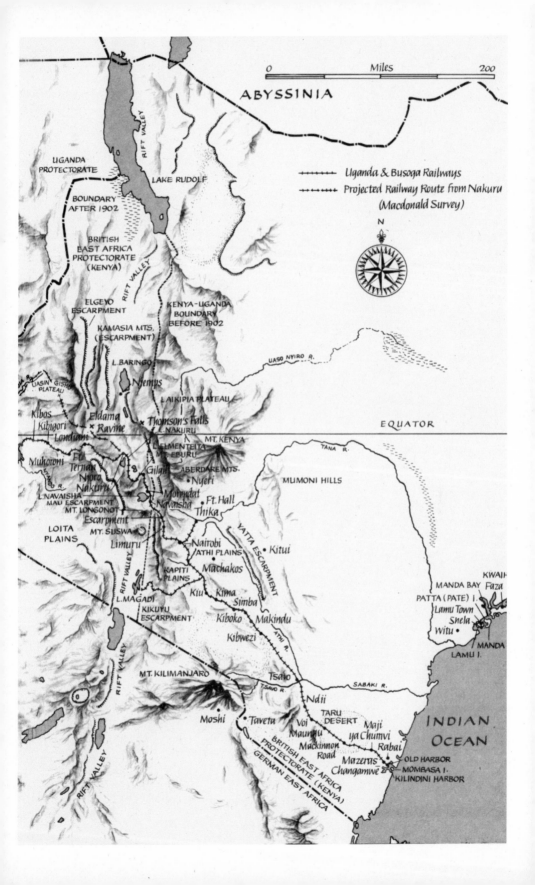

FOREWORD

What it will cost no words can express;
What is its object no brain can suppose;
Where it will start from no one can guess;
Where it is going to nobody knows.
What is the use of it none can conjecture;
What it will carry here none can define;
And in spite of George Curzon's superior lecture,
It clearly is naught but a lunatic line.

This splendid poetic rant by the radical British MP Henry Labouchere is probably better known than the railway it describes. But, in fact, the line from Mombasa on the Indian Ocean up to Uganda and to what became Nairobi, was a great success. The result of one of the most complicated episodes in ninteenth-century imperial, and indeed railway, history was the creation of what became two independent countries, Uganda and Kenya.

But the story does not begin in the nineteenth century. In his thorough and eminently readable book, replete with fascinating stories and personalities, Charles Miller goes back over a millennium to describe the story of the coastal civilization round Mombasa and the island of Zanzibar, which was intimately linked with Oman on the Arabian peninsula through the vagaries of the monsoon winds that enabled sailors to sail rapidly for half the year and equally speedily the other way for the other half. But until the late nineteenth century, the interior, inhabited by warring tribes, was treated by the inhabitants of the coast as a source of slaves.

European imperialism had come early to the coast with the Portuguese in the early sixteenth century, but by the middle of the nineteenth century, the whole of East Africa had become a cockpit for the rival Imperial ambitions of the British, the French, the Germans and even King Leopold II of Belgium, who personally owned the whole Congo. All realized that, as one British official put it: "stations in the interior are untenable without a territorial footing on the coast". The whole unappetizing process of imperialism in East Africa was described by the historian Margery Perham as "a lot of greedy, quarrelsome children in a school playground... Britain was the rather aloof child in the corner", for until the late 1880s the British were unwilling to commit government money, let alone troops.

Eventually, belatedly, the British—or rather imperialists like Lord Rosebery and the Marquess of Salisbury—woke up to the fact that, as Miller puts it, "whatever Power dominates Uganda dominates the Nile; the master of the Nile rules Egypt; the ruler of Egypt holds the Suez Canal, and, indirectly, the key to India". It did not help opponents that the Germans were building a railway from the coast through what is now Tanzania and that the French had sent an expeditionary force east into Sudan.

Construction of the six hundred miles of the railway itself was a triumph of guts, engineering ingenuity and sheer persistence, involving major obstacles such as the Mau escarpment that was 9,000 feet high requiring twenty even viaducts, as well as horrors like the Taru, not a desert, but "more like a dense forest of wire-bristled, man-high, scrubbing brushes". The result, compounded by a two-year drought, was sweeping epidemics of diseases such as smallpox in what was a truly imperial venture. Virtually all the equipment, including the rails, sleepers, bridges and the locomotives, was imported from India, as were most of the workers, for the locals were thought of, not unreasonably, as idle, useless and prone to desertion. The Indians remained, to be the forbears of the thousands thrown out by Idi Amin and who have proved such a positive source of immigrants to Britain.

However, the most dramatic episode was the battle at Tsavo—which translates as slaughter in the local language—against two aged, enormous eight-foot lions who killed over a hundred workers before they were shot by a railway engineer. One Lieutenant-Colonel Patterson needed no fewer than seven bullets to kill one of them, though it is said he was prouder of the long and complicated bridge he built over the river itself.

There may have been logic to this lunacy, but alas, the railway has decayed. Today, as one Kenyan railwayman puts it, "If you are in a hurry in this country you take a bus not a train" and the Chinese have just begun construction on a replacement which, hopefully, will reduce the journey from Mombasa to Nairobi from thirteen to three hours.

                                        – Christian Wolmar & Nicholas Faith, 2015

PROLOGUE:
DAMNOSA HEREDITAS

On December 11, 1895, the British India Steam Navigation Company's two-thousand-ton S.S. *Ethiopia* crept at three knots beneath the dour battlements of Fort Jesus as she made one of her infrequently scheduled calls at the east African port of Mombasa. On the boat deck stood one of the few debarking passengers, a tall, trimly built man in his mid-thirties who carried himself with the diffident self-assurance of Victorian England's upper class. His name was George Whitehouse, and he looked about him with interest as the *Ethiopia*'s anchor chain rumbled out from its hawsehole. Shielding his eyes from the sun, Whitehouse took particular notice of the great fleet of Afro-Oriental sailing vessels which were crammed into the claustrophobic Old Harbor, and which now seemed to be huddled about his own ship like a plague of waterborne locusts. For the most part, these craft were huge Arab dhows from the Persian Gulf, but others quickly moved out of the throng and attached themselves, leechlike, to the *Ethiopia*'s hull. They were cargo lighters and flimsy dugouts, manned by Swahili and Bajuni boatmen who wore sarongesque kikois and seemed engaged in a shrieking contest. When one of the dugouts made fast below the passenger gangway, Whitehouse clambered down and stepped awkwardly aboard.

The distance from shore was less than five hundred yards, but the leaking cockleshell had nearly swamped when Whitehouse finally jumped on to a flight of slime-coated concrete steps leading to the wharf at the edge of the town. Here, a small mob of ragged Arabs, Swahilis and Africans immediately began to clout and kick and claw and gouge and bite each other for Whitehouse's gear. One man tried to make off with a Gladstone bag but was stopped when someone else kneed him in the groin and vainly demanded ten rupees from Whitehouse for apprehending the thief. Presently the feebler contenders were driven off and Whitehouse followed a bleeding, laughing procession of luggage bearers along the wharf to the foot of Vasco da Gama Street. This narrow alley was Mombasa's principal thoroughfare, the only one, in fact, worthy of the name. It climbed a somewhat steep incline which Whitehouse was relieved to discover he did not have to negotiate on foot. The private British company which had administered east Africa before that region officially joined the Empire had laid down a dainty cobwebbing of rails in Mombasa to accommodate a sort of Toonerville pushcart service for the convenience of the city's few whites. Each vehicle, driven by African manpower, was a midget tramcar with a pair of back-to-back seats beneath a canvas awning; one could call it a trolley with a fringe on top. Such a carriage now awaited Whitehouse.

The Vasco da Gama Street branch of the line wound its way upwards between two closely packed rows of buildings: warehouses, Government offices and coral-lime residences occupied mainly by Mombasa's wealthier Arab and Indian families. These homes stood two or three storeys high. Their windows were barred and shuttered, and their arched doors—made of mvule, a rocklike indigenous timber—had ham-sized iron padlocks to guard against breaking and entering. From the upper end of the cramped boulevard rose a diminutive sun-bleached minaret toward which the tramcar clacked laboriously in a formidable traffic jam.

Whitehouse could not decide whether the density of this throng was more arresting than its color. Collisions were barely avoided with lurching Swahilis who wore gaudy kikois or nightshirt-like kanzus and brightly striped vests. The tramcar was continually nudged by white-robed Arabs perched on bobbing Muscat donkeys that were slightly smaller than Great Danes. Sometimes there would be a halt of five minutes or longer, as a string of heavily laden camels, driven by a bean-pole Somali in a brilliantly-hued wraparound cloak, plodded across the tracks ahead. Female garb seemed to glow. Indian saris ran a silken spectrum. The Swahili women were swathed in enormous envelopes of Manchester cotton bearing all manner of gaily printed patterns: caged lions, pineapples, horses, palm trees, monkeys on poles. Even the women who glided by in the grim black buibuis of purdah suggested the carrying out of exotically sinister errands. Tiny gold studs flashed from nostrils, ankles and necks. Bald heads of both sexes, shaved for cleanliness and coolness, reflected the intense glare of the sun. Everyone seemed to be eating a betel-nut sandwich; the nut was encased in a green leaf and the chewers spat big gouts of scarlet juice into the street, itself long stained in that hue. The smell of fresh human excrement rose from open drains to challenge

Whitehouse's breathing. Beggars with corkscrew limbs and missing faces thrust their dirt-caked bowls from a hundred hidden doorways. The scene was one of torpid vitality, bespeaking Asia more than Africa.

Not far from the minaret, Vasco da Gama Street crested the bluff, some sixty feet above the Old Harbor. Whitehouse gave the tram-car driver a handful of pice and made his way to the Customs House where he would pass through the wringer of the bureaucracy which had already taken root in England's newest colonial possession. Within five minutes he found himself almost awash in perspiration. His white linen trousers, waistcoat and jacket hung from his body like wet dishrags; his cork topee and red flannel spine pad were sodden lumps of blotting paper. This was not caused entirely by the sun; thanks to the Indian Ocean monsoon, the heat in Mombasa, even during December, could seldom be called intolerable. But Victorian England's greatest contribution to discomfort in the tropics, the corrugated iron house, easily did the work of a Turkish bath. Whitehouse noticed that the Goan customs clerk sat behind a lectern-like desk with a forty-five-degree slope which allowed his sweat to cascade freely to the ground without smearing the ink on the quadruplicate entry forms he filled out.

Leaving the Customs House, Whitehouse walked to another corrugated iron kiln a few hundred yards away. Designed to resemble a bungalow, it stood beneath an outsize Union Jack. This was the Mombasa residence of Sir Arthur Hardinge, H.M. Commissioner for the British East Africa Protectorate, who normally made his headquarters on the island of Zanzibar. Whitehouse was made welcome here with the few amenities that the indigent administration of a remote colonial outpost could afford. They were few indeed. Rare was the European in Mombasa who served his guests a steak dinner, all local "beef" having been butchered from camels which had died in the streets. Vegetables, even when boiled, presented a risk to untrained stomachs. Tea was deprived of its flavor with tinned milk. But one could at least have a good wash; Whitehouse squeezed into a galvanized tin tub, not much larger than a bucket, and sloshed himself down with tepid muddy water. Another luxury awaited him on the veranda: a tray bearing a choice of whisky and Holland beer. Whitehouse decided on the latter. Like all malt drinks shipped from Europe down the Red Sea, this beer had been spiked with a chemical preservative which tended to act like the blow of a closed fist. But it was no less refreshing.

The veranda, too, offered a sort of balm. Here, on one of the town's highest points, Whitehouse could fully appreciate the natural ventilating system of the monsoon as it coasted steadily in from across two thousand miles of Arabian Sea and Indian Ocean to blunt the vindictive edge of the equatorial sun. Encircling the house, the veranda also offered something like a gull's-eye view of Mombasa itself. What Whitehouse saw was an island, some ten square miles in area. Much of it was masked off by coco palms, mango, almond and baobab trees and an occasional stand of acacias; but the city's actual layout—what there was of it—came easily into perspective. Nearby, along the crest of the bluff, the unprepossessing Government House was duplicated in miniature by perhaps two dozen more corrugated iron boxes, in which Mombasa's European officials and businessmen made their homes. A few of these houses boasted English-style gardens which seemed gratuitous amid the surrounding profusion of bougainvillea, oleander, frangipani, jacaranda and Nandi flame. A cricket pitch had been laid down here; now and then a bush pig or a baboon would scamper across its grass, although Whitehouse had yet to see any of the puff adders which, according to old Africa hands aboard the *Ethiopia,* proliferated squirmingly on the island.

To the north and west, in the direction of the narrow Macupa creek separating Mombasa from the mainland, the African quarter sprawled out in sleepy disarray. Some fifteen thousand Africans and Swahilis, the bulk of the town's population, lived here, in primitively tidy wattle-daub shanties that were roofed with the plaited coconut leaf called makuti. (A few families had substituted flattened paraffin tins which afforded equal measures of status and sweat.) In this section, Whitehouse also noticed scattered fanfares of color: fruit and vegetable stalls that spilled over with tomatoes, chillies, maize, beans, cassava, limes, lemons, mangoes, guavas and the small but supremely juicy Zanzibar oranges. About two miles due west, behind a green-gold fringe of coco palms, he was able to make out the azure blanket of the vast inlet known as Kilindini—Swahili for "deep water."

Strolling to the other side of the veranda, Whitehouse looked directly down the bluff at the Arab town, a huddle of stone and coral-lime houses lying almost in the shadow of Fort Jesus. The Old Harbor itself was barely visible for the screen of fish weirs and the forest of dhow masts that sprouted from the water. At least three hundred Persian Gulf bagallas and booms bobbed sluggishly at their moorings, looking bloated and deformed with their swollen waists and towering sterns. Under canvas, these craft cut a different figure, and their arrival in Mombasa every autumn was something of an extravaganza. Not many sights could match the ungainly splendor of some twenty to thirty dozen seagoing fat ladies lurching crazily toward port, their lateen sails inflated into great crescent-shaped balloons by the urgent northeast monsoon. At these times, the dhows' vaulting poop decks would be emblazoned with bright pennants that snapped jauntily from barber-pole jackstaffs and from the oversize basketlike toilets which swayed precariously beneath after rails. Turbaned crews would set up hideous dins on ceremonial drums, gongs and conch-shell horns. The Persian Gulf fleet was an ambassador from a pre-Biblical age.

Indeed, Mombasa's entire cyclorama reeked of the past. Yet the city had also begun to show a few ravages of the Industrial Revolution and the disruptive ways of the white man. Its streets and natural surroundings brought together sophistication and savagery, vitality and languor, comfort and peril, loveliness and squalor. The blend of these ingredients gave forth the heady pong of romance.

But Whitehouse was in no mood to appreciate it. He had looked on far too many tropical vistas to wax lyrical over Mombasa, and while he was by no means esthetically numb, his professional reflexes tended to transform scenes of natural glory into mathematical equations and the laws of physics. For Whitehouse was neither painter nor poet nor novelist nor travel writer nor gentleman hunter nor naturalist. Strictly speaking, he was not even a colonial official, although he did draw his salary from the Foreign Office. Only a few weeks earlier, he had been appointed Chief Engineer in charge of building a railway from the coast to Lake Victoria in Uganda. And, as he looked about him, he might well have wondered whether Whitehall had not saddled him with an impossible task.

What Whitehouse saw in Mombasa was the gateway to an enigma. The right of way through the interior seemed shrouded in a dense fog of ignorance. His superiors in London had been able to give Whitehouse little more than a guess as to the path the tracks must follow. All he had as a guide were the findings of a preliminary survey which had been completed three years earlier. A great deal of time and effort, it was true, had gone into that undertaking; the leader of the survey party was an engineer of recognized competence. Yet no one had tried to pretend that the recommendations were anything but tentative. Railway experts who studied the projected route agreed unanimously that it amounted to a sketch map that would require substantial filling in before construction could begin.

Ordinarily, a sketch map might barely have sufficed. Whitehouse himself, while building railways in South America, Mexico, India and South Africa, had become familiar with the not infrequent necessity of adapting original survey routes to unforeseen demands of terrain. Now, however, he was being told to carry his tracks across six hundred miles of land which in effect had been given no more than a cursory glance. In all likelihood he would find that certain sections of the route traversed country that had not even been explored. This handicap could also be overcome, but it needed time, and Whitehouse had not the time to spare. Every memorandum he received from the Foreign Office reiterated the urgency of reaching the lake with the utmost despatch. He had been given four years to complete the task, but the Railway Committee was openly voicing the expectation that this deadline could be met much earlier.

Whitehouse was not completely handcuffed and blindfolded. Caravans of the private company had made numerous journeys to the lake along a trail originally laid down by Arab and Swahili traders, and much of the projected railway route followed the same track. But what little Whitehouse could learn of the rough corridor was sobering at best. Directly behind Mombasa lay a desert. Although not large as deserts go—its area was only about twenty-five hundred square miles—it was waterless and poorly mapped. As a rule, caravans tried to skirt it. The railway must cross it. Beyond, the route punched through some three hundred miles of gradually rising savanna and scrub country that teemed with lions, whined with tsetse flies and breathed malaria. After this came a ragged volcanic highland region that was bisected, as if with a cosmic meat cleaver, by the fifty-mile-wide Great Rift Valley. Explorers had described the Rift as offering an unsurpassed vista of natural grandeur, but Whitehouse could only think of it geologically, as a fault in the earth's surface which challenged him to perform an engineering miracle. And even if his construction gangs could somehow manhandle the rails over the valley's near-vertical, two-thousand-foot escarpments, there remained still another hundred miles to the lake, a last lap consisting mainly, it was believed, of spongelike quagmire.

This fragmentary information was the limit of Whitehouse's familiarity with the route he was expected to follow. To all practical purposes, the tracks of the railway would be laid down across a six-hundred-mile question mark.

Indeed, the scant knowledge which Whitehouse's own Government possessed of its new African colonial hinterland had prompted many Englishmen to question the need for building a railway through this howling wilderness. Why was it urgent to reach the lake? Why must the lake be reached at all? Who would benefit from the line? How would it pay for itself? Was the British taxpayer to underwrite the estimated £3 million cost of construction without expecting a return? These questions had been put in Parliament, with unusual acerbity, by a strong minority of Liberals, Radicals and Irish Nationalists. Characterizing the railway as a "gigantic folly," this articulate and influential body of British public opinion had been unmoved by the assurances of Lord Salisbury's Unionist Government that the line would stimulate commerce, open east Africa to settlement and destroy the slave trade. Above all, the Opposition had repudiated—and furiously excoriated—the chief rationale for building the railway: that it would serve as an arm of imperial strategy, enabling Britain to control the upper waters of the Nile and thereby maintain her hold on Egypt and the Suez Canal. Here was rampant jingoism at its most brazen.

For in the last analysis the issue was not the railway at all but east Africa itself. Deft maneuvering in 1894 and early 1895 by Liberal Imperialists under the then Prime Minister, Lord Rosebery, had secured for Britain nearly half a million square miles of territory between the Indian Ocean and the upper Nile. Salisbury's Tory Unionists had since come into power and consolidated Rosebery's gains, successfully concluding a long and intense battle with a decisive victory for the Empire over the coalition of opponents known as the "Little England" faction. Parliamentary debate on annexation of the region had witnessed a flood tide of British anti-imperialist sentiment. Acquisition by Britain of overseas territories had never before been the focus of quite so heated a controversy; east Africa touched off clashes as bitter as any in England's political history. So fierce had been the struggle to thwart establishment of the Uganda and East Africa Protectorates that even the question of Irish Home Rule had for a time been relegated to secondary importance. Opposition Members had demanded to know how it was possible to justify the occupation of what they called Britain's "damnosa hereditas." By what right did England assert mastery over thousands upon thousands of unlettered African tribesmen? How could Lord Salisbury and his Cabinet, quite obviously in the dark as to east Africa's potential, if indeed it had a potential, maintain so lofty and unyielding a stand that the country must be held? What resources did the land offer? Where were its markets? How could white men make their homes in a part of the world where the rays of the sun alone were known to shorten life? What strategic purpose would retention accomplish except to buttress a costly and self-serving imperial vainglory?

Even before it became British soil, east Africa for a century had brought England nothing but aggravation. Leaders of Government since Pitt's first ministry in 1783 had consistently sought to avoid official responsibilities in the region. Why, then, almost overnight as it were, had this measureless and apparently profitless spawning ground of disease and death been deemed indispensable to the security of the Empire?

What circumstances, in fact, could ever have involved Britain with east Africa in the first place?

PART I:
FLUTE OUT OF TUNE

MOMBAZA

1

IVORY, APES AND OWEN

*"A good Lamu man has a thousand
wiles; so a bad Lamu man,
what will he be like?"*

The same monsoon breezes which air-conditioned Mombasa for George Whitehouse also served, over many millennia, as the key to foreign exploitation of east Africa. As far into the past as human knowledge can grope, this seasonal wind has been breathing back and forth across the Indian Ocean with metronome regularity. Local sailors know the monsoon by its two Swahili names. Between October and April, when blowing down from the northeast, it is called the kazkazi; when it veers on a 180-degree angle and retraces its invisible path for the next six months, it becomes the kuzi. Although brisk and at times vigorous, neither kazkazi nor kuzi can be called tempestuous, and both drive as steadily as well-tended dynamos. Until the age of steam, one could think of the monsoon as a sort of meteorological paving machine which converted the Indian Ocean into a boulevard for whatever maritime nations chose to ply it in their pursuit of commercial or imperial expansion on the east African coast.

For many centuries, political domination of this land was not considered worth the effort of the outsiders. Trade was the major inducement. Over a period of more than four thousand years before the birth of Christ, merchant sailors from India, the Persian Gulf and the eastern Mediterranean were utilizing the monsoon in a spirited commerce with east

Africa's coastal inhabitants. What drew these venturesome businessmen were natural resources at once exotic and profitable. A single dhow of eighty tons could take on sufficient elephant tusks to furnish every room in a maharajah's palace with ivory chairs and tables, enough rhino horns to keep a dozen sultans in aphrodisiacs for a year. Slaves and concubines were easily obtained on the coast. There was a thriving trade in tortoise shell, favored by cabinet makers for inlay work. The perfume manufacturers of the Orient paid huge sums for diminutive flagons of the ambergris spewed up by stranded whales on beaches between Mogadishu and Mombasa. Just behind the Benadir coast—present-day Somalia—lay an inexhaustible wealth of cinnamon, frankincense and myrrh; Cape Guardafui, at the tip of Africa's "horn," was long known as the Cape of Spices.

Far to the south, at the port of Sofala, in what has since become Mozambique, the dhows took on cargoes of gold which had been extracted from the almost legendary mines of Ophir in the interior. It is believed that Ophir was the ancient and hardly less mysterious city of Zimbabwe, whose ruins still baffle archaeologists. But the working of gold is known to have been one of Africa's earliest industries. Perhaps the most familiar and probably the most beguiling reference to this trade is found in the Book of Kings: "And Hiram sent in the navy ... with the servants of Solomon. And they came to Ophir and fetched from thence gold, four hundred and twenty talents, and brought it to King Solomon ... once in three years came the navy of Tharshish bringing gold and silver, ivory, and apes and peacocks."

By way of payment, the foreign merchants brought in cotton cloth, axes, spearheads, knives, flint glass, ghee, wheat, rice, sesame oils, wines and other manufactured or processed goods. In modern eyes, these imports may seem to suffer by comparison, at least for their lack of glamour, but to the industrially immature peoples of the coast they were of inestimable value. Neither party to a barter contract was likely to feel that he had been euchred. Kazkazi and kuzi wafted with them the sweet smell of success.

To Europe, this trade wind was something of a trade secret for nearly five thousand years, although the curtain was drawn back briefly some time between the first and third centuries A.D., when an Alexandrine Greek sailor made a long voyage down the coast. His book, *The Periplus of the Erythraean Sea* (meaning a pilot's guide to the Indian Ocean) described the flourishing east African commerce in detail, but it did not bring on a stampede of gold- and ivory-hungry Europeans. The anonymous author had picked the wrong time to write his prospectus, for the so-called dark ages were then overtaking the West, while a not dissimilar stagnation was concurrently settling over the coast itself. No one is altogether sure how the latter hibernation came to pass, although a principal cause was probably a prolonged period of raids on the coastal towns by warlike tribes from the interior. At about this same time, east Africa also lost one of its larger export outlets, southern Arabia, which staggered in the throes of a lengthy economic depression touched off, it is believed, by the bursting of a great reservoir which transformed the already harsh existence in that land to bare survival. Such disasters were not conducive to trade, and east Africa as a member of the Indian Ocean community fell into a coma that lasted more than five hundred years.

*

What awakened the coast from its uneasy slumber was Islam—or more specifically, the death of the Prophet in 632 and the ensuing clashes among splinter groups asserting rightful succession to Mohammed's spiritual stewardship. Persia and Arabia in particular did not seem big enough to hold the two main sects, known as Shias and Sunnis, whose bitter conflicts resulted in a wave of Sunni migrations to east Africa that were not unlike the later Puritan exodus to New England. It is hard to say which dhow was the Muslim *Mayflower*—we have evidence of amoebic settlements springing up on the Benadir coast and the Lamu archipelago as early as the seventh century—but all these pilgrim fathers were responsible for the first foreign-ruled dominion in east Africa.

Known as Zinj—a Persian word meaning land of the black people—this realm was not really an empire as we understand the word. Perhaps it would be better described as a loosely knit confederation of some dozen-odd city-states, scattered like small change along two thousand miles of littoral and seldom if ever pledging allegiance to a single ruler. At first predominantly Persian in culture, Zinj gradually took on an Arab personality with a steady influx of immigrants from sheikdoms along the Red Sea, the Hadramaut and Oman. All these colonists, Persian and Arab alike, gave the coast a remarkable face-lifting.

From the very outset, Zinj enjoyed a robust economic health. The settlers cultivated the land and harvested the sea, but the lifeblood of their prosperity was the same foreign commerce that had attracted their forbears. This trade underwent certain marked changes. While gold, ivory and spices continued as the leading exports, they now fetched higher prices, partly because of a tariff system and probably because Persian and Arab middlemen could bring to bear a keener business acumen than had less shrewd African merchants. The greater profits in turn permitted a vastly broader range of imports, which reflected the colonists' high living standards and cultivated tastes. The dhows brought in carpets and silks from Persia, cut gems, bracelets, necklaces and gold and silver ornamentation from India, silver plate and tempered steel swords from the Levant. Fine porcelain, in great demand, arrived in the holds of Chinese junks which made regular voyages to the coast for several centuries. Splendid mansions mushroomed. Built of wood, cut stone or coral and lime, these houses had pillared verandas and arched porticos, and they girdled spacious courtyards that glowed in smotherings of oleander, jasmine and roses. Indoor furnishings bragged tastefully. Alongside the polished crystal glassware on any well-set table lay silver cutlery and emerald-encrusted gold fingerbowls. Retiring for the night, one mounted a silver stepladder to reach an elevated bedstead of ivory-inlaid rosewood. Gold-embroidered silk robes were everyday garb. Thumb-sized rubies set off the silver hilts of the curved, razor-sharp jembias worn at every waist. Some towns had their own mints, which struck coinages of silver and copper. The historian Basil Davidson has likened such places as Kilwa, Pemba and Mombasa to "'city empires' in the same sense as medieval Venice or Genoa."

*

While it must not be supposed that Zinj was a millionaires' club, few went hungry. Ibn Batuta, the great fourteenth-century Moroccan traveler, describes the typical diet of the typical town of Mogadishu: "The food of these people is rice cooked with butter ... With it they serve side dishes, stews of chicken, meat, fish, and vegetables. They cook unripe bananas in fresh milk, and serve them as a sauce. They put curdled milk in another vessel with peppercorns, vinegar and saffron, green ginger and mangoes." As an afterthought he remarks that the citizens of Mogadishu are "very fat and corpulent." Even the poverty-stricken could find the living easy. Ibn Batuta mentions a Kilwa sultan who literally gave the silks off his back to a beggar, and threw in a substantial gift of slaves and ivory. Almost apologetically, Ibn Batuta adds that in Kilwa "the majority of presents are of ivory: gold is very seldom given."

Despite (or possibly because of) its opulence, Zinj was often depicted by outsiders as a bizarre never-never land. This image may or may not have been deserved, although it must have resulted at least in part from the same notions of Africa that inspired medieval European cartographers to people the continent with comic-strip bestiaries. One Masudi, who traveled down the coast in the tenth century, declared that Zinjians rode oxen that could gallop as swiftly as horses. A fifteenth-century writer named Abu al-Mahasin had an alarming account of an ape invasion; in Mombasa, he said, "the monkeys have become rulers ... When they enter a house and find a woman, they hold congress with her ... The people have much to put up with." Even the one European to report, none other than Marco Polo, asserted that the inhabitants "are so stout and large-limbed that they have the appearance of giants. ... They have big mouths and their noses are so flattened and their lips and eyes so big that they are horrible to look at. Anyone who saw them in another country would say that they were devils." Perhaps this extravagance can be forgiven since Marco Polo never traveled within a thousand miles of Zinj.

The settlers themselves do not seem to have been put out of countenance by foreign misrepresentations, being occupied as they were with concoctions of their own. Most city-states had what might be called historical societies whose records, largely endless catalogues of begats and battles, uniformly reveal a singular gift for fabrication. Perhaps the most representative is the so-called Pate Chronicle, which covers events in the Lamu archipelago from the year 1204 to the late nineteenth century, long after the Zinj era itself had ended. This work would do credit to the *Thousand and One Nights*. We read of how a Pate sultan, fleeing from enemy dhows, scribbled hastily on a piece of paper and threw the note overboard, causing a shoal to spring up and halt the pursuing fleet; of how a maiden, about to be raped by a soldier, called out to the earth, "Open that I may enter," whereupon the earth obeyed and the soldier "gave up the profession of arms" on the spot. There is the islands' own Robert the Bruce, an aspiring explorer whose expeditions unfailingly ended in shipwreck, and who was pondering a new career when he observed the successful perseverance of a cockroach trying to scale a bathroom wall. "I have been outdone by that cockroach," declared the young man, "for it fell twice and tried a third time. God has sent it to teach me a lesson. I must set forth again." He did, and discovered an island of silver ore.

But the Pate Chronicle—indeed, all local histories—are largely records of scheming and aggression, lavishly spiced with episodes in which "Bwana Bakari stayed at Amu and the Pate people did not like him and made a plot to dethrone him." ... "When Fumoluti seized his sword he struck Suleimani, who ran away and fell, outside, split in two halves." ... "Thus it was that Pate conquered the country of Manda in one day..." For Zinj may have been history's most quarrelsome assemblage of feudal states. Diplomacy suggests a kaleidoscope of shifting alliances and palace coups animated by lust for power, relish for intrigue, damaged pride and simple orneriness. The Lamu archipelago was one of the busiest arenas of conflict, with its islands and towns of Lamu, Shela, Pate, Manda and Faza forever at one another's throats—a condition that might correspond roughly to hostilities among the five boroughs of New York. No one here, at least according to the chronicles, was ever to be trusted: "A good Lamu man has a thousand wiles; so a bad Lamu man, what will he be like?" ... "The Pate people weave discord, then it is unravelled, and they ask, 'Who is it that began the quarrel?'" A war could be fought because of someone's failure to open a city's gates to visitors. One Manda elder, offended because he had not been notified of a council meeting, betrayed his country to Pate. A persistent call to arms rose from flaws to the title to the ceremonial brass horn of Lamu, which was pilfered from its rightful owners, whoever they may have been, with tedious regularity. Hostilities once broke out when Pate shipwrights at work on a dhow ignored warnings that their hammering disturbed the sleep of a Manda prince.

There was a lyrical quality to all these affrays. When surprise attack was deemed discourteous (which is to say impossible), declarations of war could take the form of verse, with opposing generals shouting metric insults for the better part of a day. Wars could end abruptly if the combatants became bored or if a heavy run of turtles called for the services of all available fishermen. Cease-fires were arranged with no more trouble than it took to shake a bag of sequins, recognized throughout Zinj as a flag of truce.

To whatever extent one chooses to believe the chronicles and other imprecise records, this was life in Zinj for nearly five hundred years: commerce, gracious living, intrigue and war in an atmosphere of Arthurian pageantry. It was a quaint and unorthodox little realm, apparently possessing fewer obnoxious features than do most imperial undertakings. Zinjians may have thrived on armed conflict, but they fought only among themselves and evinced little desire for territorial aggrandizement. What they had they held, and if one town forced another into subjection for a few years, the second community would have its turn in due course. One might almost say that these city-states saw their struggles as a sort of diversion, in which few innocent bystanders came to harm. It was all, so to speak, in the family.

Zinjians were also unique in that they made no real effort to impose their ways on the original inhabitants. Islam and Arab customs did come to shape the character of the coast, but the process was not one of decree; it came instead from absorption through widespread intermarriage among settlers and Africans, producing the people and the lingua franca called Swahili. Here, too, the Zinjians showed a striking aspect of their imperial personality: an indifference to racial immaculacy; their Swahili descendants were accepted on an equal footing in all walks of life. Certainly repression and inhumanity existed, mainly in the form of slavery, but this was not a Zinj or even an Arab innovation. Nor did the sale of slaves run into large numbers. (That would come under a different rule.) If Zinj could not be called a Utopia, it nonetheless gave a respectable account of itself as empires go.

"Even the birds of the heavens were shot down."

The decline and fall came abruptly. In 1497, while making his famous voyage to the East, Vasco da Gama cast an eye over Zinj and recognized a worthwhile claim for the King of Portugal. As a result, the ensuing two centuries bore witness to Europe's first imperial venture in eastern Africa. Portugal regarded the coast not so much as a land to be developed but as the site of convenient provisioning stations for her own caravels bound to and from India. Little more was asked of Kilwa, Mombasa, Lamu and the other coastal cities than the supply of fresh water and stores for the transient ships. The little more, however, consisted of fealty to the Portuguese monarch and annual tribute payments amounting to three thousand mizcals of gold (slightly less than $1,000) per town. These requirements were enforced with an energy so draconian that it was not long before the Portuguese had won for themselves the most noisome image ever achieved by a conqueror of east Africa. It is almost an axiom of the imperial dynamic that irrespective of an overlord's unpopularity, many of his customs become absorbed by the subject peoples, but Portuguese rule in east Africa is an exception. One indication of the singular loathing for Pax Lusitania may be seen today in the all but total absence of anything Portuguese in the artifacts or behavior of the present inhabitants of the Kenya and Tanzania coasts. Apart from one or two more or less indestructible forts and the pastime of bullfighting on the island of Pemba, one would not know that Portuguese ships had even passed by.

By the accounts of their own chroniclers, the Portuguese appear at times to have found a certain sanctimonious enjoyment in mutilating the coast. After Kilwa "had been taken without opposition," wrote a member of the force commanded by Dom Francisco d'Almeida in 1505, "the Vicar-General and some of the Franciscan Fathers came ashore carrying two crosses and singing the Te Deum. They went to the palace, and there the cross was put down and the Grand-Captain prayed. Then everyone started to plunder the town..." Father Monclaro, a monk who accompanied the expedition of Francisco Barreto somewhat later, remarked casually that "we went to Pate, which was our principal destination, with intention to destroy it because of the harm which is done there to the Portuguese." Perhaps the most pleasure was taken in the sack of Mombasa, whose inhabitants had also resisted. Wrote a factor named Duarte Barbosa of Almeida's attack on the port in 1505: "The king of this city refused to obey the commands of the King our Lord, and through this arrogance he lost it, and our Portuguese took it from him by force ... They slew many of his people and also took captives many, both men and women ... Of gold and silver great booty was taken here ... and the town was left in ruins."

As soon as he was able, Mombasa's refugee sultan wrote a warning letter to his counterpart in Malindi: "This is to inform you that a great lord has passed through the town, burning it and laying it waste. He came to the town with such strength and was of such cruelty, that he spared neither man nor woman, old nor young, nay, not even the smallest child ... He not only killed and burnt men but even the birds of the heavens were shot down. The stench of the corpses is so great in the town that I dare not go there." This letter may possibly account in part for the fact that Malindi was the only coastal state to accept Portuguese conquest supinely. Within a decade of their arrival, the new rulers had sufficiently sacked, looted, burned, raped, tortured and beheaded to have transformed the entire coast into a banked volcano. It was only a matter of time before surly submission would give way to open revolt.

The first major outbreak occurred in 1586, when a Turkish admiral named Ali Bey sailed into Mombasa with a nondescript but heavily armed fleet of xebecs, galleys and dhows, and announced that he had been sent by the Sultan of Turkey to deliver the coast from the infidel. Although Ali Bey was in fact a notorious corsair who had been despatched by no one but himself, his arrival was greeted with great joy and voluntary donations of manpower. Within a few weeks he blasted the Portuguese from nearly all of their settlements and departed, drunk with success and the honors of a grateful populace and laden to the gunwales with loot. Caught napping, the Portuguese could retaliate only by sending a squadron from India to level the cities which had given aid and comfort to the Turk. This in turn served merely to whet Ali Bey's appetite for further action and a dividend of booty; in 1589 he returned to Mombasa, proclaiming his intention to drive the Portuguese from the coast forever. He might in fact have done so had not the Viceroy of India, on learning the news, acted swiftly and ordered an amphibious task force to Mombasa: twenty warships would blockade the harbor and hold Ali Bey under siege until troops landed and recaptured the town.

At this juncture, a deus ex machina of sorts materialized across the creek on the mainland: a sizable and bellicose Bantu tribe known as the Zimba, who sought entry into Mombasa in return for their services as anti-white mercenaries. The Mombasans did not know whether to cheer or hide, for the Zimba were celebrated cannibals who had been eating their way up the coast for a thousand miles, "sparing nothing," a Portuguese friar wrote later, "but such Cafres as adjoined themselves to their company in that design." There was no reason to believe that their hunger had been satisfied, but with several hundred Portuguese cannons trained on Mombasa just outside the harbor, the inhabitants had little option but to take the Zimba at their word. Accordingly, the gates of the city were thrown open and the Zimba promptly devoured everyone in sight, with the exception of a few dozen men and women who leaped into the sea, where they were disposed of by sharks and Portuguese arquebuses. Ali Bey also managed to survive, only to be captured by the first wave of assault troops and sent to Lisbon in chains, while the Zimba were wiped out shortly afterwards. Sophisticated weaponry had prevailed. Dislodging the imperialists was not going to be a simple affair.

*

But the oppressor's rule continued uneasy, and threats to the Portuguese did not spring only from Zinj and its sympathetic Muslim neighbors. It is at this time, in fact, that we see Britain's earliest and most tentative move toward east Africa. By the end of the sixteenth century, both England and Holland had begun to extend their mercantile arms eastward in fierce competition for control of trade in India and the Spice Islands. Portugal, having arrived there first, responded with bared fangs. In 1591, Sir James Lancaster, one of Queen Elizabeth's knighted filibusterers, took three ships to the Indian Ocean with the express purpose of breaking the Portuguese monopoly. The attempt began to bear fruit nine years later with the formation of the British East India Company, but Lancaster's maiden voyage almost came to grief near Zanzibar. Here he found "need to take good heed of the Portugals: for while we lay here the Portugall admiral of the coast from Melinde to Mozambique, came to view and to betray our boat if he could have taken at any time advantage, in a gallie Frigate of ten tunnes with 8 or 9 oares on a side. Of the strength of which Frigate and their treacherous meaning we were advertised by an Arabian Moore which came from the king of Zanzibar divers times unto us ..." According to Lancaster, the Portuguese also launched an anti-British propaganda campaign among the Zinjians; from other friendly "Moores" he learned "of the false and spitefull dealings of the Portugals toward us, which made them beleeve that we were cruell people and man-eaters."

Portuguese hostility was of course justified, for Lancaster had not come to east Africa on a goodwill mission; whenever possible, he himself sought to cut out prizes from among enemy shipping. He was also attracted by the coast, and his description of Zanzibar could not have failed to whet the interest of his fellow mercantile adventurers. "This place for the goodnesse of the harborough and watering," he wrote, "and plentifull refreshing with fish, whereof we tooke great store with our nets, and for sundry sorts of fruits of the countrey, as Cocos and others, which were brought to us by the Moores, as also for oxen and hennes, is carefully to be sought for by such of our ships, as shall hereafter passe that way." These remarks, published in Hakluyt's *Principal Navigations*, constitute the earliest known documentary evidence of Britain's reluctant preoccupation with east Africa's elusive potential as a commercial and strategic asset. Other British captains who stopped at coastal ports in 1608 and 1609 gave similarly favorable descriptions of harbor facilities and the abundance of provisions. They also commented on the continuing absence of Portuguese hospitality. Their visits, however, were premature by nearly two centuries.

*

Meanwhile, Portuguese proconsuls were experiencing few serene moments among their Jacobin subjects. Mombasa's behavior remained so fractious that by 1593 construction had begun on Fort Jesus, the colossus of all European defense works in eastern Africa. But Fort Jesus proved more useful as a status symbol than as an instrument of security. Before long it was in enemy hands, the adversary this time being one Yusuf bin Hassan, who also went by the name of Don Geronimo, having been ostensibly converted to Catholicism in his youth and later appointed Sultan of Mombasa as a reward for his good behavior. A double agent par excellence, Don Geronimo bin Hassan bided his time until an opportune moment in 1631, when he gathered three hundred Arab and Swahili soldiers, massacred every Portuguese in the city and took possession of the fort. News of his revolt touched off a general uprising along the coast, and although the Portuguese were able to recapture Fort Jesus by 1635, the beginning of the end of their empire was at hand.

For other bastions had also been crumbling. To secure the route to India, Portugal had not only annexed Zinj but certain strategic ports on the Persian Gulf, where she established large military and naval bases. By the early seventeenth century, these strongholds began to slip from the conqueror's grasp. In 1622, Persian armies re-entered Ormuz, and in 1651 a staggering blow was struck when the key city of Muscat fell to the Omani Arabs who had previously made it their capital. The loss of Muscat did not merely deprive Portugal of a strategic imperial linch-pin. It also gave new hope and heart to the subject peoples on the east African coast, who recognized in Oman an ally that could put a permanent end to their subjugation. Soon the imams of Muscat were receiving and responding to calls for succor, and in 1729—after a seventy-year struggle during which Fort Jesus exchanged hands like a baton in a relay race —the Portuguese were finally driven from the coast. Or, more precisely, from their Zinj holdings, for they retired south only as far as present-day Mozambique, to lick their wounds and build a more enduring if not more popular imperial edifice. But they never went back to Zinj.

"It is to me as clear as the sun that God has prepared the dominion of East Africa for the only nation on earth that has public virtue enough to govern it for its own benefit."

Zinj did not rise from its own ashes, for the Portuguese had thoroughly smashed up the once tight little empire. "In less than a hundred years of destructive effort," Davidson has remarked in his book *Africa in History,* "they had gone far to ruin the work of centuries." As late as 1811, a British naval surgeon visiting the coast could still observe that "the very touch of the Portuguese was death." However, the vacuum left by the European invaders was instantly filled by the Omani liberators. East Africa they regarded as theirs by right of conquest, although for the most part they preferred to rule in absentia, collecting the customary tribute from marionette sultans. This system of proxy government was not a success, for despite their religious and cultural bonds with Zinj, the Omani Arabs were foreigners. The coast people might welcome deliver-ance from Portugal, but subjection was subjection even if the overlord happened to be a fellow Muslim, and the imams of Muscat soon discovered that in their new colonies they held a tiger by the tail. For more than a century it required all their energies to keep from being eaten.

Not unexpectedly, the fountainhead of dissent was Mombasa, which by now had well earned the name Mvita, the island of war. Here, the Omani had committed a prodigious blunder in selecting as administrators a ferociously aristocratic family named Mazrui, whose members, considering themselves the rightful rulers of Mombasa, had no more intention of genuflecting to Muscat than they had to Lisbon. They complied with the ordinances governing fealty and tribute by ignoring them, except on the not infrequent occasions when an irate imam would seek to collect back taxes with an expeditionary force. The Mazrui would then show their teeth, lining the roofs of the city with spearmen, archers and tubs of boiling oil. Fort Jesus would bristle with whatever carronades, serpentines, culverins, falconets, blunderbusses and hackbuts the defenders could gather. As often as not, the Mazrui would hurl back the invader. When they failed, however, they would surrender with grace, reek with loyalty and wait with patience for the imam's Baluchi mercenaries to depart, at which moment they would renew their defiance. They knew how to express derision inventively. One Mazrui governor replied to a stern demand for overdue tribute with a handful of gunpowder, a ragged coat of mail and a wooden vessel used for measuring corn. The Dauphin of France had hardly showed more disdain when he sent his gift of tennis balls to Henry V.

Mazrui insurgency was successful largely because the Omani rulers—occupied as they were with staving off a continual two-pronged assault by fanatical Wahabi nomads from the desert and marauding Jawasmi pirate navies on the Persian Gulf—could ill afford the luxury of a permanent garrison in Fort Jesus. The best that Muscat could usually do was seek other friends on the coast. This was by no means difficult, since the Mazrui enjoyed little more popularity than did the imams, and because the old Zinjian relish for feuds and conspiracy had not flagged. Thus the ancient sport of intercity combat continued. The most savagely fought engagement was probably the battle of Shela. It took place around 1800 and saw Lamu substituting for Oman against Mombasa and Pate, although during a lengthy prelude of scheming, marked by the traditional exchanges of slander, there was some uncertainty over who was going to fight whom. Despite the enemy's numerical superiority, Lamu emerged the victor, thanks to the skillful application of witchcraft, if we are to believe the Pate Chronicle. According to that document, a Lamu sorcerer "made a brass pot and a brass gong and buried them underground. When he had made this charm the Pate people and the Mazaru'i were driven back and utterly overcome." This was confirmed many years later by a centegenarian eyewitness to the affray, who declared that the buried pot and gong "paralyzed the enemy so that they could not fight," while the spells cast by Pate and Mombasa were "nullified" by Lamu matchlocks. During the 1890s, the bleached bones of many of the battle's victims could be seen in the dune grass at Shela.

The victory, however, was only less stunning than it was rare. Mombasa for the most part held the upper hand in war as well as in peace; and with their free hand to misbehave, the Mazrui rather than the imams were considered the real power to be reckoned with on the coast.

*

After more than a century of enduring affront and frustration from its colonies, Oman suddenly found the tables turning in its favor, owing to an unrelated conflict, writ large, between two other imperial powers. On January 25, 1799, a letter was despatched from Cairo to Seyyid Sultan bin Ahmed, the reigning Imam of Muscat, "to inform you of the arrival of the French army in Egypt. As you have always been friendly you must be convinced of our desire to protect all the merchant vessels you may send to Suez." The letter was signed "Bonaparte" and enclosed another message, to be forwarded to Tippoo Sahib, the Anglophobic Sultan of Mysore in southern India. To this ruler, Napoleon spoke of his "numerous and invincible army, animated with the desire of delivering you from the iron yoke of England," and further urged that Tippoo Sahib "send to Suez some competent person who enjoys your confidence, and with whom I can confer."

It hardly need be said that Napoleon was not unduly troubled over the safety of Oman's merchant marine or the territorial integrity of Mysore. He was then preparing to invade India, and to succeed, he needed assistance. If Seyyid Sultan and Tippoo Sahib could be won over, Napoleon might bring off his master plan. Briefly stated, the objective was to send Mysore enough weaponry so that Tippoo Sahib could divert a substantial British force southwards while the French army, using Muscat as an advance base, kicked down India's back door. Tippoo Sahib was known to be ready and willing, if not yet able, to make common cause with the French; for twenty years he had been seeking arms from France to hurl against the hated British Raj. Seyyid Sultan, whom Bonaparte called "friendly" (possibly because he had a French physician), might have been described just as accurately as a cat that could jump either way. Yet the strategic location of Muscat gave that city such importance as a staging area in any attempt to wrest India from Britain, that Napoleon's goal of ruling the East could almost be said to have hinged on Seyyid Sultan. As for the Imam's response, Napoleon had reason to be sanguine. Seyyid Sultan was a typical Arab Machiavelli who had gained the throne by placing the rightful ruler, his brother, under preventive detention and then mislaying the key to the prison cell. He could not be expected to reject an entente which promised to resolve his dilemma with the maverick Mazrui.

But Seyyid Sultan was never given the opportunity to enlist with Bonaparte, for the letters from Cairo were intercepted by the British Agent in Mocha and forwarded instead to the Marquis of Wellesley, Governor General of India. Wellesley acted swiftly. While a British army was incorporating Mysore into the Empire (and liquidating Tippoo Sahib in the process), Seyyid Sultan found himself undergoing gentler treatment with the state visit of a high-ranking Indian Government official. In this instance, diplomacy was deemed more useful than military force, since a hub of British Indian policy had been to cultivate friendships, wherever possible, with the countries lying on the more exposed flanks of the land and sea routes to the East. Indeed, only a few months before Napoleon made his abortive overture, Wellesley had concluded a treaty with Seyyid Sultan, in which the latter pledged himself to British interests in India.

Under the terms of the pact, the Imam expressly forbade French ships and French citizens from entering Oman for the duration of Anglo-French hostilities, "nor shall they get even ground to stand upon, within this state." To reinforce the ban, it was further agreed that a factory of the British East India Company—with a large sepoy garrison—would be built at the port of Bandar Abbas on the Persian Gulf. But the most important clause had yet to be written. Early in 1800, Seyyid Sultan consented to the posting of "an English gentleman of respectability" as the full-time British Agent in Muscat. Whether or not the Imam realized it, Oman had become a client state of England.

Thanks, moreover, to Oman's own satellites in Mombasa and the other descendant-cities of Zinj, the treaty gave Britain her first foothold in east Africa. No one could have been expected to foresee that this tenuous extension of influence would eventually expand into an empire. At the turn of the nineteenth century, England's only real preoccupation with Africa lay at the southern tip of the continent. In 1795, the Cape of Good Hope had been wrested from its Dutch colonists, but not with a view to settlement or exploitation of natural resources. The sole purpose of the annexation had been to forestall a possible French move toward India from the south Atlantic. As for suzerainty over the east coast, and the grim terra incognita that sprawled out behind Mombasa, the mere thought of such a political-economic albatross would have been looked on as madness. Both the Foreign Office and the East India Company saw the treaty with the Imam simply as assurance that Oman would be placed out of bounds to Napoleon. As for Seyyid Sultan, he welcomed the alliance as his long-awaited chance to deal with the Mazrui from a position of strength. Yet the signatories could exercise only so much control over the future course of events, while the treaty they drew up proved to be the initial impulse in a long political chain reaction which, in the end, virtually forced east Africa down England's throat. The better part of a century was needed for this to happen, and twenty-nine consecutive British Ministries would fight it off manfully before yielding; but when the treaty was signed, the handwriting went on the wall.

*

The most perceptible shape of things to come was seen as early as 1824, when England established her first east African colony without knowing she had done so. This episode revolves around the so-called "Owen Protectorate," and illuminates a clash of outlooks which would simultaneously shape and confuse British policy in pre-colonial east Africa: a struggle between what might be called the schools of philanthropic expansionism and the more cautious imperialism by remote control.

The principal role was played by the Royal Navy's Captain William FitzWilliam Wentworth Owen, in command of two ships charting the east African coast for the Admiralty. On December 4, 1823, Owen's junior vessel, H.M.S. *Barracouta*, put into Mombasa for stores. Although the port was then under blockade by an Omani fleet preparatory to another siege, the Muscat admiral did not challenge *Barracouta*'s entry. The British warship was in a sense representing Oman and could be expected to do more harm than good to the Mazrui cause. But the defenders hoped otherwise. Thanks in no small measure to the Anglo-Omani treaty, they now found themselves with their backs closer to the wall than ever before, and in the visiting man-of-war they recognized an opportunity to beguile England away from the Imam. Hardly had *Barracouta*'s anchor taken hold on the harbor bottom than a delegation of Mazrui sheiks, garbed in their most splendid silks, appeared at the water's edge, seeking permission to board. Their objective was quite simple. Over cups of coffee served to them on the tarpaulin-shaded quarterdeck, they begged *Barracouta*'s commander, Vidal, for British protection against Oman. In return, said the senior sheik, Mombasa itself would be ceded to England.

To Vidal, the appeal was eloquent, enticing and altogether out of the question. Even if the squadron's orders had not been rigidly apolitical, Britain remained bound by treaty and interests to Oman. No low-ranking officer in his senses would put his career on the block by tampering with an instrument that touched on the security of India. Yet Vidal could at least find room to sympathize with Mombasa's hard-pressed defenders, and he sought to remove the sting from his reply by declaring that he needed twenty-four hours to consider the request. Next day, down with fever, he sent his first lieutenant, Thomas Boteler, ashore, with orders to decline the Mazrui proposal as gracefully as possible.

The meeting took place under lock and key in a small room in Fort Jesus. Before Boteler could get in a word, he was subjected to an outpouring of impassioned Mazrui oratory. "In an impressive manner," he later wrote, "they dwelt on the reiterated efforts of the Mombassians to maintain their small territory ... and on the heart-rending idea ... that their struggles must prove unavailing ... and their lives probably be sacrificed to the resentment of the Imaun of Muscat." At length, the senior sheik "concluded by requesting, in the name of himself and of the people of Mombas, that I would hoist on their castle the British flag"; whereupon he produced a gaudy banner of Mazrui design which seemed intended to resemble the Union Jack. This gave Boteler his chance to announce Vidal's polite but firm rejection of the offer, and the cordial tone of the meeting vanished instantly. Boteler even became concerned for his personal safety as Mazrui tempers flared. "So urgent were their importunities that I would grant their request, that at last I almost thought they would make me hoist the English flag, whether I would or not." But he managed to return to the *Barracouta* intact, and the vessel departed.

By now, the Mazrui had arrived at the conclusion that only one course remained open to them: they must run up the Union Jack regardless of the consequences, and in short order their inventive version of the flag was whipping defiantly over Fort Jesus. The sight left the Omani blockade commander with a conclusion of his own: Britain had betrayed her ally.

At about the same time, Captain Owen appeared to be confirming this impression at an audience with the incumbent Imam, Seyyid Said bin Sultan, while his own ship, H.M.S. *Leven*, stood at anchor in Muscat harbor on a courtesy call, if courtesy is the word. An intensely devout man, Owen can be seen in some respects as considering himself divinely ordained to strike a blow for freedom in Britain's recently declared war against slavery, and he now took pains to make this manifestly clear. After presenting Seyyid Said with a Bible translated into Arabic, he proceeded to hector the Imam on Oman's obligations to assist England in curbing the Indian Ocean slave traffic. He then ordered Seyyid Said to outlaw the trade in his domains within three years. And having delivered that ultimatum, he announced his intention of sailing at once to Mombasa, where he would bestow his official blessing on the Mazrui struggle for independence. "I should feel it my duty to my King to grant it to them," he wrote, "in which my principal motive would be the suppression of that hellish traffic."

On February 7, 1824, Leven worked into the Old Harbor while Owen gazed with some puzzlement at the flag flying over Fort Jesus. The following day, he was received at the fort by the rebel leaders, who admitted to having raised the flag without authorization and then went on to repeat their plea for British protection. Owen had little reason to esteem the Mazrui—he described the senior sheik as "an old dotard who had outlived every passion but avarice"—yet he had recognized in their revolt an opportunity to loosen the stranglehold of the slave trade on the coast. Accordingly, he informed the sheiks that, subject to the approval of his own Government, he would be pleased to welcome Mombasa into the Empire, and that in the meanwhile he "should have no objection to holding the place," provided that slavery be abolished forthwith. The exulting Mazrui accepted the terms on the spot, ceding not only Mombasa but some two hundred miles of coastline which may or may not have been theirs to give away. When the meeting adjourned, Owen ordered the Union Jack struck and replaced at once by an authentic flag, which climbed ceremoniously up the staff while a bosun's pipe squealed, sideboys stood to attention, a marine guard presented arms and the Leven's officers doffed their cocked hats.

*

In bullyragging Seyyid Said and granting even pro tem protection to the Mazrui, Owen had committed a breathtaking act of insubordination. It amounted to open defiance of the Imam, the Governor General of India, the Directors of the East India Company, the Lords of the Admiralty and the Foreign Office. But the scope of his disobedience did not perturb him. In a somewhat unsailorlike despatch to the Admiralty, he asserted that "I have been influenced by no personal motive nor interest whatever ... nor even by that which might be supposed to have the greatest charm for one in my profession, viz. the hope of obtaining some marked expression of their Lordships' approbation, but solely and conscientiously my endeavours have been so to use the powers given to me as should most conduce to the Honour of God and my King ..." Nor did he doubt for a moment that official endorsement of his annexation would be forthcoming: "It is to me as clear as the sun that God has prepared the dominion of East Africa for the only nation on earth that has public virtue enough to govern it for its own benefit and for the only people who take the revealed word for their moral law." Perhaps Owen's only real trouble was that he had been born three quarters of a century too soon.

Upon weighing anchor, Owen left behind his third lieutenant, a youthful South African named John James Reitz, as the first Governor of British East Africa. The Mazrui, in turn, faithfully honored their emancipation obligations under the agreement until Leven's royals disappeared below the horizon, at which moment they resumed their slaving with vigor. This was disconcerting to Reitz, hardly in a position to uphold Pax Britannica with an armed force composed of a midshipman, a marine corporal and three seamen. But he did protest lustily, which was all he could do, and the Mazrui, who genuinely liked the young officer, sought to placate him as best they could, giving him, among other things, a sizable plot of land which he named English Point. But Reitz was not a man to be won over with soothing words and gifts. Nor was he to be deterred from a projected inspection tour of England's new mainland possessions, despite Mazrui warnings that the summer rains were due and that the fever-breathing swamps would eat him alive. He put this down less to the sheiks' solicitude for him than to their obvious distaste for the idea of a British officer discovering the full extent of their slave dealings. On May 4, Reitz crossed Macupa Creek and vanished into the mangroves. On the 29th he returned on a litter, dying of malaria—"in a most awful state of delirium," as Owen subsequently learned. Today, one of Mombasa's larger inner harbors is named Port Reitz in his memory.

Command of the Protectorate now devolved on Mr. Midshipman George Philips, and relations with the Mazrui thenceforth became strained, if for no other reason than that the venerable intriguers could not have taken happily to rule—albeit nominal rule—by a beardless sixteen-year-old. They came to appreciate Philips even less when the youngster somehow managed to capture a slave dhow, liberate its human cargo and establish the first of the many freed-slave colonies that came to flourish along the coast under British guardianship some six decades later. Each of the former slaves was given a small plot of land on which he built a tiny grass hut and cultivated his own maize, millet and cassava crops. One visitor described this community as "a picture of perfect content," which may or may not have been gilding the lily slightly. Yet all things considered, England had no cause to be ashamed of her maiden imperial venture in east Africa.

*

For the time being, however, the enterprise amounted to little more than bravery and honor in a vacuum, for Seyyid Said had not been idle since Owen's visit—although he waited tactfully for several months before lodging a courteous but indignant protest with the British authorities in India. They reacted with consternation—and not merely to Owen's boorishness, or even to the flouting of the treaty. For Owen could hardly have been unaware, when he defied Seyyid Said, that he was throwing a heavy spanner into a fragile piece of political machinery. It so happened, as Owen well knew, that for over a decade, Britain had been seeking the Imam's cooperation in suppressing the Indian Ocean slave traffic. Just a year before *Leven* entered east African waters, the Bombay Government had managed to obtain Seyyid Said's signature on an agreement which put a limit on the area of the seaborne trade. This was a small concession, to be sure, but it nonetheless represented an important first step on a long and thorny diplomatic path. Since Seyyid Said held a near-monopoly on the slave market in east Africa, the task of winning his consent, without force, to the liquidation of that ownership would, to understate the case, be delicate. The very last thing the Foreign Office or the East India Company required at this juncture was the unsolicited assistance of a religious zealot. No time was lost, therefore, in disavowing the annexation and shattering Owen's dream of evangelical empire. Midshipman Philips was returned to sea duty, the flag was hauled down from Fort Jesus, and in due course Seyyid Said dislodged the Mazrui from Mombasa. Britain's awkward moment in east Africa was happily forgotten.

Or so it seemed at the time. As events were to prove, England might have saved herself infinitely greater embarrassment—and tribulations multiplied a hundredfold—had she simply allowed the Union Jack to keep flying over the Old Harbor.

2

BALOZI BEHIND THE THRONE

*"The stench at night is so gross
or crass one might cut out a slice
and manure a garden with it."*

In 1828, during one of his periodic campaigns against the Mazrui, Seyyid Said made a brief stopover at another of Muscat's coastal possessions, the island of Zanzibar. So attractive did he find this place that he made it his capital not long afterwards. Even more than the Anglo-Omani treaty, Seyyid Said's move to Zanzibar hastened Britain's entry into the east African arena.

From a strategic standpoint, the Imam's decision showed wisdom. Zanzibar was situated only twenty-five miles from the mainland, and its capacious harbor afforded more than adequate room to mobilize naval task forces against any fractious east African community. Mombasa in particular lay only two or three days' sail from Zanzibar when the kuzi was blowing, little more than a week with the kazkazi; under any circumstances, the journey from Muscat to Mombasa required at least a month at sea. A tactician by heritage and training, Seyyid Said could instinctively recognize a natural base of operations. Yet even if Zanzibar had not suited his military needs quite so well, the Omani ruler would in all likelihood have established the hub of his empire on the island just the same. During his 1828 visit he came down with what can only be called a case of love at first sight for Zanzibar, and he never recovered. This is not surprising. After thirty-seven years in a pitiless wilderness of rock and sand that had been flayed alive by sun and wind since time immemorial, Seyyid Said could have been expected to look on Zanzibar's emerald coco palms, ivory beaches and languid climate as a sort of geophysical tranquilizer. Small matter that the island was not in fact quite that much of a Nirvana; to Seyyid Said it seemed a veritable Riviera by comparison with the Siberia of Oman. Zanzibar became not just a forward command post but a year-round home, and the Imam of Oman soon came to be better known as the Sultan of Zanzibar.

*

Seyyid Said also treated the island as a business proposition. Zanzibar was not only blessed with a large harbor; its abundant springs were a much-sought fresh water supply for merchant vessels. These two factors alone offered commercial possibilities. The soil showed even more promise, being ideally suited to the growing of cloves, previously the virtual monopoly of the East Indies. Seyyid Said lost no time in introducing the clove industry to Zanzibar by decreeing that whenever a coco palm fell, three clove trees must be planted in its place, unless the landowner wished to have his property confiscated. Seyyid Said himself cultivated forty-five clove plantations, and by the end of his reign Zanzibar was well on its way to becoming the world's leading clove producer.

As a further business stimulus, taxes were held to a minimum; the only tariff imposed was a five percent import duty. This encouraged Indian traders, long active on the coast, to enlarge their Zanzibar branches, and the island soon established itself as east Africa's bargain center for ivory, hides and gum copal. Acting in tandem with the low duty, these products also served as a magnet to a large clientele from Europe and the New World, seeking new outlets for their textiles and manufactured goods. Trade with the West brought diplomatic relations as well, although, oddly enough, Britain did not make the first move in that direction. In 1833, Zanzibar and the United States signed a commercial treaty, and four years later a U.S. Consulate was opened. Britain established her own Consulate in 1841, and was followed in due course by France, Portugal, Italy, Belgium and Germany.

The business of these Consulates was primarily the business interests of their importers, who brought to Zanzibar more than a million dollars in cotton cloth, metalware, rum and beads every year. Increasingly, the forest of sharply raked dhow masts in Zanzibar harbor became punctuated with the contrastingly squared-up yards of brigs, barks and other ships out of Salem, New Orleans, Liverpool, Bristol, Marseilles, Bremen, Lisbon and Genoa. Between 1859 and 1871, foreign merchant shipping rose in tonnage from 18,000 to 27,000 tons. By the late 1850s a British Consul could write that Zanzibar "bids fair to become the chief emporium of trade on the east coast." In less than a generation, Seyyid Said was able to build an international supermarket on his drowsy little island.

*

The Sultan's factories, however, were far removed from the retail outlet. A business trip to the most distant production center might take as long as two years. Behind the fringe of Oman's coastal possessions lay the interior: unnoticed, untouched, unclaimed. Its cellar-dank rain forests, measureless, undulating savannas and thorn-carpeted bush regions swarmed with elephants; during the early nineteenth century, a single tusk could often weigh one hundred pounds or more. The hinterland was also a bottomless reservoir of slaves. After a six-month ivory- and slave-gathering expedition, a merchant might easily spend the rest of his life in prosperous retirement. Mindful of the revenues accruing to his own treasury from the import duties on these commodities, Seyyid Said hastened to exploit the east African interior as the prime supplier of Zanzibar's wealth. Carrying the Sultan's letters of authority and his blood-red flag, Zanzibari trading caravans began thrusting inland to open up avenues of commerce to the coast.

A typical caravan consisted of several hundred men, armed with matchlock rifles and spears, led by three or four Arab or Swahili traders working in partnership. The rank and file was usually a mixed bag of Swahili and African, the latter mostly slaves in a semi-wild state. Discipline on the march was lax and an expedition often suggested an annual outing of bindlestiffs. Porters deserted, fought like wild dogs for the lightest loads, lived like vultures off the land. Yet these ivory and slave caravans were the real pioneers of east African exploration. The Europeans who made the so-called discoveries of the nineteenth century followed trails which, almost without exception, had been blazed for them by Zanzibari Arabs and Swahilis.

There were three principal conveyor belts. The southern route led from Kilwa to the lightly forested and densely populated regions near Lake Nyasa, a distance of about two hundred and fifty miles. Farther to the north, the traders opened a corridor extending from the port of Bagamoyo, just opposite Zanzibar itself, to Ujiji, a scrofulous handful of thatch and elephant-grass hovels on the eastern shore of Lake Tanganyika. Since the journey across this monotony of bush was twice the distance of the march to Lake Nyasa, caravans on the Ujiji trail were serviced by a sort of halfway house called Kaze (today the town of Tabora), where the traders put up one of their few permanent settlements away from the coast. Kaze was a model city of sorts. Its Arab population came to no more than two dozen, plus a small handful of Indian merchants. All did well by themselves. Wrote Sir Richard Burton, the celebrated explorer-eroticist, in 1860: "The houses, though single-storied, are large, substantial, and capable of defence. Their gardens are extensive and well planted; they receive regular supplies of merchandise, comforts and luxuries from the coast; they are surrounded by troops of concubines and slaves whom they train to divers crafts and callings ... even the poorest keep flocks and herds." In 1861, Burton's onetime companion John Hanning Speke passed through Kaze and observed that the inhabitants "looked more like great farmers, with huge stalls of cattle attached to their houses."

Kaze was also a fork in the road, where the more venturesome caravan leaders turned northwest on the third main highway, along the farther shore of Lake Victoria. This march took them through Karagwe, a fertile, well-watered land whose merry monarch, Rumanika, offered a hospitality that came as a breath of fresh air after hundreds of miles of sullen stares from justifiably hostile petty chiefs. Rumanika not only liked to receive presents (and the traders could be lavish when it suited their purposes), but from all accounts seems to have genuinely enjoyed entertaining guests. When Speke and Captain James Grant stopped at Rumanika's capital in 1862, the king, according to Speke, "was delighted beyond all measure with what he saw of us," and tried to press on the explorer all the ivory he could carry "as a lasting remembrance of the honour I had done him in visiting Karagwe in his lifetime." The Zanzibari entrepreneurs were made no less welcome. They found Karagwe an ideal place to trade, rest and take on supplies for the final leg of their trek to the almost mythical kingdom of Uganda at the very top of the lake. The first Arabs to reach Uganda (or Buganda as it was then known) in the early 1850s were the first foreigners ever seen by the inhabitants, and the wealth of ivory and slaves they found here made the thousand-mile tramp from Bagamoyo more than worth their while. Some caravans pressed even farther north, to the aboriginal monarchy of Bunyoro near Lake Albert. Trade in this land, however, had for the most part been pre-empted by Egyptian merchants who brought their own expeditions south from Khartoum. Nonetheless, the Zanzibaris found themselves quite satisfied with the profits accruing from Uganda.

The most important by-product of the long-haul caravan trade was the empire it created for Seyyid Said: approximately one million square miles (which is to say ten percent of all Africa), embracing the whole of present-day Tanzania plus sizable regions of Malawi, Zambia, the Congo, Uganda and Kenya. Like Zinj, this was an empire in name only. Seyyid Said and his successors never displayed any real interest in settling or developing their immense fief. Apart from Kaze, Ujiji and one or two other caravanserais, no colonial or administrative roots were put down in the Zanzibari hinterland. The Arabs saw the country merely as a great vein of precious ore, which they mined with no thought to any possible depletion of resources. Still, it was theirs, by the age-old law of imperial conquest: guns. As long as the sultans' caravans could ply their trade without massive, concentrated interference, there was more than a ring of truth in the boastful saying of the times: "When the flute plays in Zanzibar, they dance on the lakes."

*

Overlordship of this vast realm came naturally to Seyyid Said. A stout but energetic bludgeon of a man, he had succeeded to the Omani throne in time-honored Arab fashion, by planting a knife in a pretender's stomach during a palace reception. This had happened in 1806, when Seyyid Said was fifteen years old, and the ensuing five decades of his rule never softened him. It was his nature to surround himself with military force. When an enemy—whether Mazrui, Wahabi or Persian—became troublesome, Seyyid Said usually took personal command on the field of battle. His navy, in addition to the customary assortment of armed dhows, also boasted a full-rigged, three-decked, seventy-four-gun flagship (it had the picturesque Arabic name *Liverpool*), a sixty-four-gun frigate, two corvettes and six sloops of war. Seyyid Said also owned a private armed yacht, the *Kitorie* (named for Queen Victoria), and when he went aboard he was not just the honored sovereign but the nakhoda—the captain— barking out orders to the crew as if he had been a seaman all his life, which in fact was the case.

Seyyid Said, in short, was born to lay down the law, and in Zanzibar he functioned largely as his own prime minister, cabinet and legislature. He was also the judiciary. At twice-daily meetings called barazas, he gave his personal attention to all his subjects, rich and poor alike, who came to him with petitions, claims and grievances of every imaginable nature, and he handed down decisions with all the finality of a traffic court magistrate. There were few appeals. Yet Seyyid Said cannot be described as a bullying oriental tyrant; if anything he was the reverse. Undeniably he looked on obedience and fealty as only his due, loved a good fight and was hardly a man to be crossed; yet among Arabs of the era he held an uncommon regard for fair play and considered it not just imprudent but dishonorable to misuse the royal prerogative. If the verdicts he delivered in baraza usually went unchallenged, it was not because litigants feared his ire; they simply respected his impartiality. "Justice he valued above all things," wrote his daughter, the Princess Salme, in her memoirs, "and in this respect he knew no difference of person, not even between one of his own sons and the lowest slave."

Such words are only to be expected from a fond daughter, but less biased observers tended toward similar judgements. For all his outrage with Seyyid Said's slave dealings, Owen could nonetheless remark on the ruler's "mild and gentlemanly manners." The English traveler William A. Shepherd spoke of the Sultan's "honesty of purpose, kind feeling and decision of character." Johann Krapf, the missionary-explorer whom we shall presently meet, had an audience with Seyyid Said in 1843 and wrote that he was shown "a condescension and courtesy which I had not met with at the hands of any oriental ruler." Although regal at all times in his bearing, Seyyid Said dressed without ostentation, shunning the jeweled rings and gold-faced robes favored by most Eastern poten-tates. Even his dagger hilt was of silver rather than gold; for a Sultan, this almost amounted to flaunting beggardom. He also possessed that peculiar Arab generosity that could be at once breathtaking and embar-rassing. A British naval officer, during a visit to Zanzibar, happened to make a casually complimentary remark to Seyyid Said on the trim appearance of the *Liverpool,* and found himself, despite his protests, the ship's new owner. Shortly afterwards, *Liverpool* was enrolled in the Royal Navy as H.M.S. *Imaum.*

Above all, Seyyid Said was a compulsive paterfamilias who enjoyed nothing more than to dandle grandchildren on his knee and spoil them beyond redemption. To house his uncountable progeny he built two enormous palaces in Zanzibar. These were multi-storeyed Xanadus whose many spacious, high-domed rooms overflowed with Persian car-pets, floor-to-ceiling gilt-framed mirrors, rosewood beds, ivory-inlaid tables and chairs, proliferating assortments of glass and chinaware, and a multitude of clocks which chimed away independently of any hour. Since the palaces accommodated not only the Sultan's wives, children and grandchildren but his seventy-five concubines and an army of retain-ers and slaves, domestic life had a madly hectic flavor. Princess Salme describes one of the royal homes thus: "Two large, separate flights of stairs lead ... to the rooms on the first floor. Crowds of people are continually going up and down these stairs, and the crowding is often so great that it takes some minutes before one can get to the staircase at all ... The kitchen is put up in the open ... The numberless cooks quarrel and fight continually, until one of the head cooks steps in, dealing blows right and left, and restoring order for a time. The quantities of meat boiled here are enormous, the beasts being always cooked whole. Fish of so large a size was often brought as had to be carried by two negroes ... Thirty to forty porters, sometimes as many as fifty, came in daily laden with fruit." One could escape this regal pandemonium in the park-like palace gardens, where peacocks, flamingoes and gazelles wandered among clouds of jasmine, oleander and frangipani. And, wrote Princess Salme, "there is a splendid view of the sea ... which delighted me much."

*

Through less lyrically myopic eyes, Zanzibar would be seen more like Camelot in a sewer. The city was typically coastal-Arab: a closely packed, reeking suffocation of dirt-caked stone and coral-lime houses divided into a crossword puzzle of dark, fetid alleys whose open drains, abundant night soil and busy vermin helped erase any image of oriental glamour. The great missionary-explorer David Livingstone, who simply called the place "Stinkibar," remarked that "the stench at night is so gross or crass one might cut out a slice and manure a garden with it." Dr. James Christie, an English physician who visited the island in 1869, wrote: "Countless millions of ants and beetles, millions of rats and armies of wild dogs aid in removing the garbage of the town and suburbs, and the rain sweeps away to the ocean much of the filth of the place. Thus ... the lanes leading to the shore become impassable to any but natives, from deposits of filth and rubbish." If the bustling, dhow-filled harbor evoked adventure and thriving commerce, it also produced other reactions. "No stranger ever lands at Zanzibar," continued Dr. Christie, "without expressing extreme disgust at the odious state of the sea-beach ... To some it occasions nausea and vomiting, and both olfactories and optics are most painfully affected. Except at high tide no one ever thinks of boat exercise, and it is only at that time that European ladies can approach the shore."

A perpetual hazard arose from the island's deceptively balmy tropic airs, which breathed a deadly halitosis on city, soil, streams and vegetation. Whatever hot-country affliction one may have dreaded most—whether malaria, bilharzia, yaws, leprosy, jungle rot or blackwater fever—Zanzibar nourished more than enough to go around. Cholera alone took a total of 50,000 lives during outbreaks in 1858 and 1869; this represented one-sixth of the island's population. The highly touted freshwater springs were not all that fresh. Captain George Lydiard Sulivan, who served on and off for two decades with the Royal Navy's anti-slavery squadron, declared that the high dysentery rate aboard the warships could be attributed directly to the drinking water supplies taken aboard at Zanzibar. "No one," wrote Livingstone, "can truly enjoy good health here."

Certainly the handful of Consuls, merchants and other whites residing in Zanzibar had not been drawn by tourist literature. They were there because they had to be, although it was sometimes not hard at first to succumb to the island's outward charms. Typical was the reaction of one British Consul, Christopher Rigby. Hardly had he taken his post in 1858 than he was informing his diary that "the climate is really delightful here now, the air is so clean and pure, and no heat all day. I take long rambles over the island every morning. It is the very perfection of rich tropical scenery. Here nothing is dry and parched up as in India. The country is ever fresh and blooming ... with soft green turf and clumps of large mango-trees, groves of oranges, cloves, etc ... The evenings at this season are lovely, so cool, calm and bright." It is not long, however, before we find in Rigby's writing such adjectives as "unwholesome," "muggy," "detestable." By 1861 he was told he must leave Zanzibar if he wished to remain alive.

Traders were obliged to do business in unremitting squalor. Retail transactions could be especially trying. Sulivan describes a shopping visit to one of Zanzibar's largest emporia, French Charlie's, which was situated "in one of the narrowest and dirtiest streets of that pestilential town." To enter this place, wrote Sulivan, "requires a strong constitution and a well-scented pocket-handkerchief ... The first things that attract the eye are great piles of mildewed bags and rusty preserved-meat tins stored against the wall up to the cobweb-covered ceiling ... The ground of this shop—it has no flooring—might be taken for the model of a battlefield, or for a plan of Africa with its hills and valleys ... but with a far larger population represented by millions of ants, while the wild beasts are replaced by innumerable spiders and cockroaches. Into this shop we were compelled to go, for it was the only one in Zanzibar that could supply what we wanted."

The island's whites could not wind up their affairs too quickly. "Every merchant," wrote Burton, "hopes and expects to leave Zanzibar forever ... every agent would persuade his employer to recall him." Nothing whatever, he said, relieved the oppressive drabness of Zanzibar life: "there is no society, no pleasure, no excitement." Burton was not entirely correct in this, since transients could attend occasional band concerts at the German Consulate or partake of an infrequent salt-horse dinner aboard a visiting naval vessel. But such meager delights only magnified the loneliness of their blank and brutal exile in a purgatorial Eden.

Romance, indeed, was the least likely pleasure to be found on Zanzibar. The fabled sex life of the East tended to lose its capacity for arousal on a visit to the town's red-light district, the venereally adorned Lal Bazaar, where the girls, according to Burton, had "faces like skinned apes." More hygienic involvements could be equally risky; one such liaison came near to touching off a major disaster. In 1866, a young German merchant named Heinrich Reute had a clandestine affair with Princess Salme. Eventually, perhaps inevitably, he made her pregnant, and when this was discovered by the Royal Family, Salme's days became numbered—no sin being quite so deadly in upper-class Arab eyes as sexual relations with an infidel. Fortunately for the Princess, a sympathetic Royal Navy officer managed to smuggle her off the island on his warship. Reute, whose status as a foreign national was thin armor under the circumstances, followed shortly afterward and in due course married her. But to her own family, Salme was officially dead, and the enormity of Reute's act placed the island's entire white community in grave danger for many months. A British man-of-war had to be sent to Zanzibar to inhibit any possible massacre of Europeans.

It can be said that Zanzibar carried the mark of Cain. The harbor and its beach were studded with whatever bloated corpses or part-corpses might have escaped the attention of the sharks—affording, in Dr. Christie's words, "sights ... sufficient to shock even those who have been familiar with the dissecting-room." For murder was endemic on the island, and the harbor served as a convenient repository for the bodies of men, women and children who came to unwitnessed but grisly ends in the unlit alleys after nightfall. These unfortunates were usually the victims of lawless slave traders from Arabia and the Persian Gulf known locally as "Northern Arabs" and dreaded by the townspeople. Not content merely with the human cargoes they could pick up in Zanzibar's open market, these slavers would scour the city at night, seizing anyone careless enough to go into the streets without an armed escort. Those who resisted got the blade of a jembia between the ribs and were pitched into the harbor. The submissive ones were bound and gagged, taken to caves along the shore and later transported secretly to the slave dhows. There were bold snatches in broad daylight as well; few cared to challenge a Northern Arab as he enticed a little boy or girl with a piece of fruit. The Sultan's own slaves were not safe from the marauders, and even the white residents, although never taken captive, could not always count on their nationality or color to immunize them from street hooliganism. Once, for no particular reason, a mob of Northern Arabs gathered threateningly outside the U.S. Consulate. When the Consul, a retired navy captain, ordered them off the grounds, they tried to break into the building and murder him. Only the presence of a British cruiser in the harbor and the timely arrival of a detachment of bluejackets kept the stars and stripes flying and their custodian in one piece.

*

Even Zanzibar's wealth was tainted, and its imperial might, beneath the veneer of county-fair palaces and arcadian gardens, a fragile thing. If the inhabitants of the lake regions did indeed dance to the airs of the Zanzibar flute, it was decidedly a danse macabre, and the flute itself was very much out of tune. For more than anything else, slaves brought Zanzibar its prosperity. By the middle of the nineteenth century, an incumbent Sultan could consider it a bad year if his annual income from duties on the slave traffic fell below $100,000—the equivalent of at least ten times that amount today, and under any circumstances nothing short of fabulous for so shabby a monarchy as Zanzibar. And slaves were also, inevitably, Zanzibar's festering sore: the cause of the empire's ultimate decline and fall. For it was slavery that first brought east Africa to England's special attention.

"It is like sending up for a large block of ice to London in the hot weather; you know that a certain amount will melt away before it reaches you ... but that which remains will be quite sufficient for your needs."

The situation could hardly have gone unnoticed, for just as Seyyid Said was shifting the concentration of his affairs from Oman to Zanzibar, Britain was setting in motion the crusade of national conscience that would change the social face of the planet. Although slavery had been under attack in England since the seventeenth century, the abolitionist movement was little more than an exercise in do-goodism until the late 1700s, when Adam Smith pronounced human bondage economically unsound and John Wesley's evangelism began stirring outrage across the land. By 1772, a self-taught lawyer named Granville Sharp had forced a test case in the English courts; its outcome was the abolition of

slavery in Great Britain. Despite the power of West Indian sugar planters who bought seats in Parliament and exercised considerable influence
on policy, the anti-slavery movement rapidly developed muscle after
this behind the no less politically sophisticated William Wilberforce. In
1807, with the support of the pro-abolition Whig-Tory Ministry of All
the Talents, Wilberforce, a socialite turned evangelist, rammed through
a bill which outlawed the slave trade in the British Empire. By 1833,
slavery itself had become illegal wherever the Union Jack flew. Meanwhile, the abolitionist flames had begun to spread across the Channel;
however reluctantly, Portugal, Spain and France signed anti-slavery treaties with England. It was not long before the institution had acquired a
gamy image among all enlightened Europeans.

In England itself, where the conviction of divine mission was fast
becoming a knee-jerk reflex, the country's Anti-Slavery Society emerged
as a force in the political arena; it was a daring prime minister who would
deliberately court that group's displeasure. Indeed, there was seldom
reason for Government to cross swords with the Society. As the British
historian, Sir Reginald Coupland, has observed, "the subject of the Arab
Trade ... could scarcely be debated when all were agreed in condemning
it ... Ministers needed no spur from Parliament or the public to press
their attack on the Trade." As one might expect, the movement was all
but drowned in its own sanctimoniousness—not for nothing were its
leaders called the "Saints"—but it was no less right. For the first time
in history, an entire people had declared of their own free will that they
were indeed their brother's keeper. The loftiest achievement of Victorian
England was the example she set in spearheading the world assault on
the edifice of slavery. If this meant British Governments poking their
noses into affairs that were none of their own, well, then, by Jove, they
would make it their business. Among the first of the slaving countries to
feel the weight of British righteousness was Zanzibar.

*

In eastern Africa, the effort might just as easily have been focused elsewhere. Egypt was tunneling slaves down the Nile from the Sudan in
hordes, and there was a tremendous Red Sea traffic from Abyssinia to
western Arabia. Zanzibar, however, became Britain's prime target; and
the selection was not unwise, for at least two reasons. First there was
the Anglo-Omani alliance which, it was felt, would prove useful as an
opening wedge. To Seyyid Said, England's friendship meant more, as we
shall see, than just a weapon against the Mazrui. Therefore, if he could

not be persuaded to give wholehearted cooperation to an anti-slavery campaign, it was reasonable to assume that at the very least he would refrain from offering full-scale resistance. Indeed, Britain envisioned an even larger role for the Sultan. As the historians Ronald Robinson and John Gallagher put it, in their *Africa and the Victorians*, "the Foreign Office expected him to be the Wilberforce of East Africa." Seyyid Said never quite met that lofty standard, but in the end he proved surprisingly compliant.

The second reason was simply that Zanzibar operated the Indian Ocean's largest and most smoothly functioning slave production machine. This was a veritable land-sea conveyor belt almost three thousand miles in length, which moved as steadily as does a present-day automobile assembly line, although conversion of raw material into finished product was not, of course, anywhere nearly as complex. Lord Lugard, the colonial administrator and empire builder whom we will meet in a subsequent chapter, describes from close-up observation the most commonly practiced slave gathering system in action. "At first," he writes, "a slave trader comes as a friend and settles down in the country by the permission and with the goodwill of the natives. He calls himself a *Mzungu* (white man), and the deference he exacts from his followers invests him with the appearance of being in reality a great chief ... He soon becomes a *beau ideal* to the savage. They imitate his dress, assume his name in lieu of their own; they covet his guns and powder ... Meanwhile he has made himself acquainted with all tribal quarrels ... He espouses one side, and to that alone he sells arms. By-and-by a bargain is struck, and he joins his allies to make war on a neighbouring tribe, who have done him no wrong. His guns and his superior intelligence are irresistible. His share of the booty consists of the captives, and perhaps *largesse* of ivory as well ... He has now become, not merely the *beau ideal*, but a dreaded power in the land, whose friendship must be won at all hazards by presents of women and ivory. Chiefs are eager to be in alliance with him, and he has no difficulty in recruiting his band of 'Ruga-Ruga,' whom he will arm with guns and despatch to raid for slaves. To be enlisted in this body becomes the ambition of the young bloods. Our slaver need no longer command his forays in person; his 'Ruga-Ruga' are his dogs of war, ripe for carnage, revelling in blood. What can any individual chief of a petty tribe do now? The slaver's foot is on his neck, and he must yield to his every demand."

Besides outright captures and a great deal of kidnapping, many slaves were also bought in the interior. Beads or lengths of cloth, usually calico or the cheap U.S. cotton appropriately called merikani, formed the most widely accepted media of exchange. Children fetched the highest prices, being more adaptable to bondage and easier to capture when they tried to escape. Rates varied, but tended to decrease the farther inland a caravan traveled. According to Henry M. Stanley, the price at Ujiji in 1876 for girls between the ages of thirteen and eighteen could run from eighty to two hundred pieces of calico, while men aged between eighteen and fifty brought no more than fifty pieces. These rates were rather steep, Ujiji being a relatively settled area; prices would plummet in disturbed regions. The Rev. Horace Waller, who served for five years as a missionary near Lake Nyasa, remarked in 1871 that "I have seen children of the age of from eight to ten years bought for less corn than would go into one of our hats." But under any circumstances the slavers obtained their wares cheaply enough. Even two hundred lengths of merikani were worth little more than five dollars. The girl who fetched that price on Lake Tanganyika would bring $25 in the Zanzibar market, $100 in Muscat. The estimated average net profit on every slave sold was sixty percent.

After raids, kidnappings and over-the-counter sales had milked a region, the trader prepared to depart. The slaves were fastened together at the neck with heavy wooden yokes (or at the ankles with iron fetters), the headman gave them the order to pick up their massive loads of ivory, and the caravan plodded off. It seldom moved directly to the coast, however, proceeding to other areas where the yield was known to be rich. Half a dozen such side journeys over as many months might be made before a caravan leader gathered all the wares he could handle—sometimes as many as a thousand slaves—and was ready to go to market.

There was no need for the anti-slavery propaganda machine to embroider its accounts of bestiality on the march. "The subject," wrote Livingstone in his journal, "does not admit of exaggeration. To overdraw its evils is a simple impossibility." One could trace the passage of any slave caravan simply by following the vultures and hyenas that shredded the flesh from an endless, winding line of putrefying cadavers. Livingstone's journals bristle with such observations as: "we passed a woman tied by the neck to a tree and dead" ... "we came upon a man dead from starvation" ... "we passed a slave woman shot or stabbed through the body." Some idea of why these casualties occurred is furnished by A. J. Swann, a retired sea captain who for ten years ran a mission steamer on Lake Tanganyika. In his book, *Fighting the Slave Hunters in Central Africa,* Swann wrote of a chance meeting with a slave caravan. "The head-men in charge were most polite to us ... Addressing one, I pointed out that many of the slaves were unfit to carry loads. To this he smilingly replied: 'They have no choice! *They must go or die.' ...* 'What do you do when they become too ill to travel?' 'Spear them at once!' was the fiendish reply. 'For if we did not, others would pretend they were ill in order to avoid carrying their loads. No! We never leave them alive on the road; they all know our custom.' ... 'I see women carrying not only a child on their backs, but, in addition, a tusk of ivory or other burden on their heads. What do you do in their case when they become too weak to carry both child and ivory? Who carries the ivory?' 'She does! We cannot leave valuable ivory on the road. *We spear the child and make her burden lighter.* Ivory first, child afterwards.'" Added Swann: "I could have struck the demon dead at my feet."

Livingstone estimated that for every five slaves in a caravan, one reached the coast alive. He also believed that for every African captured by slavers, ten others were killed. Considering that approximately 20,000 slaves were pried out of east Africa each year, the total annual depopulation figure may have approached a quarter of a million; Verney Lovett Cameron, the naval officer turned explorer, thought it was closer to half a million. In a land of some ten million people this was a demographic catastrophe that did not go unremarked by the Victorians. Visiting the Lake Tanganyika region in the 1850s, Speke wrote: "How the shores could be so desolate strikes one with much surprise. Unless ... this beautiful country has been harassed by neighbouring tribes and despoiled of its men and cattle to satisfy the spoilers and be sold to distant markets, its present state appears quite incomprehensible." In one of his letters, Livingstone described making a 120-mile march near Lake Nyasa without seeing a single human being. Sulivan was plainly aghast. "What country in the world," he wrote, "could stand such a drain on its population?" Waller put it more coolly when he commented: "It is like sending up for a large block of ice to London in the hot weather; you know that a certain amount will melt away before it reaches you ... But that which remains will be quite sufficient for your needs."

These mortality rates apply to the overland trek alone, and perhaps the dead ones were the fortunate ones, for upon arrival at the coast, the remaining slaves learned that they had completed only the first stage of their journey. At Kilwa, Bagamoyo and other ports, dhows stood at anchor, waiting to ship the goods to their ultimate destination. No one traveled first class. A slave dhow, though seldom more than 100 feet long, could accommodate as many as 600 involuntary passengers, crammed below decks in specially constructed bamboo tiers with about three feet of headroom. Here, one neither sat nor knelt nor squatted, but achieved a crippling combination of the three. Sulivan tells of liberating several children, aged between five and eight, "doubled up with their knees against their faces, in the position, they told us afterwards, that they had been in for many days ... They were a week ... before they could stretch their legs." Meals on board consisted of a daily handful of rice and a cup of stagnant water. Sanitation facilities were of course nonexistent.

The dhows in fact were waterborne pesthouses. An article from the *Times of India* in 1872 describes conditions aboard a typical Zanzibari slaver after its capture by a British warship. "The hold, from which an intolerable stench proceeded, was several inches deep in the foulest bilge water and refuse. Down below, there were numbers of children in the most loathsome stages of small-pox and scrofula of every description ... On examination by the surgeon, it was found that there were no less than 35 cases of small-pox in various stages." Surviving slaves also told the *Times* reporter that when the outbreak was discovered, "all the infected slaves were at once thrown overboard, and this was continued, day by day, until ... forty had perished in this manner." Consul Rigby once accompanied a Royal Navy boarding party to the deck of another captured dhow with 112 girls in the tiers. A detachment of seamen was sent below to free them, but according to Rigby, "each man as he went into the hold fainted away."

The first major port of call was Zanzibar. Here, wrote Rigby, the slaves "are frequently in the last stages of lingering starvation and unable to stand. Some drop dead in the custom-house and in the streets. Others who are not likely to recover are left on board to die in order that the owner may avoid paying the duty which is levied on those landed." The hardier ones, however, went on the block in Zanzibar's celebrated slave market, where, for the first time since their capture, they received something akin to humane treatment, since it was necessary to pretty them up for customers. Although the men were usually given no more than a brisk rubdown with oil, aimed at making them appear brand-new, special care was lavished on the women. They were draped with cotton robes and hung with bangles, earrings and bracelets; generous layers of henna and kohl were smeared on their faces, hair and eyelids. It was a spectacle combining honky-tonk and Grand Guignol.

By the mid-nineteenth century the Zanzibar market had acquired international notoriety, and was a must for any sea captain, merchant, explorer or missionary making a tour of the city. Few foreign visitors failed to record their impressions of the market. Perhaps the classic description was written in 1811, by the Royal Navy's Captain Thomas Smee. "The show commences," he wrote, "about 4 o'clock in the afternoon. The slaves ... are ranged in a line commencing with the youngest and increasing to the rear according to their size and age ... When any of them strikes a spectator's fancy ... a process of examination ensues which for minuteness is unequalled in any cattle-market in Europe. The intending purchaser, having ascertained there is no defect in the faculties of speech, hearing, etc., that there is no disease present, and that the slave does not snore in sleeping which is counted a very great fault, next proceeds to examine the person: the mouth and the teeth are first inspected, and afterwards every part of the body in succession, not even excepting the breasts etc. of the girls, many of whom I have seen handled in the most indecent manner in the public market by their purchasers: indeed, there is every reason to believe that the slave-dealers almost universally force the young females to submit to their lust previous to their being disposed of."

These more carnal parts of the auction seemed to arouse the most indignation and capture the most attention among the European visitors. Sulivan, writing of the women in the market, tells us that "their bodies are painted, and their figures exposed in proportion to their symmetry, with barely a yard of cloth around their hips, with rows of girls from the age of twelve and upwards exposed to the examination of throngs of Arabs, and subject to inexpressible indignities by the brutal dealers." One is almost tempted to wonder whether, beneath their moral outrage, the proper Victorians were not also the slightest bit titillated from witnessing such scenes. If so, they were no less genuinely revolted. And certain sexual aspects of the Zanzibar slave market did not even excite: such as the fairly common sight of little boys dying slowly as they stumbled in pain through the streets, intestines dangling from jagged holes in their crotches. These were the results of botched Arab attempts to produce eunuchs. It was believed that no more than one in twenty survived the gelding.

*

Perhaps it is puzzling that Africans should have capitulated so supinely to the Arab-Swahili scavengers. But apart from the fact that slaver firearms seldom left them much choice, it should be noted that not all tribesmen did submit without a fight. A little-known sidelight of the slavery era in east Africa is the record of certain black rulers who gave the Zanzibaris as good as they got. The names of such tribal guerrilla leaders as Myungu of Manyoni, Simba of the Congo and Songoro of Mwanza are probably meaningless today, even to the most heritage-conscious Afro-American, but they were names dreaded by the Arabs for the ferocity with which they resisted caravan raids. And these counterattacks, being essentially defensive, were mere pinpricks alongside the first strikes launched against Kaze during the 1860s by a ruler named Manwa Sera. According to Speke, who passed through the region in 1861, "Manwa Sera, I must say, was as fine a young man as I ever looked upon"; and he was apparently quite prepared to fling down the gauntlet to all Zanzibar when the Kaze Arabs tried to depose him. "This I could not stand," he told Speke. "The merchants were living on sufferance only in my country. I told them so, and defied them to interfere with my orders, for I was not a woman to be treated with contempt." The slavers accepted the challenge, to their regret. For five years, caravans in the Kaze neighborhood were uniformly and frightfully mauled in full-scale attacks by Manwa Sera's warriors. Even a 400-man army, recruited by one of Zanzibar's most bellicose slavers, was ambushed and routed. It was not until 1865 that the Arabs finally managed to capture Manwa Sera and behead him.

But Kaze did not enjoy law and order for long. By 1870, the slavers found themselves opposed by the Unyamwezi warlord Mirambo, who actually carved out his own empire across the Bagamoyo–Ujiji route. Mirambo has been called the "Napoleon of Central Africa," and if the sobriquet seems extravagant there is no question of the authority he wielded in his bush dominion. By all accounts, Mirambo would have stood out in any society. J. B. Thomson of the London Missionary Society described him thus: "He is a man of about 40 years old, 6 ft. 10 or 11 in., not stout but well made and firm, very active, and has none of the put-on dignity which native chiefs so often put on. He is very quick, shrewd and never at rest. His features are small, but he is quiet and kindly in manner ... He does not drink: beer and brandy he will not look at. He punishes his people if they drink too much." Cameron wrote in 1873 that "I cannot but admire the pluck and determination shown by Mirambo."

Courage and class were not Mirambo's only assets. He also possessed an advantage seldom given to African rulers of the era: guns in huge quantities. These he had captured, traded or filched (he even kept them in working order in a well-equipped arms repair shop), and they enabled him to raise a black army so formidable that it brought two thousand Baluchi troops from Zanzibar to protect Kaze. The reinforcements proved a waste of effort. For a decade Mirambo waged relentless war against the Arabs, trouncing them with such regularity that during one period Zanzibar disclaimed overlordship in the Kaze region. Of all the African resistance encountered by the Arabs, none came closer than Mirambo's to silencing the Zanzibar flute.

They didn't behead Mirambo. He died in bed, or a reasonable fac-
simile thereof, in 1884. Although his empire died with him, the ravages
that he and other rulers inflicted on the slavers would seem to refute at
least in part the notion that Africans were no more than dumb, helpless
animals in the face of Arab firepower. Nonetheless, for all their personal
courage, most African chiefs showed little moral outrage over slavery
and did not conspicuously object to conniving with the traders. This
only stood to reason, for they themselves had been taking slaves from the
captives of their own wars many centuries before superior civilizations
introduced the techniques of mass marketing to the land.

*

As for the Arabs, they did not, of course, regard the system as any more
reprehensible than did their cultivated contemporaries in South Carolina
and Georgia. No Arab ever thought of defending or even rationalizing
slavery. It was there. It always had been. And, paradoxically, one could
even find virtues in the institution, albeit of a backhanded sort. The treatment of slaves in transit was undeniably monstrous, but once arrived at
his destination, a slave was more than likely to find his new life far less
trying than the dark and deadly struggle with nature that had been his
lot in bush and forest. The woman whose nightmare journey from the
interior ended in the cushioned and perfumed security of a harem—or
even the plodding monotony of a plantation—was relieved forever of
the specter of drought, flood, wild beast or tribal raid. The lowliest of
manual laborers were fed two or three times daily; to many, this was
unheard-of luxury. If Waller could assert that "a man will not ill-treat his
slave ... any more than he will his horse," he was not being altogether
fair to the Arab slaveowner, who for the most part held a surprisingly
humane regard for his property. Among other things, the Koran expressly
forbade cruelty to slaves, and while this prohibition was honored in the
breach during transport, and although sadistic masters were by no means
unknown, the vast majority of slaveholders simply preferred, out of what
can only be called plain decency, to see their workers contented.

This was particularly so on Zanzibar, where even Rigby conceded
that slaves led "an easy life." A young mother bought by a Zanzibari
Arab was almost never separated from her child. Most slaves on the
island were given their own garden plots, plus two days each week to
tend them—or simply to doze in the sun if that was their preference.
The sultans, moreover, generally took it upon themselves to see that the
strictures of the Koran were adhered to; if brutal treatment were brought

to their attention, the offending owner's slaves would be set free. But in any case cruelty was the exception to the rule. Slaves often became salaried retainers in their masters' households and not infrequently married into the family. (If a slave wed a noblewoman, however, he remained in bondage and had to address his spouse as "Highness" or, at least, "mistress.") Many, after a given period of servitude, were totally emancipated. Some did not even have to wait that long. Alexander Mackay, the pioneer Uganda missionary, wrote of one Arab who purchased two hundred slaves simply for the purpose of liberating them. As often as not, the slaves would decline their freedom, for they had come on a good thing and knew it. The explorer Joseph Thomson, who detested slavery as only a nineteenth-century Scots Presbyterian could, had to remark of the Zanzibar slaves that "it would seem as if this class here is a particularly comfortable position, and enjoys ten times more liberty than thousands of our clerks and shop-girls ... a jolly-hearted crew they are, whose motto in life is 'beer, women, and ease.'"

Even the villains of the piece, the dreaded traders, could be seen from a certain perspective as only part ogre. Murder for murder's sake was in fact a luxury they could not afford, every dead slave being one less marketable item. When they speared a baby or tossed a smallpox victim to the sharks it was only to keep the bulk of their highly perishable commodity moving as swiftly as possible. At least this is how they saw their work. By their tradition and religion it was in no way evil, and the slavers were not without their own peculiar sense of right and wrong. At the very least they could never have been accused of holding the European's ideas of racial mastery. Blacks were taken only because they were available in huge quantities and because the Koran ruled out the enslavement of fellow Muslims. If they could have got by with it, the Arabs would cheerfully have made slaves of all east Africa's whites.

Actually, the slavers' relations with the Europeans were as a rule surprisingly cordial, at times even warm. Some whites, of course, would have no part of this. "I could never see a slave-dealer," wrote Sulivan, "without a strong desire to hang, or at least horsewhip him." Yet Sulivan himself was not above accepting help from the monsters. At one time, when his men were on short provisions, the nakhoda of a slave dhow offered him a gift of fowls and coconuts, which he eagerly accepted. Few explorers were not in some way or other indebted to the slavers; more than one European expedition traveled long distances in the company of a slave caravan, with the Arab leader acting as guide. Burton and Speke, on their journey to Lake Tanganyika in 1858, received valuable information on the geography of the country from Snay bin Amir, the Arab slaver who had first reached Uganda and later raised the army against Manwa Sera. Burton spoke of the "open-handed hospitality and hearty good-will of this truly noble race," and if one does not care to take the word of a self-acknowledged Arabophile, one can turn to any number of European contemporaries for confirmation. Wrote Speke: "These Arab merchants are everywhere the same. Their warm and generous hospitality to a stranger equals anything I have ever seen elsewhere." Passing through Kaze, Cameron "could not speak too highly of the behaviour of the upper classes of Arabs" in that town.

There is even the scourge of the slave trade himself, the man more responsible for its eradication than any other single individual. Writing in 1868 to Lord Clarendon, the British Foreign Secretary, Livingstone told of how, on meeting a slave party near Lake Bangweulu, he "was at once supplied with provisions, cloth and beads," and of how the slavers "showed the greatest kindness and anxiety for my safety and success." In this same letter, Livingstone went so far as to take what could almost be called an approving tone toward the traders' profession: "I was glad to see the mode of ivory- and slave-trading among these men, it formed such a perfect contrast to that of the ruffians from Kilwa." He even added that the slavers enabled him to write the letter, on a piece of paper "borrowed" from an Arab.

Other missionaries, who had no more reason to love Arabs than did Livingstone, constantly wrote of how slavers, fully aware that they were hastening their own unemployment, took pains to do the Christians kindnesses large and small. Mackay often mentioned hospitality, gifts and badly needed supplies received from slave traders. It was the pure charity of Zanzibari slavers that kept Livingstone alive for many months in Ujiji while Stanley conducted his long search.

And it was a Swahili slaver named Hamed bin Mohamed who ordered his own men to lead Stanley to Livingstone. This man, better known as Tippu Tib ("he who blinks," in reference to a nervous tic), was the Rockefeller/Croesus of the slave industry; the wealth he amassed in the quarter century during which he milked a region half the size of Europe of its people will never be measured. (The volume he handled, though, is suggested by the size of his caravans; some consisted of two thousand porters and one thousand armed guards.) If anyone should have headed the list of those most wanted, alive or dead, among the slave barons, it was Tippu Tib. Yet few figures, white, black or brown, in nineteenth-century east Africa, commanded more respect.

Stanley describes him thus: "He was a tall, black-bearded man of negroid complexion, in the prime of life, straight, and quick in his movements, a picture of energy and strength. He had a fine, intelli-gent face ... the air of a well-bred Arab and [was] courtier-like in his manner ... I came to the conclusion that [he] was a remarkable man, the most remarkable man that I had met among the Arabs, Wa-Swahili and half-castes in Africa." Tippu Tib was also a conspicuously devout Muslim. He belonged to a sect which did not even permit smoking, and his personal life (apart from twice-daily visits to his concubines) was almost monastic. Except on one occasion when he came down with fever in the bush, he never rode a horse or donkey but always walked. This practice was cultivated both to remind himself of his insignificance in the eyes of God and to keep in shape. He had a passion for physical fitness, which he once demonstrated to Stanley in a curious way while accom-panying the explorer's 1874–75 Congo river expedition. When the two caravans finally separated, Stanley gave Tippu Tib a farewell party, in which the high point was to be a footrace. The slaver trained for this event by jogging up and down the river bank for several hours, and then went on to beat Stanley's assistant, Frank Pocock, by three lengths.

He was always prepared, of course, to field any questions designed to shame his profession. A favorite rejoinder to missionary critics was that Abraham and Jacob had been slave owners. Once, when a European reproached him for rescuing an African village from a cannibal raid and then enslaving his beneficiaries, he shrugged his shoulders and replied: "Which would you rather be, a slave or a meal?" And although he took the characteristically callous Arab attitude toward slaves, the mortality rate in his caravans was the lowest in the east African trade. He was never sent to the gallows, or even horsewhipped, but lived to a ripe old age as one of the pillars of the Zanzibar community, plowing his slave profits into real estate and continuing to pleasure his concubines twice a day even as a septuagenarian.

*

Tippu Tib was only the most conspicuous example of the enormous socio-economic-military-political power wielded by the slavers. He per-sonified a phenomenon which even the staunchest abolitionists had to acknowledge as a deeply rooted and integral part of the Zanzibari way of life. Sir Leopold Heath, the admiral commanding the Royal Navy's east African anti-slavery squadron, freely declared, as late as 1871, that the trade satisfied "a want which, sanctioned by the religion of the country, has grown almost into an instinct." This instinct blocked the anti-slavery path like a concrete wall.

"You have put on me a heavier load than I can bear."

The respectability of slavery was perhaps the principal reason that eradicating the Indian Ocean traffic ran into more snags than the same undertaking on the Atlantic. The west African trade basically served the needs of countries which in varying degrees had voluntarily committed themselves to outlawing human bondage. Such was not the case in a predominantly Muslim world which saw no transgression in the practice of enforced servitude and which regarded the selling of slaves as a calling no less honorable than medicine or the law. Just as much to the point, the economies of the east African coast and the Persian Gulf states were geared almost entirely to slave labor; for most of the nineteenth century there was simply nothing to replace it. The concept of labor by free, paid workers was totally and utterly incomprehensible to the Arab mind; one could not expect the idea to take hold in a year or even a generation. England had taken it upon herself, so to speak, to condemn an apartment building whose tenants would have nowhere to go when demolition was completed. Wiser British statesmen, aware of this, knew also that to bring down the edifice with one swift blow was to invite catastrophe.

A particularly sensitive spot was the most exposed nerve on the southern route to India. During the first half of the century, Zanzibar, despite its autonomy and growing commercial stature, remained in theory at least no more than a province of Oman. And so long as Oman might jeopardize even vaguely the slender thread of communication between England and the East, it was considered imprudent to antagonize Zanzibar's Sultan—who was still Oman's Imam—with combustible instant emancipation projects. Certainly no one wished to experiment with such undertakings while Napoleon hovered in the wings. Thus, the first assaults launched against the Indian Ocean slave trade amounted to little more than love taps. In 1812 and 1815, the Bombay Government approached Seyyid Said with tactful suggestions that any assistance he might wish to offer Britain in curtailing the traffic would be "greatly appreciated." No less courteous, Seyyid Said replied that Bombay could not be serious, and there the matter rested until 1822, when it was at last deemed safe to apply a small amount of pressure. This bore fruit in an agreement, known as the Moresby Treaty for the British naval officer who delivered it to Seyyid Said, which forbade the Sultan to sell slaves to Christians, and prohibited his slave dhows from sailing beyond specified points south and east of Zanzibar.

The principal object of the Moresby Treaty was to cut off the supply of slaves to India and Mauritius (particularly the former), and its terms were stiffened some years later with the broadening of the prohibited area. Seyyid Said assented to these restrictions without noticeable enthusiasm, but they produced a less than spectacular shrinkage in the volume of the slave traffic. Although some slaves were emancipated through the edict against ownership by Christians, their freedom was not altogether edifying since its most visible manifestation was the spawning of freed-slave gangs that roamed the streets of Zanzibar for years, committing murders on a large scale and generally matching the Northern Arabs as terrorists. (At night, said Burton, "a man found in the streets may safely be determined to be either a slave or a thief—probably both.") Furthermore, there simply were not enough Christians in the Sultan's possessions to give the treaty damaging effect. By 1845, however, Britain was prepared to throw a harder punch.

Although cushioned in the regally deferential euphemism, "assisting His Highness with his enlightened views," the terms of the new proposal came in like a flying brick: the slave trade in the Oman–east African empire will henceforth cease, period. Seyyid Said's response was at least equal to the occasion. When the British Consul, Captain Atkins Hamerton, formally presented the draft to the Sultan, the latter is said to have cried aloud: "All is over now! This treaty and the orders of Azrail, the Angel of Death, are the same!" The melodramatics, however, left Britain unmoved. "You will take every opportunity," wrote Lord Palmerston, then Foreign Secretary, to Hamerton, "of impressing upon these Arabs that the nations of Europe are destined to put an end to the African Slave Trade, and that Great Britain is the main instrument in the hands of Providence for the accomplishment of this purpose: that it is vain for these Arabs to endeavour to resist the consummation of that which is written in the book of fate."

In point of fact, however, the treaty was neither that fatal nor that final. Seyyid Said had no intention of accepting it without a fight, and he hastened to send one of his most trusted counselors to England to plead for a less severe death sentence. The envoy, one Ali bin Nasur, was known to be a hard bargainer. As Seyyid Said's Governor in Mombasa, he had once saved members of the coastal Wanyika tribe from famine by lending them large stores of Government-owned grain and accepting as security their wives and children, whom he promptly sold into slavery. But since that sort of diplomacy could not be expected to go down well with the British, Ali bin Nasur adopted other tactics. On arriving in England, he presented Queen Victoria with a pair of emeralds, four bottles of attar of roses, two pearl necklaces, ten cashmere shawls and four Arab steeds. In public, he also brought to bear what was apparently a considerable personal charm. Not every day did London society have the opportunity to lionize an authentic Arab prince, and Ali bin Nasur received a gratifying regal treatment. The press described him as "that enlightened Arab statesman, Envoy Extraordinary to H. M. the Imam of Muscat, to the court of H. B. Majesty," and he himself was showered with dazzling gifts that included at least one gold chronometer.

Most significantly, Ali bin Nasur's diplomatic path was eased by both the Foreign Office and the East India Company. They had come to entertain second thoughts about the wisdom of an outright ban which would have the effect simply of bringing the slave trade under new and less governable management. Ottoman Turks, Persians and Red Sea Arabs were ready, willing and able to take up the Zanzibar slack. Thus, Ali bin Nasur could return to his master with a modified treaty.

Whether it had been worth the journey was another matter. While the terms grudgingly permitted the continued movement of slaves in the Zanzibari coastal domains—a seven-hundred-mile ribbon of littoral between Kilwa and Lamu—it was also stipulated that "His Highness the Sultan of Muscat hereby engages to prohibit under the severest of penalties, the export of slaves from his African dominions." What this meant was the end of the lucrative Persian Gulf market, which accounted for the vast bulk of Zanzibar's slave revenues. The "severest penalties" referred to the teeth in the treaty, which gave British warships "permission to seize and confiscate any vessels the property of His Highness or of his subjects" found to be carrying slaves north of Lamu or south of Kilwa. In short, the agreement remained onerous. "You have put on me," Seyyid Said told Hamerton, "a heavier load than I can bear." Yet Hamerton, who for five years had enjoyed the Sultan's confidence as well as his personal friendship, was finally able to prevail on him to accept the disaster with Mohammedan fatalism. In 1847, the regulations became law.

*

All that remained was to enforce them. During the nineteenth century, words like "seize" and "confiscate," especially when associated with England's fleet, had a fine martial ring that evoked the image of a righteously terrible iron fist. But for the first two and a half decades after the signing of the 1847 treaty, British iron along the east African coast proved sadly malleable. Sulivan has made some illuminating remarks on why the effort brought less successful results than might have been expected. A member of an old naval family, Sulivan had a distinguished career that included service aboard the Royal Yacht *Victoria and Albert* and conspicuous bravery during the Crimean War. But his heart seemed most in his work when he was hot on the spoor of the slavers, and his book, *Dhow Chasing in Zanzibar Waters*, offers a somewhat ponderously drawn but no less vivid picture of the frustrations confronting the navy's anti-slavery campaign in the Indian Ocean.

To begin with, the treaty bristled with exquisitely worded but firm regulations which Sulivan and his fellow officers sometimes looked on as drawn up with a view to inhibiting their searches and seizures. No fewer than 211 separate clauses governed procedures to be observed on boarding. A particularly stern article directed that no legally seized vessel could be destroyed until her ship's papers had been removed; this made for huge complications because few nakhodas ever carried such documents, much less knew what they were. On the rare occasions when papers were produced, one could seldom identify them as such. In those days, few officers understood more than two or three words of rudimentary Arabic or Swahili, while the navy's hired interpreters as often as not served as double agents in the pay of the slavers. Papers, wrote Sulivan, "might have been, for all we knew, Bills of Sale for the [slaves] ... or warrants for their execution; or, more probably, directions as to where our boat was, how to avoid it, or to cut the throats of every Englishman if they could get the chance."

The treaty also contained at least two loopholes big enough to sail a dhow through. Since the transport of slaves remained legal along the Sultan's coastal possessions, what should have been the most hazardous stage of the voyage to the Persian Gulf became instead a safety zone in which Northern Arabs could taunt the British with relative impunity. Time and again, officers of the squadron would watch the dhows as they put boldly into Zanzibar to discharge or take on slave cargoes and then depart, under the very noses of a very impotent navy. Sulivan recalled one occasion when a dhow passed within pistol shot of his own warship in the harbor, "her upper deck so covered with slaves ... that not a square foot of it was visible. As she passed, every face on board her was turned toward us, and the Arabs from the raised or poop deck abaft, gave a most derisive cheer, followed by laughter." Another article forbade interference with what were described as "domestic slaves." How was an officer to tell the difference between a common field hand and a cook, or a laundress or a gardener, when the slavers could claim that large numbers of captives were domestics? Remarked Sulivan: "I am sure that every officer who has been on the African coast... will agree with me, that not one in a thousand of those on board [the dhows] are 'domestic slaves,' or ever return to Zanzibar territory again."

The nakhodas, who were nothing if not inventive, also transformed many slaves into passengers simply by draping a few lengths of merikani over their waists and shoulders. Other slaves were told to impersonate members of the crew, and it mattered not that an officer could invariably see through the pretense. "The stamp of the negro sailor himself," wrote Sulivan, "who is so differently treated on board the dhows, and whose intelligence is evidently so superior to any other negroes found there, and the absence of the look of submissive despair in the expression of his countenance, are sufficient to distinguish him." But try to prove this. Demonstrative legal evidence of treaty violations was elusive at best, particularly with the likelihod that crooked interpreters would not support the navy. Even the slaves were loath to reveal the masquerade, for had not the Arabs told them that these English sailors were not out to liberate black men but to eat them? That useful myth, which gained wide currency along the coast, was reinforced when steamships joined the squadron. After the unsuccessful pursuit of one dhow which took cover in shoal water, Sulivan learned that "on seeing [the cruiser] the Arabs said, pointing to the smoke from our funnel, 'White man is lighting a fire to cook nigger with,' and by this they persuaded the poor creatures to risk jumping into the water when they grounded."

Hardly less frustrating than the small print in the treaty were the obstacles thrown up by European nations pledged to the anti-slavery cause. France and Portugal had territorial possessions on nearby islands or along the coast to the south of the Sultan's domains. They also had naval forces of a sort, and might have been expected, at the very least, to lend moral support to the British squadron. Quite the contrary. To furnish plantation workers on the French islands of Reunion, Mayotte and Nossi-Be, French colonial officials devised a system which they described as "free labor emigration." Slaves were bought at Kilwa, "liberated" and then enrolled on the spot as long-term "volunteers" for the plantations. The Portuguese made scarcely any effort to conceal an active and lucrative involvement in a huge slave trade carried on in their precariously held territories around Mozambique. Holding passports identifying them as "free negroes," Africans were shipped out of Portuguese coastal ports in a volume that may have exceeded Zanzibar's. According to Sulivan, these "free negroes" made a practice of hiding under piers in Mozambique harbor whenever his ship was anchored there; at night, they would swim out and seek British protection. On one occasion the

local police chief demanded that Sulivan yield up several of these runa-
ways. "He said that they were not slaves, but 'free,' to which I replied
that, if so, they had a right to come on board. 'No!' said he, 'they would
require passports.'" The policeman undoubtedly had the law on his
side, but he did not get his "free negroes" back, Sulivan having already
decided, "apart from the probability of their being flogged to death, that
it would have been a disgrace to the flag, and dishonorable on my part,
to surrender them."

The unkindest cut of all came from fellow Englishmen: the officers
of the Indian navy, which dragged its feet conspicuously on patrol. As in
the Arab countries and Persia, slavery had become deeply imbedded
in the Indian way of life, to such an extent, in fact, that the influence
of powerful slave-owning and slave-trading interests made itself felt at
fairly high levels of the Raj. Officers of the Indian fleet could jeopardize
their careers by overzealous pursuit of dhows. When one of their warships made a seizure, like as not the action would be challenged in the
Indian courts. "Very few captains," wrote Sulivan, "took the trouble
to capture slavers, in fact, I have heard them say they put the helm the
other way and went clear of the dhow whenever they came across one."
In 1871, Admiral J. H. Cockburn, a veteran of the east African station,
complained to a Parliamentary committee about "the known fact that
the East India Government do not encourage their agent in his efforts
for the destruction of the inhuman traffic." For nearly two decades, such
protests fell on deaf ears.

Finally, there were the outright violations, for it hardly need be said
that the treaty was observed with the same scrupulousness that Americans gave the Volstead Act. Seyyid Said, a man of honor, made genuine
and sometimes effective efforts to enforce the regulations, but after his
death in 1856, far less painstaking compliance was forthcoming from
his son Majid, who ruled—and looked the other way—until 1870.
And even token observance of the treaty was never expected from the
Northern Arabs. Under only the most nominal jurisdiction of the Zanzibar Government, they carried on the bulk of the deep-sea traffic. These
traders were the navy's open enemy, and the battle against them was, to
understate the case, an uneven contest. On the west African coast, the
British anti-slavery effort was carried out by two dozen warships. To
halt the Indian Ocean traffic, the navy could seldom spare more than
four cruisers at any time. From a watery Augean stable several million
square miles in area, this insignificant force was expected to sweep two
thousand slave dhows, and the task was patently impossible.

*

Yet the navy pursued the Northern Arabs with untiring zeal, for their dhows were where the action was, if indeed it could be called action. A large share of this exasperating work was given to the ships' boats: pinnaces, cutters, gigs and other midget utility craft that served as the squadron's eyes and ears, and occasionally its fists. Setting up base camps on small coastal islands, these cockleshells hovered about estuaries, inlets, deltas, mangrove swamps and in fact some thousands of square miles of shoal water that the deep-draft cruisers could seldom approach. From time to time they even made extended offshore patrols which could last two weeks or longer, and which were not pleasure cruises. When the men were not bailing for their lives in rain squalls of insane ferocity they were endur- ing the hammerblows of a vindictive sun and moistening tar-paper throats with a daily cupful of dysentery-flavored water. Their diet consisted of gamy salt junk and dry, weevily hardtack, served out sparingly. A sailor who came down with fever had no naval surgeon to treat him. Bandages for wounds often had to be improvised from ship's biscuit saturated in seawater. Serious cases could either be written off as dead or taken to the Portuguese hospital in Mozambique, which amounted to the same thing.

Yet Sulivan, who spent long months on these patrols as a midship- man during the late 1840s, writes of the experience as "a most delightful kind of life," and for an adventurously inclined youngster it could have seemed a perilous but exhilarating blend of Captain Bligh's launch voyage and Huck Finn's raft expeditions. Despite the oppressive climate and cramped quarters, the health of the boat crews was, as a rule, quite good, owing in large measure, says Sulivan, to "the extra allowance of spirits, which was to be served daily ... having in it a due proportion of quinine, or bark, which indeed was the condition of their receiving it at all." There were diversions, too. Patrol vessels sometimes put in at the Comoro islands in the Mozambique Channel, where the crews were welcomed by a friendly local officialdom which had appointed itself to such titles as the Duke of Devonshire, Lord Augustus Fitzroy, Lord Rodney and Admiral Blankett. Resplendent in hand-me-down British army uniforms of Peninsular War vintage, they greeted their guests with formal speeches which included several words of English, and bestowed further honors that could be alarming in their sincerity. Sulivan describes how "the commander-in-chief of 'all the forces' ... gave the order, '—— sent arms,' at which some of them came to the saluting position, and some levelled their old flint-locks at us with dangerous precision, had they been loaded, which they had not been perhaps for many years."

Life could be particularly agreeable on the island base camps. Here, all lived in tents, and the crews' daily routine, apart from keeping watch for slave dhows, consisted mainly of infrequent maintenance chores at a portable blacksmith's forge and carpenter's bench. At least as much time was given over to dozing, whist and bird shooting. The officers had a beer ration and used the empty bottles to barter with mainland inhabitants for fowls, eggs and vegetables. From these they concocted a stew called "kettler," which was shared among all ranks; Sulivan says he was never certain whether one ate or drank it. Every morning a party collected bucketsful of oysters from the coral beds on shore; in the evening all hands cast lines and nets for fish. They caught more than they needed, salting down the surplus which was given to the cruisers that sometimes anchored nearby.

Such arrivals were red-letter events, if Sulivan's description of one visit is any measure. "An invitation was sent in the following terms:— 'The governor and officers of the island request the pleasure of Captain Parker and officers of H.M.S. *Pantaloon* at dinner.' ... A guard of honour was drawn up ... and a substitute for a band was supplied by two or three fifes, with a tin pot for a drum ... The banquet consisted of 'kettler soup,' a variety of fish, 'kettler entrées,' fowls, salt junk, pressed vegetables, and yam, with plum pudding *à la* lower deck, and an ample supply of beer and rum ... After dinner the party left the tents to witness a game of 'rounders' played by the boats' crews ... A very jovial evening was then passed, every one of us being compelled to sing, whether he could or not, the rule adopted being 'That he who could not sing should be made to sing, or else drink a pint of salt and water.' The toasts were various, concluding with 'God Save the Queen.' After which Captain Parker and the officers re-embarked, with the same guard of honour, and with the addition to the band of ALL the pots and pans that we possessed."

From time to time there was even a naval engagement of sorts. The squadron concentrated much of its effort along the Benadir coast north of Lamu, where fewer legal obstacles could be thrown up by the slavers. Here, interception tactics were simple enough against dhows that kept too close to land. A ship's boat, concealed behind a coral outcrop, would wait for the slaver to sail by and then swoop down on him. The nakhoda was now boxed in, his ungainly craft no match for the tiny but highly maneuverable and heavily armed cutter or pinnace that cut off his retreat, while dead ahead lay the open gunports of the waiting cruiser. He had two alternatives. He could either heave to and surrender or run the dhow ashore through the usually mountainous surf, although the latter course meant trusting in Allah, writing off the dhow and salvaging whatever slaves he might, in the hope of moving them farther north by land.

Almost invariably the slavers opted for the rocks, hotly pursued by two or three ships' boats whose crews performed prodigies of seamanship in the juggernaut breakers. Not often did they have the chance to attack, and their zeal in these amphibious operations was at once bloodthirsty and boyish. Midshipman Sulivan took part in one landing under the command of an officer so diminutive in stature that he had to be carried from his boat to the beach, by a six-foot coxswain "who, whether for his own convenience or the commander's, had lifted him in the most unceremonious way possible, and tucked him under his left arm ... in which most undignified position ... he was waving his sword in his usual energetic manner ... exclaiming, 'Come on, come on, my lads, skirmishers advance!'—'Fall in on the beach!' &c."

These assaults, however, were seldom rewarding, for the dhow crews generally managed to escape into the thorn scrub with the few slaves who had not drowned in the surf. More successful forays took place to the south of Kilwa, a sodden region laced with labyrinthine swamps and other hidden waterways. In this area, the dhows could retreat up several convenient rivers and defend themselves under the guns of their own prepared fortifications on the banks. Going in after them, like a pack of hound dogs, would be the task force of launches, pinnaces, paddle-box boats, whalers and barges, each nearly awash under the weight of a ponderous muzzle-loading cannon, plus as many as two dozen sailors and marines armed with cutlasses and muskets. While twelve- and twenty-pound balls from the fort threw up great waterspouts all about them, the dwarf squadron, bravely gaudy with white ensigns, would advance in line abreast, its own artillery returning the Arab fire with shell, grape and canister. Within a few hours, the guns of the fort would usually be silenced, the dhow set afire and her slaves brought aboard the awaiting cruiser for transportation to Aden, the Seychelles, India or a free-slave community on the coast.

*

Still, the pickings were lean, and by the early 1870s it was becoming clear that the effort to halt the oceangoing slave trade with three or four warships was something like trying to stem the flow of the Nile with a fish weir. During a record two-year period between 1867 and 1869, the navy had seized 116 dhows and liberated 2,645 slaves, a respectable

enough figure until one learns that the number of slaves illegally transported during the same period came to slightly less than 40,000. In the
spring of 1870 alone, no fewer than 400 dhows were intercepted; of
these, only eleven could be condemned legitimately as slavers. In 1871,
Admiral Cockburn, the squadron's new commander, reported that "the
trade is as busy and profitable as ever it was ... It is a matter of sneer
and jeer by the Arabs, our impotent effort to stop that horrible abomina-
tion ... Even the Sultan says the English will talk and bully, but can't or
won't stop the trade." A year later, John Kirk, the British Vice-Consul,
wrote that "never, since coming to Zanzibar, have I seen so many large
dhows come in, crowded with slaves ... There is every sign of the Slave
Trade being on the increase ... The means at our disposal [to outlaw it]
under the existing treaties, are obviously useless." Admiral Heath put
the case even more bluntly. "I think we have gone on for twenty-five
years," he said, "and done no good whatever." Britannia did not appear
to be ruling Zanzibar's waves.

*"The Prince was made to understand
that he ... had no chance if Her
Majesty's Government were against him."*

The most curious aspect of the navy's setbacks is that they did little
damage to British prestige on the east coast. All this time, paradoxically, Britain was quietly but steadily increasing the range and depth of
its influence in the Sultan's possessions, while Zanzibar itself was being
drawn, willy-nilly, toward the status of a British satellite state. Indeed,
it can be said that the foundations of the British Empire in east Africa
were laid down during the humiliating quarter century that followed the
signing of the loophole-riddled treaty of 1847.

Perhaps, however, it would be more precise to say that a trap was
being sprung on England, for the building of the imperial framework in
east Africa was anything but a deliberate or even conscious act of British policy. Zanzibar and the Sultan's mainland dominions during the
mid-Victorian era must be viewed in their proper perspective, which is
to say, through a wide-angle lens that renders them all but invisible. The
ferment of the commercial-industrial revolution that spewed up such issues
as Corn Law repeal, Chartism, Reform bills, factory acts and poor laws;
the global convolutions which exploded in the Afghan War, the Crimean
conflict and the Indian Mutiny; all these events made up a tremendous
flood tide that left Zanzibar and east Africa in a stagnant backwater.

Any suggestion that England might have been seeking to plant the Union Jack over such a quagmire would have appalled every responsible Prime Minister and Cabinet member of every major party. Until the final two decades of the century, the least conspicuous feature and the least desired goal of British imperial thinking was territorial expansion in Africa.

It should be borne in mind that this was an era which saw Britain's ideology of empire taking its shape largely from the Palmerstonian credo of world domination through free trade and moral influence—although backed up, when necessary, by the threat of force. British policy in east Africa, such as it was, turned on two objectives: to put down the slave trade and to utilize Zanzibar's geographical positions (as well as its ties with Oman) as a sentry post guarding the southern route to India. Hand in glove with these aims went a third policy: tacit yet uncompromising rejection of any colonial acquisitions. As early as 1838, Palmerston himself had swiftly rejected a proposal that Mombasa be bought or annexed from Seyyid Said and used to serve anti-slavery interests. If such outposts were to be employed effectively, he said in a Foreign Office memorandum, "you must begird with them the whole circumference of Africa." Still, it was the very nature of the first two goals that made realization of the third impossible. Had she been trying, Britain could hardly have devised a more jimmy-proof method of locking herself into east Africa.

The commitment to the suppression of the slave trade can be seen as chiefly responsible for this. Although the 1822 and 1847 treaties brought no appreciable reduction in the traffic itself, their long-run effect was to undermine the sovereignty of the sultans in other ways, leaving a power vacuum that had to be filled. Despite his natural reluctance to preside over the dissolution of his own profits, Seyyid Said had not found the Moresby or Hamerton agreements an unmixed curse, if for no other reason than that in accepting them he felt assured of Britain's continued friendship. Thanks to the alliance born of necessity in the Napoleonic War, no European nation had enjoyed a longer or more cordial relationship with Oman than had England. If the conditions of amity sometimes seemed harsh to the junior partner, he could still take comfort in the knowledge that Big Brother was truly big. For Seyyid Said not only welcomed support in ousting the Mazrui from the coast, but stood in desperate need of insurance against his arch-enemies, the shahs of Persia, with whom Oman had been continually at war for centuries. By the mid-nineteenth century, Oman's military resources had become seriously strained from deployment in east Africa as well as Arabia. Without visible ties to a strong European power, the Sultan felt, he would be hard pressed to hold his desert kingdom against Persia's armies.

Thus, in 1854, when Persia launched a surprise invasion of Oman, Seyyid Said had every reason to expect the immediate assistance he sought from England. Indeed, he was confident that Britain would strike back with fury, since the East India Company's installation at Bandar Abbas had been destroyed by the invaders. But it was not to be. At that time, the Foreign Office was involved in negotiations with Persia herself, on a small but ticklish border question. Since Persia offered a natural corridor between Russia and India, and since England and Russia were mired down in the Crimean War, the last thing British diplomacy sought in 1854 was a move that might throw Persia into the enemy camp. The upshot was that Seyyid Said received an unsolicited and catastrophic lesson in power politics. The defeat and humiliation he was compelled to take from Persia may or may not have hastened his death in 1856; but it did blunt the edge of Omani power. It also helped set the stage for two successive crises in which Britain was forced to intervene, asserting her de facto mastery and unwittingly tightening the east African noose around her own neck.

*

As early as 1844, Seyyid Said had made known his wish to reorganize the administration of his two principal domains—which shared few common interests and much mutual distaste—along the lines of a confederation. Thus, after his death, Zanzibar and Oman, although nominally one, were in fact ruled separately by two of the Sultan's sons, Majid in Zanzibar and Thuwaini in Oman. The arrangement was far from satisfactory to Thuwaini, who claimed that Oman was the parent state and that he must therefore be acknowledged as sovereign in both Arabia and east Africa. Majid, of course, did not share that view. Although he was a peace-loving man who showed more interest in his harem* than in Arab-style eye gouging, and was further handicapped by recurrent hemorrhages and epilepsy, he had no intention of becoming his brother's puppet. Early in 1859, when news arrived that Thuwaini was preparing an expedition to take Zanzibar by force, Majid drew his own sword and the island rallied to him. Loyalty demonstrations went on day and night, often dissolving into skirmishes when some over-exuberant warrior accidentally blew out a comrade's brains with his muzzle-loader. This

---

* Majid's most enduring achievement during his reign was the construction on the mainland of a pleasure dome community called Dar es Salaam, the Haven of Peace, today the capital of Tanzania.

was the closest Zanzibar came to war. Hardly had Thuwaini's dhow fleet rounded Ras el Hadd on the eastern tip of Arabia than a British cruiser bore down, heave-to signals flying from her main truck. Curious and apprehensive, Thuwaini complied. Within minutes his flagship was boarded by a political officer of the Indian Government who forthwith suggested that the Omani ruler reconsider his strategy. Thuwaini did, and the fleet returned to Muscat. The withdrawal was carried out, Thuwaini explained, "with a view to exhibiting my sincere friendship and respect for the British Government."

He spoke as though he had been given a choice. The Indian Mutiny had only just been crushed, and neither Bombay nor the Foreign Office could have been expected to sit by idly and allow an Arab catfight to encourage possible resurgence among unreconstructed sepoys—and certainly not to threaten the lifeline between England and India. Shortly after Thuwaini had been ordered home, both he and Majid were invited to submit their grievances to Lord Canning, India's Governor General, and in 1861 a final decision came down. Canning had earned the nickname "Clemency," for his forbearing treatment of the mutineers, but Thuwaini found nothing lenient in the "Canning Award," as it came to be known. For the judgment legally divorced Oman and Zanzibar and recognized each as an independent sovereignty. Thus Thuwaini's dream came to an end, as did the old Omani empire, while the British, who had taken it upon themselves to sever the knot, could only find themselves that much more firmly implanted in their unofficial and unwanted responsibility for east Africa.

*

Britain's growing authority also made itself felt during a concurrent outbreak of violence on Zanzibar: the abortive coup by one of Seyyid Said's younger sons, an Anglophobic bruiser named Barghash bin Said, who had little use for the easygoing ways of his voluptuary brother. As with all palace revolutions in Zanzibar—and few members of island royalty were considered worth their salt if they did not attempt the role of usurper— Barghash's bid combined the elements of a cloak-and-dagger novel and a Keystone Kops movie. Discovering the plot, Majid acted with less than his customary lethargy and threw a cordon of his shabby Baluchi troops around Barghash's town house. To counter this, two of the pretender's sisters, Salme and Chole, arranged the Prince's escape in the dead of night—a plan which almost went awry when Barghash wasted precious minutes by angrily refusing to don the woman's robe and veil they had brought for his disguise. Finally, however, he consented to the costume and made his way to a nearby royal plantation called Marseilles, while his sisters retired to their own house and indulged in the nineteenth-century upper-class female pastime of swooning.

Meanwhile, discovering that Barghash had eluded him, Majid rushed several thousand soldiers to Marseilles. For the next twelve hours or so, cannon and musket balls zipped harmlessly among the clove trees and coco palms, while Majid's troops resolutely hung back from launching a frontal assault. Barghash, with five hundred of his own supporters, had fortified himself in a sugar factory, and neither Majid nor the Baluchis cared to make a hand-to-hand test of the defenses. At last, in exasperation, Majid broke down and appealed to the one man who seemed in a position to quell the revolt: Consul Rigby. Without delay, Rigby brought in a small armed party from a British warship in the harbor and smashed open the factory gates, only to find that Barghash had slipped back into the city. Rigby then turned back, deployed a platoon of marines around the town house, rapped on the door with his walking stick and demanded immediate surrender. Minutes later, the door opened and Barghash emerged, weeping with rage and shame. He spent the next two years as an exile in India.

*

Both the Canning Award and Barghash's insurrection are footnotes printed in history's smallest type size, but they underscore the ever-widening role played by British diplomacy in England's unspoken over-lordship of Zanzibar. The Consuls in particular were becoming more and more the true powers behind the throne. As often as not these men were officers seconded from the Indian army, but they were also civil servants of a high caliber, exercising an almost unique function in Anglo-Zanzibari relations. The duty of Britain's "Balozi" (as European Consuls were known) far exceeded what was normally expected of a friendly nation's accredited representative. Tacitly, yet specifically, he was charged with imposing his country's will on the host kingdom—if possible with the carrot, if necessary with the stick. Hamerton had taken pains to cultivate a warm personal rapport with Seyyid Said; this not only made the bitter pill of the 1847 treaty easier for the Sultan to swallow but enabled the Consul to win from Seyyid Said a degree of enforcement that might otherwise not have been forthcoming. (Later, on Seyyid Said's deathbed, he was to call repeatedly for his English friend.) When Rigby stared down Barghash with the unique imperiousness of a

British colonel, he was acting in theoretical accordance with the wishes of the reigning Sultan, but it is revealing that Lord Russell, then the Foreign Secretary, also justified Rigby's intervention on the grounds that the revolt had "threatened the immediate destruction of British property and the prospective annihilation of British trade." And, had England wished to see Barghash rather than Majid as head of state, one can easily picture Rigby reminding Majid that a Consul could not rightfully interfere in Zanzibar's domestic affairs.

It is no less significant that Barghash spent his exile on British soil, returning home only when the Indian Government recommended that Majid issue a decree of clemency. Moreover, on Majid's death in 1870, it was the British who chose the new Sultan—none other than Barghash himself. Wrote H. A. Churchill, Rigby's successor as Consul: "The Prince was made to understand that he ... had no chance if Her Majesty's Government were against him." Nor was the selection an act of carelessness. During Barghash's exile, Indian officialdom had brought into play Britain's singular gift for outward deference to whistle-stop royalty, treating Barghash not as a prisoner but as an honored guest, with a large mansion, a staff of servants and the freedom of Bombay. This diplomacy brought the desired results. Barghash's loathing for people and things English was soon replaced by respect and affection.

*

Yet despite his change of heart and readiness to comply with consular edicts, Barghash remained very much his own man. No vacillating hedonist like Majid, he stood forth as a figure hardly less commanding than his father. He was a born ruler, with instincts more aggressive than temporizing. "An open threat he resents," wrote Vice-Consul Kirk, "and his reckless obstinacy of temper at once rises to resist it." A photograph taken in the 1870s shows a broad-shouldered truck driver of a man whose turban and silken robes only accentuate his bulk. A bushy black beard frames a countenance at once judicious and ruthless. The eyes are half closed, yet they take in everything. There is the suggestion of a smile but the corners of the mouth are turned down. One thinks of a Mafia Don, oriental style. If Barghash fancied a plantation, he would make a preposterously low offer and, on the owner's rejection of the bid, simply confiscate the property. He set himself up in a palace called Beit el Azab— quite aptly, the House of Wonders, a colossal display case of mahogany paneling, marble floors, Aubusson carpets and superbly hideous Victorian furniture. Barghash was a man accustomed to getting what he wanted.

But land hunger and ostentation showed only one facet of Barghash's character. In personal finances he made a point of living within his income, no minor accomplishment for nineteenth-century royalty anywhere, slightly short of miraculous among Arab princes. He could be both considerate and generous as well; every year he turned over at least one of his private dhows to indigent pilgrims lacking transportation for the haj to Mecca. A lively sense of fair play usually canceled out his high-handed covetousness; he restored the integrity of the one-man judicial system which Majid had made into something scandalous even for Zanzibar. He utilized a sound business instinct to advance the island's well-being; among other things, he established a steamship company whose four vessels not only competed with the powerful British India line but brought in grain supplies which sold at prices far lower than those charged by gouging Banyan merchants. His civic-mindedness easily matched Seyyid Said's. Most of the revenues from customs duties and his own private estates went into such municipal improvements as badly needed street lighting, a police force and Zanzibar's first water-supply system. Like his father, Barghash devoted nearly every hour of his waking day (which began at four in the morning) to personal management of the island's affairs.

Briefly, Barghash ruled as well as reigned; so when the inevitable showdowns with Britain came, the fur was bound to fly. Barghash would emerge the loser, of course, sometimes a justifiably bitter loser. But despite Britain's not always honorable conduct toward him, he remained for the most part a staunchly faithful friend. That he did so may be attributed largely to the dean of all Her Britannic Majesty's Consuls on Zanzibar.

*

Dr. John Kirk first went to Africa at the age of twenty-five as physician-botanist with Livingstone's 1858–63 expedition to the Zambesi. Back in England by 1865, he was contemplating the offer of a poorly paying job as director of the Bombay Botanical Gardens when his friend Livingstone brought influence to bear, with the result that Kirk returned to Africa as Agency Surgeon and Vice-Consul in Zanzibar. In 1870, the year of Barghash's accession, Consul Churchill left the island in ill health; Kirk took the post in an acting capacity, to be appointed to the full consulship in 1873. His sixteen-year incumbency saw Britain rise to the pinnacle of her invisible rule over the island and coast. For the extent of this mastery, Kirk himself was chiefly responsible. As the instrument of his Government's interests in east Africa he was the de facto Sultan of

Zanzibar from 1870 to 1886, epitomizing the Palmerstonian concept of domination through influence rather than annexation. No other Balozi ever wielded anything like Kirk's power, power he can be said to have gained both from an awareness of his duty to the Crown as well as from a genuine, and at times even parochial, concern for Zanzibar's welfare. It was an attitude that was not lost on the island's nominal rulers.

For if any white man of the era came close to calling "Stinkibar" his real home, it was Kirk. He even brought his wife to the disease-ridden island, where she in turn bore him four healthy children. The family lived in a small but well-kept house just outside the town; its grounds were spacious enough to accommodate not only a private chapel which Kirk built but a tidy profusion of tropical shrubs and trees which he personally cultivated with professional skill. His diplomatic green thumb also came into evidence from the very start. Hardly had he taken up his official duties in 1866 than he received a request—command is the better word—from Barghash, to attend an ailing elder sister. (Barghash's preference for Western medicine over the local quasi-magic therapies suggests the extent to which he had been influenced by the British during his exile.) When Kirk made his house call, he found the usurper manqué living in law-abiding seclusion on a country estate, and the two men took an instant liking to one another. Kirk wrote enthusiastically to a friend of Barghash's hospitality and warm nature, observing that "the Prince, you must know, is a great cook. He in person superintends the cuisine and I had an ample and elaborate breakfast." More to the point: "Barghash is a jolly good fellow, I would willingly do what I can for him." These words do not merely come in sharp contrast to Rigby's earlier description of Barghash as "a sullen, morose, discontented character" who "detests all Europeans." They also say something about Kirk's own tendency to seek out the better side of the Sultan's personality.

The mutual regard which this first meeting nourished between prince and diplomat augured well for harmonious relations when Barghash finally came to the throne. Good will, however, may not have been conspicuous at the outset, for the new Sultan launched his reign, somewhat unexpectedly, on the wave of an inflammatory quarrel with the fever-wracked Churchill. The dispute had arisen largely from Barghash's not entirely surprising objections to the anti-slave trade treaties and from Churchill's disapproval of what he deemed a hostile element among the Sultan's Arab advisers. The Consul, in fact, became so incensed that he delivered to Barghash what almost amounted to an ultimatum: "You complain ... that the treaties signed by your father are more than you can bear. Shall I, then, convey this sentiment to Her Majesty's Government, and advise them under the circumstances to withdraw the Agency from Zanzibar, and leave your Highness to your own devices?" Churchill even went so far as to suggest officially that Barghash's removal, "on the first pretext," would be "desirable." For a brief period, diplomatic relations between Britain and Zanzibar were to all practical purposes suspended. At one point Barghash even made overtures to the German Consulate; in the circumstances, this could only be interpreted as a desire to remove British influence entirely.

But with Kirk in office the storm passed almost overnight. By adopting a threatening tone toward the proud Barghash, Churchill had overreached himself. Kirk, mindful that "Barghash cannot withstand repeated hints ... given in an outwardly friendly manner," took immediate steps to placate the Sultan. At every opportunity, he offered such assurances as "Your Highness will see that I am determined to support your authority," and "I shall always deem it a privilege to hold myself at Your Highness' orders." Before 1870 was out, Kirk could report to Bombay that Barghash "has shown himself particularly anxious to do nothing that could be taken as a slight to me." By March of 1871, he noted in another despatch that "so far from keeping at a distance, nothing is done by Barghash without informing me or asking my advice ... With the French, American and German consulates I find that His Highness has greatly lost favour since he has treated this Agency with proper respect and as taking precedence in everything without question." This was the first fruit of Kirk's diplomacy. It also underscored a personal friendship so firm that two years later it could withstand the severest test to which any relations with a Zanzibar Sultan could be subjected.

"I have not come to discuss, but to dictate."

What brought on the clash was, of course, the failure of the 1847 treaty, coupled with mounting pressure for more concerted action against the slavers, as a growing number of missionaries hastened the flow of atrocity tales back to their own propagandists and to the press in general. The hue and cry they raised, with Livingstone's personal and public letters setting the tone, finally brought the desired results. In 1871, an especially sympathetic Gladstone Government appointed a Select Committee of Parliament "to inquire into the whole question of the Slave Trade on the East Coast of Africa ... and the possibility of putting an end entirely to the traffic in slaves by sea."

The hearing could only have had a foregone outcome. The Select Committee was a mutual agreement society before which a procession of expert witnesses spent two weeks paraphrasing Admiral Heath's testimony that "just as it is said a drunkard can only be cured by total abstinence, so the slave trade by sea can only be put down ... by a rigid forbidding of the carrying to sea of any slaves of any description." Thus, the way was paved for Britain's final assault, which took the form of a brand-new treaty, stipulating the outright, total abolition of the sea traffic, and at last slamming shut all the loopholes.

This was finally "submitted" for Barghash's "consideration" by Sir Bartle Frere, an ex-Governor of Bombay, who had been placed at the head of a special mission to Zanzibar for that purpose. Frere was a statesman of considerable tact and forbearance, but the Foreign Office, itself usually a model of diplomacy, would have had to work overtime to find a less diplomatic moment to approach the Sultan. For Frere's arrival, early in January of 1873, came only a few weeks after Zanzibar had almost been swept away by a hurricane that not only took uncounted lives but destroyed nearly every clove tree and coco palm on the island. Even with its slave trade revenues, the Sultanate was now virtually an economic basket case. Wrote one member of the mission, the Rev. G. P. Badger, in a report to the Foreign Office: "The Sultan was moved almost to tears when he spoke of the consequences he felt sure would result ... and asked me to relieve him of the dilemma of either sealing the doom of his country or incurring the displeasure of the English."

If nothing else, however, Barghash's predicament at least gave him the opportunity to demonstrate that he could match his father's flair for the melodramatic utterance under pressure. "A spear is held at each of my eyes!" he declaimed to Frere. "With which shall I choose to be pierced?" While appealing for compromise, he also favored Kirk with at least one sample of Eastern metaphor. "When you find you have heaped a load on your camel that it cannot pass the city gate," he reminded the Consul, "do you not lessen the burden and gain your object? Now lessen this heavy burden, be it ever so little, and we are your servants, and you will gain all you desire." But the Sultan's quaint eloquence fell on deaf ears. England's patience had run out. Barghash could sign the treaty and reduce Zanzibar to beggardom, or he could reject it and become the target of Britain's wrath; he had no option but to sign. On February 11, after a month of stalling, he announced his decision to Frere: "You request that we signify either our acceptance or our refusal. In one word, No."

A combination of factors had worked to spring this surprise. For one thing, Barghash had been given the impression that France would support his defiance, thus embarrassing England and hopefully setting the stage for a compromise. Secondly, he had never quite been able to convince himself that Britain would back up her demands with real force; he had only to look back on the navy's sorry record against the slavers over the previous quarter century. While both of his assumptions later proved incorrect, still a third factor had to be taken into account: the Sultan's fiery Arab Irish was up. This was the man who by his very nature found passive submission not much less repugnant than eating pork. He was, after all, the Sultan. More than that, he was Sultan Barghash. No man would command him.

It did not take Frere long to recover from his astonishment and draw the sword he would rather have kept in its scabbard. Hardly had the envoy left Zanzibar in March than orders went out to increase the squadron to fourteen warships and to seal every slave port on the mainland. On May 31, Kirk reported to Lord Granville, the Foreign Secretary, that "where in former years over 4,000 slaves have usually been imported here by the end of May, this season only two small cargoes have been entered at the customs house—one with nineteen, the other with two slaves aboard ... The Sultan's customs house has, in fact, only realized in slave duties during the month 116 dollars against a sum of 8,290 dollars as duties for 4,145 slaves imported during the same month of 1872." At long last, Britain had closed her fist.

And yet, Barghash continued to show his teeth. Even as the navy tightened its stranglehold on the mainland slave ports, the Sultan gave no evidence of any willingness to reconsider the treaty. He seemed quite prepared to withstand the siege, come what may. He did not know what was coming. On June 2, Kirk received instructions from Granville: "You will state to the Sultan that, if the Treaty ... is not accepted and signed by him before the arrival of Admiral Cumming ... the British naval forces will proceed to blockade the island of Zanzibar."

*

Up to now, Kirk had stood on the sidelines while Frere and Barghash fought out their contest of wills on the field. The new orders, however, put the ball in his hands. On June 3, he carried it directly to the palace. In an interview with Barghash, attended by the Sultan's Wazir, Nasir bin Said, and three councilors, the Consul read Granville's instructions aloud, spelling out exactly what those instructions would mean. Kirk well knew that a blockade was the worst possible calamity that could overtake the little island, especially while it continued to reel from the clout of the hurricane, and he told this to Barghash, explaining how the tactical disposition of a sizable man-of-war force could choke Zanzibar to death. Not just the harbor but every inlet and every beach would lie within easy range of high-explosive shells. Not a dhow, not even the smallest outrigger, could so much as approach Zanzibar without the navy's leave. Admiral Cumming, if he wished, could starve or shell the island into submission. Kirk spoke forcibly. He was no longer the accommodating envoy for whom the Sultan's word was a command. "I have not come to discuss," he said, "but to dictate." Then he took his leave.

That same evening, Barghash summoned the American and German Consuls to the palace and asked for their thoughts on the possible effect of a blockade. What he heard was not encouraging, particularly when the American, Captain F. R. Webb, described his own experiences as an officer in the Union blockade during the Civil War. Next morning, Kirk was invited to the palace, where Barghash told him at once: "You may consider the treaty signed. Tomorrow I will ratify the deed with my own hand." The following day, June 5, Kirk was able to despatch to the Foreign Office a copy of the document, bearing the signatures:

JOHN KIRK
Political Agent, Zanzibar

The mean in God's sight
NASIR-BIN-SAID-BIN-ABDALLAH

The humble, the poor
BARGHASH-BIN-SAID

It was not Webb's dramatic account of the Union crackdown on Confederate shipping that had enabled Barghash to see the light, but rather the regard which the Sultan held for Kirk. To be sure, if Barghash had not accepted the Consul's ultimatum, the navy would have rammed the treaty down his throat. But to avert this was precisely why Kirk had spoken so bluntly. Had he not been genuinely concerned for Zanzibar's well-being, there would have been no need for him to particularize on the suffering a blockade would exact. Barghash in turn could hardly have failed to see this, to understand clearly that Kirk was leading no less from strength than from friendship. Still, if the point were to be brought across, a magisterial tone had to be taken, and it is not likely that any other British Consul—even Hamerton—would have dared bring it off so brazenly. In Coupland's words, Kirk himself "might not have been able to achieve the difficult task of bullying Barghash and his Arabs without offending them if his personal footing at the palace had not been so secure."

In fact, there was never any question of the special position Kirk occupied, even during the tense days following the navy's crackdown on the coastal ports. On the Queen's birthday, Barghash made a point of sending Kirk what the Consul described as "a dinner of honour—a sheep roasted whole on a gigantic charger ... pyramids of fruit and piles of confectionery." One day during the same period, Barghash, noticing one of Kirk's little daughters and her nurse near the palace, invited them in; they returned home, wrote Kirk, with "enough sugar-candy and sweetmeats to disorganize a young lady's boarding school." At the crucial showdown meeting itself, when Kirk asked the Sultan what he expected to do if the blockade cut off Zanzibar's food supply, Barghash replied, smiling, "I would come and live with you, Consul." While it cannot quite be said that with Kirk in Zanzibar Britain needed no navy to enforce her will, it is altogether probable that without him, Palmerstonian cajolery would have given way to Nelsonian force.

*

Barghash's capitulation came not only with good grace but with the same unswerving good faith that Seyyid Said had shown to the 1847 agreement. No sooner had he signed the treaty than he ordered the slave market closed forever. Three days later, on June 8, he issued a personal decree abolishing the seaborne trade and promising ruthless enforcement. This was posted on a wall of the Customs House, where, according to Kirk, "a large crowd assembled ... and read it, not without emotion." At the end of the month, Kirk was able to inform Granville that the Sultan "has done all we could possibly ask." In fact the Sultan had not even started. So conscientious was his compliance with the new laws that he dismissed the Governor of Kilwa—a member of his own family—from office and later had him thrown into the common prison for slave dealing. In 1876, on Kirk's prompting, he outlawed the mainland caravan traffic. This, the Consul told the Foreign Office, was "the most unpopular step" a Zanzibar Sultan had ever taken. "His people to a man are against him ... His Governors, ill paid, are open to other influences and have for the most part been themselves too often engaged in the traffic to look on it as a crime." Indeed, local reaction to the decree was violent; demonstrations at Kilwa and Mombasa had to be put down with armed force.

It was at this time that Kirk recommended to the Foreign Office that "if we make it seen that the Sultan's authority will be maintained ... the [laws] will be a reality. Otherwise ... we shall be forced to the kind of direct and independent interference which I hoped to have spared the Government." This is revealing, for it is a clear statement of Britain's official resolve to steer clear of any formal responsibilities for east Africa. It also shows, however, that despite her efforts Britain was simultaneously being drawn into an involvement from which she would be unable to extricate herself. Unwittingly, Kirk himself was helping to bring this about. Throughout his career, he pursued a policy only less firm than it was contradictory. His desire to maintain Zanzibar's integrity and to uphold the authority of its rulers was inevitably shaped—and diluted— by his higher loyalty to the Crown. By virtue of her pledge to outlaw the slave trade, Britain held, in Kirk's view, a vested interest in the future of the Sultanate; British interests in east Africa must therefore take precedence over the interests of all other European nations.

*

This policy did not originate with Kirk; it was Palmerstonianism pure and simple. As early as the 1840s, Robert Cogan, one of Palmerston's deputies, had described Seyyid Said "not only as a powerful political engine as regards [India], but through whose means education and morality might be introduced to an unlimited extent in ... Africa." The statement applied no less to Barghash. He was to be the willing instrument of the British civilizing mission in east Africa, a task that could be performed successfully without the burden and expense of direct British rule. This, at any rate, was how Kirk and the Foreign Office saw it. But the policy could be sound only so long as British paramountcy went undisputed by any other major European power. When the overt challenge came, England was to discover that only territorial annexation would assure her continued influence in the Sultanate.

During the 1870s, Kirk could not have known that he was preparing for that very eventuality. Not long after the new treaty became law he arranged for the posting of British Vice-Consuls in Kilwa, Mombasa and Lamu, and stationed an Agent in Ujiji. Since their principal duties were to see that the treaty regulations were enforced, these men were not so much vice-consuls as vice-proconsuls.* In 1877, Kirk took another step

---

* The Lamu man was D. C. Haggard, whose brother Rider wrote *Allan Quatermain* while on a visit to the island.

which involved England even more deeply; he persuaded Barghash to put teeth in the decree against the land traffic by reorganizing the Zanzibar army under a British officer. The Baluchis, never models of soldiery—Burton once described them as "disciplined only by their fears"—were replaced by African troops under the command of a young Royal Navy lieutenant named Lloyd Mathews, who was seconded to the Zanzibar forces as a major general. It was one of the least likely transfers of assignment in military history, but it proved an unqualified success, for Mathews trained the new army into a crack outfit which gave a good account of itself in police actions against the slavers.

More significant, however, was Mathews' unofficial, unspoken authority as an arm of British policy. A major general was no minor figure in Zanzibar officialdom, and Mathews was anything but a transient mercenary. No less than Kirk, he dedicated himself wholeheartedly to the service of Zanzibar, even to quarreling bitterly, at least once, with the Foreign Office on the Sultan's behalf. It can even be said that he gave his life for the island, dying at age fifty-one in 1901 of malaria and overwork. Though his first loyalty naturally went to the Queen, the influence as well as the affection which he won in Zanzibar could only have asserted even further Britain's unwanted mastery of east Africa. In 1890, when England at last bowed to the inevitable and made Zanzibar a Protectorate, Mathews was the obvious Foreign Office choice for Wazir. Kirk had done his work far too well.

*

As to the effect of the edicts, they damaged but did not paralyze Zanzibar's economy. This was partly because many merchants filled the revenue gap, at least to a moderate extent, with the profits from India-rubber plantations, which enjoyed a lively boom along the coast during the 1870s. But another reason was that the slave trade itself went on merrily. Not with quite the same abandon as before, to be sure—Kirk, Barghash and the reinforced squadron saw to that—yet with hardly less vigor. "It is not to be imagined," Kirk himself had warned Granville, shortly after the 1873 treaty was signed, "that contraband traffic in slaves is at an end ... On so difficult a coast ways and means will be found to evade the greatest vigilance on our part or that of the Sultan." This proved correct. The new laws in turn spawned a new, more piratical breed of slaver, generally from lower-class Arabs prepared to take great risks for the beguiling profits that accrued from the demand the stringent regulations created. Annual slave exports sometimes rose above the ten thousand figure. Moreover, the treaty itself, for all its severity, was not without one escape clause. This provided that household slaves, if they wished, could accompany their masters on sea voyages. As a result, dhows became packed with so-called domestics, ostensibly exercising their free will on pilgrimages to Mecca—whence few returned.

Thus, while the decrees of 1873 and 1876 dealt the slave trade a staggering blow, they were not immediately fatal, with resultant criticism from England. Many quarters expressed particularly strong feelings that no effort had been made to outlaw the status of slavery itself, which remained every bit as legal and respectable as it had been in the days of Haroun al Raschid. The most active protests against this go-slow policy were lodged by the missionaries, especially those near Mombasa, at Rabai and the fittingly named Freretown station. Here, large freed-slave settlements had been established, to train legally emancipated bondsmen for gainful paid labor. This work went undisturbed until the missionaries—to publicize their cause and to follow their humanitarian instincts—began to make a regular practice of harboring runaway slaves. Notwithstanding the firmness of their moral ground, it was the missionaries who had now become lawbreakers no less than the slavers. They further compounded the felony by steadfastly refusing to pay compensation to the owners.

At least once, Kirk himself had to blow the whistle on the Freretown missionaries, and though he must have found it distasteful, to remind them that "slavery being still the law of the land, the people of Mombasa had ample cause for complaint." To Granville, he wrote that "slavery is doomed, but it will be disastrous if this is attempted to be brought about by the unauthorised and irresponsible action of private parties." The warnings were seldom heeded; on several occasions, large mobs of angry slave owners threatened to put Freretown to the torch. The missionaries, however, responded with vigor. In 1880, when a particularly violent attack seemed imminent, Freretown's Lay Superintendent emulated Oliver Cromwell by exhorting his people to trust in God and keep their powder dry. This infuriated Kirk. "I told the missionaries that in case of civil war they would find themselves opposed not to the Mombasa mob, but by the Sultan's regular forces and armed ships." Nonetheless, until the end of the century, when slavery itself was at last abolished, the missionaries' defiant posture was an open jug of nitroglycerin not only in Mombasa but along the entire coast.

*

Despite the incendiary character of mission protest, however, the real issue during the 1870s and 1880s was not the abolition of slavery but of the slave trade; even with the muscle of the new laws, England remained less than satisfied with progress toward that end. It was not just a question of continued violations but of the whole approach to curbing the traffic. Could it in fact be stamped out by edict alone? Would not the illicit trade continue, through the ports and coastal land routes, so long as the interior lay untouched? For it was the vast, little-known hinterland that furnished the raw materials of slavery. Its output could not be stemmed, in the opinion of most informed Englishmen, while it was allowed to remain a no-man's land. What was needed was the European presence, the Christian religion, legitimate Western trade. This was the very theme Livingstone had hammered home tirelessly during his long struggle with the slavers. "I go back to Africa," he had declared in Cambridge in 1857, "to try to make an open path for commerce and Christianity." Other explorers also endorsed this view. Cameron spoke for many of them when in 1877 he voiced confidence "that opening up proper lines of communication will do much to check the cursed traffic in human flesh, and that the extension of legitimate commerce will ultimately put an end to it altogether."

Indeed, peaceful, profitable penetration could almost be called the key to the Palmerstonian policy in Africa: "... wishing most earnestly that civilization may be extended in Africa, being convinced that commerce is the best pioneer for civilization." These were Palmerston's own words, voiced a generation earlier. Yet even though the confident Palmerstonian world view was on the wane as the 1870s drew to a close, British interests in Africa were beginning to focus increasingly, if reluctantly, on the dimly lit netherworld that stretched behind the dhow ports.

3

THE ELMORAN AND
THE OPTIMIST

*"These eternal snows ... have so little
of shape and substance, and appear
so severed from realities, that they
take quite a spectral character."*

By the early 1880s, nearly all of the epoch-making scientific
expeditions to east Africa had been completed, and the country
itself had been divested of much of its mystery. But it had yet
to be opened up in any meaningful sense of the word. East Africa's
explorer elite had been concerned primarily with erasing history's most
tantalizing geographical *x*-factor, the source of the Nile, and since
this quest was in many respects a race, the competitors did not tarry
en route. Permanent European settlements and centers of trade were
nonexistent. Mackay hit the mark when he observed that "to talk of
Africa having been 'opened up' by the passing through it of Speke,
Grant, Stanley and Cameron is to talk of a large pumpkin being opened
up by the passing through it of a fine needle!" The Nile search, moreover, had focused mainly on the regions to the north and west of
Lake Victoria; even in 1883, when the river's headwaters had been
firmly fixed, at least three-fourths of east Africa remained a blank to
Western exploration.

Particularly blank was the country through which Whitehouse's
railway was to pass, not to mention approximately one-third of a

million square miles of bush, mountain and forest on both sides of its future right of way. This terra incognita, most of which comprises present-day Kenya, had simply not been considered worth the effort of investigation by the explorers who sought the source of the Nile. Still, it had been partially penetrated and made known to Europe as early as the fifth decade of the century, by two white men whose discoveries touched off a small storm of derision among the most learned geographers of the era. This reaction is not altogether understandable, despite the fact that neither man was an explorer by vocation.

*

The missionary Johann Ludwig Krapf went to Africa four years before Livingstone. Krapf was born near Tuebingen, Germany, in 1810, and it might be said that he had his calling literally walloped into him at the age of eleven. In his book, *Travels, Researches and Missionary Labours*, he writes of having been "so severely beaten by a neighbor for a fault which I had not committed, that it brought on a serious illness of six months' duration. Left to myself my thoughts dwelt much upon eternity." Apparently, his thoughts dwelt on travel as well, for during his teens Krapf had his heart set on becoming a sea captain. However, after learning that the cost of apprenticeship in the merchant marine was beyond his family's slender means, he found himself able to satisfy the craving for distant places and good works as a member of England's Church Missionary Society. In 1837, he was sent to Abyssinia, where he picked up odd scraps of information about the Galla tribe to the south, and formed a considerably exaggerated notion not only of their dispersion and influence but of their adaptability as Christians. "I felt," he wrote, "that [the Gallas'] conversion would produce the greatest impression on the whole of Eastern Africa."

Krapf's magnificent obsession, in fact, was to establish a chain of mission stations across the continent: a sort of equatorial theocracy which he called Ormania ("Orma" being the Gallas' own name for themselves). Therefore, he finally left Abyssinia to launch the undertaking from what he felt to be a more suitable location. This was Mombasa, where he settled in 1844, almost immediately undergoing a terrible test of spiritual fortitude when his young wife and newborn daughter died of malaria while he lay in the same room, in helpless delirium from the fever.* Eventually recovering his will and some of his health, he began working among the coast people, mainly the Wanyika tribe. By 1846 he had opened his first mission at a place called Rabai Mpya on the outskirts of Mombasa.

Krapf's religious teachings do not appear to have made a great impact on his friendly but indifferent flock. The inhabitants of one village "paid no attention to my words respecting eternity and the life to come"; another congregation "slipped away until only a few men and women remained." Yet Krapf left his mark in other ways. For one thing he was simply there, the trailblazer of all evangelists in east Africa. At the very least his presence gave the local population some idea of what future missionaries would be up to. "I explained that I was neither a soldier nor a merchant, nor an official ... nor a traveller, nor a Mganga nor Mtawi, physician, exorcist or enchanter; but was a teacher, a book-man, who wished to show ... the right way to salvation in the world to come." And, just as some Martian must inevitably be the first of his crew to step off the flying saucer and allow us to marvel at his other-worldly features and garb, "especially were my shoes, which they took for iron, my hair, which seemed to them like the hair of an ape, and my spectacles, objects of astonishment and derision." However, Krapf's greatest contribution to the white men who followed him was his removal of the language barrier. He worked long and arduous hours, "during every interval of rest," translating the New Testament into Swahili. By 1850 he had completed his classic *Outline of the Elements of the Kiswahili Language*, which was to become a standard text for many missionaries, explorers, administrators, traders and settlers.

While Krapf never forgot Ormania, the demands of the mission and the textbook generally kept him anchored to the coast; for two years his travels were confined of necessity to occasional preaching circuit tours of villages lying in the scrub country to the north and south of Mombasa. In 1846, however, he was joined by another missionary, a Wurttemburger named Johann Rebmann, who proved no less eager than Krapf himself to carry the Gospel into the interior. Rebmann's arrival, in fact, enabled a system whereby each man took turns superintending mission affairs at Rabai while the other marched deep into country which up to then had existed on maps only as flights of cartographic fancy.

---

* Mrs. Krapf's headstone can be seen in Mombasa today—although much the worse for wear following use by many visiting nineteenth-century sailors as a target for revolver practice.

Their journeys bore little resemblance to the elaborately organized and stoutly financed expeditions conducted by the more celebrated explorers. While the Church Missionary Society was eager to encourage conversions in the east African interior, only limited sums could be allocated to a pair of obscure clerics working in a corner of the world which, in the 1840s, had not yet captured enough public attention to warrant generous investment. This created a problem. East African travel during the nineteenth century usually meant paying one's way across the land, with gifts—extortion is a better word—for the ruler of every small kingdom one entered. These presents, universally called hongo, took the form of beads, copper wire and cloth, the amount being arbitrarily determined by the individual sovereign's mood and avarice. As a rule, the entry charge paid to each petty king averaged the equivalent of roughly forty dollars, and few travelers, even those who could afford a measure of lavishness, did not feel the pinch. One might always refuse to pay, but this could be dangerous. Even with rifles, no explorer wished to be harassed by hit-and-run assaults on his flanks. The ill-will of a local chief could also mean being denied guides and, when game was scarce, food. Thus the practice was to carry all the hongo possible. Even travelers on short rations tried to assign at least two dozen porters to these loads. Krapf and Rebmann, however, could not afford such luxury. Krapf mentions a two-month journey he made with one guide and seven porters. Once, setting out for Chaggaland, a region of beetling mountains some two hundred miles west of Mombasa, Rebmann's guide stared at the expedition's nine porters and told the missionary that caravans never entered that country without at least one hundred armed men. "But you are here," he marveled, "with nothing but an umbrella."

Local chiefs, on seeing so pitiful a procession stumble into their domains, might have been expected to show some compassion or at least a sense of proportion. Sometimes in fact this was the case. It has already been mentioned that Rumanika enjoyed giving as much as he did receiving, and even Krapf and Rebmann occasionally met rulers who supplied them with food in return for hongo. But it was wise not to rely on such good fortune. One of Rebmann's principal evangelizing objectives—it could almost be called a ruling passion—was to bring the Word to Unyamwezi, "by at least naming the name of Christ, where it had never been named before." This, however, meant a journey of nearly five hundred miles from Rabai, and the greed of a single chief prevented Rebmann from going farther than Chaggaland. The ruler, a man named Mamkinga, welcomed Rebmann effusively and then proceeded to milk him of every article his porters carried. "When by order of the king I was obliged to part with piece after piece of the calico which I had reserved for my further journey," he wrote, "I could not suppress my tears." But the missionary's sobs had no visible effect on his host, and there was no choice but to return to Rabai. Even this proved easier said than done. Before Mamkinga gave Rebmann permission to leave, there remained "the usual ceremony of expectorating upon the departing stranger and repeating the words 'Go in peace.' For this dirty expectoration with which first the Wanika, then the Swahili, and last of all myself, were favoured, a special payment was expected from each."

Rebmann became acclimatized to what he called "the saliva of peace," this being a common form of salutation among east African tribes. Chaggaland also drew him back many times, offering not only the opportunity to preach but a certain esthetic gratification. The missionary became quite taken with the country's natural beauty, which he likened to vistas in the Jura mountains. One Sunday in May, 1848, "it seemed to me as if Nature were celebrating with me the Sabbath. Mountains and all hills; fruitful trees; beasts and all cattle; creeping things, and flying fowl with the varied melody of their song, praised their Creator with me." And four days later, on May 11, Rebmann was treated to a sight not only surpassing in its majesty but revolutionary in its effect on African exploration. "This morning we discerned the mountains of Jagga more distinctly than ever; and about ten o'clock, I fancied I saw the summit of one of them covered with a dazzlingly white cloud. My guide called the white which I saw, merely 'Beredi,' cold; it was perfectly clear to me, however, that it could be nothing else but snow." Rebmann had just become the first European to see Kilimanjaro.

The sight did not come as a complete surprise. Arab and Swahili caravan leaders, returning to the coast from trading journeys in the interior, spoke often of a mountain whose summit was lacquered with what they thought to be silver. Seyyid Said's Governor of Mombasa had once told Krapf that the slopes were "full of evil spirits," that "people who have ascended the mountain have been slain by the spirits, their feet and hands have been stiffened ..." Therefore, if snow itself had not immediately occurred to Rebmann and Krapf, it is likely that both men at least suspected altitudes high enough to cause frostbite, and Rebmann's reaction to his first look at Kilimanjaro suggests that the presence of snow on the peak struck him as altogether plausible. But when his revelation reached Europe, he found himself being treated as a reincarnation of Baron Münchhausen.

*

It should be said that Rebmann was by no means the only African traveler whose findings evoked angered disbelief among a presumably objective scientific community. Explorers in those days, as if they were not beset by a sufficiently large sea of troubles, also faced widely circulated venom from rival experts whose pet geographical crotchets often seemed threatened by new discoveries. This climate of debunkery was inspired in large measure by conflicting theories on the source of the Nile; disputes between champions of this or that hypothesis could take on the proportions of a duel. No traveler was likely to welcome the gratuitous impiety of armchair authorities who sometimes approached the legal borders of libel and slander.* But nasty small-mindedness was not confined to the Nile controversy, and Rebmann endured his share of it, although the learned doubters may have treaded somewhat more delicately in deriding a man of the cloth.

For the most part, Rebmann's report of snow near the Equator was dismissed with condescending references to calcareous earth, refraction and other deceptive substances and phenomena that could readily create the impression of snow. From a certain viewpoint one can almost appreciate this skepticism. The writings of Rebmann and Krapf alike reveal emotional personalities and little scientific discipline; both men at times displayed an almost infantile naïveté. Yet the fact remains that a snow-peaked mountain cannot easily be mistaken for something else; and in any case Rebmann's description of Kilimanjaro hardly justified the abuse it received at the hands of supposedly dispassionate scholars. For beneath the cerebral veneer of the critiques, one reads the plain statement that Rebmann has perpetrated a hoax. The man who came closest to calling him an outright fraud was one Desborough Cooley, a pillar of the Royal Geographical Society, who wrote of Rebmann's account: "Statements such as these, betraying weak powers of observation, strong fancy, an eager craving for wonders, and childish reasoning, could not fail to awaken mistrust by their intrinsic demerits ... Those eternal snows ... have so little of shape and substance, and appear so severed from realities, that they take quite a spectral character."

Perhaps the most fitting rejoinder to Cooley came not from Rebmann but from Krapf, who remarked in his journal: "All the arguments which

---

* A respected member of the Royal Geographical Society, dissenting from Speke's Nile source theory, asserted, in so many words, that Speke had personally taken the measurements of one of Rumanika's naked wives to indulge a passion for voyeurism.

Mr. Cooley has adduced against the evidence of such a snow-mountain, and against the accuracy of Rebmann's report, dwindle into nothing when one has the evidence of one's own eyes of the fact before one, so that they are scarcely worth refuting." Krapf was not only defending his colleague here, for by the time he read Cooley's comment he too had seen Kilimanjaro. And he had also come across a snow-mantled mirage of his own.

*

As if to drive fireside geographers into apoplexy, Krapf's peak straddled the Equator itself, just beyond the frontiers of the Ukamba region, where the missionary made several lengthy journeys in search of a site for the first inland post of his Ormania chain. Ukamba was less inviting than Chaggaland. A forty-thousand-square-mile scrub-whiskered scar tissue of colossal hogback ridges, gully-slashed tablelands and grotesque boulders ten storeys high, the country afforded ideal hunting ground for bushwhackers. For the most part, these consisted of armed Galla parties who constantly harassed Krapf and helped to give him second thoughts on the tribe's potential as a congregation. There were also the region's principal inhabitants, the Wakamba, who filed their teeth to points like comic-book monsters but were usually more nuisance than peril. Krapf, who called them "very talkative, noisy, treacherous, and greedy," described a typical evening in a Wakamba village, whose residents "did not leave me a moment alone. If I wished to read, they asked if I was trying to spy into their hearts, or whether I was looking for rain and inquiring after diseases; when I wrote, they wanted to know what I had written, and whether it contained sorcery."

Yet among these people, Krapf does not seem to have been driven to his wits' end by hongo-hungry kings, and one important warlord even made a point of cultivating his friendship. The Wakamba, as it happened, possessed a degree more worldliness than did most east African tribes, having for many years taken their own ivory caravans to the coast, and in 1848, Krapf had met their ruler, a man named Kivoi, at the Rabai station. This gave the missionary a valuable entrée a year later when he arrived at Kitui, Kivoi's village. Delighted to welcome Krapf, Kivoi "introduced me to his chiefs and relatives. He made use of my presence to raise himself up in their eyes. He said: 'Did I not tell you that I would bring a Musungu to you? Now he is here; am I not a man of note since a Musungu has come to me in my country?' They all cried out with one voice: 'Truly, Kivoi is a great man, and has spoken to us the truth!' They then looked courteously at me, and took delight in inspecting my shoes, hair, hat, clothes, and especially my umbrella, which was often opened and shut up."

A traveling man himself, Kivoi appeared to comprehend if not appreciate Krapf's wanderlust, and offered his services as a sort of personal guide and lecturer. Numerous journeys made in Kivoi's company enabled the missionary to draw back the curtain on a vast portion of present-day Kenya. Krapf was the first white man to cross the Tsavo river, which would later be the scene of a nearly catastrophic obstacle to railway construction. He was the first to scale the two-hundred-mile-long Yatta escarpment, the first to explore the Tana river, Kenya's largest. He learned much about the volcanic activity in and around the Great Rift Valley, "the fire-plains of which are dreaded by the hunters." Some of the knowledge he acquired, to be sure, was twaddle. One Mkamba told him of a tribe called the Wabilikimo, who "had long feet, but short bodies, and on their backs a kind of hump; and nobody understood their language." But other anthropological blanks were filled in more realistically, if in a somewhat juvenile fashion. Before Krapf's journeys, no European had ever seen members of the Ndrobo, Embu, Meru or Kikuyu tribes. The latter, wrote Krapf, were "by no means repulsive looking." He also described a Kikuyu dance, "which consisted in each person springing as high as possible into the air, and upon his reaching the ground again, stamping with all his might with his feet and shouting out 'Yolle! Yolle!'"

Above all there was the Eldorado of African exploration, the headwaters of the Nile. Hardly less affected by the Nile fever than Livingstone, Burton or Speke, Krapf planned, on his first visit to Kivoi's country, to "inquire whether there might not be a route from Ukambani to Uniamesi to the sources of the Nile." He further hoped that this path would lead him "to those still surviving Christian remnants at the equator of whom I had heard in Shoa." Of course he did not find either, but in November, 1849—almost as if offering a consolation prize—Kivoi informed the missionary of a mountain, some six marches distant from Kitui, which he said was higher even than Kilimanjaro. Krapf had already been told of such a peak by an Embu tribesman, who claimed "that he had often been at the foot of it, but had not ascended it to any great altitude on account of the intense cold and the white matter which rolled down ... with a great noise." Similar accounts had been forthcoming from several Kikuyu, who "mentioned to me a mountain, the summit of which was covered with a substance resembling white flour."

A look at this wonder would have been a landmark event in African discovery, yet Krapf may at first have felt himself the victim of a prank, for Kivoi told him that the mountain could be seen from Kitui "only if the skies were clear"; and at that time the rains had set in heavily, reducing visibility to only a few hundred yards. However, on December 3, 1849, the clouds dispersed for a few moments, long enough for Krapf to see "most distinctly" what he described as "two large horns or pillars, as it were, rising over an enormous mountain to the northwest of the Kilimanjaro, covered with a white substance." The peak, then known variously to local tribes as ol Donyo Ebor, Kirenia, Ndur Kegnia and Kima ja Kegnia, is called Mount Kenya today. And while Kivoi had been incorrect in thinking that its broken-tooth summit rose above Kilimanjaro's flattened-out, 19,000-foot roof, his estimate was off only by some two thousand feet; Mount Kenya is Africa's second highest. Thus Krapf could write: "from personal observation ... I became firmly convinced of the existence of at least two snow-capped mountains" in east Africa, while the geographical Establishment became firmly convinced of the existence of two charlatans.

*

Although Krapf and Rebmann continued their travels, as well as their earnest if not spectacular missionary work, they soon faded into obscurity. Their discoveries, however, could not but survive Cooley's erudite bitchery. In 1862, another German, Baron Carl Claus von der Decken, mapped the Kilimanjaro region and climbed the mountain to 14,000 feet, although he failed to reach the snow line. That feat was brought off in 1871 by an English Methodist missionary named Charles New, who made the journey from the coast to Chaggaland in true evangelist fashion—with fifteen porters. When he reached the foothills and made his intent known, he was ridiculed by the local inhabitants. "The proposition," he wrote in his account of the venture, "was at first regarded as absurd. 'Who are you,' was the universal exclamation, 'that you should ascend the mighty Kilima Njaro? Haven't our people tried it again and again without success? Didn't the last *Mzungu* that came here try it, and wasn't he driven back?'" Eventually, however, New obtained guides, who dropped off one by one as the air grew cold and the oxygen thin. The last man offered a unique excuse; he "mustered courage to say, 'the ascent of this mountain is nothing to me, but I do not want *you* to be beaten.'" So New went onward and upward alone, until "the sensations ... which came over me at the idea of the profound solitude, of standing on heights to which no human being had ever before ascended, were overpowering ... Instead of exhilarating, they were oppressive." But his mood changed quickly when at last he came to the snow, "frozen as hard as the rock itself," and chopped away a few chunks to show his men. They at once decided the substance was saleable as medicine, and when New reminded them that it would soon melt, "they smiled incredulously, saying, 'Who ever heard of stones melting?'"

"An Apollo-like form and the face of a fiend."

Thus, by the 1870s, the idea of equatorial snow was no longer regarded as "spectral," and, of no less significance, a large portion of east Africa, previously a blank to the West, had been made at least partially accessible. But it was by no means all of east Africa, and in reality only the outer walls had been breached. Far beyond the peaks of Kilimanjaro and Kenya lay a topographical enigma of unmeasured vastness, on which the future of all eastern Africa might turn. For it was this region that promised the shortest route to Uganda. If it could be entered and traversed without undue obstruction, the thousand-mile journey from the coast would be neatly halved, and another spoke would be thrust in the wheels of the slavery machine.

Europeans at least knew that a corridor of sorts existed, for in fact the country had been crossed—by those very Arab and Swahili caravan leaders whose profession was now under siege. The accounts the traders brought back to the coast gradually enabled explorers to form a not altogether inaccurate picture of the region they themselves had yet to see. By the early 1880s, the principal barriers on the short route to Uganda, especially the Rift Valley, had become fairly well known and did not appear insurmountable. The most formidable obstacle, however, was not the work of climate or terrain. It was human. It was, indeed, the reason the Arab-Swahili routes across the region could not truly be called routes; only the boldest and most resourceful traders would take their caravans beyond Kilimanjaro. This same human barrier, moreover, had much to do with the European explorers' choice of the longer southern journey from Bagamoyo in their search for the source of the Nile. For these explorers could not afford delay, especially the kind of delay that might prove permanent. And bringing disaster on caravans was the particular talent of the Masai. With the possible exception of the Zulu in southern Africa, no other tribal community on the continent—perhaps on the planet—enjoyed quite so richly deserved a reputation for homicidal xenophobia.

*

During the nineteenth century, the Masai were to eastern Africa what the Apache were to the southwestern United States. For at least a superficial understanding of why, a traveler needed only to meet one of their warriors, collectively known as elmoran, in full battle dress. At first glance this killer might not have seemed very lethal, for he was not a muscular figure, sinews seemingly absent in the Masai physique. But in his very thinness there was menace, certainly nothing to suggest frailty. The man—we are about to meet him—who first reported on the Masai in detail described the moran as having "an Apollo-like form and the face of a fiend." If he stood under six feet he was considered stunted, and his lion-mane headdress, which itself appeared angrily alive, helped make one feel rabbit-like in his presence. Even when bareheaded, the moran's coiffure of pigtails, industriously saturated with fat and red ochre, bespoke not a clown but a hellish freak.

Apart from the fearsome busby, the moran's sole garment was a goatskin blanket draped over one shoulder and extending only to the waist, providing freedom to clout, slash and impale. Those actions were performed with a knobkerrie—a hardwood club that could open a man's skull at a tap—a double-edged sword called a simi encased in a red-stained oxhide scabbard, and an eight-foot spear with a two-foot blade. A moran also carried an enormous fifty-pound buffalo hide shield, emblazoned with chalk devices and quarterings which revealed his clan and age group. But a caravan leader would have been more likely to have had his eye on the spearhead, hoping to see a tuft of ostrich feathers fixed to it. This meant the warrior's intentions were peaceful, for the moment at any rate.

Clothes, to be sure, did not make the moran, but when he dressed to kill he could usually be counted on to do so. He feared only magic, having been totally impervious to physical pain ever since the day he stood erect and watched expressionlessly as the foreskin was flayed from his penis in the ceremony which elevated him from teenager to soldier. His physical trim was perfection. He could run for an entire day without stopping to catch his breath. His reflexes were swifter than those of a wounded leopard. As a moran he belonged to a military elite whose discipline and esprit matched the U.S. Marines' or the Cold-stream Guards'. Entering a hut, he would fix his spear in the ground at the left-hand side of the door, so that he could seize it instantly in his right hand when rushing out to meet an attacker. (And he never plunged the weapon carelessly into the dirt in ordinary African fashion; he brought it down smartly in two swift order-arms movements.) His regiments went into battle in long line-abreast walls, the warriors' shields overlapping in the manner of the Roman testudo. The formation itself was no less difficult to break than the British army's hollow square. Nor did many adversaries care to try, as they watched the sun strike the spear blades that leveled out from the advancing wall of gaily colored shields while the massed elmoran took up the yell which could sometimes cause an involuntary bowel movement and often decided the issue of a battle before it commenced.

A perpetual chip seemed suited to the Masai shoulder, for the people were alien to east Africa, having wandered down from the regions of the upper Nile sometime during the seventeenth or eighteenth century. Ethnically they were Nilo-Hamites, and their slim frames, prominent cheekbones, curved noses and thin lips contrasted sharply with the negroid characteristics of their predominantly Bantu neighbors. But for his color, a pure-blooded Masai might barely have passed as an Anglo-Saxon, easily as a southern European. (Even today a small but respectable body of opinion holds that the Masai are directly descended from Mark Antony's Lost Legion, citing not only physical similarities but Masai battle formations and the striking resemblance of the spears and simis to the weapons of the centurions.) In any case the tribe knew itself to be a—or more correctly, the—master race. How could it be otherwise? Had not Ngai himself, on the first day of the Creation, presented the Masai with all the cattle on earth as a personal gift? Was it not the everlasting duty of the elmoran to round up all the livestock that had been lost, strayed or stolen (mainly the latter, in the Masai view) over the ensuing ages?

Hence, continual, wide-ranging forays across the surrounding regions, which made the Masai all but unique in another respect. Most eastern and central African peoples tended to regard tribal boundaries with something like the same uneasiness that medieval geographers displayed toward the edges of the flat planet. Even such venturesome exceptions as the Wakamba walked gingerly along the relatively short and familiar path to Mombasa. Not so the Masai, whose scorched-earth campaigns showed them to be only less peripatetic than the Arab slavers and the European explorers. Borderlines held no meaning whatever for them. At least one Masai commando laid waste the country on the shores of Lake Nyasa, five hundred miles from its own land. The fortified towns of Zanzibar's coastal domains were not safe from Masai attack. In 1857, a raiding party sent Mombasa's Baluchi garrison to the cover of Fort Jesus. The port of Vanga was leveled by Masai warriors in 1859, and two years later, Mombasa went on alert again as an elmoran reconnaissance-in-force threatened the city. Only the Indian Ocean kept the Masai from invading Zanzibar itself.

It should be noted that the Masai were not conquerors but simply marauders—although this was quite enough, the license to kill having been issued to them along with the livestock and their status as lords of creation. The elmoran not only honed their collective talent as mass murderers to a keen edge but nourished a huge relish for its practice. So large indeed did violent death loom in the Masai way of life that when the warriors were not off massacring Wakamba or Kikuyu or Galla or Wanyika or Wachagga, they occasionally arranged inter-clan vendettas that could leave hundreds of their own corpses for the vultures and hyenas at the end of a day's battle.

It is fashionable today to maintain that the tribe was not quite so fearsome, that its terrible repute was simply inflated beyond reasonable proportion. This may well be true, but it would be a mistake to underestimate the Masai as a scourge. As late as 1896, when white rule was beginning to be applied forcibly throughout east Africa, the geologist-explorer J. W. Gregory, who had himself crossed Masailand, could warn: "Whether the Masai will be able to adapt themselves to altered conditions or not, it is certain that they will not do so until their military power has been broken." Wrote Charles William Hobley, one of Kenya's pioneer administrators: "It is interesting to contemplate what would probably have happened in this country if European intervention had not occurred when it did. As far as one can judge, the inroads of the Masai would have increased until most of the agricultural tribes in this land were decimated... Few can nowadays have any conception of the bloodshed for which this tribe was responsible."

*

If he lived that long, a moran's tenure lasted roughly eight years, from his teens to his mid-twenties, at which time he was retired from warrior ranks and became an old man. In this capacity he enjoyed certain perquisites reserved for the mature, including the right to take snuff, chew tobacco and marry. (Although his life as a moran had not been celibate—the warriors shared sex privileges among girls of their own age—permanent arrangements went strictly against regulations.) He was even permitted, if not actually encouraged, to cultivate a less homicidal outlook toward the rest of the world. Caravan leaders made a point of utilizing this change of heart, and would develop acquaintances with Masai elders who enjoyed the reputation of being friendly. It was important to establish such contacts, since a temporary state of peaceful coexistence could mean the difference between a caravan's safe passage across Masailand and its annihilation.

Yet a traveler in Masailand would seldom fail to register somewhat hopeful surprise at the less bellicose side of the Masai nature. Apart from their occasional clan wars, waged as much in sport as in fury, the Masai among themselves could only be described as gentle. Domestic life consisted largely of tending the beloved herds, spitting at one another and listening to elders unravel yarns from an inexhaustible wealth of folklore that blended Aesop and Joel Chandler Harris. Masai children were a pampered, frolicsome community who lived in a world of self-made toys and who traditionally greeted grownups by butting them in the stomachs with their heads. There was a neon quality to Masai dress. Hippies might have envied the moran his brightly colored love beads and the free-form grotesqueries that set off his pendulous, distended earlobes. Masai women moved about under the weight of fifty pounds and more in glittering brass wire anklets and necklaces.

Some aspects of their life, to be sure, did not charm. Nutritionists and gourmets alike would have frowned on the Masai diet, consisting almost exclusively of curdled milk stirred into a mixture of the cow's blood and urine. Masai dwellings, called manyattas, resembled nothing so much as shoulder-high dungheaps; in fact they were just that: generous layers of quick-drying manure plastered over thorn frameworks. These houses naturally attracted vast herds of flies that settled in nostrils, eyes, ears, mouths. Within two hundred yards of any manyatta, the pong was all but stupefying.

The Masai, however, took no notice of these things, for they marched to the beat of a different drummer. Theirs was a self-contained little world of its own, ever on the move under the open sky. They lived a strenuously idyllic, changelessly nomadic life in which government was indeed best because it governed least. Yet it was not anarchy. Although elders had little voice in the conduct of affairs, there were laibons—witch doctors—who delivered Ngai's edicts, usually in the form of prophecies, and who sometimes issued ordinances of their own. But for the most part, compliance with the law meant conditioned-reflex obedience to an age-old ritual and tradition which no Masai would ever have dreamed of challenging, so perfectly did they suit his life, liberty and pursuit of happiness.

*

Masailand itself was a heaving pasture of alternately rich and eroded terrain about the size of West Germany. Straddling the present-day Kenya–Tanzania border and extending northward some two hundred miles up the Rift Valley, the land provided more than ample accommodation for its 50,000 Masai and their million-odd cattle, sheep, goats and donkeys. Theoretically, if not in practice, each Masai herdsman had more than one thousand acres on which to graze his stock. Obviously, the country could have absorbed at least fifty times the Masai population, but if neighboring tribes had felt any need to extend themselves, it would not have been in the direction of Masailand. Even those caravan leaders who received permission to cross the land or skirt its boundaries were not encouraged to tarry. Nor did they. In 1878, Stanley told a meeting of the Royal Geographical Society: "If there are any ladies or gentlemen ... this evening who are specially desirous of becoming martyrs, I do not know in all my list of travels where you could become martyrs so quickly as in Masai." In all his list of travels, Stanley himself had never visited Masailand, but he knew whereof he spoke.

His advice was never more to be heeded than in 1883. Under Mbatian, probably the most charismatic laibon in Masai history, the elmoran had elevated their power and repute to what may have been its most terrifying peak. It was not a time to trespass. It was also the time when the first white man did so.

"Where only his own life is concerned, he gives you the impression of one who might be rash."

Sooner or later, of course, Masailand would have been opened to the West. As things stood, it had to be sooner. Barghash's edict against the mainland slave traffic raised interest in reaching Uganda through Masailand. In the late 1870s, moreover, a small group of Protestant and Catholic missionaries had established stations in Uganda. Although they could claim to have gained a certain amount of headway with the inhabitants, they walked an endless tightrope of latent hostility. Any day might bring a message of overt peril, and the need to extricate the churchmen quickly. But even without humanitarian imperatives, scientific curiosity over the tantalizing but barely perceived wonders of the country behind Kilimanjaro had by now become so intense that the penetration of Masailand held the highest priority in African exploration. The Nile issue having been all but settled, geographers could devote full attention to the task of ascertaining whether Masailand offered a practicable shortcut to Lake Victoria and Uganda. In 1882, the Directors of the Royal Geographical Society prepared to mount the expedition which, it was hoped, would answer that question. As its leader they chose Joseph Thomson.

*

Thomson's name usually draws a blank among people who are thoroughly familiar with the exploits of Stanley and Livingstone. Yet, on the basis both of achievement and personality, he must stand—even in the least generous estimation—as their peer. In a certain respect, he might be seen as the most remarkable figure in African exploration. It is just possible, for example, that Stanley might not have been able to traverse Masailand successfully. He was known as a man who tended to shoot his way through opposition. Had he adopted this tactic as a means of breaking Masai resistance, the result would only have been to make things much more difficult, and far bloodier, for the next expedition. One cannot easily picture the testy Burton or the aggressive Samuel Baker long tolerating Masai abuse without striking back in anger, which could well have meant the end of Burton and Baker. It is quite possible that even the tolerant Livingstone, almost always accustomed to the hand of friendship from Africans, might have found himself beyond his depth and patience among a people who practiced violence for its own sake. Thomson, on the other hand, appears to have realized from the very first that if he were to pass through Masailand in something approximating safety and a climate of good will, he must never depart from the cardinal rule of turning the other cheek.

*

And yet there is room to wonder that he should have displayed such common sense, for practical matters do not always seem to have been Thomson's strong suit. While one had to possess a taste for romance to be drawn to nineteenth-century tropical Africa, a purpose was also required, whether commercial, political, military, evangelical or scientific; but Thomson, by his own admission, was without any of these motives. "I am doomed to be a wanderer," he once wrote to his brother. "I am not an empire builder, I am not a missionary, I am not truly a scientist. I merely want to return to Africa and continue my wanderings." Not that he habitually took so somber a tone: quite the contrary, in fact. Although the term "manic depressive" was unknown in the 1880s, Thomson may have belonged in that category, with the emotional scales tipped toward a cockeyed self-confidence that had to be every bit as dangerous as his less frequent periods of confinement in the bottomless pit. Reading *Through Masai Land*, his book about the expedition, one is tempted to ask whether he should have been allowed to go off by himself without a keeper. While any writer can easily make light of his own predicaments after the fact, Thomson leaves the distinct impression that he often did face his most desperate crises with something like the airy frivolity he brings to describing them.

The book itself is one of the best ever written by an African explorer, either because of or in spite of the author's literary style. In an age when everyone expressed themselves in curlicues, Thomson's breathtakingly festooned scrollwork occasionally seems a lampoon. He gushes, he soars, his humor is that of a giggling Victorian schoolgirl. Like most of his European contemporaries in Africa, he was obsessed with the sexual habits and sparse clothing of the inhabitants. *Through Masai Land* is awash with prim or tittering assessments of what everyone in those days called "indecency." And yet, the reader somehow finds himself caught up in the work. Thomson's hyper-ornate style in no way inhibits a gift for nature writing. If he appears overly waggish at times, he is at least capable of poking fun at himself, a trait not frequently encountered among his colleagues. His drawing-room postures fail to conceal a decidedly virile personality. From behind the giddiness a real leader emerges. And the story he has to tell is high adventure all the way.

For Thomson himself is the eternal Eagle Scout, and a very youthful one at that. "When you meet him for the first time," wrote the playwright J. M. Barrie, Thomson's classmate at Edinburgh University, "you conclude that he must be the explorer's sort." Have a look at him as he prepares to leave Mombasa for the interior. He sports a pith helmet, wide-collared shirt with silk cravat, trousers tucked into buttoned-up, calf-length leather boots. A formidable Bowie knife hangs from his belt in a scabbard, a double-barreled rifle lies ready across his knee. He is seated on a wooden ammunition case, with one foot poised jauntily on a rock. His chin rests in his right hand, his eyes gaze into the back of beyond with a barely controlled rapture. His entire expression is one of immature exuberance. Even a fully grown mustache and burnsides fail to conceal his boyishness; one asks whether the whiskers haven't been pasted on. Thomson, in short, resembles a teenager playing African explorer.

This in fact is how he had passed much of his youth in Dumfriesshire, Scotland. He lived in a private world of romance and risk. When not poring through Livingstone's latest despatches or the works of Sir Walter Scott, he often appeared to be seeking out his own violent end. At one time, his mother nearly fainted as she watched him scale a beetling cliff while loudly reciting cantos from "The Lady of the Lake." What she apparently did not notice was the care he took to test each handhold before throwing his full weight on it. And in a sense, that inconspicuous precaution gives Thomson away. If he was a dreamer by nature he was a down-to-earth Scotsman by birth. If his prudence did not always win out over his recklessness, it can at least be said that the contest came close to a draw. Close enough, at any rate, so that Thomson never fired a shot in anger during the entire Masailand expedition.

"Where only his life is concerned," wrote Barrie, providing a very accurate layman's conjecture in his book, *An Edinburgh Eleven*, "he gives you the impression of one who might be rash; but his prudence at the head of a caravan is at the bottom of the faith that is placed in him." Nor were his inspirations irrational. J.A. Hunter, the pioneer east African white hunter-author, has remarked on Thomson's "uncanny instinct into the native temperament"; and while most talk about fathoming the "native" mind can be written off as so much white man's tripe, Thomson may indeed have possessed some sort of sixth sense. When they chose, which was nearly always, the Masai could be unpredictably opaque, and Thomson often showed what seemed to be, at the very least, a remarkable gift for second-guessing them.

Rock-climbing, reading and dreaming did not occupy every moment of Thomson's early years. He was an unusually bright youngster, if not downright precocious; even before he started shaving, scientific journals had published several of his papers on rocks and plant life. At the earliest permissible age, he entered Edinburgh University, to study geology, mineralogy and other natural sciences; among his teachers was T. H. Huxley, whose lectures Thomson called "sublime." The African opportunity came in 1878. Learning of an expedition that was about to leave for the Lake Nyasa region, Thomson applied for a position in any capacity without pay. A twenty-year-old volunteer scientist being too good a bargain to let pass, he was signed on as field naturalist. A few weeks after entering the interior, the expedition's leader died of dysentery and Thomson took command. This was mainly because he was the only other European in the party, but the undertaking proved eminently successful, and Thomson's book, *To the Central African Lakes*, helped win him recognition in the fraternity of professional exploration. The Lake Nyasa journey was followed in 1881 by a second expedition under the sponsorship of Zanzibar's Barghash, then seeking to exploit the wealth of coalfields rumored to lie near the upper waters of the Rovuma river. Although the deposits have yet to be located, Thomson's repute widened and in 1882 he found himself under approving scrutiny as the possible leader of the Masailand venture.

This may have been partly because he was to all practical purposes the only candidate available. Despite his accomplishments, the fact remained that Thomson was barely twenty-four years old, and the Royal Geographical Society would undoubtedly have preferred a man of Stanley's experience and years. But then, such an old hand would have insisted on an armed escort of two or three hundred men—whose wages the Society would have had to pay. Thomson, burning for the chance to join the front ranks of African explorers and supremely confident in what he liked to call his "lucky star," requested no such luxury. He was accepted.

*

So we find Thomson in Mombasa in March, 1883, ready to move out. His junior officers and personal servants appeared for the most part to show promise, when allowances were made for idiosyncrasies or minor shortcomings. The number-one headman, Brahim, also called Ali Ngombe (Ali the Bull), could be relied on to make the porters toe the mark and even win their affection whenever he chose to switch on the jovial side of his personality. He was also a sadist and trouble-maker who had engineered a mutiny in Thomson's first expedition. Makatubu, the second headman, had accompanied Thomson on both his previous journeys and had been slated for the number-one post until the porters began to balk at his low boiling point and volcanic tantrums. In his third headman, Muinyi Sera, Thomson had come across a nugget. It was the practice of expedition leaders to seek out men who had already served the greats with distinction, and Muinyi

Sera had been Stanley's headman in the historic 1875 Congo river trek. He would soon show himself to be a senile incompetent, useful only for figurehead chores.

But the key men on the staff were the interpreters; without them, Thomson might just as well have abandoned the venture. In Muhinna he was blessed with a master of Masai dialects who had made upwards of thirty trips to the forbidden land, and who would do everything in his power to sabotage Thomson's journey.* Soon, Thomson would take on an even more polished linguist named Sadi, who had accompanied von der Decken in 1862 and New in 1871. According to Thomson, Sadi had successfully conspired, out of sheer incorrigibility, to prevent von der Decken from entering Masailand, but Thomson also noted that the interpreter's perverse nature had since changed, having "gone from bad to worse."

Partly compensating for this roster of drawbacks was Songoro, Thomson's "boy," who would prove "simply perfection as an up-country servant." Finally, there was James Martin, the expedition's second-in-command. Born Antonio Martini, he was an illiterate Maltese sail-maker and jack-of-all-trades who held a vaguely supervisory post at the Freretown mission before joining Thomson's party. Thomson was to praise him highly for having "no opinions of his own," but at one point would also be "somewhat disappointed to find that Martin was not a good walker." In the light of Martin's subsequent career, the two latter evaluations are at least puzzling.

For the heavy menial work, 113 porters had been signed on. They would carry some four tons of wire coils, beads, bolts of cloth, cases of ammunition, food, scientific instruments and miscellaneous supplies— including a galvanic battery with which to astound and entertain, one of the first cameras in African travel and not a few volumes of poetry. In their own fashion, the porters were more vital to Thomson, and to any person journeying in Africa, than were the interpreters. Owing to the tsetse fly, mass animal transport of equipment and supplies was not feasible in the east African bush, and thus a curious aristocracy of riffraff had been spawned to function as beasts of burden. Collectively known as Zanzibaris, porters came from at least half a dozen mainland tribes and were Africa's equivalent of a teamsters' union. Each man received about ten rupees ($3.30) per month to carry a sixty-pound

---

* Sir Frederick Jackson, one of the first British officials in east Africa, wrote that his own maiden expedition to the interior in 1889 was "subjected to what was almost a boycott, due to the machinations of Thomson's bête noir Muhinna."

load (this regulation weight was almost invariably exceeded by fifteen pounds and upwards) and had a guaranteed daily food ration consisting of the thin maize porridge called posho. Such emoluments were hardly calculated to produce models of deportment, and did not. The average porter was a good-natured lout who sang on the march and improvised primitive games of golf and one-o-cat in camp; but he was also quick to complain over trivial inconveniences, quicker to take offense, and would go on strike without visible provocation. He was known to be a congenital liar. Constitutionally, he seemed incapable of staying awake while on sentry duty. As often as not he was a professional deserter who would sign on with a caravan to collect his three months' advance wages and then vanish into the bush before the party had traveled twenty miles.

Thomson called his own porters "a flood of vagabondage," drawn to the expedition only by the offer of a dollar-per-month bonus and the announcement—bruited in whispers along the Zanzibar water-front—that a blind eye and deaf ear would be turned to any criminal records. All things being equal, Thomson had more reliable material in his two Muscat donkeys (characteristically named Nil Desperandum and Excelsior, or Billy and Dick for short). Yet he could not afford to be choosy, as several large ivory caravans had already enlisted the cream of Zanzibar's carriers. Of even more concern, a large number of porters had also left for the interior with another expedition. This was the party of Dr. Gustav A. Fischer, whom the Hamburg Geographical Society had sent into Masailand on a mission identical to Thomson's. And Fischer had a long head start.

Thus there was no time to lose. All these expeditions were tacitly contests, and Masailand glittered more brightly than any other trophy except for the source of the Nile. Besides, in 1883 there may have been a significance in the respective nationalities of the two explorers that might not have existed five years earlier. Thomson no doubt felt relief as well as release on March 15, when his party crossed from Mombasa to the mainland and commenced its long march.

"I never doubted for a moment
that, to use Mr. Micawber's sanguine words,
'something would turn up.'"

More urgent problems than Fischer's commanding lead preoccupied Thomson during the first stage of the journey. Desertion was uppermost in his mind. With so much natural cover available and the safety of the coast easily accessible, escape did not call for the skills of a Houdini. Arab-Swahili caravan masters always exerted ruthless energy to discourage truancy: a captured deserter was usually hanged at once, seldom with the formality of a trial, or at least flogged to the point where he would have welcomed the noose. But these penalties were looked on as occupational hazards, and if porters dropped out of ivory-slave caravans in droves, Thomson could not but expect a proportionate amount of absenteeism in an expedition bound for the least inviting destination in east Africa.

His own character may have compounded the difficulty, for he was unique among caravan commanders, European as well as Arab, in never having hanged a porter. For this, contemporaries thought him less humane than insane; but he himself did not see it that way. Nor in all probability did his porters. "In the hearing of the men," he wrote, "bloodthirsty orders were given to the night-guard to shoot down without warning anyone observed to go outside camp." Thomson also used the psychological bludgeon of the Masai to keep his reluctant family together. Even on the outskirts of Mombasa, reports of nearby elmoran raiders began trickling in, and "stories about Masai in our rear ... had more effect than bushels of threats." Only two men deserted.

Yet before the coast could be considered safely beyond the reach of escapees, Thomson first had to cross a short stretch of country which had a way of giving the traveler an unpleasant surprise. "Starting at daybreak, we traversed an undulating region which seemed wonderfully fertile, and was covered with a pleasant, open forest, under the shelter of which grew a rich carpet of tender grass." Then came "an abrupt change ... The dense jungle, the grassy glades, the open forest disappear, and their place is taken by what may be called a skeleton forest. Weird and ghastly is the aspect of the greyish-coloured trees and bushes; for they are almost destitute of tender, waving branch or quivering leaf ... The wind ... raised only a mournful whistling or dreary croaking, 'eerie' and full of sadness, as if it said, 'Here all is death and desolation!' ... Through this dreadful wilderness our route now lay. The porter, wearied already with a long march, and parched for want of water, presses on panting and perspiring under a broiling sun, made worse by the glaring red soil which reflects the rays as though they came from the mouth of a furnace."

This is one of the earliest written descriptions of the Taru desert, which would present an almost insuperable obstacle to railway construction thirteen years later. Although it embraced an area not much larger than the District of Columbia, the Taru was a true Gobi to the caravan leaders who had to stagger through its grasping sea of shriveled thorn talons. To become lost and to die in the Taru was simply a matter of straying a hundred yards or so from one's party. To perish of thirst it was not even necessary to be lost. While a few cupfuls of slime could sometimes be scooped from isolated sandstone pools, the only substantial water supply lay at the summit of Mount Maungu, a great rock pimple rising from the diseased vegetation near the desert's inland perimeter. After nearly two days, Thomson and one or two men managed to scale Maungu and fill enough calabashes to carry the rest of the expedition across the last few miles.

Once clear, Thomson could enjoy a brief spell playing the tourist as he made his way through the low-lying mswaki (toothbrush) scrub near the Kilimanjaro foothills. His camera was kept busy, although attempts to photograph women were not always successful. "With soothing words, aided by sundry pinches and chuckings under the chin, I might get the length of making them stand up; but the moment that the attempt to focus them took place they would fly in terror to the shelter of the woods." Stouter hearts, however, posed, and a few even touched the galvanic battery, howling in petrified delight at its effects. For the most part the reception was friendly, enabling detailed personal accounts of local life. Among other recorded impressions, Thomson describes for "the gentle reader, who is sufficiently curious and not too bashful... the toilet of a swell M-teita damsel," taking special note of her "coating of lamp black and castor-oil which emits an aroma that gallantry compels me to call pleasing, but which, as an 'aside' ... I confess to be simply awful."

On March 31, the party entered the village of Taveta, the jumping-off place for caravans en route to Masailand. Late nineteenth-century European visitors always remarked on Taveta as a sort of Beulah-land in the bush, and Thomson agrees, only more so. He throws out his arms to the "leafy labyrinths and bosky bowers of the little African Arcadia," giving only the hint of a shocked gasp at one local custom: "Conjugal fidelity is unknown ... [the people] might almost be described as a colony of free lovers." But he hastens to add that the Tavetans, despite their lapses, are "true Arcadians ... in their peaceable habits, their great hospitality, their manly, pleasant manners, and surprising honesty." He also gushes forth on the surrounding countryside: the "splendid umbrageous canopy" of the forest, and the mountain stream whose "banks, bedecked with maiden-hair ferns and creepers, and its noble arboreal arch invite us to pause and refresh ourselves." Dominating all this is the "cloud-sucking pinnacle," Kilimanjaro itself: "There is the grand dome or crater of Kibo, with its snow cap glancing and scintillating like burnished silver in the rays of the afternoon sun, and there, on its eastern flank, rise the jagged outlines of the craggy peak of Kimawenzi. What words can adequately describe this glimpse of majestic grandeur and godlike repose?"

But Taveta lay too near the dreaded gateway for the lyrical stream to pour on indefinitely, and before long the Scotsman took over from the poet. "The whole of my beads had to be restrung into the regulation lengths of the Masai country. Unless in this form, they would not be accepted ... 60,000 strings had to be made up." The porters assigned to the chore commenced stealing the beads. Thomson seized their guns, posted a guard, issued "the usual bloodthirsty orders." The restringing proceeded apace. Now a delegation of Taveta elders arrived. The Masai cattle-raiding season was on, and the elders, who had already marveled at the galvanic battery, sought anti-elmoran magic. "To refuse is simply to make them believe that I do not want to assist them ... I brew some Eno's fruit salt, which with fear and trembling they taste as it fizzes away. Finally they retire quite satisfied." Thomson no doubt wished the Eno's might work the same spell on his own venture. Traders passing through Taveta "confirmed my previous belief that my caravan was much too small. I was assured that these traders never dreamed of entering the Masai country with less than 300 men ... I acquired sufficient ominous information to make anyone not possessed of a particularly sanguine temperament despair of even passing the threshold." But the everlasting optimist rose to the occasion. "I had great faith in my lucky star, and determined to mould my fate to my own ends."

*

On April 18, "full of buoyant hopes and sanguine aspirations," Thomson finally broke away from Taveta and the party began skirting the western flank of Kilimanjaro on the long-awaited push into Masailand. But they had scarcely returned to the routine of the march when news arrived that a two-thousand-man Masai force was heading straight in their direction. While Thomson himself had not been singled out as a target, he nevertheless adopted evasive tactics and made a ten-day detour into the kingdom of Moshi. Here, he was able to resume the tourist role; he even tried to scale Kilimanjaro, although the attempt did not come off because he could give it only one day.

The remainder of the time was spent alternately enjoying and enduring the hospitality of Moshi's ruler, a one-eyed buttertub named Mandara, already on the way to celebrity among explorers for his unbridled gluttony in levying hongo. Thomson might conceivably have escaped Mandara's cupidity, except that "with a thoughtlessness for which there can be no excuse," he invited the king to have a look at his arsenal. After marveling at the weapons and the galvanic battery (which "threw him into astonishment, till his eagle eye gleamed with covetousness, and he spat himself dry") and "ordering his chiefs to submit to the electric current," Mandara got down to business. Thomson's gift consisted of a Snider rifle, a revolver, four flasks of gunpowder and some cloth. Mandara inspected these articles with the quick but professional glance of a pawnbroker, asked if the offering were merely lagniappe for his troops and stalked off in regal dudgeon. It took a double-barreled smoothbore rifle, a tin box, a tweed suit and a pair of shoes to mollify him. Later, however, Mandara was to show a generous streak, presenting Thomson with a gold watch that he had taken from the missionary New. Thomson subsequently returned the watch to New's brother. It had cost him the galvanic battery. He was not sorry to leave Moshi.

Under way again. More unsettling news. Fischer, several marches ahead, had evidently committed some breach of etiquette which touched off the Masai's short fuse; the entire country was in an uproar. It was not the best of times to enter Masailand. But Thomson's eagerness (and perhaps his reluctance to be Mandara's guest again) overcame his better judgement and he continued to forge ahead. Almost at once he received word that a band of elmoran was approaching. The critical moment had arrived at last. Thomson ordered the men to take up the largest handfuls of grass they could hold—the visitor's sign of coming in peace. He did not have long to wait. "Passing through the forest, we soon set our eyes on the dreaded warriors that had so long been the subject of my waking dreams, and I could not but involuntarily exclaim, 'What splendid fellows!'" He was particularly struck by the elmoran "dignity," and noted that the warriors "carefully preserved their aristocratic demeanour. They indulged in none of the obtrusive, vulgar inquisitiveness or aggressive impertinence which makes the traveller's life a burden to him among other native tribes." That incredible assessment was shortly to be revised, but in the meanwhile Thomson singled out the elmoran's spokesman for special commendation. "With profound astonishment I watched this son of the desert as he stood before me, speaking with a natural fluency and grace, a certain sense of the gravity and importance of his position, and a dignity of attitude beyond all praise." According to Sadi and Muhinna, the thrust of this man's oration was grudging consent to the expedition's undisturbed passage. On May 3, Thomson at last entered Masailand.

"Leaving the forest," he writes of this day, "we suddenly emerged, at a height of 6000 feet, on a great treeless plain … quite indistinguishable from the pasture of more temperate climates. In the immediate foreground the country spread out before us in gently waving plains, diversified by low, rounded ridges, small humpy hills or volcanic cones … Such is the country … Look, now, farther ahead. Near a dark line of trees … you observe in the clear morning air columns of curling smoke, and from the vicinity strange long dark lines are seen to emerge like the ranks of an advancing army. The smoke marks the kraals of the Masai and the advancing lines are their cattle moving towards the pasture-ground. If you will now imagine a long line of men moving in single file across this prairie region … headed by myself, and brought up in the rear by Martin, while a cold, piercing wind blows in with the freezing effect suggestive of an early spring in Scotland, you will be able to form a picture of the scene which presented itself on that memorable morning."

But the bucolic glory began to dissolve rapidly when the party made camp and the Masai converged on them once more, still in peace but now demanding their rightful entry fees. "The division of the spoil … was not encouraging. The El-moran, having laid aside their spears and shields, stand ready in a hollow group. My men, advancing with the hongo, suddenly throw it in their midst, and run for their lives out of the way. With a grand yell the warriors precipitate themselves upon the articles, on the principle of 'every one for himself and the devil take the hindmost.' … A pack of half-starved wolves suddenly let loose on small animals could not have made a more ferocious and repulsive exhibition."

These second thoughts on Masai "dignity" and "aristocratic demeanour" were being accelerated by a mounting sense of alarm. "My spirits sank as I saw load after load disappear. How could we ever hope to travel many days further, if such was to be our fate?" Quickly, the camp took on the aspect of a student demonstration. "In response to repeated cries for the white Lybon, backed up by insolent attempts to tear open the door of my tent, I had to step out and bow my acknowledgements." Thomson also stepped momentarily out of character, losing his patience and nearly his life when he shoved an overly inquisitive moran away with his foot. The warrior, "fury blazing in his face and presenting the most diabolical aspect... sprang back a few steps, drew his simè, and was about to launch himself upon me. I slipped aside, however, and was speedily surrounded by the guard."

Thomson's difficulties had only begun. The following day, "I was thunderstruck by the unexpected news that the whole country ahead of us was up in arms, to oppose our further progress, and to take revenge on us for the Fischer affray ... With bitter feelings of disappointment and chagrin, I saw no further course open to me but to retreat to Taveta." Thomson also learned that the Masai planned to strike the following day, in one of their dreaded dawn attacks. It thus became imperative to retire that very night, in secret and with the greatest of haste. "An ominous silence pervaded the camp ... The night set in gloomy and dark. A black pall of clouds overspread the heavens. Some rain sputtered ... Two hours after sunset, the word was given to pack up. Not a sound broke the stillness as each man buckled on his belt, caught up his gun, and shouldered his load ... Then, when all was ready, we glided out into the blackness of night. Not an object could be seen to guide our steps, so I had to take the lead, with compass in hand and a bull's-eye lantern under my coat to enable me to read the card ... The amenities of the night were not enhanced by the occasional glare of lightning and the muttering of thunder near Kibo." This was one of the rare occasions when despair nearly overcame Thomson. But characteristically he lost little time in marshaling his spirits. "I had great faith ... in the Italian proverb, 'He who goes gently goes safe; he who goes safe goes far,' and I never doubted for a moment that, to use Mr. Micawber's sanguine words, 'something would turn up.'"

On May 12, the party was back in Taveta, Thomson more determined than ever to slip past the Masai barrier, despite the apparent unlikelihood of his being able to do so. First, however, there was a disagreeable task. Sadi and Muhinna had been stirring dissension ever since the expedition entered Masailand; Muhinna, in fact, had become so disruptive an influence that Thomson decided he must go. And, since Thomson wished to recruit additional porters in Mombasa, he would personally escort Muhinna there, without handing him his notice until arrival. On May 15, with Muhinna and four headmen, he made a dash to the coast, crossing the Taru in twenty-two hours—without water—and reaching Mombasa in six days. As this meant averaging thirty-four miles daily, Thomson could feel justified in describing the march as "a pedestrian feat which probably has never been equalled in the annals of African travelling." Nor may it have been surpassed in the annals of futility, since no replacement for Muhinna could be found and Thomson had to keep him on. One can imagine his feelings back at Taveta when he learned that the report of the impending Masai attack had been concocted by Muhinna as part of a scheme to keep the expedition from its objective. "I had ... a very strong temptation to let the knave know that his tricks had been exposed, and then swing him up on a tree." However, "I forebore both ...for the simple reason that he was indispensable to me."

Still, Thomson's faith in Mr. Micawber was vindicated in the person of a Swahili trader named Juma Kimameta, who, with a number of other coast merchants, had brought a large caravan into Taveta during the explorer's absence and was preparing to cross Masailand. Thomson "could not suppress a hurrah ... for by this time I was only too glad to stoop to the idea of joining a trading caravan." And once again a white explorer became indebted to a brown slaver. Diminutive in stature, blind in one eye, his face plowed up by smallpox scars, Juma Kimameta enjoyed a reputation for slave dealing that may have been exceeded only by Tippu Tib's. Although Thomson refers to him only as an ivory trader, he well knew Juma Kimameta's other source of income and certainly had no illusions as to the bestiality of slave caravans. ("There is no monster more savage and cruel than the Swahili trader, when the demon nature in him is let loose.") Yet the veteran hunter of black ivory could also be likened to Tippu Tib in less noxious respects. Thomson found him "far above the average in character and intelligence," and wrote that "a more thoroughly good fellow than Jumba Kimameta never lived (although he possessed all the characteristic vices of his race)." Nor was Thomson the only European to make that judgement. In any case, his delight at the opportunity to travel in company with the notorious slave driver says something not only about Juma Kimameta but about a country where a traveler needed all the friends he could get.*

Thomson soon learned, however, that safety in numbers could have its drawbacks, especially if the numbers were Muslim. On July 17, the combined forces set out, and then, almost as if conspiring against Thomson's patience, the traders began calling abnormally prolonged

---

* According to Jackson, Thomson "owed his success to Jumba's backing." Jackson knew the trader well and was saddened to witness his declining years. At the turn of the century he described Juma Kimameta as "very old, and broken in health ... He wore a pair of large horn spectacles given to him by a German missionary; one glass was missing, while the other was kept in position by string and beeswax ... Poor old chap, he soon found his influence had vanished ..."

halts. "The time was the month of Ramadan, and being good Mohammedans, they held that period sacred to fasting during the day, and to
feasting right gloriously during the night." This would continue until
the appearance of the new moon, and despite "judicious use of the
Bombastes Furioso manner," Thomson could goad Juma Kimameta
only so far. During these trying intervals, however, he was at least able
to shoot game, which not only brought welcome variety to the porters' meager posho diet but helped "let off my bile and allay the spirit
of restlessness." He also took the opportunity to read William Cullen
Bryant "as a relief from the barren occupation of cursing my fate and
wondering when all this purposeless delay would end." It was not until
August 11 that he re-entered Masailand.

"We had to eat humble pie to propitiate their lordships."

No serious incidents occurred as the caravans made their way across the
plains during the early stages of the march, mainly, perhaps, because
the big battalions had gone off on cattle raids. Anxious moments were
of course inevitable. A riot almost started when several Masai women
complained that the tourist's camera had bewitched them. Thomson
had to put aside his theodolite, since "its portentous appearance and
strangely intricate mechanism were looked upon with such feelings of
alarm by the people that they made a hostile demonstration." Occasionally a moran would rush the caravan, in the hope of stealing some
article of trade goods, but "such attempts almost wore the air of friendly
contests." For the most part the atmosphere, if electric, was not turbulent, the Masai often showing restraint and good nature. The only overt
threat of violent death did not even come from the tribe. It arose instead
during "a bloodthirsty quarrel between Martin and Makatubu, in which
the hot southern blood of the former and the unbalanced temper of the
latter got quite the better of them." Just as Makatubu pulled his revolver
on Martin, he was knocked down and tied up by Brahim and several
of the porters, while Thomson seized Martin in a bear hug until his
rage subsided.

Meanwhile, Masai deportment continued civil. Thanks to his weird
color and mysterious instruments, Thomson was treated with the
respect due a magician. No less a personage than Mbatian's daughter
offered him a donkey as a gift. He found himself constantly obliged to
spit at men and women who "flocked to me as pious catholics would

do to springs of healing virtue." At one point, his skills as an obstetrician were sought out when a Masai couple told him they wanted "a
little white boy who would be a counterpart of me." Thomson prescribed Eno's. Husband and wife "drank the effervescing liquid with
eager expectation," but with "lingering doubts whether the coveted
result was a certainty. Unfortunately I had not one of Eno's pamphlets
about me at that time, or doubtless I should have proved to their
entire satisfaction that it had never been known to fail in producing
even more astonishing results ... Bidding them good-bye, I returned
to my tent, and let out my surcharged feelings by a few steps of a
Scotch dance and sundry screams of convulsive laughter, greatly to the
bewilderment of Songoro, who thought I had gone mad."

Yet the march was not without its ominous aspects. Elmoran began
appearing in ever-growing numbers and proportionate belligerence.
They continued to greet Thomson as a laibon, but his status did not
inhibit either their demands for hongo or their invasions of his privacy.
"No one dares lay a hand on a warrior when he is determined to see
me and my things. With the greatest insolence he will push aside the
guard ... and bestow his odoriferous, grease-clad person on my bed ...
Ceremonious even in his arrogance, he will now greet me, and then
demand some beads." Less than subtly, mass war dances were held
nearly every day. "No man dared lay aside his gun."

*

By September, the files of porters had struggled into the village of
Ngongo Bagas—only about fifteen miles from present-day Nairobi—in
the soaring highland region whose mile-high altitudes swirled with icy
rain and stiletto winds. It became so cold here that Thomson gave Juma
Kimameta one of his Austrian blankets. Only a short distance from the
edge of the Rift Valley, Ngongo Bagas served as a halting place where
caravans prepared for the precarious descent of the vertiginous eastern
escarpment and the long march up the valley floor. It was not an ideal
place to linger, however, for here travelers found themselves between
the Scylla of the Masai and the Charybdis of the elmoran's most bitter
foe, the Kikuyu, who made their homes behind an almost impenetrable
defense work of forest just to the north of the caravan trail. As a rule
the Kikuyu came out second best in pitched battles with the Masai, but
they were one of the few tribes to offer genuine resistance; occasionally
they would emerge victorious. They also enjoyed a reputation for what
whites liked to call treachery, as if the defense of their land had to be

conducted in strict accordance with Marquess of Queensberry rules. By those standards, however, the Kikuyu were no more to be trusted than they themselves trusted or welcomed the Swahili slavers. Juma Kimameta's repute was particularly gamy. Even some years after his death, the Kikuyu remembered how he had lured many of their men, women and children into the open with shining trade goods and then yoked them together under the protection of his guns. He may have been singled out as the tribe's most hated visitor, and Thomson, in his company, had to endure the uneasy awareness of guilt by association.

Thus, as the expedition camped on the dark edges of Kikuyuland, the customary thorn boma, an enclosure made of nature's barbed wire, seemed inadequate protection. Instead, a stout tree-trunk palisade was thrown up around the five-acre area where the combined parties pitched their tents. But Thomson's lucky star was apparently shining overtime. Apart from one or two abortive skirmishes, the two-week stay at Ngongo Bagas was a sort of cease-fire period, and the camp itself a demilitarized zone where the traders bartered in relative security with both Masai and Kikuyu. Only when the march resumed across an abbreviated stretch of forest did a serious clash seem imminent, as grease- and chalk-smeared Kikuyu warriors, bearing all the accoutrements of battle, converged in thousands and made appropriately alarming gestures. But the test of strength did not quite come off. While the traders, who could run further amok when they saw fit than any so-called savage, were eager to cut loose with a few withering volleys from their several hundred rifles, Thomson somehow prevailed on them to forbear. Even so, the massed Kikuyu remained a real threat for several anxious hours, and "every now and then we had to make a stand and scatter them by a show of our guns."

Once at the upper lip of the Rift, Thomson could drink in briefly the spectacular plain of volcanoes and lakes which can almost be said to flow, like a fifty-mile-wide river, between the valley's two towering escarpments. Later, he inspected some of these sights at close quarters. Peering into the crater of Longonot—the Masai's "mountain of the big pit," whose lower foothills the railway would skirt—"I was completely fascinated, and felt under an almost irresistible impulse to plunge into the fearful chasm. So overpowering was this feeling that I had to withdraw myself ..." He also climbed the legendary "steam mountain," Eburu, "which we were able to identify by clouds of vapour and a curious puffing sound exactly resembling a steam-engine starting work ... Further along we came to the edge of a lava cliff... so hot that my men could not walk on it."

But as usual, the chief attraction—and incubus—was the Masai, and Thomson's march up the Rift became a perfect ordeal of harassment. By now, the aggressiveness of the warriors had reached an all but intolerable extreme. Elmoran prowled the perimeter of the heavily guarded camp at night, trying to steal, to stampede the travelers' animals and otherwise provoke. Thomson and the others could scarcely call themselves their own men when the troops came to visit. "They ordered us about as if we were so many slaves. I had daily to be on exhibition, and perform for their delectation. 'Take off your boots.' 'Show your toes.' 'Let us see your white skin.' 'Bless me! What queer hair!' 'Good gracious! What funny clothes!' Such were the orders and exclamations (anglicized) which greeted me as they turned me about, felt my hair with their filthy paws, while 'Shorè' (friend), 'give me a string of beads,' was dinned into my ear with maddening persistence ... We were within an ace of a fight, which would have been disastrous, and we had to eat humble pie to propitiate their lordships."

Thomson did not find the Masai an unmixed curse, however. "Strangely enough, in the midst of it all we made great friends with some of the elders, who delighted to sit down and talk to us, showing a frankness and absence of suspicion such as I have never seen elsewhere among Africans ... In some respects I began almost to like the Masai." Nor did his coy sense of humor desert him. "The damsels, of course, would have been without fault if they had only discarded clay and grease and used Pears' soap. Certainly there is as fine an opportunity for the introduction of that valuable article into the Masai country as there is of Manchester cottons into the Congo."

One marvels that Thomson could have kept so firm a grip on his temper and perspective. And yet, at this stage of the journey, he was in fact swinging wildly between prudence and recklessness. On reaching Lake Naivasha, where he learned that Fischer had been turned back by illness among his porters, he conceived what he called "a scheme of a perilous character": he would leave the safety of Juma Kimameta's numbers and, with only a handful of men, strike out northeast on a "flying visit" to Mount Kenya. This would take him over a range of mountains nine thousand feet high and across the Laikipia plateau, notorious as a hotbed of Masai pugnacity. The others were horrified. "'What!' said they; 'do you think you can penetrate a district with a few men, which we should be afraid to penetrate with several hundreds? ... Do you know that a few years ago a caravan was totally annihilated in that very district?' ... My only reply was that Mount Kenya *had to be reached somehow,* as all my countrymen wanted to know the truth about it."

Having failed to dissuade Thomson, Juma Kimameta and the other traders therefore prayed for him, reciting passages from the Koran and mixing cabalistic medicines as further insurance. "There are some people, I suppose, who will express astonishment that I should even have seemed to tolerate such infidel practices. All I can say to such people is, that I hope they may never be called upon to leave their comfortable arm-chairs." On the morning of October 6, after breakfasting on zebra steak, millet porridge and tea sweetened with honey, he set off.

*

At every step the excursion was interrupted by Masai brewing more earnestly for trouble than any elmoran Thomson had previously encountered. "They played with us as a cat does with a mouse, and the end would without doubt have been the same, but for a certain hazy respect and fear they had for me as a phenomenon the power of which it was not safe to rouse." For humility was not the only bolt in Thomson's quiver. There was also his intuition, which now worked around the clock, to tell him, with great accuracy, when and when not to bring his white man's magic into play. Seldom has any explorer used that fraud to better purpose. He demoralized one murder-bent band by taking out his lone false tooth and offering to remove a moran's nose in the same fashion. He convinced the members of another war party that his camera would make them invincible in battle. When he violated a local custom by shooting a zebra, the enraged Masai finally became placated on hearing the explanation that Thomson had required the entrails for a mighty spell he was casting. ("They consented to let us go on, after I had spat on them to show that I did not mean any harm ... It may be understood that I did this latter part of the ceremony with the most hearty goodwill.") Even when a stratagem backfired he could exploit it. Hoping to awe one moran, he showed him a photograph of some friends in England; the Masai immediately demanded that Thomson bring the people out of the picture, but stepped back in alarm on learning that they were asleep and might fly into an unmanageable rage if disturbed.

Most useful of all were Thomson's skills as an occult veterinarian. The year 1883 had been a bad one for Masai livestock: a savage outbreak of rinderpest was decimating the herds, the land reeked with the putrefying carcasses of cattle, and more than once Thomson was sought out to halt the epidemic. "I proceeded by laying out a small medicine-box with the lid open ... Taking out my sextant, and putting on a pair of kid gloves—which accidentally I happened to have, and which impressed the natives enormously—I intently examined the contents. Discovering the proper dawa, I prepared a mixture, and then getting ready some Eno's fruit-salt, I sang an incantation—generally something about 'Three blue-bottles'—over it. My voice not being astonishingly mellifluous, it did duty capitally for a wizard's. My preparations complete, and Brahim being ready with a gun, I dropped the salt into the mixture; simultaneously the gun was fired, and, lo! up fizzed and sparkled the carbonic acid ... Little bits of paper were next dipped in the water, and after I had spat upon them the ceremony was over, and the pieces were handed round as an infallible cure, warranted not to fail ... I thus starred it as a second Cagliostro."

And so it went. Unmolested but terribly vulnerable, the corporal's guard crossed the mountains. Temperatures, plummeting to only a few degrees above zero, proved almost too much for the porters, but not for Thomson. He reveled in the hoar frost on the grass and the junipers that carpeted the slopes. Once, finding himself in a Scotch mist, he did a "patriotic dance." The mountains he christened the Aberdare range, for the President of the Royal Geographical Society. Later, in an understandable and quite merited bid for personal immortality, he named a magnificent waterfall after himself. Another reminder of his visit is the dainty Thomson's gazelle, commonly known as the "Tommy."

The high point of the journey, of course, was Mount Kenya. On October 28, Thomson reached the banks of the Uaso Nyiro river, only fifteen miles from the peak itself, the sight of which touched off another shower of rapture. "Suddenly there was a break in the clouds far up in the sky, and the next moment a dazzling white pinnacle caught the last rays of the sun, and shone with a beauty, marvelous, spirit-like, and divine, cut off, as it apparently was, by immeasurable distance from all connection with the gross earth. The sun's rays went off, and then, with 'a softness like the atmosphere of dreams,' which befitted the gloaming, that white peak remained, as though some fair spirit with subdued and chastened expression lingered at her evening devotions. Presently, as the garish light of day melted into the soft hues and mild effulgence of a moon-lit night, the 'heaven-kissing' mountain became gradually disrobed, and then in all its severe outlines and chaste beauty it stood forth from top to bottom, entrancing, awe-inspiring ... At that moment I could almost feel that Kenia was to me what the sacred stone of Mecca is to the faithful who have wandered from distant lands, surmounting perils and hardships that they might but kiss or see the hallowed object, and then, if it were God's will, die."

It was, in fact, almost literally a case of "see Mount Kenya and die." Although Thomson had come closer to the mountain than any other white man, he was deprived of an opportunity to make an assault on the slopes, for word was suddenly received that Masai tolerance of his presence had exhausted itself and that an attack was imminent. At once the party dropped back down the escarpment, although the flight may have been more suggestive of a rush to catch an evening bus after a Sunday picnic. "We voted the whole adventure quite delightful, and heedless of everything, we light-heartedly whistled and sang or cracked jokes till the very welkin rang. Buffaloes turned up their noses and snorted astonishment; rhinoceroses, like evil spirits exorcised, fled, blowing off wind like a steam-engine."

The outing came to an end on November 10, when Thomson rejoined Martin and the main body at the village of Njemps on the southern shore of Lake Baringo. With the Masai safely behind at last, "we could ramble about without guns or attendants, doze ... under shady sycamores, and read a favourite poet." Thomson could also contemplate the final leg of the expedition, which he describes as "the most uncertain of the whole journey." Again he would take temporary leave of Juma Kimameta's caravan, which was headed north in search of ivory, and strike west to Lake Victoria, "with the agreeable knowledge that the last three caravans which had preceded me had each lost more than 100 men by violence."

To Thomson, having come through Masailand unscathed, this may have seemed a grim joke. For the Luo people (then called Kavirondo) of the eastern lake shore region were not known to be warlike by nature. They had simply been thrown into an atypical and acutely dangerous turmoil by slaver incursions and atrocities. That Thomson himself was not seeking slaves would mean nothing among a tribe whose only visitors from afar had taught them to be aggressively suspicious. Thus, on November 28, after a four-day struggle over the wind-pummeled heights of the Rift's Elgeyo escarpment, and a week's march across the buffalo-swarming "Red Plain" of the northern Uasin Gishu plateau, the party entered the Kavirondo village of Kabaras in a state of tingling apprehension.

The reception was not quite what Thomson had expected. Hardly had he passed through the opening in the stout mud wall that encircled the little cluster of tidy, thatch-roofed huts, than "I found myself surrounded by a bevy of undraped damsels, whose clothes and ornaments consisted in a string of beads." Thomson thus became the first in a long line of transient whites who were to titillate Victorian and Edwardian readers with accounts of Kavirondo as a vast nudist colony—which also abided by the most exemplary moral code. After recovering from his initial embarrassment ("I had much to do to keep my countenance, and was at a loss where to look"), he was able to offer the observation that the Kavirondo "eloquently illustrate the fact, which some people cannot understand, that morality has nothing to do with clothes. They are the most moral of all the tribes in this region, and they are simply angels of purity beside the decently dressed Masai, among whom vice of the most open kind is rampant."

Thomson was also the first to marvel at Kavirondo's bounty. He described the region as "a veritable land of Goshen" that fairly burst with sweet potatoes, maize, peanuts, fowls, eggs, honey and milk—although he did not take to the latter, for "it was discovered that the cow is made to add to the volume and flavour of the milk another animal liquid, which, as far as I am aware, has never been used in England for adulteration." But this was a minor complaint, easily forgotten, since entry into Kavirondo had not been opposed.

However, when the party reached a contrastingly barren and poverty-stricken district near the Nzoia river, the men began nervously fingering the triggers of their rifles. The expedition was now within twenty miles of demonstrating the feasibility of the short route to the lake, but it was beginning to seem as if the Kavirondo might succeed in halting Thomson where the Masai had failed. Sullen crowds, their numbers bloating rapidly, converged from all sides on the thin line of porters; Thomson often had to lower his head and literally butt a passageway through the threatening human wall. Scuffles were inevitable, and it says something about Thomson's judgement that none broke out into the pitched battle that must certainly have wiped out the party. Just once, this came within a hair's breadth of happening. During an uneasy exchange of gifts with a chief, a dispute somehow arose and so infuriated a Kavirondo blood that Thomson had to flatten him with a right cross. "The moment was very critical. All my men held their guns ready. Brahim covered the young warrior with my Express rifle, while on the other hand hundreds of warriors grasped their spears as if only waiting for a signal to precipitate themselves on our small party. As for myself, I simply folded my arms and laughed derisively, a piece of acting I have always found to have a remarkable effect on the natives, who at once conclude that I have supernatural powers of offence and defence."

But the barrier between Thomson and the lake continued to stand firm and unyielding. At a village called Serembe, barely a mile from the shore, the expedition was simply told it would not be allowed to proceed an inch farther, because "probably we would make *uchawi* (black medicine) and *stop* the Lake—whatever that might mean." Thomson got around this, however, by shooting three hippos for the protein-starved villagers, who appeared sufficiently appreciative to offer no more than token resistance when the party made its final dash on December 11 for the long-dreamed-of goal. "An hour's fever- ish tramp, almost breaking into a run, served to bring us to the edge of Lake Victoria Nyanza, and soon we were joyously drinking deep draughts of its waters." To observe the occasion, Thomson gave the porters a speech "on the heroic lines more commonly heard at a City banquet or Mutual Admiration Society than in Central Africa." Fur- ther celebration took place in Serembe that evening, when "Martin and I illustrated the 'poetry of motion' as practised in Malta and Scot- land ... Martin tried to initiate the damsels into the mysterious charm of the waltz, while I showed them ... the spirited movements of a Scotch dance."

For a few tempting moments, Thomson considered following up his victory and crossing the Nile, which lay only forty-five miles to the west. But on learning of turmoil and tribal wars in that region, he con- cluded that "to gain a little by going further I might run an immediate risk of losing all," and resolved instead to apply the not too well-worn brakes of prudence, resting on his already handsome laurels. He had, after all, done what he had set out to do; by opening the short route to the lake he had matched any exploit of Livingstone, Stanley, Burton, Speke or Baker. Thus, although "Christmas day was not marked by any feast or revelling among good things ... I was supremely happy, for I was brimful of the thought that an arduous piece of work had been completed, and that I was homeward bound."

*

New Year's Eve, a week later, was not so serene. Thomson, having been tossed and gored by a wounded buffalo, had nearly reached "the limits of my earthly existence as well as that of the year." He had been saved only at the very last instant, when a shot rang out in the best adventure story tradition and despatched the bull. Even with a gaping hole in his thigh, Thomson retained his mad buoyancy and "drank to the hopeful new year in a deep libation of buffalo soup." And although he had to endure "the humiliation of being carried— the first time I had ever sunk so low," he could still sound a sanguine note on the character improvement of his porters, who fought among themselves to be his stretcher-bearers. It was, he said, "a striking change from the time when they were the off-scourings of Zanzibar villainy, and required to be driven ... with the frequent application of the birch."

Wishing to avoid further unpleasantness with the Kavirondo, Thomson followed a more northerly route back to Lake Baringo, passing across the foothills of Mount Elgon and then through "a pathless wilderness ... with no better guide than vague notions assisted by a compass." On January 7, 1884, when the party reached the summit of the Elgeyo escarpment, he had recovered sufficiently from the bout with the buffalo to leave the stretcher and make the dizzying drop on the back of Nil Desperandum. But once on the floor of the Rift he found himself quite lost, and it was not until nearly the end of the month that the expedition reassembled at Njemps. Now more eager than ever to reach the coast, Thomson ran head-on into another frustration: Juma Kimameta had not yet returned from the north. After waiting three weeks, and with his own men on half-rations, he was left with no choice but to move out.

The decision to go may have saved his life. He was now beginning to feel the first symptoms of the dysentery which had killed the leader of his maiden expedition; by February 21 he had become so weak that he was hoisted once more to Nil Desperandum's back. On March 4, on the northern shore of Lake Naivasha, he collapsed. After nearly twelve months of outwitting Masai, Kikuyu, Kavirondo and buffalo, it appeared as if Thomson had finally met an unconquerable foe. "Martin, good soul, was in despair, and he said eloquently—though unintentionally—with his eyes: 'You are dying! and what on earth shall I do?'" Thomson himself seemed inclined almost to agree. "I could neither stand nor sit. Even milk curdled in the stomach ... I had much reason to fear perforation of the colon, which I knew would mean speedy death."

Perhaps it was only the pathological Pollyanna in his nature that kept him going. "I had not yet made up my mind to cave in, and the will, after all, has something to do with these matters ... The lamp of life flickered a little, then became more steady. I never lost hope, and the idea of my becoming meat for the hyenas was one I would never permit myself to entertain for a moment." Nor could the apparent terminal stages of the affliction prevent the poet from enjoying the scenery. As the party reached the crest of the Rift's eastern escarpment, "I got myself held up to view this grand landscape—probably unsurpassed

anywhere—and, weak and weary as I was, surveyed the glorious panorama with infinite delight, though also with a spice of awe."

And then his resistance snapped. "On the 12th of March I find the
following entry in my diary:—'After a critical three days, during which
I hovered on the verge of the grave, I have contrived to give Death the
slip by timely "joukin' roun' the corner," and to strike out on more
hopeful bearings. Appetite returning, and, after some fourteen days'
starvation, able to eat a little.' After that there appears in my journal a
blank of six weeks, which eloquently tells its own tale ... Throughout
the period represented by the blank I lay at death's door. I never knew
what it was to have more than fifteen minutes' sleep ... I became an
object fearful to look upon, with eyes sunk away deep into my skull.
A skin bag drawn tightly over a skeleton and enclosing a few indispensable organs of the human frame might express graphically my general
appearance. I was almost afraid to bend myself, lest the skin would not
bear the tension over my bones ... But enough of these details, which
can have little interest for the reader."

The worst part of the ordeal by coma was that it had to be kept top
secret. The Masai had by now started to point an accusing finger at
Thomson for the rinderpest epidemic; had they learned of his illness he
would have been speared instantly as an infectious wizard. To discourage the elmoran from prying around the grass shelter where he teetered
at the edge of death, "it was represented that the great white lybon was
hatching some infallible medicine, that he was in consultation with
the gods, and must not be seen by mortal eye." Although the Masai
believed this and kept at a respectable arm's length, they showed fewer
inhibitions toward other members of the party. After impaling a porter
on their spears and then laying his skull open because he happened
to be short of beads, they demanded that a fine be paid "for blood
having been spilt in their territory." It was not the best of surroundings
for a sickroom.

In due course, however, it began to seem conceivable that Thomson might be on the way to "joukin' roun' the corner" once more.
Although his condition remained grave; his spirits were given a lift
with the arrival of Juma Kimameta and his caravan carrying several
fortunes in ivory. But Thomson was less awed by Juma Kimameta's
wealth than touched by the old slaver's concern for him. By now very
uncertain that he would live long enough to see Scotland again, Thomson resolved that he would at least die in an attempt to reach the coast.
Juma Kimameta, on learning of the plan, begged him to reconsider.
He might as well have saved his breath, but the gesture did not go

unremarked. Thomson later gave £100 to Kirk in Zanzibar, to be spent on the trader's behalf.

En route to the coast, Thomson convalesced and miraculously recovered, despite the fact that famine had cut the heart out of much of the country on the expedition's last lap. Everyone, indeed, met the test of endurance with the jubilant second wind of the homeward bound. Thomson seemed to gain much of his own strength from watching the porters, who "worked like heroes, and pushed on cheerfully from morn till dewy eve, often parched for want of water ... They laughed at hardships, and made jokes regarding the emptiness of their stomachs ... I had taken them away as the refuse of Zanzibar rascaldom; they were returning as men." Thomson was neither the first nor the last of white explorers to pass from loathing to unreserved affection for his porters.

*

On May 24, 1884, Thomson arrived in Mombasa, having walked three thousand miles in fourteen months, and scoring what the historian Robert I. Rotberg has called "a dogged personal triumph over adversity and infirmity ... unsurpassed in the annals of African exploration." He would continue to walk for the next seven years: across the western Sudan, over the Atlas mountains, along the upper reaches of the Zambesi. And in 1895, just before dying in Scotland at the age of thirty-seven, he would say: "If I were strong enough to put my clothes on and walk a hundred yards, I would go to Africa yet!"

But before all these things happened, Thomson gave himself a priority mission. Having shown the world that the short route to Lake Victoria was open to European travel, he immediately sought to close it down. In his opinion, the Masai were not yet ready to receive white visitors. When he learned in 1885 that a young man named James Hannington was about to take the short cut, he almost made a public issue of his opposition to the journey. But Hannington no more heeded the warning than Thomson himself had listened to Juma Kimameta. Hannington was, if anything, even more recklessly brave than Thomson himself. Worse, he was a missionary, and had just been appointed Bishop of Uganda. Nothing must delay his service to the few dozen newly converted Anglicans in that 20,000-square-mile diocese. With Christian resolve, boyish zeal and fifty porters, he departed from Mombasa, strode forth across the floor of the Rift, and no Masai laid a hand on him. Even the savage game seemed to cower in the glare of his halo; at one point he actually stared down two lions and chased them to cover with a terrible roar. Not only did he cross Masailand unharmed, but he forged on—where Thomson had hesitated to tread—toward his destination beyond the Nile. And it was on the east bank of the Nile that he was murdered.

*

One of the many concerns plaguing the rulers of Uganda was an ancient prophecy that their country would succumb to conquest from the east. If Hannington, with his handful of porters, did not quite resemble an invading horde, the news of his approach more than sufficed to send a chill down the spine of the incumbent monarch, a wretch named Mwanga, who lost no time in arranging an assassination before the Bishop could cross the Nile and fulfill the prophecy. And having pushed the panic button, Mwanga lit the lights on an instrument panel whose signals, for the next decade, would flash continually in London, Paris, and Berlin.

4

CRESCENT, CROSS AND KABAKA

*"Wherever I strolled I saw
nothing but richness."*

Many years before Uganda became British soil, English explorers tended to picture the country as something like an orchid in a field of poison ivy. This reaction was to be expected. For travelers long exposed to the Masai, Kavirondo, Kikuyu, Wakamba or Wanyamwezi tribes, the tight little kingdom of the Baganda on the northern shore of Lake Victoria seemed to offer relief from a sense of imprisonment in the Cro-Magnon age. Rare was the early European visitor to east Africa who could note, as did C. W. Hobley, that "it must by no means be supposed that anarchy prevailed in any tribe, for each ... had a council of elders, who interpreted the tribal laws, and had their own methods of enforcing obedience to the tribal sanctions." And even Hobley, who was an anthropologist as well as an administrator, did not write those words until the 1920s. White men of the previous century saw only the anarchy—"blank, amorphous barbarism," as one of them put it. Yet Uganda had to be the exception. Here was a smoothly running, centralized polity with rudimentary but visible executive, legislative and judicial functions, with appropriately Victorian (or Gilbertian) titles and ceremonial, with a society divided into recognizable strata. However imperfectly, Uganda represented civilization and order. At the top of the pyramid stood an authentic monarch, the Kabaka, ruling through a combination of divine right and constitutional law. Bathing in the glow of his mightiness and reflecting it back on him were a dowager queen, the Namasole, a queen-sister known as the Lubuga (neither were blood relatives but elected officials), a prime minister, or Katikiro, and an assortment of nobles with such titles as royal butler, baker and upholsterer. These posts were more than honorary. The Katikiro presided over a parliament called the Lukiiko, composed partly of titled nobility and partly of Great Chiefs who also acted as governors of Uganda's main provinces. Although appointed by the Kabaka, the members of the Lukiiko exercised real powers within a delicate system of checks and balances. Among other things they elected the Kabaka himself; on the death of a ruler, the successor was chosen from among his sons. While a monarch could depose any Great Chief at will, it was generally considered wiser to maintain harmonious relations with the lawmakers.

Only a degree below this level were hereditary clan chiefs, who acted as custodians of the land and interpreters of its complex ownership laws. Far beneath them, a huge agricultural proletariat, the bakopi, attached itself, in true feudal fashion, to the Great Chiefs and clan rulers. In return for tilling a baron's soil and providing him with military service, each peasant received a wife or two on loan. At the very bottom rung were the slaves, taken in war. There was a place for everyone and everyone kept his place.

Uganda's material and cultural advances also came as a welcome surprise to the cultivated visitor. Before the advent of socio-anthropology, Europeans saw the African tribesman as inherently lazy and stupid, but the label did not quite seem to fit in Uganda. To be sure, most Baganda found menial labor abhorrent—this was largely a task for slaves—but they were nonetheless industrious, energetic and possessed of a crackling intelligence. Toward the end of the nineteenth century, when the British presence in Uganda had become permanently entrenched, white men marveled at the people's adaptability to Western ideas and systems. In 1892, Captain J. R. L. Macdonald, the leader of the survey party for the railway that George Whitehouse was to build, wrote that "every chief considers it a disgrace not to be able to read and write," and added that he often received letters from these men, "dated in English fashion." Another British visitor was pleasantly astonished to note that Baganda children could read books turned upside down as quickly as if held in the conventional way. Sir Harry Johnston, one of the country's first British Governors, called the Baganda "the Japanese of Africa."

But even decades earlier, white explorers had seen bountiful evidence of skills far more developed than those of any other people in east and central Africa. If a Muganda wanted to visit a distant hamlet, he usually traveled on a well-built road that was kept in constant repair. His home was no claustrophobic, dung-plastered hovel, but a spacious, beehive-shaped bungalow with solid walls of tightly woven reeds supported by a stout framework of tree limbs that had been hewed, trimmed and bent to shape. To enter an upper-class residence, one passed through two or three courtyards ringed by high fences of elephant grass or bamboo. The royal palace, itself the size of a high school gymnasium, had about twenty such enclosed plazas. There was even the precursor of the modern lavatory. When Speke visited Uganda in 1862 he found that "the sanitary orders" of the country "required that every man build for himself a house of parliament, such being the neat and cleanly nature of the Waganda—a pattern to all other negro tribes."

Clothes in Uganda were tailored from fig-tree bark that had been beaten with grooved wooden mallets to produce the look of corduroy and the texture of silk. The garments, which brought to mind Roman togas, "were sewn together," wrote Speke, "as well as any English glovers could have pieced them." Uganda music was the most sophisticated in Africa. Orchestras included harps, xylophones, flutes, horns and a proliferation of drums tuned to every note in the scale, playing compositions not much less inventive in melody and counterpoint than Bach fugues. The social graces were exquisite—it might take as long as ten minutes to bid a stranger good morning in the street—and even the coming of the impatient white man did not immediately ruffle this demeanor. As late as 1907, Winston Churchill, visiting east Africa as a Colonial Office under-secretary, could remark: "It is not in accordance with our ideas that man should kneel to man, and one feels uncomfortable to see it done. Yet it should not be thought that the action, as performed by the Baganda, involves or implies any servility. It is their good manners." Uganda's military forces were organized on modern lines. The army had its duly appointed field marshal, called the Mujasi. The navy, an armada of swift, graceful canoes with dragonlike figureheads resembling those of Viking warships, was commanded by a lord high admiral, the Gabunga. An intricate system of nationwide drum signals enabled the mass mobilization of thousands upon thousands of troops within twenty-four hours.

Even Uganda's religion, though "pagan," at least bore a resemblance to the pantheism of Greece and Rome. Lubare, the Zeus-like figure who gave the creed its name, was monarch of the upper sky and waters, with sovereignty over a host of lesser deities who carried out special responsibilities of their own. One of these latter, the demigod-king Kintu, was also the father of his country, quite literally. Every year, according to the oral traditions of Lubareism, Kintu's wife gave birth to four sets of twins; the infant boys entered the world with fully grown beards and the girls became mothers at the age of two. Hence a population explosion which helped propel Uganda to preeminence among all its neighbors.

A more widely accepted version of Uganda's beginnings is the probable migration from Abyssinia some time during the sixteenth century of a Hamitic people called Bahima to the territory north and west of Lake Victoria. Superior to the surrounding tribes in the arts of cultivating the soil and waging war, the Bahima rapidly gained ascendancy and in due course began to split up into an assortment of feudal Graustarks, including Rwanda, Burundi, Ankole, Toro, Bunyoro and Buganda (as Uganda was originally known). By the end of the eighteenth century, Uganda had become firmly entrenched as the most powerful. And despite a long-standing feud of Rome–Carthage character with the aggressive rulers of Bunyoro to the northwest, the country continued to forge ahead and refine its way of life, so that Lord Lugard could write of its people as having achieved "many advances in the scale of humanity which we are wont to accept as indications of civilisation."

This jewel of a society, moreover, was set in a diadem of roller-coaster hills, spattered with the glowing embers of tropical flowers, brightened with clouds of butterflies and sweetened with the conversation of a million tropical birds. "I was immensely struck with its excessive beauty," wrote Speke. "No part of Bengal or Zanzibar could excel it... Wherever I strolled I saw nothing but richness." Stanley called Uganda, simply, "the pearl of Africa." So lush was the land that one could barely see the capital, Rubaga, for the warm blanket of foliage that enveloped it.

*

But it was Eden after the Fall. Uganda's mighty armed forces were not mobilized to defend a peaceable family of man but to carry fire and sword across the neighboring lands in a never-ending roundup of slaves. Baganda troops, although no match for the Masai in ferocity, were savage and energetic enough to keep the people on the surrounding shores of the lake in a state of tremulous vigilance. And although slaves were the principal objective, invasions usually witnessed the slaughter of numberless tribesmen for no other reason than the Kabakas' bloodlust. Nor did atrocity come to a halt at Uganda's boundaries, since the Baganda's advanced level of civilization enabled them to refine the arts of pain and apply them to everyday life. Lesser African breeds simply killed; in Uganda's complex society the process took longer. Criminals were dismembered and then roasted alive over slow fires for capital offenses that ranged from wearing a leopard skin (high treason: the leopard was the royal animal) to stealing one of the Kabaka's cows. A ruler's son who met defeat in an election to succeed his father was usually put to death in this fashion. Misdemeanors called for the slicing off of lips, ears, noses, eyelids or hands; more serious crimes were punished by cutting away all of the wrongdoer's face except his eyes. On his first visit to Uganda in 1890, Frederick Jackson recorded "shock" at seeing one such victim, "without either lips or cheeks, and the whole of both rows of teeth fully exposed." The sight, he said, "haunted me for many days."

One did not necessarily need to break the law to be fried or mutilated. Human sacrifice was a built-in ritual of Lubareism. Mass executions highlighted the ceremonies attending a ruler's accession. When the Kabaka Mutesa took the throne in 1856, he celebrated not only by putting all his brothers to the torch but by ordering that several hundred slaves have their throats cut. Thousands might be buried alive to satisfy a royal superstition or whim. Mutesa once decreed that beads must be worn on all men's wrists and around all women's waists; male violators of the law were beheaded, females cut in half. An Egyptian political officer who visited Uganda on a diplomatic mission in 1877 remarked that the otherwise well-kept highway to the royal palace was littered with decomposing human arms and rib cages. Among the highest ranking nobles in the Kabaka's court was the Mukajanga, the lord high executioner.

In short, Uganda was fair game for the missionaries.

"We talked about many things,
principally about Europe and
Heaven. The inhabitants of the
latter place he was very anxious about."

They were slow in heeding the call. Although east Africa had begun to hum with good works by the middle of the nineteenth century, mission groups considered Uganda too remote to warrant lasting or worthwhile effort. In the early 1860s, some stations had been opened far to the south, near Lake Nyasa, but even that relatively accessible region threw up virtually insurmountable barriers of disease and poor communication. Uganda would present infinitely greater difficulties. It might take nearly a year to reach the country from Bagamoyo, and the cost of hiring porters for so long a journey put too great a strain on collection plates. Furthermore, evangelical zeal far exceeded its manpower; even missionaries could disperse their seemingly boundless energies only so far. Thus, the first three decades of Christian endeavor in eastern Africa focused almost entirely on the coast, with Uganda a cherished but neglected orphan.

This gave the Arab slavers a clear field, and they made the most of it. The first foreigners in the country, they could not fail to leave a significant mark. They introduced firepower, sodomy and a new religion. Guns revolutionized Uganda's economy and military organization. Previously, the Kabakas' armies had taken slaves for domestic consumption only, but with the arrival of the first Zanzibari caravan under Snay bin Amir in 1852, captives became a lucrative export commodity. Two males brought a musket, one female a hundred bullets. Such incentives touched off scorched-earth campaigns more devastating than ever before known, and the slave market thus gave the armed forces a new and terrible weapon. If the Arabs had not mixed generous portions of sand into the gunpowder they traded for slaves, Uganda might well have staved off foreign aggression for many years longer than it did.

Sodomy had less visible effects on the social structure, although Kabakas and some nobles took a fancy to it and gave the practice their blessing. The most profound influence, however, was exerted by Islam, a creed particularly adaptable to African outlooks. Many Baganda embraced it warmly, winking at the Koranic strictures against alcohol and anticipating a guaranteed after-life in a paradise that fairly jiggled with concubines. Kabakas, who found the latter especially appealing, saw little reason to discourage conversion, and tended to treat the slavers with esteem—to the point where the Zanzibari visitors came to wield considerable leverage at court. Not long after Snay bin Amir's arrival, a Baluchi deserter from Seyyid Said's army, one Issa bin Hussein, managed to establish himself as a sort of eminence grise in the palace of the reigning Kabaka Suna. When Speke, the first European visitor, arrived in Uganda in 1862, he found a sizable Arab-Swahili community which had not only won a substantial number of Baganda to Islam but possessed ready access to the throne. During Mutesa's reign, there was an interval when that capricious monarch ordered all his subjects to heed Mohammed rather than Lubare. The coastal traders living in Uganda might have felt less secure in their position had they realized that by undermining the country's traditional faith they had merely opened the way for Christianity. But this occurred to no one at the time.

It is somewhat curious that Speke's visit did not trigger a missionary invasion. Here, after all, was a heathen body politic being further infected by the slave-driving Mohammedans. It was a situation identical to that which had prompted Livingstone to deliver his celebrated appeal to Cambridge University in 1857, a plea that brought the vanguard of evangelists to Lake Nyasa. And with or without Islam, Uganda's plight had to be viewed as no less urgent by uplift-minded Britons. Speke might have been somewhat extravagant in his enthusiasm for the country's advanced civilization, but he by no means overlooked the warts. Probably the most widely quoted passage in his *Journal of the Discovery of the Source of the Nile* was the account of how Mutesa tested a carbine which the explorer had just presented to him. What the Kabaka did was load and cock the weapon himself, hand it to a page and order him to shoot the first person he came across outside the palace. "Which was no sooner accomplished than the little urchin returned to announce his success, with a look of glee such as one would see in the face of a boy who had robbed a bird's-nest, caught a trout, or done any other boyish trick ... I never heard, and there appeared no curiosity to know, what individual human being the urchin had deprived of life." Mutesa, however, was elated that the carbine had not jammed.

And yet another thirteen years were to elapse before a European could finally arouse the missionary establishment to its obligations in Uganda. One does not ordinarily picture Stanley, of all people, with his collar on backwards, but this is apparently the way he saw himself in 1875, when he passed through Rubaga before making his epic journey down the Congo river. For various reasons he decided then and there that Uganda was ripe for conversion, the main reason being Mutesa himself.

Although this man, as we have seen, could be a wild animal when he chose, he was not, of course, all bad. Stanley described him thus: "Mtesa is slender and tall, probably six feet one inch in height. He has very intelligent and agreeable features, which remind me of some of the faces of the great stone images at Thebes ... He has the same fulness of lips, but their grossness is relieved by the general expression of amiability, blended with dignity, that pervades the face, and the large, lustrous, lambent eyes that lend it a strange beauty... When not engaged in council, he throws off, unreservedly, the bearing that distinguishes him when on the throne, and gives rein to his humour, indulging in hearty peals of laughter. He seems to be interested in the discussion of the manners and customs of European courts, and to be enamoured of hearing of the wonders of civilisation... When any piece of information is given him, he takes upon himself the task of translating it to his wives and chiefs, though many of the latter understand the language of the East Coast as well as he does himself."

Clearly, Mutesa was on his best behavior during the explorer's visit, and it was natural that Stanley should have regarded him as a potentially enlightened Christian despot. At his audiences with the Kabaka, he wrote, "we talked about many things, principally about Europe and Heaven. The inhabitants of the latter place he was very anxious about, and was specially interested in the nature of angels. Ideas of those celestial spirits, picked up from the Bible, Paradise Lost, Michael Angelo, and Gustave Doré, enabled me to describe them in bright and warm colours... The facility with which he comprehended what was alluded to in conversation, the eagerness of his manner, the enthusiasm he displayed when the wonders of civilisation were broached to him, tempted me to introduce the subject of Christianity, and I delayed my departure from Uganda much longer than prudence counselled, to impress the first rudimentary lessons on his mind."

From these tentative discussions it was a natural step to Sunday School. "I did not attempt to confuse him with any particular doctrine, nor did I broach abstruse theological subjects, which I knew would only perplex him. The simple story of the Creation as related by Moses, the revelation of God's power to the Israelites, their delivery from the Egyptians ... the humble birth of the Messiah, His wonderful life, woeful death, and the triumphant resurrection,—were themes so captivating to the intelligent pagan, that little public business was transacted."

Stanley also translated the Gospel of St. Luke for Kabaka and court alike, but the introduction of the Scriptures touched off an animated and at times agitated theological debate among those already exposed to Islam. The Katikiro voiced the doubts of the entire Lukiiko: how could they know whether to believe the white man, he demanded, when the Arabs had already asserted that their book held the true word of God? This brought nods, murmurs and mutterings from the assembly. But then Mutesa himself stepped forward to dispel all uncertainties with his own explanation of why the truth would be found in the white man's book, his arguments founded "principally on the difference of conduct he had observed between the Arabs and the whites." This oration apparently won the day. "The chiefs unanimously gave their promise to accept the Christians' Bible, and to conform, as they were taught, to the Christian religion."

Stanley was only the first European to be "splendidly duped," in the words of one British administrator-historian, by the piety of a Uganda monarch. What Mutesa saw in his bright vision of the Christian heaven was largely a political weapon. He had at this time come to feel uneasy over the growing influence of the Zanzibari traders among his own chiefs. Uganda, moreover, was concurrently experiencing ominous pressure from Egypt, and while Mutesa himself had been professing Islam, he had no wish to see his country fall to a Muslim power. A preponderance of Muslim interests was definitely not to the Kabaka's liking, and it was natural that he should seek a Christian counterpoise. Indeed, according to the historian Roland Oliver, he "was doubtless clutching very deliberately at the straw offered by Stanley." At least, however, it can be said that Mutesa was altogether sincere when he begged the explorer to send him teachers of the new faith. "Write, Stamlee," he pleaded, "and say to the white people that I am like a child sitting in darkness, and cannot see until I am taught the right way." He could not have known, when he made this request, what he was setting in motion.

Stanley needed little prodding. Eager to keep the flames of the Kabaka's zeal burning, he wrote a forcibly eloquent letter to the *London Daily Telegraph*, describing Uganda as a mother lode of baptisms and urging that missionaries lose no time in breaching the heathen wall. By a coincidence that has yet to be explained, Stanley's message was followed almost immediately by an anonymous offer of £5,000 to the Church Missionary Society, and Uganda no longer seemed quite so remote. But the letter alone might possibly have sufficed to whet church interest, since it gained wide circulation through reprint in a number of British periodicals. One of these was the Edinburgh *Daily Review*, a copy of which happened to find its way to Berlin, where it not unnaturally caught the eye of a twenty-five-year-old Scottish civil engineer then working in that city. His name was Alexander Mackay.

"I tell them that we were once naked savages like themselves, and carried bows and arrows and spears; but when God began to teach us, we became civilised."

The great turning point in Mackay's life did not quite come as a divine lightning bolt. Barely before he learned to walk, he had been leaning toward both the church and Africa. Or, more precisely, he had been pushed in that direction. His father was a clergyman, and like many cleric parents held high hopes that his son would follow in his footsteps. His mother concurred and virtually spoon-fed the youngster on tales of Christian devotion and sacrifice among the dusky sons of Ham. Yet while both dutiful and devout, Mackay resisted the pressure, being chiefly preoccupied with an intuitive mechanical aptitude. He passed up the customary juvenile mischiefs and games to force himself on blacksmiths, carpenters, masons, machinists and any other artisans who were willing to answer his questions about their crafts. Even elderly ladies at their spinning wheels were a source of endless interrogation. At the age of nine, Mackay upset his father by asking for a printing press; but he was given one all the same, and continued, throughout adolescence and early manhood, to make clear his disinclination for the ministry.

In 1873, after four years' study of engineering at Edinburgh University, he decided to complete his apprenticeship in Germany, and it was here that his earlier upbringing began to overtake him. "Carnality and unbelief have got such a hold on me," he wrote in a letter home, "that if it were not that, now and again, in reading the word of God, I get a fresh ray of light, I would fall away altogether." Soon, he was leading Bible classes and contemplating evangelical work in Madagascar. Stanley's letter, however, changed his plans. In April, 1876, Mackay boarded ship for Zanzibar, a duly appointed missionary of the Church Missionary Society.

*

Appointed but not ordained: the greatest of Uganda's pioneer evangelists was to remain a layman all his life. Yet Mackay never found this status a handicap: quite the contrary. It is not inaccurate to describe the lay aspect of nineteenth-century mission endeavor as akin to the work of the present-day Peace Corps, and the church fully recognized that sermons were only part of its task in winning converts. Familiarity with the white man's material things would help to make his spiritual ideas less incomprehensible to the so-called heathen. If Western skills and tools were obviously superior to anything a tribesman had ever known, then it stood to reason that the religion of the men who introduced such wonders must have much to recommend it.

In due course, a missionary's bag of tricks would inevitably lose some of its capacity to command awe, but its initial impact was vital, for it opened the door. The African's fascination with things mechanical was an unmatched entree for the evangelist. During his journey from the coast to Uganda in 1878, Mackay noted how tribesmen constantly flocked around his astounding implements, particularly that marvel of marvels, the wheel. "Every day they see more wonders," he wrote in his journal. "We grind our corn with a revolving hand-mill; we produce blast by a revolving fan; we turn around articles on a revolving lathe ... I fear the king of Uganda will be so struck with awe at our endless applications of the principle of *revolution*, that he will be tempted to say, as the President of the Mexican Republic did at the Vienna Exhibition, when he was shown an engine which made a thousand revolutions per minute, 'Dat is more revolutions even dan dey make in my contree!'"

This was a correct assessment, if slightly exaggerated, for Mutesa, who had played host to Speke and Stanley, was not quite a gawking hayseed. Nevertheless, the white man and his skills remained sufficiently novel so that the Kabaka could not restrain a gasp of startled delight when Mackay presented him with a music box that plonked out an air from Haydn's *Creation*. This was followed by lectures to king and court on such topics as astronomy and physiology, with Mackay using charts of the heavens and diagrams of the human body, taken from Huxley's *Physiography* as well as standard textbooks, as visual aids. While the talks made limited sense to the audience, they nonetheless had their desired effect, which was to impress the Kabaka favorably— an indispensable objective for any missionary who sought to win acceptance among Uganda's people.

And if Mutesa had marveled, the masses were overwhelmed. Mackay lost no time in placing his skills at the disposal of the country. Uganda may have led tropical Africa in material progress, but who had ever seen a water pump, a steam-operated sawmill, a printing press, a brick kiln, a magic lantern? The house Mackay built for himself was hardly less primitive than a log cabin, but it had two storeys, plumb walls, windows, hinged doors and a balustraded staircase. These sights brought gapers from the remotest parts of Uganda. Although the Baganda made good roads, Mackay introduced them to wheeled transport: a small wooden cart, painted red and blue and drawn by a pair of bullocks. Describing the wagon's first trip through the streets of Rubaga, Mackay wrote that "at every step the crowd grew, and yelled, and screamed with delight ... I had a roaring retinue a thousand strong, a procession quite as great as if the kabaka himself had headed it." In the mission school, pupils made their first halting acquaintance with the alphabet, the carpenter's bench and a broad range of Western tools.

Mackay also hastened to introduce the Gospel, for his quasi-secular status did not disqualify him from preaching. Every Sunday, his improvised CMS flag, with a red cross on a blue field, went up over the mission house and a modest congregation gathered for the service. Here, Mackay could not only measure the spiritual results

of his temporal influence but bring to bear the special appeal which
the Christian religion itself held for the "pagan." The church offered
at least two inducements that were difficult to resist and which had
particular impact in Uganda. The first of these was the Scriptures; as
Roland Oliver has observed in his classic study, *The Missionary Factor
in East Africa*, "that He had left His words in His book was especially
impressive to a people prone to believe in divination and to whom the
art of reading appeared the greatest of human mysteries." Secondly,
Mackay's creed promised emancipation from the dread of malevolent
spirits which played so large a role in animist faiths. Christianity, to
be sure, spoke of sin and punishment, but the concept of forgiveness
inevitably struck a responsive chord among peoples hounded by
witches. In Uganda particularly, where religion rested on an all too
real system of mutilation and human sacrifice, the very idea of mercy
could not but come as something inexpressibly wonderful. Uganda was
also unique in possessing what might be called a ready-made nucleus
of Christian converts. These came largely from Rubaga's upper-class
elite, within which, in Oliver's words, "there were already some who
were accustomed to looking outwards ... who had developed a capacity
for independent thought and a sense of individual responsibility which
were fundamental to the Christian scheme of sin and redemption."

In due course, these assets would bring Uganda to pre-eminence as
the most staunchly Christian country in all east and central Africa, in
fact setting an example of devotion that would win the awed admiration
of the world. Yet the early years of mission work in Uganda witnessed
serious obstacles and not a little frustration. Even when Mackay was
joined in 1879 by six more CMS workers, the path remained thorny.
Catechists at first consisted mainly of pre-teen-age boys, many of them
pages from the palace. Calling themselves "readers," they showed both
intelligence and a real enthusiasm for the new faith. Most of what
they were required to learn, however, was not only complicated by a
language barrier that took time to be hurdled, but also flew directly in
the face of age-old tradition—of instinct itself. To comprehend even the
fundamentals of Scripture meant a long and stiff upward climb.

Part of the pupils' bewilderment has been described by one of
Mackay's colleagues, the Rev. Robert Pickering Ashe. In his book, *Two
Kings of Uganda*, Ashe tries to visualize a service as seen through the
eyes of one apprentice reader. "When I got to the Bazungu's house I saw
some strange things. Two outlandishly dressed white men, who kept
their fire on a large board which they ate off ... I was utterly bewildered
by the way which these people ate their food. I could see long things

protruding from their hands; could they be nails or some strange growth peculiar to the Bazungu? They gave me plenty of food, and then a lot of people followed one of the Bazungu and we climbed up into the roof, or rather into another house, on top of the one in which they ate their food, and then they began to sing; I have never heard singing like that before, and I did not like it much. Then they stopped and everyone knelt down, and I did too, and the Bazungu began to say words, praying to someone, some great chief, but I could see no one but ourselves. My mistress then told me I was to stay there. I did not mind for there were other boys, and I soon got used to the new life."

The missionaries also had to become acclimatized. Mackay was at times hard put to keep his composure at the Baganda notion that labor degraded. "Any amount of mere preaching would never set these lazy fellows to work ... I have made work so prominent a part of my teaching that I am called *Mzungu-wa-kazi* (white man of work). I tell them that God made man with only one stomach, but with two hands, implying they should work twice as much as they eat. But most of them are all stomach and no hands!" He was also reminded constantly of his pupils' stubborn disbelief in their own capacities. "Again and again I have heard the remark that white men came from heaven. Then ... I try to impress upon all a truth I find them very slow to believe—that they themselves can easily learn to know everything that white men know. I tell them that we were once naked savages like themselves, and carried bows and arrows and spears; but when God began to teach us, we became civilised."

Yet Mackay's journal reveals occasional patches of blue in the sky with the growth of a warm relationship between teacher and pupils. "House inundated with small boys reading with me, and watching my operations. They say my heart is good. I wish it were, and theirs also." ... "We had a very severe thunderstorm. The quantity of hail which fell was remarkable... Our boys gathered bucketfuls, and I initiated them into the pleasure of snowballing." One even has an infrequent glimpse of progress and hope. "To-day my pupils finished reading St. Matthew's Gospel. I think they have understood it all to a certain extent, and at all events they express their joy at what they have read, and their belief in the sacred Word." ... "I cannot think the day far distant when ... a Msukuma will be bishop of Unyamwezi, and a Muganda primate of all Nyanza."

*

The intermittent favor the missionaries enjoyed at the palace undoubtedly helped keep their movement alive during its infancy. Any attempt to define Mutesa's attitude toward Christianity becomes mired in contradictions, for he blew hot and cold and sometimes both at once. In his more benign moments he could appear to be a thorough convert. From time to time he went to services at the mission, whose attendance was mounting visibly, and did not consider it beneath his dignity to join with nine-year-olds in the informal critiques Mackay encouraged after the sermons. He could do things like leap up and shout: "Jesus! Was there ever any one like him?"—and apparently mean it. Not infrequently he took private instruction from Mackay at the palace, if "private" can be used to describe a meeting of court, cabinet and parliament. Like Stanley, Mackay was struck with Mutesa's healthy curiosity over his next incarnation, and by his grasp of abstract ideas, even though discussions perforce were held at the most elementary level. "[Mutesa] asked many questions on the future state. What sort of bodies, what desires, what clothing? I explained that we should all be like the angels, but I found St. Paul's own excellent simile suit best, the new body given by God to the seed-corn sowed. Mtesa quite caught this and explained it to all present."

Such a scene describes Mutesa the Good. Mackay could also record exchanges like the following: "*Mtesa*: 'They say we shall all be burnt in the fire after we die.' *Katikiro and Chiefs* (jeering and laughing): 'Oh, we shall be burnt in the fire, but the white men will be let go, eh!' Much laughter and idle talk followed these remarks, there being no opportunity in which we could well say a word. Why they should have chosen the doctrine of future punishment to make merriment of, I do not know, as in all my teaching I never preached much, if anything at all, about retribution for sin in the next world." On another occasion, "in the midst of the talk on the gods *versus* the Almighty Creator, [Mutesa] suddenly sent out for a calabash, and having got it, made some obscene observations to his chiefs. Before the talk on religion was finished, he listened to the report of the plundering batongole just returned from Busoga."

The missionaries did not always take these slights lying down, and sometimes gave as good as they got. At one meeting of the Lukiiko, Mutesa catechized his chiefs on the powers held by Nende, one of Lubareism's proliferation of deities. "'What is Nende?' asked Mtesa. Kyambalango replied, 'Nende is a man; Nende is a god.' The Katikiro said, 'Nende is an image.' 'Sekibobo!' said Mtesa, 'what is Nende?' ... Before Sekibobo could make up his mind ... Mr. Pearson, who was sitting behind the chief, called out, 'Nende is a liar.'... I proposed that

Nende be brought and set on the floor before us all, that we might see what he is. This created some merriment, while others were shocked at the idea of such sacrilege."

*

Such debates could only be meaningless, and did little to enlarge Mutesa's understanding of Christianity. Yet considering the Kabaka's background, it is altogether natural that he should have viewed the missionaries' creed with occasional scorn and more frequent confusion. The latter in particular was compounded in 1879, when another band of Christian soldiers arrived in Rubaga and took up the cudgel against Mackay. They were White Fathers,* of the order founded by Pope Leo XIII and organized by Cardinal Lavigerie, an energetic anti-slavery crusader who had once said: "to save the interior of Africa we must kindle the anger of the world!" Like CMS, the White Fathers were to play a signal role in guiding Uganda to spiritual and material uplift, but the doctrinal in-fighting between the two sects during the pioneer years nearly canceled out the good example of both. In a sense, this rivalry could be likened to a pair of children in a playground, grappling for possession of a rubber duck; but given Uganda's ignorance of Western faiths, the conflict was neither trifling nor amusing. Each mission taught its credulous congregation to love God and man and to despise the other creed, advice unbecoming enough in enlightened countries but incendiary among a people who lived by the sword. The backbiting would in time erupt into history's last authentic religious war, which in turn would help decide Uganda's fate in the larger and more sordid struggle for imperial domination of Africa.

On the coast, Protestant and Catholic missions worked in proximity and without friction; one might have expected even more harmony in Uganda, where the tiny, isolated band of Europeans could never feel altogether secure from the ever-present threat of backlash. But such was not the case when Rome and the Reformation locked horns for Uganda's soul. To be sure, priests and ministers refrained from the more extreme manifestations of hatred, and everyday life witnessed acts of cordiality, even kindness. White Fathers and CMS workers might sometimes sit down to dinner together. When CMS stores once ran short, the Catholics

---

* The name had nothing to do with pigmentation. The French Catholic missions in Zanzibar and Bagamoyo were run by an order called the Black Fathers. Many of the White Fathers in Africa today are black.

donated a supply of trade goods and refused payment. Mackay could occasionally unbend in his journal. One of the White Fathers happened to be a fellow Scot, and when he attributed recurrent indigestion to French cooking, Mackay wrote: "I felt sorely tempted to say to him: 'Och, man, I could hae forgi'en ye a' yer Popery, but what for hae ye forsaken yer parritch?'" But mainly, the two factions held aloof, placing each other in a sort of Coventry, and their good manners were a poor mask for an ugly vendetta.

Both sects fought like hungry wolves for Mutesa's favor, and neither Catholic nor Protestant passed up an opportunity to libel the other in the royal presence. Père Simeon Lourdel, Mackay's counterpart, told Mutesa that the Protestants were outlaws who had mutinied against the true church; he described his own White Fathers as authentic teachers of religion, the CMS missionaries as mere "fundis"—workmen. Another priest openly declared to Mackay that the Catholics considered it their "devoir" to slander the Protestants. Nor did Mackay show up at his best. When Mutesa asked him to describe the White Fathers' creed, his not untruthful reply was hardly designed to leave a favorable impression: "I explained to the king that they were followers of Jesus (Isa) as we, accepted the Old and New Testaments as we, but worshipped the mother of Jesus more than the Lord Himself, prayed to prophets and saints dead long ago, and taught obedience to the Pope before their own king." After Mutesa had formally greeted the new arrivals, Mackay lodged a protest with the court, "on the impropriety of having given a state reception on Sunday, to the exclusion of Divine service."

He also tried to put pressure on Mutesa himself. "I ... distinctly told the king that we could not remain here if these men were allowed to settle in the place ... I showed how impossible it was for padres to settle here without making proselytes." But Mutesa seemed indifferent to the thinly veiled threat of withdrawal, and Mackay was forced to back down, although this did not sweeten his disposition toward the Catholics: "We feel matters here have come to a crisis ... our usefulness is at an end, our medicine refused, Romish priests received contrary to our advice." This is most misleading. Mackay always exaggerated Catholic influence at the Kabaka's court; no missionary ever enjoyed Mutesa's confidence more than Mackay himself. Yet he would continually sound alerts: "I cannot but regard the presence of the Romanists ... as a warning to us to be less lax in our standard for admission into the visible Church." Or he might sniff: "Lourdel ... goes every day with some *drug* for the king. It would be a farce to call his mixtures medicines, for none of their party have any idea of medicine."

Through all this, the target of importunity, Mutesa, reacted according to his mood. He derived a certain amount of perverse pleasure from watching Catholics and Protestants call each other names, and sometimes goaded them into exchanges of insults. "Mtesa ... proposed that the Frenchmen and ourselves should first agree on religious matters, and then he would listen to us both. This was merely a *ruse* to try to get us to enter on discussion, which he enjoys, especially if it occasion ill-feeling between the disputants." But such interludes only augmented his bewilderment at the spectacle of two adult white communities, each professing to bring the true word of God and each branding the other as fraud and heretic. Was Christianity one faith or two? Or two hundred? It was enough to try his patience. "Every nation of white men has another religion," he once declared angrily to Mackay. "How can I know what is right and what is false?" No one helped him reach a conclusion.

*

Mutesa's confusion was only aggravated by the third party in the battle for his endorsement, the Arabs, who saw in the Christians a real threat not merely to their faith but to their very survival. Catholic and Protestant might go for one another's throats, but Islam and slavery were their sworn common foe. If the Arabs had any say in the matter, no missionary of either creed would gain a foothold in Uganda, and they too poured venom in Mutesa's ear. "Every fresh arrival of Arabs creates a fresh outbreak against us," wrote Mackay. "Some of them use the pretext of their religion for blaspheming the Nazarenes, while others raise rumours of English aggression, and others again merely fabricate charges against us individually." The Arabs' propaganda was at least imaginative. They told Mutesa that Mackay's CMS reinforcements were not churchmen at all but spies. Mackay had to forgo bricks for the walls of his house and use wattle and daub instead, "as the Arabs have told the king that we build *military forts* with bricks." The mission school, they said, was in reality a front for the training of an underground guerrilla army.

No Arab extravagance seemed too grotesque, no lie too big, if it would sabotage the Christian effort. The most spectacular whopper had it that Mackay was an escaped felon. This was concocted by a pair of slavers who laid before Mutesa the tale "that I had fled from England because I had murdered two men there; that I had got on board a steamer with two revolvers in my hands, and threatened to murder the captain instantaneously if he didn't convey me at once to Zanzibar; that in Zanzibar I committed more murders and had to flee from there again ... that here my presence was certainly dangerous to the king, for I was insane and only went about to kill people." The fabrication was actually lodged as a formal indictment and Mackay had to stand trial. Without difficulty he cleared himself and Mutesa swiftly dismissed the charges, but some time went by before the damage to the missionary's image could be thoroughly repaired.

Mutesa's feelings toward the coast traders were not much less ambiguous than his wavering stance on the missionaries. In some respects it can almost be said that Christ and Mohammed were one to him. Not quite, of course, for he could perceive the fundamental divergences in doctrine and was especially mindful of strictures—which put the missionaries at a disadvantage. "If we accept the Muzungu's religion," Mackay reports him telling the Lukiiko, "we must then have only one wife each; while if we accept the religion of the Arabs, we cannot eat every kind of flesh." It is not hard to guess which sacrifice the Kabaka was prepared to make.

The traders, moreover, had been in Uganda longer, and this too gave them a not insignificant edge. "The Arabs were here in my father's time," Mutesa once reminded his Great Chiefs, "and are virtually now adopted children of mine." At the social level, also, Mutesa undoubtedly found his worldly wards more engaging company than the austere, sin-sniffing Christians; in conversation, the Arabs' rich oriental eloquence had a way of casting a spell, and if Mutesa did not swallow everything he was told, he at least listened with fascination. The Arabs and Swahili had also gained integration into the Uganda community in a way denied to the Europeans, for the traders took African wives or concubines or both. Only one of Mackay's colleagues, Charles Stokes, ever "went native" in this fashion, and even then his marriage to the daughter of a Wanyamwezi chief took place after he had abandoned his missionary calling for the profession of trader and gunrunner.

But Mutesa held no undiluted love for the Muslims. Although their religion taught a non-racial brotherhood, they themselves tended to regard Uganda's man in the street as aristocratic South Carolina planters looked on white trash. The missionaries, on the other hand, made a point of inviting Baganda to their homes. Mutesa knew quite well that the traders adulterated the gunpowder they sold him, that they passed off defective flintlocks whenever they could. He was also aware that they had bought and resold his own mother (although this did not necessarily outrage the man who had had his brothers cooked). And above all the Arabs represented a vague but no less unsettling threat to his rule; it was their growing sway over the chiefs which had helped him to recognize the desirability of a missionary counterpoise. Mutesa, in short, was not in a position to place unqualified trust in Muslim or Christian.

One might wonder, then, why he tolerated either group of intruders, the alien creeds they brought with them and the influences which were inevitably disturbing the status quo. Mutesa could hardly be called a devout man, and he naturally had no wish to see the foundations of his authoritarianism undermined. At the same time, however, he recognized the manifest advantages in the Arab and European presences alike. The traders had given him an armament of fearsome power and injected fresh blood into the country's economy. The missionaries—particularly Mackay—possessed innumerable skills and devices that seemed all but magical; Mutesa was eager to exploit these to his own ends. If he exerted a modicum of political finesse, he could play one faction off against the other and thus preserve, if not bolster, his personal prestige and authority.

Yet it was a risky business, and no one was more keenly aware of this than Mutesa. The foreigners were a source not only of confusion but of fear, a fear that was by no means entirely unreasonable. Mutesa was hardly ignorant of Zanzibar's ill-defined but openly voiced claims to the interior, or of Europe's growing preoccupation with the extermination of the slave trade. In its history, Uganda had never been invaded successfully, much less conquered. Now, in only a few years, outsiders had arrived, and seemed to be boring subtly from within. There was even one period when Mutesa might have wondered whether Cross and Crescent had not actually joined forces against him.

"To establish a station and thence to push toward Mtesa."

The major threat to Mutesa's sovereignty was a curious, decade-long episode that began in 1869. And here we must make a detour of some two thousand miles north of Rubaga, to Cairo, where the Khedive Ismail, Turkey's satrap in Egypt, was setting in motion a grand design to extend his rule to the farthest reaches of the upper Nile. Ordinarily, the impending irruption might not have caused Mutesa undue concern. He was able to put an enormous, well-armed force into the field—its numbers have been estimated at between 6,000 and 150,000—against

Egyptian troops celebrated for their poltroonery. Egyptian generals were notoriously incompetent and corrupt, and it is altogether possible that Mutesa could have dealt, by superior numbers or bribery or both, with an invasion from Cairo. But to his distress and mounting alarm he discovered, as Ismail's army approached, that there were no Egyptian commanders to beat or buy off: the leaders of the Khedive's central African campaign were Englishmen. For white mercenaries were active in Africa long before the Congo upheavals of the 1960s, and Ismail's imperial blueprint was only a by-product of a new phase of England's reluctant infiltration into the continent.

*

For more than half a century, while expending all the energies they could afford against Zanzibar's Indian Ocean slave traffic, British Governments had been turning a blind or at least nearsighted eye to Egyptian slavers on the upper Nile. During the 1860s, however, the policy began to change, thanks in no small measure to the explorer Samuel Baker. A sportsman and traveler of independent means, Baker became interested in the Nile question and in 1862 outfitted an expedition aimed at linking the river to Lake Victoria. The high point of the three-year journey was Baker's discovery of Lake Albert, establishing the existence of a lacustrine chain along which the Nile flowed on its northward course. The explorer's best-selling book, *The Albert Nyanza*, not only described this accomplishment (which won him a knighthood) but threw a garish spotlight on the mass traffic in slaves carried out by Egyptian traders in the upper Nile region. For unlike the other prominent east African travelers, Baker did not penetrate the interior from the Indian Ocean coast. Instead, he moved up the Nile from Khartoum as far as the settlement of Gondokoro, then the known limit of navigation on the river, and pushed south by land from there. This route enabled him to observe the Egyptian slave trade at close hand, and while his reports did not come as a total surprise to the British Government, they generated a wave of public indignation that swept across England and could not be dismissed easily. It was not long before Ismail began to receive carefully worded suggestions from British officialdom that he consider taking action to curb the Nile traffic.

Ismail was in no position to ignore the advice. Even if colossal British and French loans had not been holding Egypt's economy on its feet, the Khedive could hardly have resisted political pressure. His government machinery wheezed with mismanagement and stank with malfeasance, his armed forces have already been described, and he himself was little more than a Barghash in Savile Row clothing. Yet Ismail was by no means a fool. Progressive and enlightened in many respects, he possessed above all a keen sense of realpolitik; as the 1860s drew to a close and construction of the Suez Canal neared completion, he became increasingly aware that the new shortcut to India would bring his own affairs under closer British scrutiny than he could have wished. There was no alternative but to take an accommodating position. In 1869, as the Foreign Office smiled approvingly, Ismail organized a large military force to undertake an anti-slavery campaign along the upper Nile. Being a slaveowner himself, he was not overjoyed at the prospect, but he did see consolation and compensation in the opportunity to annex for Egypt an unclaimed territory roughly the size of Japan. To bring this off and simultaneously retain Britain's good will, he offered command of the expedition to the man who had exposed his country's slave dealings. Without hesitation, Baker accepted.

The terms of Baker's four-year contract were generous, to say the least. He received £40,000 plus expenses, two steamers for the voyage up the Nile to Gondokoro, two thousand soldiers, ten European officers whom he personally recruited, 50,000 rounds of ammunition and permission to take his wife with him. (She had accompanied him on his first expedition.) The troops left much to be desired as fighting men but they were well led, and Baker reposed special confidence in an elite guard of Khartoum and Cairo murderers whom he affectionately dubbed the "forty thieves." Baker was also given the title of Pasha, or more grandiosely, "Governor General of the Equatorial Nile Basin." No less ambitious were his instructions from Ismail: to "subdue to our authority the countries situated to the south of Gondokoro, to suppress the Slave Trade, to introduce a system of regular commerce, to open to navigation the great Lakes of the Equator, and to establish a chain of military stations and commercial depots ... throughout central Africa."

*

This, then, was the first overt challenge to Mutesa's rule, and there was little the Kabaka could do to withstand it. After raising the Turkish flag over Gondokoro, Baker rapidly annexed Bunyoro, and almost before Mutesa realized what had happened, a foreign army was massed only a few miles from his northern borders. Nothing, it seemed, would prevent Uganda from becoming incorporated forcibly into the new Egyptian empire. But Baker suddenly came to a dead halt. To his surprise, he found himself fully occupied in Bunyoro, whose ruler, Kabarega, dissented from vassaldom to the Khedive and had to be dealt with sternly. In 1872, at the village of Masindi, Baker's troops smashed Kabarega's army in a stunning pyrrhic victory which obliged the Egyptians to retire in great haste and greater disarray. It was not the last time that Kabarega, one of history's least known and more gifted guerrilla fighters, would confound and humiliate a British commander. Thanks largely to him, Baker's anti-slavery efforts proved disappointing. Furthermore, Kabarega's unabating resistance had the effect of preventing Baker from any attempt to enter Uganda. Unwittingly, the Bunyoro king had given his arch-enemy Mutesa a breathing spell.

But it did not last long. When Baker resigned in 1873, he was succeeded in Equatoria (the name of the Khedive's new province) by no less a figure than "Chinese" Gordon, who still had slightly more than a decade to go before his heroic marytrdom in Khartoum and who seemed determined to make the most of every minute during the interval. In 1874, a worried Mutesa was receiving one of Gordon's aides, the American Colonel C. Chaille-Long, and assuring him of Uganda's good will. A year later, Gordon sent another envoy, a Frenchman named Ernest Linant de Bellefonds, who obtained Mutesa's not very meaningful promise to outlaw the Uganda slave trade. The following two years witnessed the arrival of two more emissaries, each seeking formal permission for Gordon to build forts in Uganda—although consent was hardly needed. Gordon was throwing up a chain of defense works and steamer patrols to guard his supply routes and to intercept slave caravans along the entire upper Nile; he was not likely to be inhibited by so indistinct a line as Uganda's border. The question, moreover, was academic, since the Khedive had already staked out Uganda for annexation. The walls were slowly closing in on Mutesa.

*

A hitch in Gordon's plans intensified the danger. In point of fact this new development posed an even more serious threat to Zanzibar's Sultan Barghash than to Mutesa, but it should also be viewed within the context of the Kabaka's mounting concern for the security of his kingdom. Before 1874 was out, Gordon had come to realize that his twenty-five-hundred-mile line of communication from Khartoum was a perilously frail avenue over which to take and hold Uganda, particularly since Khartoum's Egyptian Governor distrusted him and would have welcomed any opportunity to halt or delay the flow of supplies from Cairo. The only way of launching an effective invasion, Gordon concluded, would be to strike west from the Indian Ocean. "I have proposed to the Khedive," he wrote his sister in January, 1875, "to send 150 men in a steamer to Formosa Bay, 250 miles north of Zanzibar, and there to establish a station and thence to push toward Mtesa." Thus, eight years before Thomson, Gordon became the first European to attempt the short route to the lake, and Mutesa found himself confronted with the long-dreaded prospect of conquest from the east.

To carry out Gordon's bold end run, Ismail raised not one hundred and fifty but five hundred and fifty Egyptian troops and placed them under the command of another British mercenary, the Royal Navy's Captain F. H. McKillop. In September, 1875, McKillop's force boarded four warships at Suez, sailed down the Red Sea into the Indian Ocean and made unopposed landings at the Benadir coast ports of Barawa and Kismayu. Strategically the move was sound, if not inspired. Gordon had in mind, as he told an aide, "a series of small powerful military posts along a constructed road," which would "free us from Khartum and these steamers" and enable entry into Uganda with minimal opposition. Logistically, however, the plan could be seen to have flaws. In December, McKillop wrote Gordon from Kismayu that "our getting here at all was quite problematical, as we were sent away short of everything—coal, water and stores"—in other words, without the wherewithal to build Gordon's road and forts. And politically, the scheme was a disaster, since it involved nothing less than annexing to Egypt a vast portion of the Zanzibar Sultanate, which in effect meant challenging Britain.

For Ismail, whose sense of proportion was rapidly giving way to wanton greed, had accepted Gordon's proposal not only with enthusiasm but with a total disregard for Zanzibar's territorial integrity. "I have every desire to maintain good relations with the Sultan of Zanzibar," he wrote Gordon in November, "but I will not put up with any attempt on my rights, much less usurpation." Coming from the usurper himself, these were daring words, but Ismail might have brought off the annexation—and occupied Uganda—had it not been for Kirk. Late in November, after learning of McKillop's landings, Kirk sailed in a British warship to Barawa, where the Egyptian commandant informed him brusquely that he was trespassing on Turkish soil. "God says in his book," he told the Consul, "'Do not enter another's house without his permission.'" To which Kirk replied that if he was not allowed ashore by a certain hour, his ship would open fire on the town. The commandant capitulated immediately and Kirk returned to Zanzibar, where he wrote a despatch to the Foreign Office, warning that "if we hesitate to support the Sultan, we shall have to deal with a state of anarchy on the coast."

But intervention proved unnecessary. When Ismail learned that one of his officers had gone so far as to defy Britain's diplomatic watchdog in east Africa, he swiftly came to his senses and ordered McKillop to withdraw his whole force without delay. The flanking move against Uganda had been stopped in its tracks. Shortly afterwards, Gordon himself left Equatoria. He would soon return, as Governor of the entire Sudan, but by then his chief preoccupation would be the Mahdist uprising that was eventually to cost him his life. To all practical purposes, outside pressure on Uganda was removed by the end of the 1870s, affording Mutesa not inconsiderable relief.

*

Quite obviously, as we have seen, the abortive McKillop invasion placed Barghash in far greater peril than Mutesa. Yet the prophecy of apocalypse from the east had never been treated lightly by any Kabaka. And from Mutesa's standpoint, the Gordon effort, coming as it did on the heels of Baker's earlier assault from the north, had brought conquest far too close for comfort. It was natural, then, that Mutesa should have commenced seeking out spies under every bed. It was also CMS's misfortune that its Uganda mission should have been established while Gordon was still launching his probes at the country's outer defenses. Although Mutesa had requested the missionaries as a foil against Muslim influence in general and Egyptians in particular, he would have been less than human if he had not tended to identify the CMS workers with Ismail's British officers. No matter that CMS itself had appealed to Lord Derby, the Foreign Secretary, urging that Egypt be discouraged from its attempts to annex Uganda. The missionaries remained suspect.

Mackay in particular was nagged at endlessly by the Kabaka's cross-examinations. As late as 1879, when Mutesa learned that the five CMS reinforcements were entering Uganda not by the Bagamoyo caravan trail but along the route opened up by Gordon, it was all Mackay could do to convince him that the party had no plans to conquer the country. Repeatedly he told Mutesa that "neither the Queen nor Colonel Gordon had sent them, that godly men in London had asked them to come to teach him and his people." But Mutesa persisted. "Are these fellows not coming to look for lakes," he demanded, "that they may put ships and guns on them?" Although he seemed somewhat reassured when told that the missionaries were carrying only muzzle-loading rifles—this ruled them out as troops—he continued to query. "Will they bring gunpowder?" "I don't know." "Will they bring beads?" "Not likely." "What will they bring?" "I cannot tell."

At another time, Mackay writes that "in the middle of a multitude of questions about the first and second resurrections, Mtesa abruptly asked me if I knew that the Egyptians had planted a new station in his territory... 'They are gnawing at my country like rats, and ever pushing their fortifications nearer... Gordon is an Englishman, and so are you: why, therefore, do you take my country from me?' To this I merely replied that we had nothing in common: Gordon is practically an Egyptian, while we are subjects of Mtesa." It is not surprising that Mackay shared Mutesa's relief on learning of Gordon's withdrawal. "I am truly thankful to God that Colonel Gordon has determined this ... I hope we shall have much less suspicion lying on us as being implicated in bringing 'the Turks' always nearer." His wish seemed to be fulfilled when Mutesa told him "that his remarks ... that we were spies, were finished now."

But the restoration of confidence proved both premature and incomplete. Despite Gordon's departure, Mutesa could not altogether shake his notion of the CMS as a sort of CIA. His rationale, such as it was, for this continuing apprehensiveness, could be found partly in letters which Mackay and at least one other colleague delivered to him personally on their arrival in Rubaga. These were formal messages of greeting and good will, written by Derby on behalf of Queen Victoria, and although they explicitly disavowed any official connection with CMS, they stated that the mission had the approval of the British Government. In failing to recognize the distinction, Mutesa displayed both discernment and naïveté. For in a certain sense the missionaries were in fact Government agents. The frequent letters they wrote Kirk, appraising conditions in Uganda, were the Consul's most reliable means of keeping himself informed on violations of anti-slave trade decrees and other matters that might have had some bearing on Foreign Office African policy. Yet none of this activity could have been by any stretch of the imagination described as subversive or even surreptitious. Mutesa, however, could not quite appreciate this. Even the most tenuous links with the British Government seemed to have the effect of stirring his anxiety.

Some tension was reduced in 1880, when Mutesa sent envoys to England in the company of two departing missionaries. They were received, with flattering ceremonial, by the Queen, who also provided their return passage as far as Zanzibar aboard a British man-of-war. During their absence, Mutesa occasionally voiced the fear that

"Queenie," as the Baganda called her, was up to no good. "When my men return," he said to Mackay, "will they not bring her letter, asking by force that I give you land?" But Mackay was eventually able to show Mutesa pictures of the ambassadors' audience, which had appeared in the London *Daily Graphic*. These so delighted the Kabaka that he made plans to go to England and meet Queenie himself. For various reasons, however, the visit never came off, and the diplomatic mission brought no conspicuous improvement in Anglo–Uganda relations, if any such ties could be said to have existed. (One envoy, in fact, had acquired a strong anti-white prejudice while in England.) Everything British continued suspect. A CMS gift to Mutesa about this time included a set of international code flags; Mackay had to take pains to assure the Kabaka that the Union Jack had not also been smuggled in.

"Five lads were to-day enrolled in the visible Church of Christ, through baptism."

Mutesa's wariness of all foreigners was in all probability the chief reason why the missions never succeeded in winning royal endorsement of their creeds. The closest Mackay could ever come to gaining the Kabaka's official warrant was a definite maybe. Mutesa was not inept at dissembling, and often exasperated his petitioners. Once, Mackay went so far as to reproach him for "playing with us and with religion. One day you have said that our religion is the only true one, another day you adopt the religion of Mohammed, and a third day you follow the lubare." Mutesa's rejoinder was: "The Frenchmen have one religion and you have another; they cannot both be true: first agree to have one religion in Europe; and then come and I shall let you teach my people." While his envoys were in England he evaded the question altogether, stating that he could give no reply until their return. When the spirit moved him he would simply confuse the issue. "The king commenced asking questions on religion, ending in nothing as usual. After this had been going on for some time, Mr. Pearson asked if anything would be done to any of the people who embraced Christianity. Wilfully misunderstanding the question, Mutesa replied: 'Do you mean to make me a Christian by force?'"

More often, he attached conditions to any possible edict of toleration, his most persistent demand being acceptance—through marriage—into Britain's Royal Family. "After mentioning the solemn fact of all having to answer to God in the next world, Mtesa suddenly asked me if he could get a white princess by going to England!" Now it was Mackay's turn to hedge: "Prudence prompted me to answer, 'I am not an English princess, therefore I cannot give you a reply.'" The Kabaka might then cajole. "Once more Mtesa has been talking on the subject of marrying the Queen's daughter! 'I would put away all my women,' said he, 'and give you a road through the Masai country by which to bring your ships (!), if only you bring me an English princess.'" Or he could put it bluntly: "'Well,' said Mtesa, 'if you want liberty, you must fill my belly; you must give me a daughter of the Queen to be my wife; unless you do that, you shall not have liberty to teach—that is my only answer.'"

Mutesa's capricious backsliding into Lubareism was another trial. The year 1879, in fact, witnessed a widespread revival of that creed and the temporary discontinuation of religious teaching at the palace. This atavistic tendency may have been due partly to the fact that Mutesa was a sick man, afflicted with an assortment of barely controllable ailments (probably including an advanced stage of syphilis), and therefore fair game for medico-religious quackery. On more than one occasion, he welcomed the therapies of a local witch who claimed that her materia medica came from Lubare himself. "Again at dawn, or rather before it," Mackay noted in his journal one day in 1879, "the loud beating of drums and shrill cries of women let us know that the great lubare, Mukasa, was on her way to pay the king a second visit... Today, I believe, the audience was of a much more private nature... Some say that not even a single chief, nor a woman, was present." Whatever transpired during the house call was later ritualized outside the palace by a huge, noisy procession of witches and wizards, brandishing a variety of charms, including "urn-shaped things, having in the heart the umbilical cord of either the present king or one of his ancestors." Such treatments were also encouraged by the Namasole, another self-licensed healer who once prescribed banishment of all Uganda's donkeys as a cure for the Kabaka's ills. Although Mutesa lost faith in the remedy after a while, Mackay found himself without his own donkey. By 1880, he had become sufficiently exasperated with the Kabaka to exclaim in his journal: "Mtesa is a pagan—a heathen—out and out."

And if it wasn't the old-time religion it was war. "'Nyaga, nyaga, nyaga, nyo!' said the 'humane king,' as he gave the captains the orders, i.e., 'Rob, pillage, plunder!' ... This is the fifth time in the course of two years that a great army has been sent by Mtesa into Busoga ... to devastate and murder, and bring back the spoil—women, children, cattle, and goats. The crime is awful. The most heart-rending of Livingstone's narratives of the slave hunts by Arabs and Portuguese on the Nyasa and Tanganyika shores, dwindle into insignificance compared with the organised and unceasing slave-hunts carried on by this 'enlightened monarch and Christian king.' This is the man who yesterday ... uttered the sentiment, 'God hears every word I utter while I lie here.'"

*

Clearly, there was every reason for rancor toward Mutesa. Yet given the circumstances, his obstructionism could easily have been far more draconian. Although much is made in Mackay's journal of the Kabaka's denial of the right to "teach," there was not, in fact, a great deal of serious interference with the Christians' proselytizing efforts among the people. In Mutesa's more wayward moments there was nothing to prevent him from deporting the entire mission community and massacring all its readers. Indeed, he had once ordered large numbers of Muslims executed when they refused to eat meat that had not been slaughtered in accordance with Koranic law. But despite the Kabaka's suspicions and changing moods, the Christians never felt such wrath.

Mackay himself could acknowledge this. Even though separated by an all but unbridgeable gap of culture and outlook, he and Mutesa somehow managed to hit it off tolerably well. When the Arabs accused Mackay of stealing lumber to build his house, "Mtesa alone stood our friend." The Kabaka's final verdict at Mackay's "murder" trial was merely that the missionary was "a raiser of much noise and row in court." Mutesa also went to Mackay for medical treatment as often as he consulted the royal wizards. When a plague swept the country in 1881, he welcomed Mackay's list of sanitary regulations, which specified, among other measures, sponge baths for patients, burial of the dead and burning of infected buildings. Some of these recommendations were even complied with after a fashion.

It was at about this time that Mackay wrote of himself jokingly as "engineer, builder, printer, physician, surgeon and general artificer to Mtesa, Kabaka of Uganda, over-lord of Unyoro, etc." He did in fact hold those offices and others as well, including the post of royal undertaker. The latter appointment came in 1882, on the death of the Namasole, when Mutesa, "determined to make a funeral to surpass in splendour any burial that had ever taken place in the country," directed Mackay to take charge of building the coffin. The month-long project required more than half a ton of wooden planking, copper and bronze, over 3,000 yards of calico, 50,000 lengths of bark cloth and the labor of two hundred woodcutters and blacksmiths. Under Mackay's guidance and fortified with beef and beer from the palace, the workers fashioned a double casket whose outer box measured twelve by eight by seven feet. Mackay estimated the value of the cloth alone at £15,000, and deplored the ostentation. "The text is a good one from which to preach many a sermon here. Such prodigality in trying to procure a short-lived immortality, with no care at all for the immortal soul." Nonetheless his stock soared at the palace, where Mutesa "expressed unbounded satisfaction" with the finished product.

*

While Mackay's services never won Mutesa to Christianity, they at least enabled the missionaries—who were nothing if not tenacious—to ride out the Kabaka's unpredictable storms and continue their labors with a steadily growing enrollment of readers. If their task had seemed futile at first, it began to bear fruit during the early 1880s. The language gap had been filled as Mackay and his colleagues learned Luganda and the readers became proficient in English. (It took only two months, after the rudiments had been mastered, for a Muganda youngster to gain a reasonable degree of fluency.) And where the pupils had once stubbed their toes even on elementary theological questions, they were now displaying aptitude and keen perception. On March 18, 1882, Mackay was finally able to make the triumphant entry in his journal: "Five lads were to-day enrolled in the visible Church of Christ, through baptism, by Mr. O'Flaherty... Our earnest prayer is that these lads, all of them grown up to manhood, may be baptised not only by water, but by the Holy Ghost and with fire."

Had Mackay known what was in store, he might have omitted mention of fire in his prayer, but prophecy was not his vocation, and the conversion of Uganda's first Anglicans—the vanguard of a present-day enrollment of three and a half million Protestants and Catholics—too glorious an event for speculation on a murky future. More baptisms followed, readers multiplied. By 1885 the church was able to boast ten Baganda elders. And the missionaries were heartened by the news that Uganda was to have its own bishop.

*

On October 9, 1884, Mutesa died. As his successor, the Lukiiko chose a seventeen-year-old boy named Mwanga, assuming from the physical resemblance that he was undoubtedly Mutesa's son. Mwanga's reign began on a hopeful note. He was the first Kabaka in Uganda's history to observe his own accession without executing anyone; this may have been due in part to the influence of the CMS mission, where he had once spent a few days as a reader. (The Lukiiko's selection of queen-sister was also encouraging; she was actually a convert, baptized Rebecca.) Ashe had in fact once asked Mwanga what policy he would adopt toward the missionaries should he come to the throne, and wrote that Mwanga had replied, with boyish sincerity, "I shall like you very much, and show you every favour." Thus Mackay and his colleagues had reason to anticipate a new deal in church–state relations.

At his first audience, Mackay found Mwanga every inch a Kabaka, "lying on the floor on some rich carpets which the Arabs had given him... He wore a magnificent leopard skin. By his side was the magic horn (a white tusk of ivory), in his hand was a small mirror, while a larger one was placed in front of him." Mackay added that the new ruler was "very haughty," and "tried to upbraid me" for some minor infraction of protocol. This could have been the forewarning of an abbreviated honeymoon. It was not long before the missionaries had ample cause to regret the passing of the two-faced Mutesa.

"Oh, night of sorrow!
What an unheard-of deed of blood!"

Anyone reading contemporary European accounts of personal experience with Mwanga may wonder whether the writers are not being unduly harsh. All Kabakas, by upbringing and possibly by instinct, were degenerates, liars, sadists, tyrants; why single out Mwanga as the archfiend? Because in all probability he was. Accounts of the bestialities of his predecessors leave the impression that these men saw their misdeeds largely as instruments of policy. So too did Mwanga, yet he somehow cannot fail to come out as a nasty little boy who delights in pulling the wings off flies. His appearance hardly commands respect. Drawings and photographs show a face at once frail and gross: delicate, almost feminine eyebrows, heavy-lidded eyes, flaring nostrils, thick, sensual mouth rolled into the hint of a sneer. The overall impression is one of languid brutality. Yet this is not entirely fair. One can read only so much into anyone's face. And while "monster" might describe Mwanga well, it does not describe him completely. Certainly it does not explain him. That would be a task for a psychopathologist, who might throw some light not only on Mwanga's cruelties but on the inconsistent, often inexplicable, acts and policies which marked his entire reign.

Mwanga's character had more than one dimension. In some respects he was keenly intelligent; few Baganda could claim his grasp of the country's appallingly complex land laws. When the spirit moved him he was capable of displaying at least a façade of compassion. But while the people who wrote about Mwanga sometimes acknowledged these attributes, they were not disposed to show him charity—perhaps because he showed so little himself.

*

During the first year of his reign, Mwanga's behavior kept the Europeans on a tight high wire. On January 30, 1885, Mackay and Ashe were roughed up by a band of Muslims who made off with two CMS converts. Protesting to the Katikiro, the missionaries were thrown bodily from court. Shortly afterwards, a detachment of Mwanga's troops burst into the mission to search for readers. (None was found.) Several days later, Mackay learned that his two captured converts, along with another Christian, had been burned alive. The news was accompanied by a summons to the palace. Mwanga, who may have felt that he had overreached himself, hastened to disclaim any responsibility for the executions. Mackay did not believe the Kabaka and told him so, bluntly and angrily, before the entire Lukiiko. His outrage carried him beyond the bounds of discourtesy permitted even to a European, and Mackay knew he was courting dismemberment. Instead, however, he found himself in Mwanga's good graces. Possibly he had somehow managed to touch the Kabaka's conscience.

A period of uneasy amity followed, during which Mwanga went so far as to seek religious instruction. Mackay made the most of this. "Several times seen the king again. He repeatedly renewed his assurances of friendship. Set up a shelf for his clock, which pleased him much." ... "Saw king quite alone ... gave him long lesson on God's redemption. He listened well, and gave me a fat cow when I was done." Mackay also took the opportunity to submit a list of ten guidelines aimed at assisting Mwanga in the performance of his kingly duties. One rule stipulated: "No cruelties or tortures to be tolerated—e.g., roasting alive, taking out eyes, cutting off ears, hands, lips, teeth or other mutilations." Mwanga no doubt read it (or more accurately, had it read to him; he had not stayed at the mission long enough to learn English). But his good spirits could only be looked on as transient by the man who had experienced so many years of Mutesa's backing and filling. "The Katikiro shook me warmly by the hand ... and said 'I was now a great favourite.' ... I merely asked him how many days his favouritism would last."

Indeed, the truce had to end sooner or later, for Bishop Hannington was by now en route to Uganda, following Thomson's footsteps along the dreaded avenue of invasion from the east—traditionally a threat in Baganda folklore. Far more than Mutesa, Mwanga was obsessed with the hoary warning that this route was a spear-thrust into Uganda's Achilles heel. It cannot be said that his concern was without foundation. Gordon had shown that the country was especially vulnerable to assault from the east. At this time, moreover, confused but disturbing accounts of European annexations on the mainland near the coast had reached Rubaga. Yet Hannington was an entirely different kind of visitor. His affiliation with CMS, and the non-military, apolitical character of the mission, was well known in Uganda. As an evangelist, the bishop might prove a sanctimonious nuisance, but he was hardly another Gordon, or for that matter even a Thomson. Only a panic-stricken child or a paranoid would have pictured him as such. Mwanga appears to have been both.

Late in October, 1885, reports began filtering into Rubaga that white men were approaching the Nile from Masai country, and the CMS missionaries, acutely aware of Mwanga's phobia, became no less alarmed themselves. Almost overnight, the capital was transformed into a rumor factory, and none of the hearsay boded well. Mackay and Ashe tried to see Mwanga but discovered, hardly to their surprise, that they had become personae non gratae at the palace. Mwanga called an executive session of the Lukiiko and word leaked out that an assassin had been despatched to kill Hannington.

On learning this, the two missionaries immediately bribed a friendly chief to send a messenger after the thug to tell him that the plans had been changed. They had no idea whether the runner would be able to carry out his errand in time; they could only wait and pray, and work. "*Oct 26th.*—Too nervous to sleep. Up long before dawn. Ashe and I wrote to the king, craving an interview, but did not succeed in seeing him. The good Lord save our bishop ... from the hands of these assassins! ... *Oct. 29th.*—[Mwanga] has given the executioner orders to catch people *here*. It may be ourselves, or our boys, or mayhap readers, or pages coming to tell us news. At once we sent away all our boys to hide among our Christian friends. Writing out revision of St. Matthew's Gospel. Ashe busy setting it up. Time of persecution has always been a printing time."

Twenty-four hours later the suspense ended: "Oh, night of sorrow! What an unheard-of deed of blood!" The messenger had failed. Indeed, Mwanga had not sent out a killer, but a messenger of his own, with a liquidation order to be delivered to a petty chief named Luba, who ruled over a district on the east bank of the Nile. Swiftly and efficiently, Luba had complied with the Kabaka's instructions.

Ironically, it is possible that Hannington's murder might easily have been prevented—by Hannington himself. Near Luba's village, canoes waited to carry him to Uganda across the lake. It has been said that if Hannington had indicated that he planned to use this transportation, Mwanga would have had little if any reason to stop or even fear him, since the Kabaka may have interpreted the invasion legend as placing only the Nile crossing out of bounds. The CMS missionaries themselves did not dream that their bishop would choose the river (they had not even known at first that he was entering Uganda from Masailand), and had assured Mwanga of this. But Hannington had not realized the extent to which folklore had come to clamp down on the mind of Uganda's demented ruler, so he may have innocently written his own death warrant.

*

The expected reaction from England was not long in coming. As press and pulpit cried for vengeance, Lord Salisbury, the Prime Minister, weighed a Foreign Office proposal that a punitive expedition be mounted to thrash Mwanga and rescue the now beleaguered missionaries. (Even several days before Mackay received confirmation of Hannington's murder, he had written Kirk: "The English Consul is well known here. We shall look to you to aid us as you think fit.") To Salisbury, who would shortly emerge as the spearhead and architect of British imperial expansion in east Africa, there was never a moment of doubt as to where his duty lay: the Government would have no part of it.

For despite eloquent appeals and not a little pressure from influential church and philanthropic societies, the taste of Khartoum remained bitter on every politician's tongue. Only five months before Mwanga did away with Hannington, Gladstone's Government had fallen, owing largely to its reluctant, blundering and costly involvement in the Sudan—which culminated in Gordon's death when a Mahdist army stormed Khartoum and beheaded him. No politically sensitive British statesman was going to court a re-enactment of the Khartoum disaster, especially for the sake of a few obscure evangelists in a little-known and unwanted corner of Africa. The Government did act to the extent that Lord Iddesleigh, the Foreign Secretary, recommended to CMS that its missionaries in Uganda clear out on their own. But military intervention, and the consequent risk of England's becoming encumbered with an east African commitment beyond Zanzibar, was quite out of the question.

Yet the British lion's eye was now fixed on Uganda. The missionaries were, after all, Britons, and their difficulties were not dismissed lightly by the public. Other developments were also beginning to involve England with Uganda at this time; but it is not inaccurate to say that Hannington's murder and the plight of Mackay and his colleagues laid the groundwork for the eventual British annexation of the country.

*

Under the new and unwelcome spotlight, Mwanga soon found himself dogged by a mounting dread of vengeance. One might thus have expected some act of contrition from him toward the Europeans, some gesture to forestall or even halt the fist of retribution. But in his madness he seemed bent on hastening it. Several Baganda Christians advised Mackay and Ashe that a gift would allay the Kabaka's wrath. Ready to humble themselves in the cause of their faith, the two men distributed seventeen loads of badly needed trade goods to Mwanga and a number of the chiefs who had been implicated in the murder plot. This brought an immediate summons to the palace and a wild tirade from Mwanga, who promised a death sentence for any Muganda found on the mission premises. For by now, conversion had become Mwanga's bête noire. He was both humiliated and enraged by the knowledge that many of his own pages had become Protestants or Catholics. Indeed, it was only a matter of time before these boys would feel the full weight of his fury. What brought things to a head was Mwanga's fancy for sodomy and the converted pages' resistance to his amorous advances. On May 25, 1886, Mackay wrote: "What we have been in daily expectation of for a long time has now taken place—an order for the arrest of all the Christians... The Lord look mercifully on the agony of these poor black children..."

The witch hunt was carried out with an efficiency matched only by the courage of the victims. Ashe describes the typical behavior of one Christian during the roundup. "When Munyaga was captured he was in his house... The executioners came cautiously up. They saw a gun leaning against the reed lintel of the door and stopped, hesitating, believing it was the possession of a loaded gun that gave Munyaga such confidence. He, seeing their evident fear, told them they need not be afraid of the gun, for he did not mean to use it. So they came up to apprehend him. He begged to be allowed to put on his 'kansu' (white gown), which they agreed to, and then they led him away. His trial was a cruel mockery, and he was ordered to be hacked in pieces and burned. His torturers cut off one of his arms and flung it into the fire before him, then they cut off a leg, and that too, was flung into the flame, and lastly, the poor mutilated body was laid on the framework to be consumed. Ashes to ashes, dust to dust, in sure and certain hope of the resurrection of the dead." At about this time, thirty-two other converts died over a slow fire. The executioner later gave Mwanga a full account of the proceeding, and marveled that all the victims had gone to their deaths calling on God. Mwanga shrugged his shoulders and remarked that God could not have been paying much attention.

And so it went. For nearly a year, as Mwanga blew his mind on hemp and fermented banana juice and continued to bugger his unconverted pages, more than two hundred Catholics and Protestants had their limbs severed and were then broiled alive. It was, in Oliver's words, "a martyrdom as terrible as any in Christian history."* Yet conversions outpaced executions as the church went underground. A steadily increasing number of catechumens made stealthy visits to the missions at night. At the very peak of the terror, congregations of fifty and more attended services. More elders were elected, more baptisms performed. "Kiwobe came to me," wrote Ashe of one such occasion, "and said, 'Munange njagala kubatizibwa'—'My friend, I wish to be baptised.' ... 'Do you know what you are asking,' I said to him. 'Mmanyi munange'—'I know, my friend', he replied ... 'But,' I said, 'suppose people ask you if you were a reader, would you tell a lie and deny it and say no?' He replied, 'Ndiyatula munange'—'I shall confess, my friend.' Mackay and I both thought he was worthy of the rite ... so he was baptised there and then." The growth of the movement was phenomenal. Barely two months after the purge order, the CMS baptismal register carried two hundred and twenty-seven names; the number of Catholics may have been greater. Even prominent members of the Kabaka's court (including the admiral of the fleet) became converts. Europeans, learning of the

---

* Mwanga's victims became the last officially recognized Christian martyrs. In 1964, twenty-two of the Catholics among them were canonized in Rome. Assisting Pope Paul VI at the rites was Archbishop Joseph Kiwanuka, Metropolitan of Uganda. Four of the saints had been his cousins. In August, 1969, the Pope consecrated the altar of the Catholic National Shrine of the Uganda Martyrs, a few miles outside of Kampala.

pogrom and the resistance, began to look at simple African savages in a new light. "Men asked what kind of people these were," wrote Lugard, "who would thus brave death for their belief."

*

During the reign of terror, Mwanga's own fear of British vengeance did not subside, but by now he appears to have felt that if he was in for the penny he might just as well go for the pound. Therefore the missionaries, as the prime agents of subversion, had no choice but to assume that every day would be their last on earth. "It has always appeared to me," Jackson later wrote, "that full honour has not been accorded to them. They were in the field of horrors and daily facing imminent dangers and a cruel death; a position that was never sufficiently emphasized. Their conduct was heroic, nothing less." It seems almost incredible that Mackay above all should have lived. Mwanga feared him far more than any of the others, suspecting that the seditious Christian teacher also practiced witchcraft against him personally. He attributed various physical disorders (including a recurrent eye ailment) to spells cast by Mackay. There was no doubt in his mind that the missionary's sorcery was at work when, after a fire leveled the palace, he took refuge in the Katikiro's house—only to scamper out almost before entering, as a bolt of lightning knocked the building to pieces. On a number of occasions he schemed to have Mackay killed, but the plots never quite came off. What probably saved the missionary was, surprisingly, the stubborn and persistent opposition of the Katikiro. Motivated either by sentiment or superstition, perhaps by both, this man continually reminded Mwanga that Mackay had buried the previous Kabaka and the Namasole and was thus, if not sacrosanct, a risky proposition as a murder victim.

Mackay also found some security in Mwanga's reluctance to let his manual and mechanical skills go to waste, for he continued his work as craftsman by royal command. Distasteful as he must have found this, it served a purpose, placing him in a position somewhat akin to that of non-German Jews who bargained with Hitler to win freedom for a few co-religionists. On one occasion Mackay showed the palace gunsmith how to make cartridge cases in return for Mwanga's pledge to spare the lives of a large number of Christians. At another time, he cajoled the Kabaka out of an execution order with the promise to make him a hand loom and a spinning jenny. Yet his usefulness was a two-edged sword, because it also made him Mwanga's prisoner, despite a concerted effort by CMS in England to bring him out. He writes that Mwanga told him:

"A great king like me should never be without a man of skill to work for him. I will not let you go away, not even if they send seventy letters for you."

Considering the climate alone, this could have been tantamount to a death sentence. In the pre-Atabrine, pre-antibiotic nineteenth century, five years was generally considered an excessive tour of duty for any European in the tropics. Nearly a full decade of vindictive heat, unremitting attacks of fever, constant personal risk and overwork had already left an indelible mark on Mackay, and now there was the added burden of involuntary servitude to a madman. "I am almost entirely broken down," he wrote at this time, "with fatigue, anxiety, and want of sleep." He desperately needed to go, if only for a few weeks. Mwanga would have been well rid of him, too, for the value of Mackay's skill was easily canceled out by his leadership in the Christian movement. But the Kabaka cursed the alien threat to his country and refused to release him.

Mackay was not only Mwanga's captive. Even if he had been allowed to go it is entirely possible that his conscience would not have let him. By early 1887, Ashe and the others had been expelled or somehow given permission to leave, and Mackay was upholding the CMS cause alone. To desert his flock in its time of trial would have been unthinkable. As a human being he thought about it often, but excerpts from his correspondence and journal during this interlude underscore his wearily dogged resolve to stick it out—and also reveal an occasional ray of hope. "I am plodding on, teaching, translating, printing, doctoring, and carpentering. Strange medley, you will say. That cannot be helped." ... "I was astonished to hear Wakili explaining to some other chiefs that 'we Europeans are striving only for the good and peace of Africa...' This from a heathen is wonderful." ... "Praise God! St. Matthew's Gospel is now published complete in Luganda, and rapidly being bought. I merely stitch it, with title-page, and supply a loose cover. Binding, by-and-by." ... "Strange to say, the queen-mother sent me the present of a large fat cow very early to-day, without begging for anything." ... "Read three chapters of Romans, vii., viii., ix., with good class this evening. The argument they seem to comprehend. Where is ... Reichard, with his charge of extreme poverty of mental power in the negro?"

More than a year went by before Mwanga at last gave his consent to Mackay's departure. By late spring of 1887, the Kabaka's violent dementia had ebbed somewhat, with a consequent falling off in atrocities. A replacement for Mackay, the Rev. E. C. Gordon, was also on his way to Uganda, and Mackay could therefore feel free to leave—although he refused to go before making certain that an escort would be sent out to bring Gordon to Rubaga in safety. It was not until July 21, 1887, that Mackay boarded the *Eleanor*, his decaying steam launch, and set a course for the south shore of the lake.

*

He did not go far, as it was his intention to return to Rubaga as soon as conditions permitted. (One reason for his departure was an awareness that his presence might have become too inflammatory to serve the best interests of the Christians.) For nearly three years, he taught and worked with the people of Usambiro on the south shore, keeping in touch with his Uganda flock through Gordon and waiting for an opportune time to go back. He showed no desire to take his long overdue and badly needed home leave, as Stanley discovered on passing through Usambiro in 1889. The explorer was then en route to the coast from Lake Albert, where he had just brought off the controversial "rescue" of Emin Pasha, the bizarre knight-pawn of African imperialism, and he urged Mackay to accompany his party. Stanley knew and admired Mackay, describing him as "the modern Livingstone," and holding him in special regard because he "had never joined in the missionaries' attacks on me." Mackay in turn had the highest esteem for Stanley; surely, the chance to enjoy the security of the expedition's numbers and divest himself of his thirteen-year burden must have been sorely tempting. But he rejected it out of hand. He felt himself honor-bound to return to Uganda; until then, there remained much to be done on the south shore. So he stayed, although he never saw the Rubaga mission again. On February 8, 1890, at the age of forty-one, he died of fever in Usambiro.

*

Meanwhile, Mwanga had achieved something no previous Kabaka had ever accomplished: his own overthrow. For the police state he established had become intolerable even to a people accustomed to injustice and pain. Mutesa and other rulers had been able to commit their atrocities because they were commanding figures and because they had their Great Chiefs behind them. Such was not the case with Mwanga, who seemed to be showing himself constitutionally incapable of judicious action. The religious persecutions were his greatest error— less for their cruelty, which was hardly new to the Baganda, than because they alienated the chiefs. Large numbers of Uganda's ruling class having been won over to the foreign religions, they no longer felt bound to the

Kabaka by the traditional ties of Lubareism. The kingly office itself they revered—this was all that kept Mwanga on the throne—but they would not submit indefinitely when an individual monarch forbade them from worshipping as they chose.

It was Mwanga's failure to appreciate this that toppled him. In September, 1888, word leaked out that his army was about to swoop down on the country's Catholics, Protestants and Muslims and maroon them all on an island on the lake, while he himself restored Lubareism to its former pre-eminence. The plot never got off the ground. Temporarily submerging their doctrinal antagonisms, the three groups came together and stormed the palace. Scarcely before he realized what had happened, Mwanga was a Kabaka in exile on the south shore.

It would not be long before he became involved in a strange game of musical chairs on the lake. It was to be a sometimes ludicrous but always grim contest in which Mwanga would find himself dealing for the first time with a breed of European less disposed to turn the other cheek than the courageous but humble missionaries.

5

A BATHTUB FOR DR. PETERS

*"It is my conviction that ... the Zanzibar
Empire seventy years hence will be as
different from the Zanzibar of the present
day as the New Zealand of 1877 from what
it was half a century ago."*

Not many policy decisions underscore more graphically England's distaste for east African obligations through most of the nineteenth century than Lord Salisbury's refusal to aid the CMS missionaries after Bishop Hannington's murder. Yet at that very moment, thanks largely to shifts in the European political scene, Britain was almost being dragooned into asserting mastery over the land she wished no part of. The process was awkward, burdensome, dangerous and not a little humiliating. Ironically, however, it could have been carried out painlessly had Britain simply appropriated the territory eight years earlier. To have done so would in no way have violated the rights or territorial claims of the Sultan of Zanzibar. For it was Barghash himself who most eagerly sought to place his domains under the Union Jack.

Egypt's unsuccessful attempt at annexing Uganda via Zanzibar in 1875 may have alarmed Mutesa, but it opened Barghash's eyes. Nothing demonstrated so clearly to him how vulnerable his vaguely defined mainland empire was to the assault of any power, large or small, with the ambition and the few troops needed to take the country away from him. He was equally aware that what had prevented this from happening was Kirk's collision with the Egyptian force at Barawa and Ismail's consequent retreat. He had further reason for gratitude to England when, even after withdrawing, Ismail continued to seek British recognition of at least an Egyptian foothold in Zanzibar territory—only to be coldly rebuffed by Derby, the Foreign Secretary. "The Sultan is greatly delighted," said Kirk in a private letter. "He thinks that, if Derby were a Mussulman, he would have been a fit companion of the Prophet." Actually, the credit here belonged once more to Kirk, who had energetically recommended rejection of any such bid by the Khedive; but the real point was that Britain and Britain alone had kept Barghash's interior domains from becoming an Egyptian province. And Barghash knew this well.

Still, who could tell which way the political monsoon might be blowing when the next power cast covetous eyes on the Sultanate? Would England find it in her interest to step in once more? If Barghash ever were to feel secure in his possession of the mainland, Anglo–Zanzibari ties must be strengthened. The 1873 treaty was not enough; it meant no more than a British presence which could intervene or stand aside as it chose at the threat of another foreign seizure. Somehow England had to be drawn into a more active role, into a tangible stake in Zanzibar's future.

That this might further diminish the Sultan's personal power was a risk Barghash seemed quite prepared to take—and not merely, perhaps, as a matter of practical politics. Although he had been coerced into signing the 1873 treaty, his willing cooperation in its implementation could also be seen as the next-to-last step in the making of an Arab Anglophile. This process was completed in 1875, even before Britain came to his aid against Ismail. In June and July, he had made a visit to England, and the welcome he found was of a warmth seldom experienced by any foreign royalty in that country. The Queen greeted him at Windsor Castle. He was the Prince of Wales' guest at Marlborough House. In London he received the equivalent of New York's ticker-tape parade: freedom of the city at the Guildhall, followed by a state banquet at the Mansion House. Innumerable teas, balls, garden parties and formal dinners were given in his honor. He went on guided tours of Liverpool, Birmingham, Manchester and Brighton; made inspections of Woolwich Arsenal, Aldershot Camp and the General Post Office. He was the center of attraction at the Ascot races, the British Museum, the Opera (where he saw *Lohengrin*, *Acis and Galatea* and *Bluebeard*). From all accounts, he appears to have captured the imagination and the heart of everyone. During a concert at the Crystal Palace, the choir stood up to sing and Barghash also rose in a gesture of oriental courtesy, whereupon the entire audience followed his example.

Not unnaturally he was all but bowled over by the honors that fell on him like an endless cloudburst. "It is the fault of the English people," he declared somewhat emotionally in one of the many speeches he was obliged to make. "You all welcome me. You all tell me I have done something for the abolition of the slave trade ... What can I say but thank you, thank you, thank you." He could hardly have been blamed if he thought the opportune moment had arrived to win from Britain the substantive commitment which would reinforce Zanzibar's security.

In 1876 he took his first step in that direction. Although not seeking Foreign Office involvement or sanction, he made it known through Derby that he would welcome the assistance of private British capital in the development of his mainland regions. Previously, the Government had pursued a hands-off policy with respect to the support of commercial undertakings in east Africa, but the Egyptian invasion had, if nothing else, emphasized the value of opening up the interior as a weapon against the slave trade. Derby therefore passed Barghash's proposal on to Sir William Mackinnon, another in the long line of Scotsmen who planted Britain's imperial seeds in east African soil.

Mackinnon has been described by one historian as occupying "that interesting borderland between philanthropy and high finance." His British India Steam Navigation Company brought the first scheduled passenger, mail and cargo service to Zanzibar. He played an instrumental role in having the cable extended to the island from Aden. At the time of Barghash's overture he was involved with plans for a mainland road from Dar es Salaam to Lake Nyasa. (Although only seventy-odd miles were completed, the legitimate trade which the road created struck a noticeable blow against slavery; "as a philanthropic undertaking," said Kirk, "it has been eminently successful.") His interest in the Zanzibar Sultanate was at least as much humanitarian-imperial as financial, but he was not a man to turn his back on a good profit. This is what he saw accruing from the potential exploitation of east Africa's trade and natural resources, and he accordingly prepared a draft concession for Barghash's approval.

What Mackinnon asked from the Sultan was nothing less than de facto and de jure rule over the entire mainland between the coast and the lakes. Within the framework of a sixty-six-year lease, Mackinnon proposed to form a company whose management would have full powers to make all laws and to conclude treaties, not only with local chiefs but with foreign governments. The company would also levy all taxes and customs duties, mint and issue all currency, raise an army, develop public works and communications, control trade and hold exclusive rights to mineral prospecting. In return, Barghash was to receive twenty percent of any possible duty increases and a five percent royalty on mineral earnings.

The proposal was anything but lopsided. Even apart from profits, Barghash stood to come out ahead. "The terms offered," wrote Kirk, "are clearly in favor of the Sultan who has apparently all to gain and nothing to lose except his personal control and the exercise of powers requiring a supervision which ... absorbs his income and gives him nothing but incessant trouble and annoyance." Most significantly, the administration of Zanzibar's mainland domains by a private British company would constitute the very vested interest which Barghash so eagerly sought. To be sure, the British Government had no formal connection whatever with the concession, but thenceforth—regardless of Foreign Office wishes in the matter—any threat to Zanzibar's territorial integrity could only mean a challenge to Britain as well.

Curiously enough, the Foreign Office did not appear to recoil from its possible future entanglements. In May, 1877, Kirk was instructed to give Mackinnon "all proper assistance of which he may stand in need." Two months later, Derby himself went so far as to state that while his ministry "would not feel justified in giving it a formal sanction," the proposed concession nonetheless "commends itself to such support as Her Majesty's Government can properly afford to such an undertaking." To a point, this could be seen as a green light, although only a wish to strike at slavery through the interior could have overcome officialdom's long-standing aversion to a potential east African encumbrance. In any case, Kirk was elated. With Mackinnon's guidance, he wrote Derby, "Zanzibar might soon be made a prosperous and powerful kingdom, the Slave Trade totally suppressed." The Rev. G. P. Badger, who had served with the Frere mission in 1873 and now represented Mackinnon in the final stages of the negotiation, saw a future no less bright. "It is my conviction," he told the Foreign Office, "that under such management as that of the proposed Company the Zanzibar Empire seventy years hence will be as different from the Zanzibar of the present day as the New Zealand of 1877 from what it was half a century ago."

Then the entire scheme collapsed.

To this day, no one has been able to fix the cause with any certainty. Some of the individuals involved believed that Mackinnon's interest in the project cooled when he encountered difficulty in raising the capital. This in fact may have happened, although considering the scope of Mackinnon's personal commitment to commercial expansion in east Africa—not to mention his dedication to the anti-slavery cause—the case for financial timidity is less than airtight. Another possibility may be found in an eleventh-hour falling out between Barghash and Badger. The latter, a highly respected orientalist, was almost equally well known for his want of tact and patience when both were most wanted. According to Kirk, Badger tried to coerce Barghash into a hasty acceptance of the concession's fine print and only succeeded in angering the Sultan. "If the matter falls through it will be Badger's fault," wrote the Consul, in a not much less irate private letter. "He is the most undiplomatic man I ever knew ... He is making an ass of himself ... He has sent, I am told, the most insolent messages and written the Sultan a bullying letter ... The man's head seems turned." Perhaps it was; yet it is not easy to imagine Barghash spurning his long-sought opportunity in a fit of pique.

A third possible explanation is that the British Government suddenly came to realize the extent, and risk, of its commitment to Mackinnon and simply withdrew its backing. Apart from a subsequent statement by a Foreign Office under-secretary that "there is a secret history to the failure of the Mackinnon scheme that I will not commit to paper," no demonstrable evidence exists to support this conclusion. Even so, there is every reason to think Government caution at least as likely as Mackinnon's ostensible loss of enthusiasm or Barghash's willingness to sacrifice all because of an old man's rude behavior. Even so guarded an endorsement as Derby's violated nearly every canon of Foreign Office prudence in east Africa. Second thoughts and withdrawal would be only natural to a Government bound by an instinctively conservative policy to the avoidance of obligations in a part of the world where obligations seemed to bring no possible advantage and a sea of needless troubles.

But whatever the reason, Barghash failed in his bid for security, and Britain's imperial burden in east Africa was deferred.

*

Thus Zanzibar's mainland possessions remained vulnerable, and as the 1870s drew to a close, Barghash could look with increasing anxiety as European interest in east Africa mounted. In 1877, the same year that Barghash and Mackinnon almost came to terms, Belgium's King Leopold II had founded the African International Association for the purpose of fighting the slave trade, encouraging exploration and generally opening the interior to wholesome Western influences. "Our roads and posts," declared Leopold, "will greatly assist the evangelization of the blacks and the introduction among them of commerce and modern industry." Less visible beneath these lofty objectives was Leopold's ambition to annex an African empire of his own, and it is not inaccurate to describe the International Association as his front in that endeavor.

Between 1877 and 1882, Leopold mounted no fewer than four major expeditions from the coast to Lake Tanganyika. While each had some altogether laudable scientific aim (one party included four Indian elephants, being tried out as possible bush transport), none was entirely free of a certain political complexion not ordinarily associated with African travel at that time. Kirk found himself especially puzzled by one Belgian group, which departed from Bagamoyo "in secrecy and mystery." He also felt that something more than anti-slavery or natural science may have brought all four of Leopold's expeditions to a permanent settlement which their leaders established at a place called Karema near the lake shore. During his own maiden journey to the interior in 1880, Thomson visited Karema and called it "one of the most extraordinary places for a station that could be found on the lake." He was bemused to find that the European occupants "have commenced building forts and walls, digging ditches in regular military fashion as if they might expect an attack with cannon at any moment."

All this could, perhaps, have been part of the process of evangelizing the bush, but as Kirk observed at about the same time, the post was "now spoken of and held as Belgian property." He added the pertinent comment that "stations in the interior are untenable without a territorial footing on the coast." The remark was meant to be significant. Shortly after Thomson's visit to Karema, Leopold appointed Belgium's first Consul to Zanzibar. Although he took pains to inform Kirk that "our consul is not a political agent; we have no political interest properly speaking in Africa," Kirk remained skeptical. There is no telling what effect Leopold's designs might have had on the Zanzibar Sultanate had not Stanley won for the Belgian king the million-square-mile private park which was called, quite seriously, the Congo Free State. Since that domain could be entered more conveniently from the Atlantic, Leopold's preoccupation with Zanzibar's interior soon waned.

But the possibility of foreign intrusion remained real, in one form or another. Germany had weighed the pros and cons of an east African holding as early as 1875, and while the undertaking did not get off the ground, the fact remained that it had been considered. And there was always France; Barghash may not have seen her as a foe, but he was sensible enough to realize that she would not spurn any opportunity to extend her influence in the Sultanate. During the late 1870s, in fact, France made two moves in that direction—although the first may have struck on-the-spot observers as a lampoon of exploration and missionary endeavor. In May, 1878, a dedicated but eccentric thirty-three-year-old priest, the Abbé Michel-Alexandre Debaize, arrived in Zanzibar with no less ambitious a goal than to march across the continent "for the glory of God and the glory of France." Among the supplies carried by Debaize's eight hundred porters were twenty umbrellas, two dozen cases of fireworks, two loads of toy popguns, a crate of tiny bells, two suits of armor and a hurdy-gurdy. For more than a year, the poor man wandered about the interior, suffering sunstroke and blindness, before he died of fever near Ujiji. This tragicomic misadventure would have fitted no imperialist pattern except that it had been financed (to the sum of one hundred thousand francs) by a vote of the French Chamber of Deputies, a body not celebrated for handouts to starry-eyed vagrants.

But the second French bid, which came two years later, was not only realistic but nearly won Barghash himself. This was the request by a Marseilles firm for a concession not unlike that which Mackinnon had proposed in 1877. Its main difference, and one of its principal attractions, was the contractors' plan to build a railway from Bagamoyo to Ujiji. Barghash found further inducement in the offer of a half-million-dollar, interest-free loan as well as fifty percent of all mineral royalties. Had he accepted the proposition, he might in fact have found his long-desired territorial integrity under a French rather than a British wing. Then again he might not have, for Kirk, the ever faithful British watchdog in the Sultan's manger, pointed out to Barghash several deceptive clauses which absolved the Marseilles company of any responsibility to protect the interior—or even to build the railway. "The moment that these things had been explained to His Highness," Kirk wrote the Foreign Office, "the fate of the concession was not doubtful and negotiations were broken off."

This did not require a prodigious effort of persuasion, for Barghash had by no means abandoned his dream of finding a place for Zanzibar behind Britannia's shield. In 1881 he renewed his effort, not with another offer to private enterprise but a direct and open bid to Whitehall: "Finding it for the public good to make an arrangement for the government of Zanzibar after my death ... my wish and intention is that the British Government shall promise the throne of Zanzibar and its dependencies to the eldest of my sons and after him to his son ... and the British Government shall be guardian of them until they come of age." In one sense, the request was not merely harmless but reasonable, since Britain had been the deciding factor in the succession of Majid and of Barghash himself, and had also handed down the arbitrary judgment separating Zanzibar from Oman. But the proposed regency was also no more than a euphemism for a British protectorate. With the anti-imperialist Gladstone at the head of Government, the reply could only have been a foregone conclusion. Barghash may have wondered at this point which power would make the next move against him.

"Reasons of state, obscure to ordinary mortals, have made it necessary to sacrifice Seyyid Barghash."

On October 1, 1884, a new German Consul was appointed to Zanzibar. He was Gerhard Rohlfs, known not only as an African explorer of considerable accomplishment but as a zealous advocate of German colonial expansion. So outspoken were Rohlfs' imperial views that Bismarck made a point of stating to Sir Edward Malet, the British Ambassador in Berlin, that "Germany was not endeavouring to obtain a protectorate over Zanzibar." The Foreign Office may or may not have placed full credence in the disclaimer. Bismarck, who for the previous two decades had had his hands full cementing an assortment of minor Teutonic duchies and other small states into the most virile nation of continental Europe, had also turned a frequent cold shoulder to German overseas annexations. "As long as I am Chancellor," he had declared as late as 1881, "we will carry on no colonial policies." Only a few months before Rohlfs' arrival in Zanzibar, the Anglophilic German Ambassador in London had assured Gladstone's Foreign Secretary, Granville, that "it was well known that the Prince was absolutely opposed to the acquisition of colonies by Germany."

But it was also at about this time that Bismarck had launched an energetic colonial program. Impelled by a wish to stem the flow of German emigration to foreign countries, by a need for raw materials and new markets, and by a simple thirst for imperial glory, he began to make overseas claims and annexations in an almost urgent haste. Between April and July of 1884, South West Africa, Cameroon and Togoland had been brought into the Reich. Thus the Chancellor's disavowal of designs on the Sultanate was not necessarily to be taken at face value. And yet, whatever suspicions the Foreign Office may have entertained regarding German ambitions in east Africa might well have proved unfounded but for a man named Carl Peters.

*

If the story of the imperial scramble for east Africa has any villain, that role must go to Peters—at least if Britain is stage-managing the production. To this day, English historians writing about the time and place tend to depict Peters as a scheming, amoral filibusterer, a murderer of Africans and a reader of other people's mail. Even Hitler was to praise him with a faint damn, as "a model, if stern, colonial administrator." While these portrayals are not entirely inaccurate, they need rounding out. If Peters was short on ethics and long on cruelty, he was also unswervingly dedicated to his country's interests, possessed an extraordinary gift of resourcefulness and could have spared enough physical courage for half a dozen men. These things do not always come out in Peters' somewhat inconsistent background or personal appearance, both of which suggest the very antithesis of the swashbuckling African adventurer. Photographs reveal a frail, prissy, waspish fellow with a pince-nez and severely trimmed mustache, almost a caricature of some Herr Doktor Professor waxing apoplectic over a student's foolish reply to a question about Schopenhauer. Peters could have filled that part, and did: at the age of twenty-four, he received his doctorate for a paper entitled "To What Extent Is Metaphysics Possible as a Science?" He was also, quite incongruously, an unashamed Anglophile who had spent many years in London and at one time considered taking a post in India. Yet this improbable German egghead created for the Kaiser an empire twice the size of his own country. What is more, he did it largely by himself, and often without Germany's sanction. He never seems to have won the complete faith of the nation for which he so frequently put his life and colossal ego on the line.

He certainly had no official backing in 1884, when he formed a private organization called the Society for German Colonization for the purpose of annexing as much of the Sultanate as he might be able to seize. At that time, Germany had not considered staking an east African claim, and while the Society could not quite have been called an underground body, it sometimes seemed to act surreptitiously. In September, 1884, Peters and three fellow members, masked in aliases and the rough garb of mechanics, bought third-class tickets from Trieste to Aden, whence they proceeded to Zanzibar as deck passengers. Arriving on November 1, they were met by Rohlfs with instructions from his Government: "It has come to our attention that a certain Dr. Peters has set out ... to establish a German colony ... The German Consul is requested to inform him that he can claim neither German imperial protection nor any guarantee for his own life and safety." Peters is then said to have dashed off a sarcastic letter to Bismarck, suggesting that the next time the Chancellor decided to refuse his request for assistance, he might wait until such a request was forth-coming. Yet he also seems to have been aware that if his Government repudiated him as a potential empire builder it would in all likelihood be more receptive to a fait accompli. On November 10, he boarded a dhow for Dar es Salaam, crossed the strait to the mainland and vanished.

He did not remain long among the missing. Petty chiefs in the Usagara region, some one hundred and fifty miles inland from Bagamoyo, soon found themselves playing host to Peters' caravan and scrawling large crosses on sheets of paper covered with the strange symbols used by white men. Each of these documents, it hardly need be said, was a "treaty of eternal friendship," in which such and such a chief handed over "all his territory with all its civil and public appurtenances to Dr. Carl Peters as the representative of the Society for German Colonization...." At the end of five weeks, Peters had obtained the marks of twelve chiefs on deeds transferring some twenty-five hundred square miles of east African land to Germany. It was an impressive beginning, and, as Peters had correctly guessed, made him persona grata with Bismarck when he returned to Berlin early in February of 1885.

But Bismarck seemed in no haste to place his imprimatur on the treaties. In the previous November, he had called an international meeting which, in February, was still in session. Attended by thirteen European nations and the United States, its purpose was to formulate a coherent policy in the conduct of commercial and political undertakings in Africa. The most significant accomplishment of the Berlin Conference was, perhaps, the laying down of what might be called the ground rules of the impending African scramble; but the European Powers also gave their blessing to claims previously staked out by one another, including the German holdings in western and southwestern Africa. Peters' treaties, on the other hand, did not win this approval simply because Bismarck chose to withhold them from the Conference. He had two reasons for doing so. The first, as we will shortly discover, he regarded as his trump card. The second was his belief that inclusion of Usagara with Germany's already accepted claims might appear overly avaricious in the eyes of the delegates to the Conference. Accordingly, he waited until March 2, when the Conference adjourned. The next day, he personally took the new treaties to Kaiser Wilhelm I, who promptly added his own signature to those of the chiefs and issued a *schutzbrief* placing Usagara "under our imperial protection." Germany had now become a Power to reckon with in east Africa.

Bismarck did not trouble to give Barghash formal notification of the German claim until April 25. On learning the news, the thunderstruck

Sultan sent an immediate cable of protest to the Kaiser himself. "These territories," he cried, "are under our authority from the time of our fathers. We have, therefore, to ask Your Majesty to render justice ..." For Peters' treaties had in fact cut the very heart out of Barghash's interior domains. "If anywhere on the mainland His Highness exercises jurisdiction it is in Usagara," Kirk told the Foreign Office, pointing out that this region was one of the few where Zanzibar military posts had actually been established. The argument, however, made little impression either on Wilhelm or Bismarck. In drafting his treaties, Peters had taken pains to insert a clause to the effect that each of the local rulers "on direct inquiry ... declared that he was not in any way dependent upon the Sultan of Zanzibar and that he did not even know of the existence of the latter." Whopper or not, the statement was on paper, and in any case a legal claim by Barghash was not necessarily going to hold up well in a realm so vaguely defined as the one which he asserted to be under his authority. Besides which, Bismarck simply could not have cared less. By now, his move on Zanzibar territory had gone into high gear. Kirk had already cabled the Foreign Office that "Germans intend further annexation, probably Chagga," and warned that an attempt was in all likelihood being made to occupy the Witu area near Lamu.

Witu was a particularly leaky powder keg, being under the control of a unanimously self-elected "sultan" named Simba, who had for several years been showing unusually warm hospitality to two German brothers, Clemens and Gustav Denhardt. Although the Denhardts claimed only scientific and commercial interest in Witu, Kirk had received sufficient information from his agents in Lamu, who kept the Denhardts under close surveillance, to consider this "doubtful." The strong possibility of Witu's violent secession had been indicated as early as August, 1884. At that time, Haggard, the Lamu Vice-Consul, visited Witu and found that Simba's followers—"composed chiefly of all the malcontents, bankrupts and felons of the surrounding country"—were quite prepared to do away with a diplomat on Her Majesty's Service. Simba's brother-in-law openly threatened to have Haggard murdered unless he agreed to smuggle arms into Witu. "The man's manner towards me was so sinister and ferocious," Haggard later wrote Kirk, "that I could not but feel uneasy at my helpless position in a town full of savages and so securely walled that a cat could not escape." Haggard was finally permitted to leave unharmed, although Simba's brother-in-law could not resist a parting question: would Kirk be willing to smuggle the guns?

That all this was not an isolated gesture of defiance was made manifestly clear shortly afterwards, when four bulky cases labeled as scientific instruments arrived at the Zanzibar Customs House for transshipment to the Denhardts in Witu. Understandably suspicious, Barghash ordered the cases opened and found a large consignment of rifles. After the customs officer had filed down the hammer of each weapon, the guns were returned to their cases, forwarded on to Witu and followed by six hundred Zanzibari troops under orders to stand by in Lamu.

Nor was Barghash passive in his reaction to the impending German invasion of Chaggaland. General Lloyd Mathews of the Zanzibar army was instructed to take a detachment of soldiers to the region and to make treaties with the local rulers. This mission was accomplished without difficulty. On June 21, at Moshi, Mandara and twenty-four other chiefs put their marks on a declaration identifying themselves as "subjects of the Sultan of Zanzibar," and stating that "we hoist his flag in the towns of our country to prove our loyalty."

Then Bismarck bared his own fangs. Early in June, two German cruisers dropped anchor in Manda Bay near Lamu. A few days later, Clemens Denhardt announced to Kirk that Simba had consented to transform "the covenant of friendship which has existed with Germany ... into a protectorate." On June 20, Kirk was informed by Rohlfs that Germany was seeking a sea outlet, directly opposite Zanzibar itself, for the Usagara "colony." Acceptance of this, Kirk told the Foreign Office, would "undermine every Zanzibar coast claim elsewhere." But the real blow did not fall until August 7, when five German warships steamed into Zanzibar harbor.

The purpose of sending out the squadron, Malet had been assured in Berlin, was not to make war or carry off an illegal annexation but simply to "bring the Sultan to a more correct bearing." And as if by way of hastening that hoped-for change of attitude, news arrived on August 8 that Mathews' treaties in the Kilimanjaro region had been invalidated by an associate of Peters, Dr. Carl Jühlke, who had won Mandara over to acceptance of a German protectorate on condition that the protectors furnish a "better flagstaff" than the one Mathews had brought. "I love Germans above other people," Mandara was reported to have declared, "and in particular above Englishmen and Arabs." A few months later Mandara would tell two English missionaries that he had never hoisted the German flag and that he considered all Germans to be people of "mitambo"—deceit. Coming from Mandara, this had to be meaningless, but the new treaty was very real, and very alarming.

No less substantial, and a great deal more menacing, was the presence of the German squadron. One vessel in particular caught Kirk's attention. Unlike the other ships, which simply lay at anchor, this one moved about constantly in a series of strange maneuvers, entering harbor at dawn, leaving at sunset, continually flashing signals. On August 19, Kirk sent a boy out to the ship with a box of oranges for the crew and instructions to learn what he could. The intelligence revealed fully the extremity of the measures Bismarck was prepared to take in securing his claims. Aboard the mystery ship was a middle-aged Mata Hari who could have brought total destruction on the island: Frau Emily Reute, formerly the Princess Salme.

While retaining deep ties of affection and homesickness for Zanzibar, Salme had for some time been a German citizen; and although acutely aware of her ostracism by her own family, she had once dared Barghash's wrath by offering him her services as a sort of unofficial ambassadress in Berlin. "The Ruler of Germany and his family are all kind to me," she wrote, "and I have been many times to see them ... Should you wish me to act for you with the German Emperor, I can go personally to see him ... My brother, I want you to understand that the British only wish to destroy your power and your name." Despite these Anglophobic sentiments, Salme is not likely to have conspired knowingly against Barghash. However, since she had made occasional requests for a share in the financial inheritance that she considered rightfully hers, Bismarck had been able to prevail on her to pursue the matter under German protection. According to Moritz Busch, one of Bismarck's biographers, this was a callous deceit: "the trap had been very carefully prepared for Sultan Barghash"; the Princess would "go out to Zanzibar and press her claim, and an accident might possibly occur to the lady—her brother might have her strangled." And the murder of a German national in Zanzibar in those days would have given Bismarck adequate cause to order the squadron to open fire on the town. Fortunately, Kirk was able to warn Barghash and nothing came of it.

And in any case, Frau Reute had by this time lost her value as unwitting agent provocatrice and victim. On August 13, following a twenty-four-hour ultimatum by Commodore Paschen, the squadron commander, Barghash had capitulated, recognizing all German claims in Usagara, Kilimanjaro and Witu. The sound of the flute could scarcely be heard.

*

But where had Barghash's English friends been all this time? While it had certainly not been Foreign Office policy to bail Zanzibar out whenever its sovereignty was threatened, the fact remained that Britain had established herself as the power behind the Sultan's throne and did not welcome the idea of sharing that power. Under these circumstances it was quite natural for Barghash to have expected, at the very least, a gesture of resistance to Germany's encroachment. This was not forthcoming. "Reasons of state, obscure to ordinary mortals," observed Joseph Thomson sardonically, "have made it necessary to sacrifice Seyyid Barghash."

Actually, the reasons were far from obscure. In 1885, Zanzibar was not alone in its need for a strong associate, for shifts in the political winds had imperiled England's once dominant position in Europe's precariously built edifice of formal and tacit alliances. Anglo-French tensions had been mounting since 1882, when British troops, to quell a revolt that jeopardized passage through the Suez Canal, occupied Egypt, the control of whose affairs had long been shared by England and France. The Czar was making ominous moves in the direction of Turkey, where British influence was also on the wane, and a large Russian army was approaching Afghanistan, thus threatening the security of the Indian frontier. With two of the European superpowers aligned against British interests, it would have been dangerous folly to alienate Bismarck, particularly over so trifling an issue as the Sultan's mainland claims in east Africa.

Bismarck knew this quite well; he had, indeed, withheld announcement of Peters' treaties until the full impact of French and Russian hostility made itself felt in England. It was not surprising, then, that Gladstone, the scourge of British imperialism, would bless the same sin when committed by the Germans. In December, 1884, the Prime Minister had mocked his imperially inclined "forward party" minority in the Foreign Office for having suggested that Britain assert control in the Kilimanjaro region. "Terribly have I been puzzled and perplexed," he wrote his Liberal colleague, Sir Charles Dilke, "on finding a group of the soberest men among us to have concocted a scheme such as that touching the mountain country behind Zanzibar with an unrememberable name." But by early March of 1885, Herbert Bismarck, the Chancellor's son, reported to his father from London Gladstone's statement at a private dinner that "if there were no colonial movement in Germany, he would beg us to create one." Gladstone went even further in public, declaring to Parliament on March 12 that "if Germany becomes a colonizing power, all I can say is 'God speed her.'"

Salisbury, too, supported the appeasement. Taking up the reins of Government briefly in 1885, he showed not even latent signs of the conversion to the cause of east African empire which he would undergo a few years later. On August 24, he wrote Lord Iddesleigh, the Foreign

Secretary, in his most patrician manner, that "I have been using the credit I have got with Bismarck in Caroline Islands and Zanzibar to get help in Russia and Turkey and Egypt. He is rather a Jew, but on the whole I have as yet got my money's worth."

To all practical purposes, the only British voice to speak out for Zanzibar had been Kirk's. In cables to the Foreign Office in May of 1885, the Consul had sought to goad his Government into a less passive stance. "The Sultan cannot stand alone, and he will soon see that the longer he opposes German aspirations, the more he will lose ... This is what I believe the German Consul is now working for." ... "Collision in the district already annexed probable. German agents elsewhere active. Sultan helpless. Unofficial influence used to place himself under Germany ... Her Majesty's Government must be prepared for possible consequences." In August, Kirk went so far as to warn Salisbury that "the possession by Germany of a strong naval station in East Africa will ... have to be considered from a strategic point of view."

His advice went unheeded. The British Government at this time seemed bent on forestalling even the slightest act or word that might antagonize Bismarck or give heart to Barghash. As early as April, when Barghash lodged his protest with the Kaiser, Kirk received a politely worded reproach from the Foreign Office: the Sultan's cable had caused "considerable irritation" in Berlin, largely because Bismarck believed it had been sent at Kirk's instigation. Not without irritation on his own part, Kirk replied: "Protest spontaneous. Sultan wished to follow in person. I dissuaded him." Shortly afterwards, Salisbury cautioned Kirk: "You should not permit any communications of a hostile tone to be addressed to German agents or representatives by Zanzibar authorities." In August, Sir Percy Anderson, head of the Foreign Office's African department, recommended that Kirk be given explicit instructions to inform Barghash that unless he yielded to Germany he would "invite a conflict that will be fatal to his independence." Kirk could only obey. "Sultan gave way," he cabled Salisbury on August 15, "only under pressure from me." In a private letter to a friend, he added a rueful postscript: "I fear [Barghash] will drop me, and I will have the blame for what I have no power to prevent."

There was, however, at least a semblance of Government sympathy toward Kirk's espousal of the Zanzibar cause, for whatever comfort this may have given Kirk or Barghash. "Here is a very interesting letter from Kirk," wrote a Foreign Office under-secretary to Salisbury in September. "The Sultan ought not to be robbed nor the Germans benefited by sham treaties or forgeries." To which Salisbury replied: "The German proceedings are not creditable. But, if we had no motive for standing well with [Germany], I do not quite see our interest in this Zanzibar quarrel."

Actually, as Salisbury well knew, Britain's interest was considerable. The east African interior had been revealed to the world mainly by British explorers. The vast majority of the several hundred missionaries there were English. The Queen's Indian subjects controlled Zanzibar's economy through loans to finance caravan trade and through near-monopoly over the coast's retail outlets. Zanzibar itself had long been a sentry box on the southern sea lane to the East, and it was very much in the Foreign Office interest that British influence along the coast somehow be upheld as paramount despite the German intrusion. "Could we admit another occupation like that of Madagascar," asked Sir Clement Hill, one of Whitehall's Young Turks, "on our alternative route to India?" Above all, there was the commitment to stamping out the slave trade. If nothing else, that obligation alone manacled England to east Africa. Thus, after encouraging Bismarck to exercise a free hand in the Sultan's territories, British politicians soon came to realize that they too would be compelled to take similar action.

*

This would truly fly in the face of the sacrosanct hands-off doctrine, but within the Kafkaesque framework of prevailing views on high-level foreign policy it would make something like sense. Africa had at last been drawn into the European power struggle, and suspicion of other nations' designs in that part of the world had begun to condition Britain's imperial reflexes. In seeking to clarify the imperatives which actuated the scramble for Africa, historians must deal with a host of complex and not always coherent motives which held preeminence among European statesmen of the era. We know how large a role was played by the lure of new markets, natural resources, military bases, naval stations, anti-slavery, evangelism and simple vainglory. It is also useful, however, to view the scramble from a simpler perspective. Dame Margery Perham, the historian, has likened the conflict to "a lot of greedy, quarrelsome children in a school playground; none quite big enough to dominate all the others, kicking and then making up to each other, sulking, coaxing, telling each other secrets and then 'splitting', combining for a moment and then breaking up. Britain was the rather aloof child in the corner, unwilling to join wholeheartedly in the rough games and yet warily watching lest too many of these quarrelling schoolmates should suddenly combine against her." As much as anything else, it was this schoolyard mentality that hastened England's first unwilling step toward her empire in east Africa. In 1885, Germany and Britain smiled on one another. Next year, who could tell? How might some change in the European balance affect Britain's east African interests? Realpolitik dictated that Bismarck's gambit must be countered. Barghash had scarcely surrendered under the guns of the German squadron than England staked out an east African territorial claim of her own.

This was made possible through one of the more elusive polities to emerge from the Berlin Conference: the sphere of influence. The expression almost defies definition, although Lugard may have come closest to the mark when he called it "a convenient phrase during a particular phase of African history, solely because it might mean much or nothing." Mainly, perhaps, it meant that you were there— on some less than rigidly delineated parcel of African soil—and that others acknowledged your authority by virtue of your presence. During the final two decades of the nineteenth century, Africa was arbitrarily marked up into a patchwork quilt of such spheres, and although most were contested and redrawn from time to time, the principle itself helped accelerate the transformation of the continent from a chaotic conglomeration of tribal states to a chaotic conglomeration of European colonies. In 1885, the sphere of influence was seen as the means by which the Foreign Office would assert its intention to maintain British authority in east Africa.

The specific instrument which brought Britain her sphere was a Delimitation Commission, convened in December, 1885, with the purpose of giving final definition to the boundaries of the Zanzibar Sultanate. This of course would mean a drastic shrinkage in Barghash's domains and an officially recognized British presence. Bismarck, now in a position to show magnanimity, offered no objections; all parties concerned in the question (including France) were represented in the group. All, that is, except the country being dismantled, for, as Kirk observed with annoyed irony, Barghash was merely "an Oriental prince to whom are not accorded the usual rights prescribed by international law."

Despite this, Kirk himself played a role in the somewhat sordid affair. Although like Barghash he did not sit with the Commission (the British member was the future Lord Kitchener), he made his influence felt, and it can in fact be said that Britain's objective took its final shape from his recommendations. What Kirk—and the Foreign Office—sought might be summed up in a single statement the Consul made at the time: "The question to be decided is practically this: Whether we are prepared to see Germany paramount over all the Zanzibar coast ... or whether some compromise cannot be come to whereby our influence is upheld and admitted as legitimately paramount over a certain district."

The proceeding sounds more callous than it really was, since the mainland Sultanate was little more than a joke and Barghash himself anything but averse to a British foot in his door. Still, when the Commission adjourned in October, 1886, the Sultan must have felt slightly undressed. His dominions, it had been decided, were to embrace a strip of coastline seven hundred miles long and ten miles deep, extending from Cape Delgado in the south to Kipini, near the mouth of the Tana river, in the north. Barghash was also allowed to keep the islands of Zanzibar, Pemba, Mafia and Lamu, and five towns on the Benadir coast above his northern borderline. The remainder of his territory, that vast interior region where the flute had once tootled so bravely, was sliced neatly into British and German spheres of influence. Britain occupied the northern sector, which embraced most of present-day Kenya, while Germany held nearly all of what is now Tanzania. Germany also received Witu, to the north of the British sphere, and shortly afterwards gained the port of Dar es Salaam. The western boundaries of each European territory, beyond Lake Victoria, were no more sharply drawn than they had been in Seyyid Said's time. On December 7, 1886, holding up his part in the pretense that he had been given a choice in the matter, Barghash formally accepted the Commission's proposals.

*

As Britain's symbolic ratification of the agreement, Kirk was recalled—although that is not quite the word. The Foreign Office could hardly have dismissed him for upholding its own policies as masterfully as he had done; his work in Zanzibar had in fact won him a knighthood. Yet the time of the Consul's usefulness was rapidly approaching its end; in Sir Reginald Coupland's words, "the great *balozi's* day was over." In Berlin as early as June, 1885, Malet had voiced fears of future Anglo-German disharmony in east Africa while "the agent who has previously upheld the opposite system" remained at his Zanzibar post. A year later, Kirk received a private request from Lord Rosebery, Gladstone's new Foreign Secretary, to take a leave in London, where his advice "would be of the greatest value." Kirk, who had already planned something like this himself, labored under no illusions as to what the leave meant. "My return [to Zanzibar] is disliked by Bismarck," he wrote a friend, "and he has quite as much to say in our political appointments as our own Government." (This was by no means a cry of sour grapes; a year later,

Bismarck demanded and won the transfer of Kirk's successor, Frederic Holmwood, on grounds of an anti-German posture.) In any case, Kirk retired, giving reasons of health, and it is not likely that he would have wished it otherwise. His own dream of unchallenged British mastery in east Africa had gone up in smoke. To be sure, Britain remained on the spot with her sphere of influence, for which Kirk himself had fought. But the sphere, when all was said and done, was a compromise, as Kirk himself had pointed out. He was not the man to serve a policy which allowed the lion's share to be taken from the lion.

"From the Chairman downwards the business side did not always weigh heaviest."

England at least had a share in east Africa, but now she was bound to administer it. That was the sole hitch in possessing a sphere of influence: one could do with it as one pleased except let it run to seed. The Berlin conferees had stipulated that no sphere receive recognition unless the influential Power were able to show tangible evidence of what was described as "effective occupation." This term also left much room for interpretation. As often as not it meant little more than having enough troops on hand to discourage claim-jumpers, but in the final analysis it called for spending money. Which in turn could have posed a serious problem for any British Government in the 1880s, when the English taxpayer had not yet become conditioned to underwriting the white man's burden in Africa. That would transpire in due course, but for the time being no Prime Minister would willingly seek help from his Treasury to finance the development of a country whose resources may have proved not worth exploiting. Fortunately, there was a way around that.

It was known as the chartered company, the time-honored and time-tested implement which had laid the foundations of at least half the British Empire without straining England's finances. Centuries before Britain even sought overseas possessions, enterprising British businessmen had been pooling their assets, often with Royal sanction, into such joint-stock groups as the English Merchant Adventurers, the British Eastland Company, the Muscovy Company and the Levant Company, each of which played a large role in developing England's foreign trade. By the seventeenth century, chartered companies were beginning to rule the lands where they conducted their affairs. Several of the American colonies were the creations of such concerns; so too were vast regions of

Canada, carved out by the Hudson's Bay Company. Mightiest of all was the British East India Company, which had literally owned the subcontinent for nearly two hundred years: laws, treaties, taxes, administration and military forces—not to mention a tremendous commerce—were the exclusive function of this private corporation. Indeed, it was "John Company," as Britons called the Indian enterprise, which gave to England one of her most profitable overseas investments. Why could not the same system be applied to Africa, especially when it entailed no financial risk on Government's part?

Why not indeed? Only because British officialdom had acquired the habit of looking askance at the undertakings of its capitalists in Africa. At best they were seen as nuisances. On the lower Niger delta, the only part of tropical Africa which could be seen to yield a profit, Liverpool merchants (usually called "palm-oil ruffians") had stirred up the placid waters of international gentlemen's agreements and forced their embarrassed Government into burdensome territorial claims in the region. Assertion of formal British control on the Niger, with its attendant diplomatic crises, was for many years regarded as a political liability rather than an imperial asset. The temperate southern portion of the continent did indeed contain great natural wealth, but as often as not the south African potential appeared to be an incipient casus belli—thanks largely to Afrikaner hostility toward the Alexandrine ambitions of Cecil Rhodes. In any case, trade below the Sahara seemed to offer either insufficient returns or dangerous political confrontations. English entrepreneurs in Africa were by definition labeled "adventurers" in the most pejorative sense of the word.

However, the changing political climate of the 1880s saw some of these businessmen beginning to acquire a certain respectability in Government eyes. If, largely against her will, England was being dragged into a continent whose affairs she found only troublesome, might not her path perhaps be smoothed and her revenues possibly increased by the locomotive of private finance? Thus the chartered company came into its own once more. The Foreign Office would swallow its distaste for Rhodes, whose British South Africa Company would create for the Crown a dominion more than twice the size of the Ukraine. In west Africa, a like task would be performed by Sir George Taubman Goldie's Royal Niger Company. (Goldie, however, resisted steadfastly his friends' urgings that he emulate Rhodes and allow his acquisition to be called Goldesia. It became Nigeria instead.) And for east Africa, Mackinnon was the man.

*

In 1887, with the active endorsement of the Foreign Office that he had sought for so long, Mackinnon founded the British East Africa Association. A year later it was a going concern, with a subscribed capital of £240,000, a Royal charter and its name appropriately changed to the Imperial British East Africa Company, usually called IBEA. Its objective was to administer and develop not only the British sphere but the Sultan's mainland domains. For the latter task, Mackinnon had received Barghash's long-desired concession: a fifty-year-lease granting the Company de facto sovereignty along two hundred miles of the Zanzibar coastal strip between the villages of Vanga and Kipini. Barghash's tangible gain took the form of an annual £10,000 in rent, plus customs levied and gathered by the Company. His real reward, however, came in seeing the British presence at last implanted firmly. This may have struck him somewhat like building a thorn boma after nearly all his camels had been stolen, but with Allah's help—and Mackinnon's—he would keep what remained of the herd. As events proved, he did not have the opportunity to enjoy the fruits of the negotiation. On March 27, 1888, he died at the age of fifty. But Mackinnon went forward.

Like the East India Company, IBEA was a corporate dominion. It flew its own flag (bearing the company motto "Light and Liberty"), coined its own money, printed its own postage stamps, recruited its own army and built its own capital city. The latter consisted of a few corrugated iron offices, warehouses and bungalows in Mombasa, the same shantytown which George Whitehouse was to find when he arrived on his railway assignment. From Mombasa, the edicts of the Company proconsul—officially known as the Administrator—were carried out along a chain of command composed of junior officers who became more or less the law of the land in their respective districts. One of their principal tasks was to win local recognition of the British sphere; to this end they negotiated no fewer than ninety-two alliances of protection with tribal rulers on specially printed Company treaty forms. But their main objective was to open up the country and prime the pump of legitimate trade. John Ainsworth, the Company's representative at Machakos in Ukamba, wrote that "the officer in charge of a station [was] in fact a storekeeper in addition to his other duties." Machakos itself became the major market center east of the Rift Valley. Near the lake shore, a similar function was performed in the bustling caravan station of Mumias. Inhabitants traveled from distant regions to both these places to barter ivory, livestock and vegetables for the accepted currencies of cloth, beads and wire coils, and occasionally money.

To expedite the flow of these commodities, transportation and communications were improved. Wooden bridges replaced tree trunks and woven reed trestles. Some rivers were crossed by crude ferries: punts or rafts with ropes fastened to overhead cables. The hazard of caravan travel through the Taru was reduced somewhat with the building of the Mackinnon Road, which eventually extended to the highlands and traversed the Rift Valley. This rough highway not only eased the porter's task in the tsetse belt near the coast but enabled wagon transport in the non-infected regions farther inland. One of the road's most important side effects was to give Mombasa pre-eminence over Zanzibar as the gateway to the interior. A stern-wheeled Company steamer plied the navigable reaches of the Tana river. Construction began on a railway from Mombasa toward Lake Victoria; it was not the line which was eventually built, but it gave tangible shape to Mackinnon's long dreamed-of deathblow to slavery. "The ceremony of laying the first rail," recalls Hobley, who had been a junior Company officer, "was a great event for the sleepy Mombasa of those days. The East Indies squadron honoured it with its presence ... The ships made a fine show, and I well remember the band of the *Boadicea* playing the 'Boulanger' march as the fleet came to anchor."

IBEA, in fact, did everything but show a profit.

For there was really little profit to be had. One could talk of cotton and rubber plantations on the coast, of inexhaustible mineral wealth in the interior, but the latter did not exist and the former called for more capital than Mackinnon had at his disposal. For £240,000 was simply an inadequate sum with which to develop and exploit the raw wilderness of a region the size of France. Rhodes could finance his enterprise with £1,000,000, and his bailiwick north of the Zambesi fairly burst with deposits of coal, copper, lead and chrome ore. Goldie started with only £300,000, but he was working a country where trade had long been established, where palm oil alone, despite a sharp fall in prices, yielded £20 per ton. Offering only the smallest fraction of such returns, east Africa was unable to attract many investors. IBEA's few stockholders, in fact, consisted chiefly of philanthropically inclined entrepreneurs who allowed their public-spirited instincts to overcome their business sense. Sharing Mackinnon's anti-slavery zeal, they saw the Company carrying out a mission at least as humanitarian as commercial. But high-minded impulses, then as now, were not convertible assets, and Mackinnon found himself obliged, almost from the start, to dip heavily into his meager capital.

Over and above its large operating expenses, the venture had an air of impracticality about it. Some IBEA officers stationed in the interior tended to find fault with top-level management on these grounds. Frederick Jackson, who served his apprenticeship with the Company, could at times be particularly critical. "The policy ... established," he wrote, "was one of peaceful penetration and of lavish expenditure in presents and cash. The former was quite correct, but no greater mistake could be made in regard to the latter ... it cannot be disputed that it fostered the belief that the 'Kumpani' possessed a very large stock of watches, swords, clocks, etc.; and an inexhaustible supply of cash." The Tana river, he said, was not suitable for the steamer that had been built for it; the vessel would go almost out of control when sailing downstream with the strong currents. Jackson also questioned the value of building a large dock on the river: "I believe I am correct in saying that it was never used except as a nesting site ... by many Black and White, and four pairs of the beautiful little Malachite Kingfishers." The Tana project in general he regarded as "one of the extravagances of the Company that are beyond explanation."

Even less explicable was the highly touted railway, which cost £50,000 and was never completed. There were simply not enough funds or skilled labor available to carry the twenty-four-inch-gauge tracks of the grandiloquently named "Central Africa Railway" more than seven miles inland from Mombasa. "When I saw that train, with its tiny puff-puff engine and the carriages in proportion," wrote Jackson, "I refused to believe that such a child's plaything could ever have been regarded as a serious proposition of a Board of Directors composed mostly of hard-headed Scotsmen."

The Central Africa Railway did not prove a total loss. Its tracks were finally pulled up and laid down again in Mombasa, for the island's trolley service. And all the while, the near-bankrupt firm continued to bear the burden of functioning as Britain's surrogate government in east Africa, while Britain herself continued to evade responsibility for the land she had already claimed as hers. Hobley, who himself took issue with Company policy at times, could remark that "from the Chairman downwards the business side did not always weigh heaviest, and [the Directors] were undoubtedly inspired ... by the highest patriotic motives, and the great faith that the nation would eventually support them through its Government." That support was never forthcoming.

*

To the south, Peters' Colonization Society had become the German East Africa Company, and like its British counterpart, had also obtained a lease over a portion of the Zanzibar coastal strip fronting the sphere itself. But unlike IBEA, the German venture appeared to be thriving. The chief difference between the British and German territorial claims was that the former had been asserted primarily as a defensive measure against the latter; once formally established in east Africa, the Foreign Office seemed almost to lose interest in IBEA. The German colonists, on the other hand, not only enjoyed Bismarck's active encouragement but received tangible financial backing from the Reichstag. It has been estimated that the ratio of government investment in the two companies was two thousand to one, with Germany the more generous donor.

This aid went far to help launch a modest but promising agricultural economy. By 1888, Peters' associates were managing thirty large plantations in the German sphere. Describing an inspection visit to one of the newer of these communities, a place called Deutschenhof, Peters himself, in a private letter, was reminded of "a well-established German estate," and with justifiable pride went on to observe that "here and there are right and left plantations; amongst them are sugar factories, some of which are already driven by steam ... 50,000 tobacco plants have already been planted ... Everywhere there is abundant growth, like that in a greenhouse ... The fact that such progress in cultivation was at all possible in three months, bodes well for the future of our much abused East African colony." Further evidence that the Germans had come to stay is found in the Swahili chronicles of various coastal towns, which speak of the Kaiser as "our ruling sultan, the great German Bwana," and "our German Sultan, who brought peace to these lands."

Peace in fact was not quite that wonderful, for the German administrators seemed to make Prussian sternness an instrument of policy. Their conduct on the coast was particularly resented. Unlike the British, who took pains to observe all the elaborate niceties of etiquette so dear to the Arab heart, the Germans were usually impatient, often rude, sometimes brutal. By 1888 their domineering behavior and general disregard for local custom had touched off a violent uprising that threatened both spheres. The revolt was led by a dynamic Arab named Bushiri who rallied around him more than two thousand Arabs and Africans, most of them armed with breech-loading rifles. Although Bushiri himself was a man of balanced temper, he soon lost control of the rebel force, which literally went mad, cutting a swath of pillaged towns and corpses along the entire coast. Six hundred Sudanese troops under a German army officer, a joint Anglo-German naval blockade and the better part of a year were needed to capture and hang Bushiri and restore order. Bismarck's subsequent rebuke to the Company for its draconian methods hastened the demise of that organization and the eventual transfer of power to the German Government.

But the unpleasantness did not throw cold water on Germany's goal of further expansion in east Africa. By 1889, in fact, Peters had set in motion a scheme to occupy Uganda.

*

In one respect, this could be seen as highway robbery. It has already been mentioned that the western boundaries of the 1886 agreement had not been clearly defined, but Uganda was situated comfortably to the north of the line separating the British and German spheres, and hence was tacitly acknowledged by all the Powers as belonging within the British area. By all the Powers, that is, but one: Germany rested her claim to Uganda on a legalism. The border between the two spheres, Germany's African specialists quite correctly pointed out, stopped at the eastern shore of Lake Victoria; furthermore, the northern boundary of the British sphere came to a trickling halt near Lake Baringo, some two hundred miles east of the Nile. By what right, then, could Britain assert paramountcy over a country that had not even been included in the terms of the agreement? This reasoning of course gave Germany no franchise in Uganda either, but Peters—and Bismarck—would not be expected to labor the point. Nor would German public opinion; German maps of Africa in the later 1880s placed Uganda squarely and boldly within the Kaiser's sultanate. Still, anyone could draw a map. What counted was physical possession: annexation and effective occupation. Peters planned to make both possible.

*

Visitors who pass through the village of Witu today will find an unlovely slum of fly-blown mud shanties and a postage-stamp plaza fronted incongruously by two rust-caked, muzzle-loading cannons. The scene is dominated by a shapeless pile of masonry which once served as the local ruler's "palace," but which has since become an unsanitary restaurant—offering one of the best omelets the author has ever eaten. Eighty years ago, Witu was probably even less inviting. But it was the linchpin of Peters' grand design for the conquest of Uganda.

His idea arose from another of the fuzzy terms that came into the imperial lexicon after the Berlin Conference. This was called the "hinterland" doctrine. What it meant, briefly, was that effective occupation within a sphere of influence could be legally carried beyond that sphere, as far inland as possible from any coastline, until and unless halted by the recognized boundary of another sphere. The hinterland concept had been nurtured mainly by the Germans, and they had good reason for doing so. The only European sphere beyond Witu—and it should be remembered that Witu itself lay well to the north of the British zone—was Leopold's Congo, a thousand miles to the west. There was nothing, therefore, to prevent Witu's administrators from extending the effective occupation of their few squalid acres directly from the coast to Mwanga's kingdom.

True, this would mean holding Uganda by a five-hundred-mile-long thread (Jackson later called it "the thin end of a disproportionately deep wedge") but there was every reason to believe that the boldly conceived African corridor would serve its purpose. If Peters were successful, the British sphere would be neatly encircled and Germany could proceed to establish her authority in Uganda unopposed.

It should be noted that up to this time England had shown no wish to annex or even claim a vested interest in Uganda. Salisbury's firm disavowal of responsibility for the CMS missionaries following Hannington's murder had made British non-policy in Uganda all too clear. Given, however, the panic psychology of the African scramble, there was nothing more certain than that any German thrust across the Nile would eventually be countered, possibly anticipated. It was therefore essential that Peters move not only swiftly but adroitly. He intended to, and his plan was not merely to take refuge behind contestable international legalities. He could also claim an entirely apolitical and supremely humanitarian motive for entering Uganda.

"Shall our heroic countryman ...
be abandoned to destruction, and
his province, won to civilization
by German energy, become the prey
of barbarism?"

To appreciate the emotional appeal of Peters' strategy, we must shift the scene briefly to the Sudan in the early 1880s, when the religious paranoid known as the Mahdi launched a revolt against Egyptian misrule in his country. Through the sheer force of an extraordinary charisma, the Mahdi raised a vast soldiery not much less fanatical than himself, and within four years this tidal wave engulfed the Sudan. By January,

1885, Khartoum, the capital and last stronghold, had fallen—along with Gordon—and all the Egyptian and European provincial governors but one had been killed or made prisoner. The last stand was being carried out by the Governor of Equatoria, Emin Pasha. Had this man been Egyptian, Turk or Mameluke, Europe would have been indifferent to his plight. But as it happened, the Pasha was a Westerner: a forty-five-year-old German Jewish physician who had been born Eduard Schnitzer. His "civilized" origins may well have changed the course of the imperial tide in east Africa.

Like his countryman Peters, Emin does not in outward aspect conjure up the muscular colonial officer whose very word settles the fate of tens of thousands of wild men. A sterilized operating theater in Berlin seems the proper place for this diminutive, nearsighted, erudite, fastidiously dressed gentleman with the rimless spectacles and well-trimmed beard. Schnitzer, however, did not see himself that way. After a brief interlude of private practice in Germany, he had become restless and began wandering, aimlessly but compulsively, through southern Europe and into Turkey. Here, he embraced Islam, took the name Emin and moved on again, this time to Khartoum, where he started another private practice in 1875. But Khartoum soon palled, and Emin cast his eyes up the Nile. On April 17, 1876, he debarked from the river steamer at Lado, capital of Equatoria, walked into Gordon's headquarters and asked for employment. Gordon engaged him on the spot, as provincial medical officer at £50 per month. Two years later he was appointed Equatoria's Governor. Emin Effendi now became Emin Pasha.

He took up his duties with the energy of a dynamo and the talents of a Renaissance man. Emin was not merely a doctor. He was fluent in a dozen languages, versed in a broad range of scientific disciplines and possessed of a natural flair for administration. He made Equatoria a going concern. He built forts, roads and clinics, launched a diversity of agricultural, irrigation and livestock breeding schemes. "Every year," he wrote in one of his many letters to Europe, "the Equatorial Provinces send out about 22,000 cwt. of ivory to the market with an average value of £30,000. The ox-hides of the animals slain by the soldiers would in themselves suffice to stock the market in Khartoum." Equatoria showed a surplus in its revenues, and these profits Emin faithfully remitted to Cairo, unlike his Egyptian counterparts who generally pocketed the funds. He organized a network of agents who kept him au courant with affairs in the most isolated outposts of his hundred-thousand-square-mile fief. He himself traveled everywhere in the province: on horse, camel, mule or foot.

He appears never to have let up. Despite the backbreaking volume of his official duties he found time to indulge a passion for botany and zoology, sending countless specimens of plant, animal and bird life, each perfectly mounted, to museums in Europe. Whatever leisure moments he could salvage went to his Abyssinian wife and their daughter Ferida. Emin had at last found a home. "I have lived too long in Africa," he once wrote, "not to have something of the negro in me."

Emin's fellow officials did not share his enthusiasm for Equatoria. The province was notorious as an African Siberia where the Egyptian Government dumped its malcontents and misfits. The fact that Emin was neither of these did not endear him to the members of his staff, and his own personality seemed to militate against the devotion, perhaps even the respect, that had been given freely to Gordon. According to Vita Hassan, a Tunisian chemist then in the Egyptian service at Lado, "the Governor is a man who is always afraid of being overshadowed. Intensely jealous of his own authority, which he shares with no one, he is suspicious of everybody." Even the Egyptian and Sudanese troops under his command did not try very hard to conceal a latent insubordination toward this less than military figure. And it was not long before Emin found himself in need of all the loyalty he could inspire. As the Mahdist hordes swept southward into Equatoria, he was obliged to evacuate Lado and retire up the Nile. By April, 1885, he had established a last-stand capital at Wadelai, only a few hours' journey aboard his two government steamers from Lake Albert. But now Emin was all but hermetically sealed off from the rest of the world. A chance existed that he might be able to reach the east coast, but this could only have been slender. Bunyoro's Kabarega and Uganda's Mwanga would in all likelihood bar the passage through their kingdoms of Emin's huge but poorly armed garrison, along with a horde of wives, children, concubines, slaves and other camp followers. So vast a cavalcade—more than ten thousand all told—would eat the land bare. In 1886, a tentative stab was made at the coast journey. One of the European refugees who had come to Wadelai that year was the ex-Bersaglieri Major Gaetano Casati, and Emin sent him to sound out Kabarega. After an absence of several weeks, Casati staggered back into Wadelai, half dead; he had barely managed to escape from Bunyoro after Kabarega had him arrested and tortured. This ruled out any attempt to break through, and Emin resigned himself to governing the beleaguered remnant of his province. He even made it show a profit, although there was no way of sending the surplus on to Cairo; revenues were collected in ivory, and the pile of government-owned tusks soon reached a weight of seventy-five tons and a value of £60,000. Despite tattered uniforms, shaky esprit and occasional mutterings of mutiny, Equatoria was carrying on, and might well have done so indefinitely. But another European fugitive from the Mahdi, the Russian-born German explorer Wilhelm Junker, decided to brave the journey to the coast on his own. He managed to get through, arriving in Europe late in 1886 with the first hard news of the Pasha's long-rumored straits. And suddenly Emin became an international celebrity as the Western world set in motion the wheels of what may have been the most bizarre mercy mission in the annals of African travel.

*

For the thought of a lone white man caught helplessly in a snare laid by murderous black savages could not but strike a responsive chord in Europe's prideful emotionalism, and ambitious schemes for the rescue of Emin soon came into being. Yet however honorable may have been the motives of the would-be saviors, they were also tarred, inevitably, with the political brush, simply because the task of bringing Emin to safety meant entering or at least skirting Uganda, by now beginning to take on the shape of an imperial prize. It was known that Mackinnon wished to establish a post in the region just across the Nile from Uganda. With the Pasha and his garrison occupying that strategic area, Mackinnon would have ready access to trade—and the establishment of British influence—in Mwanga's kingdom. Peters' more grandiose designs have already been described.

Indeed, Germans for the most part felt that they had a prior claim to Emin's succor. He was, after all, a son of the Fatherland, and Peters played on this note for everything it was worth. Although the initiative in proposing a German rescue mission had been taken by the explorer Georg Schweinfurth, it was Peters who rapidly emerged as the driving force behind the effort. His energy and organizational skills gave birth to the German Emin Pasha Relief Committee, with an enrollment of prominent citizens that included several members of the Diet. Peters also launched a nationwide fund-raising campaign, making good use of the appeal to patriotic instincts. His literature spoke of "our German fellow-countryman, Dr. Eduard Schnitzer ... defending with his troops a last bulwark of European Culture," and posed the rhetorical challenge: "Shall our heroic countryman, left without succor, be abandoned to destruction, and his province, won to civilization by German energy, become the prey of barbarism?" By the end of 1888, the Committee had raised four hundred thousand marks, more than enough to mount two expeditions. No one was surprised at Peters' appointment as leader. On March 31, 1889, when he arrived in Zanzibar, he was almost desperately eager to plunge into the interior without a moment's delay. The sense of urgency he felt was quite understandable, since England had got off to a two-year head start in the race to save Emin.

*

The British expedition, organized by Mackinnon and led by none other than Stanley, had not been a secret. Hardly less than Germany, Britain too had been able to assert a manifest and active concern over the Pasha's fate. He may not have been a subject of the Queen, but he did happen to be in the Egyptian service, and Egypt at that time was to all intents and purposes a British possession. Yet Government itself had not in any way been involved with the rescue project: quite the contrary. In 1886, while Salisbury was rejecting the proposal for the relief of the CMS missionaries in Uganda, he was simultaneously turning a firm thumb down on a recommendation that the Treasury underwrite an Emin Pasha expedition. He went so far as to say that "it is really [Germany's] business if Emin is a German." And this despite, or, more accurately, because of, the report that the Pasha was ready to offer Equatoria to Britain in return for coming to his aid. The Cabinet gave Salisbury all the backing he needed; like the missionaries in Rubaga, Emin in Wadelai smacked too much of Gordon in Khartoum. Lord Iddesleigh minuted: "There was talk of a military expedition to assist [Emin], but this would never have done and we decidedly negatived it." Beyond making a modest financial contribution, Government even kept its hands clean of affiliation with Mackinnon's private venture, since this seemed to threaten an unwanted Foreign Office involvement in Uganda. Nor, finally, was officialdom eager to become entangled in what Iddesleigh called "any action which may by any possibility lead to our being obliged to rescue the rescuing party."

It was almost as if Iddesleigh owned a crystal ball which gave him a personal preview of the grisly farce that was to come, although prospects could not have been sunnier when Mackinnon undertook to organize the expedition. The IBEA Chairman was indubitably the right man for this task. Forming his own Emin Relief Committee, he went to work, swiftly, energetically and capably; in a few months he raised £20,000, the exact equivalent of Peters' four hundred thousand marks. To lead the party, he weighed the respective merits of Stanley and Thomson, and at the end of 1886 chose the former. Stanley immediately broke off a lecture tour in the United States to accept the offer. "When men hear a person crying out for help," he later wrote in his autobiography of this decision, "few stay to ascertain whether he merits it." Deliberation in this instance might have been the wiser course, but decisive, forceful action was Stanley's strongest suit. Taking over from Mackinnon, he outfitted the expedition on the run while he made his way from New York to Zanzibar.

There were no shortages of anything. Stanley signed on a staff of officers from a seemingly endless queue of youthful gentleman volunteers, remarking that "we might have emptied the barracks, the colleges, the public schools—I might almost say the nurseries—so great was the number of applications." For hongo payments there were nearly four thousand glass beads, 27,000 yards of cloth and a ton of copper, brass and steel wire. Bush clearing and fortifications would be expedited with 400 shovels, hoes, axes and bill-hooks. There was a 28-foot galvanized steel boat, the *Advance*, built in twelve sections, each weighing 75 pounds. Weapons included a Maxim gun (donated by the inventor himself), 510 Remington rifles, 50 Winchester repeaters, 215,000 rounds of ammunition, 350,000 percussion caps and two tons of gunpowder, to be carried by 40 pack mules and 620 porters. Some cynics suggested that Stanley had recruited an army instead of a rescue party, but they overlooked the fact that Emin's troops would need weapons to cross Bunyoro and Uganda in safety. Still, it was without doubt a formidable expedition, one of the most aggressively outfitted that had ever entered Africa. It was also a prodigious piece of one-man organization. Stanley had accepted Mackinnon's offer at the end of 1886. By February of 1887 he was ready to leave Zanzibar.

Then came the first hitch. Almost without warning, Stanley decided on a change of route. Instead of seeking to link up with Emin from the east coast, he would take the entire expedition around the Cape of Good Hope to the mouth of the Congo, proceed up that river and a tributary called the Aruwimi, and then march five hundred miles east to Equatoria. The thousand-mile journey from Zanzibar had now been sextupled in length, and people asked why. The answer was quite simple. Belgium's King Leopold had entered the picture with an offer to assist Stanley by furnishing river transport up the Congo, and the explorer had welcomed the aid. "The advantages of the Congo route," he explained afterwards, "were about five hundred miles shorter land-journey, and less opportunities for desertion of porters ... It also quieted the fears ... that behind this professedly humanitarian quest, we might have annexation projects."

There is room for argument here. At the very least, the new plan made for complications. If it discouraged desertion, it also required the hiring of six hundred more porters. To obtain them, Stanley went to Tippu Tib, who agreed to bring the men up the Congo in return for appointment by Leopold to governorship of a vast region in the Belgian King's "free" state. The cooperation of Africa's most notorious slaver in this mission of Christian succor gave the whole proceeding a somewhat gamy aspect in many European eyes. As for the absence of annexation aims, that disclaimer put a strain on veracity, simply because Leopold had instructed Stanley to sound out Emin on a proposal that he administer Equatoria as a Belgian territory with a salary of £1,500 per year and £10,000 in expenses. And, since Stanley was also representing the expansionist Mackinnon, the imperial character of the rescue mission had not only become more intense but had taken on the complexion of something like intrigue.

Another serious delay seemed to loom when Stanley reached the Congo. Here, to his dismay, he discovered that the river steamers which Leopold had promised "were now said to be wrecked, rotten, or without boilers or engines, or scattered inaccessible. In my ears rang the cry in England: 'Hurry up, or you may be too late!'" He soon adjusted to the setback, however: the expedition would crowd aboard a few available craft and proceed upstream, to a place called Yambuya on the Aru-wimi; from here, Stanley and an advance party would march to Lake Albert while the rear guard would await Tippu Tib's porters and then follow along the path already hacked out. The plan seemed altogether feasible and the upriver voyage witnessed no major difficulties. It was only on June 28, 1887, when Stanley and his advance column set forth from Yambuya, that the Emin Pasha Expedition began to come apart at the seams.

*

The trek to Lake Albert was as unfair a test of human endurance as a malevolent nature could devise. It took nearly half a year to cover less than three hundred miles. "Ever before us," wrote Stanley, "rose the same solemn and foodless Forest ... to impede and thwart our progress with ooze ... soil often as treacherous as ice to the barefooted carrier, creek-beds strewn with sharp-edged oyster shells, streams choked with snags, chilling mist and icy rain, thunder-clatter and sleepless nights, and a score of other horrors." It was a dungeon that broke the body and bent the mind. "Several of our followers who had not sickened ...

became mad with hunger and wild forebodings, tossed the baggage into the bush, and fled from us, as from a pest." On December 4, when the party emerged, Stanley could have been thankful that of his 338 porters, no more than 180 had died or deserted. On the western shore of the lake, tribesmen told him that white men were rumored to be in the north, but before he could confirm this, there were his own remaining men to look after. Most were half dead from fever, hunger and injuries. Stanley himself went into semi-coma for the better part of a month. Fort Bodo, a sort-of palisaded hospital, was thrown up a few marches from the lake. It was not until April, 1888, that Stanley was able to resume the search.

And it was at this time that a local chief came to him with an oil-silk packet containing a letter. It read: "Dear Sir, Rumours having been afloat of white men having made their apparition ... be pleased, if this reaches you, to rest where you are ... My steamer and boats would bring you here ... Yours very faithfully, Dr. Emin." A strange turn of events. Could Stanley have been responding to a false alarm? He would have none of that. Ordering the prefabricated Advance assembled, he sent one of his officers, A. J. Mounteney Jephson, out on the lake to seek the Pasha. On April 28, a small white-hulled steamer hove into sight. It was the 90-foot Khedive, one of Emin's two vessels, and Emin himself stepped ashore, accompanied by Jephson, Casati and an honor guard of Sudanese troops. Immaculate in white drill and jaunty fez, exuding informal courtesy, the long-lost Governor hardly looked like a man in need of succor. Stanley, on the other hand, did, and openly welcomed the supplies of food and clothing which Emin ordered to be taken off the steamer. "The rescuers," in Casati's words, "were rescued."

Despite this momentary reversal of roles, both Stanley and Emin were delighted to see each other. "Few men," wrote Stanley, "could have acted the part of hospitable and pleasant host so well as Emin ... He was cordial in manner, well-read, had seen much, and appeared to be most likeable." News and pleasantries were exchanged while champagne corks popped on the Khedive's well-swabbed decks. But Stanley had not grappled with the forest for a pleasure excursion on the lake, and it was not long before he got down to the business at hand. Emin flatly rejected Leopold's proposal, reminding the explorer that he was still in the Khedive's service. He seemed less unreceptive, however, to suggestions that his obligations to the Egyptian Government would not be compromised by acceptance of a post with Mackinnon. But he showed no great haste to give Stanley an answer.

Indeed, Emin did not even appear certain that he wished to be saved, and Stanley found him emerging rapidly as a sort of Hamlet of Africa.

"Until the 25th of May," the explorer recalled in his autobiography, "our respective camps were close together ... Naturally, the topic as to whether [Emin] would stay in Equatoria, or accompany me to the coast, came up for discussion frequently. But, from the beginning to the end of our meetings, I was only conscious that I was profoundly ignorant of his intentions. On some days, after a friendly dinner the night previous, he held out hopes that he might accompany me; but the day following, he would say, 'No, if my people go, I go; if they stay, I stay.'" Stanley's own theory was that Emin "had a personal objection to going to Egypt, from a fear that he might be shelved, and his life would become wasted in a Cairene or Stamboul coffee-house." Whatever the reason, however, he had been blowing hot and cold on the idea of his own rescue long before the relief expedition arrived. Through sporadic correspondence with Mackay and other missionaries, he had learned of the efforts being made in his behalf, and his responses had been mixed. In one letter, he had written: "I am still waiting for help ... from England," only to do an about-face shortly afterwards: "If ... the people in Great Britain think that as soon as Stanley or Thomson comes I shall return with them, they greatly err ... Would it be right of me to desert my post as soon as the opportunity for escape presented itself? ... The work that Gordon paid for with his blood, I will strive to carry on, if not with his energy and genius, still according to his intentions and in his spirit ... Evacuate our territory? Certainly not."

Now, with Stanley on the scene, Emin found an opportunity to temporize further. The explorer's rear column, long overdue from Yambuya, had not yet arrived, and Stanley himself resolved to go back and ascertain the cause of the delay. When he returned, the Pasha would presumably have reached a decision. On June 1, leaving Jephson with Emin, Stanley turned his face to the forest again.

Step by step, the dreadful repeat performance was acted out. "The cries of the column leaders recalled most painfully what an absence of seven months had caused us almost to forget. 'Red ants afoot! Look out for a stump, ho! Skewers! A pitfall to right! A burrow to left! Thorns, thorns, 'ware thorns! Those ants; lo! a tripping creeper! Nettles, 'ware nettles! A hole! Slippery beneath, beneath! Look out for mud! A root! Red ants! red ants amarch! Look sharp for ants! A log! Skewers below!' And so on from camp to camp." The pace, however, was somewhat less sluggish this time; after 78 days, the party reached the rear column at a place called Banalya, some 75 navigational miles east of Yambuya. But what had happened to the column? Unburied corpses lay all about; the 260-man force had been reduced to 102 half-starved derelicts. Tippu

Tib's porters were nowhere to be seen. Only one white man, William Bonny, the medical assistant, came to give Stanley the news. All the other officers had died, returned to England or gone downriver on pointless errands. Major Edmund Barttelot, commanding the rear column, had been shot and killed by a maddened Manyuema tribesman. The story of the rear party would soon burst on the outside world like a fragmentation bomb, with charges and countercharges by Stanley and several of the officers ricocheting across the pages of newspapers, magazines and even books. The affair was to become a scandal that would not subside without leaving deep scars on more than one reputation.

But for the moment there could be no crying over spilt blood. Stanley still had the remaining men of the rear column, plus his own party, and he had yet to complete the task of rescuing the reluctant Emin. Again he plunged into the forest, now over a slightly different route which offered the added hazard of hostile pigmies. One did not often see them, but one was never out of their sight, or beyond the reach of their arrows. Firing back into a somber, solid wall of vegetation was to throw away ammunition. Porters dropped silently in their tracks as the poisoned darts thunked home. Four months of this before the party broke out at last on December 20.

And now where were Emin and Jephson? Stanley was beginning to have visions of a second Banalya when, on January 17, 1889, another oil-silk packet was delivered to him. It contained letters from the two men, written a month earlier. Both had been taken prisoner north of the lake, not by the Mahdists but by Emin's own troops. Emin asked Stanley to look after Ferida; Jephson wrote: "If we are not able to get out, please remember me to my friends." But just about this time, Jephson managed to break away and reach Stanley with the details of his captivity. Emin's Egyptian and Sudanese officers had mutinied; the Pasha and Jephson had been placed under a sort of house arrest from which escape was not difficult. Then, in mid-February, Emin himself arrived with both his steamers and the rebellious officers. The latter, it seemed, had undergone a change of heart and begged Emin's forgiveness, which he readily granted. Now, at last, nothing stood in the way of a triumphant return to the coast. Nothing, that is, but Emin. He still had not made up his mind.

Stanley therefore made it up for him. Having undergone the ordeal of the forest three times, having witnessed the results of the catastrophic series of blunders at Banalya (for which he, as leader of the expedition, must bear ultimate responsibility), the explorer was no longer in a mood to humor the Pasha's whims. In his own book about the rescue expedition, Casati wrote, not altogether justly, that "Stanley's terms were harsh. He allowed us twenty days to join him, with the warning that at the end of that time he would start for the south." The brusque ultimatum had the desired effect, but the return to the coast was not a happy journey. Although they maintained an outward show of mutual courtesy and regard, Emin and his rescuer were barely on speaking terms during the entire eight-month trek. "As Stanley's guests," wrote Vita Hassan, "we were his prisoners as well; we had no illusions on that score." This is sheer nonsense, but it is undeniable that a cloud of ill will hung over the party.

Good spirits returned briefly, however, on December 4, when Stanley and Emin, leading their mile-long procession of bone-weary porters and tatterdemalion troops, finally entered Bagamoyo. Flags, bunting and a brass band enlivened the expedition's arrival. That same evening, in the handsomely appointed two-storey Government administration building, the German officers of the port laid on a gala dinner for the two heroes. Speeches were made, grudges forgotten, the champagne flowed freely. After fifteen years' absence from civilization, Emin did not quite seem to know what to make of it all. Bedazzled with adulation, perhaps the slightest bit tipsy, he strolled unsteadily to a window, fell out, was rushed to the hospital with a fractured skull. Stanley made a number of attempts to see him, but was told each time that the patient had suffered a "relapse." The "no visitors" sign was also posted on the several occasions when the British Consul in Zanzibar, Colonel Charles Euan-Smith, came over from the island to pay his respects. Imperial politics had apparently returned to the scene with a vengeance.

At the end of March, 1890, it was announced that Emin had finally made a decision: he would enter the German colonial service.

"We are witnessing the process known in private life as 'trying it on.'"

A few of Emin's countrymen did not hear the news immediately. Peters was one of these. His own Emin rescue party had now been cut off from contact with the outside world for nearly a year. Unlike Stanley, whose expedition had at least got off to an auspicious start, Peters had collided with trouble at once. His plan had been to outfit at Zanzibar, sail to Lamu and then enter the interior via Witu. At Aden he had recruited two dozen Somali porters and askaris—soldiers—who would await him at Lamu. But on arriving in Zanzibar he discovered that Lamu had been placed out of bounds to him, and that the Somalis had been sent to Bagamoyo. He also learned that it would be all but impossible to sign on more porters in Zanzibar; "the Sultan," he later wrote, "had caused it to be made known that every black man who took part in the expedition would have his head struck off at whatever time he might return to Zanzibar." Then he was informed that his own hunting rifles—shipped down from Aden—had been seized and confiscated by Admiral Edmund Fremantle, the Royal Navy commander on the east African station. The loss of these few weapons was no great calamity, but Peters also happened to be awaiting a large consignment of Remington rifles for his party, and he now had no doubt as to the fate of that shipment. Clearly, Fremantle was giving the broadest possible interpretation to his powers as the naval officer charged with carrying out the Anglo-German coast blockade against Bushiri.

As a final blow, Peters found that he, personally, had been declared contraband. He received this news when, with characteristic boldness, he boarded Fremantle's flagship and demanded an interview with the admiral. The latter, wrote Peters, "declared to me, in the plainest possible manner, that I was inconvenient to the English in Eastern Africa, and might therefore not reckon upon enjoying, with their sanction, the same right that any one else would have." In a more sporting spirit, Fremantle returned Peters' hunting rifles, and also told him that he would not be interfered with outside the blockaded area. He even added that the *Neera*, a small steamer Peters had chartered, was quite free to sail to Lamu, "provided that neither I nor contraband of war was on board." In short, the Anglo-German effort against Bushiri and the coast rebels was to be directed, with equal vigor, at Peters. "As ... the whole blockaded territory, German as well as English, was closed against me, there seemed to be no access to the interior."

Of course it was all a huge mistake. Before leaving Berlin, Peters had received off-the-record assurance that while the German Government could not give official sanction to his expedition, he had Bismarck's private blessing and therefore need not concern himself with bureaucratic obstacles. Naturally, then, Peters lost no time in lodging a complaint at the German Consulate—"where I found it impossible to get any kind of support." This was unexpected. At once he went over the Consul's head and cabled a protest direct to the German Foreign Office, which did not even trouble to reply. Instead, on May 17, Peters received a cable from his Emin Pasha Committee: "Foreign Office refuses all mediation and support."

It only stood to reason. Germany had no wish to lose Britain's cooperation in the blockade by allowing the notorious filibusterer to ravage the mainland. As for Peters himself, nonrecognition by his own Government could only have reminded him of old times. "I was now thrown back entirely on my own resources, and had to put the question seriously to myself, whether I really believed I could carry out the expedition under these circumstances, or not." But, as we have seen, Peters was not a man to be thwarted by hostile stratagems. He would defy both London and Berlin, and then present his country with another fait accompli. Bismarck would hardly decline the gift of Uganda. First, however, the Chancellor's knuckles must be rapped. In reply to the Committee's cable, he wrote: "If the Imperial Government did not wish that the German Emin Pasha Expedition should be undertaken, it should have forbidden the project ... But to have allowed the development of the project to the present point, and now to permit its being hindered ... amid the derision of all the nations represented here ... is certainly a very peculiar method of advancing German interests and German honor ... and a curious application of the 'Civis Romanus sum' of which Prince Bismarck formerly spoke in the Imperial Diet."

Having got this off his chest, Peters then proceeded to act. Bagamoyo was not closed to him, so he sailed there aboard the *Neera* and picked up his Somalis. He also managed to obtain one hundred muzzle-loading rifles and fifty breech-loaders. Fortune seemed to be smiling on him once more. "I suddenly felt penetrated with a profound certainty that the undertaking was destined to be put into practice in spite of all difficulties, and ... to be accomplished." Peters now returned to Zanzibar, and on June 1 the little *Neera* got up steam and departed from the harbor under cover of night, sailing a wildly zigzag course and keeping well out to sea to elude the blockading warships.

Peters' objective was Kwaihu, a small island just outside the blockade zone about twenty-five miles northeast of Lamu. Heavily laced with reefs, Kwaihu's bay could not be entered without a pilot, and "we had naturally not been able to procure a pilot in Zanzibar." But Peters' luck continued to run strong. On June 15, *Neera* managed to slide through the hammering breakers unscathed. Peters immediately transferred his supplies aboard a few small dhows and then began a surreptitious amphibious journey across the Lamu archipelago toward the mainland and Witu. There were one or two close shaves. At the village of Faza on Pate island, the expedition was almost challenged, but "the inhabitants took us for Englishmen, as the *Neera* sailed under the English flag. I saw no reason to undeceive them in this matter." The party also passed under the very guns of Fremantle's squadron as it combed Manda bay, flashing out signals that Peters had failed to land. When Peters reached

Witu early in July, he had managed to recruit a few more porters. And on July 26, when the party finally left Witu for the hinterland, it consisted of nearly one hundred load- or rifle-carrying Africans, a dozen of their women, sixteen camels, eight donkeys, one horse, two dogs, Peters and his second-in-command, Lieutenant von Tiedemann. In size at least, the motley band seemed just respectable enough to pass muster as an expedition.

*

The first stage of the march followed a huge arc, running west and slightly north for some three hundred miles along the Tana river; and it was Peters' conduct during this part of the journey that won him most of his subsequent malodorous fame. It cannot be said that he was blameless. No doubt the outrages laid at his doorstep have been embellished by British literary-imperial license, but Peters' own Somalis corroborated a good deal of what took place. Here is one such account: "As we passed through the various districts Dr. Peters called for the Chief or Headman, who was tied up as soon as he arrived at the camp and threatened to be flogged or killed unless he gave the caravan food or whatever was required ... Wherever the Imperial British East Africa Company's flags were flying, Dr. Peters hauled them down, destroyed some and took others home to Europe; he made treaties wherever the Company's flags were broken down, and impressed chiefs and people that they were under the 'protection of the Deutsch.'" Peters himself made no conspicuous effort to conceal his aggressions. Letters he wrote to the German press spoke openly and proudly of the iron fist he wielded on the march, and *New Light on Dark Africa*, his book about the expedition, reveals more than a little outright sadism. In Galla country, he wrote of having "again been obliged to put in practice the expedient of chaining the Sultan [a word then used frequently for "chief"] when he paid his visit." Traveling among Ndrobo tribesmen near Mount Kenya, "I took hold of one of these people with my crooked stick by one of the ear lobes that hung down to his shoulders, because he would not come on." At about this same time, "I at once had the Sultan knocked down, and fettered; then took him by the ears, and shoved him in front of me, as a kind of shield ..."

And yet a devil's advocate might just make a case for Peters. The Somali statement (given to an Englishman who obviously translated it into suitably damning phraseology) cannot be taken entirely at face value. Unlettered Africans in those days seldom had reason to prefer one European national over another, and they had a known habit of telling white men whatever they wanted to hear, for the most part as a matter of courtesy. As for Peters' unethical treaties, he certainly held no monopoly on the device of hoodwinking chiefs with meaningless words about "protection"; we have already seen how IBEA packaged its alliances, and this in fact was common practice throughout Africa. Generally speaking, the business of treaty-making in arbitrarily established and murkily defined spheres of influence was often farcical. At times it could almost take on the aspects of a game, and in this respect it should be noted that Peters could win over a district with other means than cruelty. His Lamuan interpreter, Hamiri, proved especially useful here, when describing to some tribe the difference between the British and the Germans. "The Englishmen ... he declared to be 'kidogo kabisa' (exceeding small), and would hold his outspread hand about six inches over the ground; I on the contrary, was 'mkubwa sana;' and he would hold his hand high—as high as he could, and, as his own height did not seem to him sufficient for the occasion, he would jump two or three feet from the ground." If such performances were not credible, at least they threw the unsophisticated villagers into convulsions of laughter, and into a receptive frame of mind. Peters used the device on more than one occasion.

It should be added that Peters was not alone in employing coercive methods, although he undoubtedly acted more harshly than did most of his contemporaries. One cannot deny that he did a great deal of shooting, but Stanley probably did at least as much. As for the quotations from his book, they are taken out of context, and in fact the circumstances surrounding Peters' cruelty can sometimes be seen as almost extenuating. "As I was compelled to begin the march into the interior without any real articles of barter," he wrote, "I could not pay my way, as Thomson and other people were accustomed to do ... If I could not carry out the German Emin Pasha Expedition in the usual peaceable fashion, as I had originally hoped to do, I must face the fact that I might ultimately be compelled to organize our column as a warlike band." Hence the chaining of the "sultan," who would otherwise have reneged on a promise to furnish Peters with badly needed food supplies—and "my column would have run a great risk of actually perishing through hunger." The human shield was devised in the heat of a poisoned-arrow attack following Peters' complaint that the Ndrobo chief had also backed down on a pledge to bring food. Even as he held the chief in front of him, Peters "forbade my people to fire on these people, as I wished to have peace with them."

For all this, one is not likely to admire Peters' dealings with the inhabitants along his route. He is said to have taken an African mistress and later to have ordered her hanged publicly, because, according to Frederick Jackson, she "preferred the attentions of a native to his own." And his relish for the spilling of blood was never more obvious than in November, when the party left the Tana and entered Masai country on the Laikipia plateau. Not surprisingly, Peters' conduct toward the Masai comes in sharp contrast to Thomson's. Peters had little use for the Scotsman's methods, and in fact went out of his way to shame them. "Thomson," he wrote, "commanded an expedition in Massailand, compared with which our resources must appear altogether ludicrous; and yet he had in that country submitted to a treatment which, judged by a European standard, not only falls below the notion of 'gentlemanlike,' but must be plainly designated as unworthy ... Thomson thought he could produce an impression on the Massais by all kinds of tricks ... I have tried to produce an impression on the Massais by means of forest fires, by fiery rockets, and even by a total eclipse of the sun ... But I have found, after all, that the one thing which would make an impression on these wild sons of the steppe was a bullet from the repeater or the double-barrelled rifle, and then only when employed in emphatic relation to their own bodies."

What Peters appears to have forgotten is that few if any of Thomson's contemporaries considered his tactics "unworthy"; on the contrary, his diplomacy had been universally applauded. Peters also overlooked the fact that the trickery succeeded, and that Thomson had no need, when all was said and done, even to take aim at a Masai. Peters was also the slightest bit unfair to himself in describing his own white man's magic as a total failure. At the very least, the fireworks may have saved his party from total annihilation. On Christmas Eve, 1889, after weeks of fighting off savage hit-run attacks, the harassed expedition found itself the target of a full-scale massed onslaught, and Peters treated the Masai not only to a display of his personal bravery but of holiday pyrotechnics. At about ten o'clock, when the first elmoran wave started to move in, "I came out of my tent, and, to encourage my men, called out to the Massai, 'Karibu, Elmoràn, mutakufa wote!' ('Come on, Elmoràn, you shall all die!') ... Then I had rockets brought, and one rocket after another flew hissing up into the black sky of night, giving just enough light to enable our best shots to pick out their mark among the threatening figures. A fantastic picture, which could not fail of its effect upon sensitive nerves ... This night was indeed a whimsical illustration of the biblical text, 'Glory to God in the highest, and on earth peace, goodwill toward men!' The crackling of the rockets, the roaring of my own people, and the banging of the shots, together made a din that truly appeared more consonant with the Walpurgis night of the First of May than with the solemn seriousness of the birthday of Christ."

Whatever it may have suggested, the rocket barrage served to break up the attack. One of the first sights to greet Peters the next morning was an elderly Masai woman coming toward the camp with a handful of grass, the traditional sign of surrender. "Perhaps I never approached a lady with greater eagerness than I now displayed, with an expenditure of all my gallantry, towards this repulsive-looking old Massai woman. I also caught up a bunch of grass, and took care that there should be a flower among it."

*

Not long after this incident, the news of Peters' death reached the coast. There were different versions of how he met his end, but all had one element in common: they had originated with Peters, who by early 1890 had reached the eastern shore of Lake Victoria. The intended effect of the accounts, however, could only have been minimal. British officials on the spot were not prepared to swallow whole any second- or third-hand rumors that would tend to relax the vigilance of their own watch on the lake. For by now, the implications of Peters' thrust toward Uganda had taken on alarming proportions. Although still loath to assume the responsibilities and expenses entailed in a formal commitment to Uganda, the British Government nonetheless continued to pursue its dog-in-the-manger policy with respect to other European annexations or ambitions in eastern Africa. At this time, moreover, Salisbury had begun to see the curious light that was to transform his passive if not timid east African stance into a posture of defiance; he was no longer totally indifferent to the proposition that British imperial interests might be served through the assertion of British authority in Uganda.

Salisbury's change of heart may, in fact, have been reflected in an editorial published late in March, 1890, by that ever-reliable barometer of the imperial atmosphere, *The Times*, which saw in Peters' venture an unconcealed threat. "We are witnessing," warned *The Times*, "the process known in private life as 'trying it on.' ... The Karl Peters expedition is clearly and avowedly intended to cut us off from the interior, by establishing German influence at the back of our territory ... If we are weak enough to allow these overbearing traders to carry out their intentions, we shall find that the Government of Germany finds itself obliged, however reluctantly, to recognise accomplished facts." Peters at last was forcing Britain's hand.

But action must remain unofficial at all costs, which was not difficult so long as IBEA remained available to carry the Government's burden. In his history of the Uganda Railway, the late M. F. Hill remarked that "this reliance on a small Company to fight England's battle is a peculiar illustration of the casual manner in which East Africa was secured as a part of the Empire." Casual or not, however, the Foreign Office made it quite clear that it intended to use IBEA as a pliant instrument of policy. Shortly after the *Times* editorial appeared, Whitehall's Sir Percy Anderson asserted in a memorandum that "when we gave the charter to the E. Africa Co., we understood that its main idea was to push up to Uganda." No matter that this had been the reverse of the Foreign Office's own wishes at the time. The situation was now changed, and IBEA would continue to do Britain's work. As early as mid-February, Euan-Smith in Zanzibar had cabled Mackinnon, strongly urging that the Company take steps to forestall Peters' effort, and this was followed by similar promptings from the Foreign Office in London. By April, IBEA was preparing to mount an expedition from Mombasa—despite its dwindling capital, over-extended resources and the curious fact that it already had its own man on the very borders of Uganda.

Nearly eight months earlier, in August, 1889, the Company had sent out a caravan under Jackson's command. Its mission was, if possible, to make contact with Emin Pasha (in the event that Stanley proved unable to do so) along a route far to the north of Uganda. The expedition would also map the country, make treaties and establish Company posts on the lake shore. But Jackson's instructions expressly forbade him from entering Uganda itself. And despite this, he could only have been sorely tempted to disobey orders when, on November 7, he arrived at Mumias and found waiting for him a remarkable letter from Mwanga.

*

At this juncture, one almost needs a score card to follow events on the lake since September, 1888, when Mwanga's scheme to oust the Christians and Muslims from Uganda backfired him into exile. Not unexpectedly, the alliance of Catholics, Protestants and Mohammedans proved less than enduring. Barely a month following Mwanga's forcible eviction and replacement on the throne by his brother Kiwewa, the Muslim faction began filling the new Kabaka's ears with rumors of a Christian plot to depose him. This set the stage for another palace revolt in which the Baganda Christian chiefs and the entire missionary corps followed Mwanga in retreat to the south shore. Shortly afterwards,

Kiwewa rejected a Muslim demand that he be circumcised, and he too was disposed of, making way for a third brother named Karema, who proved more accommodating. Uganda had now become, for the time being, a Muslim theocracy.

On the south shore, however, Mwanga was busily drumming up the support he needed to bring about his restoration. Oozing with penitence, he made it known to the exiled Catholic and Protestant missionaries that he was ripe for conversion. To Mackay, he wrote: "Do not remember bygone matters ... Formerly I did not know God, but now I know the religion of Jesus Christ ... Sir, do not imagine that if you restore Mwanga to Buganda he will become bad again. If you find me become bad, then you may drive me from the throne; but I have given up my former ways, and I only wish now to follow your advice." Although neither of the two sects could find the stomach to baptize the Kabaka, the Christians (with Mackay, despite the letter, as sole dissenter) did rally to his cause. By October, 1889, with the aid of Charles Stokes, the CMS missionary turned gunrunner, Mwanga had raised an army, re-entered Uganda, smashed the Muslims and built a new capital on Mengo hill near Rubaga. One month later he was out again, in hiding on a nearby island: the Muslims, allied with Bunyoro's Kabarega, had returned and scattered the Christian host. But the tables turned for the fourth time in February, 1890, with a determined Christian counter-offensive that routed the Muslims and restored Mwanga forever—which is to say nearly a year.

None of these events had transpired when Mwanga wrote Jackson. That was in June, 1889, while the Kabaka was still fretting in his first exile and seeking a means of returning to power, even if this meant calling for the aid of the despised and dreaded British. "Mwanga's letter to me was long and rambling," Jackson recalls. Much of it "recounted the circumstances of his religious conversion," but its thrust was to offer the Company what amounted to a franchise in Uganda. "I send you the news," Mwanga wrote, "that we Christians may join together ... I pray you be good enough to come and put me on my throne ... You may do any trade in Uganda, and all you like in the country under me." It was an enticing offer, since IBEA's commercial pre-eminence in Mwanga's capital could not but mean the first step toward the establishment of British political influence in Uganda.

Nonetheless, Jackson had his orders and he hesitated. Mindful of the five-month time lapse since the writing of the letter, he sent messengers to Mwanga seeking news of more recent developments. Early in December the men returned with letters not only from Mwanga but from Mackay's replacement, E. C. Gordon. Mwanga had just then been ousted from Mengo by the Muslim–Kabarega force, and pleaded even more energetically for Jackson's aid. So too did Gordon, who wrote: "Mwanga is willing to offer you the most favourable terms he can ... We think that if you help us now you will be able to ask what terms you like."

To go or not to go: it was a question that called for the most delicate judgement. Jackson finally decided to abide by the letter of his instructions. "I wrote therefore to Mwanga telling him of my decision and sending him one of the Company's flags, with the intimation that his acceptance of it would lay upon the Company the obligation to come to his assistance as a protecting power." This was to prove a serious miscalculation, although Jackson did not know at the time that Peters was closing in on him. Nor could he have realized that to the Baganda, a foreign flag symbolized total abdication of their sovereignty, and that Mwanga would probably have preferred to receive a crate of puff adders.

Having made his decision, however, Jackson struck camp and marched north to Mount Elgon on an elephant hunt. (This was not sport: the ivory was needed to pay the expedition's expenses.) On March 4, 1890, he returned to Mumias and found more mail, including a letter from Stanley, who had reached Emin Pasha. But of more immediate interest was another message from Mwanga, making his third—and by now all but hysterical—plea for Jackson's aid; he had even accepted the flag. Even more convincing evidence of the Muslim threat was a letter from the White Fathers' leader, Lourdel, who by no stretch of the imagination could be thought of as favorably disposed to a British presence in Uganda. Yet Lourdel had been able to swallow his Anglophobia and write that "we Catholic missionaries shall be very glad and very grateful to take advantage of the protection which you will be able, I hope, to grant." The most important news, however, was not on paper. Jackson called it a "bombshell." Scarcely had he arrived in Mumias than he learned that the German flag was flying over a village less than two hours' march distant.

Early in February, during Jackson's absence, Peters had passed through this place and made one of his celebrated treaties with the local chief, a man named Sakwa, "who acknowledges Dr. Peters unreservedly as his lord." The German had also left behind an open letter, declaring that all Kavirondo was now "my possession," and that "I shall deal with any infringement of the rights of Sultan Sakwa as with an infringement of my own rights." According to Sakwa, who had signed the treaty with a fatalistic shrug and now asked Jackson to run up the Company flag, Peters had not tarried in his village long. Instead, he had gone on to Mumias where, in Jackson's sputtering italics, he had "visited my camp, had *opened my letters and read them.*" And, needless to say, the information had spurred him on.

Peters later defended himself with what he may have thought was logic. "It is not a question," he wrote, "of opening letters ... but of documents which were laid before me by the acting official chief of the English station with the observation that he knew that 'my brethren,' his masters, would be glad to communicate all these facts ... to me, if they were on the spot." Then, coming down to earth, he added that it was "my simple duty to gain all the knowledge I could in any way acquire with regard to the lands that lay before us." He had indeed gained the knowledge. Taking comfort in and exploiting his head start over Jackson, Peters left Mumias and crossed the Nile. On February 25 he arrived in Mengo, and rapidly drafted the treaty that would bring Uganda into the German sphere.

Mwanga offered no opposition to the proposal. He had sought Jackson's aid only because Jackson happened to be the nearest European with troops on hand. Apart from the help this armed force would provide against the Muslims, the idea of a British presence in Mengo held no appeal whatever for Uganda's ruler. Furthermore, by the end of February Mwanga had managed to secure his own position more firmly, and the need for troops had become less urgent. Mwanga was sophisticated enough, however, to realize that he could not hold out forever against European encroachment. If he must submit to a certain amount of manipulation by one of the Powers, let it be Germany's rather than England's.

And even if Mwanga's preferences had been otherwise, it is altogether likely that Lourdel would have convinced him that Peters was the man to back. For by now, the leader of the White Fathers had taken over the position of influence that had occasionally been held, though to a far lesser extent, by Mackay during Mutesa's reign. It was the Catholic missionaries who had most energetically supported Mwanga's restoration, and while the Protestants had also aided the cause, the significance of Mackay's refusal to join them had not been lost on the Kabaka. Since his return to power it had been only natural for him to lean heavily on the priests for counsel. Ashe, now at the head of the CMS mission, carried little weight at the palace. Lourdel, on the other hand, could almost have been described at this point as Mwanga's European Katikiro, and in this purely political capacity he had joined the scramble for Uganda with a will. His aim, quite simply, was to frustrate British—which is to say Protestant—designs in Uganda while encouraging the German bid for paramountcy; Uganda's Catholics, he believed, would receive more impartial treatment under German authority. Thus he offered full coop-eration to Peters. Wrote the latter: "I came to an agreement with Père Lourdel as to the plan of our task on the very first morning. This task was to prevent the British from obtaining any influence in Uganda." On February 28, when Mwanga signed Peters' treaty, Lourdel soared to the summit of his own power behind the throne—and Uganda as a British sphere seemed lost beyond reclamation.

Meanwhile, Jackson had been trying desperately to make up for lost time and opportunity. He remained in Mumias only long enough to des-patch runners with a message for Peters, requesting that the German wait for him. On March 11, he set off for Uganda, hoping to overtake and pass his own letter. After a thirty-four-day dash over the one hundred and eighty miles separating Mumias and Mengo, he arrived at Mwan-ga's capital to find—and he could hardly have expected otherwise—that Peters had departed.*

Now, in a rage over Peters' absence, Jackson lodged his protest with Mwanga. The treaty was a gold brick, he declared, citing not only the Kabaka's acceptance of the Company flag but the geographical fine print which allegedly placed Uganda in the British sector. No European Power could possibly give legal recognition to Peters' claim, he said. If Mwanga doubted his word, let him send Baganda envoys to Zanzibar, where they would learn the truth from the British, French and German Consuls. Mwanga seemed less than impressed. "It was plain," wrote Jackson in a frustrated report to the Company, "that the king has little or nothing to say in such affairs, but is a mere tool in the hands of Père Lourdel and the Roman Catholic chiefs." Even when Mwanga agreed to send representatives to the coast, Jackson could find only cold comfort, for he knew quite well that Peters had an all but unassailable case. The Ger-man's 1884 Usagara treaties had broken more than one rule of territorial integrity, and yet they had stood up. In Uganda, no real violation had been perpetrated; only the flimsiest of legalities could be brought to bear against the German treaty. No less than Peters, Jackson understood the significance of a fait accompli.

---

* Some time afterwards, Jackson did receive a reply to the letter, although it came not from Peters but from the German's second-in-command, von Tiedemann, who chal-lenged Jackson to a duel for his "impertinence" in attempting to stop the German party. "I do not know who or what you are," wrote von Tiedemann, "but I am told you are a clerk in the English company's service. I am a Prussian officer, and I hope some day that I shall meet you and make you answerable for your insult to Dr. Peters and myself." Jackson found the letter highly amusing.

*

Early in July, with Uganda folded neatly in his pocket, as it were, a jubilant Peters reached Bagamoyo, where he discovered that he might just as well have remained in Witu. In the same manner that England had five years earlier abandoned Barghash in payment for Bismarck's good will, now Germany had for similar reasons betrayed her own Rhodes. This time it was the Germans who needed friends, for there had been a change in the plot of Europe's bizarre political drama. Berlin was facing diplomatic crises in Paris and St. Petersburg; thus an amicably disposed England would help reduce the odds against Germany, and the Kaiser, having just dismissed Bismarck, had therefore made known his willingness to renounce whatever claims he had asserted in Uganda. On July 1, 1890, the two Powers concluded a treaty whereby Uganda was placed incontestably in the British sphere and, almost as an afterthought, Zanzibar made a British Protectorate. Germany also agreed to withdraw from Witu, although her own sphere in the south would remain inviolate. As a crumb of consolation, Britain ceded to Germany the North Sea island of Heligoland, then considered useful as a naval base. Peters' hard-won treaty wtih Mwanga had become worthless.

When Peters learned all this from sympathetic officials at the German station in Bagamoyo, he was thunderstruck. "I will pass in silence," he wrote, "over the emotions these tidings excited in me. I remained two hours in the salon to regain my composure, and begged the gentlemen to say nothing more on the whole subject." In time, he had something to say to the world, declaring bitterly that "two kingdoms in Africa had been bartered for a bathtub in the North Sea." Yet the new treaty did not end Peters' usefulness in German East Africa. In 1891 he was appointed Imperial High Commissioner for the Kilimanjaro District. He served in that post until 1893, when a German judge indicted him for brutality to Africans, which led to his dismissal from the colonial service. Peters then went to live in London, but before he died in 1918, his own countrymen had forgiven him to the point of erecting his statue in Dar es Salaam. One can wonder whether a cry of rage did not burst from his grave a few years later, when the statue was moved to Heligoland.

*

Peters rates censure for many misdeeds, but not for the failure of his bold Uganda mission; "no other German, before or after Peters," Emil Ludwig has written, "conquered Africa as he did." That the conquest came a cropper was due solely to the way the European political dice fell; a single throw had won Britain all the chips. But, if those chips were to mean anything, they must be cashed in: a paper sphere of influence still had no more value than Peters' treaty with Mwanga. As of July 1, 1890, Uganda was British territory, but it would remain insecure unless Britain undertook the distasteful chore of effective occupation, and Britain still seemed far from willing to do so.

Yet the man who would assume the burden personally was then on his way to Uganda.

6

THE MAKING OF A PROCONSUL

"I inscribe this book of adventure to my son ... in the hope that in days to come he, and many other boys whom I shall never know, may, in the acts and thoughts of Allan Quatermain ... find something to help him and them to reach to what ... I hold to be the highest rank whereto we can attain—the state and dignity of English gentlemen."

Many Britons who served the Queen in the tropics during the nineteenth century were able to meet those vague but exacting standards. Not many ever reached the pinnacle quite so consummately as did Frederick Dealtry Lugard, the architect of the British Empire on the African continent and the man more responsible than any other single individual for Uganda's incorporation into that realm.* Yet in 1887, the year in which Rider Haggard wrote the above inscription, Lugard came within an ace of disqualifying himself, being then engaged in a decidedly infra dig pursuit. He was trying to commit suicide.

This hardly fitted his background or his character—although at first glance he may not have impressed. "Diminutive" is the only word for Lugard's physical stature. In group photographs he seems all but a midget alongside the people over whom he usually towered as a man.

---

* To give credit where credit is due, however, it should be noted that Allan Quatermain's real-life model was actually Frederick Jackson.

What may have revealed his true salt were his eyes, which, in the words of his biographer, Margery Perham, "really merited the well-worn adjective, piercing." In 1887 Lugard was twenty-nine years old, a captain in the Norfolk Regiment. He had served on the Afghan border, fought the Mahdists at Suakin and won the DSO in Burma. He had also absorbed fully the upper-class Briton's articles of imperial faith. Duty, honor, fair play, the almost divine rightness of the British civilizing mission: these values were his conditioned reflexes.

Temperamentally, Lugard could not have been better suited to carry the white man's burden. Like any Englishman on Her Majesty's hazardous service, he possessed the full complement of physical courage, leadership and resourcefulness—and probably more inner confidence than most. At the personal level he often displayed the somewhat mawkish sentimentality which Victorian Britons seemed to nourish as a mark of excellence. He was also able to show at least two characteristics that placed him in a special breed. One was an unorthodox racial outlook. While he never doubted that the Anglo-Saxon was a better man than the African, he never doubted, either, that the African was a man, and while he cannot be called unique in this respect he was definitely unusual. There was also his attitude toward personal responsibility, which he not only welcomed but sought out. This too set him apart. More than once he would openly defy his superiors on the issue of who was to be in charge. Throughout his life, Lugard was to feel uncomfortable as a subordinate. By instinct as well as training he had to command.

*

In 1885, Lugard's regiment returned to India from the Suakin campaign. Had he remained in India himself, his career would have stretched before him like a well-paved highway. There would be clashes with Afridis in the Khyber Pass, shikars in the forest, pig-sticking on the plains, polo matches at any number of hill stations. He could anticipate a glittering succession of formal balls at the Viceregal Palace in Calcutta, spirited betting at the Annandale racecourse in Simla, slow but certain promotion. If he survived the Kaiser's War, he would emerge with the rank of at least brigadier, with a knighthood, quite possibly, to follow. He had gone so far as to choose his lady: no ordinary accomplishment for one whose almost single-minded dedication to what Britain's officer class called "soldiering and sport" left him little opportunity or inclination for permanent female attachments. Nor was this an idle infatuation. Not a man for halfway measures, Lugard was bound hand and foot by love.

It was the lady who shattered Lugard's future in India—and in so doing, inadvertently determined the course and shape of Britain's African empire. During the summer of 1887, while on detached service in Burma, Lugard received a telegram: his beloved was critically ill in England. Obtaining leave at once, he boarded the first westbound P. & O. liner and hastened to London, where he found that the message had been somewhat misleading. The young woman was in the best of health and even better spirits, enjoying what appeared to be a lively if not intimate relationship with at least one other man. To Lugard, it was as if a Pathan musket ball had grazed his skull.

Small matter that he was not the first male in history to be spurned in this fashion. As he saw it, there was no alternative but to take his own life. Not, of course, with a revolver or open gas pipe—unthinkable for an officer and gentleman—but with honor and distinction, in the most perilously humanitarian undertaking that London could offer. Lugard therefore joined the Fire Brigade and immediately began volunteering to fight the city's worst conflagrations. However, he succeeded only in helping put out the fires, and in gaining a brief measure of celebrity when Gilbert and Sullivan put his efforts to words and music in *Iolanthe*. "The tragi-comic refrain about the quenching of a great love in fierce cascade," remarks Miss Perham, "may seem to fit Lugard's case very aptly."

Yet Lugard appears to have found the work insufficiently hazardous, for after some weeks he sought to resume his more lethal career as a soldier. At that time, Italy had declared war against Abyssinia's Emperor Menelik, and Lugard offered his services to the Italian army as a mercenary. He was not merely rejected; at Genoa, officials informed him that if he entered the Abyssinian theatre of operations he would be arrested as a spy. The warning only served to whet his interest and he bought a steamship ticket for the Italian-occupied Red Sea port of Massawa. By now, he was almost penniless and could afford only deck passage, a humiliation both acute and rare for a British officer. "The very coolies on board," he wrote in his diary, "have mattresses of sorts ... I have only a rug, and the iron ledge on which I sleep has some nuts in it." He did find moral sustenance in the generosity of a friendly Italian boatswain who "told me he knew I was a *gentilhomme*" and who literally offered Lugard the shirt off his back. But the voyage proved fruitless. Despite an altercation with an officious minor functionary, whom he confounded by replying to a barrage of questions with a rapid fire of fluent Hindustani, Lugard was not arrested in Massawa. At the same time, he discovered that Italo-Abyssinian hostilities had been suspended temporarily. He had no choice but to resume his morbid search elsewhere.

By this time, Lugard appears to have resolved that he would die in Africa, preferably in the anti-slavery cause, for him a more honorable expression of self-sacrifice than the role of fireman. Early in 1888, he accepted a post with a British commercial-evangelical organization called the African Lakes Company. He was to be commander of that group's makeshift military arm in the fever-drenched outpost of Karonga on the northwest shore of Lake Nyasa. The progress of this hard-pressed venture in philanthropy and profit had been brought almost to a standstill by the slave trading and aggression of a self-styled "sultan" named Mlozi. While that Company's small band of Europeans by no means wanted in enterprise or bravery, they did require leadership and welcomed an officer of Lugard's experience.

However, on June 16, 1888, when Lugard launched an attack on Mlozi's stockade, the fighting had scarcely begun when it appeared that his death wish had been fulfilled. The bullet that put him out of action pierced his body in six different places, even carrying some letters from a breast pocket and imbedding them in the lower part of his left arm. (He was to spend the next few years picking bits of correspondence out of his wrist.) That he lived is a tribute to what he has understatingly described as his "iron constitution," but one also suspects that the idea of self-destruction was beginning to lose its appeal. For Lugard's commitment to the anti-slavery and imperial causes had by now become something of a personal crusade. In June of 1889, he was back in England, seeking to win public support for the Company undertaking through magazine articles and speeches. In later years he would employ this method of direct appeal to popular sentiment with telling effect. Perhaps its most conspicuous result in 1889 was to bring his own accomplishments to the attention of Cecil Rhodes, then contemplating a merger with the Lakes Company. Rhodes offered to place Lugard in charge of all Nyasa operations, and Lugard was elated at the prospect. But the Lakes Company vacillated on the amalgamation, Rhodes became impatient, and Lugard, somewhat vexed with his employers, accepted another offer—from Mackinnon's IBEA.

*

Arriving in Mombasa early in December, he was sent immediately to the interior with instructions to survey and test the feasibility of a route to the Company station at Machakos that would bypass the Taru desert. The expedition lasted five months, and when Lugard returned to Mombasa in May of 1890, he was told to turn around again at once. This time his destination was Uganda.

For, as we have already seen, the struggle to gain control of that country was approaching a crisis. Britain and Germany had not yet reached their agreement (the discussions were being kept top secret), Jackson's whereabouts were uncertain and Peters' location a blank. It was quite possible that Uganda might already have passed by default into German hands. In Lugard's absence, Mackinnon had acceded to Foreign Office urgings that IBEA make a direct move on Uganda, and Lugard had been chosen for the task. The objective was to overtake or outflank Peters and establish the British presence in Uganda by concluding a treaty with Mwanga. "Whoever succeeds in doing this," the Company Administrator, George Mackenzie, had already written Lugard, "will deserve great things of his country ... You, I believe, are the man *destined* to manage it."

Although Lugard did not have to be reminded of the imperial stakes involved, he balked at his orders, and this temporizing at so crucial a moment might seem out of character. In fact, however, it merely illustrates the intensity of Lugard's aversion to playing a subordinate role. For he learned that he was not "destined" to win Uganda on his own. There had been a change in plans. Leadership of the expedition was to be placed in the hands of Sir Francis de Winton, a soldier and diplomat of long experience who had just been appointed to replace Mackenzie as Company Administrator. Lugard would serve as second-in-command. He flatly refused, and a courteous but fierce battle for the upper hand now took place between the youthful captain and the very senior major general. At one point Lugard submitted his resignation from the Company but was prevailed on to reconsider. When, for various reasons, it was finally decided that de Winton would remain in Mombasa, Lugard simultaneously exulted and reproached himself. "As usual," he wrote to one of his sisters, "I have got my way entirely, like an obstinate and self-willed man as I fear I am."

*

The expedition departed from Mombasa on August 6, and, as Mackenzie later remarked, "no caravan ever left the coast so ill-equipped." To back up any political decisions in Uganda, a powerful military force was a sine qua non. Lugard's detachment consisted of seventy Sudanese askaris and a few Somali scouts carrying museum-piece Snider rifles. Each man had been issued less than one hundred rounds of ammunition.

There was a Maxim gun that showed all the effects of its journey across Africa with Stanley's Emin Pasha expedition. "Nor had I any men," wrote Lugard, "who understood it." Belloc's satiric tribute to British imperial muscle power,

> Whatever happens we have got
> The Maxim gun and they have not

would hardly have appealed to Lugard at this time. He also observed that many of the porters "were not porters at all; they lay about in the path groaning and saying they were dying, and they deserted in twos and threes daily." After barely a week, one-third of them had vanished into the scrub.

The party's leadership offered some compensation. Two civilians, William Grant and Fenwick de Winton, the Administrator's son, had much to learn, but would prove invaluable deputies. Shukri Aga, the Sudanese officer commanding the askaris, had served under Emin Pasha in Equatoria, as had the troops themselves. The man in charge of the porters, a Somali named Dualla, had not only traveled through Africa with Stanley and other explorers but had visited Europe and the United States as a seaman; he spoke English, Arabic and Swahili as if each were his mother tongue. Lugard called him "one of the bravest and best fellows I have ever had to deal with ... extremely shrewd and intelligent ... his own master." Finally, there was Lugard himself.

Despite its handicaps, the caravan was able to proceed at a reasonably brisk pace. Lugard flanked the Taru by following the trail he had previously blazed along the Sabaki river for about a hundred miles, then turning northwest toward Kikuyuland, his first major halting place. More porters were recruited on the march. Apart from the usual fevers, along with a brief epidemic of copper poisoning when the galvanizing wore off some cooking pots, no serious mishaps occurred. There was only one brief delay: the interception of a slave caravan near the junction of the Sabaki and Tsavo rivers. The Swahili traders were disarmed and sent under guard to Mombasa, followed shortly afterwards by the liberated slaves. Not all of the latter, however, were turned loose: Lugard kept what he called his "nursery"—several of the children who were near death from starvation, and whose care and feeding he made his personal responsibility. "I do not suppose the poor little devils have had such a meal since they were born," he wrote in his diary after cooking them a chicken. The diet seemed to help; a few days later, Lugard observed that "my little children are getting on first-rate. The boy nearly died, but is pulling round. The little girls are getting quite free and happy, and one hears them speak now; before they never spoke or made any sound." The role of foster-father was to become a habit with the lonely Lugard during the next two years.

Early in October, the expedition reached Kikuyuland, and it is here that we see IBEA no less capable of wasteful delay than Lugard had been while holding out for command. Although the Anglo-German agreement was now on record, there was no assurance whatever that Mwanga would willingly accept Company authority in Uganda. The more time allowed the White Fathers to stiffen the Kabaka's spine against a British presence, the slimmer would become Lugard's chances of concluding a treaty. And yet, when he left Mombasa, Lugard had received explicit instructions to halt at Ngongo Bagas, build a fortified station and make treaties with the Kikuyu. These tasks occupied the better part of a month, and they did not serve the Company's cause in Uganda.

The pause, however, does afford the opportunity to observe the practical application of what might be called Lugard's philosophy of benevolent imperialism, described in his monumental book, *The Rise of Our East African Empire*. Unlike many of his official colleagues, Lugard looked on IBEA's treaty forms as too slick a piece of snake-oil salesmanship for unsophisticated peoples such as the Kikuyu: "I felt that I could not honourably pledge the Company's protection to distant tribes, whom they had no means whatever of protecting ... while the cession of all rights of rule ... was, in my opinion, asking for more than was fair." More equitable and equally valid was the time-honored blood brotherhood ceremony, in which Lugard participated with several Kikuyu clans. The ritual required that he and the local elder cut each other's forearms with a knife, rub the two cuts together and then eat a piece of meat that had been dipped in the mixed blood. ("Dualla, holding the meat in his hand, would cunningly substitute his finger, and so avoid the actual blood touching the meat sometimes!") Confirmation of the rite took the form of lengthy speeches pledging eternal brotherhood, as well as alliance between clan and Company. The agreement was then put in writing, witnessed and sent to England for Foreign Office endorsement. "More binding treaties could not have been executed in savage Africa." A far cry from Peters, or for that matter from IBEA.

*

Toward the end of the month, runners arrived from the coast with letters. Jackson had by now reached Mombasa, bringing news that the gunrunner Stokes was reported on his way to Uganda from the south with a large shipment of arms and ammunition for Mwanga. Should

Stokes reach Mengo before Lugard concluded a treaty with Mwanga, the Kabaka would be in a position to deal from strength; indeed he might prove unmanageable. Work on the Company stockade was hastily completed, the final blood brotherhood pacts negotiated. On November 1, Lugard moved out.

By the 14th, the caravan had traversed the Rift, hauled itself northward along the great belt of frost-laced junipers on the Mau escarpment and arrived at Njemps. Lugard halted here only long enough to mend torn loads. He had resolved to reach Mengo before the year was out, and the schedule could not be met without a sustained burst of speed, for hunger had badly reduced the caravan's pace on the march across the Rift. Lugard relied on the Uasin Gishu plateau, with its huge buffalo herds, to replenish food supplies, but on moving west from Njemps, the party came on a prairie of death: the country had been struck by an even more severe outbreak of rinderpest than Thomson had witnessed in 1883. "Through all this great plain, we passed carcasses of buffalo; and the vast herds ... which I hoped would feed my hungry men, were gone. The breath of the pestilence had destroyed them as utterly as the Winchesters of Buffalo Bill and the corned-beef factories of Chicago have destroyed the bison of America." Nonetheless, when the expedition finally marched into the Company station at Mumias on November 29, its four-week journey from Kikuyuland had broken all records previously set by caravans traveling over that two-hundred-mile section of the trail.

Although the men might have benefited from more rest, only five days—barely enough time to replenish the expedition's food stores— were spent in Mumias. It was not only Lugard's timetable that hastened his departure but also the reputation Mumias had acquired as a place where porters deserted in droves on learning that they were bound for Uganda. At this time, in fact, there was in Mumias a sizable deserter community, "a nest," wrote Lugard, "of the greatest scoundrels unhung." He enlisted (drafted is possibly a better word) a number of these men after taking away their rifles, but they managed to desert again shortly afterwards. Not so the porters who had marched from the coast; by now, characteristically, their esprit had become heartening. "The trouble I had anticipated, when they found that Uganda was our destination, was replaced by eagerness and emulation." On December 4, when the order to pick up loads was given, they stepped off westward at a smart pace.

The rains were smashing down in earnest as the caravan forded the waist-deep millrace of the Nzoia river and entered Uganda's tributary state of Busoga. The change in surroundings was as pleasant as it was sudden. From Mumias, the party had crossed a fallow landscape of wet sandpaper grass strewn with almost mountainous boulders. Now all became green and bustling. Everywhere stood date palms, lush banana groves and tidy beehive villages, while "the Great Unclad were replaced by a race of more intellectual appearance, completely clothed in voluminous bark-cloth." The physical demands of the march also became less trying; "we traveled mostly along the 'great Uganda road'—a lane with regular hedges—quite a novelty in Africa." But Lugard simultaneously found it unsettling to observe that many Wasoga carried rifles, bought or stolen from deserting porters; elaborate precautions were necessary to keep his own askaris from selling their scant supplies of ammunition. Lugard also noticed that the ruler of the country, a chief named Wakoli, "showed the utmost fear of Mwanga," although this did not inhibit him from making a blood brotherhood pact. (A coffee berry was used as a substitute.) A similar alliance was concluded several days later with a powerful sub-chief who dressed for the occasion in white robes and a leopard-skin cloak, causing Lugard to feel "quite ashamed of my karki breeches, which were in patches and tatters, with a gaping rent in front."

None of these diversions, however, slowed the pace of the march. Even a "guide," sent by Mwanga with the express purpose of delaying the party, failed to achieve that objective. It was only on December 13, when Lugard reached the Nile, that he was forced to halt. For the local chief, under Mwanga's orders, refused to lend the expedition his canoes. It was an issue Lugard did not wish to force unless necessary. He had managed to find two small, badly leaking dugouts which he thought might serve his purpose. After battling the half-mile-wide current in a solo shakedown crossing, he then commenced ferrying the entire party, in twos and threes, to the western bank. Before he had finished, however, the chief, recognizing the futility of his stratagem, "made a virtue of necessity" and donated the large canoes he had previously withheld. Exulted Lugard: "The night of December 13 saw us camped in Uganda, and we were now indifferent to whatever caressing evasions might issue from Mwanga."

But Mwanga, too, appeared to have bowed to the inevitable, at least momentarily. "The king's envoy now escorted us, and, as is usual in Uganda, his minstrels played before him on the march ... At the halts they danced the extraordinary dance of the Waganda; the little bells or hollow balls, filled with iron shot, keeping time with their tinkling sound to the motion of their bodies." On December 18, to a liquid, thumping cacophony of drums, xylophones, harps, flutes and ivory trumpets, the expedition marched through the hammering rain into the Kabaka's capital.

*"The English have come ... They eat my
land, and yet they give me nothing at all.
They have made me sign a treaty ... and
I get nothing from them in return."*

Despite the fanfare on his arrival, Lugard's reception in Mengo was
mixed. Huge crowds lined the outskirts of the city, but he could not
fail to notice that "there was an almost ominous silence as I passed
them." His vigilance was further aroused by Mwanga's hospitality. When
the men finally put down their loads and stacked their rifles, a royal
messenger arrived and led Lugard to a camp site which he said had
been especially chosen for the caravan by the Kabaka himself. Lugard
inspected the "wet and dirty hollow," strode to the crest of a neighboring
rise known as Kampala hill and informed the messenger that he would
make permanent camp there.

This touched off a flurry of almost frantic communications from
Mwanga, expressing concern for the expedition's comfort. Lugard
ignored them. Selecting Kampala hill had not merely been a matter of
elementary sanitation and tactical common sense. Lugard had come to
Uganda for one purpose: to bring the country under British authority,
and he knew that he must make this clear at the outset. "I intuitively
saw that if I was to do any good in this country it was essential that I
assert my independence from the first, and it appeared to me that even
now Mwanga was already engaged solely in finding out to what extent
he could order me about, and whether I was afraid of him." This would
never do. In Lugard's opinion, the Kabaka's uncooperativeness was in
large measure the consequence of overly deferential treatment by previous European visitors. "Mackay and Ashe relate how they knelt before
the king, when praying for permission to leave the country. Such an
attitude seemed to me to lower the prestige of Europeans, and I determined to make my own methods the more marked by contrast." As if to
drive this point home, he deliberately refrained from paying his respects
at once. "I sent courteous messages to the king with salaams, saying
we were tired and wet, and I would defer my visit to him till next day."
This was the first of many token civilities that would characterize the
mutually distasteful relationship between the two men over the ensuing
eighteen months.

The following day, as promised, Lugard went to the palace, garbed
in the most imposing uniform he could improvise from his sodden kit:
a pajama jacket with brass buttons and "a pair of comparatively sound
Melton cords." Apparently aware that this costume was not likely to

impress, he asserted the special prestige attached to a British officer by bringing his own chair with him. He also took along an honor guard of the Company's Sudanese askaris, who executed a smart present arms and bugle flourish outside the palace gates. Mwanga countered with "a band of drums and other kinds of noise," and the exchange of fraudulent pleasantries commenced.

It was not an intimate gathering; Lugard found Mwanga "surrounded by a mass of humanity packed in every cubic inch of space." Nor could the atmosphere have been called friendly. Mwanga, totally under the influence of the White Fathers and continuing to dread British vengeance for Hannington's murder, had little reason to feel amicably disposed toward the man who seemed to personify that retribution. Lugard for his part found little to admire in the Kabaka, who exuded "irresolution, a weak character and a good deal of sensuality." This impression was undoubtedly fortified by the sight of Mwanga fondling his pages throughout the conversation; Lugard later described the court as "the public scene of all the vices of Sodom and Gomorrah."

Yet the meeting somehow proceeded smoothly. Mwanga "asked no impertinent questions as to the number of my men and guns" (which he no doubt already knew), and Lugard made a point of introducing headman Dualla and Shukri Aga, the Sudanese officer. (The latter, in full-dress uniform, "'took the cake' entirely.") He also read polite letters from Mackenzie and de Winton, and delivered a few generalities touching on his own "hope of bringing peace to the country." One diplomatic gesture in particular appeared to go down well. "There was very great relief and joy in the court at there being no mention in the letters or by me of a flag ... Peters, Jackson, the French and Germans, all have talked of nothing but a flag ... I do not intend to make any childish fuss ... If I can get a treaty, the flag will come of its own accord." Presently Lugard took his leave, a considerable breach of protocol, since by custom the Kabaka always signified the conclusion of an audience. The discourtesy was also deliberate: "a final assertion that I was my own master." Yet it was less than an open affront; indeed, the meeting could be seen to have laid the groundwork for the serious political discussions to come.

Time, however, was of the essence; a treaty must be obtained without delay. For despite Germany's acceptance of the British claim in Uganda, the country was rapidly approaching an internal crisis. By now, the missionaries had polarized their respective flocks into two armed camps. The Catholics—openly hostile to Lugard—were known as Fransa, the Protestants, Ingleza, and the gulf between them all but unbridgeable. As martyrs, Uganda's Catholics and Protestants alike had gained the wonder and admiration of the world; as Fransa and Ingleza they were the church militant in its most odious manifestation. Christians in Mengo now carried their guns to church. Civil war could erupt at any moment, snapping the already fragile British hold on the country.

A treaty, as Lugard knew quite well, would not necessarily prevent the outbreak of hostilities, but at the very least it would bring him a certain degree of legal status as an arbiter. Of more immediate importance, such authority would place him in a stronger position to deal with Stokes when the trader arrived and sought to sell his rifles and ammunition; this alone might hold violence in check. The only question was whether Mwanga could be wooed away from the influence of the White Fathers and induced to sign. The possibility seemed remote. Although Lourdel, the Kabaka's Richelieu, had died of malaria some months earlier, his successor, Monseigneur Hirth, could be likened—by way of rounding out the metaphor—to a benevolent Rasputin. He would almost certainly apply pressure to prevent Mwanga from submitting to British authority. A contest of wills seemed unavoidable. But it must not be put off.

*

On December 24, accompanied by de Winton, Lugard went to the palace and formally submitted the treaty to Mwanga. This time there were no social pleasantries. "Contrary to one of the strictest customs in Uganda, every chief had come with his loaded rifle ... while outside great numbers of the hostile faction had collected." Lugard went directly to the point. The terms of the treaty were clear enough. In return for granting its protection to Uganda, IBEA would be recognized as holding certain jurisdictional rights, to be exercised through a British Resident. Freedom of trade and worship were guaranteed, the slave traffic outlawed. Although fully aware of the weakness of his position (what "protection" could he conceivably offer?), Lugard presented the treaty more as a demand than as a proposal. "I read [it] through, sentence by sentence, putting it in simple English, and Dualla rendered it most admirably in Swahili—one or other of the chiefs repeating it in Luganda. Much discussion and even uproar arose at times, but I scowled and looked as fierce as I could and insisted on reading it right through."

The meeting was then thrown open to debate. Questions were "most shrewd and intelligent," and it soon became evident to Lugard that despite the angered clamor which had interrupted his reading of the treaty, the majority was with him. This may not have come as a complete surprise. Several days earlier, Lugard had written a letter to Hirth, stating that "the support given your mission and the cordiality with which its extension is viewed will, as in any country and Government throughout the world, depend on the loyal manner in which you and the other Reverend Fathers associated with you support the authority of the Administration." This had been sheer bluff; there was no "Administration," and Lugard had possessed no official powers whatever. Yet it was not the first instance in which an Englishman had sought to gain the upper hand by raising his voice, and Hirth may well have taken Lugard's strong words at face value. In any case, it is generally believed that Hirth had advised the chiefs to cooperate, and Lugard was sufficiently familiar with Uganda politics to know that "in their hands the real executive power lay."

Given this state of affairs and Mwanga's known willingness to accept the White Fathers' counsel, Lugard might not have expected the Kabaka to balk. But with characteristic unpredictability, Mwanga did just that, having achieved "a state of great excitement and fear, for he was under the absurd impression that if he signed he would become a mere slave." But Lugard persisted. "After some discussion I asked the king if he were ready to sign ... He shuffled and I got more determined and rapped the table and told him to sign if he wanted peace ... He begged for a little delay to think it over. I said no ... at last he said he would sign."

At that moment, however, "a clamour arose from the crowd at the door, who said, I believe, that they would shoot the white men and those who signed ... De Winton says he twice heard a man cock his gun, and all say they began putting in cartridges." Lugard, whose back was to the entrance, did not know at the time that one man had actually drawn a bead on him and had started to squeeze the trigger when a chief knocked the gun out of his hands. Yet as Miss Perham has observed, "it was hardly the moment to press matters," and Lugard himself appeared to realize this. "I said that next day, being Christmas, we would do no work, but the day after I must have his reply."

It could not have been the merriest Christmas that Lugard had ever celebrated. On Christmas Eve itself, only hours after the demonstration at the palace, Mengo had been aswirl with white-robed mobs threatening to kill every European in the city. Lugard's seventy askaris, with their defective Sniders, would have been useless against thousands of well-armed Baganda. Only a full moon had prevented a massacre from taking place. Now Christmas night was approaching, and if murderous passions had abated slightly, Lugard still had little reason to believe that Mwanga himself would prove more accommodating when presented with the treaty the following day.

No one else seemed unduly concerned. Ernest Gedge, whom Jackson had left in Mengo to represent the Company's interests, gave "a magnificent Christmas dinner" rounded off with champagne that had been hoarded for the occasion. But Lugard excused himself. Somehow, he felt, he must seek to soften Mwanga's resistance before reintroducing the treaty. Darkness had already fallen, but the possibility existed that a private meeting might still be arranged. Despite a warning from one of the Anglican missionaries that this could provide Mwanga with the opportunity to have him done in, Lugard went to the palace with Dualla and requested an audience. While the two men awaited the reply, a large throng of rifle- and spear-carrying Baganda materialized. Then the war drums began to roll. Obviously the interview could no longer be private. "There was a chuckle and a suppressed jeer among the rabble as we went, till Dualla turned and faced them, and they stopped." Now Lugard was left with nothing else to do but put in a brief appearance at Gedge's party, "lest my absence be misinterpreted." He then went to his tent and tried to sleep.

Following the high-voltage tension of the previous two days, December 26 proved an anticlimax, although it had its moments. Talks were scheduled to resume at eight o'clock in the morning. The now accommodating chiefs had agreed to meet Lugard at his camp first; all would then go to the palace together. But by nine-thirty, not one chief had appeared, and Lugard became apprehensive that the Christmas interlude had witnessed a collective change of heart. Finally, however, the chiefs arrived in a body; to Lugard's relief, none carried weapons. The group then departed for the palace. Lugard was accompanied only by de Winton and three or four askaris. Grant remained behind under orders to despatch the entire Sudanese contingent should he hear firing from Mengo hill and to defend the camp itself with the Maxim. As he neared the palace, Lugard found some confirmation of his fears that Mwanga's evasiveness was continuing. "The king sent a message warning me not to come, as 'bad men' had determined to murder me. I looked on this merely as a way of putting me off."

Mwanga continued his delaying tactics with the resumption of talks. First he asked for a present. Lugard told him that would have to wait. Mwanga countered with a series of largely irrelevant questions, mainly concerning tributary states. Lugard said he could not comment until he had studied each matter separately; the treaty must be signed first. Mwanga looked at his chiefs for some indication of support. Their faces were expressionless. One is reminded of King John and the Magna Carta. At length, Mwanga appeared to realize that he had no choice but to capitulate. "The king told some one to sign for him. I would not have this, and insisted on his making a mark. He did it with a bad grace, just dashing the pen at the paper and making a blot, but I made him go at it again, and on the second copy he behaved himself and made a proper cross."

*

It was less a triumph of diplomacy than of gunboat diplomacy; we hardly recognize the man who had spared no effort to assure equitable treatment for the Kikuyu. One can appreciate Mwanga's feelings when he told a CMS missionary: "The English have come ... They eat my land, and yet they give me nothing at all. They have made me sign a treaty ... and I get nothing from them in return." Lugard himself admitted that Mwanga had been cowed: "the treaty was certainly obtained against his will—I have never said the contrary." But if he was not proud of his methods, he felt them no less justified. That invisible but indispensable cement of Empire, British prestige, had crumbled to sand in Uganda, and "this prestige it was my business to restore." Without de jure recognition of the Company's authority, de facto control would never come.

At that time, Britain feared losing Uganda to the workings of a not invalid domino theory, against which the only bulwark, for the moment at least, was the treaty. If Lugard had not applied pressure, Mwanga could have vacillated until Stokes' arrival. The latter would then have been free to sell his rifles and ammunition to Mwanga, who would have distributed them among the Fransa. This would have touched off an all-out assault on the Ingleza; outnumbered and outgunned, they would have been driven from the country. Then would come the Fransa's turn to flee, as the Baganda Muslims launched their invasion. Poised in Bunyoro to the northwest, the Muslims did not possess sufficient strength to challenge a united Christian front, but with Uganda rent by civil war, they would join forces with Kabarega, reconquer the country and install their new leader, Mbogo. Once again Uganda would be a Muslim state, fair game for federation with the Mahdists in the Sudan. Or, should the Muslim effort for some reason fail, the state of anarchy would continue, thus providing the Germans to the south with the rationale that if Britain could not preserve order it would become the simple duty of another "civilized" Power to undertake that task. Therefore, first things first: in the view of the Company and the Foreign Office, it was imperative that Lugard keep Fransa and Ingleza from each other's throats. This required legal sanction. The treaty provided it.

*

And yet, Lugard knew only too well that he wore a pitifully fragile coat of mail. Had open conflict broken out at that time, invoking a piece of paper—even forming seventy soldiers in hollow square around a malfunctioning Maxim gun—would have served only to dramatize the Company's impotence. For nearly three months following the signing of the treaty, it was only because "the Waganda set great weight on a written contract" that Lugard was able to uphold British prestige. Hardly a day went by without a major crisis. Mobs gathered, insults and threats were exchanged, guns brandished. Lugard stiffened every time he heard a shot. During one period of twenty-four hours the war drums rolled out on three separate occasions. The Company's position did not benefit from the premature return to Mengo of one of the envoys Mwanga had sent to the coast to determine the validity of Peters' treaty. This man circulated "the most extraordinary reports, saying that we were cowards who dare not fight ... that we had poisoned the Sultan of Zanzibar ... that our Maxim was merely for show, and fired single bullets like a gun." (The latter came close to the truth.) The envoy added that a large shipment of flags was on its way, "to force on the chiefs."

The chiefs, indeed, occupied much of Lugard's attention during this period. He worked continually among them to remove or at least neutralize their suspicions and religious hatreds. As a focal point of distrust himself, he did not find the task easy. Despite their acceptance of the treaty, the Fransa continued to look on Lugard as by definition an enemy; so long as they remained hostile toward him, the work of reuniting the country could not begin. Thus, to emphasize that he held no pro-Ingleza bias, Lugard adopted a policy of strict nonalignment in his dealings with both factions. As political parties, Fransa and Ingleza were constantly embroiled in struggles for land occupancy—Lugard described it as "the chronic trouble of Uganda"—and it was in large measure the responsibility of the British Resident to arbitrate these quarrels. Lugard initiated what he called a "pairing off" system, whereby two cases would be decided at the same hearing. In one dispute, justice would clearly be on the Fransa side, and would no less manifestly favor the Ingleza in the other. More often than not, this procedure miscarried, mainly because both plaintiff and defendant perjured themselves blatantly as a matter of course. ("My own belief was that the Waganda were *par excellence* the greatest liars of any nation or tribe I had met or heard of ... It appeared to be a point of honour that each side should out-lie the other.") Nonetheless, Lugard's obvious determination to remain impartial was not altogether lost on either Fransa or Ingleza.

Lugard also "endeavoured to separate in the minds of the people the two ideas of religion and nationality. I always spoke of the R. Catholics as the 'Wa-Katoliki,' and the Protestants as 'Wa-Protestanti,' refusing to acknowledge the terms 'French' and 'English,' for we were now (I said) *all* English." Although the label of Briton may not have appealed to the Fransa (much less to the White Fathers), it did have the effect of instilling at least an awareness of latent national unity. By virtue of his position, Lugard was also able to bring hostile chiefs together at various meetings, where he could sometimes observe a temporary abatement of hostilities. Of one such gathering he wrote that "all ate coffee together, and the 'deadly enemies' ... drank *pombé* out of the same bowl. They began to chaff about strength, and I left them putting the weight and playing like a parcel of schoolboys ... amid shouts of laughter."

At a more personal level, Lugard took it on himself to cultivate friendships with individual chiefs of both parties. From the outset, a mutual respect and regard had existed between Lugard and the Kimbugwe, the Fransa political whip, and this helped draw back many tent flaps in the enemy camp. Once, when Lugard remarked to the Kimbugwe that some of the Fransa leaders had placed him in a sort of Coventry, the latter "merely said that so long as all the great chiefs were my friends ... what need had I to notice the folly of a parcel of boys?" Among the Ingleza, Lugard's closest friend was a chief named Zachariah Kizito, whom he had special reason to like; this man had disarmed Lugard's would-be assassin during the December 24 mêlée at the palace.

All the while, Lugard was also able to bolster the Company defenses somewhat by fortifying the station on Kampala hill with a stockade of date-palm logs. He enlarged the garrison by offering military training to volunteer porters. These men had already shown their mettle during one threatened attack on the camp. Lugard had asked them if they would fight, and "the reply came back in a chorus, '*Eh-walla, Eh-walla. Tayari.* (Yes, yes. Ready.) Where you die we will be killed first.' I was deeply touched by their loyalty." Now, fitted out in middy-blouse uniforms, armed with Sniders and dubbed the "Zanzibari Levy," the new recruits "rapidly developed into a most serviceable body of men." They would later prove their worth in action. Additional reinforcements came at the end of January, with the arrival of Captain J. H. Williams, an artillery officer senior in service to Lugard but ready and willing to serve under his command. Williams had brought with him seventy-five more Sudanese askaris and another decrepit Maxim. He also took over the drilling of all the Sudanese, "and in a wonderfully short time," wrote Lugard, "the improvement in their smartness and general turnout was most marked."

These preparations enabled Lugard to deal with Stokes when the trader, resplendent in flowing Muslim robes, arrived in Mengo on February 5. His red beard seemed ready to take fire as he fulminated at the accusation that he had brought arms for sale, but Lugard now had sufficient force behind him—both legal and military—to stare Stokes down. "I spoke very strongly to him ... saying that the import of powder at the present moment would mean civil war," and Stokes appeared to have been won over: "he agreed it would be little better than murder." The two men became friendly at this point. Willing to assist Stokes with his legitimate trade, Lugard asked for and received an inventory of the goods which Stokes had brought with him. The list included fifty barrels of gunpowder, four seventy-pound loads of percussion caps and several hundred breech-loading rifles. Lugard kept his temper and offered to store the contraband. Stokes declined, but did not attempt to sell the arms.

*

The Stokes episode was a victory for Lugard; it can even be seen as a turning point of sorts, but it by no means ended the continuing crisis. Lugard's peacemaking efforts among the Fransa and Ingleza chiefs had not been without results. Nevertheless, they represented little more than a thin gauze dressing over a festering open sore. Despite the reinforcement of the Kampala garrison, the Company's military capacity to prevent civil war remained feeble. Increasingly, Lugard turned his eyes to the west, where he saw the only instrument that might enable him to enforce the treaty. When Stanley had "rescued" Emin Pasha on the shore of Lake Albert, the returning party had left behind eight hundred of the Pasha's Sudanese troops, partly because Stanley had suspected them of treachery. Lugard, who considered Sudanese "the best material for soldiery in Africa," pinned his hopes on somehow reaching the abandoned garrison and persuading its commander, Selim Bey, to serve under him. If this could be accomplished, he felt, he would at least be able to draw on a reliable reserve force, and Uganda's disorders, internal and external alike, might thus be reduced proportionately.

In March, a legitimate opportunity to make contact with the Sudanese presented itself. Mwanga, naturally desirous of gaining a quid pro quo from the treaty, sought to utilize Lugard's Western military training and proposed that he lead a campaign against the renegade Muslims in Bunyoro. The advantages of the undertaking were obvious. An anti-Muslim crusade was virtually the only objective on which Fransa and Ingleza could see eye to eye; it promised to halt or at least retard the spread of Uganda's sectarian cancer. And, since an invasion of Bunyoro would bring the Uganda army only a few miles from Lake Albert, there should be little difficulty in reaching the badly needed Sudanese.

By the end of the month, the expeditionary force had been mobilized, although an obstacle seemed to loom briefly when Lugard raised the question of who would command the Uganda army. According to custom, generalship was shared: in one war a Fransa would lead the troops, in the next, an Ingleza. For this crucial campaign, however, Lugard proposed that Mwanga himself assume command. The Kabaka, who "was 'knocked into a cocked hat,'" told Lugard that his advanced years ruled him out. Lugard reminded him that he, Lugard, was even older. Mwanga replied that he was unable to go because his duties obliged him to remain in Mengo. Lugard said that he also had responsibilities in the capital. "After rubbing it in till he was quite uncomfortable, I exclaimed, 'All right ... then the next biggest man in Uganda must go.' He agreed at once." The substitute was an Ingleza chief named Apolo Kagwa, whom Mwanga had personally speared during the persecutions of 1886, but who had recovered and subsequently risen to the office of Katikiro. Early in April the army was ready to march, and traditional ceremonies attended its departure. "It was a remarkable sight ... The huge drums of war were produced and beaten, while the king, surrounded by his chiefs, stood with an umbrella held over him ... Within five minutes masses of armed men began to assemble on every side, and came pouring in dense troops toward us from every direction ... Each on coming close to the king held his gun above his head, presenting the butt (as at the 'head parry'), and swore the oath of loyalty ... It looked in their mimic ferocity as though they meant to dash out the brains of his Majesty!"

The Katikiro's army marched out first, followed several days later by Lugard. The route took the troops slightly north of west, over a nearly treeless boredom of undulating hills that had been made into sponges by the heavy spring rains. The countryside carried the gashes of civil strife. Most inhabitants had fled from their villages during Muslim raids, leaving their banana groves to the elephants. Tall grass concealed the once-splendid highways. Aside from an occasional partridge, even the birds seemed to have deserted the land. But the men stepped off smartly. The Company force now numbered about six hundred, of which only half, the Sudanese and the Zanzibari Levy, carried guns; the remainder were porters. Captain Williams' two months' work with the troops "had achieved wonderful results." In maneuvers at Kampala, both the Sudanese and Zanzibaris had mastered the rudiments of extended order drill and could maintain "a tolerable line of advance." They had also learned to use the sights on their Sniders and respond quickly to bugle calls. For the sort of fighting that was expected of them, little more was required. The most serious liability was in ammunition, now down to forty rounds per man. For concentrated firepower, Lugard could rely only on the Katikiro's force, with its grab bag of forty-seven hundred flintlocks and breech-loaders, backed up by some twenty thousand spearmen.

On April 21, the joint armies of Company and Katikiro rendezvoused near the Bunyoro border. Here, the landscape underwent a change, becoming thickly wooded and littered generously with immense boulders. Another change was seen in the attitude of the Baganda chiefs. At the Katikiro's suggestion, Lugard proposed that the Company flag be carried at the head of the troops, along with the multitude of Uganda regimental colors. Not even the Fransa objected. Lugard found this heartening.

He was further encouraged to learn that the Muslims might prefer peace to war, having received a favorable response to letters which offered full pardons and a pledge that the entire Muslim community would be permitted to return to Uganda and to practice its own religion. The offer had been conditional on Mbogo's renunciation of all claims to the throne, and the Muslims appeared receptive to these terms. Through envoys, their leaders informed Lugard that they had no quarrel with the British, and voiced a willingness to hand Mbogo over into the Company's protective custody. Even when negotiations became mired down, they continued to seek a peaceable solution, at one point offering to move into German territory if Lugard could arrange their entry. Lugard, who thought the Muslims "a plucky, fine lot of fellows," agreed to write the German authorities. But then, a more bellicose faction among the Muslims emerged to produce a sudden change of heart. There would be no abandoning of Mbogo; no conditions must govern the Muslims' rightful return to their own country. The talks broke down. The issue could now be resolved only by war.

On May 5, the two armies faced each other on opposite banks of a swampy river separating Uganda and Bunyoro. Lugard estimated the Muslim force at about thirty-six hundred, including thirteen hundred of Kabarega's warriors. This gave the Christians a substantial numerical edge. The enemy, however, had dug in skillfully at the crest of a hill with a natural barricade of forest and man-high elephant grass. "Williams ... said he thought that at such a place he could oppose an army with fifty good men."

Lugard could learn little else of the Muslim position. Despite their worth as fighting men, Baganda soldiers did not take to the science of scouting. Their practice on such missions was to hide in grass and invent fictions which they would later turn in as reconnaissance reports. On this occasion, moreover, Lugard's own Somali scouts could not have crossed the river undetected. There was also disagreement over the plan of attack. Lugard proposed a series of feints at the river directly below the Muslim defenses to divert enemy fire while the main body moved upstream to launch a flank assault. But Baganda military traditions ruled out any major dispersal of forces; the time-honored offensive tactic was a massed pell-mell charge. Eventually the Katikiro was prevailed on to compromise. Under cover of darkness, he would take the army down-stream and cross the river, followed by Lugard's troops. The Muslim forces would suspect nothing, having heard the war drums sound the halt and assuming that their foe had camped for the night. At dawn the next day, the Katikiro and Lugard would lead the assault on the hill.

The crossing was effected without a hitch and the army took up its position, with the Company force in the center. Lugard had no idea what role his troops would play. The Baganda, in their rush, could be expected to outstrip the Company's more disciplined, British-modeled advance. If the charge proved successful, Lugard's men would waste none of their precious ammunition, but if the Baganda were thrown back, the three hundred Sudanese and Zanzibaris would take the full weight of the Muslim counterattack.

When the sun rose next morning, the surprise element vanished. The battle commenced with a war dance by both sides, dramatized by the waving of flags and exchanges of threats. The Katikiro then ordered his army to charge. "The Waganda went up the hill splendidly, and there was a melee for a few seconds, and then, to our dismay, we saw part of our side ... turn and come rushing down on our left pursued by the enemy. I wheeled around to support them, but the dense grass made it impossible to open fire. (The Maxim of course was useless.)" When the Company troops finally got into position to use their rifles, they were no longer needed, for the remaining Baganda had swept the hill, "the battle was already won, and we had borne, practically, no part in it." Of the Baganda, thirty had been killed and seventy wounded. Muslim casualties were estimated at between three hundred and four hundred; all had to be considered dead, "for the wounded men would be unable to escape, and would be butchered."

The victory, however, proved hollow. Lugard had planned to pursue and smash the reeling Muslims in a final engagement, then continue north to Hoima, Kabarega's capital, where he would similarly crush the Bunyoro army. Then, with the outward threat to Uganda removed, he would be free to make the short march from Hoima to Lake Albert, and hopefully, to the badly needed Sudanese. But this was not to be. Having won their battle, the Baganda had lost interest in the war. "They urged that though they were willing to follow me to a man, there was ahead of us a swamp three miles broad ... in the face of an opposing army it would be impossible to cross ... Beyond this, again, lay other swamps and rivers equally bad at this season." Lugard found it useless to argue that these obstacles could be surmounted or bypassed, useless to remind the Baganda that if the Muslims were allowed to retire without pursuit, they would simply re-form and fight another day. What had begun as a grand crusade had now degenerated into an apathetic rabble. Lugard faced the prospect of returning to Mengo with nothing accomplished. Should civil war break out, he would remain all but powerless to intervene. Emin's Sudanese seemed farther distant than ever.

However, Lugard did not return. Instead, he sent Williams back with thirty-six askaris and one of the Maxims to take command in Mengo. He himself, with the remainder of the Company troops and a number of Baganda, marched west, on a seven-hundred-mile, seven-month recruiting and empire-building campaign—an undertaking for which he was subsequently acclaimed and fiercely denounced.

"There was great joy and kissing
of my hand ... everyone temporarily
became a fool, as is right and
proper on such an occasion."

The wisdom of Lugard's western journey, from one viewpoint, is open to question. His orders called for no such venture and his presence was unquestionably needed in Mengo. Yet as Lugard saw it, his duty lay to the west. The enlistment of the Sudanese he had by now come to regard as imperative, since no other source of military manpower was available to him. Repeated requests to the Company for additional troops had brought only reproach: the expense, he was told, was prohibitive. The Directors were already nettled because Williams, on his own initiative, had burdened them with the salaries of his seventy-five askaris. To the man charged with upholding Company authority (which in effect meant British rule) in a country on the brink of civil war, this obsession with economy at the cost of security could only have been seen as mindlessly self-defeating. One way or another, Lugard was determined to enroll Emin's former troops in his own force.

Lugard found further justification for the march to the west in his own imperial horizons, which were not always confined within the limits of his official instructions. In the kingdoms of Ankole and Toro, which lay across his route to the Sudanese, he saw a no-man's land. Juridically, these countries fell within the British sphere, but no attempt had yet been made to bring them under effective occupation. By the unwritten laws of the scramble, they remained fair game for the ambitions of other Powers. Both Ankole and Toro were contiguous with German and Belgian territory. Reports had already been coming in that a German expedition, led by Emin Pasha himself, was at that very time approaching Ankole from the south. Thus there was no question in Lugard's mind that the Company must assert its presence in the west without delay.

Nor need this be a poor business risk. Indeed, annexation of the western regions promised to benefit Uganda, since that country, "impoverished by years of war—could at the moment yield little or nothing." A rich ivory trade was known to pass southward from Bunyoro through Toro and Ankole; Lugard hoped to divert part of that stream to Uganda. He had also been told of a large salt lake on the Toro-Ankole border; salt being hardly less valuable than ivory among the inhabitants of the region, Lugard believed that a measure of control over that commodity would, at the very least, defray the cost of the expedition. More than that, he saw in the salt market the potential of "a substantial revenue" for the Company. Thus, if he entertained any qualms about his unauthorized venture, he kept them well to himself as the party struck west.

*

Marching through Ankole, Lugard found Africa, Switzerland, Texas, and Surrey rolled into one. The soaring hills were a patchwork quilt of grain fields alternating with pastures grazed by longhorn cattle and fat-tailed sheep. In the plunging gorges lay mats of rain forest, lushly embroidered with orchids; on the uplands, English flowers grew in profusion. A rich land, thickly populated and for the most part friendly, Ankole came under IBEA suzerainty when its ruler, Ntali, sent his son to make blood brotherhood with Lugard. ("Ntali himself was ... too fat to walk, and avoided all locomotion.") The annexation was noted in an almost offhand fashion: "We exchanged presents, and the ceremony was complete, and this large country of Ankoli was added to the Company's territory." Armed with his new authority, Lugard continued west to the claret-hued salt lake (now Lake George), whose trade potential surpassed his expectations. "Everywhere were piles of salt, in heaps covered with grass, some beautifully white and clean." Lugard built a stockaded Company post here. Like Machakos and Mumias, it was also designed to serve as a regional market place. Salt would be bartered for local produce, which in turn would buy ivory. "I hoped that the station would not only cover all expenses, but become a valuable source of revenue to the Uganda administration."

This dividend for the Company was not gained without challenge. Banyoro invasions had reduced Toro and Ankole to vassaldom, and it was necessary to break the grip of Kabarega's warriors. Lugard did this in two major engagements, both of which should, perhaps, have seen his own force wiped out. The first clash took place a few miles north of the salt lake. Marching some distance ahead of the caravan, Lugard and forty askaris were suddenly set upon by an overwhelming mass of Banyoro warriors. "The low hills were *black* with men, as was the ground in front ... It seemed impossible we could beat these hordes; retreat was out of the question, and defeat meant annihilation." However, Lugard "had yet to learn what arrant curs these Wanyoro are." Test-firing a few rounds from the Maxim, he halted the advancing wave, and within a few minutes his own troops had turned the attack into a rout. Several days later there was a collision with an even larger Banyoro army, which directed a withering hail of musket fire at the vastly outnumbered Company force. Lugard ordered his men to counterattack, holding their fire until they reached point-blank range. The "stolid and orderly advance" proved too much for the Banyoro; all at once they turned and fled. Lugard's second victory had been won without firing a single shot. This was just as well: each man now carried only twenty rounds in his bandolier.

Six years earlier, during his fictional search for King Solomon's Mines, Rider Haggard's Allan Quatermain had met the exiled monarch of a small African kingdom and helped restore him to his throne. In the summer of 1891, as Lugard crossed the foothills of the Ruwenzori mountains and entered the kingdom of Toro, he brought Allan Quatermain's exploit to life. Toro's ruler had been forced by Kabarega to take refuge in Uganda, where he died. His son and heir, Kasagama ("an extremely prepossessing youth, both in face and manner") had attached himself to Lugard's party, and when the expedition reached Toro, he signed a treaty placing his country under IBEA's protection. This agreement and the treaty with Ntali had the effect of establishing two British-protected buffer states on Uganda's western and southern borders; both countries later became provinces of Uganda itself. In reality, the protection was a flimsy shield at the time, having been guaranteed only by Lugard without authorization, for the Company had not committed itself to so wide a dispersal of its own resources. Whether Kasagama's subjects realized this or not, they did appear uncertain as to whether their newly gained security was a cause for rejoicing or despair. "They were a poor-spirited, defence-less race ... the spirit crushed out of them by years of tyranny," and they repeatedly reminded Lugard that "if they came over to us, and we left the country, Kabarega would slaughter every one of them." Lugard was fully aware of this himself, but saw no reason to believe that IBEA would repudiate the annexation. When asked "if we had come to stay ... I replied—how could I do otherwise?—that [Toro had been] ceded to the British by the nations of Europe, and that the British flag never went back." On his departure, he was able to give further assurance by station-ing de Winton in Toro as Kasagama's adviser.*

*

Lugard moved north from Toro. By early September, the party had flanked the northeastern slopes of the Ruwenzori, forded the Sem-liki river under heavy rifle fire from Banyoro guerrillas and crossed a swamp ten miles in width to reach the western shore of Lake Albert. On September 7, the expedition arrived at the village of Kavalli's, where Emin's Sudanese made their headquarters. The scene was one of unbri-dled elation. "There was great joy and kissing of my hand (which they touched with their foreheads) ... Everyone talked at the same time, and congratulated one another, and everyone temporarily became a fool, as is right and proper on such an occasion." For two years, these men had lived in abandoned isolation. They had been forced to create their own self-sustaining community. Barracks had been built of mud and grass, cotton grown and woven on handmade looms into cloth for uniforms. The few coins they brought from Egypt formed a primitive monetary system. Records were carefully kept by clerks. It was "a noticeable—almost pathetic—attempt to maintain the status they claimed as soldiers of a civilised government."

The Sudanese, to be sure, were not paragons. They took slaves, beat their women as a matter of course, looted and terrorized the country-side. Discipline, in the Western sense of the word, meant little to them. A system of self-promotion left the army with few privates, but many

---

* De Winton never left Toro. After four months, he succumbed to malaria. "It seemed unspeakably sad," wrote Lugard, "that he should have died alone among strangers ... with no friendly voice to cheer his last moments and speak to him in the language of his own people."

corporals and sergeants and a multitude of captains and majors. This was more a matter of status than of salary, since the Sudanese had not been paid by the Egyptian Government for a decade. Yet they remained staunchly loyal to the Khedive, flew the Turkish flag and maintained a high level of esprit. Their reputation as fighting men was unmatched.

Selim Bey, their commander, was a man of colossal stature, both in physique and leadership. Like the troops under him, he took an almost feral pride in his fidelity to Egypt, and showed no disposition to serve under foreign colors. He made this clear to Lugard from the outset, declaring that "he had grown grey in the service of the Khedive, and that nothing should induce him to swerve in his allegiance to the flag for which he had a hundred times risked his life." Without the Khedive's permission, he said, he could never abandon his post in Equatoria. But Lugard would not be put off. Egypt, he told Selim, had withdrawn from the Sudan, and the Khedive had assented to the evacuation of Equatoria. To join a British force, moreover, was in effect to serve Egypt, since both countries were now allied. Lugard added that he himself had been awarded the Khedive's Star for service against the Mahdists. Would not Selim at least write the Khedive and meanwhile accept Lugard's command? If permission to serve with the British were denied, he and his troops would be free to return to Egypt. Eventually, Selim agreed, although perhaps swayed less by Lugard's arguments than by the representations of his fellow Muslims, Dualla and Shukri Aga: if they trusted the infidel Lugard, that was enough for Selim.

Lugard at last had at his disposal the most fearsome fighting machine in eastern Africa. Formal transfer of command was observed in a dress parade, as the newly enrolled Company troops passed in ragtag-bobtail review to the uneven rattle of warped snare drums and the rasp of dented bugles. "It was impossible not to feel a thrill of admiration for these deserted soldiers, as they carried past flag after flag, torn and riddled in many fierce engagements with the Mahdists." One aged campaigner, who had lost the use of both arms and his reason in combat, "wandered about interrupting all proceedings ... I had not the heart to repress his enthusiasm."

*

On October 5, the force departed from Kavalli's, and Miss Perham has already drawn the inevitable parallel between Lugard and Moses. For he was now in charge of a nation in miniature. There were not only the eight hundred Sudanese troops but their wives, children, concubines and slaves, as well as a large number of starving local tribesmen who had begged to be taken along. Each of the Sudanese soldiers had a family-cum-entourage of about ten people; some of the officers counted as many as a hundred followers. Lugard had commenced the march to the west with four hundred askaris and porters; he was returning at the head of a cavalcade numbering slightly less than ten thousand, an unwieldy, undisciplined swarm of barefoot humanity, far too cumbersome to move in a single body. Even when Lugard divided it into three separate columns, each detachment stretched over a distance of seven miles. At the end of a day's march, when the forward element of one unit made camp, the rear party had only begun to leave the previous night's bivouac area. From the cloud-ceilinged wall of the Ruwenzori, the whole expedition might have resembled three giant, decrepit earthworms.

Trisecting the beast made it only a little more manageable. Throughout the journey, the Sudanese were a thorn in Lugard's side. They abandoned their sick on the path. They forced the heaviest loads on the smallest children. They tossed away badly needed ammunition by firing countless volleys into dry grass to light their cigarettes. They committed unceasing acts of theft. Lugard once lost his temper and personally flogged an officer whom he caught in the act of striking a woman. Yet the women were hardly less callous. Mothers often left their babies on the trail, and Lugard had to post a rear guard to rescue the small derelicts. ("Most were claimed but I long had a nursery establishment myself.") When a protracted period of heat gave way to chill and heavy rains, Lugard needed the combined talents of policeman and lifeguard to bring the horde over an arterial system of swollen rivers. "It was a somewhat novel experience, even to me, to stand from 7 to 10 A.M. up to my middle in the icy-cold water, and hand over babies and children, and give an arm to each woman as they came across." Somehow, all managed to ford the streams without serious mishap, even "our marvellous old cow, which had accompanied us up and down the steepest places since we got her in Usoga, yet never went dry."

Health was a never-ending trial. The frigid weather brought on outbreaks of fever and other ailments that could not be treated properly, since the expedition's supply of medicines had long been exhausted. When smallpox struck the marchers, fantastic good luck and nothing else prevented an epidemic. Even the indestructible Lugard might have welcomed medical attention. A toothache had been hammering in his head for nearly a year. The old wound flared up again. He came down with boils, topped off by a rare attack of malaria. But he recovered from the latter rapidly—"by the violent methods which I usually adopt (with complete success) to subdue fever"—and ignored the former. The weight of his responsibility left him with no other choice. "I felt most keenly that every minute wasted by myself in illness or idleness meant suffering to those I had charge of."

Early in his career, Lugard had disciplined himself into abnormally long working days and only three or four hours' sleep each night. A few weeks before reaching the Sudanese, he had been able to note in his diary that "of late, having got abreast of my work, I have time for half an hour's lounge some days." He found no such luxury now. The small hours of every night were given to his voluminous journal and the writing of official reports which contained lengthy addenda on climate, soil, vegetation, produce, local customs and wild life. Much of this material was concurrently being incorporated into what he called his "road chart," covering almost literally every inch of the route he had traversed since leaving Mengo. A reproduction of the map was later inserted in his book, *The Rise of Our East African Empire*. Its profusion of landmarks is all but blotted out by a fine cross-hatching of descriptive commentary. These remarks are slightly difficult to read, for the dimensions of the map are twenty-five by sixteen inches, with a scale of twelve miles per inch; Lugard's original copy was twenty by thirteen *feet*. He made it with only a prismatic compass and a pocket watch.

*

In due course, the three columns became less difficult to control. During November and December, as he made his way slowly toward Mengo, Lugard threw up four forts along the Toro–Bunyoro border, and installed one or two hundred Sudanese (with their followers) in each. These forts represented frontier security. They were so situated as to serve the double purpose of halting further Banyoro raids on Toro, while simultaneously enabling the Sudanese to attack the rear of any Muslim-Banyoro invasion of Uganda itself. The remaining one hundred Sudanese troops, with Selim Bey, would accompany Lugard and bolster the garrison on Kampala hill. If reserves were needed, Lugard hoped he would be able to draw them from the forts.

Yet, as the size of the caravan dropped to a compact twelve hundred, Lugard's conscience seemed to trouble him more frequently. He had no illusions as to how the Sudanese in the forts would conduct themselves once European control had been removed. "Was it likely they would refrain from licence?" he asked himself rhetorically, recognizing that firm authority was needed to protect the local inhabitants from their protectors. But no such authority was then available and the alternative was

Kabarega. Therefore, the garrisons must stay: "There are some strange dilemmas in Africa, that our critics have no conception of!" It was the price to be paid for the effective occupation of Uganda.

"I felt wellnigh unmanned at
the destruction in twelve hours
of a year's hard work."

On December 25, less than a week's march from Mengo, a runner met the party with top-secret orders for Lugard: he was to evacuate Uganda at once; the Company could no longer afford the expense of holding the country. Lugard was directed to make another treaty with Mwanga, leave a volunteer Resident in Mengo to look after British interests, and then return with his entire force to the coast. This action, the Directors took pains to emphasize, was only temporary; as soon as finances permitted, Uganda would be reoccupied.

Lugard could scarcely believe his eyes on reading the "astounding communication." It meant abandoning Uganda to Mwanga, to the designs of the White Fathers, to the ambitions of the Muslims, to the mercy of Kabarega. Did the Directors believe that they could reassert control at will, if indeed control had ever been established? Did they truly think they could return when it suited their convenience and find everything unchanged? More to the point, did they imagine that Germany would stand aside and not fill the vacuum? "We, as a nation, could surely not dare to claim exclusive rights to the country, if we were unable or unwilling to hold it." As for a voluntary Resident in Mengo, "would you find a volunteer to go and hang himself?" To Lugard personally, the sharpest cut of the evacuation order was that he would be forced to break his word to Kasagama and the people of Toro, leaving their country open to extermination. But from any standpoint, withdrawal would be "a blow to British prestige in Africa which can *never* be recovered."

Lugard found himself with only one choice: he must ignore the orders. He would return to Toro, "found a small British kingdom" there, maintain his control over the Sudanese garrisons and thus "fulfil the pledges given to the Toru people." He hoped to pay for the enterprise with ivory and salt. It was an exercise in integrity that Rider Haggard might well have applauded. But it was also a desperate holding action, riddled with pitfalls, doomed to almost certain failure. Still, Lugard would have kept his word.

Arriving in Mengo on New Year's Day of 1892, Lugard broke the news to Williams. Rumors of the evacuation had somehow started to circulate in the city, and Williams had already told Mwanga that the reports were without foundation. But on learning the truth, he was no less stunned than Lugard, and "exclaimed that it simply *could not be done!* He said he would be ashamed to hold up his head in any society of gentlemen if he were involved in so gross a breach of faith, after his declaration to the king." He also endorsed the plan to re-enter Toro, and placed his small private income at Lugard's disposal to defray expenses. Lugard was deeply moved. "That is the kind of man my colleague, Capt. Williams, R.A., was! It was a *noble* and unselfish act, and I cannot keep silence, even though I transgress, by telling of this matter."

All that remained was to arouse British public opinion to the urgency of holding Uganda itself, and it was agreed that Lugard would "stay and run the coach single-handed while Williams went to England to 'make a buzz,' as he expressed it." This proved unnecessary. On January 7, a caravan arrived from the coast with more mail. Included was a copy of a cable from IBEA headquarters to the Administrator in Mombasa, postponing evacuation for a year. Lugard "handed the telegram to Williams, and we shook hands over it, like a couple of schoolboys."

*

It was, however, no more than a stay of execution, and before the month was out Lugard had reason to wonder whether even a year would be long enough to entrench the British presence. On January 22, a quarrel between a Fransa and an Ingleza was suddenly terminated when the Fransa picked up his rifle and shot the Ingleza through the heart. Mengo exploded. The Fransa challenged the Ingleza to fight, and although the Katikiro was able to restrain his own faction from striking back at once, the long delayed civil war now seemed a certainty.

If fighting were to break out, the strengthened Company force might well be able to intervene with some effect, but Lugard recognized that an open clash would be calamitous. Accordingly, he hastened to the palace to urge that Mwanga immediately arrest and punish the murderer. Mwanga kept him waiting outside the gates until the sun made him giddy, then invited him in and temporized. Lugard's anxiety mounted, for "everything convinced me that for some reason the Wa-Fransa did not desire a peaceful solution." He therefore left the palace and sent a message to Hirth, asking that the missionary exert his influence to curb the Fransa chiefs. Hirth said he was too busy to discuss the matter. Lugard then sent Dualla back to the palace with a letter for Mwanga, reiterating the gravity of the crisis. The letter brought only "insulting messages and threats," leaving Lugard with the conclusion that the Fransa would not be held in check and that neither Mwanga nor the White Fathers wished to halt them. He therefore rescinded his own policy of nonalignment. During his absence, Williams had confiscated a large store of Stokes' contraband arms; Lugard now drew on this supply, issuing one hundred and fifty Sniders and three hundred muzzle-loaders to the outnumbered Ingleza.

On Sunday morning, January 24, it appeared that the Ingleza would need the weapons. The Fransa were gathering in swarms on Mengo hill, waving flags and brandishing their rifles at the Ingleza position near the foot of Kampala hill about half a mile distant. In the fort on the crest of the hill, the Company troops were standing to. Lugard and Williams each manned one of the Maxims. The war drums reverberated. There were some scattered shots. A royal messenger scrambled up to the fort. He carried a last-minute appeal from Mwanga. Lugard's aid to the Ingleza had apparently brought the Kabaka to his senses, and he was now promising that the murderer would be brought to justice. The crisis appeared over.

But then a deafening fusillade crashed out from the Fransa position and the two massed factions hurled themselves at each other. In a few minutes, one flank of the Ingleza force had been turned, and the Fransa were moving on Kampala fort itself. Firing the Maxim hastily, Lugard scored a pair of freak hits on the legs of two Fransa chiefs. (One was his friend the Kimbugwe.) He then traversed to cover an open potato patch that the attackers would have to cross. The Maxim was now jamming at almost every other shot (Williams' gun had broken down with the initial burst), but the few rounds Lugard got off sufficed to hold the Fransa back. The Company bugler then sounded the charge, and "there was no stopping our Sudanese and Zanzibaris ... the enemy did not wait for them." Within minutes, the Company force had plunged down the hill and scattered the Fransa. By nightfall, Mengo was in flames, as the exulting Ingleza, deaf to Lugard's "indignant orders," observed time-honored custom and put their own capital to the torch while the routed Fransa streamed in panicked disorder toward the lake. The war had ended. But nobody had won. For Mwanga too had fled. Wrote Lugard: "I felt wellnigh unmanned at the destruction in twelve hours of a year's hard work." *

---

* Exactly seventy-four years and four months later, on May 24, 1966, the battle of Mengo hill was re-enacted as Uganda Government troops stormed the palace and sent Mwanga's grandson, Kabaka Sir Edward Mutesa II, into exile in England. The coup climaxed a long-standing political vendetta between the Kabaka, then Uganda's President, and the Prime Minister, Dr. Milton Obote, who subsequently became President himself.

"I would try and effect a settlement satisfactory to both parties, but I could not do so without the advice and assistance of the king of Uganda."

Now began a new conflict: a hot and cold running war in which Lugard found himself besieged on all sides. Having recovered swiftly from the shock of their defeat, the Fransa were gathered in the province of Buddu to the west, preparing for a massive counter-invasion. No one could guarantee that they would not succeed this time, if only because they continued to hold a vast numerical superiority over both the Ingleza and the Company force. The Muslims, still fortified by Kabarega's armies, were poised to strike from the north. Lugard saw them as his "main cause of anxiety," for with the throne now unoccupied, their long-awaited opportunity to install Mbogo could have arrived at last. The absence of a unified Christian force might well allow them to disperse enough of their own troops to hold off the Sudanese garrisons in their rear. It seemed only a matter of time before they made their move. In the east, directly astride the line of communications from Mombasa, the land was under the control of a pack of wild men called the Futabangi, the bhang smokers. (Bhang is marijuana.) They gave allegiance to no cause but their own, loved nothing better than a fight, were well armed and dangerously unpredictable. They had become, wrote Lugard, "an element of disorder ... no longer safe to despise." In Mengo itself, the Ingleza were proving uncomfortable allies. Claiming a victory they had not really won, their only wish was to seize all the country's land and offices. "They will do nothing but talk and argue," Lugard fumed in his diary, "and disagree with what I say, like a parcel of old women ... a disgusting, ungrateful, cantankerous lot, who occasionally drive me beyond all patience."

Lugard may never have felt more isolated than he did during this period. He could not even turn to his fellow Europeans among the missionaries, certainly not to the White Fathers. This galled him particularly, since it was known that he was actively seeking to negotiate with the Fransa and win them a fair settlement. But the battle of Mengo hill had been the very upheaval that the Catholic missionaries had long hoped for: the explosion that might yet throw Uganda back into the German sphere. Lugard had been informed that on at least one occasion the White Fathers "openly discussed the probability of the Germans taking the part of the Fransa faction." Hirth of course was the focal point of conspiracy, although to portray him as an ogre is neither accurate nor just. In Miss Perham's words, Hirth "had no sinister designs against the British ...

He had only one object, to extend the sway of his church. The obvious weakness of the Company made it perfectly legitimate for him to expect that it might be withdrawn and Uganda fall to some other power." Yet Lugard for his part could not have been expected to sympathize with that view. Regardless of the Company's feeble hold on Uganda, the fact remained that Lugard's authority, for whatever it may have been worth, was the legally recognized authority. Thus he could only see Hirth as an openly malign influence who, "instead of offering me friendly advice ... showed nothing but a vehement partisanship."

Not much more good will was forthcoming from Lugard's own countrymen of the CMS. At about this time, Lugard wrote of Hirth having described him and Williams as "completely under the influence of the English missionaries." In other circumstances this might have amused him, since "Mr. Ashe had similarly accused us of being 'entirely under the influence of the fascinating Fathers.'" There had been little CMS enthusiasm for Lugard since his policy of equity toward both creeds had made itself felt. At one point, the Anglican missionaries had "accused me of having struck a blow at their party which must lead to annihilation." Two years later, when Ashe published his Chronicles of Uganda, the margins of Lugard's personal copy were heavily annotated with his own angry rebuttals.

*

Lugard's one hope for restoring peace lay, curiously enough, in the self-exiled Mwanga and the possibility of allaying his fears with a view to returning him to the throne. As we have seen, Mwanga occupied a position that was both unique and contradictory. Weak and pusillanimous, he was easily dominated by whatever chiefly faction held a majority; in the hands of the White Fathers he had shown himself to be putty. Unlike any Kabaka before him, he was a paper king, usually disregarded, universally despised. And yet he also remained indispensable, simply because he embodied the heart and soul of Uganda's nationhood, as the symbol of an institution which his disrespectful subjects cherished no less than Britons revered their own royalty. Despite the flurry of coups that had occurred since 1888, the Baganda by tradition were not disposed to oust their monarchs on a whim. Although it could not be said that even Mwanga's favored Fransa held him in anything but contempt, both factions were acutely aware that they must have him back. While he reigned—although hardly ruled—the country had been uneasy enough. But unless he returned there would simply be no country.

Mwanga was, therefore, a prerequisite to Lugard's success in restoring order in Uganda; in this respect, Lugard called him the "queen bee." Without that token representation of stability residing in the office of Kabaka, the British task of effective occupation could not even begin. To be sure, Uganda without Mwanga might possibly have been held by force, with the Sudanese garrisons, if they could be brought in, functioning as an army of occupation. Lugard had not hesitated to install Sudanese troops in Toro despite his awareness that they might well commit widespread atrocities. But the action had been essentially defensive, reflecting only what might be called the emergency aspect of Lugard's views on the management of subject peoples. In point of fact, the use of armed force flew directly in the face of the doctrine that would eventually become synonymous with his name. At about this time, when he wrote that "I would try and effect a settlement satisfactory to both parties, but I could not do so without the advice and assistance of the king of Uganda," he was planting the seeds of the British African policy which came to be known as indirect rule.

Stated simply, indirect rule meant governing a country to the greatest extent possible with and through its already established systems and authorities, rather than bypassing them and imposing a colonial absolutism in which the people themselves had no voice. "An arbitrary and despotic rule, which takes no account of native customs, traditions and prejudices," was in Lugard's opinion "not suited to the successful development of an infant civilisation, nor ... in accordance with the spirit of British colonial rule." Lugard did not invent the system; he had seen it practiced in India and other British possessions in the East. But he did introduce it to Africa, where it became a cornerstone of the British African colonial edifice.

The concept was in fact a principal component of Lugard's broader belief in the exploitation of Africa's resources for the benefit not merely of Europe but of the inhabitants of the continent itself. (This view was expounded at length in Lugard's classic *The Dual Mandate in Tropical Africa*, which can almost be called Britain's African imperialist manifesto.) The soundness of indirect rule as a consistent policy can be questioned with the hindsight of today, for it often proved incompatible with many systems of tribal government. But in the 1890s it could be seen only as constructive and progressive, and ideally suited to a country like Uganda, with its already sophisticated administrative machinery. At the same time, however, the machine required an ignition key. And that key, for the moment at any rate, was Mwanga.

*

Coaxing him back was another matter. On the day of the battle, Mwanga had fled to the island of Bulingugwe on the lake, six miles south of the capital. Lugard had immediately sent envoys to Bulingugwe, urging that Mwanga return and promising honorable restoration to the throne. These efforts might have borne fruit but for Hirth, who offered to go to Bulingugwe himself and personally deliver Lugard's assurances to the Kabaka. Lugard balked. If he trusted anyone less than Mwanga, it was the leader of the White Fathers. Yet finally, with some reluctance, he permitted the missionary to go, for Hirth had seemed quite sincere. "With his hand in mine at parting he protested he would do his utmost to bring back the king." Lugard was not overly surprised, however, when Hirth wrote him to say that he had been unable to make contact with Mwanga. This of course was not true. Hirth had neither the intention nor the wish to see the Kabaka restored except on Fransa terms, which in effect would have meant splitting the country in two. Shortly after Hirth's arrival on Bulingugwe, Mwanga's small force attacked and burned a mainland Ingleza village, leaving Lugard with no option but to order a counter-attack. In the fighting, Mwanga and Hirth escaped together in a canoe, and for the next two months the Kabaka was virtually the Bishop's prisoner in Buddu. To get any message to Mwanga without its first being screened by Hirth bordered on the impossible.

However, Lugard made it a point to keep in close touch with several of the more moderate Fransa chiefs who had private access to Mwanga. One of these leaders was the Sekibobo, "incapable of treachery and deceit, a man with as straightforward and honest a heart as ever beat in a European"; and he in turn had reason to like Lugard. When his five-year-old daughter Malia had been brought to Mengo with the prisoners after the fighting on Bulingugwe, Lugard personally adopted her until she could rejoin her father. He became very fond of Malia. When the Sekibobo finally returned to the capital, he found the two eating break-fast together. Lugard was "almost as sorry to part with her as though she had been my own child; and my bare office with its piles of papers seemed to have lost the one ray of sunshine which brightened it." This sort of human touch could not help but ease considerably the path of peace discussions.

At the same time, Lugard did not hesitate to take a hard line—even to threaten—when the Fransa seemed unwilling to approach Mwanga in the interests of his restoration or when their own demands became unreasonable. On more than one occasion he warned that he might be forced to accept Muslim terms and to install Mbogo if the Fransa remained obdurate. This was a trump card that he dreaded having to deal, but it too was not without its effect in the long-range negotiations. After nearly two months, during which messages, offers, counter-proposals and rumors flew back and forth between Buddu and Mengo, a tentative basis of accommodation began to emerge. Even Hirth's efforts to enlist German support for the Fransa cause (he visited German territory at least once for this purpose) did not prevent a gradual change of heart on Mwanga's part. The end of March finally saw the Kabaka on the road back to his capital.

It was a triumphant moment for Lugard. "I rode out to meet the king, and found him being carried on a man's shoulders ... The mass of people, increasing each moment, came on to Kampala, men clearing the road with vigorous blows ... All available askaris, Sudanese and Somals, were drawn up on each side, and presented arms as we passed through their ranks, while the buglers and drummers executed a prolonged flourish, and the drums, horns and bugles of the Waganda tried to rival their row." Mwanga, however, did not seem elated by the welcome, for he had somehow convinced himself that he would be made a prisoner and perhaps be executed. Lugard found him "almost in a state of collapse," and literally held his hand as the two entered the palace. But when Lugard presented the Kabaka with a gift of cloth, the earlier apprehensions melted almost visibly. "He was immensely pleased, and I think felt really grateful for once in his life."

Lugard too had reason to be grateful. Not only had the last barrier to negotiations with the Fransa been removed, but Mwanga himself, with his sound knowledge of Uganda's tortuous land and patronage laws, would be invaluable in helping to draw up the final terms of agreement. On April 5, the Fransa chiefs consented to an arrangement whereby all offices throughout the country would be shared equally with the Ingleza, and whereby they would receive Buddu as their own province. Thus, while all tensions had by no means subsided, the threat of immediate armed conflict had been removed.

As for Mwanga, he had now become a very chastened monarch, and seemed ready to accept a further tightening of British control. At "an absolutely private interview" on the day after his restoration, he had submitted meekly to a long lecture from Lugard, appearing receptive to the Englishman's repeated assertions that the prestige and power of the kingly office would be enhanced rather than diminished if the Company's authority were given willing endorsement. Mwanga declared that "he was now under the Queen utterly (*kabisa, kabisa*); that in future he only

wished to be one with me, and take my advice absolutely ... His professions were so profuse and so emphatic that it became embarrassing."

Lugard did not feel too embarrassed, however, to exploit Mwanga's
repentance with a new treaty. On April 11, the Kabaka signed it. For the
most part, the terms did little more than reassert Mwanga's acknowledge-
ment of the instrument he had reluctantly signed fifteen months earlier,
although the Company's rights and the powers of the Resident may have
been stated more clearly and firmly. It was particularly stipulated that
"the consent of the Resident shall be obtained, and his counsel taken by
the king, before any war is undertaken, and in all grave and serious affairs
and matters of state, such as the appointment of chiefs to the higher
offices, the assessment of taxes &c." Perhaps the most significant aspect
of the new agreement was Mwanga's almost enthusiastic willingness to
accept it. He went so far as to ask Lugard personally for a Union Jack.
So too did the Kimbugwe, "saying that the Fransa faction were now most
willing and eager to fly it." Lugard complied on the spot. "So at last the
British flag flew over Uganda."

"It is enough that I have restored
him... Closer relations I do not care for."

The treaty worked no magic. The Futabangi continued to threaten in the
east. One group of Fransa repudiated the land settlement and was reported
to be raising an army. The Ingleza felt that Lugard had been too generous
with the Fransa and told him so, in "the most grossly insulting letter I
have ever received." It later developed that this communication had been
inspired by Ashe, for neither the CMS nor the White Fathers had called a
halt to their vendetta against Lugard. "The Resident of Uganda," Lugard
sighed in his diary, "is a mere slave, and penal servitude ... free from
missionaries were a state of comparative bliss—of *otium cum dignitate!*"

The most clear and present danger to stability, however, remained the
unresolved problem of the Baganda Muslims. Through a combination
of good fortune and circumstances they had not invaded Uganda while
the country lay supine. One inhibiting factor had been the total rout of
a Banyoro army, inflicted in March by the Sudanese on the frontier; this
had demonstrated clearly to the Muslims the strength that lay at their
rear. Too, a fairly influential peace element within the Muslim faction
had served as a useful brake on the more bellicose leaders. Nonetheless,
the Muslims' armed presence just across the Bunyoro border remained a
grave threat to whatever order Lugard had managed to restore in Uganda.

And even if this had not been the case, Lugard could recognize that the Muslims were no less Baganda than the Fransa or Ingleza, that they too held a vested right to live in their own country. "These people are as sincere in their belief of the acceptability of their form of worship as we are of ours ... It is not my duty to set myself in God's place, as an arbitrator of which religion is right and which is wrong." For some time, he had been exchanging envoys with Muslim leaders in a partially successful search for a common basis of negotiation. Early in May, however, reports began coming in to Mengo that the Muslims, seeking recognition for Mbogo, were cautiously reentering northern Uganda. If Lugard did not act at once, their thrust might trigger a war. On May 13, he left Mengo with a small force and marched north to meet the Muslims and, hopefully, to treat with them.

*

The mission did not promise a favorable outcome. As the party moved through the swamplands above Mengo, Lugard continued to receive unsettling reports. There were rumors of an impending alliance between the Muslims and dissident Fransa. Further news came in that the Muslim hawk element "meditated a coup," in the belief that "if they succeeded in taking my life, the British power in Uganda would collapse." Even the moderates, although still disposed to negotiate, had become wary, because "now, when their king himself, on whom the whole cohesion of their faction depended, was in question, their suspicious natures prompted doubts lest I should deal falsely by them."

Yet the mounting tension, as both sides approached each other, did not prevent the exchange of envoys. Lugard sent Dualla to Mbogo's camp to arrange and expedite a meeting, while several Muslim chiefs came to the Company command post—"nominally to bring salaams, in reality as spies." Lugard nonetheless made good use of their visit, stressing to them "how essential it was that our negotiations should be quickly concluded, in order that the people might enter into possession of their fields, and begin to cultivate them before the rains ceased, otherwise there would be famine." The chiefs appeared impressed, and Lugard found himself taken with their general demeanor, which "contrasted favourably with the Christians." Yet when Dualla returned on May 22, he did not bring encouraging news. The Muslims, he reported, "rebelled against the idea of accepting Mwanga as their king ... A very strong party ... was against us, and there was great fear lest I should attempt to seize Mbogo ... The number of their arms was probably, Dualla thought, about double ours."

The confrontation took place the following day at the Company camp, where Lugard had a grass canopy built as a courtesy to Mbogo. The Muslim pretender, garbed in flowing gold-embroidered robes, arrived with a disturbingly large retinue. Lugard "affected an easy and unconstrained manner, but Mbogo's nerves were obviously at extreme tension ... The chiefs retained their loaded arms, which is quite contrary to the custom of the country, but each man knew that the occasion was full of menace." In fact no violence occurred. Nor was anything decided. But there was a great deal of talk. Lugard had already given his word to the Muslims that if they returned to Uganda in peace they would receive a province of their own, just as Buddu had gone to the Fransa. The Muslims in turn appeared—perhaps surprisingly—receptive to the offer, but negotiations broke down on the question of Mbogo. Although Mbogo himself waived his claim to the throne, he insisted on living with his co-religionists in their new province. This demand Lugard "absolutely declined, saying that [Mbogo] would still be regarded by them as king, and there could not be two kings in Uganda"; the only outcome of such an arrangement, he said, would be war. Mbogo must therefore live in Kampala under Company protection. Mbogo asked for twenty days to consider the proposal. Lugard gave him twenty-four hours, "for I knew not what lurked behind the request." Mbogo then sought compromise. "Hour after hour he persisted, but I was stubborn as a mule ... As the sun began to set, Mbogo saw it was futile to argue, and ... gave a sort of half understanding that he agreed."

An atmosphere of celebration pervaded Lugard's camp that night. "Everyone seemed greatly delighted, and the general idea was that I had won." Lugard himself felt less sanguine. Mbogo had by no means capitulated, and one could not predict what attitude he might take when the talks were resumed the next day. A further source of uneasiness was a report that Fransa messengers had arrived at the Muslim camp, urging the chiefs "on no account to give up Mbogo, but to delay," while a Fransa detachment hastened to reinforce them. Thus, "May 24th—the Queen's birthday—dawned on an anxious time for me ... Before the day closed I should know whether my efforts meant success, or whether the country was to be plunged in a new war."

His apprehensions seemed confirmed when Mbogo arrived and "began just where he did the day before, as though we had not spoken on the subject!" Lugard countered. "I changed my tone now and spoke vehemently ... My conditions they knew ... If I were weak and yielded to entreaties, I would be false to my duty as an officer of the Queen; and if false in one matter how could they trust my assurances to themselves?"

This amalgam of the hard line, appeal to honor and quasi-sophistry eventually turned the tide in Lugard's favor. After some discussion over particulars, Mbogo accepted the terms. So too did the chiefs. Then "a curious scene took place. Amid great excitement, [the Muslims] implored Dualla and Selim Bey to take their Sultan and be surety for him. They placed one of his hands in each of theirs ... Dualla and Selim agreed, but both, with a very nice feeling, said that though they accepted the trust, all their own trust was in me alone. Therewith they placed both the king's hands in mine."

There still remained the delicate and possibly dangerous formality of reconciliation with Mwanga, but this went off smoothly. When Mbogo arrived at the capital, the Kabaka welcomed him "as though overpowered with delight. They held each other's hands and gave vent to a long-drawn guttural Oh!——oh! then Ah!——ah! in a higher note, then long low whistles as they gazed into each other's faces. This went on for a long time ... Then they fell on each other's necks and embraced, and then again began the former ceremony ... and meanwhile the same performances were going on between chiefs and chieflets and common people on every side, till the crush became so great that it was hard to preserve one's balance."

*

The amicable settlement with the Muslims may have gone further than any of Lugard's accomplishments toward entrenching the Company's authority in Uganda. For at long last, Lugard held the upper hand. It had been solely through his efforts that Uganda was an entity once more, that despite a continued simmering of hostility and suspicion, the country was nonetheless enjoying a peace it had not known for nearly five years. Things now seemed to be coming together almost as rapidly as they had fallen apart. In Lugard's person, the Company had taken a firm place behind the throne; to all intents and purposes it was the throne. Without fuss, Mengo had been divested of its function as capital. Chiefs were bringing their business, as a matter of course, to the fort on Kampala hill, by now a sizable and imposing military-administrative establishment. Here, in a spacious office of timber and dried mud, Lugard ran the country, appointing officials, adjudicating land disputes, presiding over councils— in effect, functioning as an English Kabaka. Mwanga himself gave unspoken ratification to his own figurehead status by making formal visits to the fort. He had become very friendly, and Lugard welcomed his official presence as the regal symbol of indirect rule, although he sought to avoid the personal side of the meetings. "It is enough that I have restored him ... Closer relations I do not care for." Whenever possible, he pleaded pressure of work and sent the monarch off to Williams. If Mwanga took offense at these slights he was at pains not to show it. Shortly before Lugard's departure he wrote to Queen Victoria, declaring: "I and my chiefs ... desire very, very much that the English should arrange this country; should you recall these agents of the Company, my friend, my country is sure to be ruined ... I want you to send this same Captain Lugard back to Uganda ... he is gentle; his judgements are just and true." The Kabaka also wrote the Directors of IBEA, urging that they "not be grieved by the thought that there are no profits in Uganda ... It is not so." Above his signature, he concluded: "I am your friend, who loves you."

*

By the end of May, 1892, only seven months remained before the Company would withdraw from Uganda. On June 9, a caravan led by Captain J. R. L. Macdonald of the Royal Engineers arrived in Mengo. During Lugard's absence, the question of building a railway from the coast to the lake had become a burning issue in England, and Macdonald had just completed the preliminary survey of the line. But the mails he brought for Lugard "contained no reprieve of the sentence of death to all our work, which the evacuation of Uganda at the end of the year would involve." It had been decided by now that Lugard rather than Williams should go to England to take up the public cudgel for retention, and when Macdonald left for the coast on June 16, Lugard joined his party.

The journey was miserable. Both officers rapidly cultivated a hearty loathing for each other, and Macdonald appears to have gone out of his way to inconvenience and even humiliate Lugard. When they parted near Ngongo Bagas, Macdonald promised Lugard an armed escort that never turned up, thus placing Lugard in unnecessary peril on the final lap to Mombasa. For by now, owing to injudicious dealings with various tribes by IBEA officers, the entire country between Kikuyuland and the coast was in an uproar. This further evidence of mismanagement put a cap on Lugard's growing disenchantment with the Company, but his determination to keep Britain in Uganda never flagged.

When he arrived in London on October 3, he found that he would need more than determination.

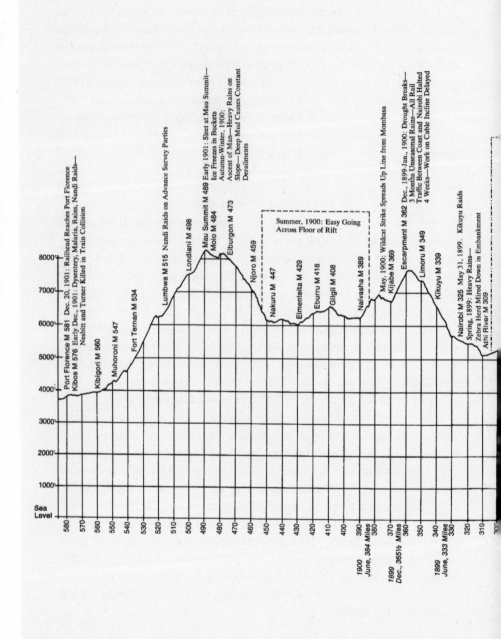

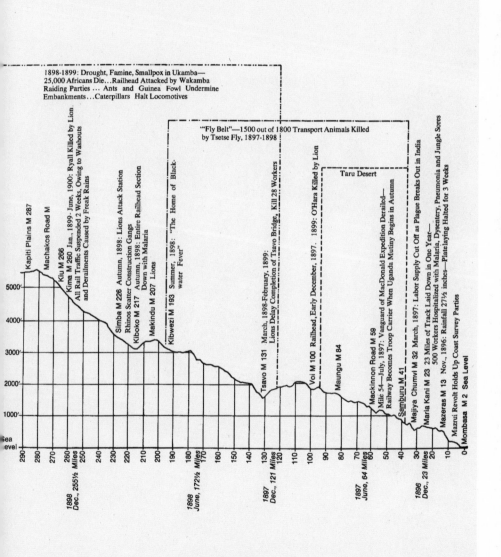

7

"CRIES OF 'OH!'"

*"Captain Lugard has a theory
which, if true, would make Uganda
colonisable. I doubt the theory."*

Had Lugard's journey to Uganda really been necessary? Were British policy makers guided by no more than a dog-in-the-manger resentment of German expansionist ambitions in eastern Africa when the Foreign Office virtually commanded Mackinnon to exercise IBEA's feeble authority over Mwanga's kingdom? Salisbury, as we have seen, had consistently shown a rooted distaste for African acquisitions or responsibilities. His 1890 agreement with the Kaiser, bringing Uganda into the British sphere, had flown directly in the face of what nearly amounted to a phobia toward any British entanglements on so politically explosive and commercially unpromising a Continent. Indeed, Salisbury occupies a somewhat ambiguous position in the history of his country's overseas expansion. In a certain respect he can be seen as having put down the cornerstone of the British Empire in tropical Africa, but at the same time it can almost be argued that he was less than an imperialist. Or rather, to put it more correctly, he is better described as a status quo imperialist than as an acquisitive muscle-flexer of the Joseph Chamberlain school. The principal consideration which governed Salisbury in his negotiation of the crucial treaty with Germany was neither saber-rattling vainglory nor a simplistic notion of colonial economics, but what must be called, essentially, a defensive instinct.

And most significantly, this had nothing whatever to do with Africa. Salisbury's sudden policy volte-face on Uganda was motivated by Britain's paramount imperial concern: the security of India.

At first glance, the idea of Uganda playing a major role in India's defense might seem akin to a suggestion that a vital strategic link exists between, say, Australia and Switzerland. One can readily understand why British statesmen valued Zanzibar, Mombasa and other coastal ports as naval stations guarding the southern sea lanes to the East. But Uganda was another matter. In what conceivable fashion could an isolated sprawl of bush, forest and mountains in the very bowels of the African continent have helped to guarantee the unchallenged supremacy of the Raj?

The answer requires a brief explanation. In 1869, the opening of the Suez Canal had reduced the sea voyage between England and India by seven thousand miles and forty days. To assure the unimpeded passage through the new short cut by her navy and merchant fleet, Britain sought to gain control of the Canal. Purchase of the Khedive's shares in 1875 was a significant stride toward that objective. By 1882, the strategic importance of the Canal had overridden all other political and economic considerations when the British occupied Egypt. In due course, however, a new specter materialized when it was suddenly discovered that the Canal had an Achilles heel some four thousand miles long—the Nile.

In May, 1889, the Premier of Italy, Francesco Crespi, negotiated a treaty with Abyssinia's Emperor Menelik which gave Italy an imperial claim—if not a recognized sphere—along the banks of the Blue Nile and in the eastern Sudan. This move did not go ignored by Britain's Consul in Cairo, Sir Evelyn Baring, the future Lord Cromer. Like Kirk in Zanzibar, Baring was the de facto ruler of Egypt. He had also been Finance Minister in India and possessed radarlike instincts for any political blip that might affect Egypt's sentry duty on the route to the East. In the Italo-Abyssinian agreement he detected a threat to the Canal, and lost no time in explaining the reason for this to Salisbury. "Were a civilised European Power established in the Nile Valley," he wrote the Prime Minister, "... they could so reduce the water-supply as to ruin the country... Whatever Power holds the Upper Nile Valley must, by mere force of its geographical situation, dominate Egypt."

Some years later, Salisbury himself was to remark that "if the world was falling to pieces around his ears, but Egypt was left intact, Lord Cromer would not ask for more." Yet Salisbury also heeded the Consul's caveat, to a degree, in fact, that witnessed a swift and complete reversal in the course of Britain's policies toward east Africa. To be sure, there was no cause for immediate concern over a European irruption in the Sudan; that country was in the hands of the Mahdists, and in 1889 no Power seemed prepared to dislodge them. But the Nile did not flow through the Sudan alone. Since the river had its headwaters in Mwanga's kingdom, Uganda suddenly became invested with incalculable strategic importance, giving rise to an axiom of the imperial geopolitics of the era: whatever Power dominates Uganda masters the Nile; the master of the Nile rules Egypt; the ruler of Egypt holds the Suez Canal, and, indirectly, the key to India.

To whatever extent this reasoning could be considered sound, there was nothing especially new in the notion of turning the Nile on and off like a faucet. In disputes with Egypt, early rulers of Abyssinia had often threatened to stem the flow of the Blue Nile, which has its source in the Ethiopian highlands, and thereby transform Egypt's delta region into a wasteland. But while such a feat would certainly have been beyond the skills and resources of medieval Amhara kings, it was at least feasible to nineteenth-century European technology, and as a phobia alone, its effect on the course of the scramble for Africa was profound. Indeed, the impact of the idea may have caused more than one statesman, particularly in Britain, to overlook at least three built-in flaws more easily recognized through the wide-angle lens of hindsight.

For one thing, if Egypt were to be entirely deprived of its water supply, it would have been necessary not only to dam the Nile in Uganda but to divert the river's two main tributaries, the Blue Nile and the Atbara, which enter the main flow more than a thousand miles north of Lake Victoria. Then, too, the gathering, transportation and assembly of the building materials for a dam on the upper Nile would have been a task of almost crippling magnitude. To be sure, it was not impossible. The river's flow is managed to a certain extent today, not only in Egypt at Aswan, but in Uganda itself, by the Owen Falls dam at Jinja, where the Nile begins its long journey north from the lake. Yet completion of the Jinja project alone—it was opened in 1954—required six years and an expenditure of £22,000,000; its builders also utilized engineering refinements and machinery unknown at the turn of the century. Considering Uganda's relative inaccessibility in the 1890s, whatever European nation might have contemplated interfering with the Nile's course in that place and at that time would have needed, in all probability, a decade and a half under the best of conditions. During those fifteen years, moreover, any number of political realignments in Europe could easily have defeated the dam's original strategic purpose. For this reason alone, one can legitimately ask whether any national treasury or legislative body would have underwritten the astronomical cost of the project.

In any case, time and expenses become little more than a quibble when a more pertinent question is raised: how could diverting the course of the Nile possibly have affected passage through the Suez Canal, which has always floated its ships on the waters of the Mediterranean and Red seas?

Yet these considerations, to the extent that they were heeded at all, did little to dispel mounting fears among many British political leaders that control of the upper Nile by a foreign nation would be an axe poised over the lifeline to India. More than any other factor, it was this concern which brought about Salisbury's change of heart toward east Africa, and his demand, when the Kaiser approached him for support against France and Russia in 1890, that Germany renounce all claims to Uganda.

*

One of the most visible side effects of Salisbury's conversion was his new and receptive frame of mind toward Sir William Mackinnon's dream of a railway to Lake Victoria; obviously, a railway was the ideal—if not the only—means of rapid troop transport should Britain's supremacy on the upper Nile be challenged. Yet Salisbury also knew that recognition of Uganda as a British sphere did not in any way assure construction of the line. In the first place, there was no one to build it. From a commercial standpoint, east Africa was generally seen as a white elephant, and England's business community was not prepared to invest in a transportation system that appeared to guarantee only huge deficits; the fiasco of Mackinnon's "Central Africa Railway" had been lesson enough. Nor could the line be expected to generate much support as an official undertaking. Even as late as 1890, the glories of the African empire had by no means entirely captured the public imagination. Were a Government railway bill introduced in Commons, it would not merely meet with the expected denunciation as a jingo adventure by the "Little England" faction among the Liberals and Radicals, and of course by the Irish Nationalists; in all likelihood, such a measure would also encounter the stiffest opposition from economy-minded backbenchers in Salisbury's own party.

At the same time, however, the railway was not without support in many quarters both inside and outside Government; and there were reasons other than strategic which seemed to argue eloquently for its construction. Anti-slavery carried the strongest emotional appeal, for it was generally believed, by no means erroneously, that the slave trade and a railway could not coexist, that the former was bound to collapse with the intrusion of the latter. A case could be made against that contention on the simple grounds that the slave trade was already doomed by virtue of the high mortality rate in slave caravans alone, and that a railway would be no more than an expensively needless coup de grâce. Yet this was a rather passive stance for a nation committed to the divine mission of eradicating a stain on humanity, and the point was not often pressed.*

Profits were the other major incentive, despite east Africa's bad odor among businessmen, for it was hardly deniable that the country possessed considerable untapped natural resources and that a trade potential definitely existed. While no one could be certain that this latent commerce justified the railway, many Britons actually on the spot were quite convinced that it did—especially since railway freight charges, estimated at about £3 per ton, were a negligible fraction of the £300-per-ton caravan porterage rates. As early as 1877, the explorer Cameron had urged construction of a line to the interior. It would, he said, "at once begin to make a return, for the present ivory trade to Zanzibar should be sufficient to pay working expenses and leave a margin for profit, without making any allowance for the increased trade." Mackay, who naturally advocated a railway as the antidote to "the barbarous and inhuman method of employing porters," also believed that material as well as altruistic benefits would be forthcoming. "I would not give sixpence for all the Company will do in half a century," he wrote, "unless they first connect the lake with the coast by a line ever so rough." Lugard dwelt at length on the same theme, declaring that "to attempt to gauge the capacity of a country before a railway is made is wholly futile, for, as has been truly said, 'A railway of itself *creates* a carrying trade,' even in civilised countries. It will open up [east Africa] as nothing else will ... by introducing trade, industry and development... Yet we hesitate to make a railway to so excellent an objective as the central [African] lakes' waterways."

These arguments did not go unanswered. Joseph Thomson, who spoke of "the hopeless prospect of developing any trade in the interior for several generations to come," naturally regarded rail transport as a

---

* Curiously enough, even the crusaders sometimes found themselves obliged to approach the subject gingerly. Although the 1873 treaty had outlawed the east African slave trade, the institution of slavery remained legal and would not be abolished until 1907. Lugard called this "a gross scandal," charging quite correctly that IBEA and even some mission groups employed slaves as caravan porters. Although for some reason he did not indict British Government officials in east Africa for the same practice (they were also guilty), he did note that a fugitive slave in a British African possession had fewer legal rights than an escaped Indian elephant.

wasteful indulgence. "If a railway was established in Uganda," he wrote, "four or five trains per annum could take all the produce we could rely upon from Uganda: and one train a month, or, say, one per week, would be sufficient for the trade to Uganda... Captain Lugard has a theory which, if true, would make Uganda colonisable. I doubt the theory, though I am prepared to believe that medical science has discoveries in store which will make things possible ... that will rob Africa of half its terrors. In the meantime, however..."

Other expressions of dissent could exasperate, as Stanley discovered in the summer of 1890 when he visited Gladstone at Hawarden with a view to gaining the Liberal leader's endorsement of the railway—more or less in principle—as an anti-slavery weapon rather than an instrument of imperial expansion. "I had brought with me the latest political map of East Africa," he wrote, "and, when the time had come, I spread it out conveniently on the table before the great man..."

> 'Mr. Gladstone,' said I, intending to be brief and to the point, as he was an old man, 'this is Mombasa, the chief port of British East Africa. It is an old city. It is mentioned in the Lusiads, and, no doubt, has been visited by the Phoenicians. It is most remarkable for its twin harbours, in which the whole British Navy might lie safely, and———'
>
> 'Pardon me,' said Mr. Gladstone, 'did you say it was a harbour?'
>
> 'Yes, sir,' said I, 'so large that a thousand vessels could be easily berthed in it.'
>
> 'Oh, who made the harbour?' he asked, bending his imposing glance at me.
>
> 'It is a natural harbour,' I answered.
>
> 'You mean a port, or roadstead?'
>
> 'It is a port, certainly, but it is also a harbour, that, by straightening the bluffs, you———'
>
> 'But pardon me, a harbour is an artificial construction.'
>
> 'Excuse me, sir, a dock is an artificial construction, but a harbour may be both artificial and natural, and———'
>
> 'Well, I never heard the word applied in that sense.' And he continued, citing Malta, Alexandria, and so on.
>
> This discussion occupied so much time that, fearing I should lose my opportunity of speaking about the slave-trade, I seized the first pause, and skipping about the region between Mombasa and Uganda, I landed him on the shores of the Nyanza, and begged him to look at the spacious inland sea, surrounded by populous countries, and I traced the circling lands. When I came to Ruwenzori, his eye caught a glimpse of two isolated peaks.

'Excuse me one minute,' said he; 'what are those two mountains called?'
'Those, sir,' I answered, 'are the Gordon Bennett and the Mackinnon peaks.'
'Who called them by those absurd names?' he asked, with the corrugation of a frown on his brow.
'I called them, sir.'
'By what right?' he asked.
'By the right of first discovery, and those two gentlemen were the patrons of the expedition.'
'How can you say that, when Herodotus spoke of them twenty-six-hundred years ago, and called them Crophi and Mophi? It is intolerable that classic names like those should be replaced by modern names, and———'
'I humbly beg your pardon, Mr. Gladstone, but Crophi and Mophi, if they ever existed at all, were situated over a thousand miles to the northward. Herodotus simply wrote from hearsay, and———'
'Oh, I can't stand that.'
'Well, Mr. Gladstone,' said I, 'will you assist me in this project of a railway to Uganda, for the suppression of the slave-trade, if I can arrange that Crophi and Mophi shall be substituted in place of Gordon Bennett and Mackinnon?'
'Oh, that will not do; that is flat bribery and corruption'; and, smiling, he rose to his feet, buttoning his coat lest virtue might yield to the temptation.
'Alas!' I said to myself, 'when England is ruled by old men and children! My slave-trade discourse must be deferred, I see.'"

Claims and rebuttals such as the above, however, amounted to little more than preliminary sparring. And the main event, public debate, was inevitable; for by virtue of Britain's east African commitments, questions that touched on any form of transportation in that region were a matter of growing national interest. In particular, the possibilities offered by a railway could not be ignored. Unlike the specter of the Nile dam that haunted the dreams of India's guardians, railways in tropical Africa had become a reality by the early 1890s, and they could be seen to work. The French had laid down seventy-five miles of track between the villages of Kayes and Bafulabe in the western Sudan. Italian engineers were surveying the right of way over a jagged mountainous wrinkle from Massawa on the Red Sea to Asmara in Eritrea. Belgium had launched construction of a railway joining the Atlantic port of Matadi and the navigable reaches of the lower Congo river. Portugal was operating a line in Angola and building another in Mozambique. Germany was shortly to begin work on a railway from Tanga to the interior of her east African territory. Only Britain seemed to be lagging, and her "forward party" element chafed impatiently. When Lugard wrote that England's hesitancy in building a railway to Uganda meant "allowing ourselves to be outstripped in the race for commercial expansion," he was appealing to what may have been the most powerful motivation behind the growth of the British Empire.

*

It was against this background that Mackinnon came forward with a proposal for Salisbury. His opportunity arose from a development which had been of the Prime Minister's own making. In 1888, Salisbury had instructed the British Ambassador in Brussels to suggest that King Leopold consider calling a conference of Powers to discuss and devise systems of concerted multi-national effort against the slave trade. The upshot was the Brussels Convention, a gathering of seventeen nations (including the United States) which sat from November, 1889, to July, 1890, and formulated a General Act embodying more than half a dozen major recommendations. Although lofty in intent, these measures could also be seen as slightly excessive, since they were directed at what was to all intents and purposes a dying institution; yet the Brussels Act won the enthusiastic endorsement of all gladiators in the anti-slavery arena. And few applauded louder than Mackinnon, whose eye fell at once on two clauses which he recognized as advancing the fortunes of IBEA— identical, in his mind, to Britain's own imperial interests.

The first was an article authorizing the signatory Powers to delegate responsibilities under the General Act to chartered companies. From a certain viewpoint, this could be seen as amounting almost to a directive that IBEA receive formal recognition as an arm of British policy rather than a pliant instrument of the Foreign Office. Even more significant was the clause which stipulated "the construction of roads, and in particular of railways ... in view of substituting economical and rapid means of transport for the present means of carriage by men." Here, just possibly, was the opening wedge to the fulfillment of Mackinnon's most ardent hope. Since Britain had in fact initiated the Brussels Convention and accepted its recommendations warmly, Mackinnon at last found himself in a position to make a strong bid, if not an outright demand, for the long-withheld Government support of his own quasi-official undertaking in east Africa.

Accordingly, on December 17, 1890, he took his case directly to

Salisbury in a long letter which utilized the Brussels Act almost as a cudgel to thwack Government into assisting the IBEA endeavor. The thrust of the letter was the railway, and Mackinnon came to the point when he stated plainly that Government could no longer evade its obligation to assist in carrying a line to the lake. What he sought, specifically, was not a grant-in-aid or a loan; he did not even ask that the Company be given responsibility for building the railway. He merely urged that the Treasury guarantee "a moderate rate of interest" on the capital needed for construction. "With such support," Mackinnon concluded, "the Company believe slave-trading would soon disappear, and they would have no difficulty in finding as much additional capital as may be necessary for ... the development of an enterprise of national importance, largely advantageous to Imperial interests."

Mackinnon's self-assured tone came in contrast to the despondency of a letter he had written Salisbury the previous April. "I feel so disheartened by the apparent lukewarmness of the support we receive from H.M. Government," he said, "... that I feel great difficulty as to our plans for the future." Salisbury had not even consented to see Mackinnon at that time, but now, his preoccupation with Uganda mounting steadily, he could look at the Company and its goals in a new perspective. The proposed railway in particular would furnish the protection he had come to regard as so essential to British mastery on the upper Nile. No less significantly, he could recognize that official assistance to the Company might just be acceptable to Parliament where a proposal for a Government-built line would in all probability be repudiated out of hand. Hardly had he digested the contents of Mackinnon's letter than he took pen in hand and wrote one of his own to the Treasury, warmly endorsing the Company's anti-slavery proposal. On February 12, 1891, Mackinnon was informed that the Treasury would guarantee the interest on a paid-up capital of £1,250,000—the estimated cost of building a meter-gauge railway from Mombasa to the lake.

This gesture of Government confidence may have enabled the Company to keep its head above water. Certainly morale soared when the news was made known, and the Directors hastened to consult three railway engineers regarding the accuracy of the Treasury estimate. All agreed that the sum was too low by at least half a million pounds; a reliable figure could not be arrived at, they said, without a survey of the proposed right of way. This neither surprised nor distressed the Directors. Obviously, a survey was called for under any circumstances, and with Government backing it could be carried out all the more expeditiously. And surely the Treasury would not cavil if its estimate fell short;

the interest-guarantee figure could doubtless be renegotiated. Salisbury had all but pledged himself to the line.

On May 20, however, during the course of a speech at Glasgow, Salisbury planted a bomb. It was all but undetectable behind a smokescreen of praise for the Company and its Chairman, "whose enterprise and philanthropic determination deserve to be mentioned with honour in any audience, especially a Scottish audience." Then he said: "Sir William is of the opinion that he cannot construct this railway without Government help, and I always speak of the Treasury with awe... Whether the Treasury will be able, consistently with the sound principles of finance which are always upheld, to give Sir William Mackinnon the assistance which he requires, or whether it must be deferred to a distant date, I do not know."

Any apprehensions the Company may have felt over Salisbury's unexpected, and seemingly gratuitous, qualifier were not unfounded. For the Treasury, after its initial smile of approval on the interest-guarantee proposal, had taken a more dispassionate look at the project and come to entertain second thoughts. These arose not only from heightened awareness that anything to do with a railway in east Africa would meet stiff resistance in Commons on straight anti-imperialist lines; besides that, there was disturbing vagueness about the entire scheme. For these reasons, Salisbury himself produced a considerably watered-down request. Instead of seeking Parliamentary authorization of the interest guarantee, his Ministry would ask only for approval of the funds for a preliminary survey. Although Mackinnon had no reason to feel elated by this sudden reversal, he no doubt appreciated the wisdom of approaching Parliament with caution. But he could not have expected the Government's next move. George Goschen, the Chancellor of the Exchequer, never ecstatic over the prospect of shoring up an insolvent business enterprise with public funds, now urged that the cost—estimated at £20,000—of the proposed survey be shared by IBEA. This drew a sharp cry of "foul" from the Directors, but they were not in a position to do more than protest, and acquiesced reluctantly, taking whatever comfort they could from the knowledge that Salisbury's Cabinet, notwithstanding its reservations, continued to support the railway.

It proved cold comfort. In mid-July of 1891, when Government's intentions regarding the survey recommendation were made known, the Liberal Opposition moved immediately to block the vote on the grounds that it was "in the highest degree contentious." This show of surprisingly stiff resistance put the cap on Salisbury's doubts of his ability to carry the issue. On July 20, the Treasury "proposed" to the Directors that they underwrite the entire cost of the survey, contingent on a Government promise to reintroduce the vote before the end of the fiscal year, and subsequently to reimburse the Company. IBEA now had its back to the wall. There was no question that Government would honor its pledge, but repayment, when it came, would be too little and too late. Three-fifths of the Company's original subscribed capital had already been devoured by east Africa. Annual expenditures were approaching £100,000, against yearly earnings of barely one-third that figure. It seemed only a matter of time before Mackinnon's venture would founder.

Yet the Directors, fully aware that they stood on a sinking ship, remained aboard, although they began dismasting the hulk to keep it afloat as long as possible. To finance the survey expedition, they voted to perform an amputation on administrative expenditures, paring annual outlays to £40,000. This in turn left them with no alternative but to pull in the boundaries of their east African holdings; henceforth, the Company's effective occupation in the British sphere would extend only as far as Kikuyuland. On August 10, orders went out to Lugard to withdraw from Uganda. Three months later, a 389-man survey party led by Captain J. R. L. Macdonald arrived in Mombasa and prepared to depart for the interior.

Sir Reginald Coupland has written of the scramble for Africa that "it was a disorderly business and it defies orderly description." This remark is no less applicable to IBEA's paradoxical situation during the summer of 1891. The Company had gone into Uganda—and nearly into bankruptcy—to defend British imperial interests, while the Government whose claims it was upholding had steadfastly withheld its own assistance. Thanks to this absence of support, the Directors had now found themselves compelled to withdraw, while simultaneously financing the survey for a railway which was intended, in the unlikely event of its authorization by Parliament, to protect the country they were abandoning. And even if construction were to proceed somehow, there was every possibility that when the line finally reached the Uganda border, that region would no longer be in British hands. Small wonder that Mackinnon was unable to refrain from a courteously sarcastic dig when he wrote Salisbury of the Directors' decision to evacuate Uganda. "It must not be forgotten," he reminded the Prime Minister, "that the Company had its rapid extension forced on it by the active efforts of its German neighbours, who apparently aimed at acquiring five-sixths of the territories now happily, through Your Lordship's diplomatic action, recognised as the British 'sphere of influence.'"

News of the evacuation was not received enthusiastically by the press, particularly *The Times*, which cried out that the skies were falling. "Withdrawal would be nothing short of a national calamity," warned a lead editorial on September 28. "Whether we desire it or not, the British East Africa Company, working under a Royal Charter, must be identified for all practical purposes with national policy. Its agents are, in the eyes of the natives, the agents of England, and their failure or retreat would be construed throughout Africa as the defeat of British policy." These alarums and excursions were followed up six days later in *The Times*' letters column, when the missionary Horace Waller, one of Britain's busiest champions of philanthropic expansionism, indicted Government for having betrayed Lugard. Describing how Lugard had established a pacifying influence in Uganda through "the individual force of his character and presence," Waller went on to pose the rhetorical question: "What will his surprise be when—just as Gordon was told to return from Khartoum and leave the people to their fate—he in turn is bidden to forsake the people whom he has made his own?" It was not the last time that the Sudan débâcle would be invoked as the Uganda controversy grew.

While it can hardly be said that these vigorous but sporadic outcries brought England to a boil of indignation, the announcement of withdrawal did take fire with the one segment of the public that proved able to keep the tottering Company on its feet a little longer. This was the church community, particularly CMS, which had reason to be concerned for the safety of its workers should British protection be removed. It is almost possible, in fact, that after its ordeal with Mwanga, CMS was even more distressed over IBEA's impending withdrawal than was the Company itself. Not long after the Directors' decision, Bishop Alfred Tucker, a prominent CMS figure who had served in Uganda and was about to return, met Mackinnon aboard the latter's yacht and responded favorably to an appeal for missionary aid. Here indeed was a reversal of roles. With £30,000, said Sir William, the Company could hold on in Uganda for at least twelve more months; if Tucker could raise £15,000 from CMS sympathizers, Mackinnon promised to subscribe £10,000 personally and go to friends for the balance. "This," wrote Tucker, "was our first gleam of hope. Time, we felt, was everything."

The gleam soon became a sunburst. On October 30, 1891, the Bishop addressed a large CMS meeting at Exeter Hall and outlined Mackinnon's proposal. The impact of his speech was reinforced by the news, just arrived, of Lugard's march to the west and his defeat of Kabarega's armies in Toro. But there was little need for dramatics; CMS clearly understood the issues at stake. Wallets and checkbooks were immediately opened;

some members of the audience contributed watches and jewelry. Within half an hour, Tucker was able to count £8,000. Several days later, the subscription total reached the required £15,000, and Mackinnon made good his own pledge—although, as Margery Perham has observed, he "well knew that, in a commercial sense, he was throwing good money after bad." On November 11, the Directors wrote the telegram that was to see Lugard and Williams exultantly shaking hands in Mengo.

"Men like Livingstone did not bring conquering armies and Hotchkiss and Nordenfeldt guns with them."

On March 3, 1892, the Government, as promised, reintroduced the survey vote with a request for a grant-in-aid of £20,000, and for the first time we see the question not only of the railway but of Uganda itself being aired in Parliament. The debate was to blossom into a marathon dialogue that ran for nearly three years, during which time one could hear the fate of an empire being decided in a surging torrent of Victorian eloquence and invective. Although the railway loomed large in the controversy—often taking center stage—it was not the main issue at stake. What really aroused Members' passions on both sides of the House of Commons was the future of Uganda. It must be remembered that despite Uganda's status as a British sphere of influence, the country was not officially under British rule. Its administration—to the extent that an administration could be said to exist—was in the hands of a private business concern, and although that might seem a fine distinction, it was in fact the crux of the dispute. If IBEA evacuated Uganda, Britain had two options open to her. She could allow the country to lie fallow politically and thereby forfeit her claim to jurisdiction, or she could immediately fill the vacuum with an official machinery of government. The latter would bring Uganda irrevocably into the family of the Queen's dominions beyond the seas, and it was that formal step of incorporation that the so-called "Little England" element in Parliament sought to thwart.

*

In the dissent voiced by British anti-imperialists of the late Victorian era, one detects a certain similarity to the position of present-day Americans who take issue with their own country's involvement in southeast Asia. It would be misleading to labor the parallel, but it can be said to exist at least in the sense that the Little Englanders resisted a policy which they believed to be legally indefensible and morally odious. There is also, however, one all-important difference between the hands-off-Africa and get-out-of-Indochina movements. This is simply that the latter appears to command tremendous and ever-growing popular support, while the former can be said to have been doomed from the very start. It should be borne in mind that as the 1890s drew to a close, most Britons could look back on the previous century as an era of almost unbroken peace during which they themselves had risen to a level of well-being that was surpassed nowhere on earth. The country had yet to endure the great European catastrophe that was to kill off the flower of England's manhood and begin to cast doubts on the infallibility of Western culture as a civilizing force. During the Uganda controversy, the majority of British voters, once they became aware of the issues, felt pride rather than shame in witnessing the expansion across Africa of what they profoundly believed was the best way of life to which any human being might aspire. Far from being despotic or draconian, Britain's presence in the aboriginal regions of the planet was seen as an influence which could only bring justice, order and hope to peoples who had crept for untold centuries through dark labyrinths of ignorance, superstition, disease and mindless hate. Certainly the Empire would bring material wealth to England as well, nor did many Britons find reason to apologize for this in an age when profits from the sweat of one's brow or brain were almost universally considered the fruit of virtue. But even though the promise of riches may in fact have been the drive shaft of imperial growth, this in no way detracted from the sincerity of the Englishman's belief in the lightness of his country's civilizing mission.

Against the emotional appeal of so lofty a concept, the Little England wing in Parliament never really stood a chance, although prior to the mid-1880s it had held the upper hand. For reasons economical and to some extent ideological, overseas expansion had fallen out of favor during some five decades of Victoria's reign. All that had changed, however, with almost startling swiftness, as European rivalries, heightened by the new spirit of nationalism, restored the imperial idea to respectability. Those who dissented suddenly found themselves in a hopeless rearguard action. Yet in England, a small band of dedicated men, numbering among them some of the nation's most respected and influential politicians, proved an astonishingly formidable opposition to the expansionists. Seasoned in the cut and thrust of parliamentary infighting, masters of the delaying tactic, they often carried their lost cause almost to within sight of victory, and the prolonged debate which they forced over the question of Uganda can be seen as the last but very spirited gap of nineteenth-century British anti-imperialism.

*

To this opposition, it was quite clear that the railway was the expansionists' foot in the door. If a line were built to Uganda, either by Government or private enterprise, there could no longer be any question of withholding the imposition of permanent British rule in that country. Ordinarily, the request for fulfillment of Salisbury's pledge to IBEA would have been no more than a formality, but the survey was obviously sewn to the coattails of a very political railway, and the question therefore became the subject of a long-winded debate which did not play itself out until nearly two days had gone by.

The tone of the Administration argument was slightly cautious, with little mention made of the railway as reinforcing Uganda's strategic position on the upper Nile. Stress was placed instead on Britain's ostensible obligations under the Brussels Act and the value of the railway as a visible expression of British humanitarianism. Introducing the motion, the Under-Secretary of State for Foreign Affairs, James Lowther, told the House that the survey was being conducted "in continuation and amplification of the policy which for many years has actuated Her Majesty's Governments and the country in dealing with the suppression of the Slave Trade in East and West Africa ... By means of a railway we should find ourselves able to substitute the locomotive in place of the caravan and the kidnapper." Without a British presence in Uganda, Lowther added, "it requires no great amount of prophecy to see that the Mahommedans and those who are on the outskirts of this Christian community ... will at once attack it. The missionaries who are now settled in Uganda will probably be the first to be sacrificed ... By adopting [the railway], we shall show that our vaunted philanthropy is not a sham, and that our professions of humanitarianism are not the merest hypocrisy."

This was bland stuff by comparison to the Opposition's scattergun counterattack. The nub of its argument was voiced by the future Lord Bryce. "A survey," he said, "involves a guarantee, a guarantee necessarily involves defence, defence involves annexation; and so what we are substantially asked to do is to take the first step towards annexation. I do not believe there is any escape from that fatal descent." A broader aspect of the same theme was expounded on with grim energy by Sir William Harcourt, a former professor of international law, who depicted British actions in Uganda as bordering on felony. "A sphere of influence," he declared, "confers no right, no authority over the people... Every act of force you commit against a native within a sphere of influence is an unlawful assault; every acre of land you take is a robbery; every native you kill is a murder." Nor did Harcourt confine himself to the juridical aspects of the question, expressing special contempt for the claim that the railway would be a weapon against the slavers. "You talk of it," he said, "as if you were going to run them off the line like a rival omnibus. You will do nothing of the kind. If you did, why, they would pull up a quarter of a mile of your railway every week, simply because you are interfering with a trade in which they have an enormous interest." Besides, he added, with more accuracy than consistency, the existence of slavery in Uganda was "extremely doubtful." Harcourt was equally unimpressed with Administration appeals on behalf of Uganda's missionaries, for whom he had little use, although he paid tribute to earlier evangelists in Africa, noting that "men like Livingstone did not bring conquering armies and Hotchkiss and Nordenfeldt guns with them."

It was also argued forcibly that construction of the railway would meet with violent resistance from local inhabitants who resented the British intrusion. An Edinburgh Member quoted from a letter written by an engineer who had recommended erecting the stations as "fortresses" and signal boxes "on the model of the Martello towers with guns raking the railway up and down." One of the more spirited attacks was delivered by Henry Labouchere, the peppery Radical bellwether who will be heard from again. Describing the Government case as "vague, general clap-trap" and dismissing the Brussels Act as "a pious opinion," he backed Harcourt's repudiation of Britain's east African claims with the assertion that "this land belongs to [the] tribes. They may be bloodthirsty, they may be savages, or what you like; but you have no right to go into the country and drive off the inhabitants because you are pleased to call them bloodthirsty." Sophistry and black humor were combined as Labouchere protested against the expenditure of public funds on Uganda's religious conflicts "to prevent these very remarkable Christians from cutting each other's throats"; after all, he observed, "the blood of the saints is the seed of the church."

Although they gave as much as they got, the Little Englanders needed more, and their biggest gun, Gladstone, seemed strangely spiked. Gladstone was in something of a dilemma; the survey might indeed be serving jingo interests, but the Liberal leader, as a fiery apostle of moral causes, could hardly offer open resistance to so lofty an aim as the eradication of slavery. He therefore contented himself with a thundering oration which in fact said little and reached its peak on a note of ringing ambiguity:

"I wish to state, in the most expressive terms that I can command, that I am determined for one to exempt myself ... from every jot and tittle of this undertaking; and yet, at the same time, I do not go so far as to deliver a final judgement." That pronouncement at least set the House to laughter. After the vote carried by 211 to 113, it was learned that Gladstone had abstained.

*

At long last, Government seemed in a position to act. It did not. The railway had become a red flag to the Opposition bull, and Salisbury dared not bring the issue to a head while he stood in danger of defeat over Irish Home Rule, the major question of the day. It was Home Rule, in fact, which proved his nemesis. The general elections in July of 1892 gave Parliament a pro-Irish majority of forty, which managed to gain a vote of "no confidence" in the Salisbury Administration, thus returning Gladstone to office. The anti-imperialist Opposition was now the Government, and with IBEA already committed to the evacuation of Uganda at the end of the year, Britain's grip on the upper Nile appeared feeble if not broken.

*

Indeed, Uganda might well have passed by default into German or French hands but for the new Foreign Secretary, Lord Rosebery. In many respects, this man would have been a welcome adornment to any Victorian Cabinet. His erudition, personal charm, patrician background, marriage to a Rothschild and stable of Derby winners made him something of a dream prince in the eyes of the public. But as Foreign Secretary in a Ministry of Little Englanders he was a fish out of water. For Rosebery, who on occasion could be heard humming "Rule, Britannia" while at work, was known to have strong imperialist leanings. These views arose to a certain extent from a supra-political belief in continuity of foreign policy, but Rosebery also shared Rhodes' horizonless visions of empire, and held firmly to the conviction that Britain must expand overseas to "peg out claims for posterity." (Interestingly, however, Rosebery was the first British statesman to speak of the Empire as a "commonwealth of nations.") He advocated imperial federation, opposed the evacuation of Egypt, and, of most significance in 1892, was an outspoken champion of a British Uganda for strategic reasons largely identical to those set forth by Salisbury. Thus his appointment to head the Foreign Office at so crucial a moment of Britain's imperial destiny seems, in retrospect, a puzzling move on Gladstone's part, although the favor Rosebery enjoyed with the Queen is believed to have weighed heavily in the Prime Minister's decision. (Some years later, Gladstone placed his selection of Rosebery in what he called a "catalogue of errors.") Rosebery himself, curiously enough, was not eager to take the post. He was then suffering from insomnia and only yielded to Gladstone's persuasion as a matter of party loyalty. And it was only natural, of course, that the Prime Minister should expect the same loyalty from his Foreign Secretary. Once in office, however, Rosebery lost no time in appearing to betray his leader on the east African question.

Late in August, Rosebery instructed Sir Percy Anderson of the African department to write a memorandum for the Cabinet summarizing conditions in Uganda. It was the Foreign Secretary's intention to present an unbiased appraisal from which an acceptable policy might be formulated, but personal beliefs soon overcame objectivity and the revisions which Rosebery made in Anderson's draft resulted in a forcibly partisan appeal for Uganda's retention. Nor did Rosebery stop at Uganda. Applauding Lugard's annexations of Ankole and Toro, he urged that Britain move even farther north to forestall threatened French and Belgian thrusts toward the upper Nile from their possessions in western and equatorial Africa. Lugard himself could not have asked for more. On September 13, the memorandum was submitted to the Cabinet, and a heated session ensued. Gladstone expressed himself as "horrified and astonished," and said he was unable to discuss the matter with Rosebery without becoming "very excited." Harcourt, now Chancellor of the Exchequer, was even more exercised. The memorandum, he fumed, was written "in the highest jingo tune"; it sought nothing less than a British invasion and reconquest of the Sudan, and he would "die a thousand deaths rather than have anything to do with it." Other Ministers were no less righteously indignant. It was almost as if Rosebery had opened a box of scorpions.

But the Foreign Secretary stood fast, and reinforced his position with a cable from the new British Consul in Zanzibar, Sir Gerald Portal, who had just met Lugard on the latter's return to the coast from Uganda. A talk with Lugard had convinced Portal that the evacuation of Uganda would not only shatter British prestige in Mengo but "must *inevitably* result in a massacre of Christians such as the history of this century cannot show." Considering Lugard's known views, the prediction may have been extravagant. Neither surprisingly nor altogether incorrectly, Harcourt saw the cable as merely another manifestation of jingo panic.

"Every sort of bogey is invoked," he told Gladstone, while invoking a bogey of his own, "to involve us in this horrible quagmire, which will be as bad as Khartoum." Even more than Gladstone, the heavily jowled, often harshly outspoken Harcourt can be seen at this time as setting the tone of Cabinet rage against Rosebery. Nor did any other Minister, it seemed, have a kind word for the renegade Foreign Secretary.

Actually, Rosebery's position might have been much more precarious as he tilted with the Cabinet. Among rank and file Liberals he was able to command a fair amount of support; Salisbury's Nile hypothesis was not entirely without appeal to the party which had occupied Egypt in the first place. It is also probable that press and public opinion stood behind the Foreign Secretary. While Britain's man in the street in the summer of 1892 could hardly have been described as sitting up nights over the fate of Uganda, he seemed, to the extent that his sentiments could be gauged, to favor retention. And of course, there was the Queen. Rosebery had taken care to bring Portal's cable to her attention, and her response was no less gratifying than it was expected. "The Queen," she wrote the Foreign Secretary, "could never support [evacuation] or anything else which lowers the dignity and power of her Empire, and she trusts to Lord Rosebery *especially* to uphold this." In the same message, she showed herself as adept as Harcourt in exploiting the specter of Khartoum: "The fate of Gordon is not, and will not be, forgotten... The difficulties are great, doubtless, in Uganda, but the dangers of abandoning it are greater."

On balance, however, the deck seemed stacked against Rosebery. Popular clamor and regal pronouncements were frail weapons against Gladstone; he was, after all, the man who had defied both the public and the Queen during the Gordon crisis. Thus the Foreign Secretary's strategy at this time could only be a holding action: deferral of an immediate Cabinet decision—at least until Lugard returned to England, so that Ministers might have the views of the man who was beginning to emerge as a central figure in the controversy. Gladstone agreed, but also revealed his awareness of what the Foreign Secretary was up to: "I admit Lugard to be a witness. I hardly attach much value to his authority. But *if you do* ... I am not certain that you mean things to remain as they are in the interval." Harcourt voiced even greater misgivings. "I can quite see," he minuted to Rosebery, "that it is the game of Lugard and Co. to play on our fears in order to force their policy upon us or induce us to give them a subsidy... There is one thing quite clear to me, that in nothing we decide or do shall we attribute any weight to Lugard's actions or opinions, or entrust him with any authority." Harcourt also stepped up the pace of his own drive for swift evacuation. Gladstone once described

Harcourt as the most difficult of the five-dozen-odd Cabinet colleagues with whom he had to work in his political career, but in the autumn of 1892 it was the overbearing Chancellor of the Exchequer who had the Prime Minister's ear. And even Gladstone's reluctant consent to wait for Lugard provided Rosebery with no comfort. Quite obviously, the Prime Minister had made up his mind; Lugard could not be expected to change it. Rosebery may have forestalled instant Cabinet action on Uganda, but he had not succeeded in setting back the Company's execution date.

One bolt remained in Rosebery's quiver. If Gladstone had been "horrified and astonished" by the Foreign Secretary's September 13 memorandum, his feelings can be imagined when he learned late in the month that Rosebery was prepared to resign unless the Cabinet yielded on Uganda. It was, said Gladstone, "the *first* time during a Cabinet experience of 22 or 23 years that I have known the Foreign Minister and the Prime Minister to go before a Cabinet on a present question with diverging views." This may have been true as far as foreign secretaries were concerned, but a showdown with another Cabinet colleague—and its possible consequences—was far from unfamiliar to Gladstone. In 1884, he had given way on the demand that an expedition be sent to relieve Gordon only after his Secretary of State for War, Lord Hartington, had threatened to quit his office. Now, with a majority of less than four dozen in the Commons, the resignation of the immensely popular Rosebery might well bring down the Government. Gladstone may have understated his emotions when he told Harcourt on September 28 that "the last days have been horrible." Rosebery himself voiced "the most heartfelt and bitter regret" at being compelled to force the issue, but he refused to budge from his position. Gladstone was thus left with no choice but to capitulate. On September 30, it was announced that Government would subsidize IBEA operations in Uganda until March 31, 1893.

This three-month reprieve may have seemed only a small victory, but, since Rosebery was playing for time, he had reason to hope. Even so, the extremity of the measures he had taken to win another breath of life for the Company did nothing to soften the Cabinet's stand against retention; if anything, the Ministers' resistance had stiffened. Britain's imperial prospects in east Africa seemed all but blotted out on October 3, when Lugard arrived in London and threw himself into the struggle to hold Uganda.

*"As a rather one-horse Company has been
able to administer I suppose the
Empire will be equal to it."*

What Lugard faced was in fact a double-barreled gun, for when
he entered the lists for the retention of Uganda he also found himself compelled to clear his own name. Not long after the battle of
Mengo hill, Hirth and the White Fathers had sent lengthy accounts
of misdeeds by Lugard to officials of their church and the French
Government. His stewardship in Uganda, they charged, was a
record of calculated religious bigotry, persecution and outright
barbarity. Hirth described the battle itself as worse than the St. Bartholomew's Day massacre. "Missions wiped out by Protestants,"
cried a message to the dying Cardinal Lavigerie. "Six Fathers prisoners ... Catholics killed, dispersed, enslaved." "What a disgrace for
France," wrote another priest, "to see her sons kept prisoners in an
English fort and reviled like low criminals!" Lugard, said the White
Fathers, was responsible for all this. He had deliberately fomented
the civil war by arming and supporting the Ingleza. During the actual
hostilities he had not only refused to protect the French missionaries, but encouraged looting, destruction of mission property and
the murder of Catholic converts. In short, Lugard was held directly
accountable for widespread atrocity and for massacre bordering
on genocide.

The reverberation from the Quai d'Orsay was mighty. On April 8,
1892, William Henry Waddington, the English-born French Ambassador
in London, was instructed by his Foreign Minister, Ribot, to lodge the
most vigorous protest with the Salisbury Government. By the end of the
month, the French press had whipped the nation into a hopping Gallic
rage. In May, during a heated session of the Chamber of Deputies, one
member declaimed that "the English should know that we will never
accept this violation of the rights of man and that we shall know as well as
they how to protect the lives and the properties of our compatriots." This
ultimatum was backed up at once by Ribot, who told the Chamber that
Britain, ultimately responsible for the acts of its chartered companies, must
pay France an indemnity for the wanton destruction of mission property
and the outrages perpetrated by Lugard on citizens of the Republic. Not
long afterwards, Waddington's chargé d'affaires, Baron d'Estournelles,
wrote what Ribot called "an interesting analysis" in which it was strongly
suggested that Lugard had been driven to his bestialities by paranoia.
It was almost as if France were rehearsing for the Dreyfus explosion.

Ordinarily, the French charges might have been disposed of with a few diplomatically phrased words of regret; perhaps they could even have been ignored. But in 1892, Anglo-French relations did not permit so easy a solution. France had long lost patience with repeated Foreign Office assurances—never acted on—that Britain would soon withdraw from Egypt. In England, no small concern existed over the eastward expansion of French west African possessions toward the upper Nile. A Franco-Russian alliance, openly antagonistic to Britain, was in the making. Thus the French Government could be expected to press its angry claims to the furthest possible limit.

But even if Ribot had not seen his country's honor besmirched, it was unlikely that the White Fathers' indictment of Lugard could have been brushed aside in England. For Salisbury's Parliamentary Opposition had recognized in the charges an opportunity to deliver the coup de grâce to the Conservative Government, already reeling under Irish Nationalist fire as the midsummer elections of 1892 approached. During the month of June, the exulting Irish Members made Uganda the subject of no fewer than nine vitriolic exchanges in the Commons. Lugard was portrayed as a jingo sadist. Pressure for an investigation mounted. One of Salisbury's last official acts before the dissolution of Parliament on June 28 was to give in to the combined French–Liberal–Radical–Irish demands. Instructions were sent to Captain J. R. L. Macdonald, who had just completed the railway survey, to proceed at once to Uganda and "draw up a Report... from reliable sources, which should explain the causes of the [civil war] and the action of British officials."

Lugard himself knew nothing of these developments until long after his departure from Uganda in June, 1892. Indeed, Britain had also been in the dark for three months, her only knowledge of the civil war and Lugard's alleged barbarities having consisted of the French accusations. The reason for this information gap was simply that the war itself had disrupted communications along the British route between Mengo and Mombasa, while the White Fathers had sent out their indictment on the southerly caravan trail through German territory. Lugard's own version, a somewhat hastily written official report, was not received in England until mid-July, by which time the damage had already been done. France was demanding Lugard's scalp.

*

In defending himself against the White Fathers' charges, Lugard was also serving his imperial cause. Were the accusations to be proved true or go unanswered, he himself would in all probability be branded by the world as an English Carl Peters. More than that, he would contribute to the image—nourished not only by France but by many Little Englanders —of the British Empire as essentially coercive, grasping and brutal. For a man who prided himself above all on his country's humanitarianism and fair play, this would have been unthinkable. Most significantly at the moment, however, failure to vindicate himself would disqualify him from any role in the fight to hold Uganda. Thus, although Lugard personally considered the French attacks "contemptible trash, obviously a mere sensational lie ... not worth replying to," he could also recognize them as a component of the larger issue of Uganda, and with Uganda in mind he set about demolishing them.

Working almost around the clock in his rooms on Jermyn Street, Lugard wrote three separate rebuttals which characterized the White Fathers' accusations as emotionally distorted, when they were not downright false. He was able to show that far from refusing to protect the priests during the battle of Mengo hill, he had on the contrary pleaded with them to take shelter in the fort—only to be spurned by Hirth. He made it clear that no priest had suffered so much as a scratch in the actual fighting, that the so-called imprisonment was no more than crowded conditions in the fort when some of the fathers later sought its security. As to his religious bigotry, he merely cited the enraged charges which had been leveled against him by Ashe and the CMS missionaries. The White Fathers themselves were produced as character witnesses, in quotations from letters they had written Lugard in Uganda, thanking him for the consideration and fairness he had shown them. One effect of this defense was to leave the White Fathers on somewhat shaky ground and to blunt, at least temporarily, the cutting edge of the official French demands. But in the context of the struggle in England, it was even more important that Lugard had shown his own hands to be clean. Macdonald's investigation, to be sure, had not been completed, and it was quite possible that Macdonald might bring in a verdict unfavorable to Lugard. Even so, from the standpoint of personal conduct, there was no longer any question of Lugard's right to an active role in the annexationist campaign.

*

Indeed, he had already waded into the battle, repeating his tactics of 1889 by appealing directly to the public through the press. On October 6, only three days after arriving in London, he had fired off his first salvo: a letter to *The Times*. It should be noted here that during the 1890s, the letter column of that newspaper, while certainly not as influential as a Cabinet post or a seat in Parliament, nonetheless had a modestly commanding political voice. Even an abbreviated paragraph of praise or dissent by an ordinary citizen could sometimes have a part in shaping public opinion or, just possibly, in guiding official policy. Lugard was hardly an obscure individual, and his letter consisted of more than one paragraph. It ran through two entire columns, in which the usual strategic arguments for Uganda's retention were set forth energetically. Lugard concluded by announcing that he had merely written a first installment. Eleven days later, *The Times* printed the second letter in its entirety. Lugard now spoke at length of Uganda and all east Africa as a potentially flourishing British colony, suited not only to the establishment of typical English farms but to the demographic relief of an already overpopulated India. He closed on an appeal to patriotism and honor: "In view of the obligations we have incurred by ... taking the initiative in the Brussels Act ... the moderate paltry sum, which will save the situation, will not be denied by the Government of the 'richest nation in the world.'"

These letters, along with the replies to the French charges, began to capture public favor. The press was taking an increasingly strong expansionist stand. (One of the more effective and less ponderous editorial protests against the evacuation policy was a Tenniel cartoon in Punch, depicting Uganda as an unmanageable but indispensable white elephant.) Yet press notices urging retention were not likely to move Gladstone, Harcourt and the Cabinet from their unyielding opposition to another jingo adventure. Less than two months remained before the start of IBEA's ninety-day countdown to eviction, and if Rosebery were to keep Britain from losing Uganda, he would need some overwhelmingly convincing demonstration of public support.

No one can say with certainty whether the Foreign Secretary was directly responsible for what happened next, although Lugard—by now something of a national hero—remarked that during this period, Rosebery "was glad to utilize me in giving effect to his opposition to the views of his colleagues." It is also known that Lugard was being urged to extend his campaign for retention by launching a whistle-stop tour of speaking engagements across Great Britain. He did not find the idea appealing at first. "No possible task could have been more distasteful to me," he later wrote, "nor was there any work for which I was less fitted ... but I saw that my duty to the country, for which I had so long been working, demanded that I should use my ultimate endeavour, no matter whether the task was congenial or not." On this note commenced one of the more remarkable opinion-molding efforts in the history of public relations.

Lugard's first speech was delivered on November 3, at the Royal Geographical Society in London. Attendance alone, said his brother, in a letter to his fiancée, "was a huge compliment to Fred. I am told 300 to 500 people, Lords and Dukes and all sorts of swells, were turned away at the door for want of standing room!" This seemed to set the tone for the remainder of the tour. Houses were equally packed as Lugard drove home the Uganda message in Manchester, Liverpool, Birmingham, Newcastle, Edinburgh, Glasgow, Aberdeen and other major cities in England and Scotland. He addressed chambers of commerce, colonial and geographical organizations, political clubs, university students, church groups and mission societies. Each meeting was presided over by a peer, bishop, lord mayor or alderman. Between speeches there were private luncheons and dinners, with lengthy press conferences sandwiched in. Wherever he went, Lugard was the man of the hour.

Perhaps the most curious aspect of the tour is that it might easily have proved a fiasco. Possibly it should have. Not unnaturally, the people who came to hear Lugard expected stirring, action-packed accounts of empire building on the dark continent, but Lugard did not oblige them. He spoke quietly and to the point, the point for the most part being Uganda's potential as a market and Britain's duty to stamp out the east African slave trade. Even the strategic aspects of retention, which may have been uppermost in his mind, were played down. "I gave addresses," he later wrote, "in almost every case nominally on geographical and commercial aspects of East Africa and Uganda, with only a mere incidental reference to the political aspect, since I thought this line more appropriate for an officer in the regular establishment of the army." The high adventure quotient, to be sure, was not entirely absent, for Stanley occasionally shared the rostrum with Lugard and could be relied on to inject a muscular note. From all accounts, however, it was Lugard's show from start to finish: "an all-important service," was a typical newspaper comment. Nor could his message have been described as totally dispassionate. The chairman of one meeting described Lugard's words as "altogether too good for these degenerate days of paper: they should be stamped in bronze or graven in stone." Obviously, the chairman had been hypnotized beyond sensible judgement, but this was the apparent effect of the soft-spoken, diminutive young man whose diffident but earnest manner seemed to breathe magic into the word "Uganda."

The magic soon began to make itself felt. Even before Lugard launched his campaign, the Foreign Office and Members of Parliament had been receiving considerable mail calling for retention. But the impact of Lugard's personal appearances had opened the floodgates for a deluge of letters and memorials. No fewer than 174 petitions came in, largely from chambers of commerce and church groups, the very bodies of opinion among whom Lugard had sought to excite active interest. It would be extravagant to suggest that this mail turned the tide for Uganda, but there is little question that it generated a climate highly congenial to Rosebery's lonely cause in the Cabinet, and placed the Foreign Secretary in a position to make what may have been the decisive move for retention.

*

"It is seldom," Miss Perham has noted, "that any colonial question comes so close to the basis of party power as did that of Uganda from 1892 to 1894... For a period, especially when the Liberal Government first took office, the destiny of this remote Nilotic region roused intense feeling in the country and nearly broke up the ministry." And that ministry could hardly have come closer to dissolution than it did in the fierce contest of wills in the Cabinet during the late fall and early winter of 1892. Gladstone and Rosebery were barely on speaking terms. One Minister, Lord Kimberley, described the Foreign Secretary as being "in a very ticklish condition." Harcourt held to his angrily intransigent insistence on unconditional evacuation. John Morley, the Chief Secretary for Ireland, said he would resign if concessions were made to the annexationists. Considering that Irish Home Rule had brought Gladstone into office, Morley's threat could be seen as not much less dire than Rosebery's had been. Sir Algernon West, Gladstone's private secretary, referred in his diary to the Uganda controversy as "this accursed thing." Mwanga's kingdom was driving Gladstone's Government to the brink of an abyss.

Some kind of accommodation seemed the only way out of the fix. It proved more than that. On November 24, the announcement was made that a Commissioner would be sent to Uganda to report to the Cabinet on conditions in that country, with a view to furnishing guidelines for policy. A week later, the Commissioner was appointed. He was Sir Gerald Portal, and the Cabinet's acceptance of the man who had so energetically endorsed Lugard's melodramatic warnings in September could not have been called mere compromise. What it amounted to was surrender, although the Cabinet did not immediately recognize this.

Curiously enough, it was the anti-imperialist Labouchere who had set the stage for the capitulation. Early in October, he had suggested that a Royal Commission go to Uganda for the purpose of assisting (and no doubt accelerating) the Company's departure. Gladstone had rejected the idea out of hand; it gave him visions of another Gordon disaster. But Rosebery had been able to recognize an opportunity for his own cause in the proposal. Thus, in November, when he reintroduced it in somewhat revised form as a means of clarifying the situation for the Cabinet, the Prime Minister was less cool. With the Uganda crisis now actually threatening to bring the Government down, prudence had begun to dictate avoidance of direct responsibility for outright evacuation. Portal had suggested that Uganda might possibly be administered from Zanzibar rather than England. Although Zanzibar was in fact a British Protectorate, hope existed that a recommendation of indirect control might prove just acceptable to Little Englanders and expansionists alike.

Two things should be noted here. One is that the Zanzibar scheme never materialized; when British authority was finally imposed on Uganda it took the form of direct rule by the Foreign Office. The other is that Gladstone and Harcourt—somewhat naïvely, it would appear— were not fully aware of the extent to which Rosebery planned to exploit Portal's appointment. One clause in the Commissioner's instructions dealt with the possibility that Uganda might prove untenable under any circumstances, but Rosebery virtually ruled this out. In a private letter to Portal, the Foreign Secretary stated that "as a rather one-horse Company has been able to administer I suppose the Empire will be equal to it." He went on to add, "as my confident though not my official opinion, that public sentiment here will expect and support the maintenance of the British sphere of influence." Considering Rosebery's stand on retention, not to mention his position as Portal's top-level superior in the Foreign Office, these words can almost be regarded as secret orders.

Not that Portal required manipulation. To be sure, his instructions gave him limited powers of decision; essentially he was to recommend rather than formulate policy. But the report he wrote could only be expected to reflect his known views, and, as Miss Perham has observed, "Rosebery ... knew his man, one after his own heart and mind." It is even more significant that when Lugard learned of Portal's selection, he broke off his speaking tour almost at once. "The day that the appointment was announced," he later wrote, "the responsibility I felt... ceased to weigh upon me."

He added, however, that he still faced "an infinity of work." Perhaps he did not realize that this was a mild way of putting it.

"I trust there will remain Members of this House who will never bow the knee to King Jingo."

When Parliament reconvened on January 31, 1893, the curtain rose on an intense debate over Uganda. The notion that the Portal mission might allay passions on both sides proved wishful thinking. For the appointment, although raising annexationist hopes, by no means assured retention, while the anti-imperialists sought not only to discredit the mission but to derail it. Labouchere led the attack. With Harcourt now in the Cabinet, the maverick Radical had emerged as the natural standard-bearer of the evacuationist forces in the Commons. All but unknown today, this remarkable personality was one of the main piston rods in the Little England engine, and yet in many ways the genial, generously bearded chain-smoker did not seem altogether fitted for the role of crusader. As an indifferent student at Cambridge Labouchere had devoted far less time to books and lectures than to London gaming houses and bordellos. For several years he had been an itinerant gambler in Mexico and had also tried his hand—with indolence and cheerful insubordination—at a number of minor Foreign Office posts. He had once managed a London theatre where audiences saw Henry Irving and Ellen Terry perform together for the first time. Invitations to parties at his home were sought out on all levels of society. "After the disappearance of Oscar Wilde," wrote Hesketh Pearson, Labouchere's biographer, "he was fairly generally regarded as the best talker in England."

Eventually, Labouchere's drifting career led him into journalism and politics. As publisher of the newspaper *Truth*, he became a sort of combined Mark Twain and I. F. Stone, deflating pomposity and exposing fraud in a literary style no less humorous than it was lethal. He was the defendant (and almost always the winner) in countless libel suits; on one occasion, the outraged victim of a *Truth* article took a horsewhip to him in the street. In Parliament, Labouchere rapidly proved himself a gadfly whose Radical sting raised many a Tory welt; few Members so frequently evoked the reaction parenthesized by the official transcripts as "(cries of 'Oh!')." He was nothing if not versatile. He could thunder outraged indignation with Gladstonian eloquence; he could be incisive, demolishing an opponent with a relentless barrage of unassailable facts. He may have been at his best, however, when hitting below the belt with a weapon of ridicule that often drew on distortions and outright misstatements. If he seldom lost a battle as a newspaperman, he seldom swung a vote as a politician, but his consummate skill with every refinement of the filibustering art made him a formidable adversary on the floor of the House. The Queen called him "that horrible, lying Labouchere," but as a rule, even his bitterest political enemies found it hard to dislike "Labby," since he himself seemed incapable of personal malice. George Curzon, the future Marquess of Kedleston, who often tilted with Labouchere in Commons, described the Radical Member during one exchange as "quite impervious to argument, which makes him one of the most perverse, but, I am free to admit, one of the most charming of men." Only one issue— imperialism—seemed to ruffle Labouchere's otherwise amiable nature, and he was a man very much to be reckoned with in the protracted duel over Uganda and the railway.

Labouchere's opening gun in 1893 came on the heels of the Queen's address to Parliament, in the form of an amendment "humbly" voicing "the hope that the Commissioner who has been sent by Your Majesty to Uganda will effect the evacuation in that country by the B. E. A. Company." He added: "I trust there will remain Members of this House who will never bow the knee to King Jingo," and then proceeded to lambaste his party leaders for having bowed their own knees. "The Government ... at first accepted evacuation," he charged, until "Lugard went about the country and the big drum was beaten"; as a result, Gladstone's Ministers were now prepared to spend huge sums on Uganda while "we have want and misery here." Special attention was reserved for Lugard, "whom we are all asked to admire," and whom Labouchere accused of "monstrous atrocities," not the least of which was having bullyragged Mwanga into acceptance of Company rule. "So far as I know, except the Zanzibaris with fixed bayonets, there was not a single man in [Uganda] in favour of the Treaty." Lugard himself was quoted directly as having told one of the White Fathers, who had just been insulted by several Baganda, that he "would dearly like to catch a man ... that I might publicly flog him." Labouchere instantly turned to the Irish Members. "I ask them what they would say if the Irish Secretary stated in this House that he would dearly like an Ulster Member, we will say, to seize hold of a Nationalist, as the right honourable Gentleman himself would like to publicly flog him."

Labouchere was only warming up. He ridiculed Lugard's claim that Uganda offered commercial possibilities: "the single fact given by Captain Lugard to justify this is, that some chief asked him when he left to be good enough to send him some opera glasses and white donkeys." As to the assertion that the country could be settled, "the only 'settlers' who will go to Uganda are those whom I cannot look upon as better than swindlers—those who would go out and dig a hole, declare there was gold in the hole, then ... sell the hole to foolish and confiding British orphans and widows." Although he was persuaded to withdraw his challenging amendment, Labouchere continued the attack. Not long afterwards, he made a motion to reduce a Supplementary Estimate by £5,000—the sum allocated to Portal's mission. He scoffed at the expansionists' Nile strategy, remarking that "our being in Egypt is used as an argument in favour of taking Uganda—just as, when they have taken Uganda, that will be used as an argument that we remain in Egypt for ever." As to the railway, "there will not be commerce for more than half a dozen trains per annum." And again Lugard came under fire: "During the occupation [of Uganda], the cause of Christianity has suffered, and to my mind that is not surprising when Christianity is associated in men's minds with Maxim guns." The motion was defeated but Labouchere was not. His protests will be heard again.

An eyeball-to-eyeball confrontation between Labouchere and Lugard was all but inevitable during this period, although neither man can be said to have emerged victorious. When Labouchere delivered his initial attack, Lugard had been seated in the visitors' gallery listening angrily as the Radical Member not only accused him of brutality and questioned his judgement but charged that he was a paid lobbyist for IBEA. (Actually, Lugard had resigned from the Company shortly after returning to England, and since that time had received no remuneration.) That very day, Lugard struck back with another of his prolix letters to *The Times*. Labouchere's printed reply to this was such that Lugard went to the offices of *Truth*, hoping to reason with his adversary in person. Apparently in fear of another horsewhipping, Labouchere leaped to a defensive position behind a large table and hastily told Lugard that the attacks were really good publicity for the imperial cause. Lugard could only throw up his hands in frustration.

Labouchere was not the only foe with whom Lugard locked horns in early 1893. He had been interviewed by most members of the Cabinet, and if the Ministers had kept up an outward show of courtesy, their general attitude did not disguise an all too manifest hostility toward the man who was increasingly coming to personify the poison of jingoism. Harcourt, who all but commanded Lugard to appear before him, was openly uncivil. Lugard's account of the meeting leaves the impression of a naughty schoolboy being reprimanded by a choleric headmaster. "I had hardly taken a seat," he wrote, "when he poured forth a torrent of invective against all African explorers, missionaries and, above all, Chartered Companies and their promoters ... I sat silent until he turned upon me and said (in effect) that he supposed that I, like Stanley, had on occasion put men to death, and that I had no legal authority to act as judge and could therefore be held responsible for my action. I replied that I had never put any man to death in Africa ... He took little notice and when he had exhausted his denunciations, I was dismissed."

It would be misleading, however, to suggest that Lugard was friendless at this time. Far from it. The Conservatives and Liberal Unionists of course stood behind him to a man. Joseph Chamberlain, on the threshold of his emergence as Britain's most bellicose champion of Empire, could be expected to speak as a self-appointed advocate for Lugard in the lower House. Lugard, he said, had done "a work of the highest responsibility and the greatest importance ... It is something for England, for the United Kingdom, to glory in that we can still boast such servants...." Even Lugard's sworn enemies at the head of the party had an occasional kind word for him. As early as March, 1892, after reading one of Lugard's reports, Gladstone had admitted to "the impression that whether these proceedings toward the natives may be juridically justifiable or not, yet ... [Lugard] is a frank man, a brave man, an able man, and an upright man." The same report had prompted even Harcourt to acknowledge having "formed the very highest opinion of [Lugard's] integrity, his intelligence, his industry, and his courage." No matter that these warm words had been uttered before the French accusations were made known; they could not but echo at least faintly a year later. And within the hostile Cabinet itself, Lugard could of course rely on the unswerving support of the rebellious Foreign Secretary.

Still, the spring and early summer of 1893 were a trying time for Lugard and the cause of retention. Although the Macdonald report had not yet come in, Lugard had no reason to expect that it would treat him gently. "As regards Captain Macdonald," he later wrote, "... I had full faith in his impartiality and honour, but it was unfortunate that the one and only man with whom I had had any personal difference in Africa should be selected as my judge!" These apprehensions were by no means baseless. Portal, who had reached Uganda late in March, had already written Rosebery to warn that Macdonald's findings would be "severe and disagreeable," but irrefutable nonetheless. By this time, Portal himself appears to have done an about-face in his attitude toward Lugard, and he said as much in a letter to Rennell Rodd, the Acting Consul in Zanzibar. "Macdonald and missionaries," he wrote, "all sitting in open-mouthed astonishment at Lugard's reports which, I fear, must be read only as vivid works of fiction... The general impression here is that the man is off his head, and I should not wonder if this were the case."

On June 27, 1893, the long-awaited report reached the Foreign Office. Macdonald's main conclusions were that Lugard's march to the west had been an irresponsible act which imperiled British interests in Mengo, and that "by adopting a high-handed policy and injudicious management of the crisis, he precipitated civil war in Uganda." The latter finding, if accepted, might not only wreck Lugard's career but deal a serious and just possibly fatal blow to the annexationists. A Cabinet subcommittee—including Harcourt—was quickly formed to study the charges, while Lugard was instructed to submit his own reply in writing. Characteristically, the defense which he presented in mid-August seemed more an attack, but Lugard did not see his own position as any too secure; the subcommittee, he wrote his brother, was "distinctly hostile— apparently they have accepted Macdonald's views."

It is indeed possible that the Cabinet group would have found Lugard's candid but somewhat heated words an altogether unsatisfactory rebuttal but for three other developments which lent considerable force to his defense. One was a long letter to Lugard from the influential Bishop Tucker, who strongly questioned Macdonald's impartiality and dismissed the hearings as "a parody of justice." Lugard took pains to have this letter circulated in the Cabinet. There was also the unmistakable anti-Lugard bias of a German journalist named Eugen Wolf, who had met Macdonald in east Africa, where the latter—quite incongruously—had invited him to assist in the investigation. On returning to Europe, Wolf was almost immediately made a Chevalier of the Légion d'Honneur by the French Government, clearly as a reward for his services to the White Fathers and the Quai d'Orsay. One result of this was a Cabinet cable to Consul Rodd, voicing "the amazement felt by Her Majesty's Government that Captain Macdonald, in making his enquiry, should have associated Herr Wolf with himself." Finally, after accusing Lugard of "high-handed" behavior, Macdonald had almost seemed to be acting out that very charge himself when, in April, 1893, he had summarily arrested Selim Bey and disarmed the Sudanese troops to quell a suspected mutiny in Kampala. Thus, as the summer drew to a close, full credence could no longer be placed in the Macdonald report. It was finally laid to rest in a pigeonhole, and the active crisis with France came to an end.*

---

* Actually, France did not entirely ease the pressure of her insistence that national honor be satisfied. Five years later, Britain would shed the irksome burden of French demands—now based more on principle than on specific grievances—with the grudging agreement to pay a £10,000 indemnity.

*

During the course of the subcommittee's investigation, Lugard had vainly urged that the members read what he felt was the most convincing testimony of all: the proofs of the book he had just completed. In writing this work, he had shown himself to be something of a literary cyclone: nearly half a million words were ground out in less than eight months—a time when Lugard had also been snowed under with magazine articles, letters to the press and a galaxy of other activities for retention. The book itself can be called a magnificent curiosity. Somewhat defiantly entitled *The Rise of Our East African Empire* (there was, after all, no such thing in 1893), it is rambling and uneven. It bristles with lengthy digressions on irrelevancies that range from tiger-hunting in India to fire-fighting in London. It contains innumerable contradictions and inconsistencies. The attention to detail is almost stupefying in its precision. (To cite just one example, the scale of costs for maintaining a Sudanese rifle regiment is broken down to the last rupee and anna in a footnote occupying nearly half a page.) At the same time, however, Lugard somehow contrives to surmount these self-made obstacles and come through with what is simultaneously a zinging adventure story and a compelling statement of the British imperial case in east Africa.

For the most part, *The Rise of Our East African Empire* is straight narrative, exhaustively tracing Lugard's early campaigns against the slavers on Lake Nyasa, his journey to Uganda, Mwanga's acceptance of the treaty, the expeditions against the Muslims, the march to the west, the civil war and the pacification of the country. While the account can hardly be called objective, it has the unmistakable ring of candor and reveals graphically the climate of unremitting crisis in which Lugard was forced to swift and often fateful decisions. From this standpoint, the book is an altogether convincing personal vindication. But Lugard was not writing to clear his own name. His major objective was to clarify the reasons for Britain's presence in east Africa, and specifically to gain public support for remaining in Uganda. This appeal said little that had not already been said, but it was eloquently put; and more to the point, it also happened to be delivered at what may have been just the right moment for the annexationist cause.

Uganda stood at this time at the crest of its abbreviated prominence as Britain's most fiercely contested political issue. Simultaneously, Lugard had taken center stage in the controversy, not merely as a champion of one faction but as a national hero. The book, therefore, was bound to be read widely—and stood fair to capture the public imagination far more effectively than any of the earlier African explorers could ever have done. Men like Thomson and Stanley and Burton, regardless of their literary skills, were to some extent specialists with limited missions, and they worked in fields seldom fully comprehensible to the ordinary reader. Lugard, on the other hand, was a public servant. His adventures could be seen, in a very real sense, as part of the public domain, the property, so to speak, of the English people. One might find superb excitement in reading Thomson's descriptions of Masailand or Stanley's account of his ordeal in the Ituri forest; experiences such as these were tailor-made for print, and both men could write rings around Lugard. Even so, the most stirring of their exploits could not evoke the sense of involvement—even of personal participation—which Lugard was able to bring to events like the treaty showdown with Mwanga or the rout of Kabarega's armies. For every Englishman had a stake in these actions. Here, in fact, was a chapter of Britain's history in the making.

Thus Lugard's Uganda experience inevitably came out as a veritable arsenal of expansionist ammunition. The book was reviewed in no fewer than 133 daily and weekly periodicals across the United Kingdom, and nearly all the comment was warmly generous. *The Daily Telegraph* saw in Lugard a man "who knew, like Caesar, how to fight with one hand and in the other to hold [the] faithfully written Commentaries." To the *Pall Mall Gazette*, Lugard was the "Bayard of African enterprise." The less than imperialist *Daily News* praised him "not merely as a traveller but as a statesman, or, at any rate, an administrator." And it was only to be expected that *The Times* would describe the book as "the most important contribution that has yet been made to the history of East Africa," adding that "the imagination will be dull to which the conflict of hostile barbarism and civilisation fail to present itself with something of the grandeur of a modern epic." Oddly enough, Lugard might have come a cropper with *The Times*. In what Miss Perham has called his "impetuous ignorance" of editorial protocol, he personally introduced himself to *The Times*' reviewer and suggested, not too subtly, that he would be gratified by a favorable response to the book. The editor, Flora Shaw, was something of a celebrity in her own right. At a time when Englishwomen did not even have the vote, she had gained considerable stature as a sort of female Walter Lippmann of imperialism, and could not have appreciated Lugard's well-intended but crude gesture. As a lady, however, she let him off with a gentle reproof. A few years later she married him.

Publication of the book also propelled Lugard into the very center of London's upper-class social life. His mail every day contained a small blizzard of invitations. He was Salisbury's guest at Hatfield, Chamberlain's at Highbury. The exclusive Beefsteak Club made him an honorary member. At luncheons, informal dinners and weekends at country estates he met such public figures as Balfour, Grey, Bryce, Asquith, Haldane and many others. It was a dazzling experience, and excerpts from title-dropping letters to his brother leave the impression of a small boy at his first county fair: "Dined with Mrs. Chamberlain on the 16th ... Sat next Duchess of X. Got on a good deal with her ... She asked me to supper. I went—and found the *fastest* performance I have ever witnessed. Ladies smoked everywhere ... Sat next Lady Randolph [Churchill] ... She has a son at Sandhurst ... Mrs. Patrick Campbell ... Colonel Brabazon ... Dined at Lady Flower's, sat next Miss Paget (daughter of Sir James, M. D.) who flooded me quite in metaphysics—I don't know *when* I've been so bowled out! ... I have just now come from dining at Marjoribanks (Liberal Whip) and met Lord Tweedmouth—he married the Duke of Marlborough's daughter ... Lady (& Lord) Curzon ... Lord and Lady Sandhurst—young Ferguson (married Lord Dufferin's daughter) ... Lady Wilton ... a Duchess of sorts ... If I meet any more Duchesses I shall have to buy a new overcoat, and goodness knows where it will stop for my dress suit isn't as new as it might be."

*

The dizzying and flattering social whirl did not, however, divert Lugard from his tireless activities as a spark plug in the annexation engine. For despite the apparent swing of public favor toward retention of Uganda, the question was far from settled. As the year drew to a close, the issue seemed more and more to hinge on Portal's report, but Portal had returned to England at the end of November, and the Government had not yet seen fit to make his findings public. And indeed, if the members of Gladstone's Cabinet appeared anxious to defer release of the report, their timidity was at least understandable, since Portal's journey had been a crucial event—tragic for him and fateful for Uganda.

"Uganda is your own child."

At the age of thirty-five, the impressionable but exceptionally brilliant (and almost impossibly handsome) Sir Gerald Portal had shown himself to be one of the Foreign Office's most promising careerists. After entering Government service in 1879, he had been Third Secretary in Rome and Cairo, performing so capably in the latter post that Lord Cromer himself had come to regard the young diplomat as his natural successor in the Egyptian proconsulship. In 1887 Portal was entrusted with the delicate mission of arranging a cease-fire between the Italian and Abyssinian armies in the very same war in which Lugard had sought action during his period of suicidal despair. Two years later he became Acting Consul in Zanzibar and was officially appointed to the office in 1891. In this capacity, Portal not only initiated many sweeping administrative reforms on the island but kept in close touch with the chaotic political developments in Uganda. He was therefore abundantly qualified to recommend guidelines for British policy toward Mwanga's subjects.

But he had very little time in which to complete the task. The Company was scheduled to evacuate Uganda on March 31, 1893, and Portal's party of eight Britons, including his elder brother, Captain Raymond Portal, could not leave Zanzibar until January 1. Since the 700-mile journey between the coast and Kampala normally took three months, Portal would thus be obliged to formulate his conclusions on Uganda's future in a matter of hours—unless he were to establish some sort of speed record for the march. He did. Despite endless outbreaks of fever, ulcers and other hot-country ailments among the six hundred porters and askaris, Portal's caravan dropped loads outside Kampala fort on March 17. The trek, which averaged twelve and a half miles per day, had been made in less than eleven weeks, and Portal could look forward to a leisurely two-week investigation.

He found Uganda in a shambles. In a despatch to Rosebery he described the country as a "whited sepulchre," and observed that politico-religious animosities, rather than having abated, had if anything intensified. The Baganda themselves, he conceded, were clearly fitted "for a leading position among the native races of Africa and as a means for the introduction of a higher civilisation," but he also remarked that "their pride is almost synonymous with arrogant conceit," and predicted "difficulties of administration" arising from their predilection for bending the truth. Mwanga's authority, to the extent that he held any, was barely acknowledged by his subjects, and only the presence of the few British officials at Kampala and the numerous Sudanese troops prevented a renewed outbreak of a "war of extermination." Portal added, however, that the Sudanese could be considered as much a curse as a blessing, since they lived off the land and held the entire country in a state of perpetual terror. Unsettled conditions, in Portal's opinion, were compounded by the position of the Catholic and Protestant missionaries, who continued to double as political bosses. "The natives

on both sides," he told Rosebery, "have acquired the habit of appealing to their respective missionaries on every possible question... There
has thus grown up a sort of dual or even triple system of government."
With a view to ending one of the graver causes of dispute, Portal sat
down with Tucker and Hirth and obtained their consent to a major reap-
portionment of land among Catholics and Protestants. A letter to his
mother, however, suggests that the moderator's task was not an easy one.
"All's well that ends well," he wrote, "but I don't wish ever again to have
a 3½ hours' skirmish with two angry Bishops—one not understanding
English and the other knowing no French."

But if the missions had contributed to Uganda's sorry state, Portal
saw the Company as far and away the worst offender. Frederick Jackson,
who met Portal at this time, remarked that the latter "always appeared
to me to be unduly biased against the Company. His criticisms were
mostly destructive, and his attitude generally was unfriendly." Considering Jackson's own not infrequent dissent from the Directors' policies,
this says a great deal, yet during the march from the coast, Portal had
seen enough to justify his antagonism at least in part. Passing through
Ukamba, he voiced suspicion that Company officers were behaving
unjustly—perhaps cruelly—toward the local populations. "It was not
pleasant," he wrote, "for an Englishman to notice that at the first sight
of a European, [the Wakamba] fled with shrieks and with every sign
of terror." Kikuyuland, he informed Rosebery, was in "a state of siege."
These indications of mismanagement along his route did not put Portal
into a charitable frame of mind toward IBEA stewardship in Uganda.
As far as he was concerned, the breakdown of government machinery
in Kampala could be attributed directly to Company ineptness and a
misguided notion of its own authority. Despite its ostensible function
as a commercial enterprise, IBEA had stimulated little trade and done
virtually nothing to improve vitally needed transport facilities; this latter
oversight was most conspicuous on the main caravan road between
Kampala and the coast. Company officers, in his view, had also concluded several treaties which they had been unable to implement, and
had at the same time created the false impression that the agreements
were endorsed by the Foreign Office. "The combination of administration and trading is fatal," Portal told Rosebery. In a private letter to
his wife he was less diplomatic, simply describing the Company as "a
disgrace to the English name."

Notwithstanding the prejudiced and highly emotional tone of these
charges, it could not be denied that the Company had introduced something less than a model of governmental authority. Nor was there any

question but that Uganda cried out for major administrative surgery. Yet the country's politico-religious cancer had become beset with so many complications that despite his strong annexationist views, Portal himself was uncertain for a time as to what specific British policy he should recommend. Even by the March 31 evacuation deadline he had not reached any firm conclusions, although on the following day he ordered the Company flag lowered and the Union Jack raised in a ceremony at Kampala fort. While this gesture at least indicated the direction of his thinking, it was not until the end of May that Portal submitted a treaty for Mwanga's signature. And even that document was not final; under its terms, Uganda would become a provisional British Protectorate pending a final Government decision. Within the scope of his own authority, Portal could do no more.

There was no longer any reason to remain in Uganda, and indeed Portal had had more than his fill of that country. Only two days before the signing of the treaty, his brother, returning to Kampala from a reconnaissance of the Bunyoro border, had died of malaria. Portal was eager to turn his back on what must by now have seemed to him an accursed land. The return journey, however, set no records. Heavy rains and continuing fever reduced the march to a stumbling crawl. At Mumias, on the other hand, nature launched one sortie which the party found almost welcome. "The whole air has been black with immense clouds of locusts," Portal wrote his wife. "Millions and millions came through... The men are catching them to eat. I tried some fried, tasteless but not nasty." But by now Portal himself had become seriously ill. On October 22, the party finally reached Zanzibar. By November 1, Portal had completed his report to the Foreign Office and set sail for England, his health shattered. On January 25, 1894, he died. "To lose two dear sons," wrote the Queen to his mother, "in so short a time ... in serving their Sovereign and country is terribly hard."

*

Two and a half months after his death, Portal's report remained on the Government's classified list, although his conclusions had seemed fairly obvious following the declaration of temporary Protectorate. Expansionists in Britain began to chafe uneasily. Was it just possible that the predominantly Little England Cabinet might be seeking to withhold— or at least delay—a recommendation that Uganda formally join the Empire? Clearly, however, the Portal report could not be relegated to the dead-letter file in the manner of Macdonald's findings. Sooner or later it must be made public, and its release may well have been hastened on March 6, when the ailing, eighty-five-year-old Gladstone resigned from office, to be succeeded by none other than Rosebery. On April 10, 1894, the long-awaited report was presented to Parliament.

While Portal's three major conclusions could hardly have astonished a single Member of either House, they were no less momentous for Britain's imperial future in east Africa. Despite his personal feelings toward what he had once called "this beastly country," and his exasperation with its political snake pit, Portal had not unexpectedly seen the retention of Uganda as vital to British interests. His report invoked all the usual humanitarian, economic and strategic imperatives of the British imperial credo in a strong plea for remaining in Uganda. The Nile hypothesis was of course given prominence. Britain's choice was clear: "All question of complete evacuation of Uganda, at all events for the present, should be set aside." Sublimely confident in the paternalistic blessings of Pax Britannica, Portal predicted that Mwanga "no doubt ... will ask for a Treaty of Protection." Accordingly, "a declaration of protectorate would probably prove to be the simplest course." Portal also sounded the death knell of IBEA. Apart from his low opinion of the Company itself, he felt, as we have seen, that any attempt to amalgamate trade and administration was like trying to mix oil and water. He was ready to pay the Directors a grudging compliment, giving them "the sole credit of the acquisition, for the benefit of British commerce, of this great potential market for British goods," but his kind words stopped there. It was Portal's recommendation "that some arrangement should be arrived at, without further delay, by which the Imperial British East Africa Company shall cease to exist as a political or administrative body." The Company's governmental role, he said, "may now be looked upon as ended."

Finally, Portal turned to the question which may have been as crucial as retention itself. The caravan road between Mombasa and Uganda, he noted, had proved no great advantage over the longer route from Bagamoyo. "Transport from the German coast to the south shore of the lake is cheaper, the road is more frequented, porters are more easily obtained, and food is more abundant ... To effect any real improvement in prosperity or commerce, efficiently to check the slave-trade, and for ourselves to reap the benefit of the material progress that may be made, there is but one course open... Transport by the 'English road,' already the shortest in actual distance, must be made the safest, cheapest and quickest... The only means of effectively doing this is by a railway."

*

Two days after the release of the Portal report, Rosebery told the House of Lords that the Cabinet was disposed to implement the recommendation that a Protectorate be established in Uganda, while Harcourt, no doubt bleeding inwardly, made a similar announcement in the Commons. Thus the lines had been drawn at last for the final showdown. But in keeping with the somewhat leisurely character of Parliamentary decision-making, the vote on the fatal question did not come up until June 1, 1894. Technically, the issue at stake was a vote of £50,000 for expenses in Uganda, but its passage would mean de facto acceptance of Uganda's incorporation into the Empire. Outlining the Government's position, Sir Edward Grey, the Under-Secretary of State for Foreign Affairs, told the House that the Cabinet had in effect accepted the first two of Portal's three recommendations. It was intended, he said, to install a Commissioner in Kampala and to buy up the Company's assets, thus establishing formal and permanent British rule in Uganda. To the surprise of many Members, however, the railway proposal had been rejected. Grey did not dispute the line's value; the difficulty, he said, was "that we do not know enough yet about circumstances and probable progress of the country to justify us in placing any proposal before the House to spend money on this particular railway."

Government's apparent timidity over the railway had no soothing effect on Little England passions. Although funds of original argument had now been exhausted by both sides, the anti-imperialists waded into the fight as if not a word had ever been spoken on the subject. Labouchere echoed his well-worn disparagements of Uganda as a noncommercial asset. Plucking items from context as usual, he drew laughter by reintroducing what Lugard himself had admitted to be a "thoughtless remark" about opera glasses, and also focused on another article in the latter's inventory. "[Lugard] expressly stated that it was the dream of every Ugandese to possess an opera glass and a white ass. Not for the present purpose taking any notice of the white asses, the cost of carrying the opera glasses ... to Uganda would be at the rate of about £300 a ton. Who would be willing in England to give that sum ... ?" Sir Charles Dilke castigated the Cabinet and the "forward" element among the Liberals as traitors to their own cause. "What power," he asked, "is forcing the Liberal Party to eat its words, its votes?" It was becoming a precedent that "we are everywhere bound to follow missions with our arms and flag," although annexations were in fact sorely injurious to Britain's real interests. "The only person," said Dilke, "who has up to the present time benefited from our enterprise in the heart of Africa has been Mr. Hiram Maxim," and he went on to suggest what England's fate might have been "if Augustine had landed in Kent with Maxim guns."

While the annexationists had also run out of fresh ammunition, Chamberlain at least injected a note of bold candor. "Some Members hold, contrary to the prevailing opinion," he said, "that it is not the manifest destiny of this country to be a great colonising and civilising Power. All I can say is that... proceeding upon that principle we have grown to our present greatness ... I greatly fear that if you are to lay down the principle that the lines of Empire are now finally settled ... you will put such a barrier in the way of the enterprise of our coun-trymen that you will virtually alter their character." The railway was Chamberlain's central theme. He accused Government of abdicating its own responsibility in seeking to foist construction off on business. "It is not a fair thing to expect of men engaged in private enterprise that they should put money into an investment which may be a very good thing in the course of years, but which cannot possibly pay for ten years, or it may be for twenty... What it comes down to, therefore, is this: Either the Government must make the railway or it will not be made at all." Chamberlain concluded on a note which may have set the truculent tone that was soon to characterize British expansionism everywhere in Africa. If England recoiled from its manifest destiny, he said, then "we would be much wiser to ... leave it to other nations to finish the work which we were too weak, too poor, and too cowardly to do ourselves."

Only fifty-two Liberal and Irish Members were prepared to accept Chamberlain's label of weakling and coward, while a Liberal–Conserv-ative–Unionist majority of 218 approved the £50,000 outlay (although not the railway). The die had been cast. On June 9, 1894, Kimber-ley, the new Foreign Secretary, cabled Sir Arthur Hardinge, the newest Consul in Zanzibar, with instructions to inform Mwanga that "the Queen has been graciously pleased to confer on him the protection for which he therein asked." On August 27, at a baraza attended by the Kabaka and his Great Chiefs, Mwanga at last became a ward of the Queen-Empress, as the Acting British Commissioner, Colonel Henry Colvile, formally proclaimed the Protectorate. "The announcement," Colvile reported, "was received with great manifestations of joy by all parties, and guns were fired throughout the day and night in honour of the event."

Although there is no record of Lugard having fired off a weapon by way of celebration, one can assume that no one in Britain was more elated by the victory than he. It would be difficult to measure precisely the extent to which his personal efforts were instrumental in bringing about the annexation. The role of a hero in the resolution of any national controversy is far too easily overestimated. In all likelihood, the chief credit for bringing Uganda into the Empire belonged to Rosebery, whose tenacity and skillful political maneuvering overcame a formidable array of what, for a time, had seemed insuperable obstacles in the Cabinet. Yet it can also be said that no single individual had toiled harder or longer, brought influence to bear with more effect or captured the public imagination more thoroughly, than had Lugard. It is quite possible that without his energy, charisma and labors, the debatable glory of possessing Uganda might have fallen to another Power—or at least have been deferred. "Uganda is your own child," wrote Goldie to Lugard. It was patently the truth.

But Lugard never saw his child again. Although he expected and coveted the appointment as Commissioner, his activities with the Company had so aroused French antagonism that the Foreign Office considered him too controversial to hold the post for which he was the obvious choice.* After being told that Whitehall sought a Commissioner in Uganda "who will start with a blank record, so far as African experience is concerned."—pure moonshine, as Lugard well knew—he reluctantly accepted an assignment with Goldie's Royal Niger Company. This was the beginning of a west African career which would gain him the Governor-Generalship of Nigeria, a knighthood and finally, elevation to the peerage as Britain's foremost proconsul on the African continent. And although he now took his leave of Uganda, the colonial foundations he laid down there would stand intact for the remaining fifty-one years of his life—and outlive him by another decade and a half.

---

* However, with a logic almost sublime in its inconsistency, the Foreign Office had sent him on a diplomatic mission to Paris in March. In effect, his duties were those of a spy: he was to meet his French counterpart, Major Parfait-Louis Monteil, a distinguished soldier-explorer, and learn from him what he could of French designs on the upper Nile. Lugard could hardly believe the instructions. "I don't speak a word of French," he wrote his brother, "and I don't see how I can conduct a very delicate matter like this and worm all Monteil's secrets out of him." Indeed, he appears to have gained no vital information ("it was diamond cut diamond"), but the two men took an instant liking to one another and Lugard was at least able to enjoy Paris as a tourist—and to bill the Foreign Office for his evenings at the Moulin Rouge. "We really had some fun," he told his brother. "These ladies of Paris take life so very lightly."

*"Our only chance is to keep the thing
quiet until our railway to Uganda
is sufficiently advanced to enable us
to send troops by it."*

In the process of introducing Pax Britannica to Uganda, the Government also dismantled IBEA. Given Portal's harsh recommendation, the new fount of authority in east Africa and the Company's own insolvency, this was inevitable. It was also felt in many quarters, however, that the liquidation itself might have been carried out with more grace, and in a spirit of fair play that, as it turned out, seemed far removed from the actual proceedings. In mid-November of 1894, the Foreign Office wrote the Directors, proposing that the Sultan of Zanzibar repurchase the Company concession for £150,000, and that Government seek from Parliament a grant of £50,000 upon cancellation of the charter. Shortly afterwards, an additional £50,000 was offered the Company for the sale of its private assets. This grand total of £250,000 would leave the Directors and shareholders with the princely sum (after erasing a £193,757 deficit) of £56,243 in return for having won Uganda and holding in trust for Britain all the territory between Mombasa and the Mountains of the Moon for six years. On March 27, 1895, aware that he had no other alternative, Mackinnon agreed to give way and accept the gratuity. Thus ended a caretaker dominion whose inefficiency was exceeded only by the energy and selflessness with which it carried out an impossible task, and whose surrogate rulers rightfully expected more honorable dealings from the Government they had served without reward.

In any event, IBEA was now a cadaver,* and there remained only the task of filling the administrative vacuum in the regions previously occupied by the Company outside Uganda. On June 15, 1895, at a formal ceremony in Mombasa, the Wazir of Zanzibar, Sir Lloyd Mathews, officially announced the establishment of a British Protectorate over the Sultan's coastal domains, pledging that "all affairs connected with the faith of Islam will be conducted to the honour and benefit of religion, and all ancient customs will be allowed to continue." In the strictest sense of the word, the coast remained foreign soil; the Sultan of Zanzibar was a landlord, receiving an annual rent of £11,000 from his British tenants. (Protocol on the coastal strip dictated that only the Sultan's red

---

* "Ghost" may be a better word, since a number of Company administrators, including Jackson, Hobley and Ainsworth, were engaged by the Foreign Office to continue their work as Government servants.

flag could fly from a staff planted in the ground; the Union Jack and all other foreign flags had to be flown from rooftops.) But the tenants of course were the de facto owners, and by mid-1896 they had incorporated into their new premises all of the former Company-held territory between the coastal strip and Uganda. This newest annexation—the future Kenya—was known officially as the East Africa Protectorate, and although it embraced nearly a quarter of a million square miles, it was generally regarded as an imperial millstone. There seemed to be only one justification for possessing such a wasteland, as many Government experts on Africa liked to call it: the new Protectorate would serve as a corridor for the railway between the coast and Lake Victoria. And the railway by this time had at last begun to take shape.

It had been inevitable that Portal's railway recommendation would prevail, and hardly less certain, despite extreme Government reluctance to invest public funds in the line, that construction would become an official responsibility. To all practical purposes, the railway had been an element of British foreign policy since 1890, when Salisbury committed his Administration—albeit half-heartedly—to financial support of the survey for IBEA. The survey expedition itself had lasted nine months, during which time Macdonald's 389-man party, like some microscopic animal, had continually subdivided itself into smaller organisms, probing the entire length of the caravan trail and many of its offshoots to cover a total distance of 4,280 miles. The project had not moved on oiled wheels. Droughts alternated with abnormally heavy rains and swollen rivers to impede progress, while famine, malaria, smallpox and cattle diseases took a severe toll of porters and baggage animals. Yet in March, 1893, when the survey was finally presented to the Treasury, the opening paragraph of the accompanying report assured Government that "there are no great, or even serious, difficulties to be overcome." In the words of Mervyn Hill, the railway's official historian, "time and events proved the paragraph to be very optimistic."

For the most part, however, facts were faced squarely. While anticipating that the railway would generate a huge traffic and have "a revolutionary effect in settling the country," the report also pointed to an initial operating deficit of about £70,000 annually for some years. Total construction cost was estimated at £3,685,400. Although this was to prove altogether inadequate, it seemed a more than reasonable figure at the time. For the line's infancy, the report projected a somewhat extravagant but not unrealistic schedule of six trains weekly; each would include one composite carriage (first- and second-class), two third-class carriages, and goods wagons with a total freight capacity of 130 gross tons. Drawn by 28-ton "F" class locomotives from India (fueled either by coal or locally obtained wood), these trains would run at an average speed of twelve miles per hour, covering the total distance between the coast and the lake in slightly over two days. Stations were to be situated no more than thirty miles apart to enable convenient watering and fueling. The recommended track width was three feet six inches rather than meter gauge, since the former was used by British railways in Egypt and South Africa.

The proposed route would be 657 miles long, running roughly parallel to the caravan trail from Mombasa and across the Rift, traversing the valley's western wall at the point where the Mau escarpment split into the Kamasia and Elgeyo ranges and then continuing west for fifty miles to the upper waters of the Nzoia river. From here, the tracks would follow the river's course southwest for another hundred miles until they reached the small gulf known as Berkeley Bay on the northeastern shore of the lake. The final hundred miles between Berkeley Bay and Mengo's port of Entebbe (then called Port Alice, for Portal's wife) would be covered not by rail but on a 200-ton shallow-draft steamer. As we shall see, this route was not without drawbacks. Among other things, it crossed the Taru desert, although an alternative right of way had been surveyed along the Sabaki river to the north. Even more serious flaws would become evident with the actual laying of the tracks. The report itself stressed the need for "a further and more detailed survey, which must necessarily take place before construction." Owing largely, however, to mounting impatience—which at times seemed to border on panic—among imperial strategists, that second survey was never made.

*

There was a certain amount of official resistance, to be sure. Even in early 1895, the Rosebery Cabinet seemed bound to the principles embodied in Grey's statement that railway construction must not be a Government enterprise, but the Administration could be seen to weaken under escalating Conservative-Unionist pressure. In the House of Lords, Salisbury began invoking the ever-reliable conspiracy to choke off the Nile. In February he spoke darkly of "four if not five Powers that are steadily advancing towards the upper waters of the Nile," and warned that Government vacillation in pushing ahead with the railway could result in Uganda's loss to a European rival—with, of course, dire consequences for the Suez Canal and India. Opposition impatience was soon rewarded. At about this time, Rosebery had appointed a committee to study the feasibility and cost of building the line. Among other things, the committee examined a proposal that a monorail system be adopted; it also advocated pinching pennies and reducing the original track width to a narrow three-foot gauge. There was some hope that the committee would recommend turning the whole project over to a private firm, but after unsatisfactory bids were received from five engineering concerns, the conclusion was reached that construction must, after all, be an official undertaking. Government found itself virtually pledged to building the railway.

But the vagaries of politics decreed against a Liberal-sponsored line. On June 21, 1895, Rosebery's Government, its majority in Commons dwindling, was defeated on a relatively minor question of munitions supply, and Salisbury returned to power. The next decade would see the Liberals in all but total eclipse as Tory expansionism carried the Empire to its apogee.

The new Government lost no time in removing the last obstacle to the railway. In August, the report of the Rosebery committee was presented to Parliament, along with a request for £20,000 to cover initial expenses of construction. Curzon, Salisbury's newly appointed Under-Secretary of State for Foreign Affairs, told the Commons that a British Protectorate in Uganda could only be seen as "absurd ... unless you had a railway to the coast," and added: "Nothing is more certain than that if we do not construct a railway to the lake, the Germans will."* (The Germans in fact had already started.) After only marginal opposition, the vote passed and Government continued to forge ahead. In September, a permanent Railway Committee was created; composed of Foreign Office officials, it would serve as a sort of board of directors, formulating policy and overseeing field operations. One of its first acts was to appoint George Whitehouse as Chief Engineer.

Shortly afterwards, the Committee recommended that the three-foot rail width be abandoned for meter gauge. This was partly because the predominantly meter-gauge Indian railways were expected to furnish the bulk of the rolling stock, but also, and far more significantly, because Salisbury was demanding a more rugged line that would meet the strategic requirements of his obsession with holding the upper Nile. There is an air of almost frantic unreality in the sense of crisis which Salisbury

---

* Curzon had what may have been a unique reason for favoring a railway through a wilderness. In 1888, he had been one of the first passengers on Russia's newly built Transcaspian line, and had written of it as a powerful sinew of the Russian imperial arm in central Asia.

appears to have felt at this time. Belgium and France, he was certain, had secretly agreed to launch a tandem drive toward the Nile valley, and on December 5, 1895—six days before Whitehouse first arrived in Mombasa— we find him privately informing the Queen that "our only chance is to keep the thing quiet until our railway to Uganda is sufficiently far advanced to enable us to send troops by it." In point of fact, Salisbury's fears were by no means entirely groundless. Three years later, a British–French confrontation would take place on the upper Nile, and the railway would loom large in Britain's military planning. But the outcome of that showdown would have been no different had the line never been built.

At the end of 1895, however, time seemed of the essence. So great was the haste to push the rails toward the lake that construction was well under way before July 2, 1896, when the actual bill authorizing funds for building the line was introduced in Parliament. By now, of course, there was not the slightest doubt that the vote would carry, but Labouchere led a corporal's guard of Radical diehards in a determined last-ditch resistance, warning that whenever Government "annexes some wretched, miserable jungle in the centre of Africa, we will be called upon to build a railroad to it." He was especially critical of the £3.6 million cost estimate, and declared that the final figure would "in all probability" come closer to £5,000,000, a prophecy that was to prove accurate almost to the last shilling. A realist, Labouchere must also have known he was beating the air, for by now the mood of Parliament was receptive only to exhortations to the fulfillment of Britain's manifest destiny in east Africa. Curzon provided them. He replied to Labouchere with a wild misstatement of facts, informing the House that "British settlers are ... already arriving ... and ... are starting plantations of coffee." He also threw down the imperial gauntlet: "We have taken over this country for better or worse," he said, "but that question is not now before the House... The whole policy of the British Protectorate in Uganda has been explained, criticised, vindicated and accepted more than once by overwhelming votes... The necessary corollary of the dominion we have established is that we should have railway communication between the interior and the seaboard." The bill passed by 255 to 75. The defeat, however, did not silence Labouchere. He and Curzon would cross swords again, and one of the latter's speeches to the House on the railway was to produce this Gilbertian rejoinder in *Truth*:

What it will cost no words can express;
What is its object no brain can suppose;
Where it will start from no one can guess;
Where it is going to nobody knows
What is the use of it none can conjecture;
What it will carry there's none can define;
And in spite of George Curzon's superior lecture,
It clearly is naught but a lunatic line.

We have yet to hear the last of Labouchere. But in the meanwhile, the imperialists had gained the upper hand. They had won Uganda and had been given carte blanche to build their long-sought railway. All that remained was to justify both.

PART II
THE LUNATIC EXPRESS

8

SLOW FREIGHT
TO ARMAGEDDON

If eleventh-hour haste had seemed to characterize the final decision and plans for construction of the Uganda Railway, it was at least to the credit of Government and the Railway Committee that neither set a specific target date for the line's completion. There was, however, a general consensus, based mainly on the informed opinion of engineers associated with the project, that the rails ought to reach Lake Victoria in four or five years—by mid-1900, perhaps, at the very latest. With the 657-mile line drawn up in Macdonald's survey as a measuring rod, this meant laying down roughly 130 miles of track a year, a not unreasonable expectation even for Africa. On December 31, 1896, slightly over twelve months after Whitehouse's arrival in Mombasa, railhead had pushed exactly twenty-three miles into the interior. If construction were to continue at that pace, the first train would make the run from coast to lake some time in 1924.

A good deal of the delay had been inevitable. In its feverish anxiety to begin construction, the Railway Committee had appeared to minimize certain major difficulties which Mombasa presented as a railway terminus. Starting the line from the island meant spanning Macupa creek, which separated Mombasa and the mainland; while this was no insuperable obstacle, it would nonetheless take time, and time was one of Whitehouse's most precious commodities. Perhaps an even thornier problem was posed by water, or rather the lack of it. During 1896, the vanguard of a huge railway labor army was to arrive from India: more than two thousand coolies, along with hundreds of Indian stonemasons, smiths, carpenters, surveyors, draftsmen and clerks. They would require ocean-sized quantities of drinking water. So too would the construction locomotives. Because of its selection as the railway's port, Mombasa had to be relied on for water supplies, not only while the tracks were being laid down on the island but far into the interior. "From what I have seen and know of the country," Whitehouse wrote the Railway Committee shortly after his arrival, "I can recommend no other plan than water trains for the first 100 miles." These trains were expected to haul a minimum of 10,000 gallons daily. The only question was where they would fill their tanks, for the silted yield of Mombasa's few ancient wells barely sufficed to meet the needs of the townspeople. A man-made drought loomed.

There was also the matter of Mombasa's suitability as a receiving point for the railway's astronomical tonnages of building materials and rolling stock. To reach Lake Victoria, over 600 miles of track were needed; this came to more than 200,000 individual thirty-foot rail lengths, each weighing 500 pounds, as well as 1.2 million sleepers (most of them steel, since creosoted teak was generally considered inadequate protection against white ants). To secure sleepers and rails, there were 200,000 fish-plates, 400,000 fishbolts and 4.8 million steel keys. The exact number of forty- and sixty-foot steel girders for viaducts and causeways was not immediately known, but the survey had shown tonnages running easily into five figures—just possibly six. Whitehouse also expected at least thirty locomotives, each weighing between twenty-five and thirty tons, not to mention a wheeled armada of tenders, brake vans, goods wagons and passenger carriages. So ponderous a bulk could never be brought ashore in Mombasa's dhow-cramped Old Harbor, which therefore meant converting the adjoining Kilindini—devoid of any facilities—into a modern port. Wharves, warehouses, machine shops and repair sheds had to be built. Even before that, it had been necessary for Whitehouse to find or improvise living quarters for the coolies and arrange suitable accommodations for his large engineering and administrative staff—in a city where lodging space (already fully occupied) consisted of a two-sto-rey flophouse ornately misnamed the Grand Hotel.

Thus, even before platelaying could begin, Whitehouse had his hands full, for over four months, with the task of setting up his base of oper-ations. At Kilindini it was necessary to build from the ground up; after acquiring about 370 acres of shorefront, Whitehouse set about trans-forming the virgin tract into a terminus-cum-reception point. It was all quite primitive at first. Arriving cargo vessels had to shift their loads of tracks, sleepers and other materials to three cumbersome 100-ton lighters, which were taken as close to shore as high tide permitted. Then there would be a wait until half tide, when a stumbling, sweating, shouting battalion of Indian coolies and African porters simply manhandled the bulky goods ashore. To offload a single lighter took nearly a day. This precarious system, moreover, was only partially workable, since it ruled out the transfer of locomotives and other rolling stock. Their delivery ashore had to await completion of a railed wooden jetty extending several hundred feet into the harbor and mounting a mobile steam crane which hoisted the vehicles directly on to the tracks.

The task of bringing in the necessary workers had also witnessed complications that militated against swift progress. "It is not anticipated," Macdonald's survey report had stated, "that any special inducements would be required to obtain Indian labour, beyond that of increased pay," but the report could not have foreseen a curious absence of enthusiasm for railway labor recruitment on the part of Indian officialdom. Somehow under the impression that the line was being built by a private company, the Indian Government took pains to protect its own nationals against any possible unfair labor practices. Before a single coolie was permitted to sign a contract, it became necessary to pass an amendment to the Indian Emigration Act, and the first small contingent of 350 workmen did not reach Mombasa until nearly two months after Whitehouse's arrival. Most significantly, however, the three-year contract itself stipulated that wages (minimum pay was fifteen rupees, or about $5.00, per month) "must not be fixed to task work." That clause alone openly invited the entire labor force to set its own leisurely pace of construction.

In time, however, some progress at Kilindini had become visible. Coco palms were felled by the hundreds to make way for sidings, turntables, machine shops, repair sheds, storage warehouses, accounts offices and a base hospital. To accommodate the supervisory staff and labor force, a ghetto of corrugated iron shanties and patchwork tents sprang up. The water shortage was relieved temporarily by damming a stream on the mainland and building a small reservoir for rainfall catchment. (Distilling machinery to convert seawater would be brought in later.) In due course, the chaste blue surface of the Kilindini lagoon acquired a patina of oil, ash and coal dust from the cargo ships, while the once immaculate ivory-white beach became a hissing, clanking, thudding factory, scarred with rails, strangled with smoke, littered with the metallic excreta of industry.

But even a fully equipped port at Kilindini would not have permitted the tracks to leave Mombasa until Macupa creek was spanned, and here the first serious obstacle arose. The original plan had simply been to throw a heavy embankment across the creek. This, however, would have blocked the passage of dhows, while a partial opening in the embankment would have created the risk of undermining. It was therefore decided instead to build a temporary wooden viaduct which would carry materials trains to the mainland until a steel bridge could be made. But with the change in plans, Whitehouse found himself in the somewhat ludicrous position of being hemmed in by trees while cabling England for wood: the only local timber of suitable dimensions and strength was situated some four hundred miles away on the escarpments of the Rift Valley—still inaccessible to bulk transport. Thus, completion of the temporary, 1,700-foot Salisbury Bridge (later renamed the Macupa Causeway) was delayed for eight months. It was not until early August of 1896 that the moat to the fortress of the interior was finally crossed.

The mainland did not go entirely ignored during the railway's captivity in Mombasa. Surveyors were feeling their way along the tentative alignment so murkily defined by the original Macdonald expedition of 1892, which the Government, in its haste to begin construction, had not seen fit to supplement. There were three main survey parties. One penetrated far into the interior, covering the route through the edge of Kikuyuland to the eastern escarpment of the Rift Valley. A second group moved out to Kibwezi, 190 miles from Mombasa, and mapped backwards across a seemingly interminable dandruff of bush country, its objective being to link up with a third party working inland from the coast. The latter reconnaissance found itself handicapped by the unexpected hazard of ambush, as the long-dormant Mazrui clan mounted a revolt against the new British Administration and spent the better part of a year shooting up the entire coast. It was only when troop reinforcements had been brought in from India that Government was able to restore order. Meanwhile, however, the progress of the coast survey, in the understated words of the Railway Committee, had been "somewhat impeded ... by the consequent inability of the Protectorate to furnish efficient guards." But even without such obstacles the three survey parties were unable to stake out a complete line until 1900, and at times the builders would nearly overtake the mapmakers. As Mervyn Hill put it, "survey and construction advanced together—the former not so far ahead of the latter." A more precarious method of planning a railway could hardly have been devised.

Nor did the initial findings encourage. "The result of these surveys," said the Railway Committee in its first report to Parliament, "... has been to show considerable divergences... There is every reason against making definite forecasts, either as to cost or time of completion, until far more is known in detail." Enough, however, had been learned to reveal disquieting surprises. After crossing Macupa creek, the route followed a serpentine path up the low-lying but sharply sloped Rabai hills directly overlooking Mombasa. "Range on range of low thickly-wooded hills succeed one another," the report continued, "and in the course of 15 miles the country rises 560 feet. From this point the country has proved to be more undulating than was expected... The roughness of the ground has precluded the laying of the surface line contemplated... The progress of the rails has had to wait on earthworks in alternate cuttings ranging up to 45 feet in depth and height." And even before work could begin on earth and rock movement, the bush and forest had to be cleared. In the Rabai hills, construction faced an all but impregnable stronghold of baobabs, mvule and thorn trees, linked by an iron grillwork of creepers and a barricade of secondary growth so dense that cutting parties could sometimes hack through no more than three hundred yards a day. Nearly two months were spent gouging out a passageway across the fifteen-mile obstacle course.

The tracks themselves advanced not much more swiftly. To the several hundred coolies who made up the railhead section, the task of platelaying was only slower than it was arduous and dreary. The men were out of their tents at sunrise every day, clambering sleepily aboard the materials train that would carry them forward to the head of the tracks. Here, rails and sleepers were quickly taken off the flatcars and stacked on the ground, while the train reversed to camp for its next load. Then the steel pathway began to inch ahead in a sort of limping leapfrog fashion. One gang placed the sleepers in rough alignment along one or two hundred yards of embankment. On their heels came teams of two men carrying thirty-foot rail lengths, slung from poles on their shoulders. When the rails had been laid on the sleepers, a third gang joined the individual track sections with rectangular steel fishplates, secured by fishbolts. Still another crew clipped the rails into the lugs of the sleepers, each rail length being tamped down with the blow of a sledgehammer and fixed even more firmly to the sleepers with steel keys driven home by keying hammers. When the entire section had been laid down, it was slued into correct alignment with crowbars. All this took anywhere from between three and six hours. By then the materials train would have returned with at least one more load of tracks and sleepers. The process was repeated all day.

Every ten or fifteen miles, the platelayers' camp would be shifted forward to the head of the tracks. The first move, at the end of September,

1896, not only reached railhead at mile 13 but also overtook the creeping advance parties, which had now been brought to a dead halt. Directly in their path lay a 400-foot-wide gully called the Mazeras ravine, which could not be bridged until the arrival of the rails enabled flatcars to deliver the necessary timbers. Platelaying had to be suspended for the twenty-five days it took to build the viaduct, and when the railhead section was finally able to move the tracks across the ravine and advance another mile and a half, a new obstacle reared its head. According to official records, the rainfall at Mazeras in November, 1896, came to twenty-seven and a half inches. For twenty-two more days, not even a sleeper could be put down. The following four months would see the rails advance another fifteen miles, covering the equivalent of two and a half city blocks daily.

During the same period, the joint effort of climate and terrain would also leave its mark on the line's 2,600 coolies. The very air was afflicted. A minor scratch from a small euphorbia thorn could go septic within hours and blossom into a festering jungle sore; rare was the Indian worker or European supervisor who did not carry at least one fist-sized blob of livid putrefaction on his arms, legs or trunk. It was a common sight to see platelayers drop their rail lengths or sleepers and stumble down embankments, frantically lowering trousers or dhotis as amoebic dysentery opened their bowels; no less often, the attacks caught them by surprise and they could only squat helplessly on the tracks. The abnormal rains did not abate until late in January of 1897, and wherever earth-moving gangs turned up the sodden laterite soil, their excavations rapidly became mosquito-breeding ponds. By December, 1896, more than 500 workers lay in leaking hospital tents, immobilized by malaria, dysentery, tropical ulcers and pneumonia. A month later, no less than fifty percent of the entire labor force was on the sick list.

Considering that the railway medical staff then consisted of five doctors and a dozen or so Indian surgical attendants, it was a minor miracle that fewer than 100 workers died in 1896, and that hospital cases could be reduced to a barely manageable ten percent by March of 1897. But just at that time, an outbreak of bubonic plague swept northwest India, and the flow of labor recruitment ground to a dead halt. The port of Karachi, where coolies embarked for east Africa, was slammed shut while medical officers established observation camps in which construction workers were quarantined. It was not until autumn that normal hiring procedures could be resumed. Since that hiatus meant withholding at least one thousand more coolies at a time when they were desperately needed, the quarantine may have delayed the progress of the rails for nearly a year.

African workers were unable to fill the gap beyond a point. During the initial weeks of construction, local labor had perforce been confined to porterage duties only, since even the most rudimentary tasks with elementary tools had seemed beyond the grasp of the few Giriama and Wanyika tribesmen who were persuaded to work on the line. It was only after long and painstaking by-the-numbers instruction in wielding— sometimes even in lifting—picks and spades that a few hundred Africans were able to join earth-moving crews. By March of 1897, the Railway Committee sounded a more hopeful note, reporting that advance labor recruiters had already signed on a sizable number of Wakamba to help build embankments near Kibwezi. But African labor was never regarded as a consistently reliable factor. Population density along the entire right of way came to no more than twelve persons per square mile at its heaviest; of these twelve, only two were adult males capable of serving construction. "Had dependence been placed on indigenous labor," stated the Committee's final report in 1904, "the works would not have been completed in twenty years."

If labor shortages impeded progress, inadequate rolling stock almost crippled it. "Economy of construction," Macdonald's survey report had emphasized, "demands abundance of rolling stock"—certainly a self-evident statement. The sole means of transporting bulk materials, workers and supplies from the coast to railhead were the very trains for which the tracks were being laid down. The Macdonald report had recommended a minimum of thirty locomotives for all-purpose haulage duties. In 1896 and 1897, Whitehouse was able to acquire 225 goods wagons from England and India, but until the end of 1897 he never had more than fifteen locomotives at his disposal. Five of these were of the "F" class used in India but specially constructed for the Uganda line. With their outsize boiler domes and headlamps, fanlike cowcatchers and ungainly 0-6-0 wheel arrangements, they suggested the Iron Horse of the old West in miniature. Despite their diminutive stature, however, these engines packed all the muscle needed to negotiate the stiff gradients and sharp curves that leaped and twisted along almost every mile of the route to the lake. But the engines, only part of an incomplete delivery, were also badly overworked. The remaining "F"s lay idle and unfinished in British yards as factory workers went on strike.

The other ten available locomotives were hoary heaps of steel that had long outlived their usefulness on Indian railways. Several of these relics—squat, pot-bellied little freaks with pipestem smokestacks and half-open cabs—proved capable only of shunting duties at Kilindini, where they clanked wearily between harbor and yards, breaking down constantly as if in protest at not having been retired. Regardless of age, moreover, all of the fifteen engines were seldom in working order at one time. At least six could almost invariably be found undergoing major repairs in Mombasa, their boilers being even more sensitive than human stomachs to brackish water. And when a locomotive was operational, it did not necessarily follow that anyone would be available to mount its footplate, man its throttle and feed its firebox. During one period, eleven of the line's twelve engine drivers tossed in malarial coma at the base hospital.

An insufficiency of locomotives did not comprise the only brake on Whitehouse's transport wheel. Even a full complement of factory-fresh engines would have been useless in the all-important function of supplying the hundreds of workers who cleared the bush and built the embankments miles in advance of railhead. Porters proved inadequate simply because there were not enough of them for the tasks at hand. Nearly all the full-time professional "Zanzibaris" were either employed in German territory to the south or had been engaged by the respective administrations of the East Africa and Uganda Protectorates to carry some ten thousand loads every year from the coast to various Government stations in the interior. It was possible to recruit a few porters from local tribes along the right of way, but the system worked badly. The men were not accustomed to carrying sixty- or seventy-pound loads over long distances, and as a rule showed themselves even more vulnerable to changes of climate than the Indian coolies. Indigenous porters, moreover, balked mightily at leaving their sharply circumscribed tribal districts, especially during planting and harvesting seasons; this alone ruled out any consistent reliance on the human backs which had always been the sine qua non of east African travel.

Whitehouse was therefore left with no choice but to bring vast numbers of animals into the service of forward transport. At one time the railway had no fewer than 800 donkeys, 639 bullocks, 350 mules and 63 camels—1,852 beasts of burden all told. Of these, more than 1,500 dropped like flies, or more correctly, dropped from the bite of the tsetse fly, since the first two hundred miles of the railway passed through one of the more heavily infested "fly belts" on the African continent. And of the few pack animals which did not succumb to trypanosomiasis, only a handful managed to survive the ravages of thirst when the tracks finally entered the Taru desert. Beyond the tsetse region and the Taru, transport animals were used successfully by railway and Government alike; the difficulty lay in bringing them across the first two hundred miles from Mombasa. Just as the old slave caravans had marked their progress with long lines of human corpses, so too did a trail of bullock and donkey cadavers, soon reduced to skeletons by vultures and hyenas, stake out the route beyond railhead. Mervyn Hill did not overdramatize when he wrote that "it seemed as if the very spirit of Africa resented the intrusion of the white man's railway."

*

Some idea of the day-to-day trials which men, animals and machines underwent during construction has been provided by the line's railhead engineer, Ronald O. Preston, who took charge of the platelaying gangs early in 1897. Preston had been building railways, harbor installations and other public works in India for eleven years, but like most of the Europeans on Whitehouse's staff, he found African railway construction totally foreign to his previous experience. So much so, in fact, that in 1948 (he had then been living in east Africa for nearly half a century) he described railhead's ups and downs in a book consisting largely of extracts and revisions from his own diaries. He called it *The Genesis of Kenya Colony*, and as a work of literary art it cannot be said to shine. Preston, who spent much of his childhood in an Indian orphanage, had little formal schooling and made no pretensions to stylistic mastery. Yet perhaps it is the book's very absence of polish that helps bring across the sinewy flavor of the railway adventure.

For Preston was involved, after all, in a virile enterprise. A contemporary photograph taken outside his tent at railhead shows a rugged man, obviously far more at home with hydraulic jacks and repeating rifles than with textbooks on syntax. Actually, the picture is dominated by Preston's wife, who sits placidly but expressionlessly on a rocker, her black straw boater, wide-sleeved white blouse and somber ankle-length skirt suggesting Maida Vale rather than the east African scrub. It should be said, however, that Florence Preston was not paying a visit. One of the few white women who accompanied railhead the entire distance to the lake, she is seen, seldom without a white parasol, in many photographs of construction. Yet her slightly incongruous presence at the entrance to the tent only serves to reinforce our impression of Preston himself. A trim but well-muscled man in his early thirties, he stares uncomfortably but directly at the camera from behind a cowboy-type black mustache. His checked cotton suit is stained and badly creased, but the rifle he holds across his knee is well oiled, and his camp chair is surrounded by a disarray of zebra skins and antelope horns. The man we see is a man of action.

Little time had been lost in introducing Preston to the scene of the action. On February 2, 1897, he had debarked at Kilindini with 300 coolies. Early next morning the party was aboard a materials train clanking toward railhead, then about thirty miles inland from the coast. The train had no passenger carriage and Preston made himself as comfortable as he could on a stack of creosoted pine sleepers in a goods wagon. It was, he wrote, "a very hot trip. No water to drink: had only coconut water and whisky. Got out of the wagon at railhead, pants, hands and netherlands badly creosoted. Met by transport officer, a real hospitable soul who invited me to tea: I gladly accepted the invite but pointing out the state of my hands asked him if I might have a bit of soap. 'Oh yes,' he replied, 'I can give you a lump of soap, but we have not a drop of water left in camp, have put the last into the kettle for tea.'"

This was the first of many dry days that Preston would experience at railhead. He soon came to welcome the scant and undetectable product of nearby waterholes, "which would catch what little rain fell and hold same till it evaporated or had been consumed by the creeping, crawling and other life in the bush. Some of these waterholes after standing for a few months would contain about equal parts of water and vegetable matter." When Preston was first offered a glass of the slime, his Indian servant "suggested straining it through the end of his turban, saying they always did that with the water they drank, but I did not appreciate the turban filter." Instead, he experimented by pouring a spoonful of the versatile Eno's into the glass. Instantly he saw the water "fiz up in hundreds of green bubbles, which on settling down left a thick green scum on the top ... with perfectly clear water below... All that was now necessary was to remove the green scum and refresh oneself with a draught of good? clear water."

The shortage of drinking water, however, was not Preston's most urgent problem at first. Being a conscientious overseer as well as a capable engineer, he saw the faltering progress of the tracks as a personal challenge, and he was naturally eager to push forward without delay. He was also frustrated at once. The platelaying section at that time consisted of 150 coolies, but when Preston called his first roll, only seventy men turned out. The eighty absentees, he learned, were not merely victims of the climate; many were also beneficiaries of the "task work" clause in the contract which stipulated a minimum monthly wage without regard to actual productivity. By 1897, the rule had proved so unrealistic that the contract had been revised to allow piecework. Even so, large numbers of coolies, either from habit or sheer inertia, appeared to prefer the old and less demanding system to the incentive of more money for more work.

When Preston arrived at railhead, he described his own platelayers as "enjoying six days rest during the week with the seventh as a holiday," and he realized immediately that some stratagem was necessary if the work were to proceed at an acceptable pace. He therefore lost no time in instructing his jemadars (foremen) to call for another turnout, explaining that he wished to learn whether the men were receiving sufficient rations. "The ruse answered": instead of 150 workers, 200 now assembled in front of Preston's tent. He then proposed that the men accept payment per mile rather than per month, "pointing out that they could ... be in a position to return to their homes with a goodly saving. The idea caught on and before many days the men settled down to their work interested and happy."

Preston was by no means the only European supervisor on the line who had to cajole his laborers into accepting piecework, but his own experiment with the psychology of the profit motive could not have come at a more opportune moment. Barely five miles ahead, a small brackish stream appropriately known as Maji ya Chumvi (salt water) flowed across the right of way. Although a special bridge-building section had been organized by now, it happened that the entire gang was down with malaria in February of 1897, and Preston received orders to throw a temporary span over the Maji ya Chumvi himself. The task did not strike him as intimidating. In India only a few months earlier, he had supervised the construction of a 300-foot lattice girder across a 200-foot gorge. Using a steam hoist, four 200-ton hydraulic jacks and a complicated system of trolleys to carry building stones, he had raised the immense span without difficulty. The Maji ya Chumvi, on the other hand, was barely thirty feet wide and its banks rose hardly more than fifteen feet above the stream itself. Bridging this creek with a forty-foot steel girder might almost have seemed a letdown to Preston. But when a pair of flatcars arrived at railhead with the girder, he found himself "up against a poser." For the train had brought no hauling or lifting machinery, and Preston was under orders to span the river without delay. For the previous few days, he wrote, "I had been regaling my headmen with various items of the programme carried out in the much talked of 300-feet span ... but here with a miserable 40-feet girder, perched on railway trucks, no derrick, tackle or jacks, and a batch of unskilled coolies, I certainly felt rather small."

To move the twenty-ton deadweight across the stream, Preston had only a few crowbars, several hundred wooden sleepers and his own ingenuity. They sufficed. He ordered the men to build a trestle of sleepers in the bed of the stream itself; these were laid crosswise to one another until they reached the level of the banks. Rails were then run temporarily across the trestle, providing a flimsy path for the flatcars carrying the girder. (The wagons had to be pushed out by the workers, as the railhead locomotive had gone to Kilindini for a shipment of tracks.) Once the girder reached its proper position, heavy teak sleepers were placed directly beneath each end, enabling the flatcars to be moved away and the temporary rails to be pulled out. After adjusting the girder's level and alignment with crowbars, the workers laid down the semi-permanent tracks and the Maji ya Chumvi "bridge" was completed. A few days later, when the first materials train crossed the river, Preston's men cheered wildly.

With the Maji ya Chumvi behind them, the tracks began to creep forward again. For a month, Preston was even able to show respectable progress; by the end of April, his platelayers, cracking along at the rate of one-third of a mile daily, had brought railhead to mile 51. In May, however, the whole creaking machinery of construction seemed about to fall to pieces once more. By now, the influx of coolie labor, previously reduced to a trickle by the Indian quarantine, had stopped entirely. At the very same time, the spring rains were setting in with an unprecedented vengeance. Some sections of the line lay beneath the heaviest rainfall that had ever been recorded in east Africa. Earthworks were washed away like mud pies. Several bridges collapsed into then-swollen rivers. For twenty-three days, all platelaying was suspended and Preston's crews were pulled back to help shore up the remaining embankments against the sodden onslaught of the deluge.

And less than ten miles from railhead lay the edge of the Taru, dry as a bone.

*

Seen through a railway engineer's eyes, the Taru desert at first appeared to offer no serious impediments to construction; in some respects it might almost have been called ideal. No cuttings and few embankments were required along the perfectly flat expanse, while the absence of waterways eliminated the time-consuming tasks of bridge and culvert building. All one had to do, it seemed, was set down the sleepers along the alignment and clip on the rails. The terrain, in fact, appeared tailor-made for a normal pace of construction, which would bring railhead out of the desert in forty days, possibly less. But the platelaying section, which entered the Taru in June, spent three months toiling across the thorn-congested skillet.

For the Taru was no lawn. In the conventional sense of the word it was not even a desert, but something more like a dense forest of wire-bristled, man-high, scrubbing brushes. "The bush clearing party ahead of us," wrote Preston, "must have had a very tough job ... and they can hardly be blamed for the thousands of jagged end stumps left jutting out of the ground, but our unfortunate barefooted coolies with bare legs were continually knocking up against these sharp stumps and suffered terribly... Before we had progressed many miles, more than half the coolies were laid up with angry ulcers on their legs, caused by the jagged ends." And whatever time may have been saved from throwing up bridges was lost again to heat exhaustion and thirst. Vast clouds of thick red dust vied with quivering heat waves to scour the throat and addle the brain. The sun's rays came down on the men's backs like a rain of lava and ricocheted up at their faces from the baking earth. Even after sunset, temperatures seldom fell below 100 degrees. On no day was it ever possible for the railhead party to move forward a single yard until the water train arrived, its tank cars filled with the tainted elixir of the Maji ya Chumvi. Since the precarious condition of the line ruled out pinpoint timetables for rail deliveries, the crews often endured long hours of dehydration before the shrill yelp of a locomotive whistle signaled the approach of the water train. On its arrival, wrote Preston, "the coolies would rush to get their mussocks filled, and as there were no taps or cocks on the tanks they would have to bale the water out ... as best they could. Owing to the ulcerated state of their bodies, these coolies carried a supply of iodoform ... with the result that their hands, arms and bodies were simply reeking ... so it is not hard to imagine the state of the drinking water after a few dozen coolies had filled their mussocks and incidentally had a semi bath while doing so."

Besides being waterless, the Taru was also devoid of game, thus preventing Preston from shooting for the pot and augmenting the men's daily diet of rice and maize meal. Not that wildlife was altogether absent. There was a species of frog that whistled rather than croaked, and the workers also "made the acquaintance of a very troublesome fly" whose bite introduced a microscopic worm beneath the skin. "In a few days," said Preston, "this develops into a full size maggot, and ... a boil like swelling appears." He added that neither worm nor inflammation were dangerous—"just give the swelling a good squeeze and the unwelcome maggot pops out"—but also acknowledged that the swarms caused the men intense discomfort. Nor did morale improve when, after reaching the seventieth mile in July, it was decided to lay the tracks on steel rather than wooden sleepers. (Timber had been used previously because the soil of the Taru was believed to contain potassium salts which corroded steel, still another error of the original survey.) At first, the coolies welcomed the changeover, since it meant that their bodies would no longer be coated with the gummy creosote that oozed from the wood. But their relief was short-lived; a few hours under the Taru sun transformed the steel sleepers into great branding irons, and it was not long before the platelayers' hands resembled barbecued hamburger meat.

It was also at mile 70 that construction of the telegraph line overtook the platelayers, and almost immediately clacked out an urgent message to the railhead telegraph officer: derailment at mile 54. Boarding a hand trolley, Preston and a jemadar hastened back to the scene. Perversely, rain had fallen the night before on one of the few spots in the Taru where an embankment had been made. By itself, the shower might have done no damage, but Preston was quick to notice the hoofprints of a rhinoceros which had crossed the tracks at this very point. The rain quickly filled the large potholes made by the rhino's feet, causing the earthwork to sag and later collapse under the weight of the oncoming train. The engine lay on its side, wheels askew, piston rods bent into hairpins. Goods wagons and flatcars sagged from the embankment like a broken spine. But it was not a supply train that had been smashed up. As he helped move the injured passengers to safety, Preston noticed that nearly all were uniformed askaris. The Uganda Railway, as if it were not sufficiently hamstrung by the Taru desert, had been called into service as a troop transport for a major British military expedition.

"Go for them! Go for them! The Swahilis are women, and will run!"

The new and unexpected role for Whitehouse's already hard-pressed staff expressed the culmination of Salisbury's obsessive concern for the security of the upper Nile. By now, in fact, his fears seemed justified, since France was making a disturbingly visible thrust in the direction of that vulnerable region. The move could not have been called sudden. As early as 1895, the Quai d'Orsay had been urging acceptance of a proposal by Captain Jean-Baptiste Marchand, a colonial army officer, that an expedition march east from French Congo–Ubangi possessions and plant the tricolor in the Nile valley. In due course, Marchand's plan became embodied in a more ambitious effort that called for a corresponding push westward from Abyssinia. If successful, the two-pronged military drive would not merely threaten the Suez Canal but simultaneously fulfill

France's imperial aim of a broad east–west sash of French soil from the Red Sea to the Atlantic. This vast exercise in annexation also promised to collide with, and hopefully to snap, the steadily advancing and even longer north—south axis of British control between the Mediterranean and Cape of Good Hope. Geopolitically, here indeed was a grand design.

On paper, the scheme was quite easily realized. Its implementation was another matter. Separated by nearly 2,000 miles of largely unexplored rain forest, bush and desert, the two French expeditions, with Marchand himself leading the force from the west, had no way of synchronizing or even roughly coordinating their movements. Once the campaign got into gear, virtually no effort was made toward that end, and what could have been a formidable challenge to British supremacy on the upper Nile was to end not with a bang but with the whimper of French humiliation. While the threat lasted, however, there was cause for real alarm. Although strategists in Paris naturally sought to keep it under wraps, an undertaking of such magnitude could not long remain a secret, and it soon saw Britain plotting her own counter-move on the equatorial chessboard.

Salisbury had made his initial maneuver in March of 1896, when the Cabinet ordered General Herbert Kitchener, Sirdar of the Egyptian army, to lead a large force southward toward Dongola in the Sudan, with a view to the long-awaited reconquest of that country from the Mahdists. The action came on the heels of a seemingly unrelated event—the Abyssinian rout of the Italian army at Adowa—which in fact provided Britain with a rationale for her immediate move. No matter that Italy's African ambitions had been the virus of Salisbury's Nile phobia seven years earlier. There was great feeling in Europe that black savages must not be permitted to work their will on the forces of enlightenment without expecting, at the very least, a show of strength from civilized nations; and Salisbury found Western indignation useful to his purposes. In a despatch to Cromer in Cairo, he spoke of being "inspired specially by a desire to help the Italians." But the same letter also revealed his real objective: "to kill two birds with one stone, and to use the same military effort to plant the foot of Egypt rather farther up the Nile." Of all people, Cromer needed no explanation of what Salisbury was up to. As the author of the Nile hypothesis, he knew quite well that Marchand and not Italy was the Prime Minister's real concern.

Yet Salisbury was not content with a southward drive alone, regardless of its military sinew. Not only the Mahdists, but more than a thousand miles of desert blocked the path to the upper Nile regions. A slightly shorter avenue ran northwest from Mombasa. The pace of

British troops marching along that route would obviously be accelerated by the railway, and, as he had made plain, Salisbury regarded that very function as the line's raison d'être. In March of 1896, to be sure, the tracks had not even been laid down in Mombasa, much less on the mainland, but the unhurried character of many nineteenth-century international crises seemed to be favoring Britain at this juncture. By early 1897, the railway's mileage, albeit barely more than a finger joint into the interior, appeared sufficient in Salisbury's eyes to serve as a base for a flanking move against Marchand from the Indian Ocean. If France could apply a pincers, so could he.

Like the Kitchener mission, the push northwest via Uganda was to be camouflaged. In April, 1897, Salisbury approached his Chancellor of the Exchequer, Sir Michael Hicks Beach, with a request for £35,000 to mount "an expedition to the east bank of the Nile to make friends with the tribes before the French get there … the ostensible reason for the despatch will be to explore the source of the Juba." Since the headwaters of the Juba river lie some 400 miles east of the Nile, Salisbury's veil of secrecy appeared reasonably opaque, although it is not likely that any interested foreign parties would have swallowed whole the statement that a heavily armed combat team was carrying out a purely scientific mission. Still, the operation itself could be seen as promising. Troop trains would carry 200 men of the expedition from Mombasa to railhead, whence they would proceed on foot to Eldama ravine on the Mau escarpment and rendezvous with three companies of the Uganda Rifles. Now five hundred strong, the force was to march north in the direction of the Juba, then swing sharply westward and form a cordon along the upper Nile in the southern Sudan. There was even some hope on Britain's part that the troops from the coast would effect a junction with Kitchener. From a geopolitical standpoint, the entire scheme appeared a counterstroke no less bold in conception than the French master plan to wrest the Nile valley from its absentee claimants.

Actually, however, the enveloping drive from Mombasa had two serious flaws. One was that after leaving railhead and commencing the push northwest toward the Sudan, the troops would be cut off entirely from all lines of supply and communication. (The Kitchener force could always rely on the Nile.) The other drawback was the terrain: between Eldama ravine and the southern Sudan lay a barely explored madness of mountains and desert which all but canceled out the possibility of swift movement so essential to reaching the arena of confrontation before the French. It was in fact a fantastically unrealistic route to follow— although given the clouds of crisis that had been gathering, strategists might have felt it worth the gamble. No one, on the other hand, could have foreseen that the principal result of the expedition, far from bolstering the British grip on the upper Nile, was to bring the Empire within an ace of losing Uganda.

*

The derailment at mile 54 was hardly an auspicious beginning, especially in the eyes of the expedition's commanding officer, who, as it happened, was the same man who had led the railway survey party in 1892. Now a major, Macdonald had already assured Salisbury of his confidence in making a successful stand on the Nile by early 1898. However, the wreckage that surrounded Macdonald's advance columns in the Taru desert in the summer of 1897 was merely the first setback he would sustain during fifteen months of unremitting ill fortune. Blame for what happened does not attach to Macdonald. No individual, in fact, can be held accountable for the forgotten but no less catastrophic anti-British convulsion known as the Uganda Mutiny. It arose mainly from the mindless oversights of a faceless military bureaucracy, and it was hastened by events beyond anyone's control.

*

The seeds of revolt had been taking root among the 1,600 Sudanese who made up the Uganda Rifles. Many of these troops were the same men who had fought under Emin Pasha and who had later joined the British forces with Lugard. Since that time they had served the Queen faithfully and valiantly. Responsible for maintaining a semblance of law and order in Uganda, they had been engaged for six years in an almost endless succession of punitive expeditions and pacification campaigns. They had played the major role in partially successful efforts to subdue Kabarega, whose raids on Uganda's northern borders had necessitated strong countermeasures which in turn had brought half of Bunyoro under British rule. Only the Sudanese were capable of holding in check the Nandi tribesmen who lived near the eastern shore of the lake and who constantly harassed the caravan road, seriously disrupting Government transport and communications. As one Protectorate official put it, the Sudanese were "a little army." But they received little reward for their labors, and their resentment was not to be discovered until too late.

"The Sudanese soldier," as described by another official, "has great qualities and serious defects. He has soldier-like instincts, is brave, physically enduring and patient; on the other hand, he is, from his very patience, profoundly treacherous." While the legitimate grievances of the Sudanese troops could hardly have been called grounds for treachery, neither were they conducive to morale. Constant campaigning, which saw them marching back and forth across the 300 miles between the Rift and the Ruwenzori, allowed the men virtually no leave. Problems of discipline often arose because many of their British officers did not understand Arabic and thought it beneath them to learn the language. A revolving-door system of officer assignment contributed further to discord. Frederick Jackson, who was Acting Commissioner of Uganda at this time and who also commanded a company of Sudanese, wrote that "the few [officers] with personality, who got to know their men and the men to know them, left, never to return. It was not known then ... that the Sudanese require 'fathering' and that come-and-go temporary officers were not what they desired." A budget-obsessed Foreign Office allotted next to nothing for the troops' uniforms and food supply. Photographs show riflemen garbed in tattered leopard skins and rag bundles which would not have survived a single washing. Inadequate rations left the Sudanese no choice but to live by plunder. Wages were held to a level that could only have been an affront even by African standards of the time. Sudanese askaris in the adjoining East Africa Protectorate received a minimum of fifteen rupees (about $5.00) per month; the Uganda troops were paid four rupees in trade goods—almost always several months in arrears owing to transport tie-ups. Jackson wrote of one occasion when suppressed giggles were heard within a formation of Uganda Rifles after he had announced that wages would be raised to seven rupees. When the men were dismissed, he asked an askari what had caused the mirth, and "was tickled at his reply: 'Effendi,' the man said, 'what is the good of raising our pay to Rs. 7 when you sometimes cannot pay us Rs. 5?'"

In many respects, these proud fighting men seemed almost to be little more than coolies with rifles, and they were thus easily exploited by a dissident element. Sir Harry Johnston, the painter-naturalist-administrator who served as Special Commissioner in Uganda in 1900, wrote the Foreign Office of his certainty that "sooner or later a mutiny amongst the Sudanese would have occurred ... quite independent of their other grievances." The reason, he said, was that these Muslim soldiers were "secretly contemptuous of the overlordship of a Christian Power," and that "the more ambitious amongst their native officers secretly conceived the idea of driving out the British and creating a great Muhammadan Kingdom in Uganda and its adjoining territories." All that was needed in the summer of 1897 was some act of British officialdom that would exhaust even the stoic patience of the rank and file.

What brought things to a head was a different rebellion, led by Uganda's most celebrated troublemaker, Mwanga, who, in Johnston's words, "had never taken favourably to British protection ... inasmuch as such control restricted him from the perpetration of the cruelties and acts of injustice in which his perverse nature delighted." Early in July, Mwanga rallied a large number of malcontents in Buddu, only to be routed almost at once and driven into German territory, where he was made a prisoner. The Sudanese who scattered the "rebel" army had been brought into Buddu by forced march from the east, where they had just concluded a successful but bone-wearying punitive campaign against the Nandi. And now, scarcely before the troops could catch their breath, they were ordered to execute an about-face and return without delay to whence they had come, as reinforcements for the Macdonald expedition. It was too much. Despite the ostensible secrecy surrounding that mission, the Sudanese knew that Macdonald's route would pass through an unknown and virtually waterless land, that they might not see their wives and children again for years—if indeed they returned at all. Protests to a ranking British officer in Kampala fell on deaf ears. Hence one is not surprised that when he met the Sudanese contingents on September 20, Macdonald described them as "much fatigued by the marches and counter-marches they had been through," and "by no means in a high state of discipline."

This understated the case. Near the breaking point, the Sudanese at last gave vent to their pent-up frustrations in a respectfully worded but no less enraged recital of grievances to Macdonald. Having been responsible for the arrest of Selim Bey four years earlier, Macdonald may not have seemed the ideal officer to treat with the men who had almost worshipped Selim; but he proved a surprisingly sympathetic listener. Lieutenant Herbert H. Austin, who had been with Macdonald on the railway survey in 1892 and was now attached to the Nile expedition, wrote that "until 9:30 that evening was Macdonald palavering and discussing all details with the native officers, with no thought for dinner, which we were all simply dying to begin on... Yet people who knew not our Chief at all, and had never worked with him, accused him of being hasty, unsympathetic and inconsiderate in his dealings with natives! We always used to say he erred far too greatly on the other side, and thought too much about conciliating naked savages." Macdonald told the men that he would take immediate steps to redress their wrongs, and his accommodating attitude went far to soothe passions. Only on one point—the expedition itself—was he unable to give way, and that question of course was the heart of the protest. Within hours, a Sudanese officer, Mbaruk Effendi, persuaded a number of men from one of the companies to desert; the group rapidly snowballed into a sizable force which stood up to the still-loyal troops in a brief but crisp exchange of rifle fire. It seemed only a matter of time before the entire Sudanese contingent would join the defectors.

At this point, Jackson himself arrived on the scene and visited the mutineers' camp under a flag of truce in an effort to win them back. He made a point of writing down each of their complaints in detail (although a heavy rain fogged his monocle and blurred his notes almost beyond legibility), and went so far as to promise unconditional pardons for the rank and file if they laid down their arms. Unlike most British officials in Uganda, Jackson enjoyed the undiluted trust and affection of the Sudanese; he may have been the only white man in the country who could have nipped the mutiny in the bud. But he was not in time; the outbreak had gathered too much momentum to be stopped. More and more men were deserting, and within a few days the rebel numbers had swelled to three hundred. Marching west toward the Nile, pillaging the countryside, they enlisted whatever scattered Sudanese units they met on their route. Hot on their heels came Macdonald and Jackson. The original expeditionary force was now reduced to eighteen Sikhs and two Swahili rifle companies, but Macdonald knew that he must intercept the mutineers. If he did not, they would push on to Kampala, rally the disaffected Sudanese at the fort, and Britain, in all likelihood, would be driven from Uganda by her own troops.

On October 16, the rebels stopped outside the Government post at the village of Luba's, the same spot where Hannington had been murdered twelve years earlier. A 100-man Sudanese garrison was now stationed here under the command of Major A. B. Thruston, one of the few British officers in Uganda who spoke Arabic fluently. Having led Sudanese troops with considerable success, Thruston felt confident that his own men would remain loyal—an optimism which proved misplaced when the garrison made him a prisoner and opened the fort to the mutineers. But the halt at least enabled Macdonald to close the gap. Hastily deploying his troops on the high ground surrounding the fort, he now had the rebels boxed in. The latter, however, were not disposed to sustain a long siege. Although their force by this time numbered more than five hundred men, they were no longer simply mutineers but outlaws, and would remain so until and unless an even greater numerical superiority over the British gained them the upper hand in Uganda. Nothing, therefore, must prevent them from linking up with the Kampala garrison. As a matter of plain survival, the Sudanese were bound to the offensive.

At dawn on October 19, they attacked, catching the British force with its guard down. On the previous day, Mbaruk and two other officers, Bilal and Suliman, had made it known that they wanted to parley with Macdonald; hence the latter had posted only one officer on sentry duty that night, not expecting trouble while the possibility of a negotiated settlement existed. Jackson recalls having been asleep in his tent when a bugle sounded the alarm. "As there was no time to dress," he wrote, "I slipped into a pair of gum boots and a coat, buckled on a revolver, and seizing a long-range and very accurate magazine .303 rifle, hurried to my post." The ensuing engagement was the fiercest fought in east Africa since the battle of Mengo hill—and far more crucial to the Empire's destiny.

"Well thought out" was Jackson's description of the mutineers' tactical planning. With darkness as a cloak, they had slipped from the fort and advanced up the slope in two columns. Mbaruk and Bilal were to launch a head-on assault, while Suliman "made a detour to their left, in order to swoop down on us along the ridge and take us in the flank." To that point, the move went off smoothly. But "poor fat Suliman," as Jackson called him, was slow in reaching his position, and meanwhile the frontal attackers had been spotted. "In order to gain time Bilal or Mbaruk began to shout that their intentions were not in any way hostile, that they only wished for a palaver, and other idle excuses." The deception proved partially successful when Suliman's force topped the crest of the ridge and advanced on the poorly defended British flank. Austin recalled that Suliman himself led the charge, shouting "Go for them! Go for them! The Swahilis are women, and will run!" But the Swahilis stood fast as Macdonald ordered them to hold their fire until the attackers came to within fifty yards—"perilously near," in Jackson's opinion. Suliman was among the first to fall in a withering fusillade which, according to Jackson, "not only checked the advance but practically cleared the ridge."

Meanwhile, the frontal attack had been hurled back by the fire of two Sikh-manned Maxim guns. But the rebels had delivered only the first of eight determined assaults on the hill, and as the morning went by it appeared certain that the British line must crack. Macdonald's troops were not only heavily outnumbered but far less well trained than the superbly seasoned Sudanese. The contest could have been likened to a battle between a platoon of militia recruits and a battalion of the Coldstream Guards. (And the Sudanese had a Maxim gun of their own.) Rout, in fact, seemed a foregone conclusion when the mutineers were reinforced by two hundred Baganda Muslims, who displayed characteristically fanatical courage. "Within two hundred yards," wrote Jackson, "several of them began as an act of defiance to wriggle their bodies as they do at a dance, in a very obscene and suggestive manner ... one, more defiant and conspicuous than the others, collapsed, while in the very act of his vigorous contortions." By now, moreover, Jackson "was not a little perturbed" to learn from Macdonald that the British ammunition reserve had been reduced to fifteen rounds per man. "Such a serious position obviously had to be kept dark, as even a rumour of it might have led to a panic, and disaster through desertions." And shortly after receiving this news, Jackson himself was put out of action by "a blow that felt as if it might have been a kick by a cart-horse." A Sudanese bullet had torn through his lungs, and he spent the next several days in gasping delirium.

At about eleven o'clock, however, he came out of his coma briefly on hearing a great cheer rise from the Swahilis and Sikhs. The effort of attempting to scale the slope under the combined barrage of British fire and equatorial sun had begun to tell on the Sudanese, and Macdonald had ordered a counterattack that decisively cleared the hill. Exhausted, the mutineers withdrew to the fort, where, in their frustrated rage, they shot Thruston and two other British officers. Although they had not been defeated, neither had they been able to break out. Macdonald could claim a victory of sorts.

*

Now commenced an eleven-week stalemate. Both sides were desperately short of ammunition and neither dared risk another major clash. The rebels, although solidly entrenched in the fort, had shown themselves unable to penetrate the encircling British line, and waited in the hope of being relieved by the Kampala detachment and possibly by other Sudanese units from Bunyoro. But the latter did not materialize, while a courageous Administration official in Kampala had been able to disarm the former. Macdonald's force, however, was not much better off, even when beefed up by 1,600 Baganda levies under the redoubtable Apolo Kagwa who had shared command with Lugard in the anti-Muslim campaign of 1891. The Baganda troops, even if they had been sufficiently disciplined to be of use in a concerted assault on the fort, were then short of percussion caps for their muzzle-loaders. Nor did another mixed bag of regulars from the East Africa Protectorate appreciably augment the besiegers' firepower. Urgent messages begging for massive reinforcements from India were carried by runner to railhead and cabled on to Salisbury. But the wheels of military administration turned with maddening slowness. Macdonald's tactics were of necessity confined to attacks, under sharp rifle fire, on large plantain groves which provided the Sudanese with their main food staple. His younger brother, Lieutenant Norman Macdonald, was killed in one such engagement.

In early January of 1898, the rebels found their opportunity to break out. The British force at Luba's had by then been depleted by another Sudanese insurrection in Buddu which obliged Macdonald to march west with two hundred men. At that time the ever troublesome Mwanga also chose to escape from detention in German territory and return to Buddu himself, professing Islam and rallying 2,000 of the region's disaffected Muslims in an anti-British jihad. While Macdonald was quelling the Buddu Sudanese and scattering Mwanga's "army," the mutineers at Luba's managed to elude the weakened besieging force and commence a swift move toward Lake Kyoga, about sixty miles to the north. The rebel objective now was to effect a junction with the Sudanese detachments in Bunyoro and thus gain the long-sought military mastery of Uganda. With a commanding lead over their British pursuers, nothing seemed to stand in the mutineers' way.

But it ended as quickly as it had begun. Late in January, Macdonald was able to leave Buddu and resume command of the original force. He lost no time in despatching a section of riflemen on a swift flanking movement into Bunyoro, where the Sudanese troops were taken by surprise and disarmed. The main British column having at last been reinforced by a large sepoy detachment, Macdonald himself led the northward pursuit of the rebels, whose pace was being reduced by the boggy terrain on the approaches to Lake Kyoga. On February 24, after making a seventeen-hour forced march through a waist-deep papyrus swamp, Macdonald's troops and the Baganda levies finally overtook the mutineers at a place called Kabagambe on the lake shore. Bayonets fixed, the Sudanese charged, only to be hurled back by the cold steel of the sepoys and the Swahili "women," who then counterattacked in force. Before the day was out, more than a hundred Sudanese corpses lay half submerged on the sodden battlefield. The remainder of the rebels had taken to the bush in confusion. The Uganda Mutiny was over.

*

By May, Macdonald was able to resume his upper Nile mission, although thanks to the mutiny this effort was now nine months behind schedule.

On July 18, 1898, from the village of Save near the northern slopes of Mount Elgon, he drew some handwriting on the wall in a despatch to Salisbury. "Your Lordship will be able to gather," wrote Macdonald, "... that the expedition is by no means on the same footing as when it originally started ... and I find that, taking transport, stores &c. into consideration, I shall only be able to keep to the field for four or five months, although I reduce the strength of my columns as far as possible." On October 21, the depleted force reached a place called Tarangole, well into the Sudan. Nearly four hundred miles, however, still separated Macdonald from his destination, and by now his troops were subsisting on a starvation diet of groundnuts. There was no other alternative but to turn back. In the end—and after almost another year—it was the presence of Kitchener's southward-moving army that brought to a close the French bid for a coast-to-coast African empire.

Thus Salisbury's railway strategy would appear, at the very least, to have been redundant as a means of defending the Nile valley.

"The inspection train traversed the long straight on the Taru desert... at the rate of 30 miles an hour, without seriously interfering with the comfort of our afternoon tea."

Although useless in thwarting French designs on the upper Nile, it is probable that the railway saved Uganda instead. Nothing else could have enabled the relatively swift movement of a desperately needed troop increment to the besieged protectorate. Despite the insatiable demands of construction, despite water shortages, despite illness among the workers, despite continuing locomotive and goods wagon breakdowns, Whitehouse somehow managed to set aside enough rolling stock for Uganda's military relief. Preston wrote that although the line's English engineers and other staff members were "keen to get away to swell the small party of defenders ... we were told that we were just as useful, even more, pushing the rails ahead so that stores and trained troops, could be rushed on as quickly as possible." During the month of January, 1898, a special train was made up every other day to carry troops from Mombasa to railhead. More than 130 miles of track had now been laid down. To cover that distance on foot would have taken upwards of six weeks for large army units encumbered with many tons of equipment and supplies. Aboard the improvised troop trains it was a matter of less than thirty-six hours. After railhead, to be sure, there remained the punishing march over the Rift Valley escarpments and the crossing of the Nile; but the major obstacle of the Taru desert had been removed, and thus a four- or five-month march from the coast to Uganda was cut by about one-third. By the end of January, the 700 riflemen of an Indian infantry regiment had reached Kampala. They were followed only a few weeks later by a 400-man Swahili battalion and an additional 400 Sikhs and Punjabis. Throughout the year, the railway continued to shovel reinforcements into Uganda—for a total of more than 28,000 troops and porters, 1,200 baggage animals and nearly 2,500 tons of military equipment.

All this martial sinew was necessary, since the quelling of the mutiny did not immediately end a state of emergency. There were scattered but dangerous pockets of resistance among those Sudanese who had not been taken prisoner at Kabagambe. Mwanga, too, was still at large. Having evaded capture after the rout of his Muslim force, he had made his way to Bunyoro and entered into an unholy alliance with his former arch-enemy, Kabarega. As long as those two unruly monarchs, supported by the Banyoro armies and the unvanquished Sudanese, were free to harass Uganda from what remained of Kabarega's kingdom, the British position would continue insecure if not desperate. "To the very last," wrote Jackson, Kabarega "was a nasty thorn in our side." By June of 1899, however, Mwanga and Kabarega were finally hunted down and deported to the Seychelles.* Although the Sudanese holdouts were not dispersed until 1901, the defeat of the two kings broke the back of the crisis. But for the railway, there is no telling how long Uganda might have continued in turmoil.

*

While the presence of the railway could only have exerted a profound influence on the course of military operations in Uganda, the emergency itself had a reciprocal effect on both the pace and the manner of the line's construction. As early as November, 1897, barely a month after the Sudanese outbreaks, Whitehouse had received an urgent communication

---

* The plucky Kabarega did not surrender without putting up a fierce fight. After being badly wounded, he was taken to a field hospital, where he lost no time in leaping from his bed and kicking a British army doctor for having attended to an African commoner before him. According to Jackson, however, the doctor took no offense, remarking later: "I didn't mind; it is not every one who can claim to have had his bottom kicked by a king."

from the Railway Committee. Although he was no doubt pleased to learn that ten more locomotives and substantial extra rolling stock had been acquired, and that coolie recruitment was to be expedited at once, he could not have been elated by the almost desperate tone of the memorandum itself. Particular stress was placed—in the form of a specific and significant instruction—on the need for haste. "When time can be thereby saved," Whitehouse was told, he would "lay out surface diversions at all places where there is even what on an ordinary railroad would be thought moderately heavy work." In other words, wherever it was found that platelaying along the surveyed right of way might be delayed by rock formations, hummocks, gullies, scarps or other topographical hindrances requiring heavy rock-cuttings or large earthworks, these obstacles were simply to be skirted and the permanent line put down at a later time. Even rivers would be spanned hastily with makeshift girder structures such as the one Preston had thrown across the Maji ya Chumvi. Bridges, station buildings and other works, although they too were to be completed as swiftly as possible, must take second priority to the all-important task of moving the rails forward with "vigour and despatch."

What this meant in effect was the building of a flimsy but very costly substitute line. While the Committee's decision to do so may have seemed justified by the unexpected turn of events in Uganda, the entire question of diversions was to become more than a minor embarrassment for the Government. In 1905, Sir Charles Eliot, who had just resigned as Commissioner of the East Africa Protectorate, held this policy to be "the chief assignable cause" of construction expenditures far exceeding the original sum granted to the railway. "Even now," he wrote, "the traveller sees everywhere traces of temporary bridges and temporary lines, and sometimes two of the latter, making three lines in all, before the final route was laid." Toward the end of construction, according to Eliot, a German official remarked, after making a trip on the line: "I am ashamed of my country. We have not built one railway to the Lake yet, and the English have built two."

Even before Whitehouse received the controversial directive, a great deal of the railway's construction had been something less than permanent, owing in no small measure to the hasty character of the survey, which at times seemed in a race with the tracks. Yet at least the tracks were being laid down, and a few signs of progress were becoming visible as 1897 drew to a close. At Voi, 100 miles inland from Mombasa on the western edge of the Taru, Preston built one of the line's first "triangles," a sort of switching spur which enabled locomotives to leave the single track and turn around. Previously, engines returning to the coast from railhead had been obliged to make the entire journey in reverse, taking almost twice the normal time. (Preston thought that the Voi triangle may have been equally useful in another way, observing that "driver and fireman were saved the discomfort of having coal dust blown in their eyes for a hundred-mile run.") From Voi, moreover, the tracks moved forward without encountering any major difficulties, and by the end of January, 1898, the platelayers—now more than a thousand strong—had made camp on the south bank of the Tsavo river, 133 miles from the coast and nearly one-quarter of the distance to the lake.

Meanwhile, late in 1897, the line had undergone its first official inspection, carried out by C. W. Hodson, Superintending Engineer of Indian State Railways. Despite, or just conceivably because of the obstacles thrown up by topography and climate, Hodson found much to praise in the work that had already been completed, and specifically approved the line as ready to carry passenger traffic.* His report was couched in the expressionless prose of bureaucracy, but at one point in his description Hodson seemed to forget himself momentarily and wax almost lyrical over what was actually the least inviting section of the route. "The inspection train," he remarked, "traversed the long straight on the Taru desert, between mile 59 and 83, at the rate of 30 miles an hour, without seriously interfering with the comfort of our afternoon tea." Then, as if startled by this burst of exuberance, he hastened to add that the interior of his carriage had acquired several thick layers of red dust.

Such accomplishments, to be sure, were hardly spectacular, but by early 1898 the Railway Committee could discern what seemed a dim ray of light at the far end of its dismal tunnel. The Taru, after all, had been conquered, and Whitehouse had performed the near-impossible in marshaling his totally inadequate rolling stock to move an army while the very rails of its transport were being laid down beneath it. To the Committee, the line appeared to be taking on the aspects of something like a fully operational transportation enterprise. The members could not, of course, have been expected to anticipate what Tsavo had in store for construction.

---

* Had there been any paying passengers, however, they would have had to wait until well into 1898, since military needs pre-empted all available rolling stock. Even Government administrators assigned to posts in the interior sometimes had to lay over in Mombasa for several weeks before places could be found for them on troop trains.

9

THE BRIDGE OVER
THE RIVER TSAVO

*"The terrible thing was to
feel so helpless."*

"It seemed an ideal spot." This was Preston's initial impression
of the railhead camp site at Tsavo. His platelayers concurred.
Their first act after setting up their tents was to plunge into the
river and divest themselves of the grime and dust that had caked their
bodies in hard layers for long weeks. They had in fact reached an oasis.
Once the Taru desert was crossed, the terrain of Ukamba that followed
had not blossomed into an equatorial Arcadia; for many miles the railway route was to traverse a gaspingly arid country not too different
from the desert itself. The land was heavily carpeted with the jagged
steel wool of wait-a-bit thorn and watered by an all but nonexistent
rainfall. Although a few tributaries of the distant Athi river crawled
across the region, they were seldom more than beds of baking stone
and sand for the better part of any year. The Tsavo was an exception. In
gentle contrast to the vast boneyard through which it flowed, its banks
were hung with a lush drapery of tropical foliage, while the swiftly
moving stream itself, if not icy, was clear and invigorating. Travelers to
and from the interior seldom failed to halt here, rest their porters and
replenish their water supplies.

But Preston soon learned that for all its charm, Tsavo was not altogether wholesome. "It never had a good name," he wrote. "All the old
caravan leaders had disliked this camp for some reason or other, and it

was a noted place for desertions ... A strange feature of these desertions was, that even on the return journey from up-country, the porters would seemingly desert ... but stranger still, some of the men who had no loads to carry would make themselves scarce." One possible explanation for this behavior might have been found in the river's name. Tsavo is the Kikamba word for "slaughter," and Masai war parties had often lashed out at the area not too many years earlier. Local Wakamba inhabitants also told Preston that the place was a breeding-ground for poltergeists, and that "a certain evil spirit had a habit of enticing the men away at night and after leading them down to the river, made away with them. At the river indeed all trace of missing natives was lost, or sometimes, an odd sandal or fez cap would be picked up."

Even the superstitious coolies, however, paid little attention to these myths, if for no other reason, as Preston observed, than that they "could desert at any time, if they were foolish enough to run away from their livelihoods." More to the point, they were only transients, whose construction would quickly overtake their own camp. The river itself needed only to be spanned with a temporary girder, and soon the rails began moving forward at the rate of more than 500 yards daily. It appeared that the evil spirit would not be given much time to work its spell on Preston and his men.

Perhaps it was aware of its limited opportunity, for it struck almost at once. Hardly had platelaying begun on the farther bank of the stream than Preston received a report that one of the coolies had vanished, leaving no trace except for a dhoti which someone had found at the river's edge. Heading up a search party, Preston soon came on the missing man—or part of him. "The skull and feet were untouched, but all the flesh had been torn away from the body. We had not far to look for the cause of the tragedy, paw marks of a lion being easily seen all round the remains." The specter of Tsavo having acquired substance, no time was lost in fortifying the coolie tents with thorn bomas. Hoping to flush out the lion before it could strike again, Preston took his Winchester and led a team of beaters through the scrub between the camp and the river. Although the men came across an occasional skeleton or isolated skull ("further evidence of the cause of the former mystery"), they saw neither hide nor hair of the marauder.

Several days later, however, at about two o'clock in the morning, a terrified cry of "sher!" (tiger) shattered the uneasy slumber of the entire railhead camp. Seizing the Winchester, Preston leaped from his tent and looked about him. "The camp was a regular pandemonium," he wrote. "Some of the men were yelling at the top of their voice, while others beat drums, the din being greatly increased by the banging of empty kerosene oil tins." It was some time before the panic subsided enough for Preston to learn that the grunt of a lion had been heard outside one of the tents, and that another coolie had vanished. With the Winchester gripped in one hand and a hurricane lamp in the other, he began butting his way through the thorn in the direction the lion was believed to have taken, but he abandoned the search after an hour. He knew that there was no longer any urgency in reaching the helpless worker, since almost invariably a lion instantly slays its prey with a single blow of its forepaw; as Preston remarked: "the act of killing the victim before devouring him is, to say the least, merciful." Little evidence of compassion, however, could be seen when the corpse was found shortly after dawn. "The remains ... were much the same as those of victim number one except that in this case even the flesh from the face had been torn off, leaving the teeth exposed which gave the skull an uncanny grinning expression."

By now, observed Preston in a nice understatement, the coolies had become "disinclined to turn out to work," but he was able to restore morale with a blend of psychology and common sense. It was certain, he told the workers, that the lion confined its depredations to the vicinity of the river bank alone, and he further pointed out that the threat would diminish in direct proportion to the speed with which the rails went forward. "The men evidently saw the wisdom of this and worked like Trojans ... We were generally fairly quick at shifting camp but this move from Tsavo was certainly a record one."

*

If Preston was soon well clear of what he called a "death hole," fortune smiled less sweetly on the engineer who followed him to take charge of building the permanent bridge over the Tsavo. This man, Lieutenant Colonel J. H. Patterson, was an Indian army officer with long experience in railway construction, and he should have completed the task without difficulty inside of four months. Nearly a year went by, however, before the bridge was ready for traffic, thanks mainly to Preston's lion and a feline companion, who at times almost seemed assigned by fate to delay the railway's progress and, if possible, to paralyze the undertaking entirely. For a while they actually succeeded, gaining a notoriety customarily reserved for the dragons of medieval legend, while Patterson emerged from the duel as something of a nineteenth-century St. George.

In *The Man-Eaters of Tsavo*, Patterson's best-selling book about the ordeal, he helped enhance that knight-errant image, while inadvertently drawing what may have been a slightly unjust caricature of himself as a pukka sahib. Present-day readers might wonder if they are not being put on by Patterson's inflated airs, creeping sentimentality and over-blown melodrama. His pages are peopled with a Victorian/Edwardian bestiary of "brutes," "treacherous-looking villains," "scoundrels" and "poor wretches." Tsavo is referred to as an "accursed spot" and the lions as "dreadful monsters." But it was and they were, while the book, for all its juvenilia, often comes very much alive as the chronicle of what can probably be called the most extraordinary stalk in the history of big-game hunting.

*

A word about man-eating lions is in order. First, however, it ought to be pointed out that the fearsome reputation enjoyed by the misnamed king of beasts is for the most part a great fraud. There exists, to be sure, a stag-gering casualty list of humans who have been killed by lions, but nearly all these victims met their deaths only after taking the offensive in one way or another, usually as hunters. Regardless of what one may have heard or seen in the movies, it is simply not in the lion's nature to attack human beings without provocation. This is due in part to the smell of man, which most undomesticated animals find singularly repugnant, and partly to an intuitive dread of the even more odious rifle or spear. Far from unsheath-ing its claws at the approach of a human, a lion is more likely to take to its heels—as in fact are nearly all dangerous African game species.* As often as not, an unarmed person can walk across miles of lion-infested bush in perfect safety, and while it is not suggested that anyone test this assertion, the plain fact is that the lion presents an all but negligible threat to human life and limb. It is only that infrequent nonconformist, the man-eater, who satisfies all the requirements of a wanton murderer.

The man-eater, it should be stressed, is a very rare phenomenon. Like many carnivores, lions find human flesh revolting; virtually the only ones who cultivate a taste for man are those who have become too old to stalk four-footed game. Yet the very fact of its advanced years increases rather than diminishes the man-eater's destructive potential. This only stands to reason. While slaying another animal requires far more physical strength than does killing a man or woman, infinitely greater mental dexterity is entailed with human quarry because the victim usually resists, not only

---

* Even the one exception, the rhinoceros, which tends to charge at anything and everything, does so less in anger than in a state of half-blind, feeble-witted curiosity.

with weapons but with conceptual thought. Thus, if a man-eating lion wishes to remain alive, it must sharpen its wits as well as its claws, giving a little extra meaning to the expression "animal cunning." Seldom have any man-eaters demonstrated those gifts to more purpose than did the pair that committed its acts of sabotage at Tsavo in 1898.

*

Tsavo was not the only place to be troubled by lions during the railway's construction and in its early years. For some reason, perhaps because of the frequent droughts and plagues which killed off much of the game in the region, man-eaters appeared along the right of way in abnormally large numbers. They virtually infested the environs of the stations at Voi, Makindu and the fittingly named Simba—often demonstrating an almost casual audacity. In 1899, near Voi, one particularly bold marauder made a night raid on a tent occupied by the family of a road engineer named O'Hara. While O'Hara's wife and two children slept beside him, the lion killed O'Hara instantly by crushing his head in its jaws, then dragged the body from the tent. At this point, O'Hara's wife woke up and ran outside, only to see the lion crouching to spring at her. A shot from an askari's rifle momentarily alarmed the beast, enabling Mrs. O'Hara and several askaris to carry her husband's body back to the tent. Within minutes, however, the lion returned, and spent the rest of the night prowling outside the entrance. Only continual (but not very accurate) rifle fire prevented it from re-entering and making off with the entire family.

Even more brazen was the behavior of a man-eater which stalked the neighborhood of Kima (Swahili for "minced meat") at mile 260. This lion so terrorized Kima's Wakamba inhabitants that in early June of 1900 they persuaded the Superintendent of Railway Police, Charles H. Ryall, to interrupt an urgent official train trip to Nairobi and defend them against the marauder. With two other Europeans, Ryall posted himself for the night at the window of his private carriage, which had been shunted to a siding where the lion was known to prowl. Each man stood a watch while the other two slept. The man-eater, however, proved not only more alert than its stalkers but far more audacious. Shortly before midnight, Ryall fell into a momentary doze and the lion immediately seized the opportunity to stride directly into the carriage, break Ryall's neck with a swipe of its paw and bound casually from the window with the corpse between its jaws. Although Ryall's mother offered a reward of £100 for the lion's pelt, a small army of volunteer hunters was outwitted for more than three months as the man-eater ravaged the area at leisure. By August, the protectorate's *Official Gazette* seemed to verge on desperation over the elusive quarry. "It is greatly to be hoped," pleaded a notice, "that somebody will, before long, be successful in putting an end to this dangerous animal." Some weeks later the lion was finally trapped, almost by accident. Yet the "Kima Killer," as it had come to be known— and, for that matter, the lion that despatched O'Hara at Voi—displayed nothing like the artfulness of the two feline bandits who for ten months held Tsavo under what can only be called a state of siege.

*

During his first few days at Tsavo, Patterson gave little thought to lions, the work at hand claiming his undivided concentration. He was responsible not only for putting up the bridge but also for the construction of the station buildings and thirty miles of cuttings, embankments and permanent track on each side of the river. The bridge alone was to be an imposing structure—for the east African bush, at any rate. It was the first major river crossing after Macupa, and plans called for a span three hundred feet long, with the rails laid down on four sixty-foot iron girders supported by three great stone piers rising at least fifteen feet above the river even when in flood. Before actual construction could begin, Patterson was kept fully occupied with a host of preliminary details: taking cross and oblique section measurements of the river, calculating water levels and rates of current, marking the positions of the abutments and piers, surveying the alignment, preparing estimates of materiel needs, and drawing up requisitions for labor and equipment to be furnished by Kilindini. "In a short time," he wrote, "workmen and supplies came pouring in, and the noise of hammers and sledges, drilling and blasting, echoed merrily through the district." The din alone should have frightened off any lions.

Patterson knew, of course, that a man-eater had been reported in the vicinity. He had reached Tsavo some days before the railhead section moved out, and soon learned of the deaths of the two coolies in Preston's gang. Yet despite the clear evidence of the manner in which they had met their ends, he was disinclined to give the credit to a lion. In his own opinion, "the unfortunate men had been the victims of foul play at the hands of some of their comrades ... I thought it quite likely that some scoundrels from the gangs had murdered them for the sake of their money." This theory in fact was altogether plausible. More than one underpaid coolie was by no means above liquidating a fellow worker if it would gain him a few rupees, and some of the men carried easily concealed but lethal multi-pronged rooting implements that left gashes almost impossible to distinguish from the furrows made by a lion's claws. Patterson's own sec-tion, moreover, seemed at times to seethe with conspiracy and dark deeds. However, as we shall see, whatever evil intent the workers harbored was directed more at Patterson than anyone else. And it was not long before Patterson himself recognized the fallacy of the mugging hypothesis.

Conversion came one day in the third week of March, when Patterson was roused from his cot before sunrise by an agitated servant who told him that one of the jemadars, "a fine powerful Sikh named Ungan Singh," had been carried bodily from his tent by a lion. Unconvinced at first, Patterson felt his skepticism dissolve as one of the victim's tentmates reconstructed the incident. "He graphically described how, at about midnight, the lion suddenly put its head in at the open tent door and seized Ungan Singh ... by the throat. The unfortunate fellow cried out 'Chow' ('Let go'), and threw his arms up round the lion's neck. The next moment he was gone, and his panic-stricken companions lay helpless, forced to listen to the ter-rible struggle which took place outside. Poor Ungan Singh must have died hard; but what chance had he? As a coolie gravely remarked, 'Was he not fighting with a lion?'" All this was confirmed without difficulty as Patter-son and several stouter-hearted workers followed a trail of clearly marked blood puddles, where the lion had "doubtless indulged in the man-eaters' habit of licking the skin off so as to get at the fresh blood." In due course, they came upon "a dreadful spectacle": a few strips of flesh, some splin-tered bones and a perfectly intact head, lying a few feet distant, "the eyes staring wide open with a startled, horrified look in them." Hastily, stones were heaped over the shreds of the corpse, "the head with its fixed, terri-fied stare seeming to watch us all the time, for it we did not bury, but took back to camp for identification by the Medical Officer."

Before leaving the scene, however, Patterson inspected the ground and reached the conclusion that not one but two lions had been at work; pugmarks everywhere indicated a violent struggle for the body. The real-ization was unsettling. Even the presence of a single lion had already begun to fray the coolies' none too steady nerves; with two man-eat-ers stalking the camp, labor efficiency would plummet. Because of the importance of a permanent bridge over the exceptionally broad Tsavo in expediting the movement of supply trains, Patterson was expected to complete his section of the line as swiftly as possible; delay could not be tolerated. Accordingly, he "vowed there and then to rid the neighbour-hood of the brutes." He had no way of knowing that he had sentenced himself to ten months of almost unendurable overtime.

The hunt commenced that very night. Its area embraced a rough circle of some eight miles' diameter, in which the several construction camp sites were scattered on both banks of the river. Obviously, Patterson could not stalk all the camps at once; but assuming quite sensibly that the lions would return to the scene of their meal the previous night, he took up a post in a scrawny thorn tree near the jemadar's tent. To greet the beasts, he carried a .303 rifle and a 12-bore shotgun, the two barrels of the latter crammed, respectively, with slug and heavy lead pellets. He was not the only occupant of the tree. Its other branches were shared by more than a dozen coolies who had become too frightened to remain in their tents. Before long their fears proved justified. A shuddering roar leaped out from an indeterminate but nearby spot in the blackness, and as the sound came closer, Patterson's "hopes of bagging one of the brutes were raised." All at once, however, the roaring stopped. For more than an hour there was only stillness. Knowing, however, that lions stalk in absolute silence, Patterson remained alert, and although his arm began to cramp from holding the .303, he patiently stroked the trigger with his finger while continuing to peer into the inky curtain that enveloped him. Suddenly there was a second explosion of roars, now mingled with screams—from a great distance. As if they had been told of Patterson's whereabouts, the lions had taken their victim from a tent more than half a mile away, and "we knew then ... that we should see or hear nothing further of them that night." The coolies' relief was audible as they slipped down from the tree. Patterson fumed in silence.

Two nights later he climbed into another tree, only yards from the tent in which the lions had foiled him. A goat was tied to the trunk as bait. After a few hours, both goat and Patterson were soaked to the skin in an unexpected drizzle. At midnight, Patterson felt "impotent disappointment" as another detonation of roars and screams "told me that the man-eaters had again eluded me and had claimed another victim elsewhere." Such was to be the pattern of calculated evasion which rapidly took shape as the lions began to harass the camp in earnest.

They did not strike at the camp every night, sometimes turning their attention to any one of several nearby Wakamba villages. A week, perhaps two or even three, might pass without incident in the railway compound, and there was always the hope that the marauders might at last have vacated the premises entirely for an even more accessible food supply. But such notions could only have been wishful thinking. Even during those intervals when no attack took place, the coolies could usually expect to be awakened at least twice every night by grunts, snarls or roars. Nor was there any way of knowing when those sounds would suddenly be punctuated by a bubbling scream.

Yet work proceeded for some time at a satisfactory pace, mainly because the coolies knew that the lions never attacked large bodies of men during the daylight hours—a slightly deceptive philosophy of safety in numbers which even provided some comfort at night. In March of 1898, the Tsavo railway community consisted of more than two thousand laborers, most of them from the vastly expanded railhead section. As long as Preston's crew remained in the vicinity, wrote Patterson, his own men "appeared not to take much notice of the dreadful deaths of their comrades. Each man felt, I suppose, that as the man-eaters had such a large number of victims to choose from, the chances of their selecting him in particular were very small." But by the end of the month, when the railhead gang made its swift departure, the list of potential targets was suddenly reduced to fewer than five hundred coolies. "A regular panic consequently ensued," and a mass walkout to Mombasa was averted only when Patterson gave the men permission to suspend work on the bridge until they had reinforced the already heavy bomas around their tents. At the very least, the new defenses bolstered the sagging morale. Inside the thorn barricades, fires blazed all night, "and it was also the duty of the night-watchman to keep clattering half a dozen empty oil tins suspended from a convenient tree. These he manipulated by means of a long rope, while sitting in safety within his tent; and the frightful noise thus produced was kept up at frequent intervals ... in the hopes of terrifying away the man-eaters."

Fortifications, fires and noisemakers, however, appeared to have only minimal effect on the lions, who continued to feed on the coolies with almost casual regularity, while Patterson's frustration mounted, since "their tactics seemed to be to break into a different camp each night." Patterson was also baffled by the man-eaters' ability to seek out and invariably find weak spots in the defenses. "How they forced their way through the *bomas* without making a noise was, and still is, a mystery to me; I should have thought that it was next to impossible for an animal to get through at all." A homicidal maniac at large in a village with only one policeman could hardly have aroused a more permeating climate of fear than did the two lions who prowled the perimeter of the Tsavo camp.

The policeman, to be sure, was not entirely without deputies, since the Tsavo construction staff included several other English supervisors. Dr. Brock, the Medical Officer, sometimes kept Patterson company in a tree at night, and a number of the jemadars carried rifles. But the full-time responsibility for apprehending the killers was Patterson's alone. And whenever the lions attacked, he could have been forgiven had he wondered whether each coolie tent contained a spy who would reveal to the pair the whereabouts of their pursuer. "No matter how likely or tempting a spot we lay in wait for them, they invariably avoided that particular place and seized their victim for the night from some other camp." By mid-April, they had become bold enough to make occasional stalks in broad daylight. Patterson once recorded their having been seen in three different spots at the edge of the camp in a single afternoon.

He could take some small comfort in the knowledge that the raiders' efforts did not meet with uniform success. One night there was a foray on a tent shared by fourteen coolies. When heads were counted later, no one was found missing; the man-eater had made off with a man-sized bag of rice. A Greek contractor, passing through Tsavo on railway business, was attacked in his tent but did not suffer a scratch; the lion apparently mistook the mattress for the man, and dragged that away instead. Another time, Patterson learned how an Indian trader who was riding his donkey near the camp after dark narrowly escaped becoming a meal. As the lion pounced, "his claws became entangled in a rope by which two empty oil tins were strung across the donkey's neck. The rattle and clatter made by these as he dragged them after him gave him such a fright that he turned tail and bolted ... to the immense relief of the terrified *bunniah*, who quickly made his way up the nearest tree, and remained there, shivering with fear, for the rest of the night."

Yet few such blunders were committed, and for the most part the lions continued to second-guess their prey with what seemed an almost human intelligence. It was only a matter of time before they discovered the camp hospital, where no one was capable of offering any resistance whatever. Although barricaded by an unusually dense wall of thorn, this enclosure proved no less vulnerable than the other bomas, and the two lions slaked their hunger on a malaria-stricken coolie while severely mauling several other patients too weak even to crawl from their beds. They also destroyed the hospital itself, ripping tent-clinics to shreds and shattering tables, shelves and countless bottles of medicine with blows from their paws. The result was that a new hospital had to be set up closer to the main tent area and protected with an even higher and thicker thorn fence. The move also gave Patterson a rare opportunity to come to grips with the man-eaters—neither of which he had as yet even seen. Knowing that lions tend to revisit newly vacated camp sites, and fully confident that his pair would return at once to the old hospital, he spent the night there. It hardly need be added that the lions raided the new premises instead, vaulting the boma as if without effort. In a further gesture of audacity, they devoured their victim only a few feet from the hospital. All that Patterson could find of the coolie the next morning were his skull and several fingers. "On one of these was a silver ring, and this, with the teeth (a relic much prized by certain castes), was sent to the man's widow in India."

Still certain, however, that an abandoned site would hasten the desired confrontation, Patterson now ordered the hospital moved again and placed the empty enclosure under surveillance that same night. Accompanied by Brock, he took a vulnerable position in a goods wagon on a siding which ran to the edge of the vacated spot. This time he was not disappointed. After a wait of several hours, during which the silence was broken only once by a snapping of dry twigs and an inexplicable dull thud, "I fancied I heard something coming very stealthily towards us. I feared, however, to trust to my eyes, which by that time were strained by prolonged staring through the darkness, so under my breath I asked Brock whether he saw anything ... Brock did not answer ... Then with a sudden bound a huge body sprang at us. 'The lion!' I shouted, and we both fired almost simultaneously—not a moment too soon, for in another second the brute would assuredly have landed inside the wagon." It was only good fortune that this did not happen. Patterson believed that the lion "must have swerved off in his spring," flustered by the twin flash and report that burst like a dynamite charge from the echo chamber of the steel wagon. The moment of confusion probably saved not only the two men but the lion as well. Next morning, a bullet was found in the dirt, less than two inches from a huge pugmark.

*

Patterson referred to the incident as "my first direct encounter with the man-eaters." In that respect alone could it have been rewarding. As a hunter, Patterson was far from being a novice. For many years he had stalked tigers in India, and tigers are generally regarded as quarry far more elusive and dangerous than lions. By any normal reckoning, he should have disposed of the two Tsavo marauders within two weeks of their appearance on the scene. But the man-eaters seemed to be operating on a calendar of their own, and a routine hunt had rapidly become a Sisyphean labor. Particularly galling was the lions' almost total indifference to any efforts to kill them or frighten them off; the crash of the rifles from the goods wagon and the banging of the oil tins on the donkey's neck were isolated exceptions. "Except as food," wrote Patterson, "they showed a complete contempt for human beings ... Shots, shouting and firebrands they alike held in derision." One night, less than thirty yards from the tent they had attacked, they leisurely ate a coolie while a jemadar in a tree emptied the magazine of his Snider at them half a dozen times. Tents, in fact, appeared to strike their fancy as the proper surroundings for a meal. Patterson mentions "a very vivid recollection of one particular night when the brutes seized a man from the railway station and brought him close to my camp to devour. I could plainly hear them crunching the bones, and the sound of their dreadful purring filled the air and rang in my ears for days afterwards. The terrible thing was to feel so helpless; it was useless to attempt to go out, as of course the poor fellow was dead ..."

During the early days of the duel, Patterson had confined his hunting to the hours after dark. While the sun was up, the man-eaters would usually lie up in the lost world of tangled undergrowth and dried-out watercourses that swept away from the camp on all sides; it was only after sunset, when they approached the camp, that one could hope to get in a shot at them. Presently, however, Patterson began to stalk in broad daylight. This was partly the consequence of personal frustration, partly because "something had to be done to keep up the men's spirits." But Patterson also found the work "exceedingly tiring and really foolhardy"; in the arid, crackling bush of Tsavo, "the hunted animal has every chance against the hunter ... If I had come up with the lions on any of these expeditions it was much more likely that they would have added me to their list of victims than that I should have succeeded in killing either of them." Yet he persisted, creeping through undergrowth so dense that his gunbearer sometimes had to lift him bodily from a stubbornly grasping snare of wait-a-bit thorn. From time to time he would even come on the lions' spoor, only to lose it when it crossed a rock formation.

The infrequent hour or so of leisure which he permitted himself brought little actual rest. On first arriving at Tsavo, he had camped in an open clearing, unprotected by any sort of boma. However, after hearing muffled scratchings outside his tent one night and discovering a furrow of pugmarks near the fly the next morning, he quickly arranged to take up quarters with Brock. In contrast to the vindictive wilderness which surrounded it, the gypsy hovel of tent canvas, tree limbs and dom palm leaves which the two men shared was not entirely without a certain domesticity. A thorn boma, more than two hundred feet in diameter, encircled the house, and a monster bonfire was kept blazing in the compound every night. The two officers' personal servants, who also lived within the security of the barricade, were on hand at all times to provide meals, drinks, clean laundry and fresh water from the river. The hut itself had what Patterson generously described as a veranda, where he was able to study his Swahili grammar over an after-dinner whisky and soda or brandy, and to enjoy what little evening breeze might have managed to complete its journey across the open hearth of the Taru. But Patterson found these pleasures "rather trying," and one can appreciate that a sense of well-being might not have come easily in a household which was more or less free of access at any time to uninvited guests who had made all too clear their disrespect for fires and disdain for lion-proof bomas. In the evenings, as a matter of course, both Patterson and Brock "kept our rifles within easy reach, and cast many an anxious glance out into the inky darkness beyond the circle of the firelight." In his own unflappable fashion, Patterson was every bit as afraid as the coolies.

"As is often the case in this world,
the impostors were greatly
in the majority."

As the weeks went by, Patterson could observe a certain amount of progress on the railway works. Preston's temporary diversions were steadily, if slowly, being replaced by sections of track on the permanent alignment. A rock cutting, hastily blasted out by the railhead laborers to a width barely sufficient to permit a locomotive's passage, had to be enlarged to prevent the destruction of bulky equipment projecting from goods wagons. Between this cutting and the river lay a dried-up watercourse. With insufficient time to bridge it, Preston had simply laid rails down the shallow but sharply sloped banks, and the daily supply train from Kilindini was converted briefly into a swaying roller coaster when it negotiated this diversion. Patterson's workers soon leveled the tracks with an iron girder across the gully.

And a start, at least, was being made on the main task of bridging the Tsavo itself. This, however, was a far less rudimentary piece of work and ran headlong into trouble almost at once. Efforts to sink for the foundations of the piers beneath the riverbed were continually frustrated by the strong current; two dams had to be built before work could proceed without interruption. Yet even when this had been done, the foundation continued to elude Patterson. "Indeed, the sinking went on and on, until I began to despair of finding one and was about to resort to pile-driving, when at last, to my relief, we struck solid rock." No sooner, however, had the problem of rock been solved than there arose the question of where to obtain the stones to build the piers themselves. Patterson found this particularly exasperating because the ground was all but littered with stone—far too hard to be worked even with rock drills. Many more days were spent combing the bush in what appeared to be another vain search, and Patterson was on the verge of requisitioning costly iron columns from Kilindini when he stumbled over the proper stones in a ravine. But the fortuitous discovery of this potential quarry merely introduced another difficulty, for the ravine was situated several miles from construction. Only a railway could have carried the huge stone blocks to the site of the bridge.

Patterson was therefore compelled to build one: a shaking, groaning narrow-gauge trolley line. Owing to the nature of the terrain, it had to cross the river twice on flimsy viaducts of felled trees which sagged alarmingly whenever the heavily laden wooden handcarts passed over them. Sometimes these makeshift spans were washed away, or they simply collapsed under the weight of the trolleys, and it was sheer good luck that none of the workers was injured or even killed outright in the many accidents that took place. Patterson himself narrowly escaped death when a cart on which he was riding jumped the tracks and plunged into the stream. The stones moved at a funereal pace on their dilapidated hearses, and it was not until early August that the huge piers of the Tsavo bridge began to rise from the river bed. What little satisfaction Patterson could derive from this barely visible evidence of work in progress was dampened by the knowledge that the bridge should already have been completed.

*

Given the presence of the Tsavo lions, however, it was almost to be expected that construction would move at a sluggish gait, and despite Patterson's efforts to shore up labor morale with his nightly stalks, the organization which he managed was not a happy ship. Happiness, indeed, had to be an elusive thing for men toiling literally at coolie wages, and without any reasonable assurance that each day they worked would not be their last on earth. The Indian laborer was no stranger to hardship or squalor; his own home in Mysore or Madras or the Punjab was a less than spectacular improvement over the scrofulous ghetto of nature to which he had been transported. Under any circumstances, moreover, the coolies building the Uganda Railway had not expected ideal working conditions; the contract had made that plain enough. But the contract had included no mention of or provision against the far from remote possibility that any one of them might be shredded into strips of bloody meat at some uncertain hour before some unspecified dawn. The coolies' quite understandable apprehension over this ever present threat could only have been reflected in the lagging pace of their work.

It would have been no less understandable had they held Patterson somewhat to blame for their predicament. For if unquestioning obedience to the white master was expected of the British Empire's lesser breeds at the turn of the century, so too was it acknowledged that the lord had an equal obligation to uphold the interests—and when necessary to defend the lives—of his darker-complected vassals. Patterson understood this quite well. "Constant night watching," he wrote, "was most dreary and fatiguing work, but I felt that it was a duty that had to be undertaken, as the men naturally looked to me for protection." Still, as the months went by at Tsavo and the lions continued to prey unhindered on the coolies, it could have appeared to the men that Patterson was not living up to his part in the rigidly defined feudal bargain.

Much more to the point, it is quite possible that Patterson compounded his record of failure as a hunter with his methods as a disciplinarian, which may have been unnecessarily harsh or petty—perhaps both. Although he appears in the book as a strict but humane overseer, that characterization is of course a self-portrait, and we can only conjecture at his image in the eyes of the coolies. It is possible that they seldom saw him when he was not carrying a small pocket notebook in which, one suspects, he unfailingly entered not only the most flagrant but the most insignificant infractions of rules. These in turn were given public airing outside his tent each day at noon, when "it was my custom to have evil-doers brought up for judgment." It should be said that such dispensations of rough justice, usually in the form of savage tongue-lashings or heavy fines—were for the most part looked on by low-caste Indians as no more than their lot; in one fashion or another they had always been ruled. This was, moreover, a time when many Caucasians considered occasional acts of discourteous or even abusive behavior toward Orientals to be a necessary function of the white man's burden. Had Patterson been playing the small tyrant in India or Burma, or, for that matter, elsewhere in east Africa, his conduct would have been accepted supinely. But in the purgatory of Tsavo, where the coolies carried a brown man's burden of mortal fear that grew heavier every day, the continual nagging to which they appear to have been subjected proved in the end to be a powder keg with a very low flash point.

It is not to be inferred from the above that Patterson was super-intending a band of angels. After finding the ravine from which the rock for the piers was to be quarried, he put in a request to Kilindini for the masons needed to dress the stone. These specialists, mainly Pathans from northern India, were paid 45 rupees (about $15.00) monthly—astronomical wages in comparison to the fifteen rupees received by the unskilled coolies. Thus Patterson could not have been overly surprised to discover, perhaps after only a few blows of the rock hammers, that many of the masons knew nothing whatever of masonry; they were simply coolies masquerading as craftsmen in order to reach the higher income bracket. Although Patterson outflanked them at once by initiating a piecework scale which would enable any real mason to draw his rightful pay while the coolies' wages dropped accordingly, he found himself faced with a counter-stratagem. "As is often the case in this world, the impostors were greatly in the majority; and accordingly they attempted to intimidate the remainder into coming down in their own standard ... in the hope of thereby inducing me to abandon the piece-work system." Given Patterson's authority and the coolies' ingrained subservience, the scheme failed. But it was not forgotten by the men.

As for the masons, they showed little if any visible gratitude for Patterson's intervention on their behalf. No more than the coolies could they have been called paragons of virtue or industry. Most of their leisure time, according to Patterson, was occupied with religious discussions so heated that he "had frequently to go down to their camp to quell disturbances and to separate the Hindus from the Mohammedans." At least once, in Brock's absence, his role as riot policeman expanded into that of doctor as he applied bandages and rough sutures to bruises and knife wounds. Despite the piecework incentive, moreover, not a few of the masons seemed to show more aptitude as shirkers than as workers. And, claiming a slightly higher social status than the common coolies, they were less averse to displays of what Patterson probably called confounded cheek. Their mixed spirit of indolence and latent defiance did not make for assembly-line efficiency in the quarry.

The most conspicuous of the malingerers, in Patterson's opinion, was one Karim Bux, "well known to me as a prime mischief-maker." This man's talents for evading toil appear to have been matched only by Patterson's inventiveness in unmasking the deceptions. A particularly dramatic test of both men's cunning took place during one of the midday magistrate's court sessions when, on summoning Karim Bux to appear on a minor charge, Patterson was informed that the defendant was dying of injuries sustained in a theological debate. "I accordingly ordered him to be carried to my *boma*, and in a few minutes he arrived in his *charpoy*, which was shouldered by four coolies who, I could see, knew quite well that he was only shamming. There were also a score or so of his friends hanging around, doubtless waiting in the expectation of seeing the 'Sahib' hoodwinked. When the bed was placed on the ground near me, I lifted the blanket with which he had covered himself and thoroughly examined him ... Having finally satisfied myself that it was ... pure *budmashi* (devilment)—I told him that I was going to give him some very effective *dawa* [medicine] ... I then got a big armful of shavings from a carpenter's bench which was close by, put them under the bed and set fire to them." The dawa brought the desired results. Within seconds, Karim Bux was out of his bed and out of sight, while "his amused comrades greeted me with shouts of *'Shabash, Sahib!'* ('Well done, sir!')." A few hours later, the humbug patient returned "with clasped hands imploring forgiveness, which I readily granted."

Whether Karim Bux was ready to forgive Patterson was another matter. As for his "amused comrades," they did not seem to benefit from the lesson. One morning several days later, after a particularly uncomfortable night of listening for lions in a tree, Patterson decided to inspect the stone quarry earlier than was his habit. He came on a scene of perfect harmony. Men were playing cards, gossiping or dozing in the shade of boulders. The quarry had become a picnic ground. It was only when Patterson fired a shot into the air that the masons hastily returned to their tasks. Unimpressed, Patterson produced his notebook and took down every man's name for fines, "besides summarily degrading the headman, who had thus shown himself utterly unfit for his position." Yet a certain spirit of impudent pluck remained. As Patterson strode away from the quarry, "two of the scoundrels tottered up after me, bent almost double and calling Heaven to witness that I had shot them in the back." They demonstrated this by turning their backs and raising their shirts to display the bleeding holes that had been made by the pellets. In fact, the wounds were the work of fellow masons who had been prevailed on to assist in the painful ruse, which Patterson recognized instantly. "Unfortunately for them ... I had been carrying a rifle and not a shot gun, and they had also forgotten to make corresponding holes in their clothing, so that all they achieved by this elaborate tissue of falsehood was to bring on themselves the derision of their comrades and the imposition of an extra fine."

It was not long after this incident that a mason awakened Patterson in his tent and furtively warned him of a plot by the workers "to put me quietly out of the way." The conspirators, it appeared, had met that very night, "all being sworn to secrecy," and it was resolved that Patterson be killed the following day while on his regular inspection of the quarry. The corpse would be tossed into the bush where, it was assumed, the man-eaters would quickly find and devour it, thus turning suspicion away from the assassins. "To this cheerful proposal every man at the meeting agreed, and affixed his finger-mark to a long strip of paper as a binding token." Not believing the workers "capable of carrying out such a diabolical scheme," Patterson laughingly dismissed his informant. The next morning, however, as he approached the quarry, the alert was sounded again. "My head mason, Heera Singh, a very good man, crept cautiously out of the bushes and warned me not to proceed. On my asking him the reason, he said that he dared not tell, but that he and twenty other masons were not going to work that day, as they were afraid of trouble at the quarry. At this I began to think that there was something in the story."

All the same, feigning a supreme confidence which he by no means felt, Patterson proceeded directly to the scene of the impending crime, where "stealthy side glances" heightened his apprehensions. Hardly had he arrived when one of the jemadars, "a treacherous-looking villain," reported two disobedient men fighting in the narrowest part of the ravine. Clearly, this was the spot that had been chosen for the dark deed, but Patterson resolved to "see the adventure through, whatever came of it." When he reached the cul-de-sac and the two culprits were pointed out to him, he took out his notebook and entered their names "in my usual manner." He could not have chosen a less appropriate gesture. "Immediately a yell of rage was raised," and some two hundred men, "carrying crowbars and flourishing their heavy hammers, then closed in on me ... I stood still, waiting for them to act, and one man rushed at me, seizing both my wrists and shouting out that he was going to 'be hung and shot for me'—rather a curious way of putting it, but that was his exact expression. I easily wrenched my arms free, and threw him from me; but by this time I was closely hemmed in, and everywhere I looked I could see nothing but evil and murderous-looking faces. One burly brute, afraid to be the first to deal a blow, hurled the man next him at me; and if he had succeeded in knocking me down, I am certain that I should never have got up again alive."

Obviously, the man did not succeed. Patterson managed to step aside and the unintentional attacker tripped over a rock. "This occasioned a moment's confusion, of which I quickly took advantage." Leaping onto a boulder which put him out of immediate reach while giving him the psychological edge of looking down, he launched a forcible harangue in Hindustani. It was the classic tableau of Empire: the lone Englishman subduing a homicidal mob of "natives" through the sheer force of his Caucasian personality. "I told them that I knew all about their plot to murder me, and that ... the *Sirkar* (Government) would soon find out the truth and disbelieve their story that I had been carried off by a lion. I said that I knew quite well that it was only one or two scoundrels

among them who had induced them to behave so stupidly ... Even sup-
posing they were to carry out their plan of killing me, would not another
'Sahib' at once be set over them, and might he not be an even harder
task-master? They all knew that I was just and fair to the real worker;
it was only the scoundrels and shirkers who had anything to fear from
me, and were upright, self-respecting Pathans going to allow themselves
to be led away by men of that kind?" Promising that the matter would
be dropped if no further plots were hatched, Patterson appeared to have
reasserted his authority over the men. "The habit of obedience still held
them," and when he called for a show of hands from those prepared to
return to work, the affirmative vote was unanimous. "I then felt that for
the moment the victory was mine, and ... I jumped down from the rock
and continued my rounds as if nothing had happened." However, since
the workers remained "in a very uncertain and sullen mood ... it was
with feelings of great relief that an hour later I made my way back, safe
and sound, to Tsavo."

The possibility exists that Patterson may not have been in any danger
at all. Another version of his adventure has been attributed to one
of Whitehouse's caravan masters in charge of transporting water and
supplies to the gangs working forward of railhead. This man is said to
have observed the entire incident from concealment in a nearby bush,
and if that is indeed the case he would certainly have opened fire and
dispersed the mob had Patterson fallen during the mass assault on him.
But as Patterson had no knowledge of a guardian angel's presence, it
took no small amount of courage to quell the outbreak by sheer bluff.
Martinet he may have been, but one could hardly have accused him of
cowardice.

The threat to Patterson's life did not end in the ravine. Hardly had
he left the quarry than the workers who had just pledged their loyalty
to him set to concocting another murder plot, which was revealed to
Patterson that same night by his timekeeper. No longer in a mood for
heroics, he strode directly to the telegraph office in the Tsavo station
building and notified the Protectorate authorities. Before the ringleaders
could invent an alibi, they were arrested by a detachment of Railway
Police and taken under guard to Mombasa for trial. Patterson was gratified to learn that "all the scoundrels were found guilty and sentenced to
various terms of imprisonment in the chain-gangs." Work on the bridge
was never again disrupted by homicidal masons. The only remaining
assassins were the lions.

*"Patterson Sahib is indeed a brave
and valiant man, like unto those
Persian heroes of old—Rustem, Zal,
Sohrab and Berzoor."*

The lions' forays had begun in the spring of 1898; the human violence occurred in September. Now the year was approaching its end and the Tsavo camp remained very much a man-eaters' chophouse. It has already been mentioned that attacks did not take place with clockwork regularity, and there had even been an extended period of grace over part of the summer. The impression that the lions had departed was reinforced by reports of killings along other sections of the line, yet one is almost tempted to wonder whether the two man-eaters were not deliberately lulling the Tsavo coolies into a false sense of security. Had this been their intention, it succeeded, for a number of stouter hearts soon took to sleeping outside their cramped, airless tents—virtually inviting an attack. It came. One night early in August, "the familiar terror-stricken cries and screams awoke the camp," the usual trash heap of flesh was found near Patterson's tent the next morning, and another coolie was taken the following night. The resumption of the siege so enraged Patterson that on viewing the carrion of one of the new victims he momentarily became something of an animal himself: "The few scattered fragments that remained of the body I would not allow to be buried at once, hoping that the lions would return to the spot the following night." (They did not.) Although it is difficult to imagine him treating a white man's corpse in this fashion, his behavior can almost be appreciated under the circumstances. And his frustration was to mount steadily in the final months of the year, for the new attacks signaled a period of incessant raiding which became known, tritely but no less appropriately, as "the reign of terror."

By now, Tsavo had become, in its own insular and insignificant fashion, a place on the map not much less celebrated than Krakatoa or Johnstown, Pennsylvania. Whitehouse had offered a reward of £100 to anyone who brought down one of the man-eaters, and the posters, prominently displayed in Mombasa and stations along the line, transformed Tsavo into a macabre boom-town camp. The river banks and surrounding bush swarmed with army, navy and civil service officers on local leave, as well as occasional wealthy "sportsmen" from England and not a few poachers and other fly-by-night opportunists. They stalked the thorn by day and sat in trees at night, banging away with their Winchesters, Remingtons and Sniders and bowling over every lion within range, including pregnant lionesses and sometimes cubs. The Tsavo station building began to reek with inexpertly cured pelts. The man-eaters continued their work undisturbed.

Patterson appears to have found the gratuitous assistance unwelcome. If he did not actually regard the destruction of the lions as a personal holy grail, he was at least discomfited by the atmosphere of kibitzing which the presence of rivals brought into the camp. This became especially evident in the amused disbelief that greeted him when he produced what may have been the largest rat-trap in the world: an iron cage built mainly of the discarded tracks from Mackinnon's forgotten "Central Africa Railway." The trap consisted of two compartments separated by a grill of steel bars. Inside one section, volunteers armed with rifles would serve as bait; the other cubicle was reserved for the lion, which was expected to lock itself in by releasing a complicated spring-wire mechanism on entering. A boma with a deliberately built-in weak spot surrounded the cage, while the latter itself was draped with a tent as a disguise. Having planned the trap and supervised its construction, Patterson naturally took pride in his brainchild and was not appreciative when "the wiseacres to whom I showed my invention were generally of the opinion that the man-eaters would be too cunning to walk into my parlour." But the critics had reason to be skeptical, since the trap could hardly have been expected to deceive a lion possessed of a purportedly superhuman intelligence. Patterson thought otherwise, and personally acted as bait for several nights. The mosquitoes kept him up but the man-eaters did not. The doubters were entertained. Patterson was not.

Nor could his disposition have been sweetened by the escalating neurosis of the workers, not a few of whom had come to believe that the man-eaters "were not real animals at all, but devils in lions' shape. Many a time the coolies solemnly assured me that it was absolutely useless to attempt to shoot them. They were quite convinced that the angry spirits of two departed native chiefs had taken this form in order to protest against a railway being made through their country." Others saw the beasts in more prosaic manifestations: hyenas, donkeys, goats and dogs instantly became lions in their eyes at night. Even humans were not altogether exempted from the coolies' fear-crazed imaginations. John Boyes, a merchant-adventurer, was nearly killed while returning to his tent after dinner with a railway official at Tsavo during the height of the panic. Armed jemadars in a nearby tent mistook the firebrand he carried for the eye of a lion. The climate of terror was infectious. Passing through Tsavo at about this time, the Administration's Hobley noted "gloom over the camp," and remarked that "everyone was in a jumpy state. I was besieged by my men begging the loan of some of my guns to protect themselves, and they clustered round my tent all night. Guns went off at intervals in the various coolie camps around us, and altogether I had a very disturbed night."

That the state of coolie demoralization was fast approaching its terminal stages must have been obvious to Patterson. One night, "some half a dozen workmen, who lived in a small enclosure close to mine, became so terrified on hearing the lions at their meal that they shouted and implored me to allow them to come inside my *boma*. This I willingly did, but soon afterwards I remembered that one man had been lying ill in their camp, and ... they had callously left him behind alone. I immediately took some men with me to bring him to my *boma*, but on entering his tent I saw by the light of the lantern that the poor fellow was beyond need of safety. He had died of shock."

Patterson's own nerves were badly frayed. Physically, he hovered on the brink of collapse. Every minute of the daylight hours was occupied alternately with supervising construction—what there was of it—and stalking for miles through the tightly knit mesh of thorn. Rare was the night he spent in his boma. After a hasty dinner just before sunset, he would take a cramped position in some tree which he thought the marauders might approach. "But all in vain. Either the lions saw me and then went elsewhere, or else I was unlucky, for they took man after man from different places without ever once giving me a chance of a shot at them." As a rule, they would seem to taunt him, boldly announcing their approach with great roars, but "once they reached the vicinity of the camps, the roars completely ceased, and we knew that they were stalking for their prey. Shouts would then pass from camp to camp, *'Khabar dar, bhaieon, shaitan ata'* ('Beware, brothers, the devil is coming'), but the warning cries would prove of no avail, and sooner or later agonising shrieks would break the silence and another man would be missing from roll-call next morning ... I was naturally very disheartened at being foiled in this way night after night, and was soon at my wits' end to know what to do; it seemed as if the lions were really 'devils' after all ..."

*

On December 1, the man-eaters scored their greatest triumph over the ragged remnants of the workers' esprit. Late that afternoon, as Patterson returned to camp from the site of the bridge, he found himself faced with a general strike. Converging on his boma en masse, the coolies

announced that "they would not remain at Tsavo any longer for anything or anybody; they had come from India on an agreement to work
for the Government, not to supply food for either lions or 'devils.'" There
is no way of knowing whether another oration by Patterson would
have swayed the men on this occasion, for at that moment the squeal
of a locomotive whistle announced the approach of the daily materials
train passing through Tsavo en route to Mombasa from railhead. The
whistle seemed to act as a signal. With a great shout, five hundred coolies
rushed to the station and threw themselves prostrate on the tracks. Frantically, the engine driver applied the brakes. He was unable, however, to
reduce speed below about five miles an hour—which was all the workers
needed to swarm over the locomotive and its four goods wagons. Patterson ordered them off, commanded the driver to stop the train; but
the latter, anxious to cross the Taru before dark, opened the throttle.
Ten minutes later, as the engine's smoke dirtied the sky to the southeast,
Tsavo's population consisted of Patterson and about four dozen coolies
who had courageously refused to abandon their work on the bridge.

The mass flight, however, brought construction to a dead halt. For
the next three weeks, the only work done by the remaining laborers
was the building of stronger barriers against the man-eaters. Bomas were
reinforced mightily. Some coolies dug pits under their tents, roofing the
excavations with sleepers and thorns. Cribs made from sleepers were
thrown up atop elevated water tanks, roofs and girders. Every stout tree
blossomed with charpoys, lashed firmly to the limbs. Still, there was
always the stray coolie to be taken, and even those who felt secure in
their new defenses could be given unnerving surprises. One inventive
worker installed his charpoy inside an empty water tank on the ground,
judging correctly that the opening would not be wide enough to admit
a lion. He had not reckoned, however, on the smaller dimensions of the
animal's foreleg, and spent the better part of a night striking matches to
ward off the claw that raked the damp air only inches from his quak-
ing body. Nor did the tree-dwellers enjoy total protection. One night a
cacophony of crashing and screams told Patterson that a branch had
snapped under the weight of its occupants. But "fortunately for them, a
victim had already been secured, and the brutes were too busy devouring
him to pay attention to anything else."

By now, Patterson had overcome his distaste for outside assistance
and had reached the point of telegraphing the Protectorate Administration for any available armed manpower. Shortly after the mass
desertion, the local District Officer arrived at Tsavo with a detachment of askaris—and a cross-hatching of claw furrows on his back,

the man-eaters having resented his intrusion. He was followed almost immediately by the Railway Police Superintendent and twenty sepoys who were promptly installed in trees. For some reason, Patterson appears to have felt that the reinforcements might improve the efficacy of his trap, and "in spite of some chaff," the thing was brought out again. Two sepoys were ordered to volunteer as bait, while Patterson joined the visiting officers in a sleeper crib, waiting for nightfall and hoping that his contraption would be vindicated at last. It was. "Nothing happened until nine o'clock, when to my great satisfaction the intense stillness was suddenly broken by the noise of the door of the trap clattering down. 'At last,' I thought, 'one at least of the brutes is done for.'" But Patterson's elation was premature, for the sepoys proved less reliable machines. Frozen with terror as the maddened lion hurled itself at the bars of the cage, they completely forgot their instructions to open fire, and it was only after several minutes of mingled encouragement and threats from the officers that they regained their wits. And "when at last they did begin to fire, they fired with a vengeance—anywhere, anyhow ... their bullets came whizzing all around us." Finally, however, a direct hit was scored on one of the door bars; it reopened the trap and the lion bounded off into the night. Justifiably or not, Patterson now lost interest in his invention, and the reinforcements were put to conventional stalking which met with "equal unsuccess." After several days, the officers were obliged to return to their respective posts, "and once again I was left alone with the man-eaters."

*

There was nowhere to go, it seemed, but up. Early in the morning of December 9, Patterson took his first step in that direction. "As I was leaving my *boma* soon after dawn, I saw a Swahili running excitedly towards me, shouting out '*Simba! Simba!*' ... and every now and again looking behind him as he ran. On questioning him I found that the lions had tried to snatch a man from the camp by the river, but being foiled in this had seized and killed one of the donkeys, and were at that moment busy devouring it not far off. Now was my chance." Taking up a heavy hunting rifle which the police officer had lent him, Patterson at once followed the Swahili into the thorn, and made his way, as silently as possible, in the direction of the man-eaters. "I was getting on splendidly, and could just make out the outline of one of them through the dense bush, when unfortunately my guide snapped a rotten branch. The wily beast heard the noise, growled his defiance and disappeared in a moment into a patch of even thicker jungle close by."

Patterson then decided to fall back on his Indian tiger-hunting experience and flush the lion out with beaters. Returning hastily to the camp, he ordered all available workmen to take up whatever drums, horns, tin pots and other noisemakers they could gather. They were then formed into a wide semi-circle around the thicket where the lion was believed to have taken cover. As the human horseshoe converged deafeningly on the target, Patterson concealed himself behind a seven-foot anthill and waited for the elusive enemy to break out. "Almost immediately, to my intense joy, out into the open path stepped a huge maneless lion. It was the first occasion during all these trying months upon which I had had a chance at one of these brutes, and my satisfaction at the prospect of bagging him was unbounded." Thanks to the din made by the beaters, the lion did not sense Patterson's presence and came to within less than fifty feet of the anthill. Patterson raised his rifle. "The moment I moved to do this, he caught sight of me, and seemed much astonished at my sudden appearance, for he stuck his forefeet into the ground, threw himself back on his haunches and growled savagely." It was impossible to miss. "As I covered his brain with my rifle, I felt that at last I had him absolutely at my mercy ... I pulled the trigger, and to my horror heard the dull snap that tells of a misfire."

The malfunction disconcerted Patterson sufficiently to make him forget for a moment that he was carrying a double-barreled weapon. In that split second, nothing could have prevented the man-eater from opening Patterson's skull with a blow of its paw. But the lion, still confused, leaped to one side. At this move Patterson regained his senses and fired the second barrel. He was rewarded instantly with the heavy thunking sound of the bullet striking home. The lion had only been wounded, however, and quickly plunged into the bush, Patterson on its heels. In a few minutes the trail vanished on a sprawl of rocks. Outwitted again, Patterson could only give up the chase and vent his fury. "Bitterly did I anathematise the hour in which I had relied on a borrowed weapon, and in my disappointment and vexation I abused owner, maker and rifle with fine impartiality ... My continued ill-luck was most exasperating, and the result was that the Indians were more than ever confirmed in their belief that the lions were really evil spirits, proof against mortal weapons. Certainly they did seem to bear charmed lives."

But the hunt had only begun. On returning to camp, Patterson stopped to examine the donkey's carcass and discovered that it had scarcely been touched. Clearly, the lions had not been given the opportunity to eat it;

in all likelihood they would return after dark. There being no large trees in the area, Patterson had his men build a machan, a rickety wooden scaffold about twelve feet high, while the dead donkey was secured by a steel wire to an ancient stump. At sunset, Patterson climbed into the flimsy perch. Since he sat only three yards from the donkey he could hope for a partially visible target—although he knew that he himself was far more vulnerable to the lions. They could demolish the machan as if it were a croquet wicket.

The sun went down in its equatorial haste and the bush became enveloped in the peculiar stillness of a tropical night that is never altogether silent. For several hours, Patterson kept an almost motionless vigil, peering intently into the thorn and gaining his night vision. Suddenly he froze, as "a deep long-drawn sigh—sure sign of hunger—came up from the bushes." Rustling sounds told him that the lion was rapidly approaching. Then the movement stopped and there was an enraged snarl; apparently the lion had seen or sensed Patterson and started to back away. "But no ... instead of either making off or coming for the bait prepared for him, the lion began stealthily to stalk *me*! For about two hours he horrified me by slowly creeping round and round my crazy structure, gradually edging nearer and nearer. Every moment I expected him to rush it." There was no use firing, for the night made the lion all but invisible. "I kept perfectly still, hardly daring even to blink my eyes."

All at once he felt an object strike the back of his neck and he almost toppled from the machan in his fright. There was a flutter of wings. An owl had mistaken him for a tree. The momentary noise drew a short rasp from the lion. It had now come so close to the machan that Patterson could make out its shape. For a few seconds, Tsavo's peril was forgotten; if Patterson were to save his own life he must fire at once. He raised the rifle and squeezed the trigger.

"The sound of the shot was at once followed by a most terrific roar, and then I could hear him leaping about in all directions. I was no longer able to see him, however, as his first bound had taken him into the thick bush; but to make assurance doubly sure, I kept blazing away in the direction in which I heard him plunging about. At length came a series of mighty groans, gradually subsiding into deep sighs, and finally ceasing altogether; and I felt convinced that one of the 'devils' who had so long harried us would trouble us no more." The silence quickly ended as "a tumult of inquiring voices was borne back across the dark jungle from the men in camp ... I shouted back that I was safe and sound, and that one of the lions was dead: whereupon such a mighty cheer went up from all the camps as must have astonished the denizens of the jungle for miles around. Shortly I saw scores of lights twinkling through the bushes: every man in camp turned out, and with tom-toms beating and horns blowing came running to the scene." Angrily, Patterson ordered them back at once. The second lion might well be lurking nearby, and there was also the possibility that the first might not have died: bullet wounds would multiply the rage and cunning of any man-eater.

Dawn showed that there had been no cause for concern. The lion was as dead as the donkey that lay beside it, and twice as large. Its corpse measured nine feet eight inches from nose to tip of tail. Eight men were needed to carry it to camp. The other workers carried the victorious Patterson.

*

He now found himself deluged with telegrams of congratulation, while visitors came from every point on the line between Mombasa and rail-head to gape at the skin and pound the hunter on the back. But Patterson could feel only partly gratified, for the second man-eater remained very much at large. It had taken eight months to kill the first lion; there was no special reason to believe that its companion could be despatched more swiftly. At about this time, Tsavo was visited by Sir Guildford Moles-worth, former Consulting Engineer to the Indian State Railways, then on an official inspection of the Uganda line for the Railway Committee. Molesworth also congratulated Patterson on his success, but "when he asked me if I expected to get the second lion soon, I well remember his half-doubting smile as I rather too confidently asserted that I hoped to bag him in the course of a few days."

For the lion was continuing to show all the casual brazenness of a veteran bandit. Shortly after the first man-eater's death, it made a direct frontal assault on a railway inspector's bungalow, and although the attack failed, the man-eater boldly paced the veranda for nearly ten minutes, seeming almost to invite rifle fire. Later, when an attempt was made to bait it with three goats tied to a 250-pound half-length of rail, the lion picked the choicest animal and carried it off in its jaws, dragging the other two goats and the rail behind it—while Patterson vainly blasted away into the night. In a subsequent encounter, Pat-terson actually succeeded in hitting the lion, but lost the blood trail in heavy bush. More than a week then went by without any attacks, and Patterson became certain that the beast had succumbed to its wound. At this point it reappeared, laying all-night siege to a tree full of coolies. Four days remained of the year 1898 as the reign of terror recommenced.

It proved short-lived, however. On the night following the man-eater's return, Patterson hoisted himself into the tree that had been occupied by the coolies and prepared for what he hoped would be the final vigil. For perhaps the first time in the long vendetta, conditions seemed to favor the hunter. The night was cloudless, a full moon provided perfect visibility and the ground near the tree was almost empty of bush. The presence, moreover, of Patterson's Swahili gunbearer, Mahina, enabled the sharing of watches and alternate hours of badly needed sleep. Mahina, in fact, was standing his own turn at about two o'clock in the morning when Patterson suddenly came awake "with the uncanny feeling that something was wrong." Mahina reassured him, however, and he was starting to close his eyes when a shadow moved at the edge of the thorn. Once again the stalk-in-reverse had begun.

Despite his danger, Patterson found it "a most fascinating sight to watch this great brute stealing stealthily round us, taking advantage of every bit of cover as he came. His skill showed that he was an old hand at the terrible game of man-hunting." In the moonlight, the lion presented a perfect target, but Patterson was taking no chances of a near miss and allowed it to come within sixty feet of the tree. Then he fired and heard the .303 slug slam home. The lion did not fall, however, and Patterson got off three more quick shots—including another hit—before his quarry reached concealment in the thorn. Now he and Mahina could only wait until daylight permitted them to take up the chase. With the sun up, they found the trail clearly marked by large bloodstains, and after following it for less than a quarter of a mile, the two men came on the man-eater in a thicket—badly wounded and doubly dangerous.

Patterson fired at once and the lion charged. Another shot somersaulted the beast, but it came up still charging. When the next shot missed, Patterson dropped the empty .303 and reached for the carbine in Mahina's hand. "To my dismay, however, it was not there. The terror of the sudden charge had proved too much for Mahina, and both he and the carbine were by this time well on their way up a tree." This left Patterson with no choice but to join them, although he would never have reached safety had not one of the lion's hind legs been smashed by a bullet. From the tree, a fourth shot finally brought the lion down, and Patterson "rather foolishly" leaped to the ground, only to face a dying charge. The fifth and sixth shots ended the duel, as the man-eater "dropped in his tracks not five yards away from me, and died gamely, biting savagely at a branch which had fallen to the ground." When Patterson examined the corpse later, he found the seventh slug which he had fired ten days earlier.

The coolies' first reaction to the exorcising of the Tsavo incubus was one of mingled jubilation and fury. They swarmed around Patterson and the lion, blessing the one and cursing the other. "So great was their resentment against the brute who had killed such numbers of their comrades that it was only with the greatest difficulty that I could restrain them from tearing the dead body to pieces." Presently, however, he was able to have the corpse carried to camp. Eight men were needed once again, as the lion measured only two inches shorter than its companion.

As trophies, however, neither animal was very presentable, the hides of both having been ravaged beyond any taxidermist's skills by years in the thorn. Nonetheless, the lions' accomplishments eventually won them a place in Chicago's Field Museum, where they can be seen today. And even before going on display, the pair also enjoyed a brief moment of immortality in the House of Lords, where Salisbury paid them a back-handed and not altogether accurate tribute. "The whole of the works [at Tsavo]," he said, "were put a stop to for three weeks because a party of man-eating lions ... conceived a most unfortunate taste for our porters. At last the labourers entirely declined to go on unless they were guarded by an iron entrenchment. Of course it is difficult to work a railway under these conditions, and until we found an enthusiastic sportsman to get rid of these lions, our enterprise was seriously hindered." Other contemporaries were less reluctant to reveal the identity of the "sportsman"—and were considerably more nattering. Typical of the unembarrassed encomiums heaped on Patterson by the press was the comment of *The Spectator* in an editorial entitled "The Lions That Stopped The Railway": "When the jungle twinkled with hundreds of lamps, as the shout went on from camp to camp that the first lion was dead, as the hurrying crowds fell prostrate in the midnight forest, laying their hands on his feet, and the Africans danced savage and ceremonial dances of thanksgiving, Mr. Patterson must have realised in no common way what it was to have been a hero and deliverer in the days when man was not yet undisputed lord of the creation, and might pass at any moment under the savage dominion of the beasts." These words, however, showed restraint alongside the panegyric delivered by the coolies, who had undergone a change of heart toward Patterson. "Instead of wishing to murder me, as they once did, they could not now do enough for me, and as a token of their gratitude they presented me with a beautiful silver bowl, as well as with a

long poem written in Hindustani describing all our trials and my ultimate victory." Extracts from the epic, composed by a foreman of masons
named Roshan, almost suggest Virgil recounting the exploits of Aeneas,
although Aeneas may seem to come out second best. Roshan first sings
of Africa,

> indeed a strange land ...
> Many rocks, mountains, and dense forests abounding in lions and
>   leopards ...
> Gorillas, ferocious monkeys that attack men, black baboons of giant
>   size, and thousands of varieties of birds ...

He then goes on to relate the progress of railway construction and the
sudden irruption of the lions at Tsavo:

> Because of the fear of these demons some seven or eight hundred of the
>   labourers deserted, and remained idle ...
> And because of fear for their lives, would sit in their huts, their hearts
>   full of foreboding and terror ...

But now Patterson appears on the scene:

> Patterson Sahib is indeed a brave and valiant man, like unto those
>   Persian heroes of old—Rustem, Zal, Sohrab and Berzoor;
> So brave is he, that the greatest warriors stood aghast at his action;
> Tall in stature, young, most brave and of great strength is he ...
> Lions do not fear lions, yet one glance from Patterson Sahib cowed the
>   bravest of them.
> He fled, making for the forest, while the bullets followed hard after him;
> So was this man-eater rendered helpless; he lay down in despair,
> And after he had covered a chain's distance, the savage beast fell down,
>   a corpse.
> Now the people, bearing lights in their hands, all ran to look at their
>   dead enemy.
> But the Sahib said "Return, my children; the night is dark, do not rush
>   into danger."
> And in the morning all the people saw the lion lying dead.
> And then the Sahib said, "Do not think of work today—make holiday,
>   enjoy and be merry."

But the second man-eater remained.

> And Patterson Sahib went forth into the field to meet him.
> And when he saw the beast, he fired quickly, bullet after bullet.
> The lion made a great uproar, and fled for his life, but the bullets
>   nevertheless found a resting-place in his heart ...
> And in the morning we followed the marks of blood that had
>   flowed from the wounded animal ...
> And when the Sahib saw the animal he fired bullets incessantly;
> But when the lion saw the Sahib, the savage animal, burning with
>   rage and pain,
> Came by leaps and bounds close to the Sahib;
> But here he was to meet his match in a brave Sahib who loaded his
>   gun calmly, and fired again and again, killing the beast ...
> Previously, many Englishmen had come here to shoot but had been
>   disappointed,
> Because the lion was very courageous and ferocious, and the Sahibs
>   were afraid;
> But for the sake of our lives, Patterson Sahib took all this trouble,
>   risking his own life in the forest ...
> My native home is at Chajanlat, in the thana of Domli, which is
>   in the district of Jhelum, and I have related this story as it
>   actually occurred.
> Patterson Sahib has left me, and I shall miss him as long as I live,
>   and now
> Roshan must roam about in Africa, sad and regretful.

It is just possible that this tribute might not have been quite as over-blown as it appears. There was nothing conventional about Patterson's lion hunt. The twenty-eight Indian laborers killed by the Tsavo man-eaters are an altogether inaccurate measure of the pair's depredations. No count was ever made of the African victims, but a conservative estimate would probably lie in the neighborhood of well over one hundred. Patterson had every reason to describe the bowl he received from the workers, with its accompanying poem, as his "most highly prized and hard-won trophy."

*

The most immediate result of the victory over the lions was the return to Tsavo of the defecting coolies and the resumption of work on the bridge.

Construction did not proceed swiftly, however. Like Preston, Patterson was without lifting machinery of any kind, and this posed a serious problem when the height of the piers reached six feet, for it was then no longer possible to raise the huge stones by manower alone. Patterson's solution was to improvise a sort of portable derrick from two thiry-foot rail lengths forming an inverted V. A block and tackle, rigged at the apex, enabled the workers to hoist the stones and swing them into position. But while Patterson found that "this contrivance worked capitally," it was in fact more suited to the unhurried construction of a pharaoh's pyramid than to the building of an industrial age railway bridge. Further delay was encountered on completion of the piers, for there seemed no way of spanning them with the girders. Patterson's primitive block and tackle hoist, adequate for the moving of 500-pound stones, would buckle and collapse under the thirty tons of a sixty-foot iron girder. He therefore borrowed a leaf from Preston's book and threw up wooden towers—built from sleepers laid crosswise to one another—between the piers. As at the Maji ya Chumvi, this shortening of distance permitted the laying down of long wooden beams and a temporary track, along which the flatcars carrying the girders were moved. When in its proper position, each girder was jacked up and placed in alignment while the truck was hauled away. The permanent rails followed in due course, and on February 7, 1899, the bridge over the river Tsavo was opened to traffic. The task should have been finished at least seven months earlier.

Quite rightly, however, Patterson took great pride in the bridge, particularly when he saw it meet its first test. Two or three days after it had been completed, premature spring rains struck Tsavo with an unprecedented fury, quickly transforming the river into a bloated battering ram that beat down anything and everything in its path. Among the first casualties were the two narrow-gauge bridges—and their tracks—from the quarry, and Patterson watched them being flicked away like twigs by the rampaging flood and twisted into a great cheval de frise. "The double tier of wreckage now swept forward, and hurled itself with a sullen plunge against the cutwaters of the stone piers, but the bridge took it without a tremor, and I saw the remnant of the temporary crossings swirl through the great spans and quickly disappear on its journey to the ocean. I confess that I witnessed the whole occurrence with a thrill of pride."

Indeed, it is probable that Patterson regarded the erasure of the Tsavo lions as a less rewarding achievement than the completion of the Tsavo bridge. If he was a big-game hunter by avocation, engineering was his profession, and engineers can derive as much esthetic gratification from the products of their training and innate talents as do painters and musicians. Seven years later, when he returned to east Africa (purely for "sport" this time) Patterson's trip from Mombasa to Nairobi could only have been a sentimental journey, especially when the train reached Tsavo. Although it was midnight and his companions in the first-class compartment were fast asleep, he made a point of waking them, "in order to point out ... by the pale moonlight, the strength and beauty of the Tsavo bridge; but I fear this delicate little attention was scarcely appreciated as it deserved. Naturally I could not expect them, or anyone else, to view the bridge quite from my point of view; I looked on it as a child of mine, brought up through stress and danger and troubles of all kinds, but the ordinary traveller of course knows nothing of this and doubtless thinks it only a very commonplace and insignificant structure."

Commonplace it undeniably was; from certain angles it might even have been called ugly. Yet one somehow feels regret that during the east African campaign of the First World War the Germans saw fit to blow it up. Until then, however, the Tsavo bridge seemed totally invulnerable to the batterings of Ukamba's corrosive climate—although in 1899 and 1900 the country almost proved the undoing of the railway itself.

10

THE FOUR HORSEMEN
AND THE IRON SNAKE

"No matter where one went
corpses strewed the tracks. Little skeleton
babies were found crying by the
dead bodies of their mothers."

While lions and homicidal workmen held up completion of the bridge at Tsavo, the advance of railhead through Ukamba was being resisted by more familiar adversaries of topography and meteorology. The pace, to be sure, had increased somewhat since the line had put the Taru desert behind it. By the spring of 1898, delays in supplying food and materials to parties working forward of railhead had been reduced considerably with the acquisition of several primitive steam-operated tractors which were immune to the tsetse fly. Weighing eight tons and burning wood fuel, "these engines," wrote Preston, "went anywhere and rolled down their own paths pulling loaded trucks after them, the dense bush presenting to them as much difficulty as a well-mown field would to a bicycle." Although one of the machines collided with the railhead locomotive and had to be abandoned with a burned-out boiler, there was no question in Preston's mind but that the new auxiliary power eased the transport burden immeasurably. And with advance gangs working more efficiently as a consequence, so too did railhead begin to hobble forward less painfully. During the summer of 1898, in fact, the platelaying crews were putting down an average of half a mile of track daily; on twenty-one separate days between June and October they covered a full mile.

One of these spurts was not without political significance, occurring as it did during a "courtesy" visit to railhead by the Governor of German East Africa. At that time, construction of the German railway from Tanga was advancing almost neck and neck with the Uganda line, and White- house appears to have felt that an impressive performance by his own workers might give Britain a psychological edge in the race to win the commerce of the lake regions. He therefore alerted Preston by telegraph of the impending visit and the latter made the necessary preparations, ordering his men to oil enough fishplates and gather enough track for two days' work if necessary. When the German Governor arrived with Whitehouse on the Chief Engineer's private train, the platelayers, wrote Preston, "were as happy as school boys and did their work on the run all day." As a result of the mile and a fraction laid down, Preston received another telegram—of congratulation—and "was informed that the Ger- man Governor had come to the conclusion that it was hopeless for them to hope to get to the Lake before us." This is a rather simplistic way of putting it, but not long afterwards, the German line did in fact come to a halt at Moshi in the foothills of Mount Kilimanjaro, three hundred miles from the lake shore.*

On September 30, 1898, the rails had reached a screen of dom palms fringing a small tributary of the Athi river. Nicely called Makindu— among the palms—this place saw the stream cross the right of way just 210 miles from Mombasa, or slightly over one-third of the surveyed route to Lake Victoria. If Preston were to maintain his pace of half a mile daily, trains would be running to the lake by the autumn of 1900. This at any rate was the view from railhead. But to members of an ever watchful and increasingly impatient Parliament, it had seemed as if the line were only one-third finished; after more than two years, they pointed out, at least half the distance should have been covered.

Although this argument carried a certain arithmetical weight, it did not take into account the unforeseen developments over which the builders had no control. At the same time, however, it was equally unde- niable that Parliament held the purse strings of construction funds, and if Westminster chose to carp, Whitehall considered it expedient to make some gesture of mollification. In late December, therefore, the Railway Committee sent an expert to east Africa to report on progress. This was

---

* By 1914, however, Germany completed another east African railway, the 700-mile Central line between Dar es Salaam and Kigoma on the eastern shore of Lake Tanganyika.

Sir Guildford Molesworth, whom we met briefly during his stop at Tsavo in the previous chapter. Molesworth spent two months on the line. He not only inspected the entire length of track that had been laid down (by the time he reached railhead it had advanced another forty-five miles) but traveled an additional four hundred miles on foot to observe preparations for carrying the line across the Rift Valley. At the conclusion of his tour he wrote a detailed report which alternately hailed the work that had been done and warned that the worst was yet to come.

Regarding construction, said Molesworth, "greater progress could not possibly have been expected. In fact, taking into consideration the very great difficulties that have been encountered, the advance of the railhead has been remarkably rapid." Special note was taken of an important accomplishment which had been brought off by Whitehouse the previous September. At that time, one of his advance surveyors, a man named Blackett, reported having come across a possible route from Nakuru to the lake which he claimed was considerably shorter than that recommended by Macdonald in 1892. Instead of angling far north, almost to the foothills of Mount Elgon, as did Macdonald's route, the new right of way sliced in a straight line across the Mau escarpment, and promised to reduce the distance from Mombasa by at least one hundred miles. On paper, Blackett's discovery seemed a windfall, but Whitehouse could not accept it without making a personal reconnaissance. His 800-mile round-trip march, wrote Molesworth, had "entailed the exploration of an absolutely unknown country, bare of supplies and traversed by no definite track." The journey was also worth the effort, for Whitehouse estimated that the new route would save 114 miles. The figure actually proved to be 75 miles, but even that meant a considerable reduction in costs, while in terms of construction time Whitehouse may have gained the Railway Committee at least half a year.

Even as an unfinished work, the railway in Molesworth's opinion was already showing itself to be a force for progress. "The porters of all up-country caravans," he wrote, "now travel as far as possible by railway, and the terrible march across the Taru desert has become a thing of the past. The civilising influence of the railway is most marked, even on the unpromising region which it has hitherto traversed. The tribes in contact with it have already commenced to trade, and a demand for European goods is springing up amongst them." But the report in no way minimized the difficulties of the task ahead. Molesworth commented at length on the problems of recruiting Africans to work on the line, the concept of organized labor being "utterly foreign to most of the tribesmen." He pointed to a sick list of nearly 2,500 patients in a labor force of 15,000. The all-important Locomotive Department, he said, "has had to contend with immense difficulties. Numerous changes have been made, owing to sickness among officers and subordinates. These changes have seriously interfered with continuity of action." Above all, he gave exhaustive attention to the harsh character of the country itself, and stated plainly that "a large and *possibly* the most difficult portion of the project has not yet passed beyond the stage of reconnaissance."

Probably the most ominous remark in Molesworth's report referred to "a great scarcity of food during the past year, owing to drought." This in fact understated the case, for drought was only one of four horsemen of a potential apocalypse arising from the perverse ecology of the country. The first blow had fallen late in 1897, when a severe outbreak of rinderpest struck down thousands of head of livestock and wild game in Ukamba and parts of Kikuyuland. This was followed in April of 1898 by the failure of the spring rains northwest of Tsavo and the onset of a two-year drought which brought in its wake a famine of near-genocidal proportions—exacerbated in turn by a rampant smallpox epidemic. Without exaggeration, it can be said that during the years 1898 through 1900, construction of the Uganda Railway proceeded across a disaster area.

*

It has been estimated that disease and starvation took at least 25,000 African lives during this period. The smallpox alone was beyond the slender medical resources of the Protectorate Administration. At Machakos, John Ainsworth, the bulky Sub-Commissioner of the Ukamba Province, found himself obliged to call for help from the neighboring Germans, whose Colonial Government laboratory rushed supplies of lymph to the stricken region. "All civil officers and members of the office staffs," wrote Ainsworth, "were instructed by the doctors how to vaccinate and by this means a fair number of natives were treated." But there was not enough lymph to go around, and the smallpox continued to run wild for nearly two years. In all likelihood, however, the drought took the heaviest toll. Under the best of climatic conditions, Ukamba's weather-weary soil produced a sparse agricultural yield. If the rains came even two or three weeks late, the anemic patches of maize and millet which fed the land would shrivel. So too would human bodies, and by the summer of 1898, when the scope of the drought was beginning to make itself felt, the hard-pressed Administration tried, mightily but vainly, to cope with the emergency. "It became necessary," wrote Ainsworth, "to bring

food to the districts and in certain areas... to open relief camps. The
Government granted a considerable sum of money for this purpose...
Information was sent all over the country to the people that they would
receive food if they came to the relief camps, but thousands died before
they either got our messages or could reach the camps."

It was not pleasant to watch the quiet massacre. Mrs. Stuart Watt, the
wife of an English missionary at Machakos, wrote that "the scenes around
our mission station were appalling. Skeletons were tottering hither and
thither with every bone and joint in their body exposed to view. No
matter where one went corpses strewed the tracks. Little skeleton babies
were found crying by the dead bodies of their mothers." Jackson, whose
train passed through Ukamba at this time, was another witness to the
impact of the blight. "I was returning from leave," he wrote, "... and
heard about it at the coast, and how the starving were begging along
the railway line, so I took with me a chop-box full of bread, and bought
more ... from an Indian. I also noticed that my servants and some forty
porters were buying every mango and banana they could lay their hands
on, and later on when we reached the famine area ... found that they
had saved the skins... The starving women and children were dreadful
to look upon, and their hunger drove them into behaving like wild beasts
directly the bread and fruit skins began to be doled out. Women and children were mixed up together, pushing and tugging, and scrambling on
top of one another in silence; poor creatures, they had not the strength
to fight and shout at the same time."

Hunger did not gnaw at the local populations alone. Porters on Uganda-bound caravans also felt the bite. So too did a growing number of
English and Indian administrators occupying permanent Government
stations at Naivasha, Eldama ravine and other locations still far beyond
the reach of railhead. The railway itself had a host of mouths to feed. By
now, there were no fewer than thirteen thousand Indians working on the
line. They required twenty-one tons of food daily, and there may not have
been a great deal more than twenty-one tons of food in the entire region;
"practically all rations have to be sent up from the coast," wrote Molesworth, "as none can be procured locally." Since the railway was already
sagging under the weight of huge rice and flour shipments for the starving
local inhabitants while simultaneous troop movements to Uganda made
additional demands on rolling stock which was badly needed for construction, the special daily food trains from Mombasa did not hasten the
progress of the rails. Work was further impeded by the poisoned arrows
of hunger-crazed Wakamba tribesmen as they launched attacks on construction parties for their meager flour supplies. Under these conditions,

it might seem curious that the Government did not lighten the railway's burden—even in the face of the risks involved—by making available what amounted to a cornucopia in the otherwise empty larder.

This was a sizable area of Kikuyuland which, owing largely to its altitude and temperate climate, had escaped the worst of the blight and fairly spilled over with maize, millet, sweet potatoes, yams, cassava, beans, bananas and sugar cane, not to mention sheep and goats in abundance. In previous years, the Kikuyu had shown only partial reluctance to sell food to the leaders of the relatively small caravans that crossed the fringes of their country. To early visitors like Thomson, Lugard and Jackson, and even to the Swahili slave and ivory traders, Kikuyuland had in fact served as a kind of storehouse where food supplies were taken on for the long march across the Rift Valley. Now, however, the Kikuyu were becoming increasingly less hospitable to the veritable stream of foreigners which the railway and the Government had spawned. It was one thing to barter a little maize flour or a few sheep to the occasional party of transients, but by 1898 the white man had made clear his intention to stay. "An iron snake will one day cross our land"; so ran the ancient tribal prophecy.* Now the snake had arrived and the Kikuyu were prepared to resist its invasion with a ferocity that could be matched only by the Masai.

*

Paradoxically—perhaps astonishingly—the Masai themselves no longer presented a serious threat, thanks in some part at least to the foresight of the great laibon Mbatian, who must have perceived that spears and simis were no match for firepower. On his deathbed, so it is believed, Mbatian had predicted plagues that would decimate the tribe and its livestock indiscriminately if the elmoran interfered with the white invaders. And by the end of 1895, the Masai had been all but domesticated as the consequence of an unexpected Government decision following an extraordinary battle. In that year, the leader of a large Swahili caravan had imprudently ordered several guards to seize two Masai girls for his evening entertainment; the result was a night attack that wiped out all but a handful of the 871-man party. News of the massacre almost immediately reached the ears of a nearby English trader named Andrew Dick, who took it on himself to organize a private punitive expedition. Virtually dragooning three French gentleman hunters into joining him,

---

* This prediction has also been attributed to the Masai; in all likelihood, both tribes shared the same vision.

Dick managed to round up a large number of Masai cattle before the elmoran struck back in force. Although hopelessly outnumbered, he put up a fierce fight, bringing down upwards of three dozen warriors before he ran out of ammunition, and then holding the others off simply by raising and aiming his empty Remington. Eventually, of course, an impatient moran called the bluff and Dick became the first and only European ever to be skewered on a Masai spear.

Government could not have been expected to tolerate the outrage for a moment. Not only had the caravan been carrying supplies for one of the Protectorate stations, but the murder of a white man by naked savages put British prestige squarely on the line. It was mandatory that the newly established Government act swiftly and firmly. So grave was the emergency that Jackson, then in charge of the Eldama Ravine station, marched across the Rift Valley to confer with Ainsworth. During the journey, a number of Masai gave him their version of the incident, and his recollection of his subsequent conversation with Ainsworth is revealing. "After greetings [Ainsworth] said, 'Well, what do you think about it?' to which I replied, 'My dear John, I have only heard one side of it, but I am, so far, of opinion that your people [of the caravan] started it, and had only themselves to blame,' to which he replied, 'I am glad to hear you say that, as I have come to the same conclusion.'"

In brief, the British public school ethic of fair play was beginning to make its influence felt on the final verdict. Further inquiries by Jackson and Ainsworth fully confirmed their original impressions. "There could be no possible doubt," wrote Jackson, "that the behaviour of the caravan as a whole was abominable, and that the Masai received the greatest provocation." Ainsworth, who shared this view entirely, was also critical of Dick for having ignored a Government request that he refrain from taking the law into his own hands. As a consequence, the Masai suffered no more than a token fine, and their new chief laibon, Mbatian's son Lenana, was outspoken in his gratitude. Wrote Ainsworth: "When I had explained to Lenana that we were satisfied that our own people were to blame ... and that on the terms mentioned we would cry quits, he came forward with obvious feeling, thanked us and exclaimed that he had heard of the white man's justice but now he knew it was a fact... This incident was practically the beginning of Lenana's friendship and loyalty to the Government."

*

The Kikuyu were another matter, and it can be said that the final decade of the nineteenth century saw this hyper-suspicious nation rise to the peak of an always acute xenophobia. Despite his disapproval of what he considered IBEA's injudicious treatment of the tribe, Sir Gerald Portal had nonetheless described the Kikuyu as "undoubtedly a treacherous, untrustworthy crowd," and his party had felt less than secure as it skirted the perimeter of their land. "The Wa-Kikuyu, as we all knew," wrote Portal, "seldom or never show themselves, or run the risk of a fight in the open, but lie like snakes in the long grass, or in some dense bush within a few yards of the line of march, waiting for a gap in the ranks, or for some incautious porter to stray away, or loiter a few yards behind... For any one to wander alone for more than two hundred yards from the stockade was almost certain death... Long before I went to their country myself I remember being told by an African traveller of great renown that the only way in which to deal with the Kikuyu people, whether singly or in masses, was to 'shoot at sight.'"

This had been written before the establishment of formal British rule, but Kikuyu demeanor did not improve under the protection of the Union Jack. Although most Kikuyu had never even seen a white man, all knew of his presence and showed little disposition to hold out the hand of friendship. In May, 1898, one clan welcomed Blackett of the advance railway survey party by attempting to poison his drinking water. Two months later, a large Kikuyu force made a dawn raid on a Swahili caravan and killed twenty porters. On learning of the attack, the British District Commissioner summoned several clan elders to his headquarters and was scornfully ignored. When he sought out the elders himself, a band of warriors threatened to spear him on the spot. Such an affront to the Queen's representative could not, of course, be treated lightly, and the upshot was a punitive expedition which accomplished little beyond the murder of an officer, whose body, according to Ainsworth, was "frightfully mutilated." The incident caused another military force to be sent out, with what can only be called marginal success. Not long afterwards, we find Ainsworth authorizing still another punitive expedition following "an unprovoked attack by the natives" on the agent of a British trading firm.

The reason that these sporadic official reprisals appear to have made little impression on the Kikuyu probably lies in the Government's ambiguous policy toward the tribe. As long as the Kikuyu remained in an inhospitable frame of mind, Kikuyuland itself was placed off limits to all outsiders not on Administration business. The victim of the abovementioned "unprovoked attack" had in fact been trespassing. Even Protectorate officials seldom penetrated far into the country. This position combined justice and expediency. The land, after all, did belong to the Kikuyu, and if they chose to bar "red men," as whites were often called at the time, they were exercising no more than their right. What was a protectorate for if not to safeguard the interests of the indigenous inhabitants? Punitive expeditions, moreover, were costly affairs that could create as much disorder as they could compel good behavior. Of special concern was the possibility that stern measures or unwelcome visitors might provoke attacks on the railway and further retard an already lagging construction schedule. Although the tracks barely passed across the outer hemline of Kikuyuland, that was enough; occasional Kikuyu raids on working parties did take place, and no one wished to see these become a regular practice. Thus, until permanent European settlement made necessary a vigorous pacification program, it was generally deemed prudent to interfere as little as possible with the Kikuyu in their own homes. This at any rate was the more or less official line, and the Government did not actually bring the full weight of its authority to bear for several years. Yet during the famine, one could not escape the fact that Kikuyuland was, so to speak, a supermarket in a boneyard. If the Administration pursued a hands-off policy, it was only a matter of time before some intrepid private person would flout the law and tap the country's desperately needed food resources—not only for the railway but for the Government itself.

"The opportunity of getting away into some hitherto unexplored part of the country, where there was a prospect of getting the adventures I wanted ... seemed too good to be lost."

In 1902, Captain Richard Meinertzhagen, the amiably bellicose British colonial army officer who will reappear in a subsequent chapter, wrote in his diary of having "met a man called John Boyes, a cheerful rogue who some years ago impersonated the Government... in Kikuyu. The Government foolishly brought all sorts of charges against him, but Boyes was acquitted... a slippery customer." That description is as accurate as any. It is no less inaccurate, for John Boyes must rank among the most shadowy of all east Africa's pre-settlement pioneers. Hardly anything is known about his first three years in the Protectorate except that he spent two and a half of them in Kikuyuland, trading with various clans and sending out large shipments of food not only to the railway but to the very Government whose laws he was openly defying. There is also some reason to believe that, as the only white man in the country, Boyes may have exercised a certain pacifying influence over the tribe. The latter, however, is merely what Boyes himself tells us in his entertaining book, *John Boyes, King of the Wa-Kikuyu.* Virtually none of the experiences he recounts can be authenticated, and one suspects that the author may not have been averse to drawing the long bow from time to time. Yet despite an occasional blood-and-thunder extravagance and some low-keyed boasting, the narrative has an unmistakable ring of truth, while Boyes himself emerges less as a "slippery customer" than as a highly intelligent hobo of fortune with a relish for action and a sharp eye to the main chance.

A Yorkshireman by birth, Boyes was twenty-four years old when he arrived in Mombasa early in 1898. He had spent the previous three years in south Africa, serving as a trooper in the Matabele war and holding a number of poorly paying jobs until he learned that profits were to be had from trading and ivory hunting in the newly established East Africa Protectorate. However, when he sought advice from a Government official in Mombasa, he was surprised to be "received with the scantest courtesy and given very plainly to understand that white men, whether travellers or hunters, were by no means welcome." This charge was neither completely just nor completely baseless. "Inconsistent" is probably the best word for official policy on new arrivals in east Africa during the 1890s. Somewhat jealous of its authority in the fledgling Protectorate, the British Administration could on occasion adopt an arbitrarily high-handed attitude toward visitors whose presence, it was believed, might in some way aggravate hostile tribes and thus retard the civilizing mission, not to mention the progress of railway construction. At other times, for no apparent reason, a trader or hunter might be given a cordial welcome. To no small extent, a newcomer's reception depended on the mood and the character of the individual bureaucrat who processed him through Mombasa or examined his credentials elsewhere. Boyes appears to have run afoul of more than his share of imperious mediocrities, and the cold shoulder he experienced on his arrival was the commencement of a long-running feud with the Administration.

Petty officialdom, however, did not keep Boyes from organizing and leading caravans to supply the British forces then occupied in quelling the Uganda Mutiny, although from a commercial standpoint the venture failed. On his final trek from Uganda to the coast, Boyes' transport animals died off and he put a sign reading "Dead Donkey Camp" on one of his abandoned wagons. This happened at the height of the famine, and as Boyes approached the outer edges of Kikuyuland on foot, he began to look on the region as the pot of gold at the end of his rainbow. He was quite aware of the railway's badly strained transport facilities and had himself passed through Government outposts which faced starvation. He also knew, to be sure, that "any parties which had gone out [to Kikuyuland] to buy supplies had always been killed by the natives," but this was incentive rather than deterrent. "Although I had lost all my wagons, I had not lost my desire for further adventure, and the opportunity of getting away into some hitherto unexplored part of the country, where there was a prospect of getting the adventures I wanted, together with the chance of making enough money to repair my misfortunes, seemed too good to be lost."

But it was almost lost on Boyes' first attempt to reach Kikuyuland. Hardly had he left Naivasha than he was brought back by a patrol which the District Commissioner had sent out to intercept him. The officer asked Boyes if he was trying to commit suicide and flatly refused to accept a letter absolving Government of responsibility for the trader's death at the hands of the tribe. It thus became necessary to enter the forbidden land from outside the Naivasha district boundary, and in due course, Boyes and his seven porters were approaching their goal through a forest of bamboo trees "as thick as wheat in a wheatfield." Nor was it long before the party suddenly found itself facing five hundred fully armed Kikuyu warriors. "Never having seen a white man before, they regarded me with something like awe ... and were at a loss how to act. The fact that I had ventured to come there alone was, in itself, quite enough to surprise and astonish them, and... I knew that if I was to succeed with them, I must keep up an attitude of fearlessness."

This bold front, in fact, set the pattern of Boyes' life for the next two years, a period during which his courage, quick wit and sheer luck were put to the test almost daily. When the flustered band of warriors took him to their leader, a man named Karuri, Boyes quickly seized the initiative as the elder began cross-questioning him through an interpreter. "I said that I was anxious to trade with him and to buy food ... As my mission was a peaceable one, I had left most of my guns in the forest to avoid trouble, but... if he harmed me, my people would come and make war on him. This pardonable untruth seemed to make the desired impression ... and when I signified my intention of making a long stay in his country, he readily agreed that his men should build a hut for me." From this moment on, Boyes seldom writes of Karuri without referring to him as "my friend."

Karuri's acceptance of Boyes may have been the latter's entrance visa, but Boyes had yet to become persona grata with the people. "The Kikuyu," he noted, "will come up to you smiling and kill you the next moment if he gets the chance," and even among Karuri's tribesmen he maintained a façade of bluff for some time—in a manner that would have done credit to Joseph Thomson. When a group of truculent warriors told him he was foolhardy in bringing only one rifle with him, he replied that it was a special type of weapon that could kill six men with a single shot. "It happened to be the old Martini-Metford, so, putting in a solid cartridge, I chose a tree that I knew the bullet would go through and fired... When they found the hole where the bullet had gone in and come out on the other side, they were considerably surprised and impressed. I assured them that that was nothing; if they would examine the side of the mountain beyond they would find that the bullet had gone right through that as well!" Boyes also cultivated an image of himself (and thus of all white men) as unkillable, by "defying the witch doctors to poison me and swallowing, in their presence, samples of what they considered their most deadly poisons without any ill effects." He was not altogether certain of what made him immune; one of several possibilities occurring to him was that "the Kikuyu had no poisons at all. It must be remembered that the African native is one of the most superstitious beings in the world, and there is no doubt that many of the deaths attributed to the action of the witch doctors were really due to pure funk." It would seem much more likely that whatever concoctions the medicine men used did not happen—by sheer good fortune—to be overly potent, but in any case, Boyes' readiness to test them at all times made a profound impression on his hosts.

His most important opportunity to gain entrée, however, arose from the internecine warfare in which the Kikuyu—"like the Highlanders in the old days"—were constantly embroiled. Not long after his arrival, Karuri's village was attacked by a hostile clan, largely out of fury over the presence of an alien. "My duty was clear. These people had brought the trouble on themselves by befriending me, and the least I could do was give them such help as I could... Seizing my rifle, I made for the scene of the fight, accompanied by a crowd of yelling savages, delighted at my decision... The attackers began to waver, and when I fired a few shots with effect, finally turned tail and bolted... The triumphant warriors returned to the village and made quite a hero of me... This incident was of the greatest value to me, as it fully established my reputation as a useful member of the community."

Following that engagement, indeed, the tribe rapidly warmed up to its honorary Kikuyu. Warriors and women alike lent a willing hand in the building of Boyes' house, a bungalow-like structure with shutters replacing the nonexistent glass panes in the windows. He soon acquired a local name, Karanjai, "meaning literally 'Who eats beans,' because I preferred that vegetable to their sweet potatoes." At first, Boyes thought the word was a greeting, and habitually repeated it whenever someone addressed him, but it was not long before he became fluent in Kikuyu. As a matter of simple strategy, however, he kept his interpreter for many months and feigned an imperfect knowledge of the language.

As suspicion gradually gave way to acceptance and friendship, Boyes worked patiently toward his main objective of supplying food to the railway and Government. The undertaking did not get off to an auspicious start; with only seven porters, Boyes had been unable to carry with him a large quantity of trade goods. That obstacle was surmounted, however, by the offer of iodoform powder. Although a radical departure from the conventional beads, wire and cloth, it had acquired the value of legal tender after Boyes treated several wounded Kikuyu following the scrape with the hostile clan. "All wanted some, and in exchange for a small quantity, wrapped in paper, would give from ten to twenty pounds of flour." Almost before he knew it, Boyes found himself with two hundred loads (about six tons) but no means of transporting them until "by dint of persuasion" he recruited sufficient volunteer porters from among the warriors. Although reluctant to leave the forest and approach Masai country, the men were willing to take the flour as far as the caravan road, where Boyes set up an open-air store. Within a few days he had sold his entire stock to railway survey parties and the leaders of Uganda-bound caravans. The price for each load was thirty rupees (about $9.00) bringing a gross profit of $1,800—"which made me highly satisfied with the result of my first venture among the Kikuyu."

Fortune continued to smile on Boyes. It was not long before his volunteer Kikuyu porters were carrying flour and other supplies directly into Naivasha, where the need for food was so desperate that Protectorate officials at that post turned a blind eye to the violations of the law and drew up a contract with the trader for a regular provisioning service. Thus Boyes may have been history's only licensed black-market operator. And his operations had barely begun.

"The beauty of a view in Nairobi depends on the more or less thorough elimination of the town from the landscape."

Boyes' adventures with the Kikuyu were being paralleled by Preston's misadventures with nature as railway construction crept forward on its iron belly through the grasping thorn of Ukamba. It was hardly surprising that the drought made its effects felt on the line with an almost vindictive inconsistency. The surrounding countryside might have been shriveling, but this did not prevent sporadic localized rainstorms from lashing out at the right of way and submerging miles of track. "The permanent way was new," wrote Preston, "embankments unsettled and shaky, and during the rains the line had to be constantly patrolled by men from the gangs." Long stretches of flatland which ordinarily presented few engineering difficulties were converted into vast puddings, and days might pass before the soil became firm enough to support earthworks and tracks. For a period of two weeks in December, 1898, all rail traffic was suspended owing to washed out embankments, and for some time afterwards supply trains were allowed to run only during daylight hours. The sudden downpours might have freakish side effects. One day, Preston was watching the three-inch-deep waters of a four-hour deluge subside into the earth, when "lo and behold, from every hole and crevice in the ground, came forth in their thousands, scorpions, varying in size from an inch to five inches ... and it was our salvation that they could scarcely drag themselves along. They had been half drowned by the flood."

The perverse weather had a less inhibiting effect on other adversaries. Harassment by lions did not cease beyond the perimeter of Tsavo. At Simba, it almost seemed as if the man-eaters were seeking to cut railhead off from its sources of supply, for they allowed the platelaying gangs to do their work unharmed and move on, only to begin attacking the station itself when it was turned over to the traffic department. Materials trains were frequently held up for the better part of a day when lions prowled Simba's tracks at sunset and kept the Indian pointsman from lighting the signal lamp. At railhead itself, work was constantly impeded by innumerable rhinoceroses. Their mere presence would halt platelaying for long hours, as there was no way to predict their behavior; Preston found them "a regular nuisance in disturbing the work, by turning up at odd times and gazing at our workmen." If the rhinos did not always take the offensive, their occasional attacks were dramatic at least. One rhino dragged the railhead hospital tent several hundred yards into the bush; due only to an almost miraculous spell of good health was the tent unoccupied, although the night watchman nearly became a casualty after being flipped ten feet into the air on the beast's horn. At another time, a large bull rhinoceros actually charged a supply train as it approached railhead, continually bashing itself against the locomotive wheels and nearly derailing the engine. The simultaneous arrival of the two lurching behemoths transformed the railhead party into a pandemonium until a well-placed rifle bullet despatched the attacker.

Smaller species of wildlife resorted to more specialized methods of sabotage. Derailments were common on sections of the line supported by wooden sleepers which, despite their coatings of creosote, did not long survive the ravages of white ants. One engine left the rails when a flock of guinea fowl undermined an embankment while feeding on the same insects. Supply trains were often brought to a dead halt and delayed for hours after running over vast swarms of locusts or caterpillars, crushing them into rivers of slippery pulp that deprived the locomotive wheels of all traction. The terrain was equally unkind. Between Tsavo and Makindu, Preston recorded "a very dreary time, the bush along this section being very dense, with large patches of spiked sanseviera, which made any attempt to push through it very painful in consequence." The thorn scrub and shriveled trees of the region could also frustrate in other ways. Once, when the railhead locomotive ran short of coal while carrying the workmen to the head of the tracks, "our poor old engine that could hardly pull six trucks with coal fuel, had a bad attack of short windedness when fed with wood fuel. Before we had got half way to railhead, the two firemen went on strike, saying that their backs were almost broken: so I put a couple of coolies to help them, but these came to me with bruised and broken fingers, so there was nothing left to be done but wait for the next load of coal." This in turn meant a full day of enforced idleness.

The thorn dispersed somewhat when the tracks reached Kibwezi at mile 196, and Preston hoped that the relatively open ground (and more especially the altitude, nearly three thousand feet above sea level) would at least improve the health of his fever-wracked workers. Instead, the new location "brought us merely an increased number of malarial-stricken patients." Hardly had camp been made, moreover, than "Kibwezi's reputation as the home of blackwater fever reached us. In record time we struck our tents." The move produced no miraculous cures—indeed, "our toll of sickness became larger and larger"—and when railhead finally reached Makindu, malaria had laid low fifty percent of the work force. Healthier surroundings, however, seemed assured when Preston shifted camp again to the bank of the nearby Kiboko (hippopotamus) stream. He found this spot "ideal ... picturesque and delightfully cool. The large flat topped mimosa trees resemble huge umbrellas and throw a generous and welcome shade during the hottest part of the day." When night fell, he also discovered "myriads of mosquitos," and within seventy-two hours the malaria rate had risen to 100 percent, making it necessary to replace the entire railhead section with fresh workers from the coast. Only Preston remained, although he too had long been a victim of the fever. "Looking up my diary I noticed that hardly a week passed without my being either laid up altogether or there was the remark 'Had to return to camp off colour.'"

*

The most remarkable feature of work on the line during 1898 and 1899 was not its absence of visible progress but just the reverse. In the face of every ambush laid by the combined forces of weather, topography, disease and wildlife, Preston's platelayers, working with dogged energy, were able to put the worst of Ukamba behind them early in 1899. By May, the tracks were approaching the highland region. Illness among the workers subsided perceptibly with a slow but steady rise in altitude. Gradually, the terrain offered less resistance as thorn gave way to open prairie and the rails began to cross the antelope-swarming Kapiti and Athi plains. Like every east African traveler before and after him, Preston marveled at the great sea of animals, and half a century later could still record his first impression with awe. "To describe what we saw in the way of game, would be put down today as exaggeration, but to put it mildly ... wherever one looked it was nothing but one moving mass of Hartebeeste, Wildebeeste, Zebra and the smaller antelope. The clang of the rails and steel sleepers would frighten the game within about a five hundred yard radius only to make the number greater and denser at the edge of the circle."

It was not all smooth sailing, to be sure. There were long delays when an occasional heavy downpour churned up the black cotton loam of the plains, and Preston then found the country not much less uncooperative than Ukamba. "Those who have had anything to do with even ox-cart transport over black soil during the rains may understand the difficulty we had to contend with in having to pass a locomotive weighing more than 50 tons over embankments of freshly thrown up black soil, with the rain coming down literally in torrents." During one such storm, plate-laying encountered the additional obstacle of a zebra herd, mired down shoulder-deep in the sodden earth of the embankment. The animals were extricated with lassos improvised from the workers' turbans. Despite all this, however, the men somehow managed to move the tracks ahead at their respectable half-mile-per-day average, and on May 24, 1899, Queen Victoria's loyal subjects at railhead celebrated the Empress of India's birthday with a record-breaking mile and a half.

Six days later, they reached mile 327, at a place known to the Masai as Nakusontelon, "the beginning of all beauty." Preston described it as "a bleak, swampy stretch of soppy landscape, devoid of human habitation of any sort, the resort of thousands of wild animals of every species." He added that it "did not boast one single tree." Nakusontelon was bisected by a small stream which the Masai called the Uaso Nairobi (cold water) and it was that name which most Europeans and Africans preferred to use. The place was not unknown to the British in 1899. Three years earlier, one Sergeant Ellis of the Royal Engineers had established a staging depot on the site for the oxen and mules used as transport animals by the Protectorate Government. Long before that, caravans had skirted the swamp en route to and from Uganda. But to all practical purposes, Nairobi was no more than a lonely sprawl of papyrus until the railway's arrival.

*

This uninviting patch of ground, in fact, played what may have been the key role in the construction of the line. After leaving Nairobi, the tracks would wind upwards on a twisting climb of nearly two thousand feet, over a distance of twenty-seven miles, to the summit of the Kikuyu escarpment, the Rift Valley's eastern wall, and then descend more than fifteen hundred feet, in a series of near-vertical plunges, to the valley floor. From an engineering standpoint, fixing the rails to the sharply pitched escarpment was recognized as potentially the most intricate and punishing task that the builders had to face. It was certainly not an undertaking that could be brought off by remote control from the coast; the precarious operation must be planned, supervised and supplied from a forward base as close as possible to the site of actual construction. Since Nairobi occupied the last stretch of level ground that the route crossed before reaching the Rift, it was the natural and obvious jumping-off place, and Whitehouse decided that it should also become the railway's principal nerve center. Within a few weeks of Preston's arrival, the entire headquarters apparatus was being railed up from Mombasa; and by early July of 1899, the placid, marshy flatland was well on its way to becoming an equatorial Waterloo Station. Patterson, who had long since left Tsavo for other construction duties, was placed in charge of the transformation process. "There was an immense amount of work to be done," he wrote, "in converting an absolutely bare plain, three hundred and twenty-seven miles from the nearest place where even a nail could be purchased, into a busy railway centre. Roads and bridges

had to be constructed, houses and workshops built, turntables and station quarters erected, a water supply laid on, and a hundred and one
other things done which go into the making of a railway township. Wonderfully soon, however, the nucleus of the present town began to take
shape." By August, a more or less regularly scheduled Mombasa–Nairobi
passenger service was in operation.

As frontier communities go, Nairobi could not be called prepossessing.
Sir Charles Eliot, who moved Protectorate Headquarters from Mombasa
to Nairobi two years later, wrote that "the beauty of a view in Nairobi
depends on the more or less thorough elimination of the town from the
landscape." With its irregular lines of weatherbeaten tents and faceless,
barrack-like corrugated iron bungalows, Nairobi at the turn of the century bore a not altogether inexact resemblance to a miniature Dachau
without walls. There was a main thoroughfare called Victoria Street
which became a canal of thigh-deep mud whenever rain fell. A proliferation of the cramped, fetid Indian shops known as dukas pockmarked the
town, and at the western end of Victoria Street sprawled a bazaar where
the Indians, in Eliot's words, "built their houses so close together that
they neutralised the natural advantages of air and light, and then allowed
the most disgusting filth to accumulate." Other points of interest were a
post office, a soda water factory and a shaky timber structure known as
Wood's Hotel which doubled as a general store and which burned down
several times before being abandoned as a poor insurance risk. Social life
centered on a singularly uncongenial heap of wood and corrugated iron
which railway officials and other British residents were pleased to call
their club. And it was not long before a city government of sorts took
shape, with the establishment of an embryonic municipal council. This
was presided over by Ainsworth, who had been directed by the Foreign
Office to transfer his Ukamba Provincial Headquarters from Machakos
shortly after the railway's arrival. The move was the first official step in
Nairobi's emergence as the principal metropolis of all eastern Africa.

But Ainsworth was not made welcome at once. In attempting to
administer Nairobi, he encountered no small hostility from the railway,
whose officials considered the town to be within their private jurisdiction and resented what struck them as a mutually exclusive dual
authority. Since it was universally recognized that whatever economic
well-being east Africa might ever enjoy would depend almost entirely
on the export of its produce by rail, the line's writ ran large. For this
reason, Government often played a secondary role in Protectorate affairs
during the years of construction, while Whitehouse managed not merely
a transportation system but what one writer has called an "*imperium in*

imperio." The railway had its own administration, its own law courts, its own police, fire and health departments. The telegraph was built and operated by the line. All land touching on the right of way or used in any fashion for railway purposes was the property of the Railway Committee. In certain respects, Whitehouse could almost be said to have owned Nairobi. Thus it was not altogether unnatural that Ainsworth's presence should have been regarded as redundant at best and an unwarranted intrusion at worst.

It was no less understandable that the railway's attitude would be resented equally by Government. "The Uganda Railway Committee," Eliot later wrote, "... had no mistrust of their own powers or diffidence in interfering, and did not even avail themselves of the valuable local assistance which was at their disposal... The Committee in their final report blandly remark that their arrangements insured harmonious working between the authorities of the Protectorate and the officers of the railway. As a matter of fact they insured a permanent squabble between the two administrations, which was most disadvantageous to the public interest." Ainsworth and senior railway officials became embroiled in more than one exquisitely courteous cat-fight over land as the latter sought to dissuade the former from putting up Government buildings in Nairobi. At the same time, however, the Sub-Commissioner and his skeleton staff did represent the Crown; one could hardly evict them. Accordingly, at an all but prohibitive rent, an inconvenient site was grudgingly allocated to the Protectorate, and the Union Jack looked down on the squalid precincts of the new provincial capital.

One can wonder at the selection of Nairobi as the seat of an important civil administration. By virtue of its swamps alone, it was the worst possible choice for any sort of urban center. The town's first Medical Officer, Dr. E. Boedeker, wrote that even among the early caravan leaders, the site "had always been regarded as an unhealthy locality swarming with mosquitoes." Eliot said that Nairobi "offers great difficulties to drainage, and it will be hard to ever make it satisfactory from a sanitary point of view." Not long after the railway's arrival, a plague broke out and Patterson took it on himself to burn down the rat-infested bazaar, giving the human occupants an hour's notice to move out. "For this somewhat arbitrary proceeding," he wrote, "I was mildly called over the coals, as I expected; but all the same it effectually stamped out the plague." There were more burnings in 1902 as another visitation struck the town. Even railway installations nearly went up in flames when a rumor arose that a dead rat had been discovered under a chair in the station waiting room. However, according to Mervyn Hill, "a matter-of-fact Traffic Manager, anxious that the railway's buildings be not added to the fires of controversy and sanitation, unobtrusively removed it and all was well and saved." In 1904, when Nairobi had grown substantially, a committee of doctors petitioned that the entire municipality be relocated, simply because it was a spawning ground of disease. Eliot concurred, but added that "it is probably too late to do this." John Boyes echoed a virtually universal opinion when he wrote that he "should never have imagined that [Nairobi] would have been chosen as the site for the future capital of British East Africa."

Yet the Foreign Office had little option when it recommended the move. The railway did not pass through Machakos, and it was mandatory that Ukamba Provincial Headquarters be situated on the line of swiftest communication with the coast. If for purely technical reasons, Whitehouse chose to make Nairobi his base of operations, then that base would inevitably attract an enormous trading community and become the hub of activity in the east African interior. The Protectorate Government simply gravitated to the focal point of authority.

"I mildly put the question to the officer as to whether he expected me to fly the Russian flag."

The establishment of scheduled rail service between Mombasa and Nairobi did not entirely relieve the critical food shortage. As the drought stalked into 1900, Boyes continued sending supplies from Kikuyuland to Government posts and railway work parties, all the while consolidating his own position with the tribe. Initially, his barter dealings had centered on a relatively small area in the neighborhood of present-day Fort Hall, but inside of a year he had been able to enlarge the number of his wholesale merchants by making extended treks and opening branch trading stations throughout most of the Kikuyu country

This was easier imagined than accomplished, since crossing the boundary line that separated any two Kikuyu clans was often an overt act of aggression that could touch off a full-scale war. But Boyes was prepared for that eventuality. Ever since having distinguished himself in the intra-tribal affray following his arrival, he had been tacitly acknowledged as Karuri's field marshal, and had in turn drilled that leader's warriors into a semi-private army. Basic training included such exercises as sentry duty, scouting, fighting in formation and launching attacks with shields locked together in Masai fashion. Boyes was also able to secure thirty rifles, with which he armed an elite guard. These troops took regular target practice and proved apt pupils, if slow to grasp the principles of sighting. Boyes found them "all right up to a hundred yards, as I had taught them always to aim low; whereas the native is apt to fire high." The guardsmen also learned the manual of arms after a fashion, became adept at saluting (Boyes hoped that that gesture would replace the saliva-drenched handshake) and were eventually outfitted in khaki which Boyes had obtained in Nairobi. At the head of this more or less formidable legion there was of course a Union Jack.

Boyes' military expeditions through Kikuyuland were not, however, the incursions of a marauder. Nor was it his wish to foment further clan hostilities; quite the contrary, "as this state of affairs was very bad for my plans of trading." Wherever he went, he urged rival clan leaders to reconcile differences without recourse to violence. "I impressed upon them that they must ... not go raiding and killing each other, telling them that it was only savages that settle their quarrels in that way. To speak of them as not being savages flattered their vanity." Flattery, however, did not always get Boyes very far, and he witnessed more spear-throwing than handshaking. As often as not, he himself was in the thick of the fray; his book spills over with accounts of ambushes and pitched battles in which Boyes' relatively disciplined troops always manage to prevail over usually hopeless odds.

And if war was the rule rather than the exception, the exceptions did not inevitably encourage, as illustrated by Boyes' most ambitious peace-making venture. This involved the bringing together of three immensely powerful and bellicose chieftains living near the foothills of Mount Kenya, some forty miles north of Karuri's district. What Boyes had in mind specifically was the rite known as pigasangi—indistinguishable in form from the blood brotherhood pacts concluded by Lugard and others, but generally binding nations rather than individuals. After an ambush-punctuated march to the region, he cajoled the three clan leaders into accepting the proposal; negotiations broke down, however, over the site of the ceremony itself. Only after long and tortuous diplomatic haggling did Boyes win consent to a market place roughly equidistant from the three chiefdoms. The participating clans then converged on the spot, and Boyes took a place with the principals at the center of the throng while the Union Jack lent an additional touch of color to the scene. But no sooner had the three nations pledged themselves to everlasting harmony than Boyes "advised the chiefs not to delay too long before returning to their homes, as the temper of the people might change, in which case there would probably be trouble."

Yet despite the limited success of Boyes' attempts to reduce inter-clan friction, they were far from being total failures. Indeed, it appears that he was able at the very least to impose a moderately effectual armed truce over sizable areas of Kikuyuland. Even the seemingly fragile *pigasangi* agreement, which he had all but forced on the three warlike Mount Kenya rulers, held together far longer than he expected. And if one is hard put to believe that a single white man could exercise even partial control over so fractious a community as the Kikuyu, it must be remembered that Boyes was very much in a position to lay down the law. Although more than a few Kikuyu clans possessed rifles, it was only the men of Boyes' shabby militia who could fire the weapons with anything resembling accuracy. "The ordinary native who has had no training with a gun," wrote Boyes, "is absolutely useless, generally turning his head the other way when he pulls the trigger." Here alone was a military edge that could not but have provided the foundation of a very firm civil authority. Backed up, more-over, by what appear to have been intuitive gifts for taking command and making friends—not to mention judicious application of white man's magic among one of the most superstition-prone peoples on the African continent—it is far from implausible that Boyes may have been looked on by most tribal leaders as a sort of super chief. The strongest of the Mount Kenya trio, one Wagombi, put it plainly enough when Boyes rejected his offer to make war on a hostile clan. "He was rather disappointed with me," wrote Boyes, "and said, 'Why all this humbug? The country is yours. What's the use of humbugging about it like a woman?'"

What may have established Boyes' authority beyond question was the result of the most serious challenge he faced from his always unpredicta-ble "subjects." This came at the end of his first year in Kikuyuland, when a large and particularly aggressive clan called the Chinga killed three Goan traders in an ambush. Mistaking their victims for white men, the raiders lost no time in letting it be known that Boyes was not indestructible after all, and some five thousand Chinga warriors took the field to eradicate the intruder. Boyes himself was on the march with his own force when the first wave approached, and he quickly ordered the men to take up a defensive position. His account of the ensuing clash reads like the scenario for a "darkest Africa" thriller. "Bands of warriors could be seen gathering all around us ... yelling their war cries and shouting what they would do to me when they got me ... Some of the natives had dressed themselves in the clothes of the ill-fated Goanese, and proudly paraded themselves in front of my camp ... It made my blood boil when I saw that they had cut off the heads of the murdered men and stuck them on poles, which they were carrying about as trophies. I knew what my fate would be if I were unlucky enough to fall into their clutches, while my anxiety was increased by the fact that our stock of ammunition was running very low..."

By nightfall, however, Boyes took the offensive with an ambush that routed the Chinga. But they rallied and counterattacked with fury the next day. "We were fighting at close quarters, and soon every man had his work cut out to defend himself. I was loading and firing from the hip, as fast as I could throw out the empty shells and shove fresh cartridges into the breech ... So closely were we being pressed that one of the savages had his spear poised over my head, and the muzzle of my rifle was pressed against his body when I fired... My followers were all equally hard pressed, and on all sides was a writhing mass of black forms, all fighting like devils." Although outnumbered by at least fifty to one, Boyes' men managed to extricate themselves, and the tide of battle turned with the arrival of the Kikuyu equivalent of the U.S. Cavalry, a huge army of blood brothers from the north. With Boyes' infantry as its doomsday weapon, this host "swept through the Chinga country from one end to the other," until the clan, "as a force to be reckoned with ... ceased to exist."

If we are to believe Boyes, the smashing of the Chinga had a profound effect on all Kikuyuland, which "settled down into a condition of quietness such as had never been known before ... and from this time on I was looked upon as practically the king of the country, all matters in dispute being referred to my judgement." Without quibbling over that claim, one can at least recognize a baronial quality in Boyes' daily life. Its only proletarian aspect seems to have been his hour of waking, six o'clock in the morning, when he would rise with the clan and then enjoy a breakfast of tea and biscuits, sometimes supplemented by maize and goat's milk, while his own men did fatigue duty around the compound. The two hours of rifle practice and close order drill which followed were usually placed in the charge of Boyes' sergeant or corporal, "who became proficient enough to relieve me of everything but superintendence of the parade." Boyes' own official tasks began at about ten, when he "held a court for the trial of any serious cases of crime, or met with the chiefs and elders in consultation with regard to measures for the general welfare of the people." At midday he would return to his house for lunch. Mutton was usually the main course ("the native mutton is some of the best in the world"), although European tinned meats and preserves might also be included on the menu. Afternoons were often given over to further meetings with clan elders. Dinner, the most leisurely repast of the day, "was served at seven o'clock, in European style, as I had been fortunate enough to get a really good Swahili cook, who could turn out a most appetising meal at very short notice. Of course,

I had to dine in solitary state, being the only white man in the country."

Boyes was actually less idle than the above daily routine suggests. After the defeat of the Chinga, he wrote, "I had time to set about improving the country itself, and got the natives to work making better roads and generally increasing the facilities for getting about the country." In seeking to upgrade farming methods, he set a personal example by laying out a large garden near his house; here, he planted various seeds purchased in Naivasha, and enjoyed "the satisfaction of finding that almost every English vegetable would grow well" in Kikuyuland's temperate climate and fertile soil. Indeed, Boyes made an important contribution to the country's future prosperity with the introduction of black wattle, which later became one of the more profitable staples in the agricultural economy of European settler and African alike. He also tried to do the work of a medical officer, although when smallpox struck his attempts at therapy were not always fully comprehended. "I saw a lot of bad cases among the people, and though I tried to get them all into isolation camps, it was practically no use. When an outbreak occurred in a family they would not report it, but continued to live and sleep together in the same hut, with the result that, in most cases, the whole family took the disease and died." There was no objection, on the other hand, when Boyes obtained some lymph from Naivasha and began mass vaccinations. "But in spite of all I could do, thousands died, many whole villages being wiped out."

The lighter side of life was not overlooked; once every week Boyes organized a huge dance outside his house, "and this day was practically a holiday, the dance taking precedence of all ordinary work." Boyes himself gained something of a reputation as a troubadour. On one business trip to the north, he had met an Ndrobo chief named Olomondo, who asked him to write something on paper, considering this to have medicinal properties. "Not knowing what to write, I lapsed into rhyme (?), and Olomondo departed the proud possessor of a poetical effusion, of which the following is a sample:

> I am chief of the Wanderobo hunters,
>   Olomondo is my name,
> Elephants I kill by the hundreds,
>   And thousands of smaller game.
> I am up in the morning so early,
>   With my bow and arrows so sharp;
> Over rivers I glide like a fairy,
>   Over mountains I fly like a lark."

Somehow, this verse later fell into the hands of a Government official, and "the joke went around that I ... was living somewhere around Mount Kenia, writing poetry for the savages."

Poetry, pomp and public works, however, played only a secondary role to Boyes' main function as provisioner to the hungry outside world. The chain of trading stations he had established in various parts of Kikuyuland was fully stocked and well managed, and supplies moved out, with conveyor-belt regularity, every four weeks. Profits had enabled Boyes to hire an abundance of carriers: "with a safari of a thousand men the long line of porters extended for about five or six miles, winding through the forest like a huge serpent." No definite figures are available, but assuming a thousand porters to be inflated by Boyes' imagination and estimating a more realistic two hundred loads per month for two years at the rate of between five and nine dollars per load, it is possible that Boyes, in his capacity of bulk caterer, might actually have grossed upwards of $40,000.

*

Although Government officers at Naivasha took no action against Boyes because he was in a very real sense their meal ticket, his activities inevitably came to the attention of higher-level officialdom, which proved less permissive. "During the early period of our occupation of southern Kikuyu," wrote Ainsworth, "we sometimes heard of a reputed powerful chief known as Kururi... Later on there were rumours at intervals of a white man living with Kururi... Native stories were to the effect that the white man had assisted the chief in raids upon other natives. [An official] thereupon proceeded to Kururi's where he found a white man named Boyes... The outcome of this was that Boyes ... was sent to Nairobi on a charge of dacoity." *

The prisoner's version of the episode leaves the impression that he found his arrest an entertaining nuisance. He too had heard rumors that white men were approaching, and assuming that they were Protectorate officials who had come to assert a long-withheld authority, told his Kikuyu that they must now obey these new rulers rather than himself. By way of demonstrating the tribe's loyalty, he assembled several hundred of his warriors and marched to the Government encampment to welcome the officers. The latter invited Boyes to breakfast and then informed him

---

* A dacoit, in Indian jurisprudence (then operating in the Protectorate), is a "native outlaw."

that his elite guard had been placed under arrest for illegally wearing the Queen's uniform. Although in fact the men's outfits were conspicuously nondescript, one of the officers "proceeded to cut some buttons off their tunics, and the rank badges off the arms of the sergeant and corporal... a needlessly insulting piece of red tape." This done, Boyes himself was given a severe reprimand for flying the Union Jack; in reply, "I mildly put the question to the officer as to whether he expected me to fly the Russian flag." Then Boyes was accused of having brought his spearmen as threat rather than greeting. By way of reassurance, he ordered the warriors to lay down their weapons, at which point "the official announced that I was to consider myself a prisoner as well. To this I merely replied, 'All right,' feeling that if I were to express the feelings of utter contempt I possessed at that moment for these two gallant specimens of British officialdom, it would be the worse for my people ... I retired to my tent and amused myself for a great part of the day with a gramophone which I had brought with me."

The next morning a formal summons was delivered. Among other things, Boyes was charged with misrepresenting himself as a Government official, waging war on various Kikuyu clans and committing dacoity. These were capital offenses, but Boyes read the bill of indictment "with some amusement," although "there was one item on the list that I could not make out, and took the first opportunity of inquiring the meaning of the word 'dacoity.'" Then a preliminary hearing was held in a mud hut furnished with a table and two camp chairs. The latter being occupied by Boyes' accusers, "there was nothing left for me but to make myself as comfortable as possible on the corner of the table ... much to the scandal of those two important officials." The charges having been read to him, he was "cautioned in the same manner that an English bobby cautions a prisoner," and several days later, under a small armed guard commanded by an askari sergeant, the defendant and his warriors were escorted to Nairobi. "The situation was ludicrously Gilbertian. Here was I, a (so-called) dangerous outlaw, being sent down to be tried... on a series of awful indictments, through a country in which I had only to lift a finger to call an army of savage warriors to my assistance... The humour of the situation was considerably increased by the sergeant in charge of the escort handing me ... the statement of the evidence against me... as he was afraid he might lose it! It struck me as distinctly amusing that I should be practically taking myself down to Nairobi, to be tried for my life, with the whole of the evidence under my arm!"

On arrival, Boyes proceeded directly to Provincial Headquarters, where the Goan clerk, unaware that the country's most wanted renegade had just entered the office, told him that Ainsworth was too busy to see anyone. "On this occasion I did not happen to be in a hurry, so telling the clerk that I would call back in about an hour's time, I went for a stroll around the town." On his return, however, he was immediately placed under a guard of sepoys with fixed bayonets, taken by train to Mombasa and imprisoned in Fort Jesus, which the Protectorate Government had made into a penitentiary. Some days later he was released on bail and escorted back to Nairobi for trial. Here, British justice was not only done but seen to be done. "After hearing the evidence against me the court acquitted me ... the judge even going so far as to say that he did not understand why the case had been brought at all, and, finally, apologising to me for the waste of my valuable time!"

In Boyes' opinion, there were "mixed motives" behind the waste of his time. "One reason, perhaps, for desiring my removal was the apprehension that existed out there that the authorities at home might think that after all the man who single-handed had reduced to peace and order a country into which no white man had successfully entered before, might not be a bad one to entrust with its future administration in the interests of the Empire. Of course, such an intrusion into the sacred official class by a common trader ... was to be prevented at all hazards." In any case, Boyes returned to the profession of common trader, continuing to supply the railway and the Administration with food until the breaking of the rains made him redundant. By that time, his distaste for officialdom appears to have abated somewhat, since he served as a guide and intelligence officer for a Government expedition into Kikuyuland. He later became a respectable member of the country's growing British settler community (but not until after another spell of lawbreaking as an ivory poacher in the Lado region of western Uganda), and by 1910 could write that "my name is little more than a legend among the Kikuyu."

One will never know the extent to which Boyes' presence among the Kikuyu may have eased the path for white settlement, but it does not seem unreasonable to assume that if he did exert any influence, it was on the whole beneficial. In any case, however, the railway was certainly indebted to him, not only for easing its burden with the food supplies which he exported in illegal abundance, but quite possibly for having forestalled massive Kikuyu interference with construction during the line's severest trial by ordeal.

"No. 2 incline was so steep that the workmen, even empty-handed, could hardly keep their feet on the loose earth embankment."

"An absolute picnic." This was how Preston described railhead's relatively short and relatively easy run across the temperate, juniper-wooded highlands from Nairobi to the summit of the Kikuyu escarpment. "There was now no lack of anything. Water and firewood we had in abundance, and the will to work, and to find joy in all things... Fever was a thing of the past... The crisp air of Limuru soon turned our thousands of workmen into a happy, healthy crowd, and our camp hospital having now become merely an encumbrance, we decided to leave this haven of rest behind... Such are the magical effects produced by an ideal climate!" Toward the end of September, 1899, the tracks reached the escarpment's crest, nearly 7,500 feet above sea level, and Preston was at last gazing down into the Rift. "The train emerges suddenly from out of the forest and away 2,000 feet below stretches... a panorama that never fails mightily to impress the new arrival. The great extinct volcanoes of Longonot and Suswa stand up out of the valley on either hand; and from the train the successive terraces that scar Longonot's side are distinctly visible ... At the base of Longonot is the grand Lake Naivasha, a sheet of water 12 miles by 11, but from your elevated perch it looks like a sheet of ornamental water in a Home-land park..."

Actually, Preston had limited opportunity to drink in the view, for he was also contemplating the less beguiling prospect of moving the track into the valley. But for the Railway Committee's obsession with haste, this would not have been an overly arduous undertaking. The permanent way itself was to be carried down the escarpment, for a distance of ten miles, on eight long viaducts with gentle gradients; building these was no more than a routine engineering task. But it was also time-consuming, and for that reason the Railway Committee had decided that platelaying could not await completion of the spans. "It was foreseen," the Committee's final report noted, "that the rails would reach and even pass a few miles beyond the summit [of the escarpment] long before the permanent works on the descent into the Rift Valley could be ready, and therefore, that unless some temporary arrangements could be interpolated, construction in the valley and beyond would be seriously impeded and delayed." This in turn meant that Whitehouse had to improvise what may have been the line's most ingenious diversion. Certainly it was the riskiest.

Photographs of the temporary alignment down the eastern Rift wall suggest a ski slope plunging 1,500 feet over the contours of four successive inclines. The first four hundred feet fell away at a gentle angle of sixteen degrees—gentle, that is to say, for anyone walking down the escarpment, but disaster for trains that were not expected to negotiate gradients steeper than two and a half degrees. All rolling stock on the first incline, therefore, was to be moved by the law of gravity. A brake drum would be placed at the top of the slope and a steel cable passed around it, the cable ends secured to engines or goods wagons running on parallel lines of track. A fully loaded truck descending the incline would thus haul an empty vehicle up, the weight of the latter controlling the momentum of the former. A far knottier problem, however, was presented by the seven hundred feet of the second and third inclines, which sloped at no less than forty-five degrees. For so steep an angle, locomotives and goods wagons had to be carried on specially constructed flatcars whose front wheels would be suspended by steel frameworks nearly ten feet below the rear axles. These carrier trucks would travel on extra heavy rails, weighing eighty pounds per yard and supported by huge wooden sleepers at a five-foot six-inch gauge to insure lateral stability. Hauling power would be furnished by another brake drum and a steam-operated winding machine which controlled a cable attached to the carriers. At the foot of the third incline, rolling stock would be transferred to the final slope and moved again by gravity and cable along the four hundred feet of the relatively negligible nine-and-a-half-degree gradient, to link with the permanent alignment traversing the valley floor. It was expected that the tracks on all four inclines would be completed by the end of November at the latest.

On New Year's Day of the twentieth century, the work had barely begun. If Whitehouse's scheme had promised more than one hurdle on paper, they were multiplied vastly in execution. The most serious bottleneck could not have been foreseen. This was the Boer War, which necessitated massive diversions of shipping to South Africa and a consequent delay of many weeks in the delivery of the drums, cables, winding equipment and carrier trucks. A further snag was encountered when the two-year drought broke without warning in the middle of what would normally have been the dry season. More than three months of uninterrupted rains transformed some seventy-five miles of newly laid embankments east of Nairobi into a sinking mud wall. All rail traffic from the coast was halted for nearly four weeks as workers frantically ballasted the line, shored up the melting earthworks and bridged rivers that had not existed previously. (One culvert consisting of an eighteen-inch pipe had to be replaced by a forty-foot steel trestle.) And as if this sea of troubles did not sufficiently inundate Whitehouse's schedule, he suddenly found himself faced with the threat of an acute labor shortage when the bulk of the Indian workers' three-year contracts expired. Although at the end of 1899 the construction force numbered 18,000 men, and although most of the Indians signed on again without delay, the loss of even a few hundred laborers was sorely felt at so crucial an hour.

And when at last the descent began, it was uphill all the way. For a time it seemed as if the simple matter of balance might defeat the entire effort. "No. 2 incline was so steep," wrote Preston, "that the workmen, even empty-handed, could hardly keep their feet on the loose earth embankment; further, owing to the sleepers being much longer and heavier, it took two men to carry one; these two men had to balance themselves, Blondin fashion, till they dropped the sleeper in position." As often as not, however, they "had the pleasure of seeing it quietly slide away and go sliding on till it pulled up 400 ft. lower down." Eventually, Preston had to station a worker at each end of every sleeper and actually sit on it until the rail section could be laid down—although the men carrying the 800-pound, thirty-foot length of steel would also lose their footing at times, allowing the rail to emulate the sleeper and smash its way to the bottom of the incline. Such mishaps were frequent because the rains turned the slope into a skidway, and because the men themselves could barely see through the dense, low-lying clouds that clung to the escarpment like wet cement. The daily platelaying average of half a mile was quickly forgotten; the workers could congratulate themselves if they were able to put down seventy-five feet of track between any given sunrise and sunset.

*

It is no small tribute to Whitehouse's ingenuity as a planner and Preston's skills as a builder that construction of the cable incline somehow circumvented the many roadblocks on its hurtling downward path and approached completion—without a single worker fatality—by the early spring of 1900. For eighteen months, the lift carried all passenger and freight traffic over the escarpment,* and enabled the rails to move ahead

---

* On November 4, 1901, when the incline was finally dismantled, the railway celebrated the occasion with a special excursion round trip between Nairobi and Naivasha. Passengers went into the valley by cable, returned on the new viaducts.

170 miles farther than they would have had the Committee awaited completion of the viaducts. But the accomplishment was not immediately appreciated in England, for at about this time the line suddenly ran out of financial steam and a somewhat sheepish Railway Committee found itself obliged to go begging to Parliament for additional funds. The £3,020,000 originally voted—and by now exhausted—had proved totally inadequate, the Committee claimed, citing increased material and labor costs as well as unforeseen demands on the facilities of the railway itself. Another £1,930,000 was needed; this would bring total construction expenses to £4,950,000—a figure which the Committee described as "final."

The Committee being in effect a department of the Foreign Office, its request was formally submitted to the Commons, on April 30, by the Under-Secretary of State for Foreign Affairs, St. John Brodrick. Torn by internal dissension over the Boer War, the House appeared to show little sympathy for the railway's plight. Indeed, it seemed odd to more than one Member that the Committee should be short of funds in view of the route having already been reduced by nearly one hundred miles. To be sure, it was expected that the vote would carry on straight party lines, but the Radicals recognized an opportunity to work an upset and strove mightily toward that end. Not surprisingly, Labouchere had something of a field day and brought all his familiar artillery to bear on the jingo venture. "I contend and have contended for several years," he said, "that this railroad would cost a great deal more than the £3,000,000 estimated, and whenever I did this, [Brodrick] jeered and laughed at me, and told me that the Foreign Office understood railroads better than I did. But if they did, they did not understand enough to make a railway ... It seems clear to me that if we ever again intend to make a railway in any part of Africa the very last men we should put at the head of it is a committee of Foreign Office clerks."

Labouchere went on to ridicule assertions by the Committee that new economies and new sources of revenue would make further Government assistance unnecessary once the additional funds were voted. A claim that passenger traffic had increased, he said, was throwing "dust in the eyes of the House of Commons," because the new riders were simply coolies who had been permitted to travel to Mombasa on leave without buying tickets. The customary flippancies were also delivered on the well-worn theme of Uganda as an economic liability whose people were anything but industrious. In Uganda, said Labouchere, "they have a fruit from which they produce an intoxicating liquor...

The Ugandese sit around and drink this intoxicating liquor, when they obtain it, until they get into a state of excitement, and as they regard fighting as the noblest attitude of man—somewhat as we do at present as regards South Africa—when they get drunk they immediately begin to fight ... and when they have injured one another to a certain extent and killed a few, they make up their little feud and sit down to drink again. Do you suppose that these people are likely to cultivate wheat? ... [Brodrick] said he would not tell us specifically what we shall gain by this railway. The fact is he could not tell us." Behind Labouchere's mixed smokescreen of lampoonery and common sense lay a more ambitious objective than the mere denial of funds to the line. Unless a specially appointed committee were to give the House a firm estimate of final construction costs in "clear business figures ... vouched for by businessmen," he urged that the line should be regarded as completed and that the remainder of the journey to Uganda be made by road. Since the two principal barriers hindering easy access to the lake—the Taru desert and the Kikuyu escarpment—had by this time been removed, the proposal was by no means without appeal to Members whose imperial passions were matched only by their devotion to sound business practices. However, the vote for the additional funds carried by a large majority.

*

The financial plasma transfusion did not witness an immediate spurt of progress in construction. One of the more embarrassing queries which Labouchere put to Brodrick on April 30 had been the question of whether the Under-Secretary had "received a telegram sent by the [railway's] British employees bitterly complaining of the way in which they are treated, and if there is not evidently almost a strike among them." The walkout was not, in fact, long in coming. To demonstrate its good faith in effecting economies after the new funds had been voted, the railway initiated a sweeping program of salary cuts among members of the junior supervisory staff, who immediately responded by staging a wildcat strike in Mombasa. It was not an orderly protest, the strikers being somewhat less than models of civic virtue. Subordinate European employees had been recruited with a minimum of screening; many were believed to have signed on because German whisky could be had in Mombasa for sixpence a quart. In the words of Mervyn Hill, the railway's historian, the line "was saddled with an unreasonable percentage of 'unemployables,' some of whom made no secret of their acquaintance with the Bombay workhouse," and such men could hardly have been expected to observe normal collective bargaining procedures. Instead, they disorganized themselves into a drunken mob, careering through the narrow alleys of Mombasa and inciting many Indian workers to join them in a march on the Kilindini marshaling yards. The Railway Police were able to restore order by breaking a few heads in a baton charge, reading the Riot Act and throwing the ringleaders into Fort Jesus—but not before a good deal of construction equipment and rolling stock had been smashed up.

By this time, moreover, the strike had moved inland as if the tracks themselves were a fuse. At various stations along the line, sections of rail were torn up and other acts of sabotage committed. Ryall, the Superintendent of Railway Police, found it necessary to leave Mombasa in order to deal with disturbances in Nairobi—although he never reached his destination, being sidetracked at Kima, where he became the first and only official in the history of labor arbitration to be eaten by a lion. Fortunately, however, the spasm of vandalism ended as quickly as it had begun. Whitehouse recognized that despite their illegal acts, the strikers had a legitimate grievance, and after discharging the "organizers," he was able to negotiate an equitable wage adjustment with the other employees. The railway resumed its faltering march to the lake.

"One can imagine what thefts would be committed on a European railway if the telegraph wires were pearl necklaces and the rails first-rate sporting guns."

Shortly before the platelayers moved out from the Kikuyu escarpment in May, 1900, Preston took an afternoon off to reconnoiter for the section's first camp site on the floor of the Rift Valley. While tramping through the silver-green leleshwa scrub of the plain, he caught sight of what appeared to be hundreds of ostrich eggs on the opposite bank of a small stream. On closer examination the eggs proved to be human skulls, a ghoulish monument to the previously mentioned Masai caravan massacre of 1895. Although, as we have seen, the Masai were no longer very much to be feared, descriptions of the infamous "Plain of Skulls" reached the workmen and so demoralized them that they refused to shift camp until Preston arranged to procure huge sheets of corrugated iron which they made into a spear-proof boma. The precaution proved unnecessary, and indeed the passage of the tracks across the Rift encountered virtually no obstacles of any sort. Apart from the need to bridge the Morendat and Gilgil rivers north of Lake Naivasha, construction might have been proceeding along the surface of a slightly moth-eaten billiard table.

Preston appears to have enjoyed something like a holiday excursion on the valley floor. No less than Thomson thirteen years earlier, he found himself awed as he passed among the Rift's towering statuary of volcanoes and its scattered carpeting of broad lakes. With no undue demands from construction he also had ample opportunity to hunt. Unlike the Athi and Kapiti plains, the Rift did not teem with game, but there was enough to keep the barrel of Preston's rifle warm as he stalked lions and leopards in the company of his dog, a little black mutt named Hero. Often the holiday took on the aspects of a cruise. Preston explored the waters of Lake Naivasha—crammed with flamingoes, pelicans and hippos—aboard a tiny centerboard sloop built by one of his fellow engineers. At Lake Elmenteita he built his own boat, a canvas sailing kayak, and used it as a sort of duck blind for the teal that settled in vast numbers near a small island. When the tracks reached Lake Nakuru, the railway yacht club gained a lifeboat that had been brought up from Mombasa on a flatcar. "With this and my own little canoe," wrote Preston, "many a pleasant and dreamy hour was spent on the beautiful sheet of water."

The vacation ended abruptly, however, in the early autumn of 1900, when the railhead section left Nakuru and Preston ordered camp to be made at Njoro near the foot of the Mau escarpment. "From Njoro onwards," he said, "we were faced with some of the heaviest work done on the railway." The ascent of the Rift's western wall did not require anything like the precarious engineering gymnastics that had been brought to bear on the Kikuyu escarpment. All that was needed was to manhandle about one thousand tons of track to the summit of a mountain range lying nearly nine thousand feet above sea level. The total distance to be covered was approximately ten miles. Early in October, the climb commenced. On New Year's Eve eight miles of line had been laid down—an average of 480 feet a day.

It was almost as if the goblins who haunted construction now sought to compensate for their leniency during the line's unimpeded crossing of the valley floor. The jagged, ravine-scarred topography of the Mau required the building of no fewer than twenty-seven viaducts, ranging in length from 156 to 881 feet, for a total distance of some two miles. Some of these bridges spanned shallow clefts, others carried

the tracks over gorges with walls higher than ten-storey buildings.*
A relentless barrage of rain hammered at the coolies as they wrestled
their 500-pound rail lengths along the right of way that crept snakelike
up the steep, craggy slope. The Transport Department wagons serving
advance work parties became so mired down in mud that their wheels
had to be removed and replaced with planks, thus transforming carts
into sleds, Preston found it "well-nigh impossible, owing to the bogey
condition of the track, to keep our locomotive on the rails... Each time
the engine went off the line it would sink up to the axles ... and give us
no end of trouble in getting it on the rails again." He was able to reduce
the difficulty somewhat by devising an ingenious "buffer beam" which
extended around the locomotive only an inch or so above the tracks,
preventing it from settling too deeply and enabling the men to lever it
swiftly back on the rails with crowbars. Nonetheless, the engine drivers could usually count on at least three derailments daily. Nor did the
buffer beam always keep a train from running amok. Jackson, visiting
construction at this time, recorded one such mishap. "My carriage did
not leave the line," he wrote, "but the engine toppled over on its side,
and the first four covered goods vans were piled up and battered in like
old biscuit tins."

Even the game on the Mau somehow seemed malevolent. Fewer animals were in evidence, but they made their presence felt in unsettling
ways. Buffalo crashed about everywhere in the dark juniper forests;
without warning, a herd might burst out and lumber across the right of
way, trampling down the embankment and scattering the work parties,
"there was something wraithlike in the forms of the black and white
colobus monkeys that sailed about in the shadowy branches overhead.
Uneasy slumber was continually interrupted by tree hyraxes—small,
furry rodents whose nocturnal mating call is the scream of a madman.
One engineer had a pet cat snatched from his lap by a leopard. "With
this exception," said Preston, "we were very fortunate in not losing any
of our pets."

When the tracks finally reached the Mau summit early in 1901, railhead was only a fraction of a degree below the Equator but 8,700 feet

---

* Owing to the Railway Committee's demands for speed, the viaducts were not
completed until long after railhead had moved forward, although it was necessary for
advance gangs to build several temporary spans from local timber. The contractor for
most of the permanent steel structures was the American Bridge Company, whose engineers, according to Hill, "introduced to East Africa a variety of novel tinned food-stuffs
which enhanced their popularity amongst those who enjoyed their hospitality and fell
heir to the surplus tins on their departure."

above sea level, and the platelaying gangs endured sub-arctic weather. The open clearing where their tents had been pitched was flayed by sleet and slashing winds; every dawn, the water in the camp buckets turned to ice. Yet it was at this time also that the rains subsided long enough for the workers to reinforce all the embankments. Trains could now labor up the Mau without leaving the rails, and the right of way on the escarpment was accordingly handed over to the Traffic Department.

The newly opened section was tested in an unorthodox manner. While inspecting the alignment, a Traffic Department engineer ordered the locomotive on his train to be coupled to the brake van in the rear so that he might have an unobstructed view of the escarpment during the descent. Before the engine could be hooked on, however, the wagons started rolling down the slope, and the official found himself the sole passenger on a runaway train that gathered speed alarmingly and threatened to jump the tracks every time it rounded a hairpin curve. He was soon forced to leap clear himself, sustaining no injuries as the embankment cushioned his fall. Pursuing the fugitive carriages in a hand trolley, Preston finally came across them more than halfway down the incline, "in a heap like toys tossed on the nursery floor." However, since the train had managed to cover so great a distance—at an uncontrolled speed of more than sixty miles an hour—without leaving the tracks, Preston considered this "a decidedly good recommendation" for the work of the railhead section.

His self-congratulation was not out of order. In scaling the crest of the Mau, Preston had carried the tracks nearly 500 miles into the interior from Mombasa. Less than a hundred miles stood between railhead and the lake, and the run would coast easily downhill. The goal now was to reach the line's western terminus at Port Florence (Whitehouse had graciously named the station for Preston's wife) before New Year's Day of 1902.

*

It was not altogether certain, however, that this could be done, thanks largely to the presence of the Nandi and Lumbwa tribes which, respectively, occupied vast tracts of country to the north and south of the route. The Nandi presented the most serious threat. Although very much like the Masai in physique, dress, customs and belligerency, they showed no discernible pride in their new status as British-protected persons, and nearly half a decade would have to pass before they could be subdued entirely. Meanwhile, Nandi spearmen waged a relentless hit-and-run warfare against the railway, which they appeared to regard as an inexhaustible source of steel and copper for the fashioning of weapons and ornaments. "One can imagine," wrote Eliot, "what thefts would be committed on a European railway if the telegraph wires were pearl necklaces and the rails first-rate sporting guns, and it is not surprising that the Nandi yielded to the temptation."

Even before railhead penetrated their country, the Nandi had made it plain that the white man was not welcome. Although held in check to some extent by the Government's Sudanese troops, the tribe was any-thing but cowed; Nandi warriors continually tore up Uganda-bound caravans and bushwhacked the railway's advance survey parties. In 1900 they had even brought off the remarkable feat of delaying steamer service on the lake. That aspect of the railway endeavor had in itself been a task of singular magnitude and difficulty. Among the assets purchased by the Government from IBEA was a 104-foot, 62-ton shallow-draft wood-burning steamer named the *William Mackinnon*. Built in Glasgow in 1895, this vessel had sailed under its own power to Mombasa, where it was dismantled and carried in sections by train to railhead, then taken on to the lake in numbered 60-pound loads on the backs of porters. By the early summer of 1900, when nearly all the sections had arrived, the hull was reassembled and the ship formally launched at Port Florence. But the *William Mackinnon* was only a shell. Most of the essential engine and boiler parts had been seized in Nandi raids, and it was not until autumn that the railway's Marine Depart-ment could obtain the necessary replacements and put the steamer into commission.

Now, barely a year later, as the railway crested the Mau and the earthwork gangs moved out toward the lake, it became necessary to post armed guards along the right of way. This was the closest the line came to fulfilling the prophecy of "Martello towers" that had been voiced in Parliament nine years earlier. Whatever violence construction had been spared at the hands of the Kikuyu in the highlands and the Masai in the Rift Valley threatened to be dealt out with interest by the Nandi on the reverse slope of the Mau.

It must be said that Nandi interference with the line was not animated solely by greed and xenophobia. Hostility to the white man's railway was exacerbated by the behavior of the brown men who laid not only the tracks but also every Nandi girl and boy they could lure into their tents. The recruitment of voluntary or involuntary African camp followers of both sexes was a fairly common practice among the

Indian construction workers, and although the Nandi were by no means the only tribe to resent this, they were among the few who resisted it forcibly. Their sense of outrage, moreover, was shared by British official-dom, which tended to be critical of the railway authorities for failing to preserve decorum among the workers. Jackson found the coolie camps a "scandal" and cited two on the western slope of the Mau as conspicuously noisome. "I passed them on foot," he wrote, "and that was enough; I never had the courage to walk through one. It was quite sufficient to view them from the line... Apart from the squalor, they were crowded with prostitutes, small boys, and other accessories to the bestial vices so commonly practised by Orientals. Complaints by the Nandi and Lumbwa natives were frequent... on account of so many of their young women being inveigled away from their homes, and har-boured in those sinks of iniquity."

This description may be a trifle lurid, since Jackson sometimes seemed to share with many Englishmen of the era an unreasoning and rather nasty prejudice toward Indians, especially those of the lower castes. (He also appears to have overlooked the degree to which "bes-tial vices" found enthusiastic if surreptitious acceptance by more than one member of his own British upper class.) Yet for all its bias, the picture is not misleading, and there is no doubt whatever that Africans along the line, most of whom regarded "unnatural" acts as genuinely revolting, harbored an entirely justifiable resentment of the railway workers. Some tribes, to be sure, were able to view the Indians' sexual habits with a certain amused detachment. Jackson himself remarked that "considering the horrible vices and corruption practised before the eyes of local natives, the effect was not so serious as it might have been; but that was due more to the good sense of the natives and their disgust ... well illustrated by a question once put to the District Commissioner at Ndii by a Mteita: '*Bwana*, are these people men?'" The Nandi, on the other hand, were not amused, and sought redress of their wrongs with the time-honored tribal penalties of pillage and murder.

Regardless of personal sympathies, British officials could not permit this, but appeals to Nandi laibons—backed up by two small punitive expeditions—had little effect. Eventually, the Uganda Administration found itself compelled to send a large force of Sudanese and Indian troops into the hostile country. The most noticeable effect of this action was the ambush of two Sudanese detachments (one was completely wiped out), followed by a night attack on a large column of sepoys who sustained heavy casualties and withdrew in what almost amounted to a rout. Now there could be no holding back. Just as railhead began its descent of the Mau, Colonel J. Evatt, the Indian army officer commanding troops in the Nandi region, received instructions from Sir Harry Johnston, Uganda's Special Commissioner, to mount a full-scale military campaign against the tribe. At the same time, Jackson was ordered to visit the Nandi's chief laibon "with a view to peace, *after* Evatt had struck such a blow that would at least make amends for the smack in the face we had so recently received."

But the invasion never took place. It was canceled at the last minute by direct order of the Foreign Office's Permanent Under-Secretary of State for Africa, Sir Clement Hill, who also happened to be a member of the Railway Committee. In both those capacities, Hill was making an on-the-spot inspection of the line's progress, and he reached the conclusion that military operations against the Nandi would impede rather than hasten railhead's advance to the lake. Jackson was stunned by this decision, which he believed to have arisen from motives of shortsighted political expediency. Hill's argument, he said, was to the effect that "the Home Government and the Foreign Office were being perpetually blamed, abused and heckled, both inside and outside the House of Commons ... about the slow progress of the railway, that it was imperative that the Chief Engineer should be in a position to announce at the earliest possible moment that the railway had reached the lake, and nothing must stand in the way of this being done." Although Jackson and other officials regarded Hill's policy as outright appeasement, the new orders remained in force; Jackson himself was given "the thankless task of patching up a peace" with the Nandi.

It is an open question whether stern measures at this time would have chastened the tribe or simply touched off even more violent assaults on the railway. As things stood, construction was able to proceed down the back of the Mau without being cut to pieces by Nandi warriors, but the hastily improvised peace treaty did not discourage the continuation of thefts and occasional attacks on working parties. The final hundred miles of the route crossed a very real danger zone.

*

Even so, the tracks advanced steadily, continuing to bypass natural obstacles with temporary diversions. Preston did not even wait for completion of the line's only tunnel, but simply threw a loop of track around the bluff where the excavation was being blasted out. Rivers were spanned more rapidly when a permanent bridge engineer joined the railhead party. By the summer's end the platelayers had put the Mau (but not the Nandi) behind them and reached the village of Muhoroni at the edge of the Kavirondo flatlands, barely thirty-five miles from their destination. Here, Preston delivered a curious pep talk. "Calling my men together I informed them that only one station, Kibigori, lay between us and the great lake and warned them that the stretch of marsh land over which we had to go, had not an over good reputation from a health point of view, [and] so induced them to promise to exert every effort to reach the lake with all possible speed. 'Right, Sir,' was their reply, 'we will, Inshalla, be there by the New Year.' So with full determination to beat all former records… we made such rapid progress … that the telegraph department was left behind." Quickly, Kibigori was passed. Turner, the railhead telegraph officer, chafed at his enforced leisure. Early in December, the tracks reached Kibos, a huddle of reed huts only six miles from Port Florence. And it was at Kibos that everything came apart.

First, a wave of dysentery swept the party. On its heels came widespread recurrences of malaria. Half the railhead work force, including Preston, was laid low. Then the skies reopened with a fury that rapidly turned the already spongy terrain of western Kavirondo into a jellied consommé. The newly laid embankments became so soft that materials trains had to be unloaded while moving; if a locomotive stopped, it would simply topple over on its side and sink into the morass. Jackson described one such train near Kibigori, "coming slowly and cautiously along, rocking from side to side, heaving gently up and down like a ship in a choppy sea-way, and squirting liquid mud for ten feet on each side of it, from under the sleepers, after the manner of a water-cart." And what little platelaying could be done in these conditions was further curtailed by new outbreaks of tribal banditry. Making little effort at concealment, Nandi warriors treated the camp as if it were a hardware store as they carried off rails, sleepers, keys and tools, while the fever-broken workers, virtually defenseless even at the best of times, could only look on dully.

Nandi buccaneering had a more telling effect than simply to delay the advance of the tracks. The tribe had already stolen so much wire that the Telegraph Department found itself unable to overtake the rails, and the result was almost to cripple delivery of materials. Without telegraphic communications, the two trains serving railhead from the forward supply base at Muhoroni had to operate on a rigidly constricted schedule if collisions were to be avoided. Neither train was allowed to leave either station until the other had completed its run. All messages and instructions to or from Preston could only be relayed verbally by the engine drivers. It was a primitive and risky procedure, made doubly hazardous by the deluge which showed no sign of abating. Eventually it had to break down, and with tragic consequences.

One night, the frustrated Turner boarded a materials train for Muhoroni, to learn for himself what progress the telegraph line might be making. He was joined by the bridge engineer, Nesbitt, whose own work had been completed and who was then preparing to leave for England. Despite his fever, Preston accompanied both men to the train and waved them off. Several hours later he was awakened by a commotion in the camp. The inevitable had occurred. Someone at Muhoroni had blunderingly despatched a third train to railhead. With sheets of rain all but erasing the beams of both locomotive headlamps, there had been no time to avert a head-on smashup. Weak as he was, Preston trolleyed hurriedly to the scene. "Poor Turner was so badly mangled as to be almost unrecognisable ... Nesbitt ... had just sufficient life to remark that he had built his last bridge, and to devoutly consign his wife to the keeping of the Almighty. In the fever-laden swamp, close to the railway line, two humble slabs were erected ... to mark the resting place of all that was mortal of Nesbitt and Turner."

*

Although severe, the reverses which construction sustained at Kibos could only be temporary. By mid-December, the rains had ended, the Nandi had vanished into the hills, the telegraph line had finally reached railhead, and nearly all the workers had recovered from their fevers. Once again the tracks moved forward, and on Friday, December 20, 1901, Preston was able to write that the men had put down "the record length of 10,400 feet of line which brought us to Port Florence Station." At four o'clock in the afternoon of the following day, there was a brief ceremony. As Preston and a few other officials of the line looked on, Florence Preston put aside her parasol, took up a keying hammer and clumsily drove home the last key in the last rail of Britain's newest imperial highway. Only a few minutes later, one of the supply trains clanked wearily to the end of the line at the very edge of the lake. One almost imagines the locomotive puffing: "I *knew* I could ... I *knew* I could..."

"I would suggest that the leading
Imperial lavatory should, in honour
of the clean slate, be called 'The Rosebery.'"

If the celebration at Port Florence had been modest, Britain's reaction to the achievement was not. *The Times* spoke for the nation in a lead editorial which energetically brandished the Union Jack while simultaneously holding up to catty ridicule the politicians who had vainly sought to sidetrack the east African extension of the civilizing mission. "Within less than five and a half years of its inception," proclaimed *The Times,* "this great and arduous undertaking has been brought to a successful conclusion. The railway is altogether 572 miles long, but its mere length conveys no idea of the difficulties which had to be overcome in carrying the steel tracks up from the shores of the Indian Ocean... The cost has been proportionately great... Yet there are few people in this country who would now question the great utility of this expenditure, though it may be interesting to remember how lukewarm was the support it received from the then Chancellor of the Exchequer, Sir William Harcourt, and other Liberals of his complexion, when the first vote was passed by the House of Commons in 1895... Then as now, the school of Radical politicians whom Lord Rosebery so aptly described the other night as 'sitting still with the fly-blown phylacteries bound round their obsolete policy,' were loath to recognise either the responsibilities which a great Imperial possession involves, or the statesmanship which demands present sacrifices to ensure the future development of a great Imperial inheritance." *The Times* went on to assure its readers that this inheritance had been more than worth the financial and physical outlay involved in building the line, citing "material evidence" from officials on the spot that Uganda's untapped natural wealth would amply repay the investment. "Nor is it a small thing, though Sir William Harcourt scarcely concealed his contempt for this aspect of the question at the time, that the *Pax Britannica* has secured order and security over a vast region of nearly 4,000,000 souls which until the advent of British rule was given over to a cruel and sterilising tyranny."

It was *The Times'* prerogative to liken railhead's arrival at the lake to a Tory election landslide, but the editorial misled in its assertion that the line had been completed. Although long stretches of the route could be considered a railway in the sense that tracks had been laid on them, those tracks were in fact no more than diversions which had yet to be replaced. Work had barely begun, moreover, on the twenty-seven via-ducts carrying the rails over the Mau escarpment. And when railhead reached Port Florence, station buildings, signal towers, water tanks and other permanent installations had been completed only as far as Nakuru. Throughout 1902, the bulk of the railway labor force* was fully occupied with the task of erecting stations and bridges, pulling up all deviations and laying track along 100 miles of permanent alignment. It was not until March, 1903, that the Mau viaducts could be opened to traffic and the line itself considered to be approaching something like a state of completion.

Just as much to the point, all this work was to cost the British taxpayer considerably more than the "final" £1,930,000 which the Railway Committee had requested in 1900. Early in April of 1902, Lord Cranborne, Salisbury's eldest son and Under-Secretary of State for Foreign Affairs, told Commons he was "afraid" it might be necessary to seek approval of an additional £600,000 in construction funds, a figure that would bring the total outlay to £5,500,000. Eight months later, the request was formally submitted to the House, and the Oppo-sition boiled over in the ensuing debate. Actually, the protest was like hurling pebbles at a castle. The Little England cause had by this time become a shambles; it could no longer even rally around Labouchere, the seventy-year-old Radical barn-burner having gone into semi-retire-ment. Even so, a few speakers managed at least to make the session a spirited one. After hearing the railway described as beneficial to local Africans, Labour's John Burns commented acidly: "If we are going to carry out philanthropic humanitarianism where it is most needed, there are women in London and the slums of other cities who might be res-cued from a calling which they pursue for economic reasons." Irish Nationalist Tim Healy was no less caustic. "I notice," he said, "that one of the bridges on the Uganda Railway is called the Salisbury Bridge, another the Devonshire Bridge and a third the Chamberlain Bridge. Now, as we owe the railway to Lord Rosebery, I would suggest that the leading Imperial lavatory should, in honour of the clean slate, be called 'The Rosebery.'"

Name-calling, of course, accomplished nothing; the vote carried overwhelmingly. For whatever its financial miscalculations, whatever its errors in planning and execution, the building of the Uganda Railway

---

* The total number of Indians brought in to work on the line between 1896 and 1903 was 31,983, an average of about 4,500 men per year.

was an achievement in which nearly all Britons could only feel pride. (One expression of this sentiment was an almost instant knighthood for Whitehouse.) The turn of the twentieth century was the high noon of the British Empire, and nowhere did the imperial sun shine more brightly than on Africa. In 1902, the Union Jack flew over 3.7 million square miles of African soil—one-third of the continent's total area. To hold and develop this vast estate called for bold schemes and intrepid men. Never since Elizabethan times had the spirit of adventure so kindled the national imagination. And in the Empire's history, few adventures could have matched the construction of what the biographer-historian Elspeth Huxley has called "the most courageous railway in the world."

Only one question remained. Had this great work of brave and dedicated men been worth the trouble?

PART III
THE RIGHT SORT

11

SUPER-SQUIRE

*"If it is necessary to remove the hat,
even momentarily, it should be done
under the shade of a thick tree."*

When they were not perpetuating the memory and glory of Queen Victoria in a multitude of cities, streets, rivers, bays and other natural or man-made landmarks, Britons generally preferred to retain indigenous place names throughout their Empire. Thus, less than a year after Florence Preston drove home the last key of the Uganda Railway at the edge of the Kavirondo Gulf, the terminus which had been named for her was reverting back to its original African name, Kisumu. At this time also, the Uganda Railway itself had become the Uganda Railway in name only, since it no longer ran to Uganda. That country, moreover, seemed on its way to a secondary role in the destiny of Britain's east African holdings, while its erstwhile poor relation, Kenya—the "wasteland" across which the railway passed—was slowly beginning to take on the aspects of an imperial promised land.*

In April, 1902, a boundary readjustment placed all Uganda territory to the east of Lake Victoria under the jurisdiction of the East Africa Protectorate. From the standpoint of local administration this move was useful, for it enabled Government to assist the political development of

---

* Although the East Africa Protectorate did not become Kenya Colony until 1920, it is common practice to use both designations in referring to the territory prior to that year.

the relatively sophisticated African kingdoms north and west of the lake without being burdened by the millstone of the "primitive" tribes inhabiting the east. Of more immediate significance, however, was the roughly simultaneous beginning of a faltering but nonetheless perceptible trickle of white settlers into the highland region of Kenya.

Strictly speaking, these pioneers did not qualify as pilgrim fathers, hence a word must be said about their antecedents. In 1894, during IBEA's stewardship, a party of some two dozen visionary hedonists from Britain and continental Europe had arrived in Lamu with the object of penetrating the interior and establishing a sort of equatorial Brook Farm near the slopes of Mount Kenya. Their proposed colony, which they called Freeland, had been inspired by the quasi-socialistic writings of a Viennese economist named Theodor Hertzka, who envisioned a society "that will guarantee to everybody the full and entire produce of his work by the unlimited maintenance of his right of doing what he pleases." It hardly need be added that the commune was doomed from the outset, and its demise appears to have been hastened by the behavior of the colonists, who never managed to get beyond Lamu. One resident of the island has described them as "a weird group of pre-existentialists" whose visit was "short and scandalous." According to another local chronicler, the Freelanders "had few plans but plenty of quaint ideas... They spent a lot of time and money drinking themselves silly and caused many disturbances by trying to convert the pretty Lamu ladies to their creed of free love. Happily they soon drank up all their funds and most of them drifted back to Europe."

Perhaps the weirdest aspect of the Freeland burlesque show was that it had entered east Africa with a tentative Foreign Office blessing, and this fact alone may have cooled the Government toward any further efforts to encourage settlement in Kenya for some years. By the early 1900s, however, it had become increasingly and disconcertingly clear that possession of a vast slab of Africa could not be justified solely by the region's function as a corridor for a railway. In 1902, Kenya hardly seemed a promising investment, with an export trade of £108,000 (mainly from ivory) buried under nearly four times that sum in imports, and total revenues amounting to £95,000 against expenditures of £311,000. Although a Parliamentary grant-in-aid erased the deficit, the British taxpayer could not be expected to subsidize the country indefinitely. The £5.5 million cost of building the railway had been burden enough, and experts saw the line continuing to lose an annual £60,000 for some years to come. Thus, the realization was growing that if the railway were ever to pay for itself, the land through which it passed must somehow be made to pull its own weight in the Empire. In 1901, Sir Charles Eliot, the Protectorate's newly-appointed Commissioner, had sounded the warning plainly. "There seems to be a tendency," he wrote in an official despatch, "to treat the railway as something apart, built in the air, so to speak, and independent of terrestrial things. But in reality a railway is intimately connected with its surroundings. It is the backbone of the East Africa Protectorate, but a backbone is as useless without a body as a body is without a backbone... Until greater effort is made to develop our East African territories, I do not see how we can hope that the Uganda line will repay the cost of its construction."

While this was clearly sound counsel, the problem of its application remained. Who could be prevailed on to take the risk of tapping the country's natural resources? On the west coast, there was a robust trade in cocoa and palm oil, but it had taken well-capitalized private companies nearly half a century to develop their plantations. In east Africa, with an Administration responsible to a budget-obsessed Foreign Office, even five years were almost a prohibitive luxury. While the soil of Kenya and Uganda, to be sure, was uncommonly fertile, African farming methods, barely adequate to a subsistence economy, were not expected to bring the regions out of the red for at least two decades. In 1893, however, the railway survey report had stated plainly that the line's "subsequent traffic ... depends entirely on the development of the country." This could mean only one thing: if east Africa and its railway were to become self-supporting in a relatively short time, the transformation must be brought about through high-volume, high-quality agricultural production, managed on modern lines and grown on European-owned farms. With that objective in view, the Foreign Office embarked—or at least went through the motions of embarking—on a program to encourage white settlement in east Africa.

Inevitably, the main thrust of this effort was directed at Kenya. Despite Uganda's undeniable potential for cultivation, its climate was torrid and its lake shores a virtual laboratory of tropical diseases, thus automatically ruling it out for permanent European colonization. Kenya, on the other hand, had at last started to awaken interest. Before rail communications were opened, the tendency had been to look on the country as an isolated trash heap, but with the completion of the line; more than one Briton began to recall that earlier trail-blazers had spoken of the Rift Valley region as tailor-made for English farms. "The soil is extremely rich," Lugard had written of the Mau escarpment in 1893, "and is covered with excellent and luxuriant pasture throughout the year, with which is mixed white clover and trefoil. The country is intersected by small streams, the rainfall is abundant, patches of forest supply bamboos and timber for building and fuel. Game roams over the acres of undulating grass, and the climate is cold and bracing." The Mau, added Lugard, was not merely ideal for ranching but "capable of producing almost illimitable supplies of grain and other produce." In 1901, Sir Harry Johnston had echoed Lugard in an official report which spoke of the highlands as "a tract of country almost without parallel in tropical Africa"—approximately the size of Belgium and "as healthy for European settlement as the United Kingdom, British Columbia or temperate South Africa." Slowly, an awareness was dawning that in the very heart of the African furnace there lay millions upon millions of acres of cool and bounteous European parkland.

Sometimes, the highlands seemed almost too good to be true. "The trouble is," said one of the earliest pioneer farmers, "to know what not to grow." Besides nourishing the growth of coffee, tea, tobacco and other hot-country produce, the rich red earth performed near-miracles with every kind of European vegetable. A single sweet potato could weigh forty pounds and more; Eliot even reported seeing Brussels sprouts over six feet high (although that phenomenon had to be a freak). Even under primitive African methods of cultivation, the land yielded two harvests each year; sometimes there were three. Herbert "Pop" Binks, who had settled in 1901, marveled at his introduction to the outskirts of Kikuyuland. "There were maize stalks twice the height of a man," he recalled many years later in his book, *African Rainbow*, "and vines of sweet potatoes, the huge flag-like leaves of arrowroot, various varieties of plantains, tree beans, bunches of bananas (one of which was a woman's load), tobacco ten feet high with eighteen-inch leaves, sugar-cane grown for beer-making, and cattle, goats and sheep in pastures lying fallow." The soil was cheap as dirt, too; an aspiring coffee or vegetable grower might buy a 640-acre farm for two rupees (about 70 cents) per acre, with payments extended over a decade and a half. Some holdings in the early years were acquired by barter with Africans—although, strictly speaking, this was quite illegal.

There was certainly more than enough land for all: at least four million acres of ungrazed pasture and unplowed arable soil, two million acres of virgin timber waiting to be felled. And, with the exception of Kikuyuland to the north of Nairobi, the country was all but unoccupied and unclaimed, thanks mainly to the sharp climate and tribal fear of the Masai. "The main point that strikes the traveller," wrote the Administration's Ainsworth in 1902, "is the sparsity of population and the large areas of good land uncultivated. It is very evident indeed that there is ample room for very extensive settlement without in any way unduly encroaching on native occupation." Eliot was no less impressed with the vacuum. "One remarkable feature of the Rift Valley and the Mau," he wrote, "is the paucity—and in large areas the absence—of native population... We have in East Africa the rare experience of dealing with a *tabula rasa*, an almost untouched and sparsely inhabited country, where we can do as we will." The phenomenon could hardly fail to whet the interest of the stock breeders, dairy farmers and produce growers with comparatively cramped acreages in Britain. It was unthinkable that this vast potential farm be allowed to lie fallow. On the slopes of the Rift Valley, the expression "white man's country" was born.

*

And yet, in 1902, the total number of white colonists in the Kenya highlands could almost have been counted on the fingers of one hand. Despite the enthusiasm voiced by the champions of settlement, there remained considerable dispute over the European's capacity for survival in an equatorial region. More than one prospective colonist was undoubtedly intimidated by various pseudo-scientific bogeymen that found no less credulous acceptance among the white men of the era than did the demons which rampaged through superstitious African societies. Apart from the more or less familiar specter of disease, climate was regarded as a potential killer. Even Lugard and other pioneer travelers who depicted the Rift as a land of near-perpetual Indian summer were unable to dispel entirely the notion that behind the deceptively genial airs there lurked every manner of lethal pollution. It mattered not, for example, that the highlands soared a mile and more above sea level. "White labour under an equatorial sun, no matter how high the elevation may be, is impossible," declared an ostensible expert from the Foreign Office after visiting Kenya in 1902. The altitude itself was believed malignant, and gave rise to numerous grim theories about the deleterious effects of the sun's vertical rays on the human brain; the expression "sea level and sanity" was long an article of faith among British residents of the highlands, who made regular holiday excursions to Mombasa. Even in 1907, when settlement in Kenya seemed to have taken firm roots, Winston Churchill, then Under-Secretary of State for the Colonies, could nonetheless voice unsettling doubts after his tour of the country. "It is still quite unproved," he wrote, "that a European can make even the Highlands of East Africa his permanent home ... The exhilaration of the air must not lead people to forget that an altitude of from five to eight thousand feet above sea level is an unusual condition, producing results, not yet ascertained, upon the nervous system, the brain, and the heart ... Although the skies look so familiar and kindly with their white fleecy clouds and passing showers, the direct ray of the sun—almost vertical at all seasons of the year—strikes down on man and beast alike, and woe to the white man whom he finds uncovered!" Until and unless the sun was shown to be benign, said Churchill, "'the white man's country' will remain a white man's dream."

Lugard himself had elaborated on the same theme, even at the risk of deterring the British immigration which he so untiringly urged. "Avoid all unnecessary exposure to the sun," he warned. "Removing the hat (to adjust it) in the sun, is a folly I see daily perpetrated... If it is necessary to remove the hat, even momentarily, it should be done under the shade of a thick tree." Along with the other explorer-soldiers who cultivated the prevailing views of the tropics as a homicidal foe, Lugard also advised the wearing of heavy flannel cummerbunds around the waist "to protect the stomach, liver, and spleen," and this counsel was heeded religiously by all Kenya settlers. Headgear, suits and dresses in the highlands were lined with red cloth as further anti-sun armor; some colonists whose houses had corrugated iron roofs wore their hats indoors, since it was believed that the metal sheets offered insufficient shield against the sun's rays. Nearly half a century would have to pass before bareheaded, bare-chested U.S. Navy Seabees in the southwest Pacific put the pith helmet, the spine pad and the flannel waistband out of fashion in east Africa forever.

Nor were climate and disease the only risks which prospective settlers had to face. The view of the highlands as a horn of plenty was by no means unanimous among experts. Perhaps the most somber picture of Kenya's commercial expectations had been painted in 1896 by the noted geologist-explorer J. W. Gregory. After completing a long expedition through east Africa, Gregory wrote a book called *The Great Rift Valley*, which remarked not only on the absence of mineral wealth in the highlands but on a probably scanty agricultural yield. Although he acknowledged that white settlement was possible and even desirable if for no other reason than Britain's humanitarian obligations to the local inhabitants, he envisioned the country as something less than an equatorial Golconda, observing, rather surprisingly, that "the natural products of British East Africa are neither numerous nor valuable." Wheat, corn and barley, Gregory admitted, could grow well in the highlands, but he pointed out that freight charges between Mombasa and London were higher than the rates between Chicago and Liverpool, "so even when the railway is made to the coast, there will be little chance of competition with the grain-fields of America." A similar problem faced livestock breeders: "the extensive grazing plains of the interior might be utilised for cattle ranches, but it is very doubtful whether these would pay at a time when, in spite of their superiority in climate and position, so many ranches are bankrupt in La Plata and the United States." All this was not to imply that settlement would be a wasted effort: "with caution, perseverance and self-sacrifice," said Gregory, it might be made to work; but "I regret ... that I cannot represent British East Africa as a land flowing with milk and honey."

*

Given such deterrents, it says something about the British colonizing compulsion that Kenya's settler population of half a dozen pioneer farmers soon began to multiply. In the twelve years between 1902 and the outbreak of the first World War, rare was the steamer docking at Kilindini whose passenger list did not include at least one settler family from England, South Africa, Australia, New Zealand, Canada and even countries outside the Empire. Previously, nearly all of the Protectorate's European residents had been missionaries, soldiers, traders and administrators; now a new breed of empire builder began to make its presence felt.

Although the settlers went to Kenya for profit—a large profit, they hoped—and although they candidly acknowledged scant interest in uplifting the country's Africans, they were far from indifferent to the role they might play in the shaping of Britain's global destiny. Elspeth Huxley, who went to the highlands with her pioneer parents in the early 1900s, has written that "imperialism was not merely a cheap planting of flags, but basically an essential driving of new furrows"; and in that sense, Kenya's colonists certainly regarded themselves as men and women with a cause. They started their farms at a time when the populations of Europe and North America were soaring, when the world demand for food often threatened to overtake the supply. Crop surpluses were unheard of; no one could have imagined such a thing as plowing back fields to stem overproduction. Every square inch of the planet's arable soil and grazing land was precious. This applied to Kenya no less than to Canada or to Kansas. In their own modest fashion, settler farm exports from the highlands would help bolster British free-trade policies and reinforce the Empire's position in the world produce market. The colonists' imperial aims did not stop here. A few of the more visionary among them had what might be called the splendid insolence to picture their insignificant community some day taking its rightful place as one of the Crown's self-governing dominions beyond the seas. But that was in the future; the immigrants must first prove their worth as tillers of the soil. Kenya, in short, was being occupied by a landed gentry that would serve the Empire by serving itself.

They were a curious mixture. In some respects they may have been the most aristocratic community of homesteaders in the history of pioneering. A large number were the younger sons of titled county families, and there was a liberal sprinkling of peers and ex-army officers. Lord Bertram Francis Gurdon Cranworth, who became the settlers' first chronicler with his book, *A Colony in the Making*, went so far as to assert that the highlands had been tailor-made for the products of the English public school system. Since Kenya's farms were worked by African labor under white supervision and since, as Cranworth put it, "for three hundred years or more the whole aim of a public-school education has been to fit a boy, not for work, but for the overseeing of work," then it only stood to reason that the Old Etonian or Old Harrovian would be "undoubtedly the best master." A few outsiders also contributed to the patrician climate. William Northrup Macmillan, a close friend of Theodore Roosevelt, was a native of St. Louis, but acquired an honorary "Sir" after starting his expansive Juja Farm on the fringe of the Athi plains. One of the country's larger coffee estates was run by the Danish Baroness Karen Blixen, better known outside Africa as Isak Dinesen.* But the highlands' blue blood came mainly from members of the English squirearchy, with the shared experience of having been "schooled early in life," as Isak Dinesen put it, "by elderly, dignified keepers and stablemen," of having become "accustomed to proud servants."

The settler community was also represented in ample numbers by men and women of humbler birth. They found ready acceptance as equals among the farming elite, for the taming of a wilderness left little room for the snobberies of Edwardian England. Ancestral castles, liveried footmen, racing stables and exquisite manners were not going to get anybody's land cleared, planted or harvested. The titled immigrants could not even claim a financial edge; thanks to primogeniture and the numerous upper-class younger sons in the embryonic colony, wealth was conspicuous by its absence. Most authorities estimated £1,500 as the minimum capital need to start a farm in the highlands (some put the

---

* Isak Dinesen left Kenya in 1931. Her coffee acreage has since become the Nairobi suburb of Karen.

figure at £3,000), but few of the early settlers arrived in the country with more than £300—as often as not representing their entire worldly goods. Thus, a sprig of the nobility was not likely to look down his nose at fellow colonists like Binks, who had been a druggist's apprentice in Yorkshire, or the Scots blacksmith James McQueen, who had abandoned his forge and anvil in Dumfriesshire because he could not stomach touching his forelock to the laird. All three were in the same boat. Cranworth might have waved the old school tie, but he welcomed rougher garb no less warmly: "It is wonderful how well they fit in. As in older colonies, there are no class distinctions. Jack is as good as his master, and thinks himself better." It was not a man's coat of arms, in short, but his character as a man that gained him the settlers' accolade, "the right sort." Irrespective of lineage, most of the immigrants met that imprecise but exacting standard.

As a rule, the settlers were big men physically, at home with guns, tools and animals, not often given to strenuous intellectual exercise; some, perhaps, might have been fair game for the snide couplet:

> Kenya born and Kenya bred,
> Strong in the arms, nothing in the head.

But they were far from being simpletons; one needed a great deal more than brawn to manage a five-thousand-acre farm. Nor could they be called esthetically numb. "These men exercise their imagination," Elspeth Huxley has said, "by creating wheat-fields out of veld and bush; see beauty in the lines of a ram or bull perfect of its kind; hear music in the swish of a reaper." The sweeping majesty of the Rift, the cloud shadows along the valley floor, the jagged white summit of Mount Kenya at dawn, the wind sighing through the leleshwa, such things were their library, art gallery and concert hall rolled into one. The settler's temper tended to be short, but his generosity seemed almost intuitive; his door was always open to the stranger. "In pioneer countries," wrote Isak Dinesen, "hospitality is a necessity of life not to the travellers alone but to the settlers. A visitor is a friend, he brings news, good or bad, which is bread to the hungry minds in lonely places. The real friend who comes to the house is a heavenly messenger, who brings the *panis angelorum*." Generally speaking, one was trusted and accepted on sight. Before going to east Africa, a man might have been a draper or a clerk or even a navvy; on the highlands he was the peer of any peer.

Provided, of course, that he was also an Anglo-Saxon, since the colonists' rough-hewn democracy seldom embraced the members of any other races or nationalities. Almost pathologically proud of their stock, Kenya's immigrant Britons viewed all lesser breeds (Americans just possibly excepted) with attitudes ranging from good-humored tolerance to aloof condescension to loutish bigotry. In this respect, one might not have called the settlers admirable, but then, the same verdict would have had to apply to most other white men of the era.

In a way, the colonists were Kenya's newest tribe. It was one thing to journey through Africa for a few months on a scientific or military expedition, however perilous, or to serve as a transient administrator, even for a dozen years or longer. An entirely different set of values came into play when a whole family cast aside the security of England to spend the rest of its days in a land that almost seemed to breathe hostility against the setting down of roots. But the new arrivals appeared suited to pioneering ways. "Most of the immigrants had come to Africa, and had stayed on there," wrote Isak Dinesen, "because they liked their African existence better than their existence at home, would rather ride a horse than go in a car and rather make up their own campfire than turn on the central heating. Like me they wished to lay their bones in African soil." Not every temperament, of course, would find the highlands congenial or even bearable, but for "the right sort" the country and its challenge and its opportunity were irresistible. The settlers had no guarantee of making quick fortunes, but they sought no guarantee. Their kind thrived on risk and savored physical hazard. Sandbach Baker had gone bankrupt as a Manchester cotton broker before becoming one of the highlands' pioneer dairymen. Dr. A. E. Atkinson threw over a promising Harley Street career to raise cattle near Nairobi. Captain Ewart S. Grogan prepared for his new life as a Kenya timber baron by walking 4,500 miles from Capetown to Cairo. The immigrants' very insolvency was a measure of the confidence which they felt in themselves and in Kenya. The only thing they asked was the opportunity to begin turning over the virgin soil in their newly chosen homes.

"A bargain comparable with buying a million tons of undelivered Sahara sand for only five bob."

The Kenya colonist made the initial stage of his African journey by rail from Mombasa to Nairobi, thence to the station nearest his holding on the Kikuyu escarpment, the floor of the Rift or the slopes of the Mau. The final lap was covered on ox- or mule-drawn wagons whose axles screamed out under the weight of disc plows, harrows, grindstones, bags of seed, rolls of barbed wire, steamer trunks, chop boxes, bedsteads, tin bathtubs, toilet seats and veritable flea markets of household goods. Practically no roads existed outside a radius of a few hundred yards from any station. The grass rose above a man's head. The ground was strewn with rocks that smashed wagon wheels, pitted with ant-bear holes capable of snapping an ox's foreleg like a dry twig. During the rains, wagons could swamp easily while being wrestled through the millraces of bloated streams. A farm no farther than fifteen miles from the nearest railway station might not be reached in a fortnight.

On arrival, the immigrant devoted little time to placing a roof over his family's head. From the outside, most settler farmhouses—with their mud-wattle walls, grass roofs and floors of red earth stamped down to the consistency of tile—did not differ conspicuously from neighboring tribal dwellings. Only the furnishings revealed the occupants' western identity. Kenya-settler interior decor was an un-beauteous amalgam of country estate and junk dealer's storeroom. Horsehair sofas and oak tallboys stood back to back with commodes and tables fashioned from empty packing cases. At meals, gazelle chops might be cooked in rough clay ovens and served on Spode china plates. Windows bespoke an elegance that few pioneer farmers could claim. Comfort and gracious living would come, it was hoped, when the highlands had been tamed. Meanwhile, the most precious articles the settlers brought with them were their plows.

Before the plows could be put to use, however, it was first necessary for the pioneer farmer to clear his land of its scabrous carapace, a task that might require four days or four months. A coarse outer beard of tall grass and dense, knotted scrub had to be shaved clean with bush knives. There were miniature forests of gum and thorn trees—often a few mammoth baobabs—to be felled and their stumps extracted like decayed teeth. Boulders and man-high anthills, harder than concrete, must be swept away. These chores in turn meant on-the-job training for the African farm hands, who were patiently taught how to wield axes, picks and hoes without amputating their legs or fracturing their shoulders. The workers also had to learn the rudiments of handling the ox teams that would drag the tree stumps from the earth with chains attached to their yokes. Even the oxen required education, being local beasts that had never known any sort of halter and that were deaf to the command of the human voice. More than one farmer harnessed his oxen by dropping the yokes on them from a tree—provided that one of the African workers could drive the animals under the branches.

When plowing finally began, the settler was likely to discover, to his exasperation, that it was a rare African indeed who comprehended the meaning of a straight line. Furrows in the infant years of pioneering on the highlands often resembled the paths left by gigantic pythons. But they were furrows nonetheless. The colonist's minute parcel of African wilderness was beginning to take on the aspects of an English farm. "My heart sang," wrote Binks, "to see the great shining discs rotating by their own friction with the earth, slicing out roots, climbing over rocks and sinking into the good earth beyond; the uncut ground was a litter of bush stubble and tussocks of grass, but on my right was the perfect seed-bed, the rubbish of years buried beneath the rich red soil to form tilth for subsequent crops."

Prospects shone even brighter with planting. Wheat, maize, barley, fruits, potatoes, beans, chillies, coffee, tea, sisal and wattle were among the marketable crops cultivated on settler farms. A widespread practice during the early years was to grow potatoes more or less for subsistence and expenses, coffee for the long-range profits. The latter was widely regarded as the Protectorate's most promising money-maker. The first seeds had been brought to Kenya in 1896, by members of a White Fathers mission, and the success of their plantation proved a beguiling incentive to the new immigrants. Coffee, to be sure, could be as much nightmare as eldorado. It required the most exquisite coddling at all times. Seedlings died almost instantly if planted even a degree off the vertical. Taller plants had to be grown alongside the delicate young trees to shield them from wind, rain and sun. At least five years must pass before any coffee plantation started producing its maximum yield; who could be certain that the capricious weather of the Rift would refrain from some catastrophic act of mischief during that crucial period? But the potential appeared limitless. "Grows like a weed" was the universal—and quite accurate—description of coffee in the highlands. One felt simultaneously elated, exhausted and anxious when the crop was finally shipped out. "In the early morning," Isak Dinesen has recalled, "while it was still dark ... I heard the waggons, loaded high up with coffee-sacks, twelve to a ton, with sixteen oxen to each waggon, starting on their way in to Nairobi railway station ... with much shouting and rattling, the drivers running beside the waggons ... In the evening I walked out to meet the procession that came back, the tired oxen hanging their heads in front of the empty waggons ... the weary drivers trailing their whips in the dust of the road. Now we had done what we could do ... and we could only hope for good luck at the big auction-sales in London."

Luck had to play a role, for nothing proceeded smoothly. The settlers had expected hardship; in a sense they had looked forward to it as a gratifying element of the rugged outdoor existence that drew them from the already conquered parts of the world. But they had not anticipated certain man-made obstacles to their progress. Most trying, perhaps, was the interval of purgatory between an immigrant's arrival in Nairobi and his actual occupation of his farm. Land may have been available for a song, but settlers soon learned that they had to burst their lungs before putting it to work. Colonization was entirely outside the province and knowledge of the Foreign Office, and its land laws, reflecting this inexperience, made for long delay and immense frustration. No holding could be occupied until a survey had been carried out by the Administration's understaffed Land Office. Weeks, even months passed, savings dwindled to the vanishing point before beacons were set up to define the boundaries of a farm. Each application for a leasehold required the approval of at least three officials who made individual inspections of the usually distant acreage whenever they could spare the time, which was seldom, from their multifarious other duties. Thwarted produce growers and stockmen fumed at their enforced idleness in the city of tents which they pitched near the railway station. (South African colonists nicknamed the improvised encampment "tentfontein.") The settler's sole daily occupation was to loiter outside the Land Office, hoping—usually vainly—for news that his title deed had been granted. Queues to the door of the building resembled breadlines.

Leisurely inspections of farms and plodding surveys were by no means the only bureaucratic barriers facing the colonists. The Protectorate's Crown Lands Ordinance (based for some years on irrelevant Canadian homestead laws) seemed at times a conspiracy against anyone who wished to profit from the soil. Land grants were hedged about with development clauses which told a farmer what he must grow in a given number of years if he wished to retain his holdings; these demands took little if any account of blights, weather and other unforeseen obstacles. Certain grazing leases expired, for no apparent reason, after only two years. Irrational restrictions added to the burden. In a country where timber abounded, settlers often had to import wood for their farm buildings and fence posts, since the Foreign Office designated nearly all the forests as private Crown property; one lumberman who acquired a substantial acreage was informed, after taking title, that he would not be permitted to fell any of the trees. No European colonist could own goats without a Government permit, although herds proliferated among the Kikuyu and Masai. Official permission was required to draw water from any stream passing through a farm. A settler could not even sell a small portion of his holding without Foreign Office permission. The seeds of a long, acrimonious and altogether unedifying feud between white colonist and white official were sown in the weed garden of red tape that choked Kenya's early land laws.

Hardly less exasperating was the recruitment of farm labor. Potential field hands abounded in neighboring villages, but most Africans were preoccupied with their own cultivation, while the sturdy young males of a clan tended to look down on planting as women's work. The very concept of wages, moreover, was usually incomprehensible in a society that simply lived on what it grew. No help in recruitment was forthcoming from the Government—this indeed was an even more serious bone of contention—and the settler found himself compelled to fall back on a tedious trial-and-error hiring system. He put up hurricane lamps outside his farmhouse after dark as help-wanted advertisements, hoping that the magic illumination would draw curious tribesmen, moth-like, to the flame. Hand-wound gramophones rasped out operatic arias and music-hall ballads as a further inducement to the aboriginal proletariat. Some colonists approached headmen directly, offering a certain number of sheep or goats in return for the services of so many able-bodied male or female farm hands; the latter were paid either in livestock or cash to the equivalent of three rupees (about a dollar) per month. Other farmers were able to obtain a scattering of laborers from tribal squatters who occupied a few acres of European land and paid their "rent" by working in the fields for several weeks or months each year. These devices, however, were not merely cumbersome; they provided no assurance whatever that a field hand would not walk off the job at the end of a week—or an hour.

Even the expected tribulations could seem excessive at times. The fate of the Kenya farmer was also very much dependent on the country's perverse meteorology. The most anxious moments of every year came in the last week of March, when the six-week "big rains" were scheduled to begin, and sometimes did not. If they failed or fell lightly, only the most meager crop could be expected. But if they arrived prematurely or were unduly torrential, the work—not to mention the investment—of months would be washed away. Tension dominated the first three weeks of March. Newly plowed fields seemed almost to shrivel in the oven heat. Dust devils swirled in voiceless fury down the Rift Valley, as if defying the greasy, swollen cloudbanks overhead to burst. The settlers themselves were not much less turbulent, often becoming prone to behavior which, as we shall see, was not without its effect on the course of Kenya's politics. On the other hand, the prompt arrival of the big rains did not necessarily guarantee that the subsequent harvest would yield a bumper crop. If produce and livestock thrived on the rich loam of the highlands, so too did innumerable parasites that waged relentless and deadly warfare against the farms. Sky-darkening locust swarms could erase a coffee plantation between sunrise and noon in a single morning. Potatoes succumbed continually to beetle-triggered blights. Poultry raisers might see a year's profits vanish overnight when marching armies of the steel-jawed black ants called siafu munched their way through hatcheries, devouring roosters, hens, chicks and eggs with swift and indiscriminate thoroughness.

Unseen armies were also at work. At a time when science had just begun to come to grips with European plant and animal diseases, a new host of killer organisms, spawned in east Africa's unfamiliar ecology and defying all attempts at isolation, went on a rampage through colonist cultivation and pasturage. Mysterious rusts were capable of leveling wheat fields the size of English counties. Livestock took a fearful hammering from grubs of indeterminate origin. Most of the oxen used for plowing carried a lethal and highly infectious pleuro-pneumonia which felled other cattle by the scores of dozens. The fertility of the grazing land was congenial not only to farm animals but to wild game; the latter bristled with ticks, which in turn transmitted a variety of murderous afflictions. East coast fever was the deadliest and most elusive of these. Almost nothing could be done to stem its ravages. For many years, the only counter-measures against east coast fever were dipping and fencing— costly, time-consuming procedures which were anything but foolproof. Up to eighty percent of all young cattle on an infected farm could be counted on to die of the disease.

Fences, as well as livestock bomas, were also erected to hold other predators at bay, with only marginal success. The settler who bought large rolls of barbed wire in Nairobi and enclosed his entire acreage soon saw the wire give way to rust or sag in the creeping embrace of proliferating secondary growth. No barrier, moreover, could keep out the game. Elephants, rhino, buffalo, zebra, giraffes, Tommy gazelles, bushbuck and duiker grazed or trampled on acres of young shoots; lions, leopards and cheetah made regular nightly forays on cattle pens. A certain official immunity was enjoyed by all these beasts. Under the game laws, a settler was permitted to shoot no more than four antelopes a month; lions, although long classified as vermin and slaughtered indiscriminately by "sportsmen," could not be shot by a farmer unless actually caught in a livestock boma.

Least deterred by enclosures were the human raiders. Among east African tribes, stock theft was generally looked on as a crime more heinous than murder, but not when committed against the alien "red men." Attempts to halt or at least check widespread rustling through the influence of Government-appointed chiefs usually proved fruitless. Keeping their faces perfectly straight, the headmen almost invariably denied any knowledge of the culprits' identity. On infrequent occasions, however, a chief might produce a criminal if pressure was brought to bear. At one time, a farmer near Kikuyuland heard a suspicious noise in his cattle boma late at night. On going out to investigate, he was knocked unconscious with a club and hospitalized with a fractured skull. When Eliot learned of the incident, he summoned a powerful Kikuyu elder named Kinanjui, whom the Administration had also designated "paramount chief" of the tribe. Kinanjui was told that if the felon were not given up within seventy-two hours, heavy fines would be imposed on all the Kikuyu. Three days later, Kinanjui returned to Nairobi at the head of a long file of Kikuyu warriors, bound together by a rope. When greeted by a puzzled Eliot, he pointed to one man and identified him as the criminal. But who, asked Eliot, are all these others? Replied Kinanjui: this one stole the sheep from the farm near Thika; that one took ten cows from the fat European's dairy; that one over there stole three oxen last month. And he continued ticking off some two dozen individual thefts. But few chiefs were as cooperative as Kinanjui, and the understaffed Administration could not always be relied on to hunt down the thieves. No head count was ever made of the cattle and sheep lifted from white farms, but theft stood only second to disease in decimating the colonists' herds.

*

Against this background of attrition by man, beast and nature, it was a minor marvel that the pioneers' livestock did not vanish entirely, that their fields did not revert to bush. Nothing seemed to go right for most of the first decade. Exports were practically nonexistent. The Protectorate's wool clip for about five years barely exceeded ten tons annually. Coffee and sisal were long in reaching full maturity, the small quantities of wheat harvested were only sufficient for local sales. Despite a lively demand for Kenya potatoes and other vegetables in South Africa, the settlers did not possess the capital needed to underwrite a marketing apparatus that would move the produce in bulk beyond Mombasa. Although the average capacity of a goods train was only forty-four and a half tons, wagons were often run empty to the coast. Even on the local market, a full trainload of produce did not always meet its delivery date;

thanks to a wildly erratic railway timetable, crops not infrequently went bad in transit. Partly as a consequence of this, Indian market gardeners with no overhead to speak of continually beat out English farmers in competition for Government food contracts. Binks likened his own holdings to "a bargain comparable with buying a million tons of undelivered Sahara sand for only five bob ... I had settled on the most productive land in the world, but I had no market for what I grew." In fact, Binks eventually capitulated, selling his farm and moving to Nairobi, where he became the colony's first professional photographer. Others only barely managed to keep their heads above water, carefully husbanding payments from infrequent produce sales or fees from moonlighting as white hunters for visiting "sportsmen"—and always hoping that the banks would extend their perilously large overdrafts. The cornucopia, in short, was clogged; at the end of 1906, things had become so difficult that it seemed as if there could be nowhere to go but up. In March, 1907, however, the big rains failed badly, touching off a three-year drought and a major depression. In 1908, the absence of rain, coupled with an especially acute labor shortage, actually caused a brief efflux of settlers. Kenya was hardly living up to its promise as a land of Goshen.

And yet, the ships from England and Australia and South Africa continued to bring in new colonists. Instead of drying up, the flow of European immigration to Kenya remained steady. Even in their darkest hours, the highlands shone as a lodestar, thanks largely to the efforts of two individuals.

*"The number of fat rosy
infants to be encountered
on an afternoon walk at
Nairobi is quite remarkable."*

A casual glance at Sir Charles Eliot did not always reveal the sort of man one would have expected to proselytize for the taming of a raw wilderness. A scholar of somewhat formidable accomplishments, Eliot had gained that accolade of the upper-class Briton's classical education, a First in Greats at Oxford. He possessed what amounted to an absolute pitch for languages; it was once said of him that he needed only to look at a man's face to understand his tongue. At Oxford, he easily won prizes in Sanskrit and Syriac, and in 1886, when he joined the diplomatic service, he had hardly arrived at the British Embassy in St. Petersburg when he became fluent in Russian. Shortly afterwards, he wrote a Finnish grammar. Language presented no problem, either, when he was transferred to Constantinople, since he had already mastered Turkish; his book, *Turkey in Europe*, was a standard work on the Ottoman Empire for many years. For relaxation, Eliot studied the habits of the sea slug; his publication of a work on British nudibranchiate molluscs won him universal recognition as a leading authority on that creature. Captain Richard Meinertzhagen, who served under Eliot in east Africa, remarked that "never did a man more closely resemble the objects of his hobby."

In 1901, after holding posts in Bulgaria, Serbia, Samoa and Washington, Eliot was made Commissioner of the East Africa Protectorate, and seldom in diplomatic history has there been a less likely appointment. In a land where nearly all the population eschewed the discomfort of clothes, he constantly voiced his shock at "indecency," declaring that tribal nakedness "is not artistic or pleasing, and is one of those African customs I would fain see done away with." The Governor of a country which had already established itself as a big-game hunter's paradise, he believed firmly that blood sport of any kind bordered on mortal sin. In a region where it was sometimes necessary to resist spear-throwing, he could declare: "Anyone who knows me must be aware that I have a horror of fighting and bloodshed, and that my constant effort has been to suppress punitive expeditions." He was particularly fond of quoting the recommendation of one District Commissioner to the effect that every British official arriving in east Africa be given several medals, and that one decoration be removed for each punitive expedition in which he participated.* Under conditions which demanded the strenuous life and tended to attract brawn rather than brain, Eliot's stewardship in Kenya almost suggests Bertrand Russell commanding a platoon of Green Berets.

And yet it can be said that Eliot's very eggheadedness helped light the flame of what was no less than a passion to domesticate this wild land. His attachment to the things of the mind was indistinguishable from his reverence for the civilization of England; it was only natural that he should wish to spread the benefits of that unique enlightenment by peopling Kenya with as many Britons as he might persuade to make their homes in the Protectorate. But Eliot did not view colonization simply as an exercise in introducing refinement to savages. He was equally quick to recognize that the highlands offered incomparable opportunities to English farmers, and, as already noted, he clearly understood that this soil must be made to produce if the country and the railway were to become going concerns.

---

* A. C. W. Jenner, the official who made this proposal, was murdered by Somalis in 1905, and subsequently avenged by a massive and costly punitive expedition.

Accordingly, he lost no time in focusing his attention on the scene of the potential profits. Almost his first official act as Commissioner was to move his own headquarters from the coast to the highlands. Although Mombasa, with its more leisurely ways and comparatively civilized amenities, would have been a more congenial location for a man of Eliot's background and tastes, he uncomplainingly established the new Government House in one of Nairobi's least inviting corrugated iron shanties.

At once his troubles began. The Administration had little more than a subsistence budget. Its undermanned staff was badly overworked. Only the mud on Victoria Street was thicker than the Foreign Office red tape which bound Eliot no less tightly than it did the settlers. The smallest decision required endorsement by Whitehall; a telephone extension could not be installed, a broken window pane replaced, without cabling London. It was all but inevitable that the tight rein should finally snap. In 1904, Eliot resigned angrily after being directed by the Foreign Secretary, Lord Lansdowne, to revoke land grants he had made to two colonists. During the interval, however, he was not idle. Even the voluminous body of administrative paperwork that seemed more suited to a European nation than the management of a remote African territory did not divert Eliot from his principal objective. To the point of becoming a nag, he took every opportunity to remind the Foreign Office that a large English colony was the only possible cure for Kenya's economic malaise.

Paradoxically, Whitehall needed the prodding. Although alive to the desirability of white settlement, the men at the head of the Foreign Office were too preoccupied with the thorny problems of international diplomacy to devote more than superficial attention to their east African stepchild. Statesmen playing no-limit poker with the foreign ministries of Germany, France, Russia, Austria–Hungary and Italy could hardly be expected to join eagerly in the penny-ante game offered by a politically meaningless patch of Africa that had been acquired almost as an afterthought. Besides, colonization was something that the Foreign Office had never tackled before; this function of imperial expansion lay beyond its competence and its grasp. "In those days," Mervyn Hill has written, "the Administration's conception of its task was to administer East Africa, not to develop it. It was concerned to enforce Pax Britannica, to impose law and order, to collect taxes." Thus, turning the land itself to a profit received a very low priority. Official records, to be sure, spill over with guarded enthusiasm for English settlement in Kenya; one even finds a few concrete incentives, particularly the offer of land at low rentals, the restriction of European taxes to a ten percent import duty and the exclusion from that impost of certain essential farm machinery. Otherwise, however, there is little to suggest that the Foreign Office regarded east Africa's development as serving any useful political purpose. And politics, when all was said and done, was the name of the Foreign Office game.

Eliot took sharp issue with that position. He saw Kenya as a wasting asset which could only be revitalized by large-scale British settlement— but only with equally large-scale Foreign Office encouragement and even more massive assistance. "It may be argued," he stated in his 1903 annual report, "that ... a colony should attract colonists: it is no business of His Majesty's Government to attract them ... This argument is true enough of an ordinary colony, but East Africa is not an ordinary colony. It is practically an estate belonging to His Majesty's Government, on which an enormous outlay has been made, and which ought to repay that outlay." For the most part, this realism fell on sympathetic but deaf ears, and if Eliot had confined himself to goading his masters, he would have accomplished little more than to stir up the air. But he also acted. Early in 1903, he was able to remove a few of the more onerous land regulations that had hobbled the earliest farmers; the result was a visible rise in the number of white immigrants. At the end of the same year, recognizing that a state of flux and discontent in the wake of the Boer War had created a sizable body of prospective Kenya settlers, Eliot sent one of his officials on a "recruiting" mission to that country. Almost immediately, every steamship arriving in Mombasa from Durban or Capetown brought in at least three dozen South African colonists; by mid-1904, their influx had raised Kenya's white population above the three hundred mark. To till the soil of the virtually empty highlands—an area twice the size of Connecticut—this figure may have seemed comically small, but under the dead hand of the Foreign Office the South African arrivals almost merited designation as a wave. Eliot's action in bringing them in constituted the first significant step toward the making of something like an authentic colony.

Even after his resignation, Eliot continued to beat the drum for Kenya. In 1905 he wrote a book called *The East Africa Protectorate*, with the express purpose of highlighting "the opportunity which [Kenya] offers for European colonisation." Written with clarity and wit, amply documented, lavishly illustrated, the book was a travelogue, real estate brochure, weather almanac and price catalogue rolled into one. It contained a small blizzard of statistics on soil content, rainfall variation, mean temperatures and wholesale prices of livestock and produce. It listed areas suitable to specific types of grazing and planting, provided useful data on land regulations and labor supply. Eliot characterized the highlands as "a country which has a singular charm for Europeans, to which they become attached, and which inspires a passionate longing for return in those who leave it." His descriptions of the scenery on the Rift evoked a rugged fairyland, and he went so far as to suggest embellishing some of the lakes with castles, "though I fear the real old African would think such erections a desecration of his favourite wilds." The fearful hazards of altitude, equatorial sun and disease, said Eliot, had been vastly inflated ("The worst climate I have ever experienced," he wrote, "is that of New York"); fever was "certainly not more prevalent and not more dangerous than influenza in England ... it will no longer sound incredible to state that European children can be reared [in the highlands] without danger ... The number of fat rosy infants to be encountered on an afternoon walk at Nairobi is quite remarkable."

Eliot also took the Foreign Office to task for its apathy in encouraging settlement. "In theory," he said, "they desire it, and have invited immigration; but there has been a woeful discrepancy between theory and practice." And this in the face of the official view which "endorses the opinion that there is no prospect of the Protectorate paying its way, or being anything but a financial burden on the Home Treasury, until it is developed by white settlers." If that policy were implemented, however, Eliot voiced undiluted certainty that Kenya's solvency would be assured. The book was a compelling reply to the doubters and quickly went into a second printing. It may have been the most effective pro-settlement broadside since Lugard's original burst of enthusiasm eleven years earlier; unquestionably, it did much to maintain the level of the colonist influx even during the later depression.

*

Still, in his unconditional commitment to the settlers' cause, Eliot stood virtually alone among Government officials, and his sudden departure left the colonists in what could have amounted to a vacuum of indifference. If Kenya's whites were to make a go of it, it appeared that they must pull themselves up by their own bootstraps—and this was a task far more easily visualized than accomplished. The soil had shown itself to be fertile beyond anyone's dreams, but the settlers seemed unable to demonstrate that it could be made to pay on anything like a profitable scale. For all their determination and agricultural know-how, they were small famers whose limited financial resources made it all but impossible to survive the inevitable errors and setbacks of pioneering an unknown country. Their lack of capital denied them the means of high-volume production, denied them a marketing machinery to facilitate bulk exports (if they could ever produce in bulk), denied them the scientific expertise needed to combat the masked microorganisms that devoured their crops and murdered their herds. Their very self-reliance and rugged individualism militated against the organization of a common front to meet common problems. Faith, courage and tenacity seemed insufficient in themselves to make the highlands self-supporting.

What the settlers needed was a fellow colonist with unlimited capital, someone who could afford to write off his mistakes and still produce on a massive scale, thus proving beyond question that Kenya had something of real value to offer in the world's agricultural market place. Such an effort, if successful, would open up a main artery of export for every other immigrant farmer. It would prime the industrial pump of the whole country. More than that, the white community had to have leadership. An individual settler may have been the master of his own fate and the boss of the Africans who worked in his fields, but in the eyes of the Foreign Office he was a cipher. Imperative to the future of the highlands was a man of uniquely commanding personality, a man with initiative and, above all, a flair for political maneuver: someone capable of orchestrating the dissonance of a few hundred separate voices into a single, resounding chorus that would be heard—and heeded—in the highest councils of Government.

In brief, the highlands needed a super-squire.

*"Send off the thresher at once.
I will pay when the money is borrowed."*

One afternoon in December of 1897, when the Ukamba Provincial Administration was still located at Machakos, John Ainsworth's American wife ran into her husband's headquarters boma and told him that a horrid, disheveled, red-bearded tramp was loitering outside the door. Graciously, Ainsworth asked the bindlestiff in for tea, and on learning that he was one Hugh Cholmondeley, the third Baron Delamere, invited him to stay for dinner. Being improperly dressed, Delamere declined with thanks, although he doubtless would have welcomed a European meal: he had just completed a one-thousand-mile journey on foot from Somaliland.

Lord Delamere went to east Africa almost by accident. He was the only Kenya settler to enter the country from the north, and the fact that he happened to follow this particular route may have settled the destiny of colonization in the highlands. His decision to go to Africa certainly spelled out his own future, for if he had never left England, he would in all probability have lived a life of brainless but affluent obscurity as a conventional lord of a conventional manor. At the age of seventeen he had inherited his father's title, and with it the family estate, Vale Royal, a generous sprawl of parkland and forest in Cheshire. He could hardly have been a more suitable heir. In her biography of Delamere, Elspeth Huxley has written that "the feudal system was in his bones and blood, and he believed all his life in its fundamental rightness." Like many youthful peers of his time, he was profligate, overbearing and very much accustomed to having his own way. He possessed a volcanic temper which was matched only by a gift for uncommonly sincere apology following every eruption. Intellectual pursuits were not to his taste. At Eton, he distinguished himself as an absentee scholar, stealing off at every opportunity to the Ascot races—he once dropped £3,000 on a single bet—or indulging a fancy for vandalism on shops in nearby towns. Although small in stature and prone to ill health, he was well muscled and afraid of nothing. As the owner of a large hunting stable, he was a keen—and even more reckless—horseman. Nearly two of his sixty-one years on earth were spent in plaster casts as the result of near-fatal falls.

It was Delamere's zest for the chase, in fact, which led him to hunting grounds more ample than England's. In 1891, shortly after his twenty-first birthday, he set sail in the company of several other titled young ne'er-do-wells for British Somaliland to shoot lions. The party had as its wet nurse a professional white hunter who wrote Delamere's trustee that "ten times my salary should not again induce me to go with such a crowd of undisciplined, foolish, wasteful, reckless youngsters," but added that Delamere at least was amenable to reason "when I can get him alone." He also told the trustee that "on several occasions [Delamere] has been made sick and ill by the sun ... I am giving you my honest considered opinion that he cannot stand the sun: some men cannot." Delamere was quite aware of this handicap, but it did not deter him from making four more expeditions to Somaliland. Nor was his relish for African travel diluted during one trip when, after being clawed nearly to death by a lion, he spent five days absolutely motionless on his back beneath a crude shelter of thorn trees to stave off sepsis. In 1896, his mother voiced a natural anxiety as he prepared to leave on his fifth journey, and he told her: "If you look after yourself, I'll look after myself, and if everyone in the world looked after their own lives, then everyone in the world would have one person looking after them."

The fifth expedition was not only Delamere's last but his most ambitious. For six of the preceding months, he had been the prisoner of a cast
after one of his horses threw him, and the enforced inactivity turned him
to reading. He may have been surprised to discover that he had a brain
as he waded through volumes on history, economics, biology and other
topics that would not long have held his attention a year earlier. During
this period he also became an admirer of Cecil Rhodes, and began to think
of white dominions in tropical Africa as possible assets to the Empire.
The result of this encapsulated education was reflected in Delamere's
decision that his next journey must have a more constructive goal than a
few dead lions. Although settlement had not yet crystallized in his mind
as a personal objective, he planned a long trek from Somaliland to east
Africa, with a view to exploration and the gathering of zoological and
botanical specimens for a museum. When his party struck inland from
Berbera on the Gulf of Aden, it included a taxidermist, a professional
photographer and an impressive array of scientific instruments.

There was also a Maxim gun, and each of the 200 porters carried
a Snider rifle. For the country through which Delamere's route was to
pass had at that time been explored by only four white men, one of
whom had not returned to describe his adventures. The region bristled with roving battalions of the Abyssinian bandits known as shiftas,
who wore the genitalia of their victims around their waists. Somali
shepherd-warriors were known to kill strangers on sight, simply for the
hell of it; Turkana tribesmen needed little coaxing to disembowel unwelcome visitors with their razor-keen bracelet-knives. Perhaps it was the
formidable weaponry carried by Delamere's men that permitted the
expedition to proceed unmolested, but even without human opposition,
the land itself proved antagonist enough. It was and still is a horizonless
frying pan of desolation: a sun-drilled moonscape of cracked earth harder
than iron, grotesque lava heaps rising to the height of ten-storey buildings, vast plains of dehydrated thorn scrub, sightless deserts and scorched
black mountains. Temperatures often climb to 120 degrees in the shade
(when shade can be found), and such articles as brass buttons and
belt buckles will sear the flesh after an hour in the sun. Thirst is the traveler's closest companion. The country may have been described best by
the late journalist Negley Farson when he called it "as close as you can
get to hell on earth."

For eleven months, the expedition crept across this hundred-
thousand-square-mile slagheap, reaching Lake Baringo at the northern
edge of the highlands in November of 1897. But Delamere was not welcomed to the future white man's country with open arms. Hardly had

camp been made than a runner arrived with a letter which read: "Sir: Please take notice that you are now on British soil. Any act of aggression on your part will be sternly resisted." The signature was almost indecipherable, but Delamere finally decoded it to read "J. Martin." This was the same James Martin whom we met when he accompanied Joseph Thomson across Masailand thirteen years earlier. Since that time, he had continued his jack-of-all-trades profession, serving as second in command of the Zanzibar army, as a caravan master for IBEA and now as a District Commissioner with the new British Administration. Apart from having learned to scrawl his signature, Martin was still illiterate and tried to conceal this by turning all paperwork over to his Goanese clerk. But the warning was real enough. Delamere had chosen to enter Kenya at the height of the Uganda Mutiny, and the size of his expedition had given rise to rumors that an Abyssinian army, at least one thousand strong, was approaching. Already depleted by the Sudanese defections, the British force in the Protectorate would have been helpless against any massed attack on its rear, and Martin was prepared to sell his own life before this happened. All parties breathed a collective sigh of relief when the identity of the visitors was revealed.

Delamere was even more elated with his first view of the highlands. Mrs. Huxley, in fact, has suggested that the seeds of his resolve to live in Kenya took root at this time. "Perhaps it was the manner of [the] introduction," she writes, "... that settled his allegiance. The contrast with the Africa he had learned to take for granted was so great that not only the beauty but the richness must have excited his imagination. Compared with the arid north, the grazing appeared Elysian. If sheep could eke out a precarious living in the barren country of the Rendile, the Gabra and the Turkana, what could they not do on these green, undulating grassy stretches?" In short, having entered by way of a sterile corridor, Delamere could not but take "a different attitude towards East Africa from that which almost every other European, at that time, possessed... He saw it, from the first, as a country of great latent wealth only waiting for development." That outlook was to be "the guiding star on which he set his course."

Although undoubtedly stricken with a case of love at first sight, Delamere also had another claimant to his affections. Before leaving on his journey, he had become engaged to the daughter of an earl, and he returned to England to marry her and settle in Cheshire. Significantly, however, the couple's seven-month honeymoon was spent in Kenya, where the groom busily collected for a museum and continued to familiarize himself with the highlands' potential for colonization. Still, he did not appear quite ready to pull up his stakes in Britain. It was only at the end of 1902 that the baronial responsibilities of Vale Royal, while providing invaluable education in the management of things agrarian, finally began to pall. In January, 1903, Lord and Lady Delamere brushed the red dust from their clothes as they stepped off the train at Nairobi, and Kenya became their home forever.

*

Shortly after his arrival, Delamere was thrown from his pony while pig-sticking on the Athi plains. During the ten months he spent on his back in Nairobi, he had ample opportunity to cultivate a friendship with Eliot. With a common dedication to a British farming community in the highlands, the two men hit it off well. Eliot went so far as to offer Delamere a post in the Administration, with the specific responsibility of promoting settlement. But although he shared Eliot's outlook, Delamere preferred an unofficial and independent role which would give him a free hand to belabor Government whenever its policies seemed to him at variance with settler interests. At this time, in fact, he had published a pamphlet rapping Whitehall's knuckles for the unrealistic land laws which were already antagonizing the small colonist community. As Delamere saw it, the Government's proclaimed purpose of making the Protectorate solvent was being defeated by "the desire of the Foreign Office to treat the country as a private estate, and settlers as small tenant farmers." Only minimal profits, he pointed out, could be expected from any country in its earliest pioneering years, and the colonist was prepared to accept these conditions. But if he were to find himself hobbled by needless artificial restraints, he might well conclude that "it will pay him better to wait until there is an immediate return to be got for the land ... and if everyone does this, who is to develop the country?" The effect of the Foreign Office regulations, said Delamere, was to make "the taking up of land by men of a free race almost an impossibility."

This relatively soft-spoken dissent from Government land policies represented Delamere's maiden venture as the settlers' self-appointed ombudsman without portfolio. Meanwhile, however, his most immediate concern was what he might accomplish in behalf of his fellow colonists as a farmer rather than a parliamentarian. He was keenly alive to the settlers' severe financial handicap, and recognized that his own apparently inexhaustible wealth placed him in a unique position to undertake dramatic, large-scale agricultural experiments which, he hoped, could help transform Kenya from colonial liability to imperial asset. As Mrs.

Huxley has put it, his goal was nothing less than "to show that in East Africa England had possessed herself of a miniature new dominion, a little New Zealand."

He started big, deciding to concentrate first on livestock and acquiring 100,000 acres of pasture which straddled the Equator at Njoro on the lower slopes of the Mau. The land had never been occupied or even grazed by the Masai. Delamere named it Equator Ranch. It cost him £200 a year in rent plus a pledge to invest £5,000 in its development in five years. Even before he had recovered from his injury—even, in fact, before the land application had been approved—he was writing his estate manager in Cheshire with detailed instructions on stocking the ranch. Among other things, the manager was told to buy two dozen English rams which were to be crossbred with a flock of local ewes. He was also directed to hire a shepherd who would double as ranch foreman and who "must not be an uneducated bumpkin as things differ greatly in a new country and new things have to be learned." In January, 1904, Delamere arrived at Equator Ranch on a stretcher. Shortly afterwards, the shepherd-foreman joined him with the English rams, and was immediately sent off to New Zealand to buy 500 merino ewes. By the end of the year, 400 of the latter had died of lung ailments borne by worms and flies, and six thousand native ewes were showing themselves almost equally vulnerable. Meanwhile, Delamere had also brought 1,500 head of cattle to Equator Ranch, and they did not fare better than the sheep. Their pastureland proved deficient in iron (this was why the Masai had never grazed it), the pleuro-pneumonia introduced by 1,000 Kavirondo oxen killed off all the imported Herefords, and a large number of shorthorns succumbed to a tick-borne cattle disease called Texas fever.

*

As if cattle sickness were not enough, Delamere also sustained heavy losses from Masai theft, although this was partly his own fault. He belonged to a more or less select group of whites who suffered from what was known locally as Masai-itis. In their eyes, the tribe could do no wrong. Delamere not only admired their courage and forthrightness, but had an unqualified respect for their intuitive knowledge of livestock, and employed many elmoran to herd his cattle and sheep. The mere fact that they consented to work for him was a high compliment, since they were hardly less independent spirits than the settlers themselves, and seldom took employment with white farmers. (Nor did they demean themselves, as other tribes did, by addressing Europeans as "bwana"; the simple patronymic was good enough for anyone.) Delamere spoiled his own Masai shamelessly, furnishing them with greatcoats to wear in cold weather and umbrellas to shield them from the sun. In return, the elmoran-herdsmen taught him all they knew about the care of livestock under local conditions and also robbed him blind. He seldom took stern measures against them, however, even though rustling depleted his herds badly and tried his patience sorely. The Masai, for their part, were at least candid on the rare occasions when he challenged them. Once, after an especially large number of cows had vanished in the usual way, he confronted an elder and demanded to know how many members of the clan were aware of the theft. He got this reply: "Delamere, the only ones who did not know of it are the children who are still in their mothers' wombs."

Undismayed by disease and rustling, Delamere embarked on dairying, and instructed his Cheshire manager to buy him still more cows. "I want to make butter, cheese, cream cheese and so on," he wrote, "for the country trade, as far as it does not interfere with the small man ... I want you to get and send out with the stock a *first-class* dairyman and his wife... It is extremely important that he should be a man who drinks nothing or practically nothing, and you *must see by personal trial* that he is capable of turning out the very highest class of stuff." When the dairyman arrived he found waiting for him a modern, completely equipped stone dairy building and a complex of milking sheds. In due course, the residents of Nairobi were eating the butter churned at Equator Ranch. By 1906, Delamere's fresh butter was being sold in Mombasa. Then the project fell to pieces as east coast fever struck. To save the herd, it was necessary to move it. Delamere by this time had acquired another holding, some 50,000 acres of hopefully less contaminated land at a place called Soysambu (Masai for "spotted rock") near Lake Elmenteita on the floor of the Rift. His sheep had already been taken to Soysambu, and now the few surviving cattle joined them. Although they did not grow fat at once, they at least seemed to stay alive.

But if the land on Equator Ranch was unsuited to grazing, surely it would grow cereals. Even before the departure of the livestock, Delamere had commenced turning over the soil on a large portion of his acreage; the first furrow on the farm's first wheatfield was three miles long. Initially, Delamere's ten-furrow disc plow was drawn by one of the steam traction engines which had served the railway during construction. The specialist driver who had been brought in from England refused to go near the thing for several days, however, certain that the boiler would explode. It did not, but its eight tons were found to flatten out the seed beds, and Delamere was eventually forced to fall back on oxen. This in turn meant taking lessons in handling an ox whip from an Afrikaner settler; for some time, the best Delamere could do was entangle his legs in the coils of the long rawhide lash. Once, a pair of neighboring colonists who came around to enjoy the spectacle took a whipping instead, as Delamere vented his frustration on them. The oxen proved a greater trial; nearly six months passed before they were broken to the plow. The effort, moreover, began to seem wasted as sowing and harvesting began and various strains of wheat succumbed regularly to the onslaught of rust. By 1908, however, Delamere managed to reap a wheat harvest that brought in a modest but no less tangible profit. His hopes rose. More plows were bought, more oxen broken in. By 1909, 1,200 acres were under wheat, and—despite the failure of the rains—Delamere saw himself on the threshold of victory over the elements. Not only could he anticipate a harvest of 2,000 bushels and a return of at least £600, but much more significantly, he would have demonstrated to the outside world that wheat was a staple of farming prosperity in Kenya. He was not given the opportunity. Yellow rust obliterated half the crop.

Delamere had now been farming in the highlands for six years. He had spent more than £40,000 on Equator Ranch and Soysambu and was deeply in debt. Only heavy loans, with the Vale Royal estate as security, had enabled him to pay for his cattle and sheep, his multitude of plows, harrows, mowers, reapers, binders, strippers, harvesters, threshers and dairying machinery. In 1909, however, after another £17,000 loan, Vale Royal went into receivership. Henceforth, Delamere would sink or swim on the earnings of his east African land, plus whatever bank overdrafts he might be able to arrange. But his optimism did not falter. A typical instruction to his Cheshire manager at this time was: "Send off the thresher at once. I will pay when the money is borrowed."

*

Possibly he had no time to worry. His day began at four in the morning, when he ate a hasty breakfast of Thomson's gazelle chops while a battered gramophone played his favorite musical selection, something called "All Aboard for Margate." He then mounted his horse (later it was replaced by a decomposing Model T Ford) for a ten-hour inspection of crops or cattle. He supervised sheep-dipping, examined calves for worms and ticks, sought out signs of rust in the cereals, checked long sections of his 150 miles of barbed wire for breaks. At work in the fields, he was easily recognizable from a distance by a well-worn cardigan, tattered khaki trousers, the most enormous pith helmet in east Africa and red hair hanging hippie-like to his shoulders as a further precaution against the sun. Even more conspicuous, at closer range, was his behavior as a task-master—particularly toward his white foremen and apprentices. "D. was exacting to a degree," one of them wrote some years later, "hardly ever satisfied, and gave one the most terrific jabs in the most tender spots. On the other hand ... he had the kindest of hearts ... Despite his roaring temper I was devoted to him, and so were all his natives."

At about three in the afternoon, he went back to the farmhouse (a grass hut fenced around by a corrugated iron boma) for lunch. After wolfing down another Tommy chop or two, he went to work for several hours on accounts, correspondence and other desk chores. Dinner, invariably consisting of more Tommy chops, blancmange and tinned peaches, was sandwiched in between rambling conferences with his Masai herds-men. Crowded into the hovel and squatting in a tight semi-circle on the dirt floor, they briefed Delamere on grazing conditions and livestock ailments that he might have overlooked, and entertained him with their bottomless fund of folk tales. By two in the morning he was ready for bed, but might not retire at once if there was paperwork to be caught up on. He always slept with a hurricane lamp burning; somehow it kept him from walking in his sleep. Certainly he needed the rest, which often came to no more than two or three hours.

Intervals of leisure or recreation were not common in the early days, but Delamere made the most of them. A favorite pastime was hitch-ing his American trotter to a buggy and racing railway trains for ten or fifteen miles as they passed his land. He seldom lost. There was also a small amount of night life. Nakuru, some twenty miles from Equator Ranch, was rapidly becoming the stockmen's capital of the highlands. Most of the cattle auctions and livestock shows were held there, and in 1908 Delamere built a small hotel to accommodate the visiting ranchers. He also used it to indulge his personal taste for vandalism and other schoolboy pranks. One night he bought all the oranges in an Indian shop, handed them out to friends and instructed them to smash every window in the hotel. He also organized rugby scrimmages in the bar, diving into the mêlée himself and running up a sizable bill for breakage. As the hotel's owner, he was compensated; as the leader of the hoodlum gangs, the damages came from his own pocket.

*

After the wheat débâcle and the staggering losses of cattle and sheep, there might have been room to fear that Kenya's agricultural future—and all hopes for a large white colony—had gone down the drain with Delamere's investments. Delamere thought otherwise. Instead of abandoning wheat, he sought to find a rust-resistant strain, and engaged a botanist who conducted experiments in a costly laboratory built on Equator Ranch. After more than two thousand plants had been discarded, a pair of sturdy hybrids emerged, one suited to growing at high altitudes, the other to low. Botany also bore fruit at Soysambu. During the early 1900s, it was not widely understood that the best breed of livestock is seldom better than the pasture on which it grazes. Delamere knew this, however, and had set about upgrading his own land. One of his major steps toward that goal was to plant English clover, lucerne and grass, which grew easily in the highlands and proved conspicuously beneficial to his imported cattle and sheep. Concurrently, he was building up his flocks by careful crossbreeding, since hybrid stock not only showed a greater resistance to disease but also yielded a fleece of outstanding quality; three crosses of Australian merino rams and Masai ewes produced a wool that matched pure merino. Cattle benefited no less from crossbreeding as Delamere resumed his dairying. Sixteen prize shorthorn bulls imported from England were joined with 600 hardy Boran animals, brought into the highlands from the grim northern frontier, to form the nucleus of a dairy herd with an annual grade-A yield of between 600 and 700 gallons per cow. The scientific method seemed to be bringing results.

Delamere did not confine himself to proving the worth of livestock and wheat. He planted vast fields of maize, barley and potatoes, worked thirty square miles of timberland, put two thousand acres under wattle and opened a plant for the disintegration of the bark, grew tobacco, planted forty acres of oranges, started a pig farm and an ostrich hatchery. (The latter proved his only real failure when the advent of the automobile put the huge ostrich-feathered ladies' headwear out of fashion.) The cost, to be sure, was staggering, but this was mainly because the entire undertaking was carried out on so great a scale, and because a small fortune was sunk in scientific experiment. For the smaller farmer, no such expenditure was necessary; the trail was being blazed for him. Other growers, ranchers and dairymen—and more to the point, the bankers who wrote the overdrafts—were gradually being shown that bulk crops and large herds could be sound investments. To insure this, Delamere took the lead in moving the colonists' produce. To market local mutton, he founded a company called Nyama, Ltd. (Swahili for "meat") which opened butcher shops in Nairobi, Nakuru and Mombasa. He also organized Unga, Ltd. ("flour") to build a mill that would grind the settlers' wheat and enable Kenya to serve the other east African territories. Although a director and principal shareholder in both companies, Delamere made a point of not taking so much as sixpence from their earnings.

There seemed to be no aspect of white settlement in which Delamere did not involve himself. He promoted the highlands to prospective farmers as energetically as any Florida real estate salesman, although he stood to gain no personal profit. Hardly had he arrived in Kenya than he had begun to beat the drum for colonization. At about that time, apparently feeling that it had nothing to lose, the Foreign Office made free offers of more than four dozen 640-acre blocks on the Mau to any applicant, the only charge being a survey fee of about £7. Without delay, Delamere set about publicizing the offer in England with long letters instructing his Cheshire manager to "help me advertise this country in any way you can." Although Delamere was not given to emotionalism in his correspondence, the promotional letters waxed almost lyrical. The available land was "the most beautiful country imaginable, with enormous timber trees, evergreen grasses and clovers, perennial streams everywhere and a temperate climate. It will grow anything and to my mind it is a chance in a thousand for a man with a little money. Settlers at present in this country say that it compares with the best of New Zealand ... Sheep, cattle, agriculture—it is a perfect country for any of them... It must be remembered that directly money is made land is sure to go up largely in value ... A South African who has had much experience was here the other day and said he wouldn't take 20 acres in South Africa for one here. My own opinion is that there is a fortune for any of the early-comers that are worth anything... If any Cheshire or Lancashire man brings me a letter from you I will see he gets a good 640 acres." Wielding Delamere's brochure, the manager addressed large meetings of farmers in both counties. The result was an eventual influx of two hundred new settlers.

*

These were the small but ambitious beginnings. No one could be certain at once what the future would bring. Much had to be done during the first decade of the century before the highland farmers could gain more than a standoff in their struggle against weather, blight and bureaucracy. Nonetheless, Delamere's experiments and investments did appear to be showing the world that an economically viable Kenya was more than just a theoretical possibility. His fellow pioneers, of course, never doubted this. Even as early as 1903, when Delamere had just arrived and when the country seemed far from congenial to the prospects of settlement, there had been no question whatever in the colonists' minds that they had come on an agricultural Eldorado. Two episodes which took place at that time served to underscore the high premium which the Kenya farmers placed on their land.

"Enough to make one
wish for a big nose and
a name like Ikey Moses."

Certain African peoples known for their intelligence and shrewdness, such as the Kikuyu of Kenya, the Ibo of Nigeria and the Ewe of Ghana, have from time to time been rather meaninglessly described by some writers as "the Jews of Africa." For a brief period at the turn of the twentieth century, it seemed as if those tribes might yield their sobriquet to the real thing. This was the consequence of a little-known British proposal—made fourteen years before the Balfour Declaration—to establish a national homeland for the Zionist movement in the Kenya highlands.

In 1902, Joseph Chamberlain, then the Colonial Secretary, made a brief tour of the Protectorate and, like all other visitors, he was struck by the fertility, the temperate climate and, above all, the emptiness of the highland region. At about the same time, in the Bessarabian capital of Kishinev, a pogrom of unusual barbarity was taking place, and when accounts of the atrocity reached Chamberlain, world Jewry found an unexpected friend. As it happened, Chamberlain held strong Zionist sympathies, and it was only natural that he should have responded warmly when the Jewish leader, Dr. Theodor Herzl,* appealed to him for aid on behalf of the Kishinev victims and their oppressed co-religionists elsewhere. Herzl had already been seeking a sanctuary for his people which he described as "an antechamber to the Holy Land, a place of apprenticeship that would serve to fit the Russian Jews to enter later into their inheritance—for an equivalent to the wilderness in which the followers of Moses spent forty years preparatory to the settlement in the land of Canaan." To this end, a Zionist commission had inspected a town called El Arish on the Sinai peninsula, but reported that the place was "more hopeless than it was when their ancestors wandered and murmured there, a desolation of stone, sand and salt." Besides this, the

---

* Not to be confused, of course, with the Theodor Hertzka of the Freeland farce.

Egyptian Government—which is to say the proconsul Lord Cromer—
was less than keen on the project, and it fell through. But Herzl had
better luck with Chamberlain. The two men met in April, 1903, and
within four months, Chamberlain had persuaded the Foreign Office to
make a formal offer of a vast tract in the East Africa Protectorate to the
Zionist movement.

When the news of the British proposal reached Kenya, the settlers
reacted as if an armada of flying saucers were descending on the country.
Protesting energetically that some of their best friends were Jews, they
proceeded, with even more vigor, to belabor the Zionists. "Feeling here
very strong against introduction alien Jews," Delamere cabled *The Times*.
"Is it for this expensive railway has been built and large sums of money
spent on country?... Is British taxpayer proprietor East Africa content
that beautiful and valuable land be handed to aliens? Have we no colonists our own race?" Delamere was speaking with comparative restraint.
At a mass protest meeting in Nairobi, a unanimous resolution opposing
the scheme warned that the colonists were "prepared to resist same by
all means in their power." Loud applause greeted one settler when he
told the audience that "I have lived and worked amongst low class Jews
in New York City... and my experience is that the poor Jew is the worst
possible man we could get in this country." The cry was also taken up
by the *East African Standard*, one of the two local newspapers, with
editorials and articles carrying such titles as "The Country's Deathblow,"
"The New Jerusalem," "The Prey of the Spoiler." One editorial sounded
an alert against "the long greasy frock-coated gentlemen who 'vould sell
you a coat' or anything—who drops into a bar and produces from the
manifold pockets of their rags anything from a comb or a piece of soap—
for neither of which they have any use—to a watch or revolver." (The
same ungrammatical warning somewhat cryptically described Russian
and Rumanian Jews as "Peruvians of the worst kind.") The *Standard*'s
letters column was even more expressive, with correspondents speaking
of the "Land of the Noses" and the "Jewganda Railway." One settler
wrote: "to read of this beautiful land ... being reserved for foreign Jewish
paupers is enough to make one wish for a big nose and a name like Ikey
Moses." Even advertisements tied in with the topic: "East Africa may be
Jewed, but you will not if you deal with T. A. Wood, Nairobi Stores."

Before one asks whether the swastika had replaced the Union Jack
on Kenya flagstaffs, several points might merit reflection. First there is
an uncomfortable but equally undeniable fact: simply that seven decades
ago, anti-Semitic slurs and jokes were not considered especially reprehensible or even improper in many otherwise enlightened European circles.

It is not very likely, moreover, that anti-Semitism, as we understand the term today, was either practiced or condoned by more than a minute handful of settlers. The nucleus of what rapidly became a sizable Jewish community in Kenya already existed in 1903. Like other Europeans of "the right sort," these colonists were not merely accepted but welcomed, being no less enterprising and no less dedicated to the ideal of a "little New Zealand" than their Gentile neighbors.* In the vitriol poured on the Jews during the Zionist furor one easily recognizes the handiwork of the small but loud-mouthed minority of sick minds found in almost any society. While it must not be supposed for a moment that Kenya's whites championed ethnic integration, it would be misleading and unjust to include Jewry in their blacklist. The real targets of settler fury in the Zionist controversy, as we are about to discover, were totally unrelated to race or religion.

The idea of a Zionist homeland, moreover, was not without enthusiasts in Kenya. While the *Standard* fulminated against the scheme, the Protectorate's other newspaper, *The East Africa and Uganda Mail*, saw the prospective new settlers as a blessing, and declared that "wherever the foot of the Jew is planted that land grows prosperous and arises to commercial importance." Eliot, who blew hot and cold on the proposal, was able, at least for a time, to look at it from a pragmatic angle favoring the Zionists. "You must understand the importance of the financial question," he wrote Delamere. "This protectorate alone costs the Government at home £256,000 per annum... As long as we go on this way we are always exposed to the risk that a radical Government may cut our vote in aid, and what should we do then? We should simply collapse, and it is better to be supported by Jews than to do that." It must be added, however, that Eliot, while holding no personal anti-Jewish bias, later joined the opponents of the scheme and backed up his change of heart by contradicting his original assertion that the Zionists would prime the country's financial pump. "Though wealthy Jews are very wealthy," he told the Foreign Office, "poor Jews are very poor, and a visit to the Jewish parts of Russia and Poland produces a most disagreeable impression of dirt and squalor... Is it in these surroundings that promising settlers will be obtained?"

---

* One of the Jewish pioneers, Abraham Block, stated several years ago that financial assistance from Delamere put him on his feet in Kenya. Block's son Jack later became the colony's Conrad Hilton, relinquishing that distinction only when he sold his Mawingo Hotel in Nanyuki to the movie actor William Holden (who renamed it the Mount Kenya Safari Club) and the New Stanley in Nairobi to Hilton himself.

And here we see one of the two authentic issues around which the controversy raged. It had no bearing whatever on religion or national origin but stemmed instead from a deep-rooted obsession with the possible effects of a "poor white" class on the colony. It was well known that South Africa had suffered severely from the presence of a large, impoverished white element with no visible means of support, often living outside the law. South Africa might perhaps be able to afford such an economic liability, but it could break the back of a country already dependent on the charity of a Parliamentary grant-in-aid. For the Jews to whom Whitehall offered a home in Kenya, far from being financiers or captains of industry, were literally paupers, their worldly goods the rags on their backs. They existed at the edge of survival in Russian and Polish ghettoes. Hardly a single one of them could scrape together enough money even for a deck passage to Mombasa, let alone the minimal two or three hundred pounds needed to start the most primitive of farms. Further intensifying the settlers' apprehensions of a mendicant population was the almost universal belief—shared by many Zionist supporters—that Jews were essentially an urban people with no aptitude whatever for agricultural pursuits. Nearly half a century would have to pass before that myth exploded with the flowering of the desert in Israel, but in the meanwhile the notion prevailed, and the colonists' fear of being overrun by parasites, while misguided, was no less real.

Perhaps most significantly, however, it is quite possible that the full force of the settlers' rage was directed at least as much at the Foreign Office as at the Zionists, and not entirely without justification. Apart from having offered generous lip service, a few token benefits and a handful of free land grants in regions it may have considered useless, Whitehall had scarcely lifted a finger to encourage or assist British settlement in Kenya. Indeed, encumbered as they were with meaningless land regulations and handcuffs of red tape, the Protectorate's pioneer farmers could almost have been forgiven if they felt at times that the home Government was conspiring to sabotage their infant colony. This view in fact was put to rhyme in the letters column of the *Standard*, by an apoplectic settler who declaimed:

> We have borne with annoyance and insult
> With justice delayed and denied
> We have borne with your laws retrogressive
> With annoyance, folly and pride
> But beware lest you add to our burdens
> The one over many to bear

> And learn to your cost and confusion
> What it is that your children will dare.

Possibly the settlers did not even see themselves as children at this time, but rather as unwanted stepchildren. And it was inevitable that that image should have come into sharper focus as they watched the Foreign Office roll out a bright red carpet for a horde of poverty-stricken aliens who could not conceivably contribute—so it was thought—to the country's well-being. With only a few exceptions, the British colonists had to pay for the land they farmed, but now an immense slab of it was to become an outright gift to the Zionists. The settlers were denied even the smallest voice in their own affairs, but the new immigrants would enjoy complete autonomy under a Jewish governor and the protection of the Union Jack. It may not have been altogether incomprehensible that tempers should have flared, that a scapegoat should have been found.

*

But if the settlers blew up a storm over the impending irruption, it was mild by comparison to the response of the invaders when Herzl revealed the British offer to the delegates of the Sixth Zionist Congress at Basle in August of 1903. For the Foreign Office proposal did nothing less than strike at the foundation stone of Zionism itself: the return of the Jews as a people to their rightful home in Palestine. To Jews on every continent, it was unthinkable that the Children of Israel might settle anywhere else than in the Promised Land, and Herzl's announcement split the Zionist movement down the middle. Leading the opposition at Basle was the Russian delegation, composed of those Jews who stood to gain most from asylum; it is no small measure of their courage that they were prepared to endure further pogroms rather than forsake, however briefly, the dream of Palestine. The debate on the offer, which took place almost concurrently with the settlers' protest meeting in Nairobi, was a chaos of impassioned rhetoric and enraged posturing. Herzl was called a traitor to his face. One woman ripped a map of east Africa from the wall. Caucuses gathered to sing the "Hatikvah" by way of dramatizing their allegiance to Palestine. The youthful Chaim Weizmann is said to have fallen out temporarily with his father and brother over the issue.

Finally the question was put to a vote: should a commission be appointed and sent to east Africa with a view to reporting on the prospects of a provisional Jewish home in that country? The balloting lasted an hour, during which time, according to the English Zionist Israel Zang-will, "each delegate's 'yes' or 'no' sounded like the hammer-strokes of destiny forging the future of the Jewish people." By a vote of 295 to 178, the proposal carried, and pandemonium swept the hall as the Russian delegation walked out en masse. Wrote Israel Cohen, one of Herzl's biographers: "many fell on one another's necks and wept, one at least, a young student, fainted; and all presented the most doleful and mournful looks as though Zion had been abandoned forever."

It had not, of course. As the Congress closed, Herzl energetically re-emphasized that the east African scheme was no more than a halfway house on the road to Palestine, and reaffirmed his own dedication to the ultimate goal with the traditional, "If I forget thee, O Jerusalem, may my right hand forget its cunning." But despite the majority that stood behind him, Herzl's troubles had only begun. The dissenters possessed sufficient influence to block any Zionist expenditure of funds for the commission's expedition to east Africa; many months passed before a private individual was prevailed on to underwrite the costs. It was not until mid-January of 1905 that the three-man commission (only one member was a Jew) finally arrived in Mombasa. During the interval, Herzl had died—some say of a broken heart over the frustrations he encountered at the hands of the scheme's opponents.

*

The region which the Foreign Office had set aside for the Zionists was a section of the Uasin Gishu plateau, five thousand square miles in area, lying some fifty miles northeast of Londiani station on the Mau. One can choose from among several different accounts of the commission's visit to that proposed homeland. According to the most colorful version, a group of settlers had previously called on Eliot and, with straight faces, requested permission to escort the Jewish party. No less gravely, Eliot is said to have replied: "I am sure that you gentlemen will be able to show the members of the commission many things they would not otherwise see." When the commission arrived in Nairobi, it was joined by the volunteer guides and the beefed-up party entrained for Londiani. Then began a long and arduous trek up the escarpment. Unaccustomed to walking on anything but pavements, the Zionists developed painful blisters on their feet within a few hours. Hardly had camp been made at sundown than a large herd of elephants crashed through the forest less than a hundred yards from the tents, and for the rest of the night, the visitors' sleep was interrupted at irregular but frequent intervals by the massive pounding of buffalo hooves and the deranged screams of tree hyraxes.

Some hours after the march was resumed the next day, a band of Masai elmoran in full war regalia converged on the little party. The three commissioners had no way of knowing that the Masai practically never entered this particular part of the country; their anxiety mounted as the warriors rattled their spears, hefted their knobkerries, stamped furiously on the ground and made other menacing gestures. It was only after the settlers approached the Masai and concluded a lengthy, cryptic parley, ostensibly in the tribe's language, that the savages withdrew to a safe distance. Then, however, they began a war dance which lasted several hours. At sunset they vanished abruptly into the forest, but the settlers took turns standing guard at the campfire until morning. Although an attack did not come, the commission members had another uneasy night, as loud grunts and an occasional roar punctuated their sleep. At breakfast, they were shown a swath of pugmarks around the encampment, and the colonist guides regaled them with tales of Patterson's ordeal at Tsavo. In due course, the expedition reached its destination, the commissioners went through the formalities of inspecting the Promised Land and returned to England. In August, 1905, the Foreign Office gift was declined with thanks.

The only substantiated part of the above episode is the rejection of the British offer. The rest of the adventure, although it enjoyed wide circulation for many years, is almost certainly the fabrication of a settler who was known for his gifts as a storyteller. While the path to the Uasin Gishu was not without thorns—the expedition did have a close call with a Nandi war party—the records of the three commissioners make no mention of harassment by Masai, encounters with lions or even the services of any colonists. Nor was their reconnaissance of the plateau carried out in panicky haste; each member made a careful inspection of the land and wrote a detailed report on its potential for Jewish settlement. Their conclusions, however, were far from sanguine: Uasin Gishu was unanimously ruled out as worthless from an agricultural standpoint. While this verdict can only be called extraordinary, for Uasin Gishu shortly became the most bountiful farming land anywhere in the Protectorate, the commissioners stood on firmer ground in noting that the region was far too small to support more than a few hundred Jewish families. That fact alone sufficed to invalidate the entire scheme. Although it was revived later by Zangwill, who aroused a certain amount of sympathy in the new Colonial Secretary, Lord Elgin, and won the enthusiastic support of Elgin's deputy, Winston Churchill, the situation by then had changed. A steady stream of

British settlers had preempted virtually all the land suitable for European colonization, and the dream of an equatorial Canaan came to an end.

Even so—and despite the schisms it had temporarily created in the Zionist ranks—the long-run effect of the proposed scheme was to consolidate the identity of the Jews as a nation. The very fact that Herzl, Zangwill and other Zionist leaders had dealt with the British Government at its highest ministerial levels gained the movement an elevated world status. And while Britain's earliest commitment to a Jewish state failed to bear fruit; there is little doubt that it smoothed the path for Balfour's landmark pledge in 1917.*

*"The position will not be tolerated
And will very soon result
in a sort of Jameson Raid."*

Another incident, concurrent with the Zionist crisis, served to show that the settlers were prepared to extend as well as defend their property. The land they sought was a vast section of the Rift Valley near Naivasha, which not only offered uncommonly rich pasture but which was bisected by the railway, thus automatically doubling its value to the stockman. It was also a traditional grazing ground of the Masai, and therefore off limits, since Government policy in the allocation of land to Europeans tended to confine leases to unoccupied areas. For the most part; the settlers had accepted the restraint with good grace and appreciated its underlying fairness; Delamere scrupulously withdrew one of his own land applications when he learned that the property overlapped a Masai pasture. But in the case of the Naivasha tract, the immigrants seemed ready to make an exception, arguing, not altogether unreasonably, that it was equally unjust to set aside a huge region for the exclusive use of a nomadic people who grazed it only sporadically. It was further pointed out that the Masai seldom sold their cattle and did nothing to improve the land, while European ranches would put it on a paying basis. Not surprisingly, Eliot took up the cudgel for the farmers. In 1904, in a despatch to the Foreign Office, he drew the distinction between "the right of the Masai to *inhabit* certain districts" and "their right to *monopolise* certain districts and keep everyone else out."

In fact, the Masai were not keeping everyone else out—at least not

---

* It is worth noting that Balfour was Prime Minister when Chamberlain made his original offer to Herzl.

the Europeans. Two years earlier, Whitehall had approved in principle a grant of 500 square miles in the Naivasha district to a well-financed British mineral prospecting syndicate, and in many quarters this apparent reversal of policy was looked on as a green light for British cattlemen. It certainly accorded with the anti-monopoly views of Eliot, who reinforced his argument with the warning that "if the Masai are kept in the best land close to the railway, and if the Europeans, who can make better use of the land and railway, settle all round them, the position will not be tolerated and will very soon result in a sort of Jameson Raid." A clash would be forestalled, he suggested, if the Masai grazing areas were simply moved some miles from the line which they never used. Most of the settlers not only concurred but went a step further, urging that the tribe be placed in a reserve. While reserves were generally welcomed by colonists as convenient for the recruitment of African labor, it was also felt in this instance that isolating the Masai would remove the last obstacle to white occupation of the Naivasha region.

But this recommendation complicated matters, since Eliot would have no part of a reserve. It was his conviction that segregating the Masai would simply perpetuate tribal customs which, although they "may be interesting to an anthropologist ... are socially and politically abominable ... a moral scandal and physically disastrous to the race." Only through contact with Europeans, Eliot maintained, would the Masai be able to rise above their own squalor, a stand which might or might not have been inconsistent with his apprehensions over a Jameson raid. The situation was further confused by Delamere's position. Unlike most settlers, he normally opposed the idea of reserves, which he called a "zoological garden policy," and shared Eliot's belief that close association with whites would accelerate African progress. But in the case of the Masai he parted company with Eliot, urging that his pet noble savages be shielded from a corrupting civilization and that Naivasha be put to gainful use by white ranchers. Eliot seemed to stand alone.

He also ran into unyielding opposition from his own officials, notably Jackson and Ainsworth, although their reasons for favoring a reserve were not likely to win settler approval. Most Administration officers tended to see themselves as custodians of African rather than white interests; Jackson, then the Protectorate's Deputy Commissioner, went so far as to recommend that the reserve chosen for the Masai be the Naivasha grazing ground itself, and that the colonists be forbidden to hold so much as a square inch of the land. Although Eliot branded this as "politically and economically a lamentable error," Jackson went over his chief's head; while on leave in England, he submitted the proposal in a forcible memorandum to the Foreign Office, which in turn indicated at least partial approval. The dispute came to a head when Eliot, assuming that the earlier grant to the syndicate meant an endorsement of ranching in the region as well, approved a land application by two private European settlers, only to see the grant canceled by Whitehall. Without delay and in a considerable huff he resigned, and the problem of what to do with the Masai remained in the air.

It was resolved, however, with the arrival of the new Commissioner. A hard-working, hard-drinking, hard-boiled, no-nonsense west Africa hand, Sir Donald Stewart believed in decisive action rather than diplomatic hair-splitting. Hardly had he taken his post when he drew up a treaty with the Masai in which the reserve prevailed—but not in the contested region. Thenceforth, the tribe would hold exclusive occupancy of two separate areas: the Laikipia plateau, well to the north of the railway, and some 4,300 square miles of the southern Rift near the German border, both zones being joined by a road half a mile in width. The way to the pastures of Naivasha had at last been cleared for the white ranchers.

"With some justice," Mervyn Hill observed many years later, "the episode has been described as an eviction." But Hill also noted that "the alternative to moving the Masai into reserves was to leave vast areas of land as the private preserve of some 45,000 nomadic pastoralists." At the same time, moreover, the Masai could hardly have been called losers, since the 4,500 square miles of Laikipia were if anything an even richer grazing land than Naivasha. Indeed, Stewart, who was by no means an admirer of the colonists, appears to have been very much alive to the possibility of some future European claims to Laikipia, for he inserted into the treaty a clause which stipulated that "the settlement now arrived at shall be enduring so long as the Masai shall exist as a race." We shall presently take another look at that durability.

*

If nothing else, the Zionist and Masai controversies left little doubt of the settlers' proprietary attitude toward Kenya. They had come to stay, as landed proprietors. Their hearts were in the highlands and the highlands, for better or worse, were their home. That claim appeared to be acknowledged in April, 1905, when the Administration of the Protectorate was formally transferred from the Foreign Office to the Colonial Office. The white community had long dreamed of this moment. Indeed, they had urged the change, since the Colonial Office not only possessed the necessary practical experience in formulating policies for Britain's overseas possessions but existed for the express purpose of advancing the interests of those territories. The transfer could mean only one thing: Government's long-overdue recognition of the Kenya farmers as respectable members of a bona fide colony rather than the no-account wards of an indifferent Foreign Secretary. Settlerdom could now expect rational land laws and a generally sympathetic hearing in London. The first step on the road to Delamere's goal of dominion status appeared to have been taken.

This at any rate was what the settlers thought.

12

WHITE KNIGHT TO BLACK PAWN

"The complete knowledge of the psychology
of their tribesmen gave the elders an enormous
advantage, which could never be fully acquired
by any European."

There was one unique aspect of British settlement in the Kenya highlands: the colonists were anachronisms. In Elspeth Huxley's words, they "were pioneering about half a century too late. They were trying to follow the tradition of the covered wagon in the era of the Ford." On debarking from their steamers at Mombasa, they found an unprecedented convenience: a railway which carried them three, four or five hundred miles to their new homes in the interior. This was not supposed to happen. In the annals of opening up blank spaces on any continent, railways had never preceded but always followed the pioneers. And, in a less dramatic but more significant way, the same applied to the machinery of government. In every other homestead community on the planet, law and order had emerged as an outgrowth of the settlers' presence; but when Kenya's immigrant farmers stepped off the train at Nairobi, they discovered the phenomenon of a ready-made administrative apparatus. Under ordinary circumstances, this built-in appendage of civilization might have been welcomed by men and women seeking to domesticate a remote African wilderness; that the Kenya settlers found their Government a decidedly mixed blessing was not necessarily a valid measure of its worth.

Anticipation of a colonist influx may have been the least important consideration in the infancy of Kenya's officialdom. The country had been experiencing bureaucracy ever since IBEA became the private care-taker of the British sphere in 1888. With the transfer of the Company function to the Foreign Office in 1895, Government departments had multiplied rapidly—both as a convenience for and rival to the burgeon-ing railway administration—and when the first settlers began coming in, there existed the makings of a Parkinsonian table of organization. Representing the Crown was a Commissioner, appointed by Whitehall and presiding over an Executive Council whose members headed up departments responsible for no fewer than fifteen separate administra-tive functions: judiciary, military, treasury, medical, trade and customs, transport, audit, public works, post office, telegraphs, port office, police, agricultural, forestry and veterinary. After 1905, when the Colonial Office took over and the Commissioner became the Governor, addi-tional wheels within wheels were continually installed in the already complicated engine. Obviously, this had to be a top-heavy edifice for so isolated and aboriginal a land as Kenya, and in fact the Adminis-tration's real activities were more imposing on paper than in practice. Apart from regulating land leases and dealing with other matters affect-ing the British colonists, the Government directed its energies toward the fulfillment of four main objectives. They were the introduction of reasonably uniform administrative and legal procedures among the two million indigenous inhabitants; the collection of hut taxes; the devel-opment of tribal agriculture; and the keeping of the peace. With these goals in view, it can be said that the early government of Kenya was largely African-oriented.

*

In local affairs, a certain amount of emphasis was placed on indirect rule, which had basked in a climate of official sanction since Lugard conducted his earliest experiments with quasi-proxy government in Uganda. A word, in fact, should be said about that country's adminis-tration, since it could be called a model for Lugard's principles. As we have already seen, the Baganda had reached a comparatively high level of political development even before the British annexation, and every effort was subsequently made to widen the scope of their autonomy. In 1901, after Sir Harry Johnston had been sent to Uganda to streamline the Protectorate's government machinery, he had recommended that the people "should be assisted and encouraged to govern themselves as far as possible without too much interference on the part of European officials." With Mwanga safely in exile, there had been no difficulty in placing nominal control in the hands of the discredited Kabaka's four-year-old son Daudi Chwa, whom Johnston described as "an intelligent little fellow" although "becoming somewhat spoilt by the adulation of his Ministers and people." Daudi Chwa exercised his sovereignty through a regency of three Baganda nobles, their appointments subject to the approval of the British Commissioner, and received further guidance and counsel from the Lukiiko.

Uganda's local government became largely the function of twenty district chiefs, whom the Kabaka appointed with the Commissioner's endorsement. Each chief wielded a modest authority. He worked closely with the British in collecting an Administration-levied hut and gun tax, arbitrated land disputes and sat as magistrate in all but capital cases. Only finance, transportation, major public works and justice to foreigners lay outside the scope of his decision-making powers. All chiefs, as well as the Kabaka and his regents, received salaries from the British, mainly to discourage independent and arbitrary assessments from the people. Similar if slightly less permissive systems were introduced in the other advanced kingdoms—Bunyoro, Toro, Ankole and Usoga—which had also been absorbed into the Protectorate. "It may be hoped," wrote Johnston, "that each district need, as a general rule, only require the appointment of a British Collector and Assistant Collector as far as local government and the collection of revenue are concerned."

Such latitude in internal self-rule, however, was withheld from the "savages" inhabiting the lands to the east of the lake. In European eyes, political institutions among the Kavirondo, Nandi, Masai, Kikuyu and Wakamba were fragmented and chaotic, altogether uncongenial to national development on modern lines; for many years, the British authorities in Kenya held their tribes on a very short leash. And yet, while Kenya's potential for indirect rule fell far short of the theoretical ideal, a certain degree of African autonomy was considered desirable, and to this end the Government sought leaders qualified to speak for the Crown at the clan or village level.

The results of the search were not always rewarding. With the questionable exception of the Masai, no peoples in the Protectorate accepted the final authority of any single individual. There were no "chiefs" as the word is usually understood by Westerners. The edifice of tribal organization, for the most part, was built on family or clan lines. The Kikuyu exemplified this, fragmenting themselves into a multiplicity of Balkan village-states, each of which was governed, after a fashion, by a council of elders. To only a lesser extent, the same system prevailed among all the other tribes. The Wakamba, wrote Eliot in an official report, "have no bond of union and, strictly speaking, no chiefs, for their *wazee,* or elders, are merely the older and richer men of each village, with very little authority, in either theory or practice ... What little influence they have is weakened by their drunken habits, and it is hardly an exaggeration to say that most of them are rarely in a condition to attend to any business." Eliot found even less leadership material among the Kavirondo, remarking that "I have never seen such a collection of filthy, decrepit, idiotic old men as a meeting of Kavirondo chiefs at Mumias."

Through a patient trial and error process, however, more or less commanding personalities were smoked out—usually from among already established clan elders—and appointed as salaried Government headmen with silver-headed staffs or brass breastplates, both embossed with the Royal arms, as badges of office. Their duties, at least on paper, included smoothing the path of hut tax collection, turning murderers and other felons over to the British Administration, and recruiting their own young men as labor whenever a Provincial or District Commissioner might decide that the tribe would benefit from a road, bridge, well or other facility. Despite this authority, the headman did not always enjoy the universal affection and esteem of his constituents, if for no other reason than that tax gatherers have never been very popular in any society. Actually, however, taxes were seldom collected by the headman in person; Eliot recommended against the practice on the grounds that these individuals might be "inclined to exaction on their own account." The responsibility devolved on the British officials; it was expected that the headman would simply assist the Europeans by furnishing a rough census of his village or district, and by explaining to his own fellow tribesmen, if he could, the purpose of the assessment.

At least two schools of thought existed on the wisdom of levying any tax on the African population. Lugard had opposed taxation without the prior introduction and acceptance of Western land tenure systems— that is, private rather than communal ownership—on which equitable assessments could be based. He believed that two or three generations would have to pass before the idea took firm root in tribal societies, and recommended as "not merely fair, but absolutely essential," that taxes be paid by Europeans, Indians and Arabs. The Kenya and Uganda Administrations, however, felt disinclined to wait sixty years or more while several hundred thousand African huts lay fallow, so to speak, as a source of revenue. Thus an annual tax of two rupees (about 70 cents) was levied on each hut in Kenya, with Uganda's ostensibly more affluent homeowners paying three rupees. "This impost," said Eliot, "occasions no hardship, and cannot be considered excessive" in view of "the advantages which natives have derived from the establishment of our rule and the abolition of the slave trade." Lugard's advice on alien taxation also went unheeded, so that the Government might encourage colonization by confining taxes on whites to the aforementioned ten percent import duty.

In the early years, tax collection from Africans conspired mightily against bookkeeping. Census taking, inevitably primitive, overlooked countless huts; many tribes and clans were simply inaccessible and could not be entered on the rolls. Payment itself tended to drive accountants up the wall. "The great aim," as one official, C. W. Hobley, put it, "was to build up a will to pay something," and Government therefore accepted taxes in kind, which took the form of cows, sheep, goats, chickens and occasionally crocodile eggs. Yet little resistance or protest was encountered. Even after cash found its way into the tribal economy, the tax dodger was a rare bird.* One of the few attempts to evade payment took place in 1906, when the Kenya rate was raised to three rupees and many inhabitants began sharing houses as a counter-measure, only to be balked by a Government decree that every adult living in a hut would be assessed whether or not he or she was the actual owner. This sort of not-too-sharp practice, however, was an exception that only proved a rule of good citizenship. Apart from the Nandi tribe, whose militant evasions will presently be examined, Africans paid their taxes promptly, conscientiously and almost cheerfully. For many years, the hut tax and the import duty comprised the Protectorate's main source of revenue. By 1910, hut tax alone was bringing Government an annual £100,000.

Concurrent with the rudimentary headman system which it created, Government was also able, gradually but perceptibly, to erect a framework of law, even to allow a small measure of African legal authority. Although Eliot acknowledged that "it often seems unreasonable to apply civilised law to simple savage life," it was inevitable that European jurisprudence would be introduced sooner or later, and the compromise embodied in the so-called "native court" helped to cushion the impact of that innovation. Functioning under the Indian Penal Code, with suitable

---

* Confusion did not vanish entirely, however. In 1907, a new coinage was introduced to replace the Indian halfpennies known as pice. As it happened, the fresh currency had been minted from aluminum, which for some reason crumbled into powder shortly after becoming legal tender. In a haste bordering on panic, the Government struck another coin, this time in nickel bronze.

accommodations to local custom, these tribunals were presided over by British officials with the aid of African assessors, and their procedures might or might not have confounded most English barristers. Witnesses performed spectacular feats of perjury as a matter of course, while the assessors sought to establish guilt or innocence by recourse to methods which Eliot described as "not exactly in conformity with the European law of evidence." Nonetheless, the coupling of Western and tribal notions of right and wrong usually saw justice prevail. In the "native court," even the least sophisticated African could expect—within the limitations of the system—a fair trial, in suits not only against fellow tribesmen but also against Europeans.

During this gradual introduction to Western legal concepts, the wheels of justice were also turning in the tradition-honored courts generally known as tribal councils. Since Government wished to preserve and encourage indigenous institutions wherever possible, these courts were not only seen as useful in local jurisprudence but viewed as potential instruments of African self-rule at the village level. It was no less clearly perceived, however, that the council's machinery needed drastic overhauling. Although many of the courts boasted something akin to a jury system, the similarity was all but unrecognizable. The panel usually consisted of two groups of elders, each enlisted by a litigant to plead his case, and their deliberations, byzantine in complexity under any circumstances, tended to become incoherent after every individual juror had consumed several gallons of fermented sugar cane. To change or at least modify this practice meant something of a showdown with the conditioned reflexes of tribal custom and ceremonial. As he attempted to streamline the Kikuyu courts, Hobley found that his major stumbling block "was to induce the elders to recognise that their function was not to represent any party in a suit, but to adopt a detached attitude towards each, and that this change of procedure was not contrary to their tribal tradition."

Perhaps to Hobley's surprise, the elders "quickly responded," accepting their new role with little fuss and a gratifying degree of natural aptitude. Many officials shared Hobley's view that the "reformed" tribal councils assured an African more justice than did Administration courts, if for no other reason than that "the complete knowledge of the psychology of their tribesmen gave the elders an enormous advantage, which could never be fully acquired by any European." Other tribes proved equally receptive to the innovation, and the eventual result was formal recognition of the tribal council as a quasi-official arm of the Protectorate Government. Owing largely to Hobley's representations, a Native

Authority Ordinance of 1912 empowered these bodies to make and enforce many of their own laws, "provided that such native law and custom is not repugnant to morality." Cases of intra-clan stock theft, assault, witchcraft, disputed bride-price agreements and other matters of customary law were adjudicated by the tribal council. It was a far cry from the more elaborate and infinitely more autonomous apparatus of indirect rule in Uganda, but the headman system and the tribal council nonetheless represented the Kenya African's first halting steps toward the ultimate management of his own destiny.

Another Government objective was to bring the African closer to the mainstream of the money economy so that he could share in as well as contribute to the country's material wealth. To this end, a number of public works and agricultural improvement schemes were set in motion among various tribes, particularly those occupying reserves. While the success of any given project rested largely on the resourcefulness and initiative of the individual tribe or clan, the main driving wheel was the local Administration official. Sparing the stick and wielding the carrot, this man aroused and sought to maintain the community's interest in raising its own living standards. But his task was not easy. From the very outset, African development faced several handicaps, not the least of which were inadequate funds, insufficient personnel and continual criticism from settlers who complained—without much foundation— that such projects denied them a major source of farm labor. Probably the biggest obstacle of all was thrown up by the tribesmen themselves, not out of hostility but from ignorance of the advantages of a cash economy and a consequent indifference to the growing of cash crops. For this reason alone, most programs did not bring spectacular results overnight. Even so, they could definitely be seen to work. Indeed, one project actually demonstrated that the African agriculturist, with the right conditions and the proper encouragement, was capable of giving the white farmer a run for his money.

It began in 1907, when Ainsworth became Commissioner of the Nyanza (lake) Province. On taking office, he found that the Kavirondo people were making only marginal use of their uncommonly fertile soil and had furnished no export produce to the railway. This apathy was not only withholding badly needed revenues from the Protectorate but had the effect of condemning the Kavirondo to a perpetual poverty. No doubt the cobwebs could have been swept away with little difficulty by imposing a farm production quota and ordering the people to meet it under penalty of fine. Apart, however, from flying in the face of British colonial policy, this was hardly the way to whet a tribe's zeal for its own self-advancement. Nor was Ainsworth the man for such methods. After a quick tour of the region, he found himself "impressed with the idea that we had a wonderful asset in the native people," and set about winning them over. And, as it proved, the tribe needed no coaxing; only the gentlest nudge in the right direction was necessary. Since a number of malaria-breeding swamps near the lake had to be cleared, Ainsworth called a meeting of Kavirondo elders and suggested to them that by performing this task they could kill two birds with one stone. "I ... explained that if their people undertook to cut a trench and so drain the swamp the land reclaimed would be available for cultivation ... and as it would be very rich soil, they might expect good crops." The double incentive turned the trick. In a few months, the onetime swamp had been plowed, planted and harvested, while Ainsworth, driving home his opening wedge, held more meetings to explain how the marketing of the new produce would benefit the tribe as a whole. It was not long, he noted, before the Kavirondo "had come to the point of appreciating the use of money in place of the old system of barter and were developing into keen traders."

Commerce flourished rapidly. With seeds furnished by the Government, cotton and groundnuts were planted and soon showed a tidy profit. There was a visible yearly increase in the sales of maize, millet and poultry products. Problems were tackled jointly by tribe and Administration, and Government was always there to lend a hand if things went awry. When one maize crop proved disappointing, Ainsworth called meetings throughout the province to win approval of a recommendation that a superior seed be introduced before the next harvest. Since this meant immediate disposal of the existing crop (some 9,000 tons) Ainsworth also arranged to have it sold in Kisumu to a German whisky manufacturer. As a further stimulus to trade, the nucleus of a road system had to be introduced, and Ainsworth sugar-coated the chore by giving it the air of a contest: "as time went on the people became quite keen, one location competing with another. A few of the more energetic headmen were given bicycles, which subsequently became quite the fashion, the result being increased trade and a desire to maintain good tracks." By 1911, when he left Nyanza, Ainsworth could write that "one way and another, the people were becoming comparatively well-to-do." He was putting it modestly. In that year, the once-stagnant province exported £44,000 in farm produce by rail. Two years later, the Kavirondo region had become the railway's best customer and proposals were afoot for the building of a branch line from Kisumu to Mumias.

This was an exceptional performance, to be sure, but it clearly demonstrated not merely the African's potential as a source of agricultural revenue but his capacity for bettering his own life. Ainsworth's methods, moreover, were anything but atypical. With only lesser degrees of success, similar programs were launched and carried out by other Administration foremen-gurus in most African regions throughout the Protectorate. Not only the Kavirondo but the Kikuyu, Wakamba and other predominantly cultivator peoples made impressive strides toward economic well-being during the first decade of British rule.

"There was an unwritten law that anyone who visited ... should leave behind one book to preserve the sanity of the next man in."

The men who implemented such programs at the grass-roots level were a mixed bag of aristocrats and roughnecks who had learned their professions the hard way. More than one had served his apprenticeship as a junior administrator with IBEA in the 1890s. A few could even claim prior African experience. Jackson had first visited the country as a trail-blazing gentleman-hunter in 1884. When Ainsworth joined Mackinnon's venture in 1889, he had already sweated for five years as a transport officer with a private trading company in the Congo Free State. James Martin had arrived on the scene before any of his colleagues. These veterans were in a position not only to carry out policy but to formulate it, by virtue both of their acknowledged experience and the fairly high-ranking posts which they held. During the early 1900s, most of Kenya's old stagers served as Provincial Commissioners (the office corresponded roughly to that of governor of a state, although with far greater arbitrary powers) and as members of the Protectorate's Executive Council, which in effect was the cabinet.* The Governor, whose term was relatively brief, leaned heavily on the knowledge of such aides. If he was a prudent man, he also made a point of not quarreling with them, for they were quite capable of doing the unheard-of and defying him

---

* Even the unlettered Martin, who never quite reached the charmed circle of provincial proconsulship, was universally recognized as one of the country's ablest District Commissioners—although he may have been the target of Sir Clement Hill's remark that administration in Kenya would suffer "so long as Civil Servants were enlisted from the gutter."

openly, as Eliot learned when Jackson (who was himself to become Governor of Uganda in 1911) derailed his recommendations for relocating the Masai. These men in fact played a unique role in the shaping of Britain's tropical African empire. Until the ascendancy of the anthropologist, Western expertise on tribal society was the almost exclusive province of the seasoned colonial civil servant; he thus became indispensable to a Government groping uncertainly toward something like an established course of conduct in its newest and least familiar overseas possessions.

Exotic associations and long-time experience with the old Africa could not be claimed by the Protectorate's younger corps of officials. The formal training they received, however, compensated at least in part for their green horns. Unlike their superiors, most of the junior officers were university graduates, and after 1907 were required, on provisional appointment to the colonial service, to attend a comprehensive series of three-month courses at the Imperial Institute in London. Initiated with the blessing of Lord Elgin, the Colonial Secretary, the crash program embraced such topics as law and administration, accounting, agriculture, surveying and tropical sanitation. Enrollment was not restricted to the tenderfeet. Senior officials on home leave were often instructed to attend the courses for their refresher value, and the orders were obeyed with much kicking and screaming in protest against being lectured on matters which had long been second nature. For a man who had gained his professional skills and knowledge in bush and forest, the curriculum no doubt seemed elementary, redundant and largely irrelevant: one certainly did not learn to make life-or-death decisions in a classroom. Yet whether or not they admitted it, the veterans found much in the courses that was instructive and up-to-date. As for the younger officials, they were furnished with a solid grounding in fundamentals that went far toward creating for east Africa's administrators what eventually became a not undeserved image as the elite of the colonial civil service.

The Imperial Institute program has been described with some wit in the reminiscences of Henry Seaton, who, as an Oxford fledgling, had been attracted to the prewar Kenya service by the £250 annual base salary. Seaton found the courses alternately illuminating, boring and alarming. "The lectures on tropical hygiene," he wrote, "were delivered by the Medical Adviser of the Colonial Office, a sick man who had served for many years on the West Coast. His tone was sorrowful and his lantern slides were horrific … When elephantiasis was projected, a strong man sitting next to me passed out and fell heavily off his chair." Surveying classes, "dry and dull, were fortunately relieved by an all-day field exercise … The professor himself had a bag of survey tools …

carried by a young and highly intelligent boy ... I mention this lad with gratitude, because our successful results were largely due to his surreptitious, skilful draughtsmanship which, for a modest bribe, he exercised on our plane tables with incredible speed." Seaton also observed that while the approach of examinations seldom caused anxiety among the aspiring satraps, all quailed at one bugbear: Islamic law, since "the lectures had been delivered by an enchanting Indian barrister, who found great difficulty in expressing himself in English." However, added Seaton, "we need not have trembled. Apparently the lecturer was in terror of losing his job; he marked all our papers 'just passed.'"

Having "just passed," the candidate could legitimately call himself an Assistant District Commissioner or Assistant District Officer or Sub-Collector or Assistant Collector—the titles were various although they generally carried the same responsibilities. But Seaton and his colleagues were also quick to discover that their formal training was not without shortcomings, and to recognize that "for the first six months of his service, a newly appointed A.D.C. was of less value than a third-grade Asian clerk." This could hardly have been otherwise, but in time the recruit would become more than worth his annual £250. It was not unusual for an apple-cheeked product of Eton and Cambridge, barely old enough to vote, only starting to shave, to find himself the absolute monarch of a region twice the size of England, and burdened with the duties of a miniature prime minister. "The modern system," as McGregor Ross, Kenya's first Director of Public Works, has written, "no doubt makes for a higher standard of performance, but in the process we lose sight of the joyous individual who was his own engineer, forester, agriculturalist, magistrate, police inspector, prison authority, commander-in-chief of (tiny) armed forces, postmaster, accountant, medical man and, at times, surgeon." These and many other tasks fell to the "bush D.O." Travel may have been his most demanding chore: "half our lives," Seaton recalls, "had to be spent under canvas." As a one-man oligarchy, the District Officer was obliged to journey many hundreds of miles every year, usually on foot, into every corner of his aboriginal domain, gathering taxes, hearing appeals from local tribunals, inspecting rudimentary public works projects, furnishing seeds for farms, and generally seeing to the welfare of the British-protected tribes whom he simultaneously ruled and served. Nor were his duties without occupational hazards. "Of a variety of very able men under whom or with whom I served in the early years," wrote Seaton, "one died of drink, two died of black-water fever, a fourth was suspected of taking drugs which, in a dangerous situation, induced unwarranted optimism; he was murdered. A fifth ended in a home for inebriates. A sixth committed suicide. A seventh suffered the pains of delirium tremens and was believed, subsequently, to have drowned himself in the Red Sea."

The high incidence of cafard in that casualty list probably resulted from assignment to several notorious hardship posts. An army or police officer patrolling the rock and desert hellscape of the Northern Frontier District might not see another European for six months or longer. At the Indian Ocean port of Kismayu in Jubaland, the soil poisoned all vegetables, and meat went rotten in hours; administrators dined on the rancid produce of tins and drank brackish river water that had to be transported ten miles in shriveling heat on the backs of camels. When Seaton was assigned to Kitui Boma in Ukamba, he found "a stark building consisting of three thick-walled rooms ... Outside, one oleander, not a blade of grass ... No vegetation was allowed to grow anywhere near habitation. The station was planned and organized to resist ever-threatening malaria and dysentery. It was bare earth all the way." Hardly more inviting was the Ukamba post of Mumoni where, according to Seaton, "there was an unwritten law that anyone who visited ... should leave behind one book to preserve the sanity of the next man in. The only other diversion the place could afford was the presence of an hermaphrodite. .. . But this poor wretch was so sick of being posed and photographed that he complained to the Provincial Commissioner, and a stern order was issued that he or she was to be left in peace."

By far the least desirable spot was Kisumu, the railway's lake terminus. Eliot all but condemned the place as a "serious and ever-increasing danger for the public health," since the harbor "becomes very easily fouled, and has no movement to speak of to refresh its sluggish waters." Kisumu was in fact a pesthouse, conspicuously vulnerable to malaria, dysentery, blackwater fever and a broad range of other tropical scourges. During construction of the railway, an epidemic of sleeping sickness swept the town and took nearly five hundred African lives. For some years, bubonic plague was endemic in Kisumu; while serving as Provincial Commissioner of Nyanza, Hobley sought to combat this with the aid of African boys who received a halfpenny for each dead rat they brought him. "The rapidity and efficiency with which they unearthed rats and killed them," he wrote, "was a revelation," but when Hobley's small change ran out, so did the boys, and rats continued to swarm through the town. In 1905, Kisumu was placed under a rigid quarantine, and the new Provincial Commissioner, Stephen Bagge, issued a directive forbidding women to live there. When Ainsworth succeeded Bagge in 1907, he had hardly taken his post than he was "forced to the conclusion that most of the officers stationed [in Kisumu] had developed what I termed a 'fear complex,' due to an obsession about the climate." The obsession was not benign. An Assistant District Commissioner had committed suicide several days before Ainsworth's arrival; within the next few months an Assistant Surgeon blew his brains out and was emulated shortly afterwards by the Provincial Treasurer. Somewhat gratuitously, Ainsworth observed that "Kisumu was not, at this time, a place for a melancholy man."

Providentially, administrative armpits like Kisumu and Mumoni did not work their grim hypnosis on everyone, and officials were usually able to reinforce their stiff upper lips with a variety of diversions. Big-game hunting was of course a much-favored pastime, not a few outposts had polo fields and cement tennis courts, there were endless rubbers of bridge at night. The club atmosphere was very much in evidence. Some stations even organized clubs, no less bona fide than the Carlton, White's or Boodle's—though far less stuffy.* Yet consolations, while welcome in any conditions, were seldom more than icing on the administrator's cake. Given the topography of the country, most Government stations offered spectacular scenic panoramas and an all but uniquely bracing climate, which whetted rather than dulled one's appetite for the multifarious tasks at hand.

For most officials, moreover, these tasks were their own reward. No record hunting trophy or winning bridge hand could ever match the gratification that came with personal involvement, however small, in helping shape a piece of the Empire. The A.D.O. who could prevail on the Africans in his district to increase their maize or potato yield for their own profit was gaining, or at least believed he was gaining, that many more faithful subjects of the King. The same contribution was made when he won a headman's cooperation in turning out a labor force to build a road on which the tribe's produce could be taken to market. As the official watched the surface being laid down, the side drains cut out, the camber formed, he could feel that he was opening not only an artery of local commerce but a direct line of good will between "his" tribe and the Crown. Likewise the administrator who sunk wells in a previously

---

* The Kismayu Club may have been the most celebrated. One guest, the English explorer-naturalist I. N. Dracopoli, remarked on Kismayu's "unusual but most excellent rule, which does not allow any member to offer another a drink without incurring a fine of Rs. 5. It might with advantage be copied in other clubs in the Protectorate, for there the habit of standing and being stood drinks has become a perfect burden, especially to those who are not blessed with an abundance of this world's goods."

arid waste, sat up nights instructing his African clerk in long division, inoculated a clan against smallpox, rid a village of a man-eating lion. All were part of doing one's bit.

Accomplishments never came easily. The smallest innovation ran headlong into tribal conservatism and superstition. Witch doctors often persuaded their clans that Government immunization programs or health clinics camouflaged lethal sorcery. Seldom did any bridge or road-building project receive more than token funds for its implementation. The work was endless, physically exhausting, often frustrating, not infrequently perilous. But it was also wholesome and constructive. Far more often than not, the "bush D.O." earned for his Government the gratitude and the loyalty of the people in the region where he held "a position," as Eliot put it, "which partly resembles that of an emperor and partly that of a general servant."

"Certain irresponsible satirists
divide the native population into two
classes: those in prison and those
who want to be."

Besides making the Protectorate's laws, Government also enforced them, or tried to. A police organization of sorts had existed in Kenya as far back as IBEA's stewardship, when the Company engaged Indian watchmen to stand guard over its warehouses at Kilindini and recruited a few other Indians to provide the façade of a constabulary in Mombasa. From all accounts, their presence did not noticeably inhibit anti-social behavior. Nor did the crime rate plummet in 1896, when the Foreign Office created an official police force. Until 1901, this department consisted of about 150 marginally trained Indian and African constables, most of them stationed in Mombasa, and one suspects that the town might have enjoyed far more law and order without them. Describing Kenya's Finest at that time, Sir Robert Hamilton, a Mombasa magistrate, wrote that "burglaries of the most daring character were committed constantly, almost under their eyes, and went undetected. The house of every European Government servant, with one exception, was broken into, or attempted ... The altar cloth was stolen from the church and the cashier's box from the Law Courts without anyone being apprehended. Indian merchants made continual complaints of the losses they suffered by robbery, and asked piteously if something could not be done." Had the police known of a solution, they might not have provided it willingly.

"On several occasions," wrote Hamilton, "I had to convict policemen of robbery from people in the streets at night, and in a number of other cases to order them punishment for being the cause of street rows or affrays in which they attempted to screen themselves by arresting unoffending people and then charging them with riotous conduct."

The absence of police esprit during the force's infancy probably stemmed, at least in part, from a generous measure of official indifference to the constables' training, appearance, equipment and welfare. Uniforms (no two were alike) ran a shabby spectrum of cast-off jackets, tattered shirts and seatless trousers. Barracks were mud hovels or shanties made from paraffin cans. There was virtually no formal instruction in elementary police procedure. Weapons may have been the laughing stock of the Protectorate. W. Robert Foran, one of the force's first officers, voiced astonishment at the rifles issued to the men. These were ancient Martini-Henrys "which had been condemned by the Royal Navy ... and then dumped into the sea as being of no further use" before they were salvaged to replace the even hoarier Sniders of the police. Forari appeared to have felt that the "new" rifles were better suited to their watery grave. "When shooting on a range at the 100 yards target," he wrote, "it was not at all uncommon for the bullet to fall at the marksman's feet."

In 1902, however, a new broom was wielded with the secondment of a British officer from a crack Indian regiment to head up the force as Inspector General. One of his first official acts was to secure the services of five British army sergeant-instructors, and the result, said Foran, "was a marked improvement in the drill, bearing, discipline and general appearance of the African ranks." The para-military corps, now known as the British East Africa Police, also began to expand, with the establishment of stations in Nairobi and Kisumu. Headquarters was transferred from Mombasa to Nairobi in 1905, and it was not long before more than 1,800 officers, sergeants and constables were serving in nearly every settled area of the Protectorate.

The process of transforming the force from an assortment of Keystone Kops into an efficient law enforcement agency was not confined to improving the performance of the lower ranks. Although a few chief sub-inspectors and inspectors were Indians who had been policemen in their own country, the majority of the officers were youthful and inexperienced British army lieutenants; in Foran's words, "they had to learn their duties by a process of trial and error, and mostly the latter prevailed." Foran himself was a case in point. While on leave from his regiment in South Africa, he entered the police almost on impulse, attracted mainly by the opportunity for big-game hunting. But he also recognized his limitations. Shortly after being posted to Nairobi, he was joined by another boyish inspector and ordered to instruct the new officer in his duties. "With only two weeks' service," he said, "this was a case of the blind leading the blind." The young men's confusion was not eased by their cramped official quarters. The Nairobi police station and jail, occupying two or three wood and corrugated iron sheds on Government Road, also accommodated Ainsworth (then Provincial Commissioner of the region) and his staff as well as the District Commissioner, the town magistrate, the treasurer and the transport officer. Compounding the traffic jam were the police's Indian clerks, who sat cross-legged on the floor, writing at tiny legless desks. Their paperwork created still another difficulty, as all of the force's records in the early days were kept in Urdu, which few British officers understood. "In view of our ignorance," wrote Foran, "... we wisely decided to let the Asian inspectors carry on, but gradually took over from them as we became more knowledgeable."

They acquired their knowledge through a rigorously comprehensive on-the-job training. On Foran's first day of official duty in Nairobi, he had to break up a fight in a pub and disarm two burly South African customers who had been using the bottles behind the bar as a shooting gallery. Hardly had the culprits been frog-marched into a cell than an equally inebriated companion, brandishing two .38 caliber revolvers, strode up to the jail and demanded the prisoners' immediate release. Foran knocked him down and locked him up. Then, while massaging his knuckles, he received a lesson in the all-embracing nature of his work when an African ran into headquarters with a report that a fire had broken out in the Indian bazaar. "It seemed I was held responsible for all fire-fighting, but no appliances existed and water had to be pro-cured in buckets ... Six shops and their contents were destroyed before we could halt the spread of the fire to others. This needed three hours' hard work."

Extracurricular activities, however, did not divert the police from their principal function of upholding the law. While serving in Nairobi, Foran may have been surprised at the relatively low incidence of crime at first, but the law-abiding climate rapidly diminished as the town grew and became infiltrated by a crooked element among the Indian residents, from whom "Africans were fast learning bad habits." Theft became com-monplace, and the undermanned police force was kept constantly on its toes—to the point where it was "rare for an African constable to be able to depend on having a full night in bed." Roundups were frequent, often centering on Nairobi's sizable red-light district near Victoria Street. Here, said Foran, the "shocking lodgings ... provided a rendezvous for bad characters and a repository for stolen goods." Searches of the district uncovered a great deal of hot merchandise, while the prostitutes sometimes lent a hand as informers: "although a blot on Nairobi's social life, yet these women were useful to the police in this way."

Less cooperative was the wildlife which habitually roamed the streets of the town at night. Foran personally shot two lions—one as it tried to enter the post office. But game was a minor nuisance alongside the human scavengers. By 1910, Kenya's police blotter showed 2,400 arrests and 1,900 convictions. Malefactors might have begun asking themselves whether crime really paid.

Probably it did, for arrest–conviction ratios tell only part of any police story. The value of property theft in 1910 was estimated at £4,758, of which the police recovered £1,998, or less than half the total. And no statistics, of course, were available on the number of criminals who got away scot-free. Crime ran riot not only because the police had to carry out their duties with a badly understaffed force, but because they were also trying to deal with a population which saw nothing reprehensible in sharing the white man's worldly goods. How could the rich bwana suffer from the loss of trifles? It was common practice among Kikuyu household servants to borrow their employers' storeroom keys, have duplicates made by Indian locksmiths from wax models, and then help themselves to generous supplies of sugar, flour and tinned goods. Cash, clothing, watches and jewelry were also fair game. Yet within the framework of their own values, Africans considered themselves no less law-abiding than anyone else. Even when arrested, many tribesmen observed a certain code of honor. Not atypical was the behavior of an Mkamba whom Henry Seaton once tried and convicted of stock theft. While being escorted, handcuffed, to the Nairobi prison, the man broke away. "Within a week," wrote Seaton, "a messenger brought in the handcuffs to me with an apology from the thief. He had had difficulty in sliding them off or he would have returned them sooner. To suppose that this was a gesture of defiance or bravado would argue a complete misunderstanding of [his] moral code."

This man was unusual only in seeking to evade his sentence, for punishment in Kenya sometimes seemed to encourage rather than inhibit lawbreaking. "Certain irresponsible satirists," wrote Lord Cranworth, "divide the native population into two classes: those in prison and those who want to be." This was almost true. Inmates of the Protectorate's two main prisons in Nairobi and Mombasa led a comfortable and even enjoyable life. They received three meals daily, had beds and blankets, and regarded the broad arrows stenciled on their uniforms as high fashion. Hard labor usually entailed light gardening, bush clearing and occasional road building. Escape presented no problem, but it was a common joke—with more than a basis in fact—that prison officers had to be on guard for Africans trying to break in rather than out. To a people who lived in cramped, squalid hovels and who were no strangers to hunger or even famine, jail could hardly have seemed much different from a resort. Even after the First World War, when Africans had begun to acquire a Western distaste for incarceration, they continued to describe the Nairobi prison as the "Hoteli ya Kingi Georgi."

Gradually, however, the police were able to make their presence felt and to a certain degree respected. The institution of an embryonic fingerprint system facilitated arrests, and while petty thieves might have looked forward to holidays in jail, they began to think twice before contemplating graver offenses. Murderers in particular learned that capital punishment was not necessarily swift. For some years, executions (carried out by firing squad) were a police responsibility, and the force's malfunctioning Martini-Henry rifles could not be relied on to perform the task with despatch. Also, said Foran, "the marksmanship was deplorably bad," even though the squad took aim from only seventy-five feet at a white card pinned over the prisoner's heart. Eventually, a British officer and a sergeant-instructor joined the squad at each end, and this "fortunately made certain that death was instantaneous," but the executions remained an acutely unpleasant duty. Foran himself took part in a large number, "always with personal feelings of intense revulsion"; it was owing mainly to his official protests that the firing squad was finally replaced by the gallows. (Nairobi's first steamroller driver also became the first Government hangman.) "But even then," said Foran, "a few more executions by shooting were carried out by the Police ... and I was again unlucky enough to be detailed to perform these grim tasks."

The police in fact were expected to perform a galaxy of chores not normally associated with following clues and making arrests, and as Foran moved across the country from station to station, he came to look on his factotum function as a matter of course. Officers might be called on to supervise road repairs or bridge construction; the police "being neither road engineers nor bridge-builders," said Foran, "the results achieved were never much about which to feel proud." The force also lent an occasional hand to the understaffed agricultural department by inspecting settler farms and reporting on their progress in fulfilling the requirements of the development clauses in the leases. Foran found this work "rather farcical" but acknowledged that "in the end the Police learned a good deal about farming." Frequently the game department, also short on personnel, would send out an SOS to a police inspector, to despatch a cattle-killing or man-eating lion. Foran welcomed those assignments.

A less enjoyable responsibility was to stand in for absent doctors. Foran, whose knowledge of surgery was limited to the removal of his own hangnails, had on two occasions to perform emergency leg amputations in the bush. His instruments were a hunting knife, a kitchen meat saw and paper clips, the latter used as clamps on the severed arteries and veins. Anesthesia in both instances was a quart of raw whisky, which rendered each patient totally numb. "The first man died on the operating table (a kitchen table)," and "it was a miracle that the second man survived this crude operation performed by an ignorant amateur." At another time, Foran doubled as an obstetrician to a settler's wife when the doctor failed to arrive for her first childbirth. The labor was going badly, the woman was almost mad with pain, and her distraught husband begged Foran for assistance. "This was asking a bit too much of a young bachelor Police Officer only twenty-four years of age, but it was clearly incumbent upon me to do all that I could to help. Armed with a medicine chest and a veterinary book … the amateur midwife proceeded to follow the instructions given … for dealing with difficult cases of cows calving down. It was no time for modesty, sentimentality or bashfulness." It was also an all-night task. By dawn, when the doctor finally arrived, mother and child were doing well. In a slightly more official capacity, Foran once found himself playing the role of marriage counselor, when the wife of another settler sued her husband for divorce on grounds of non-consummation. "The instructions included … obtaining from her a full written statement of the evidence she could give in support of her action. Both of us felt extremely bashful and embarrassed during the interview, but the intimate details of the shattered romance were recorded faithfully. It was a relief to be able to depart. Duty is duty."

"So may all the King's enemies perish."

Sometimes it was not easy to distinguish between the duties of a constable and a soldier, for police detachments occasionally joined the Protectorate's small military force in punitive expeditions against certain tribes which did not welcome Pax Britannica with open arms. Actually, it was not often that the Administration found itself compelled to apply the stern measures which Britons referred to as "teaching the natives a lesson." It might be worth mentioning, moreover, that the term "punitive expedition" did not necessarily describe a massacre, at least in Kenya during the early days. Tribal casualties, in fact, were seldom if ever the objective of such operations. "In my experience," wrote Frederick Jackson, who saw more than his share of action, "no punitive measure ever resulted in the killing of many of the enemy ... As often as not they killed as many of the punitive force, and sometimes even more. Punishment was mostly confined to an attempt to capture their stock and, failing that, to the destruction of their huts and food supplies ... Even a short stay, living on the country, and keeping them on the move, was something they did not like; and it at least showed them that the invaders were not afraid of them." In all likelihood, far more blood flowed in Chicago's gangland wars of the 1920s than in east Africa at the turn of the century. Certainly the genocide attendant on the forcible subjugation of the American Indian made Britain's punitive expeditions in Kenya look almost like a game of cops and robbers.

Almost, that is; not quite, and both sides, when they chose, were capable of barbaric excesses. Yet by comparison with other British imperial annexations in Africa, the pacification of Kenya could be described as forbearing. When one considers the protracted, bloody campaigns against the Zulu and Matabele to the south, the half-century war against the Ashanti in the west, or even the relatively minor operations against Mwanga and Kabarega in Uganda, the sporadic displays of British armed might in Kenya seem negligible. One reason for this was the Administration's distaste for punitive expeditions, an official attitude which may have been shaped by Eliot. Martial exercises, he felt, should not be "allowed to override the greater claims of justice and good policy," especially if British objectives could be achieved by showing the flag rather than brandishing the saber. "What is wanted," he wrote, "is to impress the natives with our strength and our omnipresence, or at least our long reach. This is best done by sending frequent patrols through disturbed districts, which would not cost a single life, and by establishing numerous posts with as many European officers as possible." To great extent, Eliot's counsel was heeded faithfully by his successors in Government House.

But much more to the point, the Protectorate owed its peaceful climate to an uncommonly good-natured populace. Few Europeans on the spot would have disputed McGregor Ross' observation that "the region that we know as Kenya contains tribes of a comparative geniality of character that is not found in many other parts of Africa." The Masai were the classic illustration; we have already seen how this dreaded warrior nation accepted the fait accompli of British rule without a murmur. Had they chosen to resist, they would of course have been subdued by vastly superior armed strength, but their forcible domestication would also have meant strewing the land with the corpses of the tribe's elmoran and British askaris. Elspeth Huxley was not too far off the mark when she commented that "it is probable that no country in the Empire has ever been opened up and settled with so little bloodshed and with the maintenance of such friendly relations with the native population."

It would have been more gratifying if Mrs. Huxley could have added that the achievement was brought off without firing a shot, but no Briton was ever foolish enough to make that assertion. For one thing, the Administration found it necessary to keep the tribes from each other's throats, and this task alone required guns. Before the occupation of Kenya, and for some years afterwards, war was quite literally the national pastime, both as a means of acquiring livestock and as a sport. Some Europeans even seemed to consider the practice wholesome. Writing of "constant war on a small scale" for cattle in the Lumbwa district, Binks remarked that "no permanent hard feelings were engendered between the tribes as long as raiding was not carried to excess and no women were taken to threaten the fecundity of either tribe ... It was the pleasantest form of warfare I ever encountered and let off a good deal of high spirits." Officialdom, however, took a less accommodating attitude. From the very start, it was British policy to outlaw tribal vendettas. While serving in Kavirondo during the 1890s, Hobley found that strong-arm peacemaking occupied a great deal of his time. "It took a couple of years or more," he wrote, "to teach the various [clans] that they must give up their practice of raiding and murdering each other, and, on many occasions, I had to take out the bulk of my Sudanese garrison and forcibly stamp on these internecine struggles." Eventually he saw his efforts crowned with success: "The great point about the Kavirondo ... was that they were men. Once they were beaten they readily made peace and, once they had made peace, it was peace, for within a few hours the women were in camp selling food, and one had no anxiety about a subsequent treacherous attack ... Under these circumstances mutual respect gradually supervened and we became great friends."

Not every tribe, however, accepted its uninvited new rulers in quite so sporting a fashion, and while overt African defiance of the British never brought on Armageddon, it was spirited enough to justify a regular military establishment. This was the toy army known as the Third Battalion of the King's African Rifles, with a numerical strength ranging from between 800 to 1,200 men. In prestige, the 3rd KAR was the equatorial counterpart of the Grenadier Guards. Its discipline and esprit, wrote

Cranworth in 1912, were "so high that any other body must almost inevitably suffer if judged by the same standard." The troops had not always enjoyed this elite status; their tatterdemalion and mutinous predecessors, the Uganda Rifles, have already been described. But it has also been noted that the Sudanese who comprised the backbone of that corps were incomparable fighting men; these veterans brought the same warlike traditions to the reorganized battalion in which many of them served as NCOs or "effendis"—African officers. Not much less bellicose were the Kenya tribesmen who enlisted, conceivably to find a legitimate excuse for fighting in a country where clan warfare had been proscribed. Indeed, during the 3rd KAR's undisciplined infancy, sham battles often became alarmingly authentic as one platoon would try to wipe out another in a bayonet charge. Presently, however, the battalion's two dozen British officers, through endless drill and the sheer force of their personalities, were able to replace intramural antagonisms with a gung-ho spirit that stood the men in good stead when the real shooting began.

That esprit was needed. While rebellious tribesmen might have seemed hopelessly outmatched by Maxim guns and Sniders, they knew how to give as good (or almost as good) as they got. Seasoned guerrillas, fighting on their own terrain, they showed a natural gift for tactical maneuver which not infrequently confounded the attackers. They could outnumber Government troops by as much as twenty to one, and the 3rd KAR made a practice of reinforcing its own detachments with levies of Masai spearmen. Even the elmoran, however, provided no sure guarantee of quick victory. When the chips were down, Kenya's insurgent tribal warriors often showed themselves to possess a fund of suicidal courage that approached the berserk abandon of Pathans in the Khyber Pass or of the Sudan's Dervishes. They asked no quarter and gave none. To be an askari in the 3rd KAR, one had to be "kali kabisa"—a very tough customer.

*

We get a graphic picture of the battalion in action from the diaries of Captain Richard Meinertzhagen, who served with the 3rd KAR between 1902 and 1906 after being seconded from the Royal Fusiliers in India. Meinertzhagen's Teutonic name is deceptive, for he was slightly more English than the Christmas plum pudding which his mother always sent him from Mottisfont Abbey, the family's country manor in Hampshire. Alternately buoyant and brooding, Meinertzhagen was also "kali kabisa"—in word no less than in deed. "One of my worst faults," he wrote at this time, "is blurting out what I think, often regretting it a moment later ... But there it is, I cannot help my nature." On learning that Meinertzhagen was a nephew of the Fabian socialist Beatrice Webb, an intrigued Eliot hastened to invite the young officer to dinner at Government House and to speak admiringly of his aunt. Meinertzhagen dissented. "I said I thought she was doing a great deal of harm ... and that I thought Marxian socialism a foul infectious disease. Eliot snapped at me ... I like Eliot, but after tonight I doubt if he likes me." Meinertzhagen's constant squabbles, verbal and physical, with brother officers also led him to a whimsical note of self-analysis in verse:

> They say I'm a quarrelsome fellow.
> God rot it, how can that be?
> For I never quarrel with any,
> The whole world quarrels with me.

Few British officers in Africa upheld the imperial ideal with a more Kiplingesque fervor than Meinertzhagen. None may have shown as much dedication when it came to teaching the natives a lesson—although Meinertzhagen himself did not confine that punishment to fractious tribes alone. A rabble of baboons once tore his dog to pieces, and "when my first horror was over I sat down and contemplated how I could teach those baboons a lesson." He did, with the help of thirty askaris whose rifles decimated the horde. "We killed every full-grown male, and I was pleased."

Toward human foes, Meinertzhagen and his men could be equally merciless, as illustrated by random extracts from the journals he kept while in command of a 3rd KAR company in Kikuyuland between 1902 and 1904: "There was ... a rush from the village into the surrounding bush, and we killed about 17 niggers." ... "I was surprised at the ease with which a bayonet goes into a man's body. One scarcely feels it unless it goes in to the hilt." ... "I have performed a most unpleasant duty today ... I gave orders that every living thing [in a Kikuyu village] except children should be killed without mercy ... Every soul was either shot or bayoneted ... We systematically cleared the valley in which the village was situated, burned all the huts, and killed a few more niggers." ... "We poured a hail of bullets into the trees ... and as niggers showed themselves we picked them off with rifle fire. Five fell with sickening thuds ... Adams spotted another, so I told him to fire ... and down came the fellow within a few feet of us; but he was not dead and had his short sword still in his hand. Adams, before I could stop him, blew the fellow's brains out, and so close to me was his head that a hot fid of human brain hit me in the eye as the head was split open ..."

Taken from context, the above entries suggest that Meinertzhagen found nigger-hunting grand sport. He did not. Half a century later, when preparing the diaries for publication, he wrote: "I am shocked by the account of taking human life ... I do not pretend to excuse it, but perhaps I may explain it. I have no belief in the sanctity of human life or in the dignity of the human race. Human life has never been sacred; nor has man, except in a few exceptional cases, been dignified. Moreover, in Kenya fifty years ago, when stationed with 100 soldiers amid an African population of some 300,000, in cases of emergency where local government was threatened we had to act, and act quickly. To do nothing in an emergency is to do something definitely wrong." Every one of the incidents described above arose from an emergency. The Kikuyu clans which Meinertzhagen's troops subdued had defied the Government in a manner altogether uncongenial to peaceful negotiation. Several sections of the tribe had been ambushing caravans, murdering African policemen, mutilating their corpses and challenging the Administration to do something about it. Government was left with no choice but to act.

The Kikuyu did not capitulate supinely at the approach of the 3rd KAR detachment which was sent into their district. The paths leading to their villages were riddled with hidden pitfalls in which the warriors placed sharp wooden stakes on which to impale unwary attackers. Tribesmen could ambush an invading column with the silent swiftness of a cobra striking, while the accuracy of their spears and the lethal bite of their poisoned arrows earned the unqualified respect of African askari and British officer alike. When camping for the night, Meinertzhagen's unit did not merely gird its bivouac with the usual thorn boma but added at least two outer rings of barbed wire entanglement. In combat, the Kikuyu warriors were capable of advancing under blizzards of massed rifle fire and dying on the points of askari bayonets to crack the Government defense lines. Following a typically hot engagement near Nyeri, Meinertzhagen wrote that "we decided we cannot continue operations, after our rather heavy casualties, unless we receive another 200 Masai spearmen, and until my company is made up to strength." There was no such thing as a Geneva Convention in Kikuyuland. A wounded Government soldier, unless rescued by his comrades, could generally count on being speared or clubbed to death on the field. No one liked to think much about Kikuyu treatment of prisoners. Meinertzhagen's no-quarter massacre, a barbaric reprisal by any standards (he later wrote that it "haunted me for many years") was ordered after a Kikuyu clan had committed an atrocity of its own. One suspects that Meinertzhagen may have gone temporarily insane on learning that "the natives caught a settler ... and ... dragged him to a village near the forest, where they pegged him down and wedged his mouth open; then the whole village, man, woman and child, urinated into his mouth until he was drowned."

*

While undeniably ferocious, Kikuyu intransigence seldom amounted to much more than a nuisance in official eyes; the rebellious elements of the tribe were too far removed from Nairobi and the railway to cause lasting damage. Meinertzhagen's expeditions against those clans were in a sense rehearsals for his personal showdown with the only real threat to lasting peace in Kenya—the Nandi. After more than a decade of British rule, this tribe was evincing little disposition to acknowledge the white overlord. Its attitude was largely the fruit of appeasement. We have already seen how a punitive campaign against the Nandi had been called off in 1900, out of fear that large-scale hostilities might delay completion of the railway. As a consequence of that act, the Nandi regarded themselves as victors, a superior force, and saw no reason to cooperate with Government. The tribe could put at least 8,000 spear-men into the field, and by way of asserting their national independence, these warriors staged sporadic but vigorous demonstrations against both the Administration and the settlers. By 1903, it had become nec-essary to defend the railway against Nandi raids. All stations between the top of the Mau escarpment and Kisumu were protected by barbed wire fences and entanglements. Troops of the 3rd KAR patrolled the line itself, although they were not always able to prevent Nandi flying columns from removing fishplates, fishbolts, steel sleepers and even sections of rail, which were forged into spearheads and stabbing swords. Trains were prohibited from passing through Nandi country at night; passengers bound for the lake had a weary layover in Nakuru. Armed askaris often rode locomotives and brake vans during the day-light hours, re-creating the uneasy climate of rail travel in Sioux and Apache territory a generation earlier.

For the first five years of the twentieth century, European farming near the Nandi region was hazardous in the extreme. When Meinertz-hagen was transferred from Kikuyuland to Nandi in 1904, he called the Government "absurd" for allowing any colonists in, "as the country is by no means safe." The few homesteaders who took the risk did not prosper, the Nandi stealing their cattle almost openly and with clock-work regularity. Even Delamere's Equator Ranch, although situated more than forty miles from the disturbed area, had its outer perimeter scouted by Nandi rustlers. Another stockman saw two of his Masai herdsmen and a personal servant become pincushions for Nandi spears in broad daylight, barely a stone's throw from his veranda. He himself had a close call when a pair of "friendly" elders presented him with a pot of honey. He offered some to a pet monkey which promptly spat it out; subsequent laboratory analysis in Nairobi showed the gift to con-tain a deadly poison. The Nandi also took every opportunity to express their contempt for local officialdom and its laws. On one occasion, a British District Officer is said to have sent his African clerk to a Nandi village with a formal demand for delinquent hut tax payment, only to see the clerk's head returned in a sack to the Government boma with the message: "Here is the hut tax of the Nandi."

This sort of behavior could not, of course, be tolerated indefinitely. That the Nandi had been allowed so free a rein for so long a time may have been due in part to Eliot's distaste for vigorous military action, but after 1904, with the appointment of the less forbearing Sir Donald Stew-art, Government's attitude began to stiffen. In Meinertzhagen's diary we observe the buildup of events to the inevitable collision. "There is little doubt," he wrote in June, 1905, "that the Nandi are brewing up for trou-ble and are daily becoming more daring ... Murders and raids are being reported from every part of the district, and the country is undoubtedly in a most disturbed state." Among the murder victims were an American Quaker missionary, two African policemen and one of Meinertzha-gen's own askaris. By mid-July, Stewart himself entrained for the Nandi region, summoned the tribe's elders to a baraza and warned them against further lawlessness. According to Meinertzhagen, the elders "complained that they could not hold back the young hotheads in their tribes who were clamouring for war, also that the Laibon or chief medicine man was preaching war against the Government and teaching his people all sorts of nonsense, persuading them that our bullets turn to water when fired at a Nandi, that we dare not fight them, etc." Meinertzhagen was not impressed. Nor was Stewart. "The Commissioner seems to think that a large military expedition will be necessary, and he is probably right. I should dearly like to take on the young men of Nandi and smash them up, as they are becoming too full of themselves."

Harassment continued, however. No annoyance seemed too petty to be overlooked. Nandi children pelted Meinertzhagen's house with stones, wooden clubs and arrows "which make a great noise on my tin roof." Exasperated, he ordered his men to catch a few of the young offenders. "I locked them up in the guard room and gave them bananas and a blanket each ... They were shaking with fright, thinking they would be killed. As I suspected, they had been told to do it by agents of [the chief Laibon]. I got my colour-sergeant to give each boy 7 hard smacks on the bottom, while I made the girl dig in my garden ... I dismissed them all with a rupee each." But the tribe did not confine its defiance to acts of juvenile delinquency. Meinertzhagen's detachments were continually harried on the march by Nandi war parties which usually outnumbered them by at least four to one. Exchanges of rifle fire and poisoned arrows were common. Meinertzhagen closed down the road between Nandi Fort and the Kibigori railway station, allowing only a heavily escorted mail party to make the twenty-mile journey once a week. Bagge, the Provincial Commissioner, told Meinertzhagen that tribal pillaging kept him from any constructive work with the Kavirondo, who comprised the great majority of the region's populace; "the very name Nandi stinks in his nostrils."

On August 13, 1905, Stewart finally laid it on the line: if the Nandi did not pay a fine of three hundred head of cattle within three weeks, a punitive expedition would be mounted against them. "I am convinced," wrote Meinertzhagen, "that the Nandi will roar with laughter at such a proposal."

By this time, Meinertzhagen had begun to entertain second thoughts on the wisdom of a punitive campaign. He was becoming increasingly convinced that if the chief Laibon, a man named Koitalel, were put out of the way, the mainspring in the machinery of Nandi defiance would be snapped. Koitalel, he wrote, "is a wicked old man and at the root of all our trouble. He is a dictator, and as such must show success in order to retain power ... My main reason for trying to kill or capture the Laibon is that, if I remove him, [the] expedition will not be necessary." Late in September, more than two weeks after Stewart's ultimatum deadline had passed, Meinertzhagen learned from spies that Koitalel "has just convened a representative meeting of the whole Nandi tribe, at which it was decided that the British Government was afraid of the Nandi, that no expedition would take place, and that therefore the Nandi must renew their aggressive tactics and drive all Government officials and troops from the district." The delegates also agreed that Meinertzhagen was to be their principal target, since Koitalel had told them "that the white man's bullets will be quite harmless if only he can get bits of my anatomy for his medicine, especially my brains, heart, liver, palms of the hands and eyes." To accomplish this, "he is going to pose as a peacemaker [and] entice me out to an ambush." Entertaining a similar plan for Koitalel, Meinertzhagen approved. "The situation now resolves itself into a personal quarrel between me and the Laibon, and I will bet a small sum that he falls first."

Meanwhile, preparations were under way for the long-awaited punitive expedition. The Nandi Field Force was to be the mightiest military aggregation that had ever been mobilized in Kenya, with the 3rd KAR beefed up by troops from Uganda and Nyasaland, a large police detachment and 1,000 Masai levies among others—to a total strength of over 3,200 officers and men. The diminutive phalanx also boasted two armored railway trains, and the officers adopted the practice of sending messages in French, since no code had been issued. ("It is well," remarked Meinertzhagen, "that a short telegraphic message hides many grammatical errors and lack of accent.") At Nandi Fort, Meinertzhagen did not neglect to stiffen his own defenses, issuing single-loading Martinis to his sixty porters and putting them through target practice. "To give them confidence I started them firing at 50 yards at kerosene tins filled with water, which goes up in a spout when hit ... I have christened them the 'New Army.' They are rather an undisciplined rabble but can shoot quite well and are keen as mustard ... But when it comes to using their rifles in action I am sure they will fire wildly, eager to make as much noise as possible, regardless of hitting anything."

During this interval of saber rattling, Meinertzhagen's principal objective, Koitalel, was by no means forgotten. Nor was Meinertzhagen forgotten by Koitalel, although it is hard to say which of the two men was scheming more inventively. When Meinertzhagen discovered that the Government interpreter at Nandi Fort was a member of Koitalel's family who had been planted as a spy, he at once began fabricating reports of British plans and movements which were faithfully relayed to the enemy. At the same time, his own agents were busy in the Nandi camp. Among other things, he learned from them that "a very beautiful young virgin is to be sent to me from the Laibon and she carries with her some deadly poison which she will place in my food. Should this young lady arrive she will be searched, and if poison is found on her she will get 25 of the best on her bottom with my hand." He did not keep his word. When a quick frisk revealed a packet of poison, "the poor child broke down, fell flat on the ground, seized my feet and howled for mercy. I had not the heart to punish her, so sent her back with a message to the Laibon recommending him to take the stuff himself."

The sparring came to an end on December 18. A meeting between the two men had been arranged for the following day, ostensibly to discuss peace, although neither party appears to have given that topic much thought. By now it was too late to halt the expedition, but Meinertzhagen nonetheless felt that the Laibon's removal would take the edge off the Nandi will to resist, and that the military operation would thus be less damaging to both sides. Although each man had agreed to an escort of no more than five soldiers, Meinertzhagen learned that Koitalel had also arranged for "a considerable body of men" to launch an ambush from concealment. The news did not trouble him. "Come what will, I meet him tomorrow, and during the next 24 hours I suspect that either he or I will have said goodbye to this world. I do not really very much care which of us it is."

*

It had been agreed that the meeting would be held near a place called Kaidparak Hill. On the morning of the 19th, accompanied by about 75 askaris, Meinertzhagen approached the site. Halting the men, he ordered them to await his return, covering his retreat if he was seen to be under attack. Koitalel was then observed at a distance, and Meinertzhagen left his own column, taking with him a Sudanese officer, a corporal and three askaris. The countdown began.

Meinertzhagen's official report describes the ensuing events. "We approached with rifles at full cock and loaded, also with bayonets fixed. I told my men to fire the moment treachery was apparent, but that I hoped to have a peaceful meeting. On advancing into full view of the Laibon it was clear that he had some 50 armed men around him.... The bush all round bristled with spears and shields. I halted my small party within four paces of the Laibon and asked him to come forward and shake hands. He replied that the sun was too hot, which, of course, was a ridiculous statement from a native. I also considered it wrong that a white man should have to make advances to a native, so I replied, 'Very well, we will conduct our conversation at this distance. Shall we sit down?' No sooner was this interpreted than the Laibon made a quick sign with his spear and an arrow pierced the sleeve of my shirt. The interpreter wheeled round on me, making as if to strike me with his spear, but was instantly shot by my corporal. I seized the Laibon and dragged him forward, getting scratched by his spear, and an arrow knocked off my helmet ... I am unable to state with certainty what followed. The Laibon was shot simultaneously by myself and my native officer, and several dead were left at the meeting place." The party withdrew under a hail of poisoned arrows and barely managed to reach Nandi Fort in safety. Here, Meinertzhagen was not too exhausted to declare in his diary: "So may all the King's enemies perish."

The impact of the duel made itself felt almost at once. That very night, Meinertzhagen learned from his African agents that "the death of the Laibon has completely knocked the stuffing out of the Nandi and has left them without a head ... From all accounts there will not be much serious resistance ... They now appear to have some respect for us." Actually, the tribe showed a surprisingly stiff backbone. As the Nandi Field Force deployed along the railway line and moved north into the enemy's country, it found itself pursuing a will-o'-the-wisp with fangs. The Nandi showed a gift for shrewd evasive tactics as they utilized the natural cover of tall grass and forest to great advantage. Nandi combat teams also launched more than one savage hit-and-run attack which left the invaders smarting. Meinertzhagen himself became a minor casualty when a poisoned arrow pierced the fleshy part of his thumb; in ten minutes, his entire hand turned black; nearly a week went by before he could use it normally. And almost three months passed before the Nandi finally accepted the Government's surrender terms and moved into a reserve. From that time on, they became law-abiding hut taxpayers and the colony witnessed no further serious tribal upheavals until Mau Mau half a century later. It is altogether likely, however, that the Nandi Field Force would have found itself with a much tougher nut to crack if Meinertzhagen had not disposed of the enemy's human doomsday weapon on the eve of the campaign.

The Administration seemed to agree at first, when Meinertzhagen was recommended for the Victoria Cross. Although he thought this was "making too much of so small an affair," he was even less pleased when rumors began to circulate that he had purposely lured the Laibon into a trap and shot him in cold blood without any intention of making an arrest. Furious, he demanded a court of inquiry which cleared him at once. But the rumors persisted, and although Meinertzhagen was entirely vindicated by two more courts, an uneasy Colonial Office finally concluded that his continued service in Kenya would be "undesirable." He returned in 1914, as intelligence officer with the British force which invaded German East Africa, and later fought in the Middle East with Lawrence.* In 1956, he revisited Nandi, where, at

---

* This campaign helped convert Meinertzhagen to Zionism. In 1948, at the age of seventy, while passing through Palestine, he attached himself to a Haganah patrol, killed three Arabs with a borrowed rifle in a skirmish and wrote in his diary: "Altogether I had a glorious day. May Israel flourish!"

a parish meeting, an elder named Elijah introduced him to other prominent tribesmen. "When we arrived at the final chief, a young and extremely
good-looking young man, Elijah to my horror said: 'This is the gentleman
who shot your grandfather.' This was greeted with much clapping."

"Every white man in Nairobi is a politician."

While preserving order was of course very much in the interest of the
white farmer community, the colonists often seemed less than grateful
to the fellow Britons who laid down the ground rules of harmonious
coexistence in Kenya. Wrath over Government's apparent indifference
to the settlers' future has already been noted in the outburst that
followed the Foreign Office overture to the Zionists. Other frustrations
stemmed from petty land regulations and similar bureaucratic obstacles.
These were not merely affronts and inconveniences, but manifestations
of a deeper ideological conflict which aroused bitter antagonisms
between administrator and colonist for more than three decades. It was
a struggle between what might be called benevolent despotism and
benevolent feudalism.

Officialdom was the despot. The Government literally owned east
Africa and for many years laid down its laws without the advice or consent of the people—white, black or brown—who lived there. Elspeth
Huxley has drawn a parallel between the early colonial administration
in Kenya and the government of the Soviet Union, but has also pointed
to a significant dissimilarity. "Socialism," she observes, "is a system primarily devised for the just distribution of wealth rather than for the
creation of it ... But in an undeveloped country, where wealth has still to
be created, socialism must either go forward courageously and shoulder
all the risks and losses of development (as in Russia) or it must retreat
and call upon the private individual for help." Although the British Government in Kenya opted, as Mrs. Huxley notes, for the latter course, its
unwillingness to share its powers seriously impeded the settlers' efforts
to make the Protectorate economically viable: "Once having called upon
individualism, there was a price to pay. If the individual was to take all
the risks he was entitled to ask for a certain liberty of action." That liberty, however, was not immediately granted: Government "called in the
piper and was reluctant to pay for the tune."

This at any rate was how the feudal settler looked at his dilemma.
For men and women who had committed their lives and fortunes to

Kenya, there was something that smacked of tyranny in being compelled to comply with restrictive laws framed by a transient civil servant class which was unaffected by its own legislation. As Seaton put it, "what was any Government official, in [the colonists'] view, but a bird of passage? He had no stake in the country ... He was a parasite who drew a salary provided out of local revenue and spent as much of it as he could afford in importing food and drink from Fortnum and Mason." Government had asked for English farmers to develop Kenya, but when the settlers arrived they found an Administration which appeared bent on forestalling that development. Their hopes had soared when the dead hand of the Foreign Office was removed in 1905, but the transfer of control to the Colonial Office witnessed no radical policy volte-face. As it happened, the changeover coincided with the return to power of the Liberal party in Britain, but while the Campbell-Bannerman and Asquith Ministries showed none of the revulsion for imperial holdings which had marked Gladstone's sway, it became clear that not all of the party's earlier reservations about white settlement in Africa had vanished entirely. Under the Colonial Secretary, Lord Elgin, and his successor, Lord Crewe, Government appeared quite loath to dilute its absolute authority over Kenya. As a consequence, the settlers went into politics with a vengeance.

It could hardly have failed to happen. "The settler," as Mervyn Hill has noted, "was always in contact with the Government ... The very closeness of this contact made argument inevitable, and argument meant politics." Nor were the colonists entirely new to the game. From the very beginning, the dream of someday becoming a vest-pocket New Zealand or Canada had animated them to seek a share in running the country. As early as 1902, they had petitioned the Foreign Office for appointment of a Settler Advisory Council, the plea being based on the time-tested rallying cry of no taxation without representation. But since they somehow overlooked the fact that they paid no taxes, their argument fell on deaf ears in Whitehall. Even Eliot, who advocated such a council "for the general control of local matters," found himself compelled to remark that "it is almost absurd for the present settlers to talk about their rights. They are so few ... that they can hardly logically claim to have a voice in the destinies of the country which expends hundreds of thousands on it every year." Sir Donald Stewart put it more briefly in 1904, when a colonist deputation called on him with another proposal for representative government. "Not while I'm here, gentlemen," he said, ending the interview.

But the embattled farmers were nothing if not tenacious, and they had a born leader in Delamere. "In the settlers' opinion," Mrs. Huxley has written, "he was just the man to deal with the more autocratic among the officials. He would stand up to them ... He had a quick intelligence—the brain of a debater, which seizes points in a flash and uses them to its own advantage. As a member of the Upper House he could gain access to the Secretary of State. But over and above these things he had ... the power of imposing his will on others and of inspiring faith that what he did was right." Delamere could also display a sense of proportion not always found in his fellow colonists. To be sure, this moderation often succumbed to his apoplectic temper, as we shall shortly see, but he understood no less clearly the meaning of politics as the art of the possible, and he was generally able to curb his turbulent emotions in the interests of realistic diplomacy. Once, when the settlers demanded that the Colonial Office appoint him Governor, he quashed the motion so tactfully that the act of almost unprecedented gall was quickly forgotten. Even after the bitterest outburst against any official, his thoroughly disarming apologies made it impossible for the victim to hold the slightest personal grudge. Delamere may have been the Administration's angriest and most forceful antagonist, but he was never its enemy.

The settlers also possessed the nucleus of a political machine. This body, originally known as the Farmers' and Planters' Association, had been founded in 1903 to seek a market for Kenya potatoes, but by 1905 its name had been changed to the Colonists' Association, and its function had in effect become that of a lobby. Under Delamere's presidency, the Association bombarded both the Foreign and Colonial Offices with recommendations and complaints touching on almost every aspect of policy in the Protectorate. It also continued to press for a formal settler role in the Administration, and in due course its nagging began to bear fruit. In 1905, Stewart died of pneumonia (aggravated, it is said, by alcoholic poisoning), and his successor, Sir James Hayes-Sadler, recommended to the Colonial Office that some sort of lawmaking body, with settler representation, be created. His objective may have been—at least in part—to throw the colonists a bone, to reduce the shrill clamor of their incessant kibitzing, and there is little doubt that the Colonial Office read that motive into the proposal. In any case, Elgin accepted the idea, and in August, 1907, Kenya's first Legislative Council met. It was composed of six Government officials and two "unofficials," that is, colonists appointed by the Governor. It was the embryo of a parliament, and as such could be considered a milestone in the settlers' progress toward self-rule. Delamere of course was the first unofficial member to be chosen.

Within four months he had resigned. "I object," he said, "to going back to school and it seems to me a farce that I should be asked to sit for several days listening to an estimate of expenditure which has been already definitely settled beforehand, and I cannot see that any useful purpose is to be served by my doing so." After some persuasion, he consented to take his seat again, and indeed he probably had no intention of remaining absent long, since resignation in protest proved to be one of Delamere's most useful political ploys. "No count has been kept," wrote McGregor Ross twenty years later, "of the number of times that Lord Delamere has resigned from various bodies in East Africa ... the threat has often sufficed to effect compliance with his wishes." In this, his first threat, he was seeking to dramatize what he and most other settlers not incorrectly regarded as the Colonial Office's exploitation of the Legislative Council as a political tool rather than a constitutional instrument. By allowing the colonists a token voice in their own affairs, London simply hoped to divert the tide of a mounting opposition which in time might interfere, so it was thought, with the orderly conduct of government in Kenya. The official, though unspoken, position was that the Legislative Council would enable the settlers to let off steam but exercise little if any real power. Elgin made this clear enough as the Colonists' Association began pressing for elective rather than nominative membership at the earliest possible time. "Anything except Crown Colony Government," he said in reply to one such petition, "cannot be a matter of practical policy for many years to come." Churchill also threw cold water on the instant dominion idea. "We must all admit," he said at a banquet in his honor in Mombasa, "that it will be a long time before responsible government can be granted." He added, however, that elective representation need not be ruled out "as a future goal."

On the surface, that future might have seemed generations distant. Not only did the settlers constitute a microscopic minority but splits were beginning to appear in their ranks by 1907, owing partly to the feeling of some colonists that Delamere, of all people, was not taking a sufficiently militant stand. Churchill voiced mild incredulity over what struck him as a proliferation of splinter groups. "Every white man in Nairobi," he wrote, "is a politician; and most of them are leaders of parties. One would scarcely believe it possible, that a centre so new should be able to develop so many divergent and conflicting interests, or that a community so small should be able to give to each such vigorous and even vehement expression." But the rifts were deceptive. If the settlers could quarrel among themselves over leadership, they remained united in their resolve to attain white home rule, and did not ease the pressure of their demands for constitutional advances toward that end. Nor could the Colonial Office stand totally aloof to their claims, valid or otherwise. In the final analysis, it was the plows of the homesteaders, not the pens of the administrators, which would turn the country's soil to a profit for the Empire. This self-evident fact alone gave the colonists a political leverage which in turn enabled them to wield an influence far out of proportion to their insignificant numbers. Their progress, however, was not always visible, and at times—especially during the infancy of the Legislative Council—they might have wondered whether they had not fared better under the Foreign Office. Land laws remained especially onerous. Elgin, adhering to a popular Henry George principle, sought for Government a share in the unearned increment from settler holdings. His most controversial move toward that end was the restriction of grazing leases to twenty-one years; at the end of that period, the land, including all the improvements made on it at the colonist's expense, would revert to the Crown, with no compensation to the lessee. In effect, the rancher would be evicted summarily from his own home without any assurance that he could even recover his initial investment. This disincentive to development met with such stiff resistance, not only from settlers but officials as well, that Elgin was eventually forced to back down and approve ninety-nine-year leases. (In 1915 tenure was extended to 999 years.) But the colonists continued to inveigh against other restraints. A particularly sore spot was Elgin's refusal to abolish stringent curbs on the transfer of land holdings, claiming that this would lead to "the evils of unrestricted speculation." In fact no one, least of all the settlers, wished to see the speculator run rampant through the highlands, but the farming community held that the practical effect of Elgin's policy would be to discourage any land sales whatever. Vainly did Delamere remind the Colonial Secretary of "the first principle of a successful sale, that you must get a buyer." He also pointed out that in a time of depression it might just be possible that "speculation is preferable to no business at all." Yet land transfer prohibitions remained in force for many years.

*

Numerous other obstacles worked against progress on the land. Government encouraged the building of fences around ranches rather than the increase of the livestock. An acute shortage of surveyors continued to block the occupation of farms, and queues of landless landholders remained a fixture outside the Land Office in Nairobi. Although some of the more irrational laws were occasionally repealed, others were not, and the settlers protested in appropriate pioneer fashion. One farmer whose land application was disputed by the Colonial Office built a strong fence around his farmhouse, loaded a pair of revolvers and announced that any official found "trespassing" would be shot. He held the fort for five years, at the end of which time the Government waived its claim. On another occasion, the fine print in the land laws revealed a clause designating clay as a precious mineral and forbidding its use without a mining license. Armed with this legal inanity, Ewart Grogan proceeded to stake out a claim to Nairobi; the statute was amended only minutes before he began digging an open shaft on Government Road. The Administration once ordered Delamere to change the location of a public flour mill he was building; the site, it appeared, was to become a park at some unspecified future date. Delamere is said to have responded by recruiting several dozen Africans, handing each a rupee and a box of matches and instructing them to set fire to the Land Office. When smoke began to curl up through the building's floorboards, it was hastily decided that the mill need not be moved.

Land was not the only area in which officialdom appeared to be throttling colonist enterprise. In 1903, control of the railway had passed from the Railway Committee to the Protectorate Administration, and one might have expected that whatever profits the line yielded would be plowed back into the development of the country. This was not to be: liquidation of the annual grant-in-aid must come first, and all earnings from the railway, however meager, were siphoned off into the British Treasury. Funds were not even set aside for maintenance of rolling stock and other facilities, and the result was a steady deterioration of freight and passenger service; timetables became meaningless. The worst aspect of this policy, from the settlers' point of view, was that it forced freight charges up and thus militated against the growth of the colony's infant agriculture. Railway officials themselves tended to concur. "Although a railway officer's business is to take what the traffic can bear," wrote the line's Acting Manager in 1906, "it is possibly not in the best interests of the country. The Uganda Railway was not projected as a money-earning system, its aims are far broader, the development of a new country, and if I dare offer any opinion, it is that the smaller the surplus over the working expenses for the next few years the better."

Certainly it was only right and proper that the British taxpayer be relieved of his burden, and indeed the settlers themselves were no less eager to do away with the grant-in-aid; "when they no longer exist on charity," wrote Cranworth, "the white population are likely to get a more just appreciation from the Colonial Office of their legitimate demands." But as the colonists saw it, the obligation would be discharged more

swiftly if their farm exports were allowed to grow without the artificial handicap of excessive transport charges. A heavy "down" traffic
was the sine qua non of prosperity in Kenya, but so long as the Treasury insisted on its pound of flesh, the country's industry would crawl.
This view, too, was shared by railwaymen. "If the export trade is to be
developed," stated the 1909 report of the line's Manager, H.A.F. Currie,
"... we must quote rates on the railway which will enable the settlers
to grow large quantities [of produce] with the assurance that they can
get them conveyed to Mombasa with a safe margin of profit ... I have
for years unsuccessfully advocated the reduction of down freights on
country produce in order to develop an export trade." Even Elgin, who
antagonized the colonists on land questions and other policy matters,
took their part on the railway issue, remarking that "the Treasury do
not go so far as to kill the goose that lays the golden eggs, but they delay
the hatching."

*

Land and transportation, however, were at least available. The same
could not always be said of labor, and it was over the question of labor
recruitment that the colonist locked horns most frequently—and most
furiously—with the Administration. On the face of it, the issue seemed
clear enough. European crops could not be grown without a regular and
reliable supply of African field hands. Tribal labor existed in abundance,
and farm workers could expect to receive a decent wage from the settlers. The only difficulty was that the Africans, for the most part quite
content with their subsistence economy, had little real incentive to leave
their own fields and villages. They would accept employment, perhaps,
for the few weeks it took them to earn their hut tax payments, but after
that, indifference set in. It was not uncommon for a European farmer to
lose his crop for want of manpower to harvest it; sometimes he could not
even get his fields plowed. This would never do, and the settlers turned
to the Administration for assistance. Having been invited to Kenya by
a Government which required their know-how to put the country on
its feet, the colonists assumed that that Government would at least recip-
rocate with a helping hand in labor recruitment. The enormous influence
wielded among Africans by local officials was well known. Conversant
with tribal custom, usually on the best of terms with headmen and
elders, the "bush D.O." could be expected to perform wonders in overcoming the African's natural reluctance to till another man's soil. Quite
correctly, the colonists believed that a few encouraging words from this

man to the Africans in his district would greatly facilitate the flow of labor to the white farms and ranches. It seemed no more than a simple obligation, serving the best interests not only of the settler but of the Government itself.

No such assistance was forthcoming. Encouragement, however mild, smacked of coercion. It was all very well for Churchill to declare: "I am clearly of opinion that no man has a right to be idle ... and I do not except the African native," but to Churchill's party, the Kenya labor question was a very hot potato. Already under heavy fire in the early 1900s for the conditions of Chinese mine workers in South Africa, the Colonial Office was acutely sensitive even to the faintest suggestion that it might be condoning "forced labor." Indeed, considering the out-spoken views of a small but vocal minority among the settlers, these apprehensions could at least be appreciated. "A good sound system of compulsory labour," wrote Ewart S. Grogan, "would do more to raise the nigger in five years than all the millions that have been sunk in mis-sionary efforts for the past fifty ... Let the native be compelled to work so many months in the year at a fixed and reasonable rate and call it compulsory education, as we call our weekly bonnet parades church. Under such a title, surely the most delicate British consciences may be at rest." And given such candor, it was hardly surprising that the Kenya Administration tended to stay out of the labor market.

This naturally angered the colonists, who claimed that the African population would interpret official silence as official disapproval. The hands-off policy also led to abuses, among which was the settler practice of engaging professional labor recruiters who received commissions for each African farm worker signed up. The recruiter was not always overly fastidious in the methods he adopted to earn his fee, whether this meant bullyragging chiefs and headmen or masquerading as a Government official. Settlers themselves sometimes harried local administrators in person. "District officers stationed in combined black and white areas," wrote Seaton, "... were under pressure to recruit farm labour for which there was never any sanction. Their position was very difficult. Tension at times rose high." Backlash thus became inevitable. Officials sought to keep the recruiters from approaching the Africans in their districts. One top-level Government officer went so far as to advise the Kikuyu, the principal labor source, against working on European farms. A crisis was in the making.

It came to a head in 1908, when a deputation of settlers, led by Delamere, met in Nairobi with Hayes-Sadler to seek a clarification of Administration labor policy. Two years earlier, a Masters and Servants

Ordinance had laid down minimum wage and ration levels and established other working standards on white farms, but it did not spell out to the colonists' satisfaction the Government position on recruitment, and labor shortages had become acute. There was also a noticeable shortage of tempers at the meeting, which happened to be held in the last week of March, when the big rains were due but showed no signs of arriving. Delamere may have set the tone of the discussions when he told Hayes-Sadler: "I feel so strongly about this matter that I cannot speak about it." Nor, apparently, could Hayes-Sadler. Known to settlers and officials alike as "Flannelfoot," this man may have been the least articulate civil servant ever to hold a high post in the British Empire. His fumbling, incoherent statement so baffled and enraged the deputation that it met again the same day and converged on Government House in what almost amounted to a mob. According to Hayes-Sadler's official report, "Lord Delamere ... addressed me in an excited and offensive manner ... [He] burst out with: 'to-morrow, to-morrow, it is always to-morrow, we are sick of to-morrows; we are not schoolboys, we demand an immediate answer on the spot and nothing else,' or words to that effect." Delamere's tantrum is said to have been followed by shouts of "Resign!" from the throng. A colonial Governor being the direct representative of the Crown, this was tantamount to demanding the King's abdication.

The Colonial Office did not take it lying down. Delamere was immediately suspended from the Legislative Council for six months. In London, Churchill called the meeting an "organised demonstration of an insulting and disorderly character." Charges were made in Parliament that the settlers had tried to coerce Hayes-Sadler into adopting a forced labor policy. This was altogether untrue; their purpose had simply been to learn the Government's position on recruiting, if indeed a position existed. But there could be no denying that the farmers had given a consummate performance as hooligans. A highly confidential despatch went out from the Colonial Office to Hayes-Sadler, describing the settler community as "a source of danger to the order and good government of the protectorate," and seeking "an expression of your opinion as to the desirability and feasibility ... of repatriating them." Perhaps characteristically, Hayes-Sadler submitted a tardy and inconclusive reply, in which he also admitted that the highlands had suffered a "serious falling off in the supply of labour." Nothing ever came of the expulsion proposal, but the very fact that the colonists could verge on becoming persona non grata in their own home only dramatized the intensity of their feelings toward officialdom on the labor issue.

"I am convinced that in the end the Africans will win."

The farmers' confrontation with Hayes-Sadler also underlined a more fundamental question: in whose interests was Kenya being governed? Despite the occasional punitive expedition against some unruly tribe or clan, it can be said that most officials in the Protectorate considered themselves primarily responsible for advancing the rights and welfare of the African population. But this was sharply at variance with the settler position that white claims must receive precedence. From the outset, the view had been expressed forthrightly by the colonists' lonely champion, Eliot, when he wrote the Foreign Secretary, Lord Lansdowne, in 1904: "I think it is well that, in confidential correspondence, at least, we should face the undoubted issue—viz. that white mates black in very few moves." In one respect, that stand was not altogether untenable, since nearly all Europeans, whether settlers or officials, agreed that even the most spectacular African agricultural advances could not match the output of white farms for many years; and farm production, after all, was not merely the mainstay of Kenya's future prosperity but in a sense its very raison d'être. Less realistically, however, the settler also argued that the African's role must be confined almost exclusively to that of field hand in white employ, that attempts to develop tribal agriculture were drying up the flow of the labor supply. Cranworth characterized Ainsworth's achievements with the Kavirondo as "exploiting ... a tribe to the detriment of the European." In vain did Ainsworth and other officials point out that the bulk of labor on colonist farms came from the most advanced reserves; in the myopically contemptuous view of the settler, such arguments simply labeled Ainsworth and his ilk as "pro-native."

Although typifying the racial arrogance of the era, this attitude was not shaped by cruel or vicious motives. The notion of the African as drone arose in large part from the settlers' legitimate need for a work force. But the white outlook in Kenya was also compounded by less edifying influences, the most conspicuous, perhaps, being a fear of "native uprisings" that bordered on psychosis. No matter that Eliot himself had voiced "little apprehension of a general uprising of natives against Europeans;" the conditioned reflexes generated by the Zulu and Ashanti wars—not to mention occasional Kikuyu or Nandi atrocities—died hard in the colonist mentality. Indicative of this uneasiness was a petition of settlers to the Colonial Office in 1905, warning of a steady erosion of white prestige, increasing African "insolence," an impending "human volcano" and the consequent need for fortifications and a "Burgher force" to protect white women and children. As late as 1912, Cranworth could write that "were the native population to make a sudden and treacherous attack on the peaceful inhabitants of [Nairobi], the garrison would be powerless to check them."

This sort of thing was poppycock; there is no other word for it. And yet, as long as the phobia persisted, it was accompanied by a no less neurotic conviction that the African must be held in a state of absolute subservience, that even the slightest display of "cheek" must be dealt with firmly. In 1907—again, the month was March—three Nairobi rickshaw boys, suspected of behaving "insolently" to several European women, were seized by a group of settlers and publicly flogged in front of the courthouse despite the enraged protests of the magistrate. At hearings of a labor commission in the same year, several European witnesses freely acknowledged the application of muscle or physical threat to keep their field hands in line. McGregor Ross wrote of one settler who "supervised his labourers ... by firing a rifle in the direction of any whom he thought to be slacking. The bullet kicked up the soil near the delinquent one and reminded him that master's eye was upon him. The inevitable mischance soon took place, of course. A labourer was seriously wounded." Such strong-arm behavior was, to be sure, exceptional; to most settlers it could only have been monstrous. But few disputed the ostensible necessity of keeping the black man in his place. Light corporal punishment of domestic help was by no means uncommon, although not indiscriminate. Compiling a list of hints for the wives of newly arrived settlers, one titled female colonist advised that women "could not, for instance, learn by experience in England when is the right time to have a servant beaten for rubbing silver plate on the gravel path to clean it, and that after several previous warnings." Wrote Cranworth: "I am ... personally convinced that for certain crimes, such as lying, petty stealing and more especially cruelty to children or animals, the whip is the best and *kindest* preventive and cure." *

It is only fair at this point to interject Elspeth Huxley's caution against "the injustice of judging men of yesterday by the standards of today." Mrs. Huxley wrote that in 1935, and it applies even more forcibly in the 1970s. If physical abuse of the black man had begun to

---

* The beating of servants, of course, came only naturally to the products of a public school system who were caned savagely and incessantly almost as a matter of routine—and usually for offenses far less grave than petty theft or ignorance of duties.

lose its respectability among whites at the turn of the century, the same could not be said for the pseudo-Darwinian notions which in large measure shaped the era's racial outlook. Asquith, the Liberals' leader after 1908, stated in Parliament that "the experience we have gained in [South Africa] ... shows that differences [in race] which are certainly implanted by nature ... sometimes seem as if they were intended by nature to be permanent." Elgin, one of the most enlightened and fair-minded men of his time, voiced uneasiness over "multiplying what we call white men's countries" in Africa; yet when it came to racial equality, he could "ask whether nature itself so permits," and answer the same question with: "So far as I know, there is no historical foundation for any such proposition." Henry Labouchere, that indefatigable champion of oppressed lesser breeds, characterized the Baganda as "without exception the very laziest of the laziest race in the whole world, the African negro."

Even the "pro-native" civil servants could not bring themselves to raise the color bar. Lugard may have been years ahead of his time when he wrote that "I would far sooner place a good reliable native in a position of responsibility than a weak or vicious European," but no prewar Briton spoke more forcibly for the ultimate authority of the white man in Africa. McGregor Ross, who incurred the lasting wrath of the settler community by habitually taking the black man's part whenever ill-treatment of African labor was suspected, had no hesitation in categorizing Kenya's Africans as "a subject race." He also opposed the sale of liquor to blacks, and when tribal political consciousness began to emerge in the 1920s, spoke of the "unwisdom" of encouraging Africans to seek the vote. Provincial and District Commissioners held no notions of ethnic fraternity; Africans were their "children," not their brothers. Men like Jackson, Ainsworth, Hobley and Seaton would be called nigger-lovers by present-day white segregationists—and indeed they were—but Black Panthers would see them as honky imperialist despots, and would also be right. Some administrators did not even regard Africans as juveniles. Captain Chauncey Hugh Stigand, who exemplified everything that was upright, honorable and compassionate in the British colonial officer, believed that "for the proper understanding of the savage African, one must not look on him as a human being, but as a rather superior kind of animal."

Possibly the best way to describe this attitude is simply to say that the white man had not yet reached that stage in his development where he could begin to question the validity of pigmentation as a guide to his conduct in human intercourse. "Segregation was observed without question," wrote Seaton. "That hated phrase 'the colour bar' was not in currency. The racial distinction was obvious and accepted as a natural order. No one bothered to think about it." And to a point, the ingrained prejudices of the settlers and administrators can be appreciated if not applauded. They had brought with them to Africa the traditions of Magna Carta and a 600-year-old Parliament. Their forbears were Shakespeare and Pitt, Wolsey and Swift, Bracton and Wren, Newton and Hogarth. They had toiled for two millennia to fashion a way of life which they regarded as a model not just for the nations of Europe but for the world. They were not likely to look up to a people who slept with their goats, beat their women, consulted sheep entrails on business matters and coated their bodies with grease and ochre. The whites of Kenya, indeed, of all Africa, could only concur in Eliot's assertion that "we are not destroying any old or interesting system, but simply introducing order into blank, uninteresting barbarism." *

Yet the business of juxtaposing two cultures was obviously a two-way street. "It has occurred to me," wrote Hobley, "to visualise mentally the opinions which the Roman invaders ... may have formed of the semi-savage inhabitants of Britain in B.C. 54 ... What must they have thought of the skin-clad Britons; with what contempt must they have compared their own elaborate Pantheism to the weird magical worship of the Druid priests ... They must have looked down on them as veritable *'washenzi'* (Swahili—savages). Would any Roman have acknowledged that these rude people had in them the makings of a great nation? I doubt it." And for all their faith in the British civilizing mission, some colonial civil servants could occasionally wonder whether it had been right to impose the white presence and will on a people who had asked for neither. Stigand, while concluding that Britain's withdrawal from east Africa would not serve the best interests of the indigenous population, also voiced doubts that Pax Britannica had worked a spectacular improvement in the African's lot. "Are we going to endeavour to civilise the native from our own point of view,"

---

* Disdain for "savages" has sometimes carried over into post-colonial Africa. Recent legislation by the Tanzania Government against Masai garb—or the absence of it— prompted a Masai member of the Kenya Parliament to remark: "If Almighty God could stomach to see the entire anatomies of Adam and Eve in their complete nudity, is it not a little prudish for an African government to have fits merely by viewing a casually exhibited Masai buttock?"

he wrote, "or are we going to leave him to work out his own future as much as possible? I would unhesitatingly give my vote in favour of the latter proceeding ... My reasons are quite simple, viz.: 1. He is richer in that condition. 2. He is happier in that condition. 3. He is a better man physically and morally in that condition." When Stigand asked himself whether Africans were better off under white rule, the answer came readily: "I think not." Colonists could share this view. "I fear," wrote the ever-candid Cranworth, "that, do what one will, never again will the native see as much happiness in the future as he has enjoyed in the past."

There was even the occasional maverick who openly took up the cudgel for the African against the settler. One of the most outspoken was the nigger-killer Meinertzhagen, who, despite his bloodlust, liked and respected the tribes with which he came into contact, violent or otherwise. "I am indeed sorry to leave the Kikuyu," he wrote in 1904, "for I have many friends among them. Their great assets are cheerfulness even in adversity, and they bear no grudge after punishment ... I found them honest and truthful ... The same cheerful young men or girls who visited me would become unscrupulous, dishonest and treacherous to the man who behaved badly to them." The Nandi gained a similar verdict. Despite their defiance, Meinertzhagen could write that "the bulk of the Nandi are a peaceful and lovable lot, enjoying jokes. I have many friends among them; they trust me and I trust them." During the actual hostilities, he borrowed a page from Lugard's book by playing foster-father to three teen-age Nandi girls as a favor to their real father, who had been supplying him with milk and eggs. In Meinertzhagen's view, Nandi country was "African land, not ours to dispose of."

Meinertzhagen also looked on the indiscriminate use of cheap black labor as "a most dangerous prospect," and crossed swords frequently with the standard-bearers of white settlement. Delamere, he wrote after one exchange, "is an enthusiast about the future of East Africa and remarked: 'I am going to prove ... that this is a white man's country.' 'But,' I humbly said, 'it is a black man's country; how are you going to superimpose the white over black?' Delamere is a quick-tempered man; he said, rather impatiently, 'The black man will benefit and cooperate.'" In a dinner coversation with Eliot, Meinertzhagen "suggested that the country belonged to Africans and that their interests must prevail over the interests of strangers. [Eliot] would not have it; he kept on using the word 'paramount' with reference to the claims of Europeans. I said that some day the African would be educated and armed; that would lead to a clash. Eliot thought that that day was so far distant as not to matter ... but I am convinced that in the end the Africans will win."*

*

While few if any colonists shared Meinertzhagen's extreme views, even fewer entertained any real animosity toward Africans. To claim that mistreatment of blacks did not occur would be foolish, any attempt to defend it a waste of time. Yet it would also be a colossal distortion to depict the white settler in Kenya as a sadistic Negrophobe. The fact that he was almost paranoically pro-white did not make him by definition anti-black. He did not dislike Africans for the simple reason that no cause for dislike existed. The very word "nigger," although hardly a compliment, was in those days not much more of an epithet than "Chinaman." If the settler's irrational fears of a "native uprising" sometimes brought on a gross abuse of his self-conferred privileges as master, far more often did he play the role of stern but fond parent. Delamere, the apostle of white settler supremacy, abided by a rigid code of justice in race relations; "when I say justice," he wrote, "I mean in a case between black and black or between white and black. I cannot myself subscribe to the belief that it is bad for a white man to be punished if he breaks the law in this country any more than at home." These were not merely words. Delamere once threw the English captain of a coastal steamer into the Gulf of Aden when the man kicked an African climbing a companionway. The secretary of the Nairobi Turf Club became the target of the celebrated Delamere wrath after canceling a race in which a Somali had entered a pony. (The secretary also received one of Delamere's equally famous apologies when the latter learned that the race had been called off only for a shortage of entries.) We have already seen how Delamere pampered his Masai herdsmen. In varying degrees, most other settlers behaved in the same fashion. "Themselves untamed, with fresh hearts," wrote Isak Dinesen, "they were capable of forming a Hawkeye-Chingachgook fellowship with a dark, untamed nomad or hunter." The less romantic farm laborers also got a reasonably square deal. Over and above their pay, and even before the law required it, all were given blankets, huts and a far

---

* In 1949, as a retired colonel, Meinertzhagen repeated the warning in a letter to another Governor of Kenya. "This morning ..." he wrote, "I renewed my acquaintance with a local chief of the Kikuyu, with whom I had been on very intimate terms when I was stationed at Nyeri in 1902 and 1903 ... He fears an outbreak of violence against Europeans ... under the direction of a secret society now in existence called 'Maw Maw.' " No action was taken on the letter.

more generous daily food ration than they could usually have expected in their own villages. If a field hand brought his family with him, the settler often paid for the extra food and lodging. Workers who were injured or became ill received professional medical attention, and if no doctor was available, the settler or his wife would substitute. Many a young bride just out of England rapidly became a skilled midwife by attending a multitude of African childbirths. Holidays might be granted so that laborers could participate in tribal ceremonies. Conversely, at harvest times, a tribe's drummers, musicians, warriors and maidens often assembled in front of the settler's house to perform an ngoma—dance— that usually lasted all night and sometimes longer. "The Ngomas," said Isak Dinesen, "were neighbourly and traditionally social functions. In the course of time, it was the younger brothers and sisters and, later on, the sons and daughters of the first dancers known to me, who came to the dancing-ground." Once, when Isak Dinesen left Kenya for a visit to Europe, the Kikuyu gave her a farewell feast attended by more than a thousand tribesmen. A fixture among the judges at settler cattle shows was the Masai chief Laibon, Lenana. It was considered a high compliment when an African named a farm animal for a European. Scores of oxen were called "Delamere."

If this sort of plantation paternalism makes the flesh crawl today, in Kenya seventy years ago it generated a robust climate of feudal good feeling which, for the most part, seemed to suit the black vassal as much as it did his Caucasian liege lord. All things being unequal, it was simply too early in history for most Africans to think of them- selves as victims of a mindless discrimination. (Among other things, they were no strangers to physical abuse from "superiors" in their own tribal societies.) They had not yet acquired the Western education that would open their eyes to a new set of values and enable them to realize just how short was the end of the stick they held. Until then, with his bottomless fund of patience and intuitive good will, the African farm worker found little cause for complaint. The flogging of the Nairobi rickshaw boys made hot copy. It was far less typical of black–white relations in turn-of-the-century Kenya than the humdrum vignette of a settler's afternoon social call on an African village. "I passed through the narrow entrance to the group of huts," wrote Binks, "raised my hand and exclaimed 'Jambo!' The greeting was returned. A child brought a stool, placed it in the centre of the clearing and invited me to rest. The children ... placed their heads against my stomach ... I placed my hands upon their heads in token of good-fellowship. A man came in through the entrance to the circle of huts carrying a newly-born lamb and was followed by its bleating mother. A calabash of milk was offered me which I drank sparingly ... When at last, in the last golden light I left, I shook hands with the man and we first spat on our hands to show our trust and respect for one another."

"To be within measurable distance of an Indian coolie is very disagreeable."

If only a handful of whites bore grudges against Kenya's Africans, an even smaller minority was prepared to tolerate the third major element of the country's population. Like the American pioneers of the old West, the British colonists in east Africa had to cope with Indians. The latter of course did not live in tepees, nor were their names Sitting Bull or Geronimo, but Chaturbhai Patel, Ramji Kanji, Purshottamdass Bootamal and so forth. In the eyes of most of the white settlers, the only good Kenya Indian may have been a dead one.

A fairly large percentage of the six or seven thousand Indians living in Kenya in the early 1900s had been coolies on the railway who chose to remain in the Protectorate. Some continued to work on the line, others had become clerks, masons, cabinet makers, teamsters, leather workers and tailors. A few were market gardeners and an even smaller number had entered professions as draftsmen, physicians, lawyers and bankers. The vast majority, however, were "duka wallahs"—the operators of tiny shops that sprang up like mushrooms across the country and sold every imaginable article of cheap merchandise from blankets to badly fitting shoes to hurricane lamps to patent medicines to bottled mineral water to individual cigarettes and individual matches. Irrespective of calling, Kenya's Indians worked hard and kept largely to themselves. They were also universally and utterly despised.

If for no other reason than their own country's overpopulation, Indians had been given substantial encouragement by British officialdom to settle in Kenya. "Indian trade, enterprise and emigration," wrote Sir Harry Johnston in 1901, "require a suitable outlet. East Africa is, and should be, from every point of view, the America of the Hindu." In 1902, Indian farmers were formally invited, by a Kenya Government Notice, to take land in the Protectorate. An Administration official visited Calcutta in 1906 to discuss the possibilities of Indian immigration with the Viceroy's Council. In the same year, overtures to Indian merchants were made by the Mombasa Chamber of Commerce. But these solicitations did not necessarily indicate hospitality as the word is usually understood. Few

expected that the Caucasian residents of Kenya would welcome the huddled masses of an Asiatic horde.

For when all was said and done, the Indian was the pariah of the
British Empire. In more generous moments, the white settler in Kenya
might view his Indian counterpart as a figure of fun. Everyone enjoyed
quoting the telegrams of semi-literate "Babu" stationmasters on the
railway. One favorite was the message clacked out from Elmenteita to
Nairobi when Delamere boarded a train with a bull terrier and her
litter: "The Lord is on the train with one bitch and four sons of bitches.
No ticket. Please collect." SOS calls were equally entertaining: "Please
inform station-master Makindu serious mix-up. Approach with caution
or beware trouble and life dangers. Four lions with consorts aggressively on platform and completely in charge of my official functions."
But the Indian as jester played a minor role alongside the Indian as
leper. It was repugnant enough that a conquered race should seek to
live on terms of equality with Anglo-Saxons, but the Indians also had
the effrontery—the absolute bloody cheek—to claim a civilization much
older and in some respects superior to Britain's. As Eliot put it: "the
average Englishman ... tolerates a black man who admits his inferiority,
and even those who show a good fight and give in; but he cannot tolerate dark colour combined with an intelligence in any way equal to his
own." That combination of course made the Indians doubly damned,
and the white settlers exerted every effort not only to hold them at arm's
length but wherever possible to deprive them of any influence outside
their own community.

*

Like most of their grievances, the settlers' case against the Indians
wedded fact and fiction. A great point was made of asserting that race
did not enter into the question; it was simply a matter of character. "If
the Indian in the Protectorate," wrote Cranworth, "were represented by
the type so dear to tourists, we would welcome him with open arms. It
is not because his skin is black that he is unpopular; it is because he is
a foul liver, a drunkard and a thief." That accusation, while base, was
not altogether baseless: a fairly large number of Kenya's Indians had in
fact been spurned as human refuse in their own homes. In Elspeth Huxley's words, "it was wrong to encourage the lowest caste ... as it would
have been to dump thousands of illiterate, poverty-stricken and frequently diseased Englishmen from the workhouses of industrial cities,
without resources, organisation or training, into any populated part of

Africa, and leave them to scrape a living as and how they could." True enough, but when the early settlers argued from this position of logic, they seldom troubled to make any distinction between the untouchable and the "type so dear to tourists," thus slandering what was for the most part a self-supporting and conspicuously industrious—if rather drab—lower middle class. And whenever a "respectable" Indian turned up, which was continually, the white colonist somehow seemed to be looking the other way.

A weightier charge was that the Indians constituted a public health hazard by ignoring the most elementary rules of sanitation and personal hygiene. Plague, venereal disease and a host of other communicable ailments were directly attributed to the Indians, as the result of what Cranworth called "living conditions under which no English farmer would dream of keeping his pigs." The point was fairly well taken; for evidence, one needed only to visit the fetid, rat-crawling, typhus-breeding bazaars of Nairobi, Mombasa, Kisumu and other towns. Yet it was both misleading and scurrilous to label a community of six thousand people as a walking virus—and that in effect was the tone of the indictment.* One suspects, moreover, that the fastidious Anglo-Saxon may have been more appalled by the Indian's odor than by his germs, as witnessed by Cranworth's exquisitely haughty sarcasm in describing a railway compartment. "Into it one would at once spring," he wrote, "were it not that the next similar compartment is crowded with about six Indians of the usual or baser sort, and that an inspection reveals to our olfactory senses that our compartment has recently had occupants of the same kind. I would like to urge on the management that certain compartments, first and second class, be reserved for Indians only. It is, I believe, recognised that the effluvia of hot Europeans is most offensive to the Asiatic, and in his interest I urge that it is most unfair that he should be subjected to them!" Lady Delamere put it more succinctly when she remarked that "to be within measurable distance of an Indian coolie is very disagreeable." No doubt it was.

---

* Jomo Kenyatta has given the whites credit for venereal disease. Describing how major events in Kikuyu history are chronicled in the names of tribal age groups, he wrote in 1938 that "the Gikuyu have been able to record the time when the Europeans introduced a number of maladies such as syphilis into Gikuyu country, for those initiated at the time when this disease first showed itself are called *gatego*, i.e. syphilis." Both Kenyatta and the settlers probably allowed their prejudices to overcome their objectivity. In all likelihood, it was the Arab and Swahili slavers who first injected the spirochete into the east African bloodstream.

Other anti-Indian charges were also two-sided coins. The colonists stood on fairly solid ground in pointing to a large number of Indian thieves and fences who were turning many Africans to crime. It was both accurate and farsighted to warn that the presence of Indian clerks and artisans would retard African progress into those occupations (although the alarm, sounded as it was by the settlers, could not but have a slightly hypocritical ring). Less substance, however, could be found in the assertion that the Indians made little if any contribution to the country's development, being basically merchants rather than agronomists and repatriating their profits rather than investing them in Kenya. In point of fact, the Indian was not much less close to the soil than the Briton, as evidenced by his small but flourishing market gardens whose produce often gave lively competition to white settler crops. Nor did the image of economic scavenger hold up. The very presence of the dukas went far toward priming Kenya's commercial pump. As early as 1902, after an inspection visit to the Protectorate, F. L. O'Callaghan, a member of the Railway Committee, spoke warmly of the Indian role in the Kenya economy. Africans, he said, "must be taught to trade, and so far the best teacher is the small Indian trader." In 1905, while serving as Acting Deputy Commissioner, Ainsworth noted in his official report that "up to within recent times, European capital and enterprise have been almost entirely absent ... fully 80 per cent of the capital and business energy of the country is Indian."

Whatever the merits of the anti-Indian testimony, it hardly justified relegating Kenya's Indians to the status of second-class settlers. "Is it possible," asked Churchill, "for any Government with a scrap of respect for honest dealing between man and man, to embark on a policy of deliberately squeezing out the native of India from regions in which he has established himself under every security of public faith?" To the white colonists, it was not only possible but desirable, and they embarked on a squeezing-out campaign with vigor, concentrating mainly on two objectives.

One was to keep Indians out of the colony's politics, and here, although a minority in the Legislative Council, the settlers demonstrated what the sheer force of an intimidating presence could accomplish. In 1908, Hayes-Sadler recommended that an Indian be nominated to represent his community on the council, and the Colonial Office endorsed the proposal, its staunchest advocate, Churchill, proclaiming that "there can be no reason for excluding this large and meritorious class. Begin early to instill good principles in the East Africa Protectorate!" The Administration accordingly cast about for a nominee, and its choice could hardly have been more acceptable to the white colonists. Steamship owner, merchant, contractor, philanthropist, A. M. Jevanjee had already presented Nairobi with a statue of Queen Victoria (unveiled by the Duke of Connaught), and one newspaper was to call him "as enthusiastic an imperialist as you would find in a day's march." Yet if the settlers evinced any pleasure in the selection of this "type so dear to tourists," their cheers did not rise above a whisper. While they could not legally block Jevanjee's entry into the Council, neither was there any requirement that they encourage him, and he quickly took the hint from their silence. In McGregor Ross' words, Jevanjee "concluded that the presence of one solitary Indian member, in a Council otherwise European and largely hostile, served no useful purpose. He withdrew and was not replaced." Twelve more years would have to pass before another Indian was nominated.

Even greater energy was devoted to throwing up an Indian-proof wall around the highlands, with a view to keeping the region lily-white. To a point, one might have discerned a certain justice in the segregation policy, stemming as it did, at least in part, from the then-universal misconceptions of equatorial climate and its effects on the frail Caucasian. Stated the 1905 report of a land commission chaired by Delamere: "Considering that only a comparatively small area [of Kenya] is suitable for European settlement it is desirable that land within that area should be reserved for the support and maintenance of a white population." Elsewhere, the report noted, lay "an enormous area of land eminently suited" to Indian needs. Fair enough, on the face of it; but to suggest that a region the size of Belgium could not accommodate the occasional "type so dear to the tourist" who could afford to buy land and farm there was to reveal the closed fist of bigotry.

The Indians' response was a mass protest meeting in Mombasa in 1906. Grievances were aired, resolutions passed and 20,000 rupees subscribed to finance a delegation to London seeking Government guarantees against discriminatory land laws. The commission's aims were modest enough: "not to obtain equal rights with the Colonials in British colonies in Africa," explained Jevanjee in a letter to *The Times of India*, "but only to secure fair treatment of the Indian subjects of the King-Emperor." For their pains, the petitioners were rewarded with an official despatch from Elgin, assuring them, in exemplary bureaucratic prose, that "it would not be in accordance with the policy of H.M. Government to exclude any class of His subjects from holding land in any part of a British Protectorate; but that, in view of the comparatively limited area in the Protectorate suitable for European colonisation, a reasonable discretion will be exercised in dealing with applications for land on the part of natives of India and other non-Europeans." Two years later, Elgin reaffirmed his forthright ambiguity: "It is not consonant with the views of H.M. Government to impose legal restrictions on any particular section of the community, but as a matter of administrative convenience grants in the upland area should not be made to Indians." One can legitimately ask how the administrative machinery might have been sabotaged had a handful of Indians sought leases in the Rift or on the Mau.

In any case, the effect of both statements, known individually and together as the "Elgin Pledge," was to transform the highlands into a private white country club. Considering Elgin's known apprehensions over a white settler oligarchy in Kenya—not to mention his earlier post as Viceroy of India and his generally favorable attitude toward Indian colonization in east Africa—the "pledge" might better have been termed a surrender.

*

If nothing else, however, it underscored the ever-growing power which the European colonists were able to exercise from their small but firmly grasped foothold in the local Administration. They carried weight simply because their presence was indispensable. Officials might see them as an exasperating and sometimes insufferable rookery of enfants terribles, but without the produce of their farms—however meager—Kenya would be doomed for many years to hobble about as the sick man of the Empire. If the Protectorate was to pay for its railway and liquidate the grant-in-aid, if it was ever to take its place as a productive member of the British imperial family, only the soil of the highlands, tilled by a corporal's guard of cantankerous Englishmen, would bring about that transformation. Both the Kenya Administration and the Colonial Office knew this all too well.

Much more to the point, the settlers knew it. As the keystone of the country's prosperity they held an ace in the hole which they played for all it was worth to gain their own ends, never relinquishing their pressure for a stronger voice in Kenya's affairs. They pounded on the doors of the Legislative Council until colonist membership in that body increased from two to four seats. In 1911, the fragmented Colonists' Association was disbanded and a new and far more sophisticated lobby called the Convention of Associations came into being. Led by Delamere, it was composed of settler-elected delegates who convened periodically in Nairobi as an unofficial opposition and soon became a sort of shadow legislature known throughout the Protectorate as the "settlers' parliament." At once articulate and strident, the Convention set its sights on the next step toward white self-rule: elective rather than nominated membership on the Council. In 1912, the "no taxation without representation" slogan was revived with the introduction of a poll tax on Europeans. In 1913, the unofficial on the Council dramatized their stand by resigning in a body, and within three years elective representation was granted in principle. Only the war delayed its immediate, formal implementation.

Even with elected membership, to be sure, settlerdom was never to see its dream of dominion status realized. Armed as it was, however, with the knowledge that the country could not do without it, the unofficial white minority was able to exercise its political acumen and loud voice to such purpose that before the first decade of the twentieth century was out, the colonists had come to dominate—and at times to dictate—Government policy in Kenya. Churchill had perceived their top-heavy influence as early as 1907, when he made an observation that was later paraphrased in a different context: "Never before in colonial experience has a council been granted where the number of settlers is so few."

UGANDA RAILWAY.

THE HIGHLANDS OF
BRITISH EAST AFRICA
AS A
WINTER HOME FOR ARISTOCRATS

HAS BECOME A FASHION.

SPORTSMEN in search of BIG GAME make it a hobby.

STUDENTS of NATURAL HISTORY revel in this FIELD of NATURE'S own MAKING.

UGANDA RAILWAY, BRITISH EAST AFRICA
ARRIVAL OF THE FIRST COOK'S EXCURSION. AND THE RESULT OF CAREFULLY PRESERVING THE BIG GAME

UGANDA RAILWAY Observation Cars pass through the Greatest Natural GAME PRESERVE in the WORLD.

For reliable information, etc. address

PUBLICITY DEPT., UGANDA RAILWAY
DEWAR HOUSE, HAYMARKET

13

HAPPY VALLEY

"It would be hard to find a country where the conditions were more favourable ... to a practical experiment in State Socialism."

While Kenya's settlers were causing official migraines in Nairobi and London, the region which had first drawn Britain into the east African interior seemed all but forgotten. With the adjudication of European territorial claims below the Sahara and the cessation of Uganda's own religious fratricide, an era of almost unprecedented peace had settled down on the once volatile kingdoms to the north and west of Lake Victoria. Under the nominal rule of the sub-teen Kabaka Daudi Chwa, the British Administration in Uganda had relegated the Grand Guignol spectacles of Mutesa, Mwanga and Kabarega to the files of dim memory. Much more significantly, however, political stability also enabled the country to forge ahead on the road to an economic condition which would not inaccurately have been described as prosperity.

Uganda's outlook had been favored from the start by at least two factors unique in east Africa. One was the absence of a white settler population to blow up racial storms and otherwise interfere with Government's exclusive concentration on African progress. Uganda, wrote the Governor in 1904, "will never be a white man's country in the sense that South Africa and parts of [Kenya] have proved to be." (This self-evident fact may have been voiced with some satisfaction, since the incumbent happened to be the unfortunate Hayes-Sadler.) The people themselves were the other asset. Eliot, the white man's patron saint in Kenya, wrote of Uganda as "a black man's country, like our West African colonies," and observed that "in few parts of the world inhabited by dark races will the missionary, schoolmaster and engineer find so good a reception, for [Uganda] has a large and unusually intelligent population, who show a striking readiness to adopt European ideas and inventions. For the same reason it offers an extensive market for European goods, and the prospects of creating a considerable trade are encouraging."

Even so, the sledding was rough at first. Like Kenya, Uganda carried the burden of payments on a grant-in-aid (largely the result of emergency outlays to quell the 1897 mutiny); in 1900, the debt to the Treasury stood at more than £200,000. In the same year, the country's revenues of £81,000 were swamped by £251,000 in expenditures, while the value of agricultural exports—the only real promise of solvency—barely reached £20,000. In themselves, these financial handicaps may not have been a great deal more than what was to be expected in any fledgling tropical possession, but two other factors threatened for a time to make Uganda's deficit permanent.

The first was unforeseen: an epidemic of sleeping sickness that lasted nearly a decade and seemed, at one point, on its way to rivaling the Black Death of medieval Europe. No one knew the cause of the malady, much less its cure, although the symptoms were all too clear. The victim was simply overtaken by lethargy. Standing required more effort than he could expend; presently he was unable even to sit or squat, and in due course he lost the physical energy to remain alive. Mwanga in his most genocidal moods could not have hoped to match even a small fraction of the casualties which the plague inflicted. Shortly after it broke out in 1901, Sir Albert Cook, Uganda's most distinguished pioneer doctor, asked chiefs from stricken villages to send him a twig for every person who died. When the runners began arriving at Cook's hospital in Kampala, he thought at first that they were carrying bundles of kindling wood. In the ensuing six months, more than 40,000 men, women and children succumbed to the disease while the medical world looked on helplessly.

There was a breakthrough in 1903 when a British medical commission led by Sir David Bruce managed to isolate and identify the lethal organism as a trypanosome carried by a species of tsetse fly. But the cure remained a mystery. At one point, English laboratories produced a drug which offered high hopes. Cook treated forty-five patients with it; twelve hours later, all were dead. By the end of 1903, fatalities had risen to 90,000. Entire villages on the lake shore were wiped out. Tens of thousands living in the infected areas were removed by the Protectorate Government to huge hospital camps, but even close medical attention could not stem the ever-mounting mortality rate. Deaths were often hastened by leopards, hyenas and other predators who prowled the camps by day and devoured their human prey alive after nightfall; the torpid victims did not even possess the strength to cry out. By early 1906, 200,000 Africans in a population of less than half a million had felt the tsetse's fatal sting. It was not an incentive to expanded cultivation and mass agricultural exports.

While less spectacular as an obstacle, inadequate transport facilities may have retarded Uganda's progress even more effectively than did trypanosomiasis. The country which caused the railway to be built had no rail connection of its own with the coast, and although this missing link did not quite strangle economic growth, it had the effect of holding exports almost to a standstill for many years. All produce from Uganda had to be carried to railhead at Kisumu in the holds of cargo ships, and movement was laggard at best. At the time of the boundary revision in 1902, merchant shipping on Lake Victoria consisted of the midget steamer *William Mackinnon*, a privately owned steam launch, a broad-beamed cutter named *Winifred* and a German schooner. The total cargo capacity of this limping fleet would barely have filled the five wagons of a single railway goods train every month.

The funereal pace of waterborne cargoes was due partly to the fact that the ships served ports in German territory as well as Uganda. In theory, the *William Mackinnon* could circumnavigate the lake in a week, but the voyage usually took twice as long. All captains made a practice of anchoring in convenient inlets each night rather than risk the possibility of heaving to in one of the abbreviated but insane williwaws that pounced on the lake without warning and turned its ordinarily placid surface into a procession of mammoth battering rams. The *William Mackinnon*, once described by Jackson as "a champion roller," was almost disastrously vulnerable in these storms. Nor could one expect to see lost time made up during the day. Visibility and speed were often reduced sharply by the lake's unique living fog. "Patches of black," wrote Stigand, "hover over the water like rain clouds. These are caused by myriads of 'lake fly,' masses of which are swept about by the breeze ... If we strike one of these clouds, the deck will become covered with them, and cabins must be shut up." Swift passages were also ruled out by poor charts (the lake was not completely surveyed until 1906) which failed to reveal numerous rocks and sunken reefs. Sometimes it became necessary to alter course hastily about twenty miles south of Entebbe, when seagoing cannibals from the Ssese islands launched their war canoes in a surprise attack. There was little on Lake Victoria that did not seem to conspire against the expeditious movement of freight.

The burden was lifted slightly in 1904, when the steam tug *Percy Anderson* and several lighters were transferred from Kilindini and railed to the lake, while another steamer, the 600-ton *Sybil*, was launched in the same year. But deliveries continued to lag far behind schedule. Even aboard the brand-new *Sybil*, the relatively short 180-mile run from Entebbe to Kisumu could take four or five days, and another week might pass before her cargoes were offloaded, since the port was without a deep-water pier. Shipping also sustained a major setback in 1906, when *Sybil* piled up on an uncharted reef, jettisoned her cargo and spent nearly six months in drydock. By the end of that year, backlogs of produce had accumulated in small mountains on the docks of every lake port. Seldom did any exports reach the Kisumu rail terminus less than three months late.

*

With manpower decimated by sleeping sickness and transport hobbled by the caprices of a few malfunctioning arks on the lake, it says something about Uganda's Administration and people that they were able nonetheless to cultivate the land, sell its produce and realize substantial returns. Even during the lean years, few doubted that Uganda could look to a rosy future. One of the Protectorate's most ardent boosters was Winston Churchill, who passed through in 1907 and found himself far more impressed with prospects north and west of the lake than on the Kenya highlands. "Concentrate on Uganda!" was the message he took back to Britain. In his book, *My African Journey*, Churchill marveled at the "unequalled fertility" of the land, its "extraordinary waterways" and its "tropical products for which the demand of civilized industry is almost insatiable." The country, he said, "is alive by itself. It is vital; and in my view, in spite of its insects and its diseases, it ought in the course of time to become the most prosperous of all our East and Central African possessions, and perhaps the financial driving wheel of all this part of the world."

Politically, Churchill saw Uganda as a Utopia of indirect rule: "Under the shelter of the British flag, safe from external menace or internal broil, the child-King grows to a temperate and instructed maturity." In the Kabaka's palace, beneath portraits of Queen Victoria and King Edward, he took tea with the eleven-year-old Daudi Chwa, "a graceful, distinguished-looking little boy" who, after overcoming his initial shyness, confessed to a passion for football.* Thanks, said Churchill, to an English tutor, the youthful monarch "will probably become a well-educated and accomplished man." From the standpoint of human relations, Churchill "rejoiced" that the climate did not permit the intrusion of "a petty white community, with the harsh and selfish ideas which mark the jealous contact of races and the exploitation of the weaker." His general enthusiasm for the country even moved him to envision Uganda as a vast socio-economic laboratory. Uganda's wealth, he declared, should belong to Uganda's people and not be exploited by "divers persons across the sea, who have no concern, other than purely commercial, in its fortunes." Development of agricultural commerce must therefore be the function of Government rather than of outside interests. "Indeed, it would be hard to find a country where the conditions were more favourable ... to a practical experiment in State Socialism."

Churchill's boyish exuberance may at times have been trying on the local Administration. "Last night he kept me awake for some time," wrote the Governor, Sir Hesketh Bell, in his diary, "by what appeared to be a long soliloquy in his bath ... while performing his ablutions he was dictating to a clerk." Bell also remarked that Churchill "seems to have a good many preconceived ideas about Uganda which I shall have to knock out." Unquestionably, in strewing superlatives across the land, the distinguished young visitor sometimes allowed his rhapsodizing to obscure his common sense. He may have been at his least realistic when, with characteristic foresight, he perceived the headwaters of the Nile as a major source of industrial power but simultaneously pooh-poohed the expense of the project and described its engineering problems as no more complex than those attendant on the construction of a mud pie. "It would be perfectly easy," he enthused, "to harness the whole river and let the Nile begin its long and beneficent journey to the sea by leaping through a turbine. It is possible that nowhere else in the world could so enormous a mass of water be held up by so little masonry ... at an inconceivably small cost." In fact, the "little masonry" proved to be the Owen Falls dam, a concrete colossus eight storeys high and half a mile long, which cost £22,000,000 and took six years to build. Nonetheless, the

---

* On returning to England, Churchill received a letter and two snapshots from Daudi Chwa. The letter, written in an awkwardly fastidious hand, announced that "our football are going on very nicely, and the other day the Budu boys came to play football with my boys, and we beat them ... The words on the fortographs mean I am your friend."

simple fact that the dam did get built attested to Churchill's vision, even though he had to wait five decades before seeing the not so impossible dream become reality.

Uganda's agricultural prospects probably found Churchill at his most prescient. While the country's climate ruled out large-scale growing of European vegetables, the soil was tailor-made for coffee, cocoa, tea, sugar cane, tobacco, rubber and cotton. The latter in particular caught Churchill's eye. "A hundred thousand intelligent landowners occupying twenty thousand square miles of suitable soil," he wrote, "are eager to engage in [cotton] cultivation;" there was little doubt in his mind that "cotton alone can make the fortune of Uganda." This proved correct, although the forecast was somewhat daring at the time.

Cotton had got off to a painfully slow start. The plant was not indigenous to Uganda. It had probably been introduced by Emin Pasha's Sudanese troops in 1889, and while the seeds thrived under the country's rich loam and abundant rainfall, the absence of a mass market had stimulated virtually no production until 1904. At that time, a private company distributed modest quantities of seed to some two dozen chiefs, who produced about forty-five tons of unginned fiber. Of this output only ten tons, valued at £236, managed to make the precarious lake voyage to Kisumu and the rail jorney to Mombasa. But even so meager an export volume proved sufficient to encourage applications for seed by 500 more cultivators, and Hayes-Sadler expressed official hope of "an extensive cotton industry springing up" across the country. Actually, "creeping up" might have been a better way of putting it. Farmers had to learn planting and growing methods from scratch, and their trial-and-error procedure, along with primitive hand gins, made for a shabby finished product. Many of the varieties of seed introduced, moreover, proved either inferior or unsuited to local conditions. At the time of Churchill's visit in 1907, it looked as if the industry was ready to collapse under its own inertia.

At this point, the Administration stepped in, with the Uganda Cotton Ordinance of 1908, a drastic emergency measure drawn up by Governor Bell. Cotton fields growing all but one type of seed were to be plowed under without delay. A directive went out ordering the destruction of every hand gin in the country; these were replaced by machine gins. Stringent regulations were put into effect controlling the sale of locally produced cotton and prohibiting the export of grades which did not meet rigid quality standards set by Government. The Administration also initiated crash training programs in cultivation and ginning and opened an experimental seed farm. The new broom was wielded with vigor as chiefs throughout the Protectorate enforced Bell's rules conscientiously—and perhaps harshly at times. The ordinance also brought almost immediate results. At the end of 1908, with an export of 3,900 four-hundred-pound bales valued at £51,000, cotton had taken its first step toward fulfilling Churchill's prediction.

*

Its ascendancy, however, was by no means certain so long as transport remained clogged. This applied not merely to export shipments across the lake; the movement of cotton crops from fields to ports was at least equally sluggish, largely because no interior rail arteries existed. "Unfortunately," wrote Bell in his 1908 report to the Colonial Office, "the area of territory in which cotton can be profitably grown is limited to the distance over which it can be cheaply transported to the ports on Lake Victoria ... Every peasant in the country appears to be willing to grow cotton on condition that he is not obliged to carry his crop on his head for more than a two days' march." A railway indeed was long overdue. As early as 1901, Sir Harry Johnston had recommended the building of a 250-mile line from Lake Victoria to Lake Albert, the northern shores of which were easily accessible to a cotton-producing region west of the Albert Nile. The route, Johnston also told the Foreign Office, would "traverse a country producing great quantities of food, and inhabited by a settled and civilized people." The plea fell on deaf ears.

It was revived, however, by Churchill, who was quick to recognize transport as Uganda's principal hobgoblin and to press—with partial success—for improvements. Following his visit, he lost no time in brushing off the dust of Johnston's Victoria–Albert proposal—"to join together these two noble reservoirs with all their respective river connections." The railway, he emphasized, need not be elaborate; it was a mistake to think of pioneering African lines in the same context with European railways: a more apt comparison was "with a jogging, grunting, panting, failing line of tottering coolies, men reduced to beasts of burden ... the most painful, most degrading, slowest and feeblest method of transportation which has ever disgraced the world." After describing the projected route in some detail, Churchill ventured to envision "a time—not, I trust, remote ... when the Mountains of the Moon are scarcely four days' journey from Mombasa."

As in the case of the Owen Falls dam, this project also saw Churchill's eloquence wasted until the 1950s, but he encountered far less delay in winning Government acceptance of his second railway proposal, which met an even more urgent priority. Some of Uganda's richest cotton potential was to be found in the soil of the Busoga district, particularly along the banks of the Nile between the river's headwaters and the shores of Lake Kyoga about 100 miles to the north. Without a rail link, however, the land could not be opened up commercially, and Churchill urged the building of a line extending at least to the Nile's navigable reaches. This in turn would permit access to Lake Kyoga, "with its long arms and gulfs stretching deeply into the whole of the fertile regions to the south-west of Mount Elgon," and enable steamers to bring in produce from along 250 miles of coastline. Mainly as the result of Churchill's representations, the Treasury agreed to a £200,000 loan for construction of a sixty-mile railway to the port of Kakindu on the Victoria Nile, where steamers from Lake Kyoga could offload their cargoes. Early in 1910, work began on the Busoga Railway, as it was called.

It would have been completed in less than a year but for the absence of rail communications with Mombasa and a consequent delay in shipments of materials—compounded by the boggy character of the terrain guarding the approaches to Lake Kyoga; nearly two years went by before the line could be opened to traffic. But the sharp rise in cotton exports from the region amply proved the new railway's worth, while a stern-wheel tug and several lighters on Lake Kyoga opened a flourishing trade by tapping not only the resources of the Mount Elgon region but the produce of eastern Bunyoro. It is quite probable that without Churchill's efforts and the resultant Busoga rail artery, the commerce of nearly a quarter of Uganda would have lain fallow for many years.

*

Meanwhile, other tentacles of communication were steadily reaching out across land and water. Telegraph wires could be seen everywhere, hanging from the branches of trees rather than poles, since dead wood did not long resist the ravages of white ants. The postal system, too, had become a smoothly functioning machine, with an occasional unwanted by-product. "Huts were built at intervals of a mile," wrote Bishop Tucker of the CMS, "along all the principal roads ... A letter despatched say 100 miles in the interior is placed in the hands of a native runner, who at once, having tied it to the end of a split reed, starts at full speed holding aloft the missive and shouting at the top of his voice, 'A letter, a letter, it is burning in my hand—a letter, a letter.' As he draws near the first hut on the road he finds a messenger standing ready ... For important communications such a postal service was invaluable. But ... not infrequently I have been roused up at one or two o'clock in the morning with the cry,

'A letter, a letter—it's burning in my hand', and upon opening the letter I have found it read something like this: 'TO MY FRIEND THE BISHOP. How are you, Sir. How have you passed the day? All is well here; there are no evil tidings to tell. Farewell. May God take care of you. I am, your friend who loves you, SAMWILI.'"

*

No less visible, and much more important, was the concurrent growth of transport in areas elsewhere than Busoga. Early in 1907, the Lake Victoria merchant fleet had been beefed up with two brand-new steamers, one of which, the 1,100-ton *Nyanza*, almost rated designation as a superliner. The export-import flow was extended as far as the Sudan border when the Government launched two small steamers on Lake Albert to open a cargo-passenger service along 150 miles of upper Nile between the ports of Butiaba and Nimule. Not long after the Busoga feeder became operational, Uganda gained another rail artery which joined Kampala with the steamer dock on Lake Victoria. Although only six miles long, the toy line accelerated the shipment of goods—previously moved by hand cart on an ancient monorail—to and from the Protectorate's commercial nerve center. The road network also grew. If the coveted railway to Lake Albert was prohibitively expensive, Uganda's budget could at least absorb construction of a main trunk highway following roughly the same route and built expressly for motor traffic. In 1909, Bell was able to report that work on the road had passed the halfway mark and that a pair of Government-owned two-ton Albion lorries was already carrying produce along more than 100 surfaced miles. Something of an experiment, the trucks had lived up to Bell's expectations. "These cars," he wrote, "are run by kerosene oil, and only a very small amount of petrol is required to start the engines... I have had no hesitation in ordering additional vehicles of a similar type ... By the construction of good metalled roads ... and by the use of motor wagons ... the distressing system of human porterage may soon become a thing of the past. The natives of Uganda will cease to act as beasts of burden."

While hardly breathtaking, these advances nonetheless went far toward removing the cork from Uganda's transport bottle. They could barely keep pace, however, with agricultural production. By 1913, it had become necessary to build two more steamers and another tugboat to cope with a burgeoning lake traffic, while the African drivers of thirteen motor lorries were hauling more than 200 tons of farm produce over nearly 500 miles of metaled roads every month. It almost seemed as if cotton growth alone would threaten to swamp the ships and stall the trucks. Between 1913 and 1914, Uganda farmers, cultivating more than 10,000 acres, produced 27,000 four-hundred-pound bales of lint cotton worth £317,000, plus cotton seed fetching slightly over £13,000, for a total value of £331,000—nearly 65 percent of all Uganda exports for that period and six times the value of the 1908 breakthrough crop. Despite impressive strides in the growth of other agricultural staples, notably coffee, tea and rubber, cotton was undisputed king in Uganda. On the eve of the First World War the fiber had carried the country to within a year of erasing its debt to the British Treasury, and by the 1920s would bring annual export earnings approaching £5,000,000 into the mainstream of Uganda's own economy.

The performance hardly jibed with Henry Labouchere's earlier assertion that "a worse speculation could not be presented to the public than the investment of public funds in Uganda."

"The land won't run away."

During Uganda's advance toward economic well-being, Kenya did not stagnate, but progress in that country may have been partially obscured for a time by the meanderings of one of the highlands' typically convoluted land controversies. It will be recalled that when the Masai were evicted from their Naivasha grazing lands in 1904, the Government granted them two reserves in a treaty drawn up by Sir Donald Stewart which proclaimed the regions to be Masai property so long as the tribe "shall exist as a race." By 1908, the race had shown no signs of vanishing, but the treaty, for several reasons, was beginning to appear less durable. Among other things, a fairly sizable number of Masai had never moved out of the Rift, but continued to graze their herds on settler farms or Crown land; according to the official history of the reserve, they had become "a general nuisance." Then, too, the choice Laikipia land in the north had proved insufficiently spacious—even after the Administration had extended its boundaries twice. A further complication was the half-mile-wide road connecting the northern and southern reserves; this had rapidly become a corridor of tick-borne cattle diseases, forcing the Government to place it under quarantine and thus divide the tribe into two disunited halves.

Although these difficulties were far from insignificant in official eyes, they could almost certainly have been surmounted without invalidating the 1904 agreement. As it happened, however, one overriding factor seemed to promise a breach of promise. By 1908, in the words of the official history, settlers had begun to "cast envious eyes on the grazing-grounds of Laikipia." That year, in fact, witnessed much discussion of the feasibility of relocating the northern Masai. Stewart's earlier premonitions of colonist land hunger had not been farfetched.

The ensuing episode might have been written by Lewis Carroll. At first, any move seemed out of the question. An ironclad clause in the treaty—which no amount of covetousness could amend—specified that Laikipia would remain strictly out of bounds to white farmers unless the Masai themselves asked for some new arrangement. But it was the settlers' good fortune to hear such a request when, at the end of 1908, the Masai's chief Laibon, Lenana, told the Government that he wished to see both sections of the tribe reunited in the southern reserve. The petition was not, apparently, made out of any desire to oblige the colonists, but rather for Lenana's own convenience: he lived in the southern zone and had seen his authority over the Laikipia wing begin to erode. In 1909, he met with Hayes-Sadler, and it was agreed that the northern Masai would move south. To accommodate the tribesmen and their herds, some 9,200 square miles on the Loita plains (more than twice the area of Laikipia) were added to the southern region. The few settlers then farming on Loita were immediately promised three acres of Laikipia for every two they vacated.

At this point, however, bureaucracy intervened. Hayes-Sadler was transferred to the West Indies and the new Governor, Sir Percy Girouard, sought formal confirmation of Lenana's agreement. Early in 1910, another meeting was held at which not only Lenana but the northern Masai elders gave their consent to the move. Routes were then mapped out by Government officials and the evacuation began. Almost at once, it was halted in its tracks by a cable from Lord Crewe, who had just succeeded Elgin as Colonial Secretary. Both the Masai and Kenya Administration, it appeared, had jumped the gun: the move could not be carried out until a treaty, no less binding (if that is the word) than that of 1904, had been signed by all parties concerned. "Nothing must be done," wrote Crewe in a departmental minute, "without a searching inquiry, all the more as there is no conceivable urgency. The land won't run away." Beneath a nuclear cloud of dust, and in a confusion bordering on chaos, the vast herds of cattle and sheep were turned around and driven back to Laikipia. Late in May of 1910, a third meeting was called, and all elders agreed once more—by now somewhat impatiently—to go south. All, that is, but one.

This person was Legalishu, the leader of the northern Masai. Jackson describes him as "a spare and wiry little man with a long and rather sulky-looking face, but of undeniably strong character," who "controlled his men in a manner I never saw equalled off a military parade ground." Legalishu also lived up to the first five letters of his name in a Philadelphian sense of the word. Wearied of official backing and filling, and reluctant from the first to vacate Laikipia, he now complained that the extensions to the southern reserve were not large enough. The Government accordingly invited him to appoint tribal representatives who would inspect the region. On receiving their unfavorable report, he then declared: "If you wish us to go, we will go, but we do not want to go." This statement, as Legalishu was no doubt aware, could be interpreted broadly or narrowly. Uneasy over a possible violation of the 1904 treaty, the Administration chose the fine print and the move was called off. In Mervyn Hill's words, Crewe "had thrown a spanner into the works."

It was removed less than a year later, when Lenana died. His last words are said to have been: "Tell the Government to look after my children ... Tell my people to obey the Government as they have done during my life. Tell the Laikipia Masai to move with their cattle to the Loita plains." Since the Masai set the highest store by the deathbed wish of any chief Laibon, Legalishu was left with no option but to reverse his earlier stand. At the end of May, 1911, a treaty was drafted, signed by the Masai elders and formally endorsed by the Colonial Office, while another 2,000 square miles were added to the southern reserve. Early in June, the great exodus got under way again.

Napoleon's retreat from Moscow may have been a dress parade by comparison. Planned routes were forgotten as ten thousand Masai, 175,000 cattle and over a million sheep sprawled out across the Rift and its two escarpments like nails spilled from a giant's keg. In some areas the march was reduced to a crawl by waist-deep mud as heavy rains set in. Other routes proved waterless and devoid of pasture. Cows and sheep died in droves when rinderpest broke out. Many families gave up trying and simply squatted on settler farms in the valley. Government officers attached to the move despaired of keeping even a semblance of order. One gave vent to his frustrations in doggerel:

> Oh dear, will it never be finished for ever?
> This Promised Land exodus, how it does pall!
> There's Ol-Beress in the deuce of a mess;
> He can't keep his cattle at all.
> The settlers abuse us, there's none to excuse us.

The furrows are broken, their crops trampled lie.
Oh! powers that be, any kazi* give me
Except further tramps with the giddy Masai.

By mid-August, the situation had so deteriorated that Ainsworth was called in from the lake province to take charge. Recognizing at once that the evacuation would become a rout if not carried out in relays, he ordered the bulk of the Masai back to Laikipia. This decision was followed by another cable from another Colonial Secretary, Lewis Harcourt, who showed himself no less a champion of African rights than his father had been during the railway debates of the 1890s. As a consequence of complaints over the alleged inadequacy of the grazing on the Loita plains, Harcourt suspended the move until the northern section reaffirmed its "full and free assent" to be transferred. Legalishu lost no time in seizing this opportunity to reverse himself again and Laikipia was declared to be a Masai reserve until the end of time, which proved to be nine months. In May, 1912, Harcourt also underwent a change of heart. Having been informed to his satisfaction that the Loita grazing was superior to Laikipia's (in fact it was not), he directed that the evacuation be carried out after all.

Legalishu countered immediately with a move that no one could have expected. He engaged a Nairobi lawyer who obtained a temporary injunction restraining the Government from carrying out its eviction order. The Masai case was then fed into the slowly grinding mill of the law, and another year went by before it was dismissed. Undismayed, Legalishu appealed, and in December, 1913, the case was thrown out again—on a point almost as delicate as it was astonishing. The verdict held that the East Africa Protectorate was, juridically, a foreign country in its relations with Britain, that all agreements between the Masai and the Colonial Office were therefore treaties between two nations, and as such "not cognisable" in the courts. Although the tribe could have appealed this rather slick decision once more—to the Privy Council—its funds were by now exhausted. Nothing remained but to accept the verdict and depart from Laikipia. The latter presented no difficulty. Some months earlier, almost as if subconsciously aware of what the court's decision would be, the northern Masai, on their own initiative, had migrated without fuss into the southern reserve.

*

---

* Work

Officially, the settlers had been no more than bystanders during the entire seesaw charade, but the evidence suggests that the weight of their influence—exerted on Masai and Government alike—probably decided the outcome. More than one official smelled a rat. From the very beginning, Ainsworth felt "inclined to suspect that outside pressures had been brought to bear on [Lenana]." Jackson, who favored the move, nonetheless called it "a sorry show," and all but declared outright that at least one important statement by Legalishu had been distorted to indicate the northern Masai's approval of their own ouster. McGregor Ross hinted that Lenana's deathbed wish might have been no more than a "convenient report." The behavior of the colonists tended to reinforce these suspicions. They made no secret of their wish to occupy Laikipia, or of their opposition to any move which might forestall them. When the Laikipia Masai went to court, an angry rumor circulated among the settlers that Ainsworth had suggested the action to Legalishu. "I hope this is untrue," wrote Delamere to the Protectorate's Chief Secretary, "as I believe in his wrong-headed way Mr. Ainsworth has had the interests of the country at heart. But he has always denied the rights and benefits of the civilization to which he should be a prop ... and it is possible that he has taken up this attitude with regard to the Masai movement." Ainsworth took "extreme exception" to the charge, and subsequently received an apology from the instigator of the rumor,* but the colonists had showed their hand. No words were minced by the official history of the reserve, which stated flatly that "the suggestion to move the Masai was undoubtedly made in the interests of European settlers."

Just possibly, the relocation was carried out entirely on Government initiative so as to give the settlers access to an especially productive region and thus increase the volume of livestock produce exports. This, however, was simply not the pattern of Colonial Office behavior at the time; colonist demands were seldom heeded unless political pressure was applied. Government, moreover, possessed only fragmentary awareness of Laikipia's agricultural value, while the white ranchers knew it to be an unmatched pasture. As one settler put it, "a European requiring a stock farm cannot go wrong in acquiring land formerly occupied by Masai, who are experts in choosing grazing grounds." In the eviction of the tribe from its second home, one finds it difficult not to detect the fine Caucasian hand of the colonists.

---

* Ainsworth made it clear, however, that he considered the Masai right in seeking legal redress. "If they really thought that they were being unjustly treated," he wrote, "it was a much more civilized way of doing things than going into rebellion."

*"It is a great encouragement to think
that at last we have a man at the head
of affairs who is really interested
in the country and wants it to prosper."*

If the settlers were indeed responsible for the Masai highway robbery, the act at least testified to their buoyant morale. During 1909, as the clumsy machinery of the second Masai move began to gather momentum, the country also experienced the last of its three consecutive dry seasons. At the end of March, 1910, the unexpected arrival of the big rains brought a long succession of punctual seasons and bountiful harvests. At about the same time, the high tide of the labor shortage appeared to be receding, as Africans began to cultivate a greater collective taste for the blankets, khaki trousers, bicycles and other manufactured goods they could buy with farm wages. Settlers took new heart also from the mounting success of Delamere's experiments with rust-resistant cereals, livestock cross-breeds and marketing schemes. As earnings rose, moreover, so too did the value of the farms. A good yield in a single season could enable a planter or rancher to meet his bank overdraft (or at least part of it) and still retain profits to plow back into the development of his own holding. He could buy a new thresher or disc-furrow plow, invest in dairying machinery or concrete dams and iron pipeline for irrigation. He might acquire more acreage and add coffee, sisal or wattle to his existing crops. He could build up his herds and flocks by importing high-grade rams from Australia, pedigree bulls and prize pigs from England. These improvements in turn were not slow in bringing additional profits. It seemed possible that Kenya was about to round the corner.

*

Not that spirits had ever really flagged. Even during the worst of the drought, the country's homesteaders and prospective colonists had remained supremely confident in their land and its potential. Symbolizing this optimism, a single week in 1908 had witnessed the largest mass arrival of white settlers ever to debark at Kilindini—and one of the more courageous pioneering gestures since Delamere had committed his fortune to the highlands. The immigrants, 280 Transvaal Boers, were headed for the Uasin Gishu plateau, intending to transform its wind-whipped virgin prairies into the promised land which the Zionists of 1903 had failed to recognize. Led by a bearded Gentile Moses named van Rensburg, they may not have realized fully the task that faced them, for

Uasin Gishu was by far the Protectorate's least known farming region. It also happened to be the least accessible. The pathless route from railhead at Nakuru climbed three thousand feet up one of the most vertiginious and heavily forested slopes of the Mau. The way was blocked by alternating layers of juniper and solidly packed bamboo. Torrential rains often embedded the party's ox-drawn wagons up to their axles in mud; sometimes several days would pass before three spans of oxen—48 beasts in all—could extricate a single wagon. The total distance was less than 75 miles, but it took four days to cover the first seven miles out of Nakuru. The entire journey lasted two months.

Once on the plateau, the colonists had to start small. The capital of any single Transvaal family probably did not exceed £50, and for some time, all eked out a Robinson Crusoe existence. Apart from salt, tobacco and ammunition, they paid cash for nothing. Houses were built of grass, mud and rough stone, the latter hand-quarried by the settlers themselves. They baked their own bread from maize flour ground in small hand mills, brewed coffee made of roots, tailored their clothes from the skins of the game they shot for beef; even shoes were made of giraffe hides. Barter with the Nandi brought in an occasional cow in exchange for tobacco. A little money trickled in as some of the men hired out as assistants on distant English farms while others earned a few rupees as transport riders, carrying freight and mail between the railway and various outlying settlements. Very slowly, the land was cleared. Not everyone had a plow, but harrows were fashioned from the trunks and limbs of acacia trees, with wooden pegs used for nails. With their small savings, the settlers were gradually able to engage a few Nandi as farm hands; in due course they saw their fields planted and harvested. And as they sowed, so too did they reap: within less than a decade of their arrival, Uasin Gishu was to become an ocean of cereal—the biggest wheat-growing region in the Protectorate. The new colonists had performed a dramatic and risky act of faith, but they found the odds with them. For richness of soil, the land they had chosen was unsurpassed anywhere in Kenya.

*

The Transvaalers had also chosen the right time to make their new homes. It was not only the weather that favored settlers after 1909; so too did the new Governor, Sir Percy Girouard. A dapper, monocled French Canadian, Girouard had succeeded Lugard as High Commissioner of Northern Nigeria, and was the first Governor of Kenya since Eliot to take up the cudgel for the colonists. In his view, the white farmers were not merely to be tolerated as a necessary evil; it was vital that they be given active encouragement, that their cause be advanced as serving the best interests of the Empire. High priority, therefore, went to patching up the long-standing settler–Administration vendetta.

The intensity of the cold war is said to have been brought home to Girouard, in a curious way, almost immediately after he took office. He was a physical fitness enthusiast and made a practice of taking pre-breakfast jogs outside Nairobi. One morning, so the story goes, he ran across a young Englishman working out on the same path and greeted him cordially, only to hear the reply: "Oh, go to hell, you bloody settler." It later transpired that the young man was a member of Girouard's own staff who had not yet met his chief. Whether or not this little drama ever took place, it is a matter of record that Girouard lost no time in inviting Delamere to Government House for an informal but exhaustive discussion of the country's problems. The men liked each other on sight, and Girouard was glad to accept Delamere's reciprocal invitation to Equator Ranch. These gestures by the Governor and the leader of his "opposition" were generally interpreted as the dawn of a less acrimonious and more constructive day in the settler–official relationship. Lady Delamere voiced the hopes of all whites when she wrote: "It is a great encouragement to think that at last we have a man at the head of affairs who is really interested in the country and wants it to prosper." Girouard lived up to expectations simply by making it a matter of policy to seek out settler views rather than have them brought to his attention in irrational demands or unedifying demonstrations. Animosities, to be sure, did not vanish overnight, nor were certain points of bitter dispute ever removed, but there was no mistaking that Kenya's political climate had changed from one of coexistence to concord. "Indeed," wrote Cranworth in 1912, "now it may be said that ill-feeling is almost if not entirely obliterated."

But more than harmony was needed to put the country on its feet. When Girouard took office, he found Kenya deeply imbedded in what the *East African Standard* called "an inextricable financial morass." Although the Protectorate's annual revenues had reached £250,000 in 1909, expenditures had mounted to the half-million mark. Even the annual grant-in-aid (about £130,000 at the time) was little more than a fragile thumb in a dike that threatened to burst at any moment. Although agriculture held the long-range cure for the country's economic sickness, the medicine was locked up, so to speak, in a strongbox of outside neglect. If farm exports were to bring Kenya out of the red, a vast public works program had to be set in motion. The railway in particular cried out for maintenance and development. Deterioration of rolling stock had reduced the outward movement of produce to a crawl. Overseas shipments from Mombasa were hobbled by the absence of a deep-water pier at Kilindini. After nearly ten years, no branch lines had been built to tap such productive regions as Kikuyuland and northern Kavirondo, although as early as 1904, Eliot had stated that "in order to make the Uganda Railway pay ... it is absolutely necessary to provide feeders for its traffic." The railway, as Churchill put it, was "only a trunk, without its necessary limbs and feeders."

Other essentials of a modern infrastructure were not much less urgently needed. Government agricultural and veterinary services were sparse, rain churned the few existing roads into impassable ribbons of mucilage, there were only two hospitals worthy of the name, public education did not exist. But all these things cost money, and Kenya had not the money to spend. Four-fifths of the country's total annual revenues were instantly swallowed by the routine demands of public works, police and army, while the remainder was sucked into the seemingly bottomless pit of repayments on the grant-in-aid. All yearly revenue increases automatically reverted to the British Treasury, leaving Kenya without the elbow room of even a small surplus. This debt placed the Protectorate under what was in effect a double rule: that of the Treasury as well as the Colonial Office. The Treasury, moreover, had all but disqualified Kenya from eligibility for any loans until the grant-in-aid was liquidated and the budget balanced. Since it was practically impossible to meet either of those conditions without a massive infusion of the loan capital that would permit desperately needed development projects to stimulate the economy, Girouard seemed trapped in a squirrel cage.

He found his way out, tackling the railway first. Not far from Nairobi, near the fringes of Kikuyuland, lay a broad and uncommonly lush expanse of farming country where a few settlers had already started growing coffee and sisal with promising results. Their progress, however, seemed threatened by the absence of any rail link with the line to Mombasa. Although barely thirty miles separated the farms from Nairobi, the transport of produce by ox-drawn wagons over dust-choked, pothole-riddled dirt paths could occupy a week or longer, become stalled entirely during the rains. Shipping schedules and delivery contracts were seldom met, and profits often became losses. The lack of a railway branch discouraged wider settlement of the land; prospective farmers naturally wanted assurance that their crops would be moved with something like swiftness. Farther north, moreover, on the rich red soil of Kikuyuland, tribal cultivation promised another substantial market—if it could be reached. Girouard was determined to open up the entire region, but he was also mindful of the Treasury's almost certain reaction to any proposal that it invest money in a branch line. A mild stratagem was therefore not out of order.

Girouard made his first move by asking for the moon: funds to build a 120-mile feeder line from Nairobi to the foothills of Mount Kenya, and as he no doubt anticipated, the request was rejected out of hand. He then lowered his sights and sought approval of the building of what he called a "tramway" running only as far as Thika, where most of the new European farms were situated. Apparently impressed with Girouard's conversion to thrift, the Treasury endorsed the modest proposal, and the "tramway"—which happened to be built to the same gauge as the main line—became the country's first operating feeder branch. Its opening immediately assured a steady and rapid flow of sisal and coffee exports. New farms multiplied around Thika, land values rose from ten shillings to three pounds per acre, and the whole region soon became a major revenue earner. In due course, the tramway was also to penetrate Kikuyuland and finally reach Mount Kenya, as one of the railway's busiest and most profitable branch lines.

A much more important step was taken toward solvency when, after prolonged negotiation, an agreement was arrived at with the Treasury allowing less severe conditions for the erasure of the grant-in-aid. Under the new terms, generally called the "half and half" arrangement, only half of every annual increase in revenues would be earmarked as a grant-in-aid installment, while the other half could be turned to public services and other expenditures for Protectorate needs. Although something less than a windfall, the new funds enabled Girouard and his own treasurer to perform a minor miracle on the bookkeeping high wire and balance the budget within three years. In 1912, the Treasury made its last grant-in-aid; Kenya was finally removed from the charity rolls. But even before discharging that debt, Girouard, with the colonists' aid, had been able to score an even greater triumph. In 1911, the Treasury's ruling on financial aid had in effect been defied when Girouard prevailed on the Colonial Office to raise a direct loan from Parliament. Pleased with the budget performance, taking new note of mounting settler productivity and correctly assuming a speedy end to the grant-in-aid, Parliament had required little coaxing. While the loan was modest (only £250,000) it hastened completion of the Thika "tramway" and allowed construction to begin on the badly needed deep-water pier at Kilindini. Exports would soon move swiftly as a result.

The real significance of the loan, however, was that Kenya had never received one before. Up to 1911, England seemed almost resigned to

accepting the country as little more than an imperial millstone, a recip-
ient of alms that would not be worth the risk of investment for many
years. That outlook could be seen to undergo a drastic change with Parliament's gesture of confidence in Girouard—and more to the point, in
the settlers' increasingly evident ability to make the land pay. The loan
symbolized the beginning of the breakup of a decade-long logjam.

*"The motley collection of so-called
racehorses was equalled only
by the class of owners and jockeys."*

Fortune seemed to be smiling on the highlands at last. As profits began
to come in, the colonists—Kenya had more than 3,000 Europeans by
1911—not only set about improving their farms but began looking to
their own creature comforts. Slowly but perceptibly, the grass and corrugated iron shanties of the pioneering years were giving way to stately
English country houses with walls of mortised cut-stone, Elizabethan
half-timbered façades and lead-mullioned windows that overlooked terraces, lawns and formal gardens. The old packing-case furniture was
broken up and fed into huge stone fireplaces in commodious drawing
rooms. Oil paintings replaced rifles on walls, leopard and zebra skins
went into storerooms as Persian carpets arrived from London. Profits
also permitted a more generous measure of leisure: in 1911, Kenya farmers spent £23,000 on agricultural implements while drinking up £30,000
worth of whisky, gin, brandy and beer. A climate of animated gracious
living was steadily permeating the white homesteads on the Rift and the
Mau. The highlands had got off to a good start toward the swinging life-
style which would presently win the region the nickname "happy valley."
    This may have reflected itself most visibly at first in a heightened
enthusiasm for recreation, although the settler had always played nearly
as hard as he worked. Farming amid the largest concentration of big
game on the planet offered limitless opportunities to bag lions and
leopards, collect record elephant tusks and buffalo and antelope horns.
Traditional English sports seemed to thrive on African soil. Kenya's
first cricket match had been played in Nairobi in 1899, and since that
time cricket pitches had been virtually strewn across the highlands. So
too had tennis courts, football fields and golf courses. The Protectorate
had six of the latter, at least three of which boasted the unique hazard of
lions in the rough. Fly fishing caught on overnight when the icy streams
of the Aberdare mountains were stocked with New Zealand rainbow

trout. Fox-hunting was practiced with no less demented abandon than in England—even without the fox. It was not uncommon, in the frost of an early morning on the equatorial uplands, to hear the tinny blare of a horn and watch several dozen yelping hounds give chase to a terror-stricken jackal or duiker, while a mounted posse of settlers and their wives, resplendent in scarlet coats and dazzling white pith helmets, galloped hard in the wake of the pack. India contributed to the sporting life. Three polo matches were held every week in Nairobi, while pig-sticking had its devotees wherever a wart-hog appeared. The latter pastime had been introduced by Meinertzhagen and other KAR officers who used bayonets lashed to the ends of bamboo poles until the proper lances were imported. "I should think," wrote Churchill after an afternoon of spearing in the Rift Valley, "that the most accomplished member of the Meerut Tent Club would admit that the courage and ferocity of the African warthog, and the extreme roughness of the country ... make pig-sticking in East Africa a sport which would well deserve his serious and appreciative attention."

Sport could sometimes show a functional side. Farmers earned extra cash from the hides and skins of the animals they shot; a good pair of elephant tusks could pay the operating expenses of a medium-sized farm for a year. The Kisumu golf course was built by Ainsworth, who loathed the game, simply to clear several square miles of malaria-breeding vegetation. (Once this had been done, however, Ainsworth somehow became an ardent golfer.) Perhaps most significantly, active competition on the playing fields enabled settlers and officials to release aggressions that might otherwise have found less wholesome outlets. Cranworth made a point of applauding the Nairobi District Commissioner who organized a series of biennial colonist–Administration tournaments in various sports. "It is manifestly impossible," he wrote, "to feel a lasting rancour against a man with whom you have but lately fought an enjoyable game of football or polo."

*

Animosities went down the drain completely every Christmas and July, during Nairobi's race week, a joint settler–official enterprise which was also the Protectorate's major sporting and social event. Racehorses had in fact appeared on the scene before the colonists—even before completion of the railway—when Government officers held a meet at Machakos, but the founding of the East Africa Turf Club in Nairobi in 1900 gave the settlers an equal share in the sport. While the Turf

Club in its earliest years had a conspicuously swayback character, the absence of thoroughbreds was compensated for by the attendance. Nearly everyone rode to the track—a patch of bare ground near the railway station—on ponies, donkeys, camels, rickshaws, Scotch carts and two-wheeled bullock-drawn tongas. The turnout was both large and gaudy. Government officials and KAR officers glittered with medals, ceremonial swords, red sashes and plumed helmets. Settlers decked themselves out in well-worn Norfolk jackets, industriously patched riding breeches, frayed wing collars with stained regimental or school ties, and sun helmets the size of manhole covers. Their wives resembled snowmen with parasols. Asian spectators moved in an eddying spectrum of gaily colored saris, turbans and high-collared white linen chogas. Some of the Africans sported red and green blankets, others wore only their pendulous ear ornaments, brass anklets, shields and spears. It was a far cry from Epsom Downs.

So too were the races, which were nothing if not extemporaneous. The first meeting in Nairobi had even included a mule sweepstakes. Meinertzhagen, who rode in the 1903 Christmas meet, noted that "the motley collection of so-called racehorses was equalled only by the class of owners and jockeys ... The whole entertainment offered me great amusement, because it required such a deal of imagination to take it seriously ... We drove down to the course in a four-wheeled conveyance hired from the bazaar, drawn by four horses which subsequently ran in the races. None of the horses had previously been introduced to four-in-hand harness." The second race, he said, was interrupted when "a silly rhinoceros" made a half-hearted charge at the horses. "Nobody had a gun to scare him away, and we had to wait for at least half an hour before he took himself off." In one race, Meinertzhagen finished third, but deprecated his accomplishment since only five horses started. A shortage of mounts, indeed, was the bane of the Turf Club's existence during the lean years. A story has been told that the Government saved the club from temporary extinction in 1906 when lack of entries threatened to cancel a meet. Stewart is said to have called an emergency session of his officials and informed them that any man who did not wish transfer to a hardship post would do well to find "anything with four legs" and enter it. The meeting went off as scheduled and the sport of kings managed to survive.

As much as anything else, race week offered an excuse for a holiday, since few colonists could visit Nairobi more than twice a year. A certain amount of business, to be sure, was transacted. Farm implements were bought and deliveries of crops arranged; there was haggling with the

Land Office, and meetings were held among settlers to discuss prices, freight charges and wage rates. But mainly a carnival spirit prevailed. Besides the Turf Club events, special tennis, golf, cricket, football and polo matches were organized for the visitors. At a less formal level, there were rickshaw races on Government Road and the newly built Sixth Avenue,* while cockfighting took place in an abandoned shed just outside the railway yards. (Local roosters proved a fair substitute for gamecocks.) One could attend amateur theatricals, go to banquets at Nairobi's three hotels or crash any number of ostensibly private dance parties. The latter in particular provided an unsurpassed opportunity for widows and unmarried sisters, since, as Cranworth noted, "the settler from the back blocks has very likely not met a white lady since his last race meeting and is ready to see beauty in the most meagre charms."

There was also a less well-behaved side to the merrymaking. Nairobi on race week nights could often resemble Dodge City at the end of a cattle drive. Mounted farmers galloped through the town, putting out street lamps with Winchesters and horse pistols. Bearded elephant hunters in ripped shorts and reeking bush jackets strode into the pubs and stood everybody to drinks, paying the chits on the credit of the 100-pound ivory tusks they carried under their arms. Customers at any bar could be scattered two or three times a night when some horseman cantered through the doors, peppered the ceiling with birdshot and helped himself to the nearest whisky bottle without dismounting. No one tried to keep track of the fist fights; few even turned to look around when someone was tossed bodily through a hotel's second-storey window. Sport of a different kind was to be had at the "Japanese Legation," a corrugated iron bungalow on Victoria Street where a number of Yokohama prostitutes did a land-office business. The wine and champagne never stopped flowing; there was no such thing as "time, gentlemen." A hotel manager once had the temerity to tell Delamere and his party that the bar was about to close; the man was promptly locked in his own refrigerator. Providentially, he did not freeze to death. Nor, indeed, did race week casualties ever amount to anything much more serious than a few black eyes and an incalculable number of marathon hangovers. The only real sufferers were the inevitable minority of spoilsports. "Those worthy citizens," wrote Cranworth, "who write regularly to the papers to complain of the disturbance to their ordered lives should remember that what they call excess represents merely the pleasures omitted for six months but now concentrated in some five days."

---

* Later Delamere Avenue; today Kenyatta Avenue.

*

Nairobi itself had begun to cast off a good deal of its shantytown complexion as the first decade of settlement came to a close. For some years, a municipal ordinance had prohibited the pitching of tents anywhere outside a specified camping area. Corrugated iron roofs were giving way to red tile. The early Hooverville shacks were being demolished; on their sites rose more durable if not much more elegant stone structures. More than 14,000 people (including some 600 whites) lived in Nairobi in 1910, and they enjoyed pointing out to rubes from the Rift a modestly baroque complex of lumpy stone Government buildings, an airy hospital, three hotels, a Masonic temple, Anglican and Roman Catholic churches, a synagogue and numerous mosques and Hindu temples. The sprawling brick railway station was nearing completion; with its sloping roof and squat clock tower, it could have been serving rail travelers anywhere in England or India. Model T Ford trucks, Albion two-seaters and Siddeley tourers rattled and jounced along the three main thoroughfares, which themselves were lined with neatly spaced rows of tall blue gum trees. The latter had been planted by Ainsworth while serving as Sub-Commissioner, and many white residents had followed his example with tree-shaded miniature driveways to their own bungalows. Gardens sprouted everywhere, flaunting a profuse competition of temperate and tropic blooms—English roses and bougainvillea, chrysanthemums and jacaranda, iris and Nandi flame. European housewives bought their groceries in a well-stocked modern market, gossiped in a tea shop. The town had its own electric lights, telephones almost always worked, and the *East African Standard* could boast that "night soil is removed by the conservancy cart *in the night.*"

What may have been Nairobi's proudest possession at this time was a real general practitioner. Dr. Roland Wilks Burkitt, who opened his consulting rooms in 1911, was a splenetic Irishman with a bedside manner that tended to alarm and therapies that could seem unorthodox at best. His surgery was located near a pig slaughterhouse, and passersby liked to claim that they could never distinguish between the squealing of the pigs and the cries of Burkitt's tonsillectomy patients. A firm believer in cold treatments as the best medicine for any fever, Burkitt ruthlessly pulled layers of blankets from the beds of shivering old men and women, then plunged the victims into icy baths; babies were placed in drafty doorways and sprayed with watering cans. Burkitt also set great store by bleeding as the cure for a broad spectrum of maladies, and often treated his patients to religious sermons while draining them of their blood. Although he was universally known as "Kill or Cure Burkitt," there is no record of his ever having deserved the first word of the sobriquet. He was in fact a highly skilled and dedicated physician* who then stood on the threshold of a twenty-seven-year career during which count was lost of the European, Indian and African lives he saved. As Nairobi's first private doctor, moreover, he seemed an almost unique symbol of a metropolitan progress that no other community in tropical Africa could claim during the early 1900s.

Not everyone appreciated such citified pretensions, and Nairobi was by no means without its detractors. The town, said the naturalist I. N. Dracopoli, "is neither African nor European, but seems to combine in one city the discomforts of two civilisations without the advantages of either." Stigand simply dismissed Nairobi as "this horrible place." Certainly there was room for improvement. Nairobi remained very much a zoo. Residents dining out at night carried rifles as a normal precaution against the occasional lion on Government Road or Sixth Avenue; flower beds were continually trampled by zebras and rhinos, sometimes even by stray elephants. Utilities and transportation left much to be desired. The first movie projector blew half the fuses in the town. Drinking water was obtained from public taps on street corners. The streets themselves continued to flow with waist-deep mud in the rains. "All the same," wrote Isak Dinesen, "Nairobi was a town; here you could buy things, hear news, lunch or dine at the hotels and dance at the Club. And it was a live place, in movement like running water, and in growth like a young thing." At the very least, it could probably have been said that Nairobi was the most cosmopolitan hick town in the world—thanks to Kenya's vaulting reputation as a happy hunting ground for upper-crust "sportsmen" who converged on the country in droves. At the Norfolk Hotel, known locally as the "House of Lords," the guest book resembled a condensed Burke's Peerage, Almanach de Gotha and Social Register. The presence of so thick a leavening of elite could not fail to lend an urbane elegance to what otherwise would have been little more than a well manicured clearing in the bush.

---

* In 1928, Burkitt went to London to engage an assistant. The recruit, Dr. J. R. Gregory, recalls that "during luncheon he asked me if I should like to go to a theatre. Thinking of some good entertainment I accepted with alacrity, but soon I found we were on our way … to St. Peter's Hospital for Diseases of the Rectum, where we spent the afternoon watching Mr. Lockhart-Mummy operate."

"Excepting of course the food served on German liners, never have I tasted such filth."

To assure a continually increasing influx of aristocratic tourists, and the revenues they brought with them, the railway published an illustrated brochure which highlighted the country's attractions, and arranged with Thos. Cook & Son for round trip package tours between Europe and the headwaters of the Nile. The rail journey from the coast was the high spot. Four mornings every week, at eleven o'clock sharp, the Uganda Mail chuffed through the baobabs and coco palms of Mombasa on the first leg of its 580-mile struggle to Lake Victoria. At eleven-fifteen the following morning, the train was due to arrive in Nairobi, and sometimes it did. Thanks, however, to what Henry Seaton has called "the glorious inconsequence of the time-table," passengers could usually count on anywhere between six and twenty-four additional hours of travel. There may never have been another train ride quite like it.

Almost every mile of the route offered some obstacle, hidden or otherwise. Immediately after crossing Macupa creek to the mainland, the train commenced laboring up the sharp inclines of the Rabai hills, where even the faintest drizzle transformed the dust on the tracks into a fine lubricating oil which deprived the locomotive wheels of all traction. If rain fell, the engine driver had to reverse to a level stretch, wait for the boiler to cool, work up another head of steam and then literally charge at the gradient in the hope that sheer momentum would carry the locomotive to the crest. It sometimes took two or three attempts, and the process could be repeated a dozen times during the journey.

A particularly challenging slope faced drivers near the western edge of the Taru. Jackson recalled one trip in which this gentle rise defeated several strenuous efforts by the engine, whereupon "the Goanese driver ... rather shamefacedly, came along, and asked me if I would turn out my men to collect firewood, and afterwards walk to the top. To show there was no ill-feeling, I replied, 'Turn 'em out? Of course, and they will push if you want them to.'" Jackson himself seized an axe and led the African woodcutters. Washouts were common, even on the Taru and other ostensibly waterless stretches of the route. With several hundred yards of track twisted and knotted by a freak storm, there was no choice but to wait for a repair train. The latter might arrive promptly if a telegram were sent without delay from the nearest station, but communications were not to be relied on entirely. Giraffes, elephants and rhinos continually knocked down telegraph poles and snapped the wires. Not infrequently, one of the beasts would challenge a locomotive. Even an elephant was hope-lessly outmatched in these contests, but before being slain by the engine it was capable of smashing a drive shaft, cracking the boiler or bending just enough track to make another long wait necessary.

Nature was not the only saboteur. At many stops, trainmen and sta-tionmasters became embroiled in raging, interminable arguments over the disposition of some article of freight which might or might not have been cleared for delivery by the traffic manager. Bills of lading, receipts, invoices, shipping orders and other documents were consulted and brandished to a shouted counterpoint of imprecations in Hindi, Swahili and English, while passengers muttered curses of their own and waited, sometimes for an hour or longer. When the train finally lurched forward again, there was no assurance that it would proceed more than twenty yards without jolting to another halt; as often as not, signalmen forgot to throw the "line clear" signal. Although taken into account by the timetable, fueling and watering at every stop caused numerous unscheduled delays. At some stations water was piped in from distant rivers, and steam pumps and hydraulic rams broke down regularly. Wood fuel, freshly chopped and green, might prove indigestible to the locomotive boiler; during the rains the logs could not be ignited until saturated in paraffin. Some engine drivers also insisted on fueling their personal fireboxes. One, a well-known original named Sam Pike, made a practice of halting between stations, walking back along the line of carriages and demanding whisky or beer from the passengers if they wished the train to proceed. According to Foran, himself a veteran rider, "the hidden bottle was produced and handed over without further argu-ment, for Sam was a man of few words but meant what he said."

Ticket holders also contributed to the snail's pace. The railway was Kenya's liveliest social institution, and once a train entered the uplands area, few stops failed to become the occasion for leisurely exchanges of news and gossip between passengers and settlers, the latter having met the train for that purpose only. A few miles outside Nairobi, one eccen-tric Englishman, a convert to Islam, often laid out a spread of cakes, sweetmeats and coffee alongside the tracks; obliging engine drivers always stopped at this spot so that they and their riders could enjoy the impromptu hospitality. When a passenger with a rifle sighted a particu-larly handsome lion or gazelle outside the game reserve, there might be another unscheduled halt, perhaps lasting an entire morning, to permit the stalk to be completed. If the quarry was an antelope, the engine driver was rewarded for his patience with a joint of venison. Farmers on the Mau flagged eastbound trains as a matter of course, piling shotguns, bird dogs and picnic baskets into the brake van, and jumped off near some convenient lake on the floor of the Rift for a day's duck shooting; when the evening train picked the hunters up, the crew shared the bag.* Visiting dignitaries satisfied their appetites for game and scenery aboard private trains. "Everything moves on the smoothest of wheels for me," Churchill wrote his mother; "... a special train with dining and sleeping cars at my disposal ... We sat... on a seat in front of the engine with our rifles & as soon as we saw anything to shoot at—a wave of the hand brought the train to a standstill." It did not seem to matter that on the railway's single line of track, this practice meant throwing regular "schedules" into even greater than the customary disarray.

For all its diversions, the train ride to Nairobi offered minimal amenities. Churchill might have had his own diner, but ordinary mortals, if they did not take sandwiches with them or buy fruit from Swahili vendors at Changamwe, went hungry for eight or ten hours, sometimes longer, on the 103-mile stretch between Mombasa and Voi. Without one's own supply of soda water, beer or whisky, thirst while crossing the Taru became considerably more than a minor discomfort. Dark goggles were also advised on this section of the route as protection against the desert's red dust which penetrated every compartment in billowing red clouds. It was only natural that passengers would welcome the evening stop at Voi, where supper was served in one of the Dak bungalows which substituted for dining cars at two or three stations. The Dak bungalow was the Howard Johnson's of east Africa and looked every bit the oasis with its wine stewards, white-jacketed waiters and barmen. There was also a visitors' book in which passengers were invited to record their impressions of the fare. Critiques ranged from "the chef is a true artist" to "excepting of course the food served on German liners, never have I tasted such filth." The latter assessment was probably the more accurate. At Voi, the main course almost invariably consisted of iron boiled beef, rubber mashed potatoes and something that the menu called cabbage. All entrées were garnished with insects; diners ate with one hand while the other fanned away hordes of mosquitoes. An all but stupefying aroma of garlic permeated the premises. Yet the tolerant could usually come up with some kind word for dinner at Voi. "At least," remarked Foran, "your soup went down into your throat and not into your lap, as so often proves the case in railway dining cars."

---

* Local rail travel was generally lackadaisical. Settlers going from one station to another on the Rift usually paid their fares—when they remembered to do so—on arrival. One farmer is said to have journeyed to London on a second-class ticket between Nakuru and Elmenteita.

After brandy and cigars (the latter held the mosquitoes at bay) on the bungalow's veranda, passengers returned to their compartments, where bedding had now been laid out on upper and lower berths. For those who did not wish to join all-night bridge tournaments or stay up to gaze at the moon over Kilimanjaro, sleep came easily; after the trials of the Taru and Voi, the swaying motion of the train tended to do the work of a knockout drop. The first stop at dawn was usually Simba station at mile 229, where everyone stumbled to the platform, bleary-eyed and gummy-mouthed, for the ceremony of brewing morning tea or cocoa. Water was obtained from the locomotive boiler by adopting one of two techniques. Stigand described both: "The first is to make yourself very agreeable to the driver, and then inadvertently show him the teapot. The second method is, concealing the pot from his view, to make remarks calculated to raise his anger. If you do either of these things sufficiently well, the driver will probably find that he can dispense with a little steam and water, and turn on some handle inside the machine. Only if you have practised the first method, though, will he warn you to stand clear, which will be a sign to have the pot ready."

Whichever device was utilized in its preparation, the sunrise tonic brought all passengers to full consciousness—and readiness for the journey's pièce de résistance on the final hundred miles to Nairobi. Flanked on the north by the broken-tooth peak of Mount Kenya and by the pink-white mushroom of Kilimanjaro to the south, the train was now clattering out of Ukamba's eroded half-desert and approaching the Kapiti and Athi plains. Braving the showers of red-hot embers that poured from the locomotive smokestack, passengers climbed to the roofs of their carriages for an unobstructed view of the most massive and varied assemblage of game species anywhere on earth. To an English country squire whose estate might have been stocked with a few dozen deer, it was a revelation to look out on what almost seemed an ocean of zebra, giraffe, impala, Thomson's gazelle, Grant's gazelle, kob, hartebeeste, wildebeeste, oryx— hundreds upon endless hundreds of thousands of ruminants. As far as the eye could see to the southwest, the gently undulating prairies were nearly invisible beneath their thick-piled living carpet. Almost oblivious to the fire-breathing missile that lurched past, the uncountable herds grazed and gamboled as if man had never contaminated their placidly monotonous lives with his presence. The zebra nearest the tracks might raise their heads momentarily as the train thundered by, but would return at once to munching the grass, altogether unperturbed. Government had marked off the Kapiti and Athi plains as a game reserve, and by an unfathomable intuition the denizens knew that rifles would not molest them here.

"The array of porters and of tents looked as if some small military expedition was about to start."

The legal immunity of the Athi and Kapiti plains game did not frustrate those "sportsmen" among railway passengers who visited Kenya to elevate social status or satiate personal blood lust by killing animals. For many years, the bagging of east African trophies was not much less de rigueur to the world's white upper crust than the European grand tour, and since the practice furnished Kenya with one of its principal sources of revenue, vast expanses of the Protectorate were set aside for hunting. The word "safari" had caught on as a lure for affluent tourists; its cost seemed no object. To emulate Allan Quatermain on a four-month packaged expedition through Edwardian East Africa, one usually paid about $2,500—an amount that would be far greater today. Figures of two and three times that sum were not uncommon. Big game was big business because it was big logistics. Even the least bloodthirsty hunter was expected to carry a minimum armament of three rifles and a thousand rounds of ammunition, plus an assortment of colored rockets for signaling at night. These had to be packed in tin-lined cases and shipped to Mombasa a month in advance for customs clearance. The ordinary £50 hunting license, as a rule, was not considered sufficient; much red tape had to be unraveled to obtain special permits for individual giraffes and elephants with tusks exceeding a specified weight. Porters (at least thirty per hunter) had to be hired, along with headmen, gun bearers, askaris, cooks, syces and personal servants. There were tents, blankets, ground sheets, mosquito nets and water filters to be bought, medicine chests to be stocked with the proper drugs and syringes, chop boxes to be filled with tinned goods, preserves and other delicacies. Substantial supplies of salt and moth-killer were needed to preserve skins. Since few visitors had the time, inclination or ability to cope with these details, Kenya rapidly gave birth to a modest but thriving safari industry. "One who wished to do so," wrote the *Chicago Tribune* cartoonist John T. McCutcheon after accompanying the Carl Akeley expedition in 1909, "could telegraph ahead ... and then, with only a suit-case, he could arrive, with the certainty that everything would be in readiness."

The wealthiest visitors usually went to the firm of Newland and Tarlton, which ran private expeditions like high-priced circuses and pampered its customers like the royalty they often were. Penetrating darkest Africa on a Newland and Tarlton safari was something akin to taking a swank regiment out on dress parade. The clients and their professional white hunters rode at the head of the column, which often consisted of a hundred or more porters and askaris, the former sporting dark blue jerseys with the letters "N & T" sewn in red on the chests, the latter uniformed in blue blouses and white knickerbockers. (Each porter also wore two pairs of brand-new boots around his neck. These were required by the Government but uncomfortable on the march.) Camp exuded opulence. The capitalist huntsmen lived in capacious double roof ridge tents, removed the grime of a day's stalk in collapsible canvas bathtubs, slept under Jaeger blankets on inflated rubber mattresses and enjoyed vintage wines with every meal. During the actual hunt, the use of saddle horses or mules held exhausting tramps through tall grass or dense bush to a minimum. The quarry was stalked by skilled African trackers and virtually coaxed to within rifle range. Trophies were skinned, salted and cured on the spot by expert skinners, then hastened by runner to Nairobi and shipped onward to London for mounting by Rowland Ward of Piccadilly. It can be said that Newland and Tarlton—in fact all safari enterprises—did everything to please the visiting crown or merchant prince but squeeze the trigger for him. Indeed, they were even prepared to perform that service if nerves failed at the crucial moment.

More than one old hand deplored this sissifying of a virile adventure. "To my mind," wrote Stigand, "champagne, armchairs and seven or eight course dinners with Goanese cooks and every modern luxury are out of place, and spoil the charm of the wilds." Not surprisingly, Stigand was echoed by Theodore Roosevelt, who made his celebrated east African expedition in 1909 and remarked that "our tents, our accommodations generally, seemed almost too comfortable for men who knew camp life only on the Great Plains, the Rockies and in the North Woods." But Roosevelt, as was only to be expected, experienced more than his share of discomfort and physical danger, and so too did nearly all the transient members of a somewhat less than effete international haut monde. For all its sybaritic trappings, an east African safari was not the best of insurance risks; one's lineage and bank balance mattered little to a wounded lion or stampeding elephant. And for most amateur hunters, this was what made the journey worth the expense. Challenge was the name of the game.

*

Some of the more inventive tourists, notably the Americans, saw big game as the opportunity for stunts. One Buffalo Jones, who entertained his British cousins by lassoing lions and rhinos, was described by

Frederick Jackson as "a very fine-looking elderly man, who might well have remained content with his reputation in America, instead of getting himself up for effect like 'Uncle Sam' and parading the streets of Nairobi with an escort of cowboys, just as if they were about to enter the arena of a wild west show." Another lariat artist was a man called Tarpon Dick, who not only roped wild animals but dragged them into Nairobi and branded them on the rumps in front of the Norfolk Hotel. (At one time he also lassoed "Sir" Northrup Macmillan, who was watching the performance from his rickshaw, but in this case the iron was spared.) Paul Rainey took a pack of trained bear hounds into the bush and turned them loose whenever a lion was reported in the vicinity. The dogs' success was remarkable. "A lion that roared after midnight," wrote Jackson, "sounded not only its own death-knell but that of any other that was with it." Jackson added, however: "Whether [Rainey's] method of killing them is sport or not, is a matter of opinion." Rainey was also a pioneer in big game movie photography, using several sturdy but cumbersome pneumatically operated cameras; when pumped up, the air contained in each contraption was enough to expose thirty feet of film. Binks was once engaged as Rainey's cinematographer in a lion hunt; when he asked what he should do if the air supply gave out while the lion was charging, Rainey told him to throw the camera at the beast.

Other film experiments were more colorful than Rainey's, if less successful. In 1909, a man named Boyce went into the Rift Valley to get the world's first aerial photographs of big game, using twenty-nine electrically operated movie cameras suspended from captive balloons and box kites. After several trial balloon ascents in Nairobi (with settlers and Africans volunteering as human guinea pigs), Boyce moved the carnival from the Norfolk to the railway station, his porters blasting dissonances on rented bugles and waving tiny American flags. The specially chartered train was decorated with red, white and blue bunting which promptly took fire when the locomotive began spewing embers from its smokestack. No damage, however, was sustained by the cameras and their airborne rigs, which were reassembled as soon as the expedition reached the valley floor. Boyce began working with a single balloon, which was inflated every morning and allowed to ascend several hundred feet. The camera's basket mount was secured by rope to a mule, which in turn was driven in the direction of whatever herds Boyce wished to photograph. In theory the system was foolproof, but flaws quickly became apparent after the balloon left the ground. One was the prevalence of unpredictable air currents in the valley; they caused the balloon's basket to perform a St. Vitus dance and played havoc with the camera's primitive shutter and focusing mechanisms. The balloon itself also conspired against picture-taking, simply by its presence. Herds vanished at the sight of the weird object careering about overhead, and after three days, not an animal could be found within camera range. It was also at this time that the balloon made its own escape, when an exceptionally muscular thermal current lifted it and the mule into a cloudbank on the Mau escarpment. Neither was ever seen again. Nor, one must assume, were any of Boyce's pictures.

*

Not all Americans put on vaudeville acts. Many, in fact, hunted in Kenya with objectives considerably less frivolous than "sport." Although there were no longer any mountains, lakes or rivers left to discover, the land which had so recently been opened up still offered innumerable treasures to the naturalist; it is likely that more scientific expeditions marched across east Africa in the first ten years of the 1900s than had been seen during the entire previous century. Of these, the two largest were led by Americans. The imposing elephant family that greets visitors to the American Museum of Natural History in New York—as well as the museum's lifelike bronze groups of lions, buffalo and Nandi spearmen—are among the fruits of the expedition organized by Carl Akeley in 1909. Included in the two tons of equipment carried by the party's sixty-five porters was a complete portable darkroom in which Akeley processed thousands of feet of film, probably the decade's best motion picture record of African game in its natural habitat. Rainey, Boyce and other camera trail-blazers were novices by comparison. And Akeley's own venture was dwarfed by the mammoth caravan which Roosevelt headed up in the same year for the Smithsonian Institution. Roosevelt himself, on first inspecting his 500 bearers and askaris, remarked that "the array of porters and of tents looked as if some small military expedition was about to start." Indeed, at least from the standpoint of firepower, the trek might have been likened to a re-enactment of San Juan Hill. During the ten months in which Roosevelt marched from Mombasa to the upper Nile, the barrels of his three rifles practically never stopped smoking. He personally shot no fewer than 296 animals, including nine lions, eight elephants, thirteen rhino (of which nine were the rare white type) and six buffalo. The expedition's total bag came to upwards of a thousand specimens of 164 different species, ranging from bull elephant to Naivasha pygmy mouse. The four tons of fine salt which the porters carried for curing skins could have been only barely adequate to their task.

Roosevelt's scientific objectives notwithstanding, this performance bordered on slaughter and evoked more than one shocked reaction from the conservation-minded, particularly in Kenya. Jackson, who otherwise looked on Roosevelt with something akin to hero worship, found it "a matter of great regret to learn from Colonel Roosevelt's own showing ... that he was so utterly reckless in the expenditure of ammunition, and what it entailed in the matter of disturbing the country; and that he so unduly exceeded reasonable limits in certain species." Cranworth commented on "the devastation that is done in the name of or on behalf of museums," and asked: "Do those nine white rhinoceros ever cause ex-President Roosevelt a pang of conscience, or a restless night? I for one venture to hope so."

This was the only unfavorable criticism leveled at Roosevelt during his visit. It may be, in fact, that he was the most honored guest— including Chamberlain, Churchill and the Duke of Connaught—to be welcomed in Kenya before the First World War. No doubt a certain ulterior motive lay beneath the red carpet that was rolled out for him. The expedition, as Foran noted, "brought the Protectorate a mass of invaluable free publicity" which "was chiefly responsible for attracting ... many keen sportsmen from almost every corner of the world." But it was more than his former high office and value as a drawing card that made Roosevelt persona uncommonly grata. "He proved to be the simplest of men," wrote Hobley, "frank in speech, devoid of any side, and, if a man had anything to say, he at once felt at ease and soon forgot that he was addressing a man who had lately been President of U.S.A." Jackson called it a "privilege and a pleasure to receive and entertain that great man ... It was only natural to expect him to be a very remarkable man, but I did not expect to find him quite the most interesting one I have ever met ... In a man who had held the position he had, and carried the weight he did, the thing that surprised me most was that he showed so much on the surface—his spontaneous outspokenness was simply delicious." Jackson was also captivated by Roosevelt's humor, although he noted that the celebrated grin was less than ogrish: "when he laughed he only showed the teeth of his lower jaw, and not a whole mouthful as represented in most caricatures."

As Acting Governor at the time, Jackson personally escorted Roosevelt from Mombasa to Nairobi aboard his own private train. (Roosevelt called the line a "railway through the Pleistocene.") The two naturalists spent most of the trip on the cowcatcher of the locomotive (an American Baldwin, to Roosevelt's delight), holding long discussions on the protective coloration of the game that grazed near the tracks. In the highlands,

Roosevelt received an almost royal welcome. At Equator Ranch, where he was Delamere's guest, he found that the latter had already written specially to England for two Swedish elk hounds which he hoped would help the ex-President track down a bongo—east Africa's most elusive antelope. (The dogs failed in their mission, but Roosevelt's son Kermit bagged two bongos without assistance.) During Roosevelt's fairly long stay in Nairobi, where he worked on several magazine articles and the manuscript of his book, *African Game Trails*, banquets were held in his honor almost every night.

Roosevelt paid back the compliments with interest. He was, after all, very much in his element and very much among his own kind. The terrain had a distinct déjà vu quality: "Again and again, the landscape struck me by its likeness to the cattle country I knew so well. As my horse shuffled forward, under the bright, hot sunlight, across the endless flats or gently rolling slopes ... I might have been on the plains anywhere, from Texas to Montana." More gratifying still were the fellow Anglo-Saxons who not only fêted him but seemed to personify his doctrines of the strenuous life and benign but firm Caucasian mastery of the world. Even aboard ship en route to Mombasa, he was busily admiring the imperial personality of the British officials on the passenger list, likening them to the Americans who "have reflected such honor on the American name" in the Philippines, Cuba, Puerto Rico, Panama and Santo Domingo. Special tribute was reserved for the army officers who were "going out to take command of black native levies in out-of-the-way regions where the British flag stands for all that makes life worth living ... Moreover, I felt as if I knew them already, for they might have walked out of the pages of Kipling."

*

The settlers, however, drew Roosevelt's warmest praise. It could hardly have been otherwise: "No new country is a place for weaklings," and the Britons who had gone out to tame Kenya were "frontiersmen of the best kind." Delamere in particular: "Indeed I do know," Roosevelt told Lady Delamere in a bread-and-butter letter, "that you and D. have the large outlook, that your success comes from the feeling that you have taken the lead in adding to the Empire the last province that can be added to the white man's part of it." He voiced similar admiration on meeting Harold and Clifford Hill, two of the country's foremost farmer-hunters: "We instinctively understood one another, and found that we felt alike on all the big questions, and looked at life, and especially the life of effort led by the pioneer settler, from the same stand-point. They reminded me, at every moment, of those Western ranchmen and homemakers with whom I have always felt a special sense of companionship and with whose ideals and aspirations I have always felt a special sympathy." Those words could have applied to any of the colonists whom Roosevelt met during his stay.

He was no less struck by the increasingly visible fruits of the settler effort. With every farmer's door open to him, he had ample opportunity to compare the country's agricultural progress with earlier pioneer cultivation and ranching on the American frontier. Kenya passed the test. The owner of a typical 500-acre mixed farm on the edge of the highlands "was growing all kinds of things of both the temperate and tropic zones: wheat and apples, coffee and sugar-cane. The bread we ate and the coffee we drank were made from what he had grown." On a neighboring ranch, "there were numerous outbuildings of every kind, there were flocks and herds, cornfields, a vegetable garden, and, immediately in front of the house, a very pretty flower garden, carefully tended by unsmiling Kikuyu savages ... Within the house, with its bedrooms and dining room, its library and drawing-room, everything was so comfortable that it was hard to realize that we were far in the interior of Africa." To be reminded, however, Roosevelt needed only to glance out of any farm window: "The wild velt came up to the door-sills, and the wild game grazed quietly on all sides within sight of the houses. It was a very good kind of pioneer life."

"Hooray, hooray! We're off to G.E.A."

The pioneer life was also starting to show a tidy profit. With the passing of the drought, with Girouard's fiscal reforms, with an ever-continuing influx of new farmers, Kenya in the five years before the First World War found herself the proprietor of a bustling stall on the world produce market. Next to the yield of the mammoth agricultural nations, the statistics of colonist output were minuscule, but the quality of their production assured volume sales, especially at a time when the demand for many staples outstripped the supply. Coffee's performance, stimulated in part by the opening of the Thika "tramway," may have been the most dramatic. The two years between 1909 and 1911 alone saw production of the high-grade Kenya coffee bean rise from 442 to nearly 800 tons, with a corresponding price jump from £45 to £80 per ton. In 1907, highland coffee exports were valued at £270; by 1913 the figure had vaulted to £18,000. It was only the start. Within fifteen years, Kenya's annual coffee crops would reach 10,000 tons, worth more than £1,000,000.

Other crops fared hardly less well. Thanks to the hybrids emerging from the test tubes of Delamere's laboratory, the local wheat market thrived; in bushels per acre, Kenya wheat output in 1912 was twice Canada's, at least its equal in quality. Plans were afoot in the same year for large-volume wheat exports; only the war delayed completion of a grain elevator at Kilindini. Maize production, 4,600 tons in 1910, rose to 6,000 tons the following year. Although maize was grown primarily for regional consumption, a railway freight charge reduction in 1910 enabled planters to sell 20,000 bags in Europe, and to lay the groundwork of a lucrative overseas maize trade. By the 1920s, maize exports of 1,000,000 bags would fetch £500,000 annually. The country's wattle not only provided the railway with the bulk of its fuel, but the unusually high tannin content of the bark created a flourishing export commerce. Sisal, first imported from German East Africa in 1902, showed itself to mature more rapidly than the Central American plant, while concurrent political unrest in the Caribbean raised both the world demand and the world price. By 1914, 7,500 acres of Kenya land were under sisal, which brought upwards of £20 per ton at London auctions. To protect its own trade from competition in the highlands, the Germans imposed a stiff duty on exports of sisal buds and shoots to Kenya. They were locking the barn door after the horse had been stolen: in just over a decade, overseas markets would be paying £500,000 annually for Kenya sisal crops.

Herds and flocks were also beginning to earn their keep. European wool brokers continually pressed Rift Valley sheep ranchers for their crossbreed merino fleece. In 1909, second cross merinos produced an average of five pounds of wool per clip; by 1912 the yield had reached eight pounds, while the fleece of third cross flocks was selling at nearly a shilling per pound. Regional beef and mutton sales extended outwards when Delamere's Nyama, Ltd. opened a refrigerating plant in Mombasa and secured a contract to supply incoming ships with mutton; during one period, upwards of 500 wethers were railed to Kilindini weekly. Butter from a cooperative creamery supplied all of Kenya and Uganda and laid the foundations of a sizable dairy industry production with a quality which in time would be excelled only by that of Denmark.

Kenya also sprung a surprise in proving herself not entirely destitute of mineral resources. In a somewhat forbidding and desolate part of southern Ukamba near the German border, there lay a thirty-square-mile body of water called Lake Magadi. At first glance it seemed frozen over. Indeed, one could almost walk on the solid white substance that coated its surface—at the risk of burning the feet even through leather soles. The "ice" was in fact crystalline soda, and although it was believed to be marketable even before any chemical analysis had been made, the inaccessibility of the lake ruled out bulk transport without prohibitive cost. In 1909, however, a private company sent an expedition to Lake Magadi, and the party's consulting chemist reported the deposits to be of an almost unmatched purity, easily convertible to commercial soda ash. He estimated, moreover, that the lake itself contained at least 200 million tons of the soda. The problem of transport vanished in 1911, when the Magadi Soda Company was formed and construction began on a 100-mile branch railway connecting with the main Nairobi–Mombasa line. Government granted a large site at Kilindini for a conversion plant and docking facilities. The rail extension was completed in 1913, and the company's directors estimated an initial soda traffic of 80,000 tons for the following year. Owing to the war, that export was delayed, but subsequent years were to see soda ash output rapidly reach annual tonnages of six figures, with yearly values of well over £1,000,000.

*

The most reliable measure of the growing jackpot was the railway's "down" traffic. In 1913, the General Manager's annual report stated that the "flourishing" east African trade had "outstripped the transport capacity of the railway." This may have been putting it gently. In the decade between 1904 and 1914, freight carried by rail from the interior to Mombasa rose from 5,700 to 76,900 tons, an increase of more than 1,300 percent. Approximately half of that total export traffic—shared by Kenya, Uganda, German East Africa and the eastern Congo—came from the highland farms. "Down" volume, to be sure, did not overtake "up" freights during this period, indicating what was in fact an unfavorable balance of trade. Yet in terms of the protectorate's national income, the gap could be seen to narrow spectacularly. In 1903, expenditures had stood at £311,000, revenues at £95,000, leaving a £216,000 deficit. By 1912, however the balance sheet showed expenditures up to £772,000, while revenues, soaring by nearly 700 percent, had reached £729,000 and erased all but £43,000 of the arrears. By any standards this was no mean performance. Even Lloyd George, Chancellor of the not always sympathetic Exchequer, could tell Parliament in 1912 that "there is no doubt at all about the enormous possibilities of this great country."

If that was the case, nearly all the credit belonged to the insignificant squirearchy of obstreperous nuisances who had somehow transformed a quixotic dream into what was beginning to look more and more like a sound investment.

*

On August 4, 1914, the curtain began to descend on the first act of Britain's imperial adventure in east Africa. The main business before Kenya's Legislative Council on that day was the question of whether there should be a closed season on duck hunting on Lake Naivasha, but the debate came to an abrupt end when a messenger entered the Council chamber with a cable which he handed to the Speaker. A state of war, it appeared, existed between Great Britain and Germany.

The immediate reaction to the news was a wave of confusion that swept from Mombasa to Lake Victoria. East Africa had been caught with its defenses down. Hardly anyone had taken notice of the brief item that had appeared six weeks earlier in the *East African Standard*, on the assassination of an obscure Austrian archduke, while accounts of the subsequent mounting crisis in Europe had been fragmentary even in Nairobi. His Majesty's armed forces in Kenya and Uganda on the eve of hostilities numbered about 1,900 askaris and some five dozen British officers. The Royal Artillery consisted of six Maxim guns mounted on Model T Fords; two of these weapons had jammed for Lugard in 1891 and had continued to malfunction faithfully ever since. There was also something called the Uganda Railway Volunteer Reserve, a body of 100 men commanded by one of the line's assistant accountants; they had been given occasional rifle practice to meet an emergency which everyone knew would never arise.

To hold off this assortment, the enemy on the other side of Mount Kilimanjaro was slightly better prepared. The Germans had an army of about 2,000 men, but they were backed up by forty modern field pieces, seventy machine guns and an air force. The latter consisted of a biplane which had been brought into the country as a feature of an exhibition celebrating the opening of Germany's Central Railway to Lake Tanganyika; although it had crashed on its first flight, this did not prevent an outbreak of extemporaneous air-raid warnings in Nairobi. For several days, residents of the town identified everything they saw in the sky—from locusts to the planet Venus—as a fleet of bombers.

But the British were quick to rally. East Africa's three KAR battalions were rushed out from isolated posts in Kenya and Uganda and deployed along the German border. An armored train patrolled the railway line along its vulnerable section east of the Rift. Martial law was declared and a handful of German nationals placed under arrest. A recruiting office opened in Nairobi, while sandwichmen with enlistment placards marched up and down the platform of the railway station. Delamere

rode off into the bush at the head of a volunteer elmoran patrol, scouting the Masai section of the border. Most other settlers answered
the call with equal fervor. No sooner did the news of the war reach
a European farm than the owner seized his elephant gun or carbine,
mounted his horse or mule and galloped off to Nairobi. In barely a fortnight, the town was swarming with "regiments" of volunteer cavalry
raised by ex-army officers or farmers with extra-loud voices: Wessell's
Scouts, Bowker's Horse, Arnoldi's Scouts. The Uasin Gishu Boers, who
had fought their British neighbors fourteen years earlier, formed themselves into a mounted commando called the Plateau South Africans.
Delamere's brother-in-law, Berkeley Cole, took command of 800 Somali
horsemen eager for a piece of the action.

It is probable that only the Somalis looked like soldiers of the King.
The European troops brought to mind an oversized sheriff's posse. Their
uniforms were faded khaki trousers or shorts, sleeveless bush jackets and
battered pith helmets or broad-brimmed terai hats bristling with ostrich
plumes and fish eagle feathers. Their horses and mules were caparisoned
with blanket rolls, water bottles, coffee pots and iron skillets. Even after
becoming merged as the East African Mounted Rifles—what Mervyn
Hill has called "this quaintest of regiments"—the irregular units did
not lose their picaresque character entirely. Just before departing for the
front, they passed in review for the new Governor, Sir Henry Belfield,
looking as smart as could be expected until somebody raised a cheer,
causing the regimental mules to bolt and transforming the dress parade
into pandemonium. But order was presently restored and the squadrons
trotted off, pennons snapping jauntily from makeshift bamboo lances.
Their objective, hopefully, was the key town of Tabora on the German
Central Line, and the men took up their war song, to the tune of "Marching Through Georgia," with bellicose good cheer:

> Hooray, hooray! We're off to G.E.A.
> Hooray, hooray! The squareheads we will slay.
> And so we sing this happy song
> Upon this happy day
> As we go marching to Tabora.

The carnival atmosphere quickly vanished, however, in a cloud of
gunsmoke. These pages are not the place for an account of the forgotten
but grim east African campaign of the First World War. Suffice it to say that
two years had to pass before Tabora fell (to Belgian rather than British
troops), and that German East Africa did not become the British territory

of Tanganyika until 1918. For that new addition to the Empire, Britain paid a price of nearly 50,000 English and African lives.

Yet there was reason for the volunteers to feel buoyant at the outbreak of hostilities. Not that they welcomed the war itself, which could hardly have come at a less timely moment in their task of reclaiming the wilderness. What had raised spirits was the unquestioned success of that trail-blazing effort. Barely a decade had seen Kenya's white settlers extricate themselves from the red and put the Protectorate on a paying basis, while Uganda's African cotton growers had performed a like service for their own country. No one, to be sure, had become a millionaire in Kenya or Uganda—nor did anyone expect to—but by 1914, few Englishmen were prepared to deny that the two countries had been worth more than the colossal nuisance of occupying and holding. Far from having encumbered herself with a colonial white elephant, it was beginning to look as if Britain might have taken title to an uncut imperial emerald. The troopers who took their amateurishly hell-for-leather departure from Nairobi also ushered out a pioneering era. The Empire's long and prosperous future in east Africa had been assured beyond the slightest doubt. For all of forty-nine more years.

BIBLIOGRAPHY

Allen, R. K. Unpublished historical notes, Lamu archipelago.

Anonymous. Unpublished historical narrative, Lamu island.

Ashe, R. P. *Chronicles of Uganda*. London: Hodder & Stoughton, 1894; reprinted 1971 by Frank Cass, London.

———. *Two Kings of Uganda*. London: Sampson, Low, 1890; reprinted 1970 by Frank Cass, London.

Austin, H. H. *With Macdonald in Uganda*. London: Edward Arnold, 1903.

Baker, Sir Samuel White. *The Albert N'yanza*. London: Macmillan, 1866; reprinted 1962 by Sidgwick & Jackson, London.

———. *Ismailia*. London: Macmillan, 1874.

Barrie, Sir James M. *An Edinburgh Eleven*. 3d edn, London: Hodder & Stoughton, 1896.

Beard, Peter Hill. *The End of the Game*. New York: Viking, 1965.

Beloff, Max. *Imperial Sunset*, vol. 1, *Britain's Liberal Empire, 1897–1921*, New York: Knopf, 1970.

Binks, H. K. *African Rainbow*. London: Sidgwick & Jackson, 1959.

Boteler, Thomas. *Narrative of a Voyage of Discovery to Africa and Arabia, Performed in His Majesty's Ships* Leven *and* Barracouta, *from 1821 to 1826, Under the Command of Capt. F. W. Owen, R.N.*, vol. 2. London: Richard Bentley, 1835.

Boyes, John. *John Boyes, King of the Wa-Kikuyu*. London: Methuen, 1911; reprinted 1968 by Frank Cass, London.

Burton, Sir Richard. *The Lake Regions of Central Africa*. London: Longman, Green, Longman & Roberts, 1860.

———. *Zanzibar: City, Island and Coast*. London: Tinsley Bros., 1872; reprinted 1967 by Johnson Reprint Corp.

Cameron, V. L. *Across Africa*. London: Daldy, Isbister, 1877.

Casati, Gaetano. *Ten Years in Equatoria and the Return with Emin Pasha*. London: Frederick Warne, 1891.

Christie, James. *Cholera Epidemics in East Africa: An Account of the Diffusion of the Disease from 1820 till 1872.* London: Macmillan, 1876; to be reprinted by Frank Cass, London.

Churchill, Randolph S. *Winston S. Churchill*, vol. 2, *Young Statesman, 1901–1914.* Boston: Houghton Mifflin, 1967.

Churchill, Winston S. *My African Journey.* London: Hodder & Stoughton, 1908.

Coupland, Sir Reginald. *East Africa and Its Invaders.* Oxford: Clarendon Press, 1938; reprinted 1965 by Russel & Russel, New York.

The Exploitation of East Africa. London: Faber & Faber, 1939; reprinted 1967 by Northwestern University Press, Evanston.

Cranworth, Lord. *A Colony in the Making.* London: Macmillan, 1912.

Cross, Colin. *The Fall of the British Empire.* London: Hodder & Stoughton, 1968.

Davidson, Basil. *Africa in History.* London: Weidenfeld & Nicolson, 1968; New York: Macmillan, 1969.

Dawson, E. C. *James Hannington, First Bishop of Eastern Equatorial Africa.* London: Seeley, 1887.

Dinesen, Isak. *Out of Africa.* New York: Random House, 1937.

———. *Shadows on the Grass.* New York: Random House, 1961.

Dracopoli, I. N. *Through Jubaland to the Lorian Swamp.* London: Seeley, Service, 1914.

Eliot, Sir Charles. *The East Africa Protectorate.* London: Edward Arnold, 1905; reprinted 1966 by Barnes & Noble, New York.

Fage, J. D. *An Atlas of African History.* London: Edward Arnold, 1958.

Farson, Negley. *Last Chance in Africa.* London: Victor Gollancz, 1949.

Foran, W. Robert. *A Cuckoo in Kenya.* London: Hutchinson, 1936.

———. *The Kenya Police, 1887–1960.* London: Robert Hale, 1962.

Forbes-Watson, R. *Charles New.* Edinburgh and London: Nelson, 1951.

Freeman-Grenville, G. S. P. *The East African Coast: Select Documents from the First to the Earlier Nineteenth Century.* Oxford: Clarendon Press, 1962.

Gardner, Brian. *The African Dream.* New York: Putnam, 1970.

Goldsmith, F. H. *John Ainsworth, Pioneer Kenya Administrator.* London: Macmillan, 1955.

Gregory, J. R. *Under the Sun.* Nairobi: The English Press, n.d.

Gregory, J. W. *The Great Rift Valley.* London: John Murray, 1896; reprinted 1968 by Frank Cass, London.

Grogan, E. S. *From the Cape to Cairo.* London: Hurst & Blackett, 1900.

Hamilton, Genesta. *Princes of Zinj.* London: Hutchinson, 1957.

Hardy, Ronald. *The Iron Snake.* London: Collins, 1965; New York: Putnam, 1965.

Harlow, Vincent, and Chilver, E. M. *History of East Africa*, vol. 2. Oxford: Oxford University Press, 1965.

Heminway, John Hylan, Jr. "A Double Quantum of Thyroid." Unpublished manuscript, Princeton University.

———. *The Imminent Rains*. Boston: Little, Brown, 1968.

Hill, M. H. *Permanent Way*. Nairobi: East African Railways & Harbours, 1949.

Hobley, C. W. *Kenya: From Chartered Company to Crown Colony*. London: H. F. & G. Witherby, 1929; reprinted 1970 by Frank Cass, London.

Hollingsworth, L. W. *A Short History of the East Coast of Africa*. London: Macmillan, 1957.

Hollis, A. C. *The Masai, Their Language and Folklore*. Oxford: Clarendon Press, 1905.

Hunter, J. A., and Mannix, Daniel P. *Tales of the African Frontier*. New York: Harper, 1954.

Huxley, Elspeth. *Red Strangers*. London: Chatto & Windus, 1939.

———. *White Man's Country*. London: Chatto & Windus, 1935; reprinted 1968 by Praeger, New York.

———. *The Flame Trees of Thika*. New York: Morrow, 1959.

———. *The Mottled Lizard*. London: Chatto & Windus, 1962; New York: Morrow, 1962 (American edition published under the title *On the Edge of the Rift*).

Hyam, Ronald. *Elgin and Churchill at the Colonial Office, 1905–1908*. London: Macmillan, 1968.

Ingham, Kenneth. *A History of East Africa*. London: Longmans, Green, 1962.

Jackson, Sir Frederick. *Early Days in East Africa*. London: Edward Arnold, 1930; reprinted 1969 by Dawsons of Pall Mall, London.

Johnston, H. H. *The Kilimanjaro Expedition*. London: Keegan Paul, Trench, 1886.

Jones, K. Westcott. *Great Railway Journeys of the World*. Brattleboro, Vt.: Stephen Greene Press, 1965.

Kenyatta, Jomo. *Facing Mount Kenya*. London: Seeker & Warburg, 1938.

Krapf, J. L. *Travels, Researches and Missionary Labours During an Eighteen Years' Residence in Eastern Africa*. London: Trübner, 1860; reprinted 1968 by Frank Cass, London; reprinted 1968 by Johnson Reprint Corp.

Livingstone, David. *The Last Journals of David Livingstone*. Edited by Horace Waller. London: John Murray, 1874.

Loftus, E. A. *Thomson: Through Masai Land*. Edinburgh and London: Nelson, 1951.

———. *Johnston on Kilimanjaro*. Edinburgh and London: Nelson, 1952.

———. *Gregory: The Great Rift Valley*. Edinburgh and London: Nelson, 1952.

Lord, John. *Duty, Honor, Empire: The Life and Times of Colonel Richard Meinertzhagen.* New York: Random House, 1970.

Ludwig, Emil. *Genius and Character.* New York: Harcourt, Brace, 1927.

Lugard, F. D. *The Rise of Our East African Empire.* London: Blackwood, 1893; reprinted 1968 by Frank Cass, London.

———. *The Dual Mandate in British Tropical Africa.* London: Blackwood, 1922; reprinted 1965 with introduction by Margery Perham by Archon Books, Hamden, Conn.

Macdonald, J. R. L. *Soldiering and Surveying in British East Africa.* London: Edward Arnold, 1897.

Mackay, J. W. H. (Mrs. J. W. Harrison). *The Story of the Life of Mackay of Uganda.* London: Hodder & Stoughton, 1891.

Marsh, Zoe. *East Africa Through Contemporary Records.* Cambridge: Cambridge University Press, 1961.

Marsh, Zoe, and Kingsnorth, G. W. *An Introduction to the History of East Africa.* Cambridge: Cambridge University Press, 1957.

McCutcheon, John T. *In Africa.* Indianapolis: Bobbs-Merrill, 1910.

McDermott, P. L. *British East Africa or Ibea.* London: Chapman & Hall, 1893; reprinted 1971 by Frank Cass, London.

Meinertzhagen, Richard. *The Diary of a Black Sheep.* Edinburgh: Oliver & Boyd, 1964.

———. *Kenya Diary, 1902–1906.* Edinburgh: Oliver & Boyd, 1957.

Moorehead, Alan. *The Blue Nile.* New York: Harper & Row, 1962.

———. *The White Nile.* New York: Harper & Bros., 1960.

Morris, James. *Pax Britannica.* New York: Harcourt, Brace & World, 1968.

New, Charles. *Life, Wanderings and Labours in Eastern Africa.* London: Hodder & Stoughton, 1874; reprinted 1971 by Frank Cass, London.

Oliver, Roland. *The Missionary Factor in East Africa.* London: Longmans, Green, 1952.

Owen, W. F. W. *Narrative of Voyages to Explore the Shores of Africa, Arabia and Madagascar.* London: Richard Bentley, 1833.

Patterson, J. H. *The Man-Eaters of Tsavo.* London: Macmillan, 1907; new edn, 1947.

Pearson, Hesketh. *Labby.* New York: Harper & Bros., 1937.

Perham, Margery. *Lugard: The Years of Adventure.* London: Collins, 1956.

Peters, Carl. *New Light on Dark Africa.* London: Ward, Lock, 1891.

Preston, R. O. *Descending the Great Rift Valley.* Nairobi: Colonial Printing Works, n.d.

———. *The Genesis of Kenya Colony.* Nairobi: Colonial Printing Works, n.d.

——— *Oriental Nairobi.* Nairobi: Colonial Printing Works, 1938.

Richards, C. G. *Krapf: Missionary and Explorer.* Edinburgh and London: Nelson, 1950.

Richards, Charles, and Place, James. *East African Explorers*. London: Oxford University Press, 1960.

Robinson, Ronald, and Gallagher, John (with Alice Denny). *Africa and the Victorians*. New York: St. Martin's Press, 1961.

Rodwell, Edward ("The Watchman"). *Coast Causerie*. Mombasa Times, 1945.

———. *Ivory, Apes and Peacocks*. Mombasa Times, 1948.

Roosevelt, Theodore. *African Game Trails*. New York: Scribner, 1910.

Rose, Kenneth. *Superior Person: A Portrait of Lord Curzon and His Circle in Late Victorian England*. New York: Weybright & Talley, 1969.

Ross, W. McGregor. *Kenya from Within*. London: Allen & Unwin, 1927; reprinted 1968 by Frank Cass, London.

Routledge, W. S., and Routledge, K. *The Akikuyu of British East Africa*. London: Edward Arnold, 1910; reprinted 1968 by Frank Cass, London.

Rowland, Peter. *The Last Liberal Governments*. London: Cresset Press, 1968; New York: Macmillan, 1969.

Ruete, Emily ("Salme"). *Memoirs of an Arabian Princess*. New York: P. F. Collier, 1890 ("Once A Week Library," vol. I, No. 20).

Schiffers, Heinrich. *The Quest for Africa*. New York: Putnam, 1957.

Seaton, Henry. *Lion in the Morning*. London: John Murray, 1963.

Speke, J. H. *Journal of the Discovery of the Source of the Nile*. Edinburgh and London: Blackwood, 1863.

———. *What Led to the Discovery of the Source of the Nile*. Edinburgh and London: Blackwood, 1864; reprinted 1967 by Frank Cass, London.

Stanley, H. M. *How I Found Livingstone*. New York: Scribner, Armstrong, 1872.

———. *Through the Dark Continent*. New York: Harper, 1878; reprinted 1969 by Greenwood Press, New York.

———. *In Darkest Africa*. New York: Scribner, 1890.

———. *The Autobiography of Henry M. Stanley*. Boston and New York: Houghton Mifflin, 1909; to be reprinted by Frank Cass, London.

Stigand, C. H. *The Land of Zinj*. London: Constable, 1913; reprinted 1966 by Frank Cass, London.

Sulivan, G. L. *Dhow Chasing in Zanzibar Waters*. London: Sampson Low, Marston, Low & Searle, 1873; reprinted 1967 by Dawsons of Pall Mall, London; reprinted 1968 by Frank Cass, London.

Swann, A. J. *Fighting the Slave-Hunters in Central Africa*. London: Seeley, 1910; reprinted 1969 by Frank Cass, London.

Thomas, H. B., and Scott, Robert. *Uganda*. London: Oxford University Press, 1935.

Thomson, Joseph. *To the Central African Lakes and Back*. London: Sampson Low, Marston, Searle & Rivington, 1881; reprinted 1968 by Frank Cass, London.

———. *Through Masai Land.* Boston: Houghton Mifflin, 1885; reprinted 1968 by Frank Cass, London; abridged edition reprinted 1962 by Northwestern University Press, Evanston.

Tucker, A. R. *Eighteen Years in Uganda and East Africa.* London: Edward Arnold, 1908.

Watt, Mrs. Stuart (Rachel S.). *In the Heart of Savagedom.* London: Marshall Bros., 1913; London and Glasgow: Pickering & Inglis.

Weisbord, Robert. *African Zion.* Philadelphia: Jewish Publication Society of America, 1968.

Wild, J. V. *Early Travelers in Acholi.* Edinburgh and London: Nelson, 1954.

———. *The Uganda Mutiny, 1897.* London: Macmillan, 1954.

OFFICIAL DOCUMENTS AND PERIODICALS

Foreign Office. 1894; Africa No. 2: Reports Relating to Uganda, by Sir Gerald Portal.

———. 1897; Africa No. 4: Report on the Progress of the Mombasa–Victoria (Uganda) Railway, 1896–97.

———. 1897; Africa No. 7: Report by Sir A. Hardinge on the Condition and Progress of the East Africa Protectorate from Its Establishment to the 20th July, 1897.

———. 1901; Africa No. 7: Report by His Majesty's Special Commissioner on the Protectorate of Uganda.

———. 1904; Africa No. 11: Final Report of the Uganda Railway Committee.

Parliamentary Debates: 1892, 1893, 1894, 1900.

Sikio and *Spear* (publications of the East African Railways Corporation).

NOTES

While this book can make no pretense to scholarship, a certain amount of research was necessary in writing it. The following four works were indispensable to me. Although each focuses on a specific individual or theme, taken together they comprise a detailed and reliable history of the period covered in my own book.

Sir Reginald Coupland's *The Exploitation of East Africa* was intended originally as a biographical account of Sir John Kirk's career in Zanzibar. In fact, however, it is a definitive study of the east African slave trade, the British efforts toward curbing the traffic and the partition of the Sultan's mainland dominions following the German irruption. The book also contains valuable sections on the explorers and missionaries, the frustrated Ismail–Gordon annexation attempt, and the abortive Mackinnon concession of 1877.

Lugard: The Years of Adventure, by Margery Perham, can be said to pick up the narrative thread from Coupland, since Lugard's five years as a shaper of the British imperial destiny in east Africa saw him deeply involved in every aspect of the European struggle for that part of the continent. The author, although a formidably erudite Africanist, is anything but a pedant; her book moves with the pace of a suspense yarn, and its numerous personalities—notably the central figure—come very much alive. I feel a particular debt to Miss Perham for having so readably unscrambled so many complexities of the scramble for Africa.

M. F. Hill's *Permanent Way* is the official history of the Uganda Railway through the Second World War; the chapters on the line's construction are essential to any conscientious study of the undertaking. The book is almost equally useful as a narrative of the scramble, while the account of subsequent British administration and settlement in Kenya and Uganda has special value because of the indispensable role played by the railway in the development of those countries. Getting through this work can be hard sledding; in his own way, Hill has written a sort of east African

War and Peace. The sequence of events seems arranged like a maze, the sheer mass of statistics tends to intimidate and the volume itself weighs nearly a ton. But I have managed to read it at least three times.

White Man's Country, Elspeth Huxley's biography of Lord Delamere, may also be the classic work on white settlement in the Kenya highlands. It is written with all of Mrs. Huxley's abundant gifts as journalist, historian and novelist, not to mention the special authority she can claim as a member of the settler community for many years.

The following chapter-by-chapter discussion of important sources includes works that were hardly less useful to me than the four above. A complete list of all references consulted, with full citations, can be found in the Bibliography.

PROLOGUE

For the reconstruction (or perhaps the razing) of Mombasa at the time of Whitehouse's arrival in 1895, bricks and straw came mainly from the writings of people who appear in this book. With the exception of Delamere, every Englishman going to Kenya in Victorian and Edwardian times had to pass through Mombasa, and few failed to record some impression, pleasant or otherwise, of the town. Stigand's *The Land of Zinj* offers a wealth of detail on the shipping in the harbor, the

architecture of the Asian and African quarters and the garb and customs of the inhabitants. Among others, Preston, Boyes, Patterson and Binks (the last in his *African Rainbow*) have written entertaining accounts of the multifarious inconveniences and discomforts that transients had to endure. Hobley's *Kenya: From Chartered Company to Crown Colony* tells us what everyday life in Mombasa was like for the relatively permanent European residents. It could have been worse. It could also have been better.

1, IVORY, APES AND OWEN

Elementary but instructive background to the Zinj era, the Portuguese occupation and the Omani succession will be found in L. W. Hollingsworth's *A Short History of the East African Coast*. The culture and prosperity of the Zinj empire come under expert scrutiny in Basil Davidson's *Africa in History*. G. S. P. Freeman-Grenville's *The East African Coast: Select Documents* contains passages from the *Periplus*, Ibn Batuta and his contemporaries, the Portuguese narratives and Sir James Lancaster's account of his voyage in 1591. The Pate Chronicle (more commonly known as the *History of Pate*) appears in its entirety both in Freeman-Grenville and Stigand. It was the latter, in fact, who made the only English translation of this work, while serving as an administrative officer on Lamu. He was assisted by a local hafiz (one who can recite the entire Koran from memory) named Bwana Kitini, who may well have added some embroidery of his own to the already inventive text. The flavor of early coast legend has also been preserved by Edward Rodwell, a prolific Mombasa journalist and historian whose many works include two engaging little collections of regional lore entitled *Coast Causerie* and *Ivory, Apes and Peacocks*.

The events surrounding the short-lived "Owen Protectorate" were much more complicated than my necessarily telescoped account. Coupland describes the episode with scrupulous attention to detail in *East Africa and Its Invaders*, while a less scholarly but quite engrossing version will be found in Genesta Hamilton's *Princes of Zinj*. Owen wrote about the undertaking in his *Narrative of Voyages*, and the same adventure is seen through the eyes of Thomas Boteler in his similarly titled *Narrative of a Voyage of Discovery*.

2, BALOZI BEHIND THE THRONE

Coupland's *The Exploitation of East Africa* was the principal source consulted in this chapter, particularly with regard to Kirk's role in stemming the tide of the slave traffic and his influence with Barghash. Roland Oliver's *The Missionary Factor in East Africa* contains interesting sidelights on Kirk's troubles with the Freretown evangelists. Ronald Robinson and John Gallagher, in

their *Africa and the Victorians*, provide illuminating background to the Palmerstonian spirit which animated the nineteenth-century British anti-slavery movement. Most of the on-the-spot battle action is taken from Sulivan's *Dhow Chasing in Zanzibar Waters*. First published in 1873, this book was reprinted in 1967 by Dawsons of Pall Mall for its Colonial History Series, with a very good biographical introduction by Donald H. Simpson, Librarian of the Royal Commonwealth Society.

Contemporary writings on slaver misdeeds would probably overflow from the shelves of any small-town library. The most celebrated atrocity stories are found in Livingstone's *Last Journals*, as well as in his many private letters. Lugard's description of slave-gathering techniques, based on personal observation in the Lake Nyasa region, appears in *The Rise of Our East African Empire*. Swann recalled his conversation with the caravan headmen in *Fighting the Slave Hunters in Central Africa*. There is an excellent profile of Tippu Tib in *Tales of the African Frontier*, by John A. Hunter and Daniel P. Mannix; Stanley's cameo of the trader will be found in his *Through the Dark Continent*. The classic account by Thomas Smee of merchandising slaves in the Zanzibar market first saw print in 1844, in the *Transactions of the Bombay Geographical Society*, but is more readily accessible in Coupland's *East Africa and Its Invaders*.

The best-known work on nineteenth-century Zanzibar is Sir

Richard Burton's *Zanzibar: City, Island and Coast.* Dr. Christie made his ghoulish observations in *Cholera Epidemics in East Africa*, passages from which are quoted in *Princes of Zinj.* In the latter book, Lady Hamilton has written a very colorful description of island ways, and gives us three-dimensional character sketches of Seyyid Said and Barghash. Salme's picture of the bustling palaces was drawn in her *Memoirs of an Arabian Princess*; quotations from this work will also be found in both *Princess of Zinj* and *A Short History of the East African Coast.*

3, THE ELMORAN AND THE OPTIMIST

Large segments of the journals kept by Krapf and Rebmann during their penetrations of the east African interior appear in Krapf's voluminous *Travels, Researches and Missionary Labours.* New described his ascent of Kilimanjaro in *Life, Wanderings and Labours in Eastern Africa.* Thomson's *Through Masai Land*, published in 1885, was reprinted in 1968 by Frank Cass of London, with an excellent biographical introduction by Professor Robert I. Rotberg of Harvard University. Additional background on Thomson is provided in *The Exploitation of East Africa*, while less formal but perhaps more revealing opinions of his personality are expressed by J. M. Barrie in *An Edinburgh Eleven* and by John Hunter in *Tales of the African Frontier.* In Frederick Jackson's *Early*

Days in East Africa and Harry Johnston's *The Kilimanjaro Expedition*, there are fine portraits of the greedy Mandara. Jackson also has a great deal to say about his good friend, "little Martin"; the two were closely associated while serving IBEA and the Protectorate Government. Hannington's tragic journey is related in *James Hannington, First Bishop of Eastern Equatorial Africa*, a biography by E. C. Dawson, who draws heavily on the missionary's private journals. Among the more worthwhile studies of the Masai is A. C. Hollis' *Masai Language and Folklore.* The author was a turn-of-the-century Protectorate official whose knowledge of anthropology and fascination with the tribe's folk tales combined to produce something of a classic. Not everyone saw the elmoran as a menace; Jackson dissented sharply from the majority view, asserting that the Masai's bellicose image was largely the invention of Arab-Swahili traders who sought "to keep the door closed as long as possible and their happy hunting-grounds free of poachers." But Harry Johnston and J. W. Gregory (the latter in *The Great Rift Valley*) were among the Europeans who described close shaves with the Masai following Thomson's expedition. And long before that journey, in 1874, New had written of how he barely avoided being bushwhacked by elmoran raiders in Ukamba. Hobley voiced his own opinion of the Masai threat in *Kenya.*

Apart from Thomson's trek and the Emin Pasha expedition, this book is concerned only marginally with the major explorations of the era, but the classic works of the more celebrated travelers should not be overlooked. Probably the best known are Livingstone's *Last Journals*; Stanley's *How I Found Livingstone* and *Through the Dark Continent*; Burton's *The Lake Regions of Central Africa*; Speke's *What Led to the Discovery of the Source of the Nile*; and Baker's *The Albert N'yanza*. All are masterfully written, and their flavor of high adventure has not been diluted even in our sophisticated times, especially when it is remembered that a nineteenth-century African explorer was more completely sealed off from his world than any present-day astronaut who can at least keep in touch by radio and television. Selections from these and a number of other books will also be found in an excellent pocket-sized anthology entitled *East African Explorers*, edited by Charles Richards and James Place. Countless third-person works, of course, have been written about the early travelers and their discoveries. None, in my own opinion, has ever surpassed—or is ever likely to match—Alan Moorehead's *The White Nile*.

4, CRESCENT, CROSS AND KABAKA

Uganda's pre-colonial past and ancient mythology are dealt with informatively in *An Introduction to the History of East Africa*, by Zoe Marsh and G. W. Kingsnorth, and in H. B. Thomas' and Robert Scott's *Uganda*. Lugard furnishes brief but substantial background material in *The Rise of Our East African Empire*, while Harry Johnston's official *Report by His Majesty's Special Commissioner on the Protectorate of Uganda* (1901) is helpful on the Bahima migrations. Among early European visitors to Uganda, Speke may have written the best description of the country and its customs in *Journal of the Discovery of the Source of the Nile*. Stanley's entertaining account of how he brought the light to Mutesa is related in the explorer's *Autobiography*. The principal source for the section on Gordon's frustrated invasion of Uganda was *The Exploitation of East Africa*. Baker recounted his achievements and tribulations on behalf of the Khedive in *Ismailia*.

For a proper appreciation of the influence wielded by Protestant and Catholic missionaries at the courts of Mutesa and Mwanga, Roland Oliver's landmark study, *The Missionary Factor in East Africa*, is mandatory. The Kabakas' unpredictable whims are well treated by Ashe in his *Two Kings of Uganda* and *Chronicles of Uganda*. Lugard, Jackson, Hobley and Eliot, to name only a few, are among the Europeans whose works portray Mwanga as an archfiend. The greater substance of this chapter, however, is based on *The Story of the Life of Mackay of Uganda*, by the missionary's sister, who made abundant use of Mackay's journals and correspondence.

5, A BATHTUB FOR DR. PETERS

The fine print of the first Mackinnon concession and the breakdown of negotiations with Barghash are examined minutely in *The Exploitation of East Africa*, which also describes the various European attempts to establish footholds in the Sultan's mainland dominions, and includes a detailed account of the sudden German thrust at Zanzibar. Both *Africa and the Victorians* and Margery Perham's *Lugard* contain lucid analyses of the motivations underlying British official behavior during the entire scramble. There is a brilliant profile of Carl Peters in Emil Ludwig's *Genius and Character*, while Heinrich Schiffers, in *The Quest for Africa*, recounts Peters' filibustering adventures with far more appreciation than British writers are usually prepared to give. Jackson's *Early Days* has several amusing anecdotes about German machinations on the coast and some charming personal recollections of Kirk.

If there is a definitive work on IBEA, it is P. L. McDermott's *British East Africa or Ibea*. (The abbreviation was once considered as a possible name for the Protectorate, although Lugard suggested Equatoria.) McDermott was an assistant secretary with the Company and had ready access to all its documents, as well as the directors' authority to write the book. Perhaps the most objective evaluation of IBEA's accomplishments will be found in *Permanent Way*.

Stanley's *In Darkest Africa* takes the reader on every agonizing and frustrating step of the Emin Pasha expedition. The quotations in my condensed account are from that book and the *Autobiography*. Nearly every European involved in the tragi-comic "rescue" mission felt compelled to write about it; Casati's version appears in *Ten Years in Equatoria and the Return with Emin Pasha*. Among popular histories of the expedition, Schiffers gives a dramatic replay in *The Quest for Africa*, although it does not have quite the zing of Alan Moorehead's superlative reconstruction in *The White Nile*.

Peters and Jackson not only raced each other to Uganda but vied for honors in writing of their respective experiences. In my view, the latter contest is a draw. Despite a somewhat cumbersome Germanic style, Peters' *New Light on Dark Africa* is a spirited narrative with a fine air of urgency about it. In *Early Days*, Jackson traces the events in a more leisurely but no less vivid fashion. Jackson's delightful memoirs, incidentally, were published in 1930 and reprinted in 1969 in the Dawsons of Pall Mall Colonial History Series, with a well-documented biographical introduction by H. B. Thomas, a widely respected authority on east African history. It is a pity that Peters' book has not also been reissued. It ought to be read as a sequel to Jackson's—or the other way round, if one prefers.

6, THE MAKING OF A PROCONSUL

Lugard's forbiddingly gargantuan and altogether marvelous epic, *The Rise of Our East African Empire*, was consulted throughout this chapter, and backstopped by Miss Perham's biography. The quintessence of the English gentleman, as seen by Rider Haggard, is part of the dedication in *Allan Quatermain*.

7, "CRIES OF 'OH!'"

For whatever coherence this chapter can claim, the credit belongs largely to the guidelines furnished by Miss Perham in *Lugard*, which also contains the bulk of the private papers quoted. Another extremely useful source—particularly on the Nile theory and Salisbury's conversion—was *Africa and the Victorians*. Most of the oratory was taken, of course, from Hansard, although Stanley's exchange with Gladstone appears in the *Autobiography*. Portal's experiences and recommendations are found mainly in his official report; certain passages are also quoted in *Permanent Way*. Revealing character sketches of many figures in the annexation controversy—notably Salisbury, Gladstone, Harcourt and Labouchere—have been drawn by Kenneth Rose in *Superior Person*, a superior biography of Lord Curzon. Labouchere also comes under a separate and well-deserved spotlight in Hesketh Pearson's *Labby*.

8, SLOW FREIGHT TO ARMAGEDDON

The blizzard of statistics in *Permanent Way* fails utterly to obscure that book's splendid handling of the struggle with nature that marked the entire course of the Uganda Railway's construction. All these trials are brought into more immediate focus by various official documents, especially the Railway Committee's first and final progress reports, submitted to the Foreign Office in 1897 and 1904 respectively. Also useful is the 1897 report of Sir Arthur Hardinge, Commissioner of the East Africa Protectorate, who throws much light on the difficulties of securing porters and animal transport in the interior. For the more human side of the adventure, however, one must turn elsewhere. The first-hand narratives, particularly Preston's and Patterson's, are far and away the best sources, with additional color supplied by that ubiquitous and ever observant official passenger, Frederick Jackson. The Kenya Police's W. Robert Foran, although he had no part in construction, arrived in east Africa early enough to become acquainted with many of the railway's builders; his book, *A Cuckoo in Kenya*, contains quite a few vivid descriptions of the hardships those men faced. A much more recent account of the construction ordeal is Ronald Hardy's tautly written informal history, *The Iron Snake*, which makes good use of the journals of a railway caravan master named Robert Turk.

There are several first-rate eye-witness views of the Uganda Mutiny, notably in Jackson's *Early Days* and Herbert Austin's *With Macdonald in Uganda*. Both *Permanent Way* and J. V. Wild's *The Uganda Mutiny* reconstruct the complex events of that outbreak with painstaking documentation, while Harry Johnston, in his 1901 official report, has some interesting observations on the rebellious Sudanese officers and their quasi-nationalist motivations. The broader imperial objectives of the Macdonald expedition are well treated in *Africa and the Victorians*.

9, THE BRIDGE OVER THE RIVER TSAVO

It is almost impossible to write at any length about the Tsavo episode without referring continually to the central figure and his baroquely thrilling book. Many valuable sidelights, however, have been contributed by contemporaries of Patterson who passed through Tsavo around the time of the siege. Jackson, Hobley and John Boyes draw particularly graphic pictures of the devastation which the man-eaters wrought on property and morale, while Preston, as we have seen, was personally involved with one of the lions for several days. Among present-day writers, Ronald Hardy has rec-reated very credibly the atmosphere of gnawing tension in the camp, although for some reason he has chosen to portray Patterson as a tyrannical, raving egomaniac, which

might be hitting just a bit below the belt. While one suspects that Patterson may have been something less than a scoutmaster in labor relations, his occasional harsh behavior toward the Indian workers has to be judged against the background of the almost unprece-dented attrition which seriously jeopardized completion of the bridge.

Foran's *The Kenya Police*, along with an article in *Spear*, the railway's official magazine, were the main sources for the account of Ryall's death at Kima. Patterson, who happened to be in Voi when O'Hara was killed, probably has the most accurate version of that tragedy, although many others have written about it. The epic poem will be found in the appendix of Patterson's book.

10, THE FOUR HORSEMEN AND THE IRON SNAKE

The best eyewitness accounts which I have read of the drought and famine in Ukamba are those of Jackson, Ainsworth and Mrs. Stuart Watt; the last described the suffering at Machakos in her book, *In the Heart of Savagedom*. Nearly every individual writing about east Africa in the 1890s has his own version of the Dick incident; mine is a sort of montage which draws on Jackson, Hobley, Ainsworth, Preston, Boyes, Mervyn Hill and McGregor Ross, the last in *Kenya from Within*. Both Jackson and Ainsworth give the most reliable information on the truce with the Masai. Substantial extracts from Ainsworth's official reports and personal memoirs are to be found in F. H. Goldsmith's excellent biography, *John Ainsworth, Pioneer Kenya Administrator.*

In *Tales of the African Frontier,* John Hunter writes of John Boyes, whom he knew personally, as a man who "under somewhat different circumstances ... might well have been another Rhodes or Clive." As for Boyes' narrative, it is hard to say how much of the writing is actually his own. The manuscript was edited by a fellow-settler named C.W.L. Bulpett, and the polished style hardly bespeaks Boyes' very limited formal education. But there is no question that the events recounted were real enough, while Boyes' descriptions of Kikuyu customs, although less than anthropological, show him to be a keen observer.

Among the better known and more reliable works on the Kikuyu are W. S. and K. Routledge's *The Akikuyu of British East Africa* and Jomo Kenyatta's *Facing Mount Kenya.* The latter book, written in 1938 while the author was a student of Bronislaw Malinowski at the London School of Economics, is of special interest for its free-wheeling anti-British rhetoric, which the President of Kenya has soft-pedaled in recent years. Kenyatta is also the only individual I can think of who calls the Kikuyu the "Gikuyu"; a Gikuyu himself, he is in a position to know. Another commendable study of the Kikuyu is *Red Strangers,* a novel by Elspeth Huxley which

describes most compellingly the disruption of tribal ways brought about by the arrival of the whites.

Few Britons visiting the infant Nairobi failed to remark on the place with affectionate disgust; the comments of Ainsworth in his memoirs and Eliot in *The East Africa Protectorate* are particularly worthwhile, since both men played major roles in giving the town a face-lifting. *Permanent Way* contains a very helpful if somewhat complicated explanation of the plans for the cable incline on the Kikuyu escarpment, as well as a balanced account of the wildcat railwaymen's strike. In James Morris' *Pax Britannica,* an informal wide-angle portrait of the Empire at the time of Queen Victoria's Diamond Jubilee, one almost shares the cocky imperial pride that Britons took in achievements like the completion of the Uganda line.

11, SUPER-SQUIRE

Of all the European colonial enclaves in tropical Africa, none has come under more painstaking, exhaustive and critical scrutiny than the British settler-official community in the Kenya highlands. The sources consulted in Part III of this book are an almost invisible fragment from a voluminous bibliography of colonist-administrator records, but they do embrace a broad spectrum of experience and opinion. Generally speaking, *White Man's Country* and *Permanent Way* should be seen as the principal guides, since there is scarcely a single factual or controversial aspect of settlement that these books do not touch on.

White Man's Country, certainly, is the definitive work on Delamere, who has been canonized by innumerable contemporaries (such as Cranworth) and consigned to perdition by nearly as many others (such as McGregor Ross). For my descriptions of the early pioneering years, I have also relied to great extent on Mrs. Huxley's warm personal recollections of her childhood in *The Flame Trees of Thika*. If one borders on heresy in suggesting that Mrs. Huxley can evoke the robust flavor of early settlement in Kenya at least as skillfully as does Isak Dinesen, this is not meant to disparage the lean but elegant genius of the writing in *Out of Africa* and *Shadows on the Grass*. Hardly less helpful on this period were Binks and Cranworth. The former's *African Rainbow* is a charming rags-to-rags memoir, replete with amusing (occasionally sidesplitting) anecdotes about the setbacks sustained by the colonists. In *A Colony in the Making*, Cranworth furnishes a wealth of data on agriculture in the highlands, while simultaneously revealing the settler's character at its gallant best and bigoted less than best. Churchill's warnings about the terrible effects of the sun's rays are sounded in *My African Journey*. Gregory devalues Kenya's commercial prospects in *The Great Rift Valley*.

Both Mrs. Huxley and Mervyn Hill tell us a great deal about Sir Charles Eliot's character, his cold war with the Foreign Office and his achievements on behalf of colonization; the same authors also go into considerable detail on the Zionist settlement scheme. Eliot, however, is his own best advertisement in his official reports and *The East Africa Protectorate*, while the most amply documented source for the Herzl–Chamberlain episode has to be Robert Weisbord's scholarly but engrossing *African Zion*. Weisbord also has a diverting account of the goofy Freeland venture; two unpublished manuscripts which I read during a recent visit to Lamu gave me a local angle on that "colony."

The complexities of the first Masai move and its attendant controversy receive expert attention from Mrs. Huxley, Hill, Hobley, Ainsworth and McGregor Ross among many others. But Jackson's comments are the most revealing—by virtue of their absence. So bitter was the dispute between Jackson and Eliot on the Masai reserve that Lady Jackson expunged all mention of Eliot from her husband's memoirs while editing them for *Early Days*. It is also of interest to note that Eliot's book contains no reference whatever to Jackson. One does not know whether to laugh or groan at the spectacle of two of Britain's most intelligent and honorable colonial servants placing each other in personal coventry.

12, WHITE KNIGHT TO BLACK PAWN

Trying to lift quicksilver with a fork may be a simpler task than pinpointing any clear-cut British policy toward the indigenous inhabitants and white settlers in its east African possessions during the first decade of the twentieth century. To both the Foreign Office and Colonial Office, the period was one of trial and error; in *Elgin and Churchill at the Colonial Office, 1905–1908*, Ronald Hyam sheds much light on the conflicting ideas—and often contradictory actions—that were spawned in this climate of uncertainty. Even so, however, discernible patterns of policy occasionally emerge in the writings of administrators on the spot. Harry Johnston's comprehensive 1901 official report on Uganda includes a very helpful outline of the mechanics of indirect rule through the Kabaka's regency, the Lukiiko and the chiefs. The problems and progress of "native administration" in Kenya are treated with thoroughness by Hobley and Eliot. Ainsworth's recollections of his role in the Kavirondo agricultural development program underscore the importance of the British official's personal presence in helping any tribe make the transformation from subsistence to cash economy. Reading Henry Seaton's *Lion in the Morning* was something of a picnic. One is certain that Seaton approached his crushing responsibilities with the same good cheer that gladdens his many reminiscences of life as a "bush D.O."

Foran's informal history, *The Kenya Police*, furnished most of the material (including the quotation from Sir Robert Hamilton) for the law and order section of this chapter. All of the writers mentioned above have nothing but the best to say about the 3rd KAR—except that Meinertzhagen's praise is sometimes punctuated with irate snorts over tendencies to cannibalism and other breaches of discipline among the askaris under his command. My own profile of Meinertzhagen is based almost entirely on his journals, which he published in 1957 under the title of *Kenya Diary, 1902–1906*. Background to the Nandi campaign will be found in *Permanent Way* and *White Man's Country*, although for some inexplicable reason neither Hill nor Mrs. Huxley gives Meinertzhagen credit for the vital role he played. For more about this most forthright of men, John Lord's biography, *Duty, Honor, Empire*, is warmly recommended.

In the no-holds-barred arena of Kenya politics, the free-for-all can be seen through the eyes of Britain's top-level statesmen in *Elgin and Churchill at the Colonial Office*, but ringside seats are also available in *White Man's Country* and McGregor Ross' *Kenya from Within*. It can be said, in fact, that the two latter books fight a sort of private duel, Mrs. Huxley presenting the settlers' case with restrained but formidable logic, while Ross no less ably wields the lance of sarcasm and the bludgeon of statistics. The play-by-play account is narrated by Mervyn Hill, who, despite a pro-settler bias, manages to remain commendably fair to both sides. The most interested—and easily the most interesting—spectator is Winston Churchill; simultaneously irked and entertained by the tussle, he favors it with some of his liveliest Churchillian prose in *My African Journey*.

There are very good accounts of the settlers' showdown with Hayes-Sadler in *White Man's Country* and *Elgin and Churchill at the Colonial Office*. Grogan's outspoken views on forced labor were voiced in his book, *From the Cape to Cairo*, which also relates some grisly encounters with cannibal tribes during that epic walk, thus providing at least a hint of where the author developed his beliefs in iron-fist control. (Interestingly, the word "nigger," which appeared when the book was first published in 1900, was changed to "native" in the second edition two years later.) Although Grogan never showed any doubts as to the rightness of his prejudices, he managed to win a surprising measure of affection from Kenya Africans. He even stayed on after independence and, as a contented and respected nonagenarian, left his bones in the highlands in 1968.

Of all contemporary writings on the race question, Stigand's book is probably the most illuminating and unusual, simply because the author sought to present that theme "as much as possible from the native point of view rather than from that of the white man." Even though the attempt did not quite come off, Stigand merits an "A" for effort and open-mindedness.

The events leading to the "Elgin Pledge" are well covered from the settlers' standpoint by Mrs. Huxley and at the Colonial Office level by Ronald Hyam. *Permanent Way* offers a balanced assessment of the Indians' uneasy position in Kenya, while Ronald Preston, one of the few Britons in the Protectorate who liked and respected the Indians, acknowledges their contribution to the country's prosperity in *Oriental Nairobi*. Others taking up the cudgel for the Indians are McGregor Ross, in a positively scathing indictment of white colonist prejudice, and Winston Churchill, who correctly depicts the Indians as a victimized community. It should be added, though, that Churchill was the man who later dismissed Gandhi as a "half-naked fakir."

13, HAPPY VALLEY

Although *My African Journey* is quoted extensively in the Uganda section of this chapter, most of the hard facts and figures will be found in *Permanent Way, Uganda* and *Elgin and Churchill at the Colonial Office*. The latter is specially informative on Bell's overhauling of the country's infant cotton industry. *Tales of the African Frontier* contains an encapsulated but dramatic piece about Sir Albert Cook's work during the sleeping sickness epidemic, based largely on Cook's *Uganda Memories* (which I regret that I have not read). Tucker's description of early mail "deliveries" appears in his *Eighteen Years in Uganda and East Africa.*

All of the writers mentioned in connection with the second Masai move have valuable accounts of that episode. Ainsworth and Ross, being the only individuals directly involved, probably speak with the greatest authority, although the entire affair is riddled with contradictions. The ever reliable *Permanent Way* and *White Man's Country* provided most of the background to Girouard's accomplishments and Kenya's sudden rise to prosperity. Nearly all writers cited contributed to the pictures of sport, social life, the railway excursion and Nairobi's growing pains. "Kill or Cure" Burkitt has been the subject of countless anecdotes and fabrications; my own sketch was drawn mainly from *Under the Sun,* an affectionately witty memoir by Burkitt's long-time assistant, Dr. J. R. Gregory. Patterson was undoubtedly consulted by many

a transient hunter for his helpful if somewhat awesome catalogue of weapons and other safari gear, which appears as an appendix to *The Man-Eaters of Tsavo.* Jackson's personal recollections of the zanier visitors are among the most diverting parts of his book. Binks has an uproarious description of the Boyce Balloon-ograph Expedition, as does John T. McCutcheon's *In Africa.* With the exception of Patterson and one or two others, most people writing about big-game stalks tend to make me drowsy, and I think the most tiresome of all these narrators has to be Theodore Roosevelt in his *African Game Trails.* But whenever Roosevelt leaves the dreary subject to comment on the country around him and the people who live there, we recognize a nature writer of real gifts and a very keen judge of character.

Daudi Chwa's letter to Winston Churchill and Churchill's letter to his mother from the railway carriage appear in volume II of Randolph S. Churchill's *Winston S. Churchill.*

INDEX